Thinking the Unconscious

Since Freud's earliest psychoanalytic theorization around the beginning of the twentieth century, the concept of the unconscious has exerted an enormous influence upon psychoanalysis and psychology, and literary, critical, and social theory. Yet, prior to Freud, the concept of the unconscious already possessed a complex genealogy in nineteenth-century German philosophy and literature, beginning with the aftermath of Kant's critical philosophy and the origins of German idealism, and extending into the discourses of romanticism and beyond. Despite the many key thinkers who contributed to the Germanic discourses on the unconscious, the English-speaking world remains comparatively unaware of this heritage and its influence upon the origins of psychoanalysis. Bringing together a collection of experts in the fields of German Studies, Continental Philosophy, the History and Philosophy of Science, and the History of Psychoanalysis, this volume examines the various theorizations, representations, and transformations undergone by the concept of the unconscious in nineteenth-century German thought.

ANGUS NICHOLLS is Claussen-Simon Foundation Research Lecturer in German and Comparative Literature in the Centre for Anglo-German Cultural Relations at Queen Mary, University of London.

MARTIN LIEBSCHER is Senior Lecturer in the Institute of Germanic & Romance Studies in the School of Advanced Study at the University of London.

Thinking the Unconscious
Nineteenth-Century German Thought

Edited by
Angus Nicholls and Martin Liebscher

CAMBRIDGE UNIVERSITY PRESS
Cambridge, New York, Melbourne, Madrid, Cape Town,
Singapore, São Paulo, Delhi, Tokyo, Mexico City

Cambridge University Press
The Edinburgh Building, Cambridge CB2 8RU, UK

Published in the United States of America by
Cambridge University Press, New York

www.cambridge.org
Information on this title: www.cambridge.org/9780521897532

© Cambridge University Press 2010

This publication is in copyright. Subject to statutory exception
and to the provisions of relevant collective licensing agreements,
no reproduction of any part may take place without the written
permission of Cambridge University Press.

First published 2010

A catalogue record for this publication is available from the British Library

Library of Congress Cataloguing in Publication data
Thinking the unconscious : nineteenth-century German thought / [edited by]
  Angus Nicholls, Martin Liebscher.
    p. cm.
  ISBN 978-0-521-89753-2 (Hardback)
  1. Philosophy, German–19th century.   I. Nicholls, Angus (Angus James),
  1972–   II. Liebscher, Martin, 1972–   III. Title.
  B2741.T45 2010
  127.0943´09034–dc22
                                          2010000059

ISBN 978-0-521-89753-2 Hardback

Cambridge University Press has no responsibility for the persistence or
accuracy of URLs for external or third-party internet websites referred to in
this publication, and does not guarantee that any content on such websites is,
or will remain, accurate or appropriate. Information regarding prices, travel
timetables, and other factual information given in this work is correct at
the time of first printing but Cambridge University Press does not guarantee
the accuracy of such information thereafter.

Contents

Notes on contributors   page vii

    Introduction: thinking the unconscious   1
    ANGUS NICHOLLS AND MARTIN LIEBSCHER

1. The unconscious from the Storm and Stress to Weimar classicism: the dialectic of time and pleasure   26
   PAUL BISHOP

2. The philosophical significance of Schelling's conception of the unconscious   57
   ANDREW BOWIE

3. The scientific unconscious: Goethe's post-Kantian epistemology   87
   ANGUS NICHOLLS

4. The hidden agent of the self: towards an aesthetic theory of the non-conscious in German romanticism   121
   RÜDIGER GÖRNER

5. The real essence of human beings: Schopenhauer and the unconscious will   140
   CHRISTOPHER JANAWAY

6. Carl Gustav Carus and the science of the unconscious   156
   MATTHEW BELL

7. Eduard von Hartmann's *Philosophy of the Unconscious*   173
   SEBASTIAN GARDNER

8. Gustav Theodor Fechner and the unconscious   200
   MICHAEL HEIDELBERGER

9. Friedrich Nietzsche's perspectives on the unconscious   241
   MARTIN LIEBSCHER

10. Freud and nineteenth-century philosophical sources on the unconscious 261
GÜNTER GÖDDE

Epilogue: the "optional" unconscious 287
SONU SHAMDASANI

Works cited 297
Index 324

Notes on contributors

MATTHEW BELL is Professor of German and Comparative Literature at King's College London. He is the author of *Goethe's Naturalistic Anthropology: Man and Other Plants* (1994); and, most recently, *The German Tradition of Psychology in Literature and Thought, 1700–1840* (2005).

PAUL BISHOP is Professor of German at the University of Glasgow. His publications include *The Dionysian Self: C. G. Jung's Reception of Friedrich Nietzsche* (1995); *Nietzsche and Antiquity* (edited, 2004); *Friedrich Nietzsche and Weimar Classicism* (with R. H. Stephenson, 2005); and the recent study *Analytical Psychology and German Classical Aesthetics*, in two volumes (2007–8).

ANDREW BOWIE is Professor of Philosophy and German at Royal Holloway, University of London. His books include: *Aesthetics and Subjectivity: From Kant to Nietzsche* (1990; 2nd edition 2003); *Schelling and Modern European Philosophy* (1993); *From Romanticism to Critical Theory: The Philosophy of German Literary Theory* (1997); *Introduction to German Philosophy from Kant to Habermas* (2003); and *Music, Philosophy, and Modernity* (2007).

SEBASTIAN GARDNER is Professor of Philosophy at University College London. His publications include: *Irrationality and the Philosophy of Psychoanalysis* (1993); and *Kant and the Critique of Pure Reason* (1998).

GÜNTER GÖDDE is a practising psychotherapist, a lecturer at the Berliner Akademie für Psychotherapie, and a scholar who works on the history and theory of psychoanalysis. He is the author of numerous publications on the history and theory of psychoanalysis, including *Traditionslinien des Unbewussten: Schopenhauer, Nietzsche, Freud* (1999), and *Mathilde Freud* (2003). He is also (with Michael B. Buchholz) the editor of a three-volume history of the concept of the unconscious and related discourses, entitled *Das Unbewusste* (2005–6).

Notes on contributors

RÜDIGER GÖRNER is Professor of German and Head of the School of Languages, Linguistics and Film at Queen Mary, University of London. Recent publications include: *Rainer Maria Rilke: Im Herzwerk der Sprache* (2004); *Thomas Mann: Der Zauber des Letzten* (2005); *Heimat und Toleranz: Reden und Reflexionen* (2006); *Das Zeitalter des Fraktalen: Ein kulturkritischer Versuch* (2007); and *Wenn Götzen dämmern: Formen ästhetischen Denkens bei Nietzsche* (2008).

MICHAEL HEIDELBERGER is Professor of Philosophy at the University of Tübingen, Germany. He is the author of numerous publications on the history and philosophy of science, including an intellectual biography of Gustav Theodor Fechner, entitled *Nature from Within: Gustav Theodor Fechner's Psychophysical Worldview* (2004).

CHRISTOPHER JANAWAY is Professor of Philosophy at the University of Southampton. Among his many publications are included: *Self and World in Schopenhauer's Philosophy* (1998); *Willing and Nothingness: Schopenhauer as Nietzsche's Educator* (edited, 1998); *The Cambridge Companion to Schopenhauer* (edited, 1999); *Schopenhauer: A Very Short Introduction* (2002); and *Beyond Selflessness: Reading Nietzsche's Genealogy* (2007).

MARTIN LIEBSCHER is Director of the Ingeborg Bachmann Centre for Austrian Literature and Senior Lecturer in the Institute for Germanic & Romance Studies, University of London. His publications include: *Nietzsche-Studien: Gesamtregister*, volumes I–XX, 1972–91 (2000); *Kontinuitäten und Brüche: Österreichs literarischer Wiederaufbau seit 1945* (edited with H. Kunzelmann and T. Eicher, 2006); and *Nationalism versus Cosmopolitanism in German Thought and Culture 1789–1914: Essays on the Emergence of Europe* (edited with M. A. Perkins, 2006).

ANGUS NICHOLLS is Claussen-Simon Foundation Research Lecturer in German and Comparative Literature and Acting Director of the Centre for Anglo-German Cultural Relations at Queen Mary, University of London. His first monograph is *Goethe's Concept of the Daemonic: After the Ancients* (2006). He is co-editor of *ANGERMION: Yearbook for Anglo-German Literary Criticism, Intellectual History and Cultural Transfers* (volume I, 2008), and guest editor of a special section on *Goethe and Twentieth-Century Theory* in *The Goethe Yearbook*, volume 16 (2009).

SONU SHAMDASANI is Reader in Jung History at the Wellcome Trust Centre for the History of Medicine at University College London. His books include *Cult Fictions: C. G. Jung and the Founding of Modern Analytical Psychology* (1998); *Jung and the Making of Modern Psychology: The Dream of a Science* (2003); *Jung Stripped Bare by his Biographers, Even* (2005); and *Le dossier Freud: enquête sur l'histoire de la psychanalyse* (with Mikkel Borch-Jacobsen, 2006).

Introduction: thinking the unconscious

Angus Nicholls and Martin Liebscher

> In the entire world one does not speak of the unconscious since, according to its essence, it is unknown; only in Berlin does one speak of and know something about it, and explain to us what actually sets it apart.[1]

So wrote Friedrich Nietzsche in 1873, as part of his ironic response to the success of the *Philosophy of the Unconscious* (*Philosophie des Unbewussten*, 1869), written by the Berlin philosopher Eduard von Hartmann. If the influence of a concept can be gauged by the way in which it is received by the public at large, if not in academic circles, then Hartmann's volume, which ran to some eleven editions during his lifetime alone and was seen by some as introducing an entirely new *Weltanschauung*, might be regarded as marking one of the pinnacles of the career of *das Unbewusste* (the unconscious) during the nineteenth century.[2] Although Hartmann's understanding of the unconscious was, like Freud's, subjected to a scathing critique at the hands of academic philosophy and psychology, it nevertheless took some half a century or so for Freud to supersede Hartmann's public role as the chief theorist and interpreter of the unconscious for the German-speaking public. Today the concept of the unconscious is arguably still first and foremost associated with Freud and with his successors such as Carl Gustav Jung and Jacques Lacan; in short: with psychoanalysis in general. And although the existence of "the unconscious," or of unconscious affects, continues to be questioned within large sections of the human and psychological sciences, it is indisputable that many people in the Western world still subscribe to the notion that they have, in some form or another, "an

---

[1] [In der ganzen Welt redet man nicht vom Unbewussten, weil es seinem Wesen nach ungewusst ist; nur in Berlin redet und weiss man etwas davon und erzählt uns, worauf es eigentlich abgesehen ist.] Friedrich Nietzsche, *Nachgelassene Fragmente, Sommer 1872 bis Ende 1874, Werke: Kritische Gesamtausgabe*, part 3, vol. IV, ed. Giorgio Colli and Mazzino Montinari (Berlin: Walter de Gruyter, 1978), 262.
[2] On the popular success of Hartmann's *Philosophy of the Unconscious*, see chapter 7 of this volume, by Sebastian Gardner.

unconscious" – generally understood to be an active component of one's mental life that escapes one's direct awareness, but which may nevertheless influence one's behavior.

It is well known, especially in the German-speaking world but also to a lesser degree in the Anglophone territories, that Freud was not the first person to offer a detailed theoretical account of what is called "the unconscious." Yet there has until now been no detailed study in English of the various ways in which the unconscious was conceptualized or "thought" by German-speaking intellectuals during the nineteenth century. The central purpose of this volume is to fill this gap by providing an in-depth account of key figures in this conceptual history, not only in terms of how they may or may not have influenced Freud and the origins of psychoanalysis generally, but also in terms of their independent historical and contemporary relevance for other fields such as philosophy, literature, and aesthetics. In accordance with this analytical framework, this volume has also been edited with a strong commitment to the philology of the German language, in an attempt to avoid the frequent mistranslations and misinterpretations that occur when analyzing cultural traditions in foreign languages (Anglophone mistranslations of Freud being perhaps the best-known case in point).[3] For this reason, all quotations from the German primary sources appear in the original German in the notes, and where a term has a particular resonance in German that cannot be captured in English translation, the original German term appears in brackets in the main text.

Nietzsche's remarks, although directed first and foremost at Hartmann, also touch upon a series of irreducible philosophical questions with which this volume is confronted. If, by its very definition, "the unconscious" escapes our conscious awareness, then how is it possible to "think" about it at all? If we do in some way manage to "think" the unconscious, does it not thereby cease to *be* unconscious, thus defeating the purpose of the entire enterprise? Would it not be better to withdraw completely from any rational or "conscious" analysis of the unconscious, leaving the way free for other modes of expression – the visual arts, poetry, or music – to bring unconscious affects to light? If it is difficult or impossible to "think" the unconscious, how can it even be an object of knowledge expressed in the substantive form "*the* unconscious"? And can one in fact assume the ontological existence of "*the* unconscious," or is this "object" or "realm" merely an invention of Western (in this case particularly but not exclusively German) thought? In short: does the unconscious exist

---

[3] On this subject see the Introduction to Bruno Bettelheim's study *Freud and Man's Soul* (New York: Knopf, 1982).

Introduction: thinking the unconscious 3

only in the West, only among certain socio-economic or cultural groups, or, as Nietzsche ironically suggests, "only in Berlin"?[4]

In answer to these questions, the chief English-language precursor to this study – Henri F. Ellenberger's magisterial *The Discovery of the Unconscious: The History and Evolution of Dynamic Psychiatry* (1970) – proceeds on the assumption that "*the* unconscious" is, more or less like the brain, an aspect of human subjectivity which has an objective existence in all members of the human race, regardless of ethnicity, geography, and cultural or religious difference. Yet in light of the fact that the human sciences and the humanities in general necessarily play a role in creating their own object – the "human," understood not only as an empirical or biological organism but also as a thinking subject capable of self-reflection, self-definition, and therefore also of self-transformation – this study remains open to the possibility that theorists of the unconscious actually invent or *think* the non-empirical "object" or phenomena which they attempt to describe.[5] In this sense, the notion that the unconscious was "discovered" necessarily forecloses upon the question as to whether "*the* unconscious" or "unconscious phenomena" actually exist objectively and independently of their theoretical elaborations. Thus, despite its invaluable contribution to the history of Western psychiatry and psychoanalysis, Ellenberger's study must be regarded as being methodologically inadequate. In light of this fact, the title of this volume – *Thinking the Unconscious* – attempts both to express and to preserve the fundamental ontological instability of its theme.

Two further important questions raised by the title of this study – why "German" and why the nineteenth century? – necessitate an account here of how and why the question of the unconscious became a central theme of German thought from 1800 onwards, and this account must commence, not at the beginning of the nineteenth, but at the beginning of the eighteenth century. Arnim Regenbogen has correctly pointed out that the history of the unconscious can be understood both as the history of a philosophical problem (*Problemgeschichte*) and as the history of a concept (*Begriffsgeschichte*).[6] Where and when this problem and this

---

[4] Similar questions are also raised by Elke Völmicke in *Das Unbewusste im Deutschen Idealismus* (Würzburg: Königshausen & Neumann, 2005), 14.
[5] On the status of the "human sciences" in this respect, see: Michel Foucault, *The Order of Things: An Archaeology of the Human Sciences* (1966; London: Routledge, 2002), 375–87; Bruce Mazlish, *The Uncertain Sciences* (1998; New Brunswick, NJ: Transaction, 2007), 1–36; Roger Smith, *Being Human: Historical Knowledge and the Creation of Human Nature* (New York: Columbia University Press, 2007), 1–61.
[6] See Arnim Regenbogen and Holger Brandes, "Unbewußte, das," *Europäische Enzyklopädie zu Philosophie und Wissenschaften*, ed. Hans Jörg Sandkühler, vol. IV (Hamburg: Felix Meiner, 1990), 647–61; here 647. See also, Thomas Mies and Holger

4   Angus Nicholls and Martin Liebscher

concept first arose is, however, a matter that could endlessly be debated. Some, for example, have found ideas relating to the unconscious in the ideas of Gautama Buddha (c.563–483 BCE); in Plato's (427–347 BCE) theory of the recollection of divine memory (*anamnesis*);[7] in the works of Plotinus (204–269 CE); in the theological writings of St. Augustine (354–430 CE) and Thomas Aquinas (1225–74); in German mystics such as Meister Eckhart (1260–1328) and Jakob Böhme (1567–1624); and even in poets such as Dante Alighieri (1265–1321) and Shakespeare (1564–1616).[8] With this myriad of sources and possible historical and cultural origins in mind, Ludger Lütkehaus has rightly observed that any comprehensive historical exploration of the unconscious would necessarily have to overstep national and even European boundaries.[9] Nonetheless, if our central concern here is the discourses on the unconscious which took place in nineteenth-century German thought, then the origin of the problem which these discourses seek to address is relatively easy to identify.

Petites perceptions and the unconscious: Descartes, Leibniz, Wolff, and Platner

The problem turns out to have originated in seventeenth-century France. When René Descartes (1596–1650) posits, in his *Meditations on First Philosophy* (1641), the central dualism of modern European thought – according to which being is divided into the categories of thinking and extended substance (*res cogitans* and *res extensa*) – he associates *res cogitans* or thinking substance exclusively with consciousness. The famous proposition *cogito ergo sum* ("I think therefore I am") thus relates the core of human being – in other words, the soul – exclusively to thought and therefore to consciousness. Since conscious thought alone guarantees the existence of the human subject, then it is literally impossible, in Cartesian terms, to conceive of unconscious mental states, since to be without consciousness would mean to lack any being whatsoever, as

---

Brandes, "Unbewußte, das," *Enzyklopädie Philosophie*, ed. Hans Jörg Sandkühler, vol. II (Hamburg: Felix Meiner, 1999), 1657–65.
[7] See Plato's dialogues entitled *Meno*, *Phaedo*, and *Phaedrus*.
[8] See, in this connection, Lancelot Law Whyte, *The Unconscious before Freud*, 2nd edn. (London: Julian Friedmann, 1978), 77–86; George Frankl, *The Social History of the Unconscious* (London: Open Gate, 1989); M. Kaiser-El-Safti, "Unbewußtes, das Unbewußte," *Historisches Wörterbuch der Philosophie*, ed. Joachim Ritter *et al.*, 12 vols. (Basel: Schwabe, 1971–2004), vol. XI, 124–33; here 124–5; David Edwards and Michael Jacobs, *Conscious and Unconscious* (Buckingham: Open University Press, 2003), 17–27.
[9] Ludger Lütkehaus, ed., *"Dieses wahre innere Afrika": Texte zur Entdeckung des Unbewußten vor Freud* (Gießen: Psychosozial Verlag, 2005), 11.

Descartes observes: "it could be that were I totally to cease from thinking, I should totally cease to exist."[10]

Descartes' definition of the human subject as *res cogitans* offers both a functional and a material definition of consciousness. In *functional* terms, Descartes outlines a structure, substance or ground within human subjectivity (that is, the soul) in which mental contents are cognized; while in *material* terms consciousness refers to those mental contents themselves which are apprehended: in everyday parlance the "facts," "stream" or "field" of consciousness.[11] In the British empiricism of John Locke and David Hume, the latter (material) sense of consciousness is maintained, while the former is regarded as being unsubstantiated. Consciousness, for Locke, is merely the "perception of what passes in a man's own mind," while for Hume it is the "inward sentiment" that arises from one's perceptions and ideas.[12] Since, however, the self or "I" to which these perceptions belong cannot be proven to exist on an empirical basis, the question as to the substantial ground of consciousness is regarded as being unanswerable, the self being, according to Hume's well-known formulation, nothing more than a "bundle" of different perceptions.[13]

In Germany, by contrast, Descartes' functional or substantial conception of consciousness received a more positive reception in the *Monadology* (1714) of Gottfried Wilhelm Leibniz. At the same time, however, Leibniz attempted to replace Cartesian dualism with a monism that would unify thinking and extended substance. For Leibniz, the entire universe is constituted of simple, immaterial, and indivisible unities known as monads, all of which are capable, albeit to vastly differing degrees, of having perceptions.[14] Every monad is unique and develops according to its own internal law, being endowed with what Leibniz variously calls appetite or striving. Each monad strives to achieve what it regards, from within the limitations of its own position in the universe, to be the apparent good.[15]

---

[10] René Descartes, *Meditations on First Philosophy*, ed. and trans. John Cottingham (Cambridge: Cambridge University Press, 1996), 18 (II, 27). See also: Johannes Oberthür, "Verdrängte Dunkelheit des Denkens: Descartes, Leibniz und die Kehrseite des Rationalismus," *Das Unbewusste*, ed. Michael B. Buchholz and Günter Gödde, 3 vols., vol. I: *Macht und Dynamik des Unbewussten: Auseinandersetzungen in Philosophie, Medizin und Psychoanalyse* (Gießen: Psychosozial Verlag, 2005), 34–69; here 40.

[11] A. Diemer, "Bewußtsein," *Historisches Wörterbuch der Philosophie*, vol. I, 888–96; here: 891.

[12] Quoted in ibid.

[13] David Hume, *A Treatise of Human Nature*, ed. David Fate Norton and Mary J. Norton (Oxford: Oxford University Press, 2000), 165.

[14] Gottfried Wilhelm Leibniz, *Monadology* (§§1–3), trans. Nicholas Rescher (Pittsburgh, PA: University of Pittsburgh Press, 1991), 17; see also Nicholas Jolley, *Leibniz* (London: Routledge, 2005), 5.

[15] Leibniz, *Philosophical Essays*, ed. and trans. R. Ariew and D. Garber (Indianapolis, IN: Hackett, 1989), 181. Quoted in Jolley, *Leibniz*, 67.

In being immaterial and directed towards the good, monads are seen by Leibniz as mirroring the qualities of God,[16] and in this respect they are at least theoretically capable of representing the whole universe, albeit only from their own particular points of view. The development of monads occurs in complete isolation: described by Leibniz as being "windowless," they are neither susceptible of alteration by external sources, nor do they have direct relationships with other monads.[17] Thus, although separate monads may seem to interact with one another causally, Leibniz's doctrine concerning the *harmonie préétablie* (pre-established harmony) between all forces or substances ensures that each monad develops independently and yet in perfect harmony with other monads.[18]

In Leibniz the ontological status of the human self, subject, or soul is thus secured by virtue of its status as a monad. Since the monad is constantly active and functions at all times as a mirror of the entire universe, it is (even during sleep) continually subject to perceptions about this universe; yet these perceptions are characterized by wide differences in terms of their clarity and distinctness, ranging from those of which the subject is completely unaware on the one hand, to those which are clear and distinct on the other, with endless gradations of clarity and distinctness existing between these two extremes.[19]

On the lower end of the scale of consciousness, there exist what Leibniz calls, in his *New Essays on Human Understanding* (*Nouveaux essais sur l'entendement humain*) both *petites perceptions* (small perceptions) and *perceptions insensibles* (unnoticed perceptions).[20] As its title suggests, this text (completed in 1705 but not published until 1765) constitutes Leibniz's most comprehensive response to John Locke's *Essay Concerning Human Understanding* (1690). Locke had expressed doubts concerning the Cartesian idea that the essence of the soul lies in its thinking activity, arguing that certain non-conscious states – like, for example, the state of sleep – demonstrate that the soul may experience interruptions in its thinking, and that it is therefore not purely to be identified with the activity of thought. In this way, Locke rules out the possibility that "any thing should think, and not be conscious of it."[21]

In response to Locke's argument, Leibniz proposes "there is in us an infinity of perceptions ... of which we are unaware because these

---

[16] Leibniz, *Monadology*, §56, 24.
[17] Ibid., §7, 17.
[18] Ibid., §78, 27.
[19] Ibid., §14, 18.
[20] Leibniz, *New Essays on Human Understanding*, ed. and trans. Peter Remnant and Jonathan Bennett (Cambridge: Cambridge University Press, 1996), 55.
[21] John Locke, *An Essay Concerning Human Understanding*, (London: Penguin, 1997), 113; (see book 2, chapter 1, §§10–19).

Introduction: thinking the unconscious 7

impressions are either too minute and too numerous, or else too unvarying, so that they are not sufficiently distinctive on their own." Thus, for example, what we experience as "the roaring noise of the sea" is actually the cumulative sensation of many individual waves crashing on the shore. Although each of these individual waves does not on its own create a sufficient impression to enter our consciousness, when combined they may in fact enter our conscious awareness. In this situation we are made conscious of the cumulative effect of the waves, but not of their discrete, individual existences. Similarly, when one has become habituated to living by a waterfall, the noise which it creates may escape our conscious awareness, fading into the background of our everyday existence.[22] In both the *New Essays* and the *Monadology*, Leibniz distinguishes between these *petites perceptions* (often termed simply *perceptions*), and what he calls *apperceptions*. Perceptions occur at a low level of consciousness and do not entail reflexive consciousness or thought, and for this reason Leibniz holds that even "beasts" may have perceptions. Apperceptions, by contrast, are perceptions of which the subject has a conscious or reflexive awareness, and which may be said to amount to conscious thoughts.[23]

Leibniz's theory of *petites perceptions* or perceptions without consciousness is normally seen as having inaugurated the German philosophical discourse on the unconscious.[24] Yet here a particular caution with regard to the use of terminology is in order. It is clear from Leibniz's argumentation that his notion of *petites perceptions* does not demarcate a type of perception that is radically different from what he calls apperceptions or perceptions of which one is reflexively aware; in fact, it may be argued that the difference consists only in the intensity, clarity and distinctness of these perceptions rather than in their fundamental type. As we shall see, this has led some to suggest that in the case of Leibniz, the term *unbewusst* (unconscious) might well be replaced by that of *unterbewusst* (beneath consciousness), designating a field of perception which merely exists beneath a particular threshold of conscious awareness, but which could easily become conscious upon the focusing of one's attention.

This is certainly the sense in which Leibniz's idea of *petites perceptions* was interpreted by two of his most important successors in the German tradition of psychology – Christian Wolff (1679–1764) and Ernst Platner (1744–1818) – both of whom are also seen as being key figures in the history of the unconscious. In his *Rational Thoughts on God, the Soul of Man, and Also All Things in General* (*Vernünfftige Gedancken von Gott, der Welt und*

---

[22] Leibniz, *New Essays*, 54–5.
[23] Ibid., 134; Leibniz, *Monadology*, §14, 18.
[24] See, for example, Lütkehaus, *"Dieses wahre innere Afrika,"* 19; Regenbogen and Brandes, "Unbewußte, das," 648; Kaiser-El-Safti, "Unbewußtes, das Unbewußte," 124–5.

der Seele des Menschen, auch allen Dingen überhaupt, 1720), Wolff defines consciousness as the self-reflexive knowledge that we represent things to ourselves as being external to us, and as the ability to differentiate individual things from one another (§§728, 729). Wolff argues, for example, that when he holds a mirror in front of his face, he is conscious of the fact that he is holding the mirror, that he sees his own image in the mirror, and that the mirror is an object which is differentiated from himself as well as from other objects in his immediate surroundings (§729). Were he not capable of such differentiation, then he would not be conscious of these objects, since "when we do not notice the difference between the things that attend us; then we are not conscious of the things that fall into our senses."[25] Similarly, when one is reading a book, although one may hear a conversation going on the background, if one does not pay attention to the conversation then one is not conscious of it (§729). Consciousness is thus defined by Wolff in Cartesian terms: in relation to clarity and distinctness. If we fail to differentiate between the things that occur to our senses, this leads to what Wolff terms (§731) "darkness of thoughts" (*Dunckelheit der Gedancken*).[26]

Wolff's consideration of obscure or dark thoughts did not go unnoticed by his philosophical successors, and led, albeit indirectly, to the raising of aesthetic questions which would later re-emerge in German idealism and romanticism. In 1759, the Swiss mathematician Johann Georg Sulzer (1720–79) opined that philosophers should pay the closest attention to the dark areas of the soul (*die genauste Aufmerksamkeit auf die dunkeln Gegenden der Seele ... richten*).[27] Yet as Hans Adler has pointed out, Sulzer's project was arguably couched in Enlightenment terms: that of exploring, conquering, and in a sense domesticating the dark areas of the soul by exposing them to rational analysis.[28] It was the German philosopher Alexander Baumgarten (1714–62) who thought that these dark areas of the soul called for a different method of consideration than that normally deployed by traditional metaphysics. Already in the first edition of his *Metaphysica* (1739), Baumgarten sees obscure or dark

---

[25] [Wenn wir den Unterschied der Dinge nicht bemercken, die uns zugegen sind; so sind wir uns dessen nicht bewußt, was in unsere Sinnen fället.] Christian Wolff, *Vernünfftige Gedancken von Gott, Gesammelte Werke*, ed. J. École *et al.*, part 1, vol. II (Hildesheim: Georg Olms, 1983), 455.

[26] Ibid., 457.

[27] Johann Georg Sulzer, *Kurzer Begriff aller Wißenschaften und andern Theile der Gelehrsamkeit, worin jeder nach seinem Inhalt, Nuzen und Vollkommenheit kürzlich beschrieben wird*, 2nd edn. (1759), §206, 159; quoted in Hans Adler, "Fundus Animae – der Grund der Seele: Zur Gnoseologie des Dunkeln in der Aufklärung," *Deutsche Vierteljahrsschrift für Literaturwissenschaft und Geistesgeschichte* 62 (1998): 197–220; here 203.

[28] Adler, "Fundus Animae," 203.

Introduction: thinking the unconscious 9

perceptions (*perceptiones obscurae*) as being the foundation of the soul (*fundus animae*), and in the fourth (1759) edition of the *Metaphysica* this Latin construction is replaced with the German *Grund der Seele*. In §1 of Baumgarten's *Aesthetica* (part 1: 1750; part 2: 1758) those perceptions which are obscure, dark, or inferior (*gnoseologia inferior*) are associated with the particular, sensitive, and sensuous modes of cognition (*cognitionis sensitiuae*) found in poetry, as opposed to the general, clear, and distinct modes of conceptual cognition found in philosophy; while the analysis of inferior, obscure, or sensuous cognition belongs to aesthetics – otherwise known as the theory of the liberal arts (*theoria liberalium artium*) – clear and distinct cognitions belong to metaphysics.[29]

A less innovative reception of Wolff can be found in the work of Ernst Platner, whose *Philosophical Aphorisms* (*Philosophische Aphorismen*, 1776) is widely regarded as the first German text to use the word *Unbewußtseyn* (unconsciousness).[30] Platner inherits the essentially Leibnizian epistemological framework of Wolff. The soul (*Seele*) is regarded as a substance (*Substanz*) and a power (*Kraft*) which brings forth impressions or ideas (*Wirkungen, Ideen*). Since power or *Kraft* is defined solely in terms of activity (*Thätigkeit*), the soul must always be active; otherwise it would cease to exist. This leads Platner to argue that the soul continues to have ideas during sleep, and that "the soul is not always conscious of its ideas" (*Die Seele ist sich nicht ihrer Ideen immer bewußt*). Following Leibniz and Wolff, Platner refers to those ideas with consciousness (*mit Bewußtseyn*) as apperceptions, and to those without consciousness (*ohne Bewußtseyn*) as dark or obscure representations (*dunkle Vorstellungen*). In this way, the life of the soul is seen by Platner as being an unbroken series of ideas or impressions, which wax and wane between apperceptions and perceptions, waking and sleeping (*Wachen und Schlaf*), consciousness and unconsciousness (*Bewußtseyn und Unbewußtseyn*).[31]

Kant's anthropology and the "dark map of the mind"

With the possible exception of Leibniz, Immanuel Kant arguably determined the way in which unconscious phenomena were understood in nineteenth-century German thought more than any other philosopher of the eighteenth century. Although Kant's opposition to some of the ideas

---

[29] Alexander Gottlieb Baumgarten, *Aesthetica*, §1 (1750), quoted in ibid., 206.
[30] Kurt Joachim Grau, for example, describes Platner as the creator of the word "unbewußt." See Kurt Joachim Grau, *Bewusstsein, Unbewusstes, Unterbewusstes* (Munich: Rösl, 1922), 63. See also Lütkehaus, "*Dieses wahre innere Afrika,*" 20.
[31] Ernst Platner, *Philosophische Aphorismen nebst einigen Anleitungen zur philosophischen Geschichte* (Leipzig: Schwickertscher Verlag, 1776), §11–19, §25, 5–9.

of Leibniz and particularly to the latter's notion of pre-established harmony is well known,[32] there is nonetheless, in the early (pre-critical) Kant, a positive reception of Leibniz's ideas of *petites perceptions*. The earliest example of this is to be found in Kant's *Attempt to Introduce the Concept of Negative Magnitudes into Philosophy* (*Versuch, den Begriff der negativen Grössen in die Weltweisheit einzuführen*, 1763), part 3 of which attempts to apply the mathematical concept of negative magnitude to psychology, and especially to the coming to be and passing away of thoughts. How is it, Kant asks, that at one moment he can be thinking of the sun, and the next minute this thought disappears, only to be replaced by new thoughts? His answer is that, just as in physics a force is cancelled by an opposing force of equal or greater intensity, so too in our minds are thoughts negated or cancelled by mental contents which oppose them. This argument is then advanced in terms of clarity and distinctness: "the clearer and the more distinct a certain idea is made," according to Kant, "the more the remaining ideas are obscured [*verdunkelt*] and the more their clarity is diminished."[33] Those thoughts which are, in Kant's words, *verdunkelt* (darkened or obscured) would thus appear to bear some similarity to Leibniz's *petites perceptions*, as well as to the "dark thoughts" (*dunkle Gedancken, dunkle Vorstellungen*) of Wolff and Platner respectively. For this reason it is no coincidence that Kant invokes Leibniz in this context, opining that

There is something imposing and, it seems to me, profoundly true in this thought of Leibniz: the soul embraces the universe only with its faculty of representation, though only an infinitesimally tiny part of these representations is clear.[34]

Kant's consideration of so-called "dark" or unclear thoughts (*dunkle Vorstellungen*) receives its most detailed treatment in his *Anthropology from a Pragmatic Point of View* (*Anthropologie in pragmatischer Hinsicht*, 1798),[35]

---

[32] See Kant's *The Employment in Natural Philosophy of Metaphysics Combined with Geometry, of which Sample I Contains the Physical Monadology* (1756), *Theoretical Philosophy, 1755–1770*, trans. David Walford and Ralf Meerbore, *The Cambridge Edition of the Works of Immanuel Kant* (Cambridge: Cambridge University Press, 1992), 47–66; see also the editors' introduction to this piece on pages lii–liv.

[33] Ibid., 234 (translation altered); [in je höherem Grade eine gewisse Idee klar oder deutlich gemacht wird, desto mehr werden die übrige verdunkelt und ihre Klarheit verringert]. Kant, *Werke in sechs Bänden*, ed. Wilhelm Weischedel, 6 vols. (Darmstadt: Wissenschaftliche Buchgesellschaft, 1960), vol. I, 810–11.

[34] Kant, *Theoretical Philosophy, 1755–1770*, 237. [Es steckt etwas Großes, und, wie mich dünkt, sehr Richtiges in dem Gedanken des Herrn von Leibniz: Die Seele befasset das ganze Universum mit ihrer Vorstellungskraft, obgleich nur ein unendlich kleiner Teil dieser Vorstellungen klar ist.] Kant, *Werke in sechs Bänden*, vol. I, 814.

[35] Although this text appeared in 1798, towards the very end of Kant's career, it originally emerged from much earlier sources. As Manfred Kuehn and John H. Zammito

section 5 of which is entitled "On the representations that we have without being conscious of them" (*Von den Vorstellungen, die wir haben, ohne uns ihrer bewusst zu sein*). Here Kant takes issue with Locke's doubts about the existence of unconscious perceptions or thoughts by positing two levels of consciousness: indirect or mediated (*mittelbar*) consciousness and direct or unmediated (*unmittelbar*) consciousness. Kant asks us to imagine that we see a human figure on a meadow in the distance; although at such a distance we cannot distinguish the person's eyes, nose, and mouth, we nonetheless make the *assumption* that what we have before us is a human being. Yet, according to Kant, in this example we are strictly speaking unconscious (or at least not *directly* conscious) of that person's individual parts (eyes, nose, mouth, etc. ...), which also means that we are unconscious or only indirectly conscious of that person as a whole. If we fail to represent to ourselves what Kant calls, in relation to the above example, the "part-representations of a whole" (*Teilvorstellungen eines Ganzen*), then we must also fail to achieve a clear and distinct representation of the object before us, since clarity consists in distinguishing an object from its surroundings, while distinctness lies in knowledge of the entire object in terms of all its parts. Conscious or unmediated representations are thus characterized by clarity and distinctness, and lead to knowledge, while mediated representations, of which we are conscious in only an indirect way, are described by Kant as being *dunkel* (dark or obscure).[36]

This argument prepares the way for one of the most influential and highly metaphorical passages on "unconscious," "dark," or "obscure" representations (*dunkele Vorstellungen*) to have appeared in the German language. Kant describes as "immeasurable" (*unermeßlich*) "the field of sensuous intuitions and sensations of which we are not conscious, even though we can undoubtedly conclude that we have them."[37] This leads him to conclude that our clear and distinct representations represent only "infinitely few points" (*unendlich wenige Punkte*) on the field of consciousness, to the extent that "only a few places on the vast map of our mind are illuminated" (*auf der großen Karte unseres Gemüts nur wenig Stellen*

---

have noted, Kant's interest in anthropology began with his course in physical geography (inaugurated in 1758), as well as with his first lecture course on anthropology in the winter semester of 1772–3. Manfred Kuehn, *Kant: A Biography* (Cambridge: Cambridge University Press, 2001), 406–9; John H. Zammito, *Kant, Herder and the Birth of Anthropology* (Chicago: University of Chicago Press, 2002), 284–92.

[36] Kant, *Anthropologie in pragmatischer Hinsicht, Werke in sechs Bänden*, vol. VI, 417–18. Translated by Robert B. Louden as *Anthropology from a Pragmatic Point of View* (Cambridge: Cambridge University Press, 2006), 23–4.

[37] [das Feld unserer Sinnenanschauungen und Empfindungen, deren wir uns nicht bewußt sind, ob wir gleich unbezweifelt schließen können, daß wir sie haben ... sei ... unermeßlich]. Kant, *Anthropology*, 24; Kant, *Werke in sechs Bänden*, vol. VI, 418.

illuminiert sind).[38] This passage would go on to inspire, either directly or indirectly, an array of Romantic speculations on the unconscious,[39] one of the most interesting of which is the novel by Jean Paul (Johann Paul Friedrich Richter, 1763–1825): *Selina or on the Immortality of the Soul* (*Selina oder über die Unsterblichkeit der Seele*, 1827). Here Jean Paul argues that "we make ... much too small or much too narrow measurements of the kingdom of the self, if we neglect the enormous kingdom of the unconscious, this true inner Africa," a metaphor which has led Ludger Lütkehaus rightly to posit a relationship between the discourses of European colonialism and the supposed "conquest" of the unconscious.[40]

Despite the suggestiveness of Kant's "dark map of the mind," he goes on to argue that, although "the field of obscure representations is the largest of the human being," it actually "belongs only to physiological anthropology, not to pragmatic anthropology, and so it is properly disregarded here."[41] While *physiological* anthropology, in Kant's view, describes only "what nature makes of the human being," *pragmatic* anthropology investigates what man as a "free-acting being makes of himself, or can and should make of himself."[42] The purpose of pragmatic anthropology is thus to prepare the way for what Kant calls practical philosophy or ethics: that of understanding human nature in order that we may change it by instituting moral laws arrived at by reason alone. This important distinction does not, however, prevent Kant from describing, almost as an aside, what physiological anthropology might be like. In this connection he opines that

often we are ourselves a play of obscure representations [*dunkeler Vorstellungen*], and our understanding is unable to save itself from the absurdities into which they have placed it, even though it recognizes them as illusions. Such is the case with sexual love, in so far as its actual aim is not benevolence but rather enjoyment of its object.[43]

[38] Kant, *Anthropology*, 24; Kant, *Werke in sechs Bänden*, vol. VI, 418.
[39] In this connection, see chapter 4 of this volume, by Rüdiger Görner.
[40] [Wir machen ... von dem Länderreichtum des Ich viel zu kleine oder enge Messungen, wenn wir das ungeheure Reich des Unbewussten, dieses wahre innere Afrika, auslassen.] Jean Paul, *Selina*, quoted in Lütkehaus, *"Dieses wahre innere Afrika,"* 77. For Lütkehaus's discussion of the unconscious and colonialism, see 7.
[41] Kant, *Anthropology*, 25; [So ist das Feld dunkler Vorstellungen das größte im Menschen ... gehört die Theorie selber doch nur zur physiologischen Anthropologie, nicht zur pragmatischen, worauf es eigentlich hier gesehen ist.] Kant, *Werke in sechs Bänden*, vol. VI, 419.
[42] Kant, *Anthropology*, 3. [Die physiologische Menschenkenntnis geht auf die Erforschung dessen, was die Natur aus dem Menschen macht, die pragmatische auf das, was er, als freihandelndes Wesen, aus sich selber macht, oder machen kann und soll.] Kant, *Werke in sechs Bänden*, vol. VI, 399.
[43] Kant, *Anthropology*, 25; [öfter aber noch sind wir selbst ein Spiel dunkeler Vorstellungen, und unser Verstand vermag nicht, sich wider die Ungereimtheiten zu retten, in die ihn

Here Kant's emphasis seems to have shifted from dark or obscure representations to something altogether more elemental: sexual desire. In Kant's mature critical philosophy, such desires are regarded as belonging to the broad class of inclinations (*Neigungen*), which, considered merely on their account (that is, in abstraction from their relation to the moral law), have no proper place in ethics. Ethics as such is referred to by Kant as pure moral philosophy (*reine Moralphilosophie*), and is to be prioritized over practical anthropology, being "cleansed of everything that may be only empirical and that belongs to anthropology."[44] Thus, while Kant seemed to have opened the door to what might be called "dark," "obscure," or even "unconscious" desires in §5 of the *Anthropology*, this door is, if not closed altogether, then certainly on the way to being shut by the time of the *Groundwork of the Metaphysics of Morals* (*Grundlegung zur Metaphysik der Sitten*) of 1785. And it is precisely this door to the unconscious which Kant's nineteenth-century successors in the related movements of German romanticism and German idealism would try to pry open. This is not to suggest that Kantian ethics takes no account of what Kant refers to as the empirical component of ethics and the possible unconscious desires which may underlie them; rather, it is to maintain that, as is arguably the case with respect to the critical philosophy in general, Kant's primary interest is to explore the nature of reason and to identify the rational grounds of thought and action. In short: Kant was more attuned to light than to darkness, and therefore shied away from direct consideration of the unconscious.

The faculties and divisions of the Kantian subject

Despite the fact that Kant's discussion of dark, obscure, or unconscious representations (*dunkele Vorstellungen*) certainly emerges from the tradition of Leibniz, Wolff, and Platner, his position on this issue represents a marked departure from these earlier thinkers. As John H. Zammito observes:

What would differentiate Kant from the Wolffian school was his abandonment of the idea that all the mental faculties could be arrayed in a single *continuum*

---

der Einfluß derselben versetzt, ob er sie gleich als Täuschung anerkennt. So ist es mit der Geschlechtsliebe, so fern sie eigentlich nicht das Wohlwollen, sondern vielmehr den Genuß ihres Gegenstandes beabsichtigt.] Kant, *Werke in sechs Bänden*, vol. VI, 419.

[44] Kant, *Groundwork of the Metaphysics of Morals*, ed. and trans. Mary J. Gregor, in Kant, *Practical Philosophy*, ed. Mary J. Gregor, *The Cambridge Edition of the Works of Immanuel Kant* (Cambridge: Cambridge University Press, 1997), 44; [eine reine Moralphilosophie zu bearbeiten, die von allem, was nur empirisch sein mag und zur Anthropologie gehört, völlig gesäubert wäre]. Kant, *Werke in sechs Bänden*, vol. IV, 12–13.

of cognitive clarity and distinctness for the idea that there was a categorical *disjunction* between sensibility and understanding.[45]

In the *Anthropology*, Kant's distinction between the faculties of sensibility (*Sinnlichkeit*) and the understanding (*Verstand*) – a distinction which is outlined at greater length in the first *Critique* – appears almost immediately after his discussion of dark or obscure representations. In §7, Kant contrasts sensibility with the understanding, arguing that only the latter, when conjoined with sensibility, can offer us cognition and therefore knowledge. While sensibility is merely passive, providing us with only the raw sensory data relating to external objects, the understanding is active and discursive, bringing concepts (such as, for example, unity and causality) to bear upon the data provided by sensibility.[46] In this way, Kant argues that we can only have access to *phenomena* (things as they appear to us, filtered through our cognitive faculties) rather than to *noumena* (things as they may be "in themselves," independently of our cognition of them). In §§8–11 of the *Anthropology*, Kant makes it clear that sensibility is not to be held directly responsible for the darkness or obscurity of our representations, arguing (for example, in §9) that while the senses do not in themselves confuse things, it is the understanding which may err if it judges too hastily.[47] Thus, if we refer back to Kant's earlier example of the human figure standing at a distance from us in a meadow, it is the understanding which judges this figure to be a human, but without the necessary sensory data which would make this into a conscious (in the sense of clear and distinct) object of knowledge.

Although the exact date of Kant's discussion of unconscious representations in the *Anthropology* is difficult to determine, through a comparative analysis of arguments which appear in the first and second versions of the "Transcendental Deduction" (*transzendentale Deduktion*) of the first *Critique*, Arnim Regenbogen argues that this development must have taken place in the time between these two versions, that is: between 1781 and 1787.[48] In the "A" version of the first *Critique* (A100–103), imagination (*Einbildung*) has the role of synthesizing representations and of conjoining sensibility with the understanding. Kant sees the activity of the imagination as being executed a priori; that is, as making possible the synthetic unity of experience. On this basis, he assumes (at A117) that "all representations have a necessary relation to a possible empirical

---

[45] Zammito, *Kant, Herder and the Birth of Anthropology*, 52.
[46] Kant, *Anthropology*, 29–30; *Werke in sechs Bänden*, vol. VI, 424–425.
[47] Kant, *Anthropology*, 35; *Werke in sechs Bänden*, vol. VI, 433.
[48] Regenbogen and Brandes, "Unbewußte, das," 649.

Introduction: thinking the unconscious 15

consciousness: for if they did not have this, and if it were entirely impossible to become conscious of them, that would be as much as to say that they did not exist at all."[49] Kant reiterates this view in §24 of the *Prolegomena to Any Future Metaphysics* (*Prolegomena zu einer jeden künftigen Metaphysik*, 1783), where he states that there is no level of psychological obscurity or darkness (*Dunkelheit*) that cannot be regarded as a form of consciousness, since obscure or dark representations are only those which have been prevailed over by their stronger or more intense counterparts.[50]

Things change, however, in the "B" version of the "Transcendental Deduction." At B132–136, Kant establishes what he calls the "original-synthetic unity of apperception" (*ursprünglich-synthetische Einheit der Apperzeption*), the "I" which accompanies and makes possible all representations that are given to me.[51] This "I" or thinking subject is, says Kant, an *object* of inner sense or intuition, yet at the same time this "I" is also a *subject* that thinks discursively through the operations of the understanding. As Kant makes clear at B150–156, this dual function of the "I" – as both the intuited *object* of inner sense, and as the active thinking *subject* made possible through the understanding – leads to what must be regarded as a split or divided "I." Since the "I" as a thinking subject (as apperception) is dependent on the faculty of the understanding, it can have no direct cognitive access to itself as object, in intuition.[52] This, according to Kant at B153, is because the understanding has no capacity for intuitions, and can therefore not take intuitions "up into itself" (*in sich aufnehmen*), leading him to conclude (at B158) that "the consciousness of oneself is … far from being a cognition of oneself" (*das Bewußtsein seiner selbst ist also noch lange nicht ein Erkenntnis seiner selbst*).[53]

A similar point is also made in §7 of the *Anthropology*. Here Kant argues that, although "it is true that I as a thinking being am one and the same subject with myself as a sensing being,"[54] full self-cognition

---

[49] Kant, *Critique of Pure Reason*, ed. and trans. Paul Guyer and Allen W. Wood, *The Cambridge Edition of the Works of Immanuel Kant* (Cambridge: Cambridge University Press, 1998), 237; [Alle Vorstellungen haben eine notwendige Beziehung auf ein mögliches empirisches Bewußtsein: denn hätten sie dieses nicht, und wäre es gänzlich unmöglich, sich ihrer bewußt zu werden: so würde das so viel sagen, sie existieren gar nicht.] *Werke in sechs Bänden*, vol. II, 174.
[50] [keine psychologische Dunkelheit, die nicht als ein Bewußtsein betrachtet werden könnte, welches nur von anderem stärkeren überwogen wird]. Kant, *Werke in sechs Bänden*, vol. III, 174.
[51] Kant, *Critique of Pure Reason*, 246–8; *Werke in sechs Bänden*, vol. II, 136–40.
[52] Kant, *Critique of Pure Reason*, 256–9; *Werke in sechs Bänden*, vol. II, 147–52.
[53] Kant, *Critique of Pure Reason*, 260; *Werke in sechs Bänden*, vol. II, 153.
[54] Kant, *Anthropology*, 33; [Ich, als denkendes Wesen, bin zwar mit mir, als Sinnenwesen, ein und dasselbe Subjekt.] *Werke in sechs Bänden*, vol. VI, 430.

remains impossible. This is because the "I" of apperception or reflection (*Ich der Reflexion*) is not equipped to cognize itself as "inner experience" (*innere Erfahrung*) which is described as "a manifold of empirical inner intuition" (*ein Mannigfaltiges der empirischen inneren Anschauung*).[55] Thus, if Kant's definition of unconscious representations is applied to the cognitive state of affairs described here, then it would seem that, since clear and distinct *cognitive* knowledge of the self and all its parts is not possible, then parts of the self remain, in Kant's terms, dark (*dunkel*), obscure, or unconscious.

The divided self which is presented in the "Transcendental Deduction" of Kant's first *Critique*, in his writings on moral philosophy (including the second *Critique*), as well as in his *Anthropology* – a self which combines the natural necessity of physiological sensations, inclinations, and intuitions on the one hand with the discursive spontaneity of the understanding and the freedom associated with reason on the other – persists in the final part his critical philosophy: the *Critique of Judgment* (*Kritik der Urteilskraft*, 1790). This text can, alongside the *Anthropology*, be seen as having exerted a profound influence upon how ideas relating to the unconscious were theorized in nineteenth-century German thought, especially in relation to aesthetics.

In the second part of the *Critique of Judgment*, entitled the "Critique of Teleological Judgment" (*Kritik der teleologischen Urteilskraft*), Kant explains how a natural organism like a bird, in displaying harmonious and proportionate relationships between its constituent parts, gives rise to a sense of teleology or objective purposiveness (*objektive Zweckmäßigkeit*, §61, B267–268/A265–266). Since, however, we can only know things as they appear to us rather than as they are "in themselves," we cannot know whether this apparent design exists in nature as an objective reality; rather, our judgment relating to the objective purposiveness of this bird is seen by Kant as being reflective (§75), in that we cognize the bird through the reflective concept of an organism or organized being (*organisiertes Wesen*, §66), according to which the parts of the bird (for example, its wings, and feathers) are seen as having interrelated functions which exist teleologically in relation to the whole.[56]

When we view such a bird, we may also deem it to be *beautiful*, and in so doing, we endow it with what Kant calls *subjective* as opposed to *objective* purposiveness. While the objective purposiveness of the bird exists in our thinking of it in conceptual terms as an organism whose integrated parts

---

[55] Kant, *Anthropology*, 32; *Werke in sechs Bänden*, vol. VI, 430.
[56] Kant, *Critique of the Power of Judgment*, ed. and trans. Paul Guyer and Eric Matthews, *The Cambridge Edition of the Works of Immanuel Kant* (Cambridge: Cambridge University Press, 2000), 247–8; *Werke in sechs Bänden*, vol. V, 319.

are designed to help it survive and prosper, *subjective* purposiveness suggests a form of harmony which is without any apparent use or purpose, but which gives rise to certain feelings of pleasure (*Wohlgefallen*) that correspond with the term "beauty" (*Schönheit*, §17, B62/A61). The beautiful object in nature thus suggests a pleasing design at work in nature, but a design for which we can have no corresponding concept, since aesthetic judgments do not proceed by way of rules and concepts, but rather arise from what Kant calls (§9, B29/A29) the "free play" (*freies Spiel*) of our cognitive powers (*Erkenntniskräfte*).

For Kant, beauty in nature is prior to beauty in art. Yet like beauty in nature, the beautiful work of art must appear to be purely spontaneous and free from any "arbitrary rules" (*willkürliche Regeln*), producing in us the idea of a purposiveness which is free in the sense of being subject only to its own internal laws (§45).[57] In §46 of the third *Critique*, Kant insists that such beautiful works of art emerge from what he calls genius, defined as the talent or natural gift (*Naturgabe*) which "gives the rule to art" (*welches der Kunst die Regel gibt*).[58] This talent, which Kant describes as the inborn productive faculty of the artist, belongs to nature, and cannot be taught, conceptually reconstructed, or even explained by the artist or genius himself. Thus, as Kant observes of Homer (§47), he does not know how his ideas come into being, and so cannot teach his mode of composition as a method.[59]

In Kant's third *Critique* we once again find a human subject that is split, and one which is now, in addition, not transparent to itself, in that the artist's genius is given to him by the hand of nature (*von der Hand der Natur erteilt*, §47) and he cannot, therefore, explain on a conscious or conceptual level how he produces beautiful works of art.[60] Beauty in nature and the phenomenon of genius thus suggested to Kant that there may be a deeper, inherent relation between nature (or its supersensible ground) and the subject, than he had considered in the first *Critique*, while also pointing to a creative and possibly unconscious (in the sense of obscure or uncognized) role played by nature in human subjectivity and creativity.

As Andrew Bowie observes, Kant's aim in the third *Critique* is to "link the harmony manifest in aesthetic apprehension of natural objects with the idea of natural teleology, thereby revealing the ultimate connection of nature as a whole to the ways in which we think about it."[61] Yet these

---

[57] Kant, *Critique of the Power of Judgment*, 185; *Werke in sechs Bänden*, vol. V, 404–405.
[58] Kant, *Critique of the Power of Judgment*, 186; *Werke in sechs Bänden*, vol. V, 405.
[59] Kant, *Critique of the Power of Judgment*, 187–188; *Werke in sechs Bänden*, vol. V, 408.
[60] Kant, *Critique of the Power of Judgment*, 188; *Werke in sechs Bänden*, vol. V, 408.
[61] Andrew Bowie, *Aesthetics and Subjectivity from Kant to Nietzsche*, 2nd edn. (Manchester: Manchester University Press, 2003), 32.

speculative questions gestured beyond the bounds of Kant's critical philosophy, which explains how subjectivity makes cognition possible, while deliberately remaining silent about what nature and human subjectivity may be like "in themselves" as well as how they may be interrelated, since (according to the very terms of Kant's project) such questions are absolutely impossible to answer. Thus, as Birgit Althans and Jörg Zirfas have observed, although the unconscious is a theme which runs through Kant's metaphysics, his moral philosophy, his anthropology, and his aesthetics, it never became an explicit question for consideration in any of Kant's works, precisely because it could not be further developed within the framework of Kant's system.[62]

But in response to the highly suggestive arguments of the "Transcendental Deduction," the third *Critique* and the *Anthropology*, Kant's successors in nineteenth-century German thought stepped beyond the bounds of the critical philosophy in what were radically speculative, innovative and (in some cases) completely fanciful ways, actively theorizing about the role played by nature in the human subject, a role which they often described through the term *unbewusst* (unconscious). It is the nineteenth-century German responses not only to Kant's suggestive discussions of unconscious phenomena, but also to those found in figures like Leibniz, Wolff, Platner, and Baumgarten, that form the central subject of this volume.

Reflections on recent scholarship, on methodology and on terminology

In recent years, as yet untranslated German-language scholarship has sought to offer a systematic account of how the concept of the unconscious and related ideas developed during the three centuries prior to its becoming the cardinal term of psychoanalysis. Volume I of the monumental three-volume project entitled simply *The Unconscious* (*Das Unbewusste*, edited by Michael B. Buchholz and Günter Gödde, 2005–6) examines philosophical, medical and psychoanalytic theorizations of the unconscious from Descartes to the present;[63] while other studies – like Odo Marquard's *Transcendental Idealism, Romantic Philosophy of Nature, Psychoanalysis* (*Transzendentaler Idealismus, romantische Naturphilosophie, Psychoanalyse*, 1987); Wilhelm W. Hemecker's

---

[62] Birgit Althans and Jörg Zirfas, "Die unbewusste Karte des Gemüts – Immanuel Kants Projekt der Anthropologie," *Das Unbewusste*, ed. Michael B. Buchholz and Günter Gödde, vol. I (Gießen: Psychosozial Verlag, 2005), 70–94; here 72.

[63] Michael B. Buchholz and Günter Gödde, eds., *Das Unbewusste*, 3 vols., vol. I: *Macht und Dynamik des Unbewussten: Auseinandersetzungen in Philosophie, Medizin und Psychoanalyse*; vol. II: *Das Unbewusste in aktuellen Diskursen: Anschlüsse*; vol. III: *Das Unbewusste in der Praxis: Erfahrungen verschiedener Professionen* (Gießen: Psychosozial Verlag, 2005–2006).

Before Freud: Philosophical-Historical Preconditions of Psychoanalysis (Vor Freud: Philosophiegeschichtliche Voraussetzungen der Psychoanalyse, 1991);[64] and more recently, Elke Völmicke's The Unconscious in German Idealism (Das Unbewusste im deutschen Idealismus, 2005) – offer intensive analyses of how eighteenth- and nineteenth-century thinkers like Kant, Goethe, Johann Gottlieb Fichte (1762–1814), Friedrich Schelling (1775–1854), Arthur Schopenhauer (1788–1860), and Friedrich Nietzsche (1844–1900), among others, either conceptualized the unconscious or may have influenced the origins of psychoanalysis by other means.

Some of the conceptual and terminological issues at stake in the present volume are highlighted in the introduction to Völmicke's book, and especially in her thoroughgoing critique of the earlier approach favored by Odo Marquard. Marquard's study is based on the premise that certain categories and concepts found in psychoanalysis – like, for example, the unconscious, repression (Verdrängung), defense (Abwehr), and resistance (Widerstand), among others – are philosophical categories which can already be found in German idealism and Naturphilosophie.[65] Transcendental philosophy, by which Marquard means the respective systems of Kant, Fichte and Schelling, offers a genetic-historical theory of the "I" or subject. What unites all three of these systems, according to Marquard, is the different ways in which they lead to what he calls (following Schelling) the depotentialization (Depotenzierung) or the reduction of autonomy of the rational "I" or subject. In being characterized by a series of tensions and contradictions – between the rational, free and autonomous self and the self of sensuous intuitions and natural-physiological proclivities (Kant); between the self-positing "I" or subject and the "not-I" upon which the identity of the "I" depends (Fichte); and between the self as conscious reason and unconscious nature (Schelling) – transcendental idealism leads to the empowerment (Ermächtigung) of what is variously conceived of as the not-I (Nicht-Ich), the non-rational (Unvernunft), and drive-nature (Triebnatur) within the subject. In Marquard's view, this empowerment of the "not-I" gives rise to a continuous tradition – beginning with Kant, and developing via Friedrich Schiller, Friedrich Schelling, Carl Gustav Carus, Arthur Schopenhauer, and Friedrich Nietzsche – before entering the work of Freud. While Freud's attention to this tradition was blocked by the decidedly non-idealist scientific-medical culture of the late nineteenth century, Marquard contends that psychoanalytic categories *are* philosophical categories, because they *were* the philosophical

---

[64] Wilhelm W. Hemecker, *Vor Freud: Philosophiegeschichtliche Voraussetzungen der Psychoanalyse* (Munich: Philosophia, 1991).
[65] Odo Marquard, *Transzendentaler Idealismus, romantische Naturphilosophie, Psychoanalyse* (Cologne: Dinter, 1987), 1.

categories of transcendental idealism before they *became* the psychoanalytic categories of Freud.[66]

Taking issue with Marquard, Völmicke's study underlines some of the radical discontinuities between the concept of the unconscious in both the German Enlightenment and in German idealism and the use of this term by Freud. As we have seen in the cases of Leibniz, Wolff, and Platner, as well as in Kant's *Anthropology*, unconscious (in the sense of dark or obscure) perceptions are merely weaker or lesser forms of consciousness which theoretically are capable of becoming conscious; while as Andrew Bowie shows in chapter 2 of this study, the unconscious in the early Schelling revolves around the connections between subjectivity, nature, and freedom, and the capacity of art to unveil these connections. These various formulations are indeed difficult to equate with "*the* unconscious" in its various Freudian manifestations, and this diversity of unconscious phenomena in the German tradition has, in turn, led to diversity in the German terminology.

In a study published in 1922, Kurt Joachim Grau offers an account of this terminology which remains useful and provocative today. *Das Unbewusste* (the unconscious), according to Grau, refers to an area of mental life of which the self can have no consciousness or knowledge at all. For this reason Grau, who was a harsh critic of Freud, expresses doubts as whether it is meaningful to talk about "*the* unconscious" at all, since by definition we can have no experience of this realm as an object. The term *unterbewusst* (beneath or under consciousness) is associated by Grau with the *petites perceptions* or *dunkle Vorstellungen* of Leibniz, Wolff, and Platner – referring to those perceptions of which we are not directly aware, but which are "in" consciousness and which can, under the right conditions, come to our awareness. Finally the term *bewusstlos* (without consciousness) simply refers to non-living objects without mentality. Grau sees Ernst Platner as being the first person to use the term *Unbewusstsein* (unconsciousness) in his *Philosophical Aphorisms* of 1776.[67] To the best of our knowledge, the first German dictionary entry on the term *unbewusst* appears in Adelung's dictionary of 1780, in which it is simply defined as referring to things which are unknown. The substantive masculine form *der Unbewusst* (an interesting early variation on the eventual standard neutral usage, *das Unbewusste*) is simply described in Adelung as being the condition of not knowing something (*Der Zustand des Nichtwissens*).[68]

---

[66] Ibid., 1–5, 131.
[67] See Grau, *Bewusstsein, Unbewusstes, Unterbewusstes*, 63, 82, 89, 154.
[68] Johann Christoph Adelung, *Versuch eines vollständigen grammatisch-kritischen Wörterbuches der hochdeutschen Mundart, mit beständiger Vergleichung der übrigen Mundarten, besonders aber der oberdeutschen, Vierter Teil, von Sche–V* (Leipzig: Breitkopf, 1780), 1220–1.

Introduction: thinking the unconscious 21

A glance at the *Oxford English Dictionary* reveals that the word "unconscious" can, in the English language, carry a variety of meanings depending on context: not knowing or being heedless of something; not being endowed with or having temporarily lost consciousness in the sense of mentality; performing certain tasks or operations in an automatic way that does not require one's direct attention; and finally the sense of *the* unconscious, associated with Freud and psychoanalysis. The term "subconscious" approximates the German *unterbewusst*, referring to partial or imperfect awareness, or to perceptions which are below the threshold of consciousness but which are capable of becoming conscious.

Although there exists in nineteenth-century British philosophy a number of thinkers – such as, for example, Herbert Spencer and William Hamilton[69] – who discuss different levels of consciousness and forms of latent mental activity that might be described as unconscious, the idea of "*the* unconscious" has, since Freud, often been received with skepticism in Anglophone philosophy.[70] This has led to a tendency to refer to a variety of "unconscious mental states" in the sense of automatic or latent forms of cognition, rather than to a single substrate or realm associated with "the unconscious."[71] This state of affairs suggests a version of the nominalism versus realism debate, whereby empiricist positions would accept a variety of states associated with latent or "unconscious" mental processes, while also denying any common ground or essence to which they might be reduced. A historical analysis of the unconscious must keep in mind these tensions, while also being aware that in some cases – such as Kant's "dark map of the mind," Jean Paul's eminently colonial "true inner Africa," or Freud's bourgeois-European understanding of the unconscious as a kind of "entrance hall" (*Vorraum*) – what we are dealing with is not only the history of a concept but also a history of culturally and historically conditioned metaphors.[72]

With regard to methodology, Elke Völmicke rightly points out that any attempt to find the roots of psychoanalysis in German idealism or in other pre-Freudian sources already constitutes a prejudice or preunderstanding concerning what the concept of the unconscious may

---

[69] See Herbert Spencer, *Principles of Psychology* (London: Longman, Brown, Green and Longmans, 1855); William Hamilton, *Lectures on Metaphysics and Logic*, 2 vols. (Edinburgh: Blackwood, 1859). Both of these texts are discussed in Regenbogen and Brandes, "Unbewußte, das," 653–4.
[70] The classical case in point is Alasdair MacIntyre's critique of Freud in *The Unconscious: a Conceptual Analysis* (London: Routledge and Kegan Paul, 1958).
[71] See Georges Rey, "Unconscious Mental States," *The Routledge Encyclopedia of Philosophy* (London: Routledge, 1998), 522–7.
[72] As is suggested by the title of a study by Günther Bittner: *Metaphern des Unbewussten: Eine kritische Einführung in die Psychoanalyse* (Stuttgart: Kohlhammer, 1998).

actually mean in those sources.[73] This type of teleology can readily be found in studies such as Ellenberger's *Discovery of the Unconscious*, Lancelot Law Whyte's *The Unconscious Before Freud*, as well as in Hemecker's *Before Freud* (*Vor Freud*), all of which proceed on the basis that history of the unconscious moves towards its decisive end-point in the works of Freud. As an alternative to this approach, Völmicke suggests that, when investigating pre-Freudian sources on the unconscious, one must endeavor methodologically to suspend or bracket out the psychoanalytic concept of the unconscious, in order that one may see the pre-Freudian sources in their own independent historical and philosophical contexts.[74] This does not amount to dismissing in its entirety the notion that there may, in some cases, be significant similarities between pre-Freudian notions of the unconscious and Freud's own theoretical constructs, and for this reason this volume does (especially in chapter 1, by Paul Bishop) include analyses that might be regarded as teleological in their approach. Yet at the same time, one must deploy a high degree of self-reflexivity with respect to the pitfalls of teleology in intellectual history. If we accept that, to use the hermeneutical language of Hans-Georg Gadamer, Freud's idea of the unconscious and its various manifestations in popular culture still belong to our Western cultural *horizon* – the collection of pre-understandings and presuppositions which constitute our historical world-view – then this type of self-reflexivity presents us with a task that is extremely challenging but also eminently worthwhile.

While the early phases of the historical period covered by this volume are addressed in great detail (albeit in German) by the respective studies of Marquard and Völmicke, the later stages of the nineteenth century are examined (again only in German) by Hemecker's *Before Freud* and Günter Gödde's *Tradition-Lines of the "Unconscious": Schopenhauer, Nietzsche, Freud* (*Traditionslinien des "Unbewussten": Schopenhauer, Nietzsche, Freud*, 1999). In what is probably the most detailed existing study on nineteenth-century philosophical sources on the unconscious and their possible influences on psychoanalysis, Gödde understands these sources in terms of what he calls three tradition-lines (*Traditionslinien*) of the unconscious.[75] This approach allows him to offer a relatively differentiated account of exactly which nineteenth-century philosophical discourses on the unconscious exerted an influence on Freud and which did not. Gödde is well aware that this story does not begin in the nineteenth century, and it is arguably the case that at least the early phases of each

---

[73] Völmicke, *Das Unbewusste im Deutschen Idealismus*, 17; see especially fn. 25.
[74] Ibid., 17–18.
[75] Günter Gödde, *Traditionslinien des "Unbewussten": Schopenhauer, Nietzsche, Freud* (Tübingen: edition diskord, 1999), 25–8.

of his tradition-lines can already be found, albeit to differing degrees, in some of the eighteenth-century sources that we have encountered in this chapter. Certainly the first of these tradition-lines – that of the *cognitive* unconscious, according to which perceptions only enter consciousness when they are characterized by sufficient levels of attention and intensity – can be found in Leibniz, Wolff, and Platner, as well as in elements of Kant's *Anthropology*.[76] Chapter 8 of this volume, by Michael Heidelberger, examines two of the chief nineteenth-century theorists of this cognitive tradition: Johann Friedrich Herbart and particularly the father of "psychophysics," Gustav Theodor Fechner.

The second tradition-line examined by Gödde – which he describes variously as "romantic" and "vitalist," and which he sees as having emerged from the aesthetic theories of German romanticism and *Naturphilosophie*, all of which take into account the aesthetic dimensions of nature, as well as the non-rational, biological, or natural elements within the human subject[77] – is explored in chapter 1 of this study (Paul Bishop on the aesthetics of the Storm and Stress and Weimar classicism), in chapters 2, 3, and 4 (Andrew Bowie on Schelling's aesthetics and *Naturphilosophie*; Angus Nicholls on Goethe; and Rüdiger Görner on German romanticism), and in chapter 6 (Matthew Bell on Carl Gustav Carus). As we have seen, certain elements of this tradition-line can already be located in Kant's aesthetic approach to the themes of beauty, nature, and genius in the third *Critique*.

The fact that two of the chapters associated with this second tradition-line are substantially devoted to Goethe (chapters 1 and 3, by Bishop and Nicholls respectively) requires a brief note of clarification. Perhaps more than any other German literary figure of the nineteenth century, Goethe – the iconic author of *Faust* and arguably the central figure of modern German literature – is seen to have exerted an enormous influence upon Freud, who claimed to have embarked on his medical career after listening to a public lecture, the text of which was (albeit incorrectly) attributed to Goethe.[78] Yet the centrality of Goethe in the history of psychoanalysis is a contested issue: some, like Bishop, see a deep-seated affinity between Goethe and Freud on the unconscious; while others, like Nicholls, see this purported affinity as being part of the historical mythology of psychoanalysis, which is based upon a fallacious teleology according to which earlier sources are seen as leading to Freud. These two chapters also demonstrate a theoretical precept of this volume: where teleological relations between earlier and later figures are

[76] Ibid., 29–34.
[77] Ibid., 35–56.
[78] For further details concerning Freud's claim, see chapters 1 and 3 of this volume.

explicitly posited (as is the case with regard to Bishop's view of Goethe's relation to Freud), this teleology is at the same time explicitly questioned (as is the case in the chapter by Nicholls).

Finally, a third tradition-line – which Gödde describes as "drive-related" and "irrational" (*triebhaft-irrational*), and which focuses on the sexual and sometimes destructive drives within the human subject[79] – is examined in chapter 5 (Chistopher Janaway on Schopenhauer); in chapter 7 (Sebastian Gardner on Eduard von Hartmann); and in chapter 9 (Martin Liebscher on Friedrich Nietzsche). Kant arguably recognizes such drives in his discussion of sexual desire in §5 of the *Anthropology*, only to turn away from what he sees as being "physiological" questions, in keeping with his preference for the "pragmatic" and "practical" dimensions of rational human behavior.

In the final chapter of the present volume, Günter Gödde examines the question as to whether, and if so to what extent, these three tradition-lines and the thinkers within them may have influenced Freud's various conceptualizations of the unconscious. Here a good measure of skepticism with regard to Gödde's posited tradition-lines is in order. It is certainly not the case that such tradition-lines represent completely independent and hermetic developmental streams within the greater flow of nineteenth-century German intellectual history, as Gödde occasionally seems to suggest. In fact, some of the thinkers examined in this volume arguably belonged to more than one "tradition-line" at once, and were in intense dialogue both with their forebears and contemporaries. Gödde himself points out, for example, that the works of Schelling can be seen to have contributed to both the "romantic/vitalist" and the "drive-related/irrational" tradition-lines of the unconscious.[80] Likewise, Sebastian Gardner's contribution to this volume (chapter 7) questions Gödde's view that the works of Eduard von Hartmann are *only* to be situated within a "drive-related/irrational" tradition-line of the unconscious, suggesting that elements of his work may also correspond with what Gödde's terms the "romantic/vitalist" tradition-line. The pitfalls of Gödde's approach demonstrate that if we make use of such tradition-lines without the appropriate level of reflexivity and skepticism, we run the risk of projecting our own clear-cut teleologies and schemata onto the messy and diffuse realities of intellectual history. Yet as Gödde's contribution to this volume shows, an appropriately tentative and heuristic deployment of such tradition-lines can also provide us with a differentiated answer to the question as to whether and to what extent nineteenth-century sources actually influenced the origins of psychoanalysis.

[79] Gödde, *Traditionslinien des "Unbewussten,"* 57–80.
[80] Ibid., 37–46, 57–60.

Sonu Shamdasani's Epilogue to this volume returns us to the question raised at the beginning of this chapter: is "*the* unconscious" a scientific object or phenomenon which was "discovered" and which can be interpreted and examined, or is it rather a non-empirical construct or effect of various discourses which originated in the nineteenth century, and which found their ultimate institutional realization in the psychoanalytic movement? In posing this question, Shamdasani explores some late nineteenth-century critiques of the concept of the unconscious that appeared both within and outside of the German-speaking world.

1 The unconscious from the Storm and Stress to Weimar classicism: the dialectic of time and pleasure

Paul Bishop

Nature! We are surrounded and embraced by her – powerless to leave her and powerless to enter her more deeply. Unasked and without warning she sweeps us away in the round of her dance and dances on until we fall exhausted from her arms. She brings forth ever new forms: what is there, never was; what was, never will return. All is new, and yet forever old. We live within her, and are strangers to her. She speaks perpetually with us, and does not betray her secret.[1]

Thus begins, in what could be read as a vivid evocation of the intertwining of the twin forces of Eros and Thanatos, the fragmentary text "On Nature," the text – allegedly written by Goethe[2] – that made Freud, or so he later claimed, decide to study, not law, but medicine, after he had heard it read at a public lecture by Carl Brühl (1820–99).[3]

---

[1] [Natur! Wir sind von ihr umgeben und umschlungen – unvermögend aus ihr herauszutreten, und unvermögend tiefer in sie hineinzukommen. Ungebeten und ungewarnt nimmt sie uns in den Kreislauf ihres Tanzes auf und treibt sich mit uns fort, bis wir ermüdet sind und ihrem Arme entfallen. Sie schafft ewig neue Gestalten; was da ist war noch nie, was war kommt nicht wieder — Alles ist neu und doch immer das Alte. Wir leben mitten in ihr und sind ihr fremd. Sie spricht unaufhörlich mit uns und verrät uns ihr Geheimnis nicht.] Goethe, *Scientific Studies*, ed. and trans. Douglas Miller, *Goethe's Collected Works*, vol. XII (New York: Suhrkamp, 1988), 3–5; here 3; *Werke: Hamburger Ausgabe*, ed. Erich Trunz, 14 vols. (Hamburg: Wegener, 1948–1960), vol. XIII, 45; (hereafter cited as *HA* followed by volume and page numbers).

[2] Or, rather, the text that is attributed to Goethe, but it is now thought to have been written by the Swiss theologian Georg Christoph Tobler (1757–1812). Nevertheless Goethe saw in the text an accurate summary of his early *Naturphilosophie*. For further discussion of this text, see Imre Hermann, "Goethes Aufsatz *Die Natur* und Freuds weitere philosophisch-psychologische Lektüre aus den Jahren 1880–1900," *Jahrbuch der Psychoanalyse* 7 (1974): 77–100; and Henry F. Fullenwider, "The Goethean Fragment 'Die Natur' in English Translation," *Comparative Literature Studies* 23 (1986): 170–7.

[3] See Freud's "Autobiographical Study" ("Selbstdarstellung," 1925), in Sigmund Freud, *The Standard Edition of the Complete Psychological Works of Sigmund Freud*, ed. James Strachey and Anna Freud, 24 vols. (London: Hogarth Press, 1953–74), vol. XX, 8 (hereafter cited as *SE* followed by volume and page numbers); Freud, *Gesammelte Werke*, 19

At the opening of this volume, which takes us on a chronological journey – from Schelling, the late Goethe, and romanticism, via Schopenhauer, Carl Gustav Carus, Eduard von Hartmann, Gustav Theodor Fechner, to Nietzsche and Freud – through the concept of the unconscious in nineteenth-century German thought, where should one begin? The history of the concept of the unconscious reveals itself to be a complex and much-contested one, and the story of that complexity and contestation has been told by a variety of narrators.[4] In a sense the "discovery" (or the "invention," depending on one's point of view) of the unconscious is bound up with the "discovery" of consciousness itself. Within the context of this volume's focus on the nineteenth century, the purpose of this chapter is, first, to provide a brief overview of ideas relating to the unconscious in mid to late eighteenth-century German thought; and second, to gauge to what extent these ideas – as mediated by Friedrich Schiller (1759–1805) and especially by Johann Wolfgang von Goethe (1749–1832), the two chief proponents of the Storm and Stress and Weimar classicism – may have influenced the most renowned nineteenth-century German-language theorist of the unconscious: Sigmund Freud.

As its name suggests, the movement known in the English-speaking world as the Storm and Stress[5] – also called *pré-romantisme*, associated with the idea of "sensibility" (*Empfindsamkeit*), and active in the period of the "age of genius" or *Geniezeit* of the 1770s – was not so much a program as an attitude, a state of mind, or (in the eyes of its critics) a pathology.[6] Coinciding chronologically with the later phases of the Enlightenment, it represented its antipode: by questioning the primacy of reason, by emphasizing the non-rational emotions of individual subjectivity, and by

---

vols. (Frankfurt am Main: Fischer, 1952–87), vol. IV, 34 (hereafter cited as *GW* followed by volume and page numbers).

[4] See, for example, Lancelot Law Whyte, *The Unconscious before Freud*, 2nd edn. (London: Julian Friedmann, 1978); Henri F. Ellenberger, *The Discovery of the Unconscious: The History and Evolution of Dynamic Psychiatry* (New York: Basic Books, 1970); in relation to the eighteenth century, see George S. Rousseau, "Psychology," *The Ferment of Knowledge: Studies in the Historiography of Eighteenth-Century Science*, ed. George S. Rousseau and Roy Porter (Cambridge: Cambridge University Press, 1980), 143–210; and, in relation to German literature in particular, see Matthew Bell, *The German Tradition of Psychology in Literature and Thought, 1700–1840* (Cambridge: Cambridge University Press, 2005).

[5] This is the conventional translation of *Sturm und Drang*, also the title of a play (1776; performed 1777) by F. M. Klinger (1752–1831).

[6] For further discussion, see Barbara Becker-Cantarino, ed., *German Literature of the Eighteenth Century: The Enlightenment and Sensibility*, The Camden House History of German Literature, vol. V (Rochester, NY: Camden House, 2005), esp. the contributions by Becker-Cantarino (1–31), Kai Hammermeister (33–52), and Robert Holub (285–307). See also David Hill, ed., *Literature of the Sturm und Drang*, The Camden House History of German Literature, vol. VI (Rochester, NY: Camden House, 2002).

celebrating the relationship between humanity and nature, it anticipated, as the French term suggested, romanticism's search for a reason beyond reason. Perhaps its most iconic and (for the purposes of a brief, generic description of the movement) illustrative text is Goethe's novella *The Sorrows of Young Werther* (*Die Leiden des jungen Werthers*, 1774), the story of an artistically-inclined yet psychologically unstable young man who is given to reveries about nature, and who commits suicide ostensibly due to a combination of factors: unrequited love for an already betrothed woman; a failure to realize his vague yet vaunting artistic ambitions; and a fundamental inability to reconcile his internal fantasies and desires with the restrictive expectations of his society. Here it is also worth mentioning, in line with the theme of this volume, that Goethe claimed to have written his *Werther* "unconsciously" (*unbewußt*) and "like a sleepwalker" (*einem Nachtwandler ähnlich*).[7]

Equally, if in different ways, the literary movement or period known as "German classicism" – often also referred to as "Weimar classicism" due to the fact that both Goethe and Schiller resided in this town during important and productive periods of their lives – remains a contested one in German literary scholarship. Whereas some see it as being more or less exclusively coterminous with the friendship and eventual collaboration of Goethe and Schiller, which began in 1794 and ceased with Schiller's death in 1805, others argue that the movement had earlier and more diverse origins, and should therefore not be confined to Goethe and Schiller; while still others question whether "German" or "Weimar" classicism should be referred to as a movement or epoch at all.[8] Most agree, however, that Weimar classicism is at least in part a reaction to and also a development of tendencies already found in the Storm and Stress. Whereas the Storm and Stress, perhaps generically

---

[7] Goethe, *Sämtliche Werke: Briefe, Tagebücher und Gespräche*, 2 parts, 40 vols., ed. Hendrik Birus *et al.* (Frankfurt am Main: Deutscher Klassiker Verlag, 1985–2003), part 1, vol. XIV, 639. This edition of Goethe's *Sämtliche Werke*, otherwise known as the *Frankfurter Ausgabe*, will hereafter be cited with the letters *FA*, followed by part, volume and page numbers.

[8] For further discussion of German classicism, see Elizabeth M. Wilkinson and L. A. Willoughby, "Missing Links or Whatever Happened to Weimar Classicism?" *Erfahrung und Überlieferung: Festschrift für C. P. Magill*, ed. Hinrich Siefken and Alan Robinson (Cardiff: Trivium Special Publications, 1974), 57–74; Hans Robert Jauss, "Deutsche Klassik – eine Pseudo-Epoche?" *Epochenschwelle und Epochenbewußtsein*, ed. Reinhart Herzog and Reinhart Koselleck (Munich: Fink, 1987), 581–85; Dieter Borchmeyer, *Weimarer Klassik: Portrait einer Epoche* (Weinheim: Beltz Athenäum, 1994); Gerhart Hoffmeister, ed., *A Reassessment of Weimar Classicism* (Lewiston, Queenston and Lampeter: Edwin Mellen, 1996); Simon Richter, ed., *The Literature of Weimar Classicism*, *The Camden House History of German Literature*, vol. VII (Rochester, NY: Camden House, 2005); Rolf Selbmann, *Deutsche Klassik* (Paderborn: Schöningh, 2005); and Volker C. Dörr, *Weimarer Klassik* (Paderborn: Fink, 2007).

embodied in the character of Werther, had emphasized the potentially transgressive qualities of individual subjectivity and genius – while also rejecting, on a formal level, the prescriptive aesthetic tendencies of the French neo-classicism which had preceded it – Weimar classicism expressed the need once again to bring subjectivity and genius within formal bounds derived from the aesthetic models of the ancients. As we shall see, for the Weimar classicism of Schiller, the unconscious inspiration of the genius is, in and of itself, insufficient for the production of great and morally instructive works of art: such inspiration must also, Schiller thought, be accompanied by self-reflection and the capacity to bring such emotions within clear, formal boundaries. Thus, while the Storm and Stress had valorized the breaking of psychological, aesthetic, and perhaps even social boundaries, Weimar classicism called for their at least partial reinstitution, leading Goethe famously to declare late in his life – in a polemical remark directed against some of his German romantic contemporaries – that while classicism is health, romanticism is sickness.[9]

It is impossible here fully to outline, let alone to resolve, the complex debates that surround the opposed yet related movements of the Storm and Stress and Weimar classicism. Yet it should be pointed out that the gestation of arguably *the* key nineteenth-century German literary text dealing with unconscious affects and desires, and perhaps the single most important German literary text for Freud – Goethe's *Faust*, and especially Part One of the tragedy – spans both of these periods or movements.[10] Goethe's great drama was begun in fragmentary form during the 1770s, before being revised and completed partly as a result of Goethe's collaboration with Schiller from 1794 onwards, seeing its first publication in 1808, three years after Schiller's death. Similarly, many of the key aesthetic texts written by Schiller which have important implications for the concept of the unconscious – in particular his *On the Aesthetic Education of Man in a Series of Letters* (*Über die ästhetische Erziehung des Menschen in einer Reihe von Briefen*, 1795) and the essay "On Naive and Sentimental Literature" ("Über naive und sentimentalische Dichtung," 1796) – emerged from his years of collaboration with Goethe.

---

[9] [Classisch ist das Gesunde, romantisch das Kranke.] Goethe, *FA*, 1, XXV, 11–13.
[10] For further discussion of psychological aspects of Goethe's "main work," see Sabine Prokhoris, *The Witch's Kitchen: Freud, "Faust," and the Transference*, trans. G. M. Goshgarian (Ithaca, NY and London: Cornell University Press, 1995); Irene Gerber-Münch, *Goethe's Faust: Eine tiefenpsychologische Studie über den Mythos des modernen Menschen*, Beiträge zur Psychologie von C. G. Jung, series B, vol. VI (Küsnacht: Verlag Stiftung für Jung'sche Psychologie, 1997); and James Simpson, *Goethe und Patriarchy: Faust and the Fates of Desire* (Oxford: Legenda, 1998).

The decisive factor that links both the Storm and Stress and German classicism to the unconscious and, in turn, to Freud is also, as we shall see, a central theme in Goethe's *Faust*: the relationship between time and pleasure. Both Goethe and Freud were aware that pleasure is fleeting and transient, and both recognized that one of the deepest human desires is to secure and retain pleasure at all costs, in spite of time and decay. The view that this desire to sustain pleasure over time is often unconscious and irrational, the idea that such desire should be channeled and redirected in useful and socially acceptable ways, and the notion that the ontological basis of this unconscious desire inheres in a materialist, yet non-reductionist, understanding of nature, constitute central features of the Storm and Stress and German classicism that persist, sometimes in a subterranean or unacknowledged form, in the work of Freud.

Countless remarks by Goethe about the unconscious – "what the genius, as a genius, does happens unconsciously"; "human beings cannot remain long in a conscious state, they are compelled to return to the unconscious, for that is where our roots lie"; and "all our most sincere striving / succeeds only in the unconscious moment"[11] – do not amount to a systematic theory of the unconscious, yet clearly acknowledge its significance.[12] Just as the Storm and Stress (in its emphasis upon unrestrained subjectivity and emotion) and German classicism (in its attempts to bring such subjectivity within formal bounds) outline opposed, yet interrelated, ways of viewing life, so too do the irrationalism of the Storm and Stress and classicism's struggle to give *Gestalt* or form to one's experience arguably inform psychoanalysis. At the beginning of this chapter it must be pointed out, however, that the roots of these ideas lie ultimately not in the eighteenth, but rather in the seventeenth century.

---

[11] [Ich glaube daß alles was das Genie, als Genie, thut, unbewußt geschehe.] Goethe to Schiller, March 6, 1800, in Friedrich Schiller, *Werke: Nationalausgabe*, ed. Julius Petersen and Gerhard Fricke, 50 vols. (Weimar: Hermann Böhlhaus Nachfolger, 1943–), vol. XXXIX, 51 (hereafter cited as *NA*, followed by volume and page numbers). [Der Mensch kann nicht lange im bewußten Zustande oder im Bewußtsein verharren; er muß sich wieder in's Unbewußte flüchten, denn darin lebt seine Wurzel.] Goethe, conversation with F. W. Riemer, August 5, 1810, in *Werke: Weimarer Ausgabe*, ed. Johann Ludwig Gustav von Loeper, Erich Schmidt, and Paul Raabe, 4 parts, 133 vols. in 143 (Weimar: Böhlau, 1887–1919), *Anhang: Gespräche*, vol. II, 324 (hereafter cited as *WA*, followed by part, volume and page numbers). [All unser redlichstes Bemühn / Glückt nur im unbewußten Momente], Goethe, *HA*, I: 325.

[12] For further discussion of Goethe's therapeutic ambitions and as an exponent of *Lebenskunst*, see Frank Nager, *Goethe: Der heilkundige Dichter* (Frankfurt am Main and Leipzig: Insel, 1994); and John Armstrong, *Love, Life, Goethe: How To Be Happy in an Imperfect World* (London: Allen Lane, 2006).

Descartes, Leibniz, Wolff

By emphasizing the primacy of the *cogito*, of rational thought, of "clear" and "distinct" ideas, René Descartes (1596–1650) – a figure who, by common consent, stands at the beginning of the period called modernity[13] – acknowledged and demarcated the existence of the opposite: of "confused" and "obscure" ideas, for "all the properties we discover in the mind are only diverse modes of thinking" (*omnia, quae in mente reperimus, sunt tantum diversi modi cogitandi*).[14] But then, long before Descartes, Augustine (354–430) had urged his listeners and readers to search within themselves – "Go not outside, return into thyself: truth dwells in the inner Man" (*noli foras ire, in teipsum redi; in interiore homine habitat veritas*)[15], which presupposed there was something there to find: "For what is so much in the mind as the mind? ... Let the mind know itself, and not seek itself as though it were absent."[16] Whereas Augustine's theological premise involved the belief in the soul, and philosophical researches concentrated on the problem of memory and time,[17] the modernity of Descartes lay in his promotion of consciousness to a position of supremacy, in effect identifying the soul and consciousness.[18] This step is extremely significant, as Friedrich Seifert has argued,[19] for if consciousness (*cogitatio*) constitutes the essence or the nature of the soul

---

[13] For a technical interpretation of Descartes as "legislator of modern times" (in a Nietzschean sense), see Laurence Lampert, *Nietzsche and Modern Times: A Study of Bacon, Descartes, and Nietzsche* (New Haven and London: Yale University Press, 1993). For a popular discussion of Descartes in relation to contemporary developmental psychology, see Antonio Damasio, *Descartes' Error: Emotion, Reason and the Human Brain* (1994; London: Vintage, 2006); and Paul Bloom, *Descartes' Baby: How the Science of Child Development Explains What Makes Us Human* (London: Heinemann, 2004).

[14] Descartes, *The Principles of Philosophy*, book 1, §53, *Œuvres*, ed. Charles Adam and Paul Tannery, 12 vols. (Paris: Cerf, 1897–1913), vol. VIII, 25; *A Discourse on Method; Meditations on the First Philosophy; Principles of Philosophy*, trans. John Veitch (London: Dent; New York: Dutton, 1969), 185.

[15] Augustine, *De vera religione*, 39 (72), in Augustine, *De doctrina christiana; De vera religione* (*Opera*, vol. 4.1; *Corpus christianorum, Series Latina*, vol. 32), ed. Josef Martin and Klaus-D. Daur (Turnholti: Brepols, 1962), 234.

[16] [Cognoscat ergo semetipsam, nec quasi absentem se querat], *De trinitate*, 10. 8, in: Augustine, *On the Trinity: Books 8–15*, ed. Gareth B. Matthews, trans. Stephen McKenna (Cambridge: Cambridge University Press, 2002), 53; Augustine, *De trinitate* (*Opera*, vol. 16.1; *Corpus christianorum, Series Latina*, vol. 50), ed. W. J. Mountain (Turnholti: Brepols, 1968), 325.

[17] See *Confessions*, book 11.

[18] See *Objectiones Quartæ*, "Quartæ Responsiones," 345, in Descartes, *Œuvres*, vol. VII, 246.

[19] Friedrich Seifert, "Psychologie. Metaphysik der Seele," *Mensch und Charakter, Handbuch der Philosophie*, Abteilung III, ed. Alfred Baeumler and Manfred Schröter (Munich and Berlin: Oldenbourg, 1931), 72–85. See also Kenneth Dewhurst and Nigel Reeves, "The Emergence of the Psychological Sciences," in their edition of Friedrich Schiller, *Medicine, Psychology and Literature* (Oxford: Sandford Publications, 1978), 109–41.

(*essentia sive natura animae*), then all of those rich and various psychic functions attributed to the soul become correspondingly downgraded, ignored, or repressed. No longer the "divine spark" within the individual human being, the ego – the subject of the *cogito* – becomes a mere mathematical point, and consciousness is no longer an object in itself, but that for which something else is an object.[20]

Descartes' purely formal conception of consciousness is a significant shift away from the ancient conception of the soul as εἶδος (*eidos*), or as *forma substantialis*, and from this new position a path leads to Immanuel Kant's conception of the "synthetic unity of consciousness," or the "transcendental unity of apperception" – the idea that consciousness consists in a formal organization of preexisting categories of thought and sense data. But already prior to Kant, in the philosophy of Gottfried Wilhelm Leibniz (1646–1716), consciousness acquires – and thus, by implication, so does the unconscious – a new quality: it becomes *dynamic*. For Leibniz, "that which does not act does not merit the name of substance,"[21] which means that "substance is a being capable of action."[22] By defining the soul or consciousness as a creative, energetic act – "the soul is active of itself"[23] – Leibniz attributed similar dynamic qualities to those less clear, less distinct modes of perception he dubbed *petites perceptions*.[24] In turn, and as is pointed out at some length in the Introduction to this volume, Kant would come to speak of these modes of perception as *dunkle Vorstellungen* or "obscure representations."[25] In a beautiful passage in his

---

[20] "By the word thought, I understand all that which so takes place in us that we of ourselves are immediately conscious of it" [Cogitationis nomine, intelligo illa omnia, quae nobis consciis in nobis fiunt, quatenus eorum in nobis conscientia est], *Discourse* 77; *Principles of Philosophy*, book 1, §9; *Œuvres*, vol. VIII, 7.

[21] [ce qui agit point ne mérite point le nom de substance.] Leibniz, *Theodicy: Essays on the Goodness of God, the Freedom of Man and the Origin of Evil*, ed. Austin Farrer, trans. E. M. Huggard (London: Routledge and Kegan Paul, 1951), §393, 359; *Essais de Théodicée sur la bonté de Dieu, la liberté de l'homme et l'origine du mal* (1710), *Opera philosophica*, ed. Johann Eduard Erdmann (1840; Aalen: Scientia, 1959), 617.

[22] [la substance est un être capable d'action], *Principes de la nature et de la grâce, fondés en raison* (1714), §1; Leibniz, *Philosophical Writings*, trans. Mary Morris (London Dent; New York: Dutton, 1956), 21; *Opera philosophica*, 714. From this position a path leads to Johann Gottlieb Fichte's (1762–1814) fusion of the ego and the will in his identification of the *ego cogitans* with the *ego agens*; Fichte describes this primary activity of the ego as "positing" (*setzen*). See Fichte, "Second Introduction to the *Wissenschaftslehre*," chapter 1, in J. G. Fichte, *Introductions to the "Wissenschaftslehre" and Other Writings (1797–1800)*, ed. and trans. Daniel Breazeale (Indianapolis, IN: Hackett, 1994), 106–18 (esp. 108, 110–15).

[23] [l'âme est active par elle-même]. *Théodicée*, §322; *Opera philosophica*, 598.

[24] *Nouveaux essais sur l'entendement humain* [1703]; *Opera philosophica*, 196–7; Leibniz, *New Essays on the Human Understanding* (1700; 1765), in Leibniz, *Philosophical Writings*, 148–50. For a clarification of these terms, see Bertrand Russell, *A Critical Exposition of the Philosophy of Leibniz* (1900; London: Routledge, 1992), 167–8, 281.

[25] See Kant, *Anthropologie in pragmatischer Hinsicht*, book 1, §5, in *Gesammelte Schriften* (Prussian Academy Edition), 29 vols. (Berlin: Reimer; de Gruyter, 1902–1980),

Principles of Nature and of Grace, founded on Reason (1714), Leibniz (in anticipation of Kant and his successors) evoked the entire range of possible conscious and unconscious perceptions with the following image:

> Each soul knows the infinite, knows everything, but confusedly. Just as when I am walking along the shore of the sea and hear the great noise it makes, though I hear the separate sounds of each wave of which the total sound is made up, I do not discriminate them one from another; so our confused perceptions are the result of the impressions which the whole universe makes on us.[26]

As this passage (like others in Leibniz's writings) makes clear, the categorization of thoughts and perceptions into "clear" and "distinct" on the one hand, or "obscure" and "confused" on the other, itself divides thought from sensation – and, ultimately, the mind from the body – in a way that stands completely at odds with our everyday experience. Rather than refining even further the conceptual apparatus developed by Leibniz, his chief follower, Christian Wolff (1679–1754), conceived psychology, not just as "rational psychology" – as "the science of whatever is possible through the human soul"[27] – but also as "empirical psychology."[28] This empirical approach drew on such English thinkers as Francis Bacon (1561–1626) and Thomas Hobbes (1588–1679), from whom a line of English and Scottish thought stretches, via John Locke (1632–1704), David Hume (1711–76), and David Hartley (1705–57), to James Mill (1773–1836), J. S. Mill (1806–73), and Alexander Bain (1818–1903). Within this tradition of thought, the workings of the psyche should be approached just as any other scientific subject should be; J. S. Mill, for

---

vol. VII, 135; *Anthropology from a Pragmatic Point of View*, trans. Mary J. Gregor (The Hague: Martinus Nijhoff, 1974), 16. See also Immanuel Kant, *Lectures on Metaphysics*, trans. and ed. Karl Ameriks and Steve Naragon, *The Cambridge Edition of the Works of Immanuel Kant*, vol. X (Cambridge: Cambridge University Press, 1997), 47.

[26] [Chaque âme connoît l'infini, connoît tout, mais confusément. Comme en me promenant sur le rivage de la mer, en entendant le grand bruit qu'elle fait, j'entends les bruits particuliers de chaque vague, dont le bruit total est composé, mais sans les discerner, nos perceptions confuses sont le résultat des impressions que tout l'Univers fait sur nous.] *Principles of Nature and of Grace*, §13, *Philosophical Writings*, 28; *Opera philosophica*, 717.

[27] [scientia eorum, quae per animam humanam possibilia sunt]. *Psychologia rationalis* (1734), "Prolegomena," §1, in Christian Wolff, *Psychologia rationalis*, ed. Jean École, *Gesammelte Werke*, vol. VI (Hildesheim: Olms, 1972), 1; Robert J. Richards, "Christian Wolff's Prolegomena to Empirical and Rational Psychology: Translation and Commentary," *Proceedings of the American Philosophical Society* 124, no. 3 (June 1980): 227–39; here 234. For further discussion, see Richard J. Blackwell, "Christian Wolff's Doctrine of the Soul," *Journal of the History of Ideas* 22, no. 3 (July-September 1961): 339–54.

[28] "Empirical psychology is the science that establishes principles through experience, whence reason is given for what occurs in the human soul" [Psychologia empirica est scientia stabiliendi principa per experientiam, unde ratio redditur eorum, quae in anima humana siunt]; *Psychologia rationalis* (1732), "Prolegomena," §1; see also §4 and §7, in Christian Wolff, *Psychologia empirica*, 1; see also: Richards, "Christian Wolff's Prolegomena," 230.

example, posited the notion of a "mental chemistry."[29] Moreover, Wolff introduced the idea of *psychometry*, a mathematical approach to our experiences of pleasure and pain in relation to our apprehension of the perfection or imperfection of any given object.[30] Although some, such as Kant, still doubted or disputed the validity of psychology as a discipline distinct from philosophy, Wolff was articulating a more broadly held preoccupation with the workings of the mind (both conscious and unconscious) that had left well behind the theological assumptions of Scholastic thought and was taking a deeper, and more praxis-oriented, interest in the age-old problem of the relation between "mind," or "soul," and "body."[31]

How to solve the dualism found in Platonic thought and reinforced by the distinction between "thinking substance" (*res cogitans*) and "extended substance" (*res extensa*) in Descartes' philosophy was a problem that exercised Descartes himself, and his specific solution was to suggest the pineal gland as the site where mind and matter can interact. In the twelfth of his *Letters on the Sensations* (*Briefe über die Empfindungen*, 1755), the German philosopher Moses Mendelssohn (1729–86) developed the idea of an interchange or *Wechselwirkung* between the soul and the body.[32] This proved to be a fruitful notion: in his *Hamburg Dramaturgy* (*Hamburgische Dramaturgie*, 1767), the great German dramatist, writer and critic Gotthold Ephraim Lessing (1729–81) discussed how the mimetic skills of the actor enabled a change of "soul" to bring about a change in his "body."[33] And similar ideas were common currency in the eighteenth century: Christian Garve (1742–98), the translator of Adam Ferguson (1723–1816) into German, for example, argued that the passions of the soul produce corresponding passions in the body; Georg Stahl (1660–1734), who conceived of the human body, not as some sort of Cartesian machine, but as an organism animated by a kind of vital principle, variously called *activitas vitalis*, *agens vitale*, or *energia vitale*, argued

---

[29] See Mill's *System of Logic* (1843), where he states his "laws of association." J. S. Mill, *Collected Works*, ed. F. E. L. Priestley and J. M. Robson, 33 vols. (Toronto: University of Toronto Press; London: Routledge and Kegan Paul, 1963–91), vol. VIII: *A System of Logic Ratiocinative and Inductive: Part II*, book 6, chapter 4, §1 and §3.

[30] [Theoremata haec ad Psychometriam pertinent, quae mentis humanae cognitionem mathematicam tradit et adhuc in desideratis est.] *Psychologia empirica*, §522, 403.

[31] For a discussion and selection of relevant texts, see Joan Wynn Reeves, *Body and Mind in Western Thought: An Introduction to Some Origins of Modern Psychology* (Harmondsworth: Penguin, 1958).

[32] Moses Mendelssohn, "On Sentiments," Letter 12, in *Philosophical Writings*, trans. Daniel O. Dahlstrom (Cambridge: Cambridge University Press, 1997), 52.

[33] Lessing, *Hamburgische Dramaturgie*, Letter 5. For a discussion of the impact of Lessing's theories on his dramatic praxis, see Matthew Bell, "Psychological Conceptions in Lessing's Dramas," *Lessing Yearbook* 28 (1996): 53–81.

that the soul "builds" the body;[34] and Albrecht von Haller (1708–77), the author of the influential didactic poem *The Alps* (*Die Alpen*, written 1729, published 1732), explored the expression of various passions in the body.[35] Thanks to Jakob Friedrich Abel (1751–1829), the author of *Introduction to Psychology* (*Einleitung in die Seelenlehre*, 1786) and *On the Sources of Human Representations* (*Über die Quellen der menschlichen Vorstellungen*, 1787) and a teacher of philosophy at the Hohe Karlsschule, the contemporary debate in general and the work of Garve, Haller, and Stahl in particular became mediated to a pupil at this school: the young Friedrich Schiller.

Schiller and Herder

Through Schiller's early medical writings, which include the *Philosophy of Physiology* (*Philosophie der Physiologie*, 1779) and the *Essay on the Connection between the Animal Nature of Man and his Spiritual* (*Versuch über den Zusammenhang der tierischen Natur des Menschen mit seiner Geistigen*, 1780),[36] and also through his later writings on aesthetics – including "On Grace and Dignity" ("Über Anmut und Würde",1793) and *On the Aesthetic Education of Man in a Series of Letters* (*Über die ästhetische Erziehung des Menschen in einer Reihe von Briefen*,1795)[37] – we can trace the extent to which the philosophical-physiological convictions of the Enlightenment fed into the tradition of German classical aesthetics.[38]

According to Schiller's medical dissertation, "an admirable law of supreme wisdom" dictates "that very noble and loving emotion enhances

---

[34] G. E. Stahl, "Über den Unterschied zwischen Organismus und Mechanismus" (1714), in *Über den mannigfaltigen Einfluss von Gemütsbewegungen auf den menschlichen Körper* (Halle, 1695). See also Stahl, *Über die Bedeutung des synergischen Prinzips für die Heilkunde* (Halle, 1695); *Über den Unterschied zwischen Organismus und Mechanismus* (1714); *Überlegungen zum ärztlichen Hausbesuch* (Halle, 1703), ed. Bernward Josef Gottlieb (Leipzig: Barth, 1961), §71, 49.

[35] Albrecht von Haller, *Elementa physiologiae corporis humani*, 8 vols. (Lausanne: Marci-Michael Bousquet & Sociorum, 1757–66).

[36] For further discussion, see Wolfgang Riedel, *Die Anthropologie des jungen Schiller: Zur Ideengeschichte der medizinischen Schriften und der "Philosophischen Briefe"* (Würzburg: Königshausen & Neumann, 1985); Walter Hinderer, "Schiller's Philosophical Aesthetics in Anthropological Perspective," and Steven D. Martinson, "*Maria Stuart*: Physiology and Politics," in *A Companion to the Works of Friedrich Schiller*, ed. Steven D. Martinson (Rochester, NY: Camden House, 2005), 27–46; 213–26; and Rüdiger Safranksi, *Friedrich Schiller oder die Erfindung des Deutschen Idealismus* (Munich: Hanser, 2004).

[37] For translations of, and commentaries on, these seminal texts, see Jane V. Curran and Christopher Fricker, eds., *Schiller's "On Grace and Dignity" in its Cultural Context: Essays and a New Translation* (Rochester, NY: Camden House, 2005); and Elizabeth M. Wilkinson and L. A. Willoughby, eds., *On the Aesthetic Education of Man* (Oxford: Clarendon Press, 1982).

[38] For further discussion of Schiller's aesthetics, see Frederick Beiser, *Schiller as Philosopher: A Re-examination* (Oxford: Clarendon Press, 2005).

the beauty of the body, whereas base and hateful ones produce bestial distortions,"[39] thus bearing witness to the principle, first articulated by Aristotle,[40] and turned into a commonplace by Sallust,[41] that attaches priority to the psychological over the physiological; or, in other words, "the soul shapes the body" (*die Seele bildet den Körper*).[42] In "On Grace and Dignity" Schiller reformulates this principle enunciated in his medical treatise when he writes that "finally mind even *constructs* itself a body and the *form* itself must join the *play*."[43] Schiller then extends this principle to all movements when he says that "an active spirit gains influence over *all physical movement* and finally comes indirectly to the point of changing even the set forms of nature, which are not accessible to the will, through the power of sympathetic play."[44] "In such a human being," Schiller adds, "everything comes down to character," leading him to conclude that "one is very right in saying that in such a form, everything is soul" (*daher sagt man sehr richtig, daß an einer solchen Gestalt alles Seele sey*).[45]

Schiller's ideas on the relation between body and soul become, filtered through the *Trieblehre* or "doctrine of the drives" in his *Aesthetic Letters*, an almost typological distinction in "On Naive and Sentimental Literature" ("Über naive und sentimentalische Dichtung," 1796). Whereas the "ideal" (*idealisch*) or "sentimental" (*sentimental*) attitude consists in "the elevation of reality to the ideal," in the "real" (*wirklich*) or "naïve" (*naiv*) condition "the human being functions together with all his powers as a harmonious unit … and … the whole of his nature expresses itself completely."[46] A few

---

[39] [ein bewundernswürdiges Gesetz der Weisheit]; [daß jeder edle und wohlwollende [Affekt] den Körper *verschönert*, den der niederträchtige und gehäßige in *viehische* Formen zerreißt] (§22). Schiller, *Medicine, Psychology and Literature*, 279–80; Schiller, *NA*, XX: 68.

[40] See *De anima*, book 2, chapter 4: "The soul, then, is the cause and principle of the living body," Aristotle, *De Anima (On the Soul)*, trans. Hugh Lawson-Tancred (Harmondsworth: Penguin, 1986), 165; compare Schiller, *NA*, XX: 131.

[41] Sallust, *De conjuratione Catilinae*, 1:2.

[42] Schiller, *Medicine, Psychology and Literature*, 280; Schiller, *NA*, XX: 68.

[43] [endlich *bildet* sich der Geist sogar seinen Körper, und der *Bau* selbst muß dem *Spiele* folgen]. Quoted in Curran and Fricker, *Schiller's "On Grace and Dignity,"* 135; *NA*, XX: 265.

[44] [ein reger Geist verschaft sich auf *alle* körperlichen Bewegungen Einfluß, und kommt zuletzt mittelbar dahin, auch die festen Formen der Natur, die dem Willen unerreichbar sind, durch die Macht des sympathetischen Spiels zu verändern]; quoted in Curran and Fricker, *Schiller's "On Grace and Dignity,"* 142; *NA*, XX: 274.

[45] [An einem solchen Menschen wird endlich alles Charakterzug.] Quoted in *Schiller's "On Grace and Dignity,"* 142; *NA*, XX: 274. An off-shoot of this way of thinking is physiognomy, a "science" developed by Johann Kaspar Lavater (1741–1801) in his multi-volume work, *Physiognomic Fragments to Encourage the Knowledge and Love of Humankind* (*Physiognomische Fragmente zur Beförderung der Menschenkenntnis und Menschenliebe*, 1775–1778).

[46] [die Erhebung der Wirklichkeit zum Ideal]; [wo der Mensch noch, mit allen seinen Kräften zugleich, als harmonische Einheit wirkt, wo mithin das Ganze seiner Natur

years later, in his correspondence with Goethe, Schiller expressed his irritation with the position taken by the Romantic *Naturphilosoph* Friedrich Wilhelm Joseph Schelling (1775–1854) in his recently published *System of Transcendental Idealism* (*System des transzendentalen Idealismus*, 1800) about the relation between nature, art, consciousness, and the unconscious.[47] In contrast to Schelling, Schiller declared that "unconsciousness combined with reflection constitutes the poetic artist," thus locating the unconscious at the heart of his conception, but also – and now more classically – giving equal status to *ratio*.[48]

Schiller's earlier dictum that "the soul shapes the body" reflects the increasing awareness in the course of the late eighteenth century that the unconscious can exercise a somatic influence – the core idea behind what psychoanalysis calls a "symptom."[49] Not that the effects of the unconscious were, in eighteenth-century eyes, always nefarious. For Johann Gottfried Herder (1744–1803), philology – another rapidly developing science at the time – suggested that the motor of human history, human civilization, and human progress, was itself something primordial and irrational: language. In Herder's view, "language was an unconscious collective growth," rising spontaneously from the people (*Volk*), and from the soil.[50] Yet it would be a mistake to read Herder retrospectively

---

sich in der Wirklichkeit vollständig ausdrückt]. Schiller, *On the Naive and Sentimental in Literature*, trans. Helen Watanabe-O'Kelly (Manchester: Carcanet New Press, 1981), 39; *NA*, XX: 437. In the terminology of Erich Jaensch (1883–1940), the former attitude characterizes the integrated (*integriert*) type, the latter the unintegrated (*disintegriert*) type. Where Schiller and, subsequently, Jaensch expounded their typology on the basis of the individual's relationship to nature, the characterologist Ludwig Klages (1872–1956) predicated his chief distinction between the "biocentric" (*biozentrisch*) and the "logocentric" (*logozentrisch*) or "egozentrisch" (*egozentrisch*) on the relationship of the individual to life. See Marga-Elfriede Jansen, *Die ausdruckskundlichen Studien Schillers und ihre Beziehung zu Ludwig Klages* (Braunschweig: Technische Hochschule Carolo-Wilhelmina, 1944), 63.

[47] In Schiller's paraphrase, Schelling had argued that "in nature one starts from the unconscious in order to raise it to consciousness, whereas, in art, one proceeds from consciousness to the unconscious" [in der Natur von dem Bewußtlosen angefangen werde um es zum Bewußtsein zu erheben, in der Kunst hingegen man vom Bewußtsein ausgehe zum Bewußtlosen]. *The Correspondence between Schiller and Goethe, from 1794 to 1805*, trans. L. Dora Schmitz, 2 vols. (London: George Bell and Sons, 1877), vol. II, 371; *Der Briefwechsel zwischen Schiller und Goethe in den Jahren 1794 bis 1805*, ed. Manfred Beetz, 2 vols. (Munich: Goldmann, 2005), vol. I, 851.

[48] [Das Bewußtlose mit dem Besonnenen vereinigt macht den poetischen Künstler aus.] *Correspondence between Schiller and Goethe*, vol. II, 372; *Briefwechsel zwischen Schiller und Goethe*, vol. I, 852.

[49] For further discussion of Schiller's use of the psychological concept of the unconscious in his writings with specific reference to *The Robbers* (*Die Räuber*, 1777–80; pub. 1781), see Gerhard Oberlin, *Goethe, Schiller und das Unbewusste: Eine literaturpsychologische Studie* (Gießen: Psychosozial Verlag, 2007), 105–72.

[50] Lewis W. Spitz, "Natural Law and the Theory of History in Herder," *Journal of the History of Ideas* 16 (1955): 453–75; here 457.

and see his outbursts – such as, for example, "Heart! Warmth! Blood! Humanity! Life! ... I feel! I am!"[51] as he typically enthused – as no more than an apologia for a narrowly conceived nationalism. This is because Herder's "vitalistic understanding of nature and of human nature in particular," as Lewis W. Spitz describes it, involved an important focus on the body. In his *Sculpture* (*Plastik*, 1778) Herder emphasized how, in the aesthetic experience, all of the senses work together, so that "the eye is only the initial guide, the reason of the hand; the hand alone reveals the *forms* of things, their concepts, what they *mean*, what *dwells* therein."[52] And *another* new science of the eighteenth century, aesthetics, founded by Alexander Gottlieb Baumgarten (1714–62) in his *Aesthetica* (vol. I, 1750),[53] aimed to investigate and thus, in a sense, to rehabilitate precisely those sensations excluded from the (neo-)Platonic dualism of Cartesian rationality: "aesthetics (the theory of the free arts, epistemology of the lower senses, the art of beautiful thought, and the art of the analogue of reason)," said Baumgarten, is "the science of sensory knowledge."[54] In the second half of the eighteenth century, then, the unconscious becomes something bodily, something dynamic, and something vitalist.

Goethe ... and Freud

Thanks to the essay "On Nature," which was mistakenly attributed to Goethe, but which allegedly inspired Freud to take up a career in

---

[51] [Herz! Wärme! Blut! Menschen! Leben! ... Ich fühle mich! Ich bin!] *Auch eine Philosophie der Geschichte zur Bildung der Menschheit* (1774), section 2, §2, in Johann Gottfried Herder, *Werke*, 10 vols. (Frankfurt am Main: Deutscher Klassiker Verlag, 1985–2005), vol. IV, 9–107; here 64; and "Zum Sinn des Gefühls" (1769), in *Werke*, vol. IV, 235–42; here 236. See also Spitz, "Natural Law," 455–6.

[52] [Das Auge ist nur Wegweiser, nur die Vernunft der Hand; die Hand allein gibt *Formen*, Begriffe dessen, was sie *bedeuten*, was in ihnen *wohnet*.] Herder, *Sculpture: Some Observations on Shape and Form from Pygmalion's Creative Dream*, ed. and trans. Jason Geiger (Chicago: University of Chicago Press, 2002), 64; *Werke*, vol. IV, 243–326; here: 280. Similarly, the "economies of pleasure" explored in Herder's essay "Love and Selfhood" ("Liebe und Selbstheit," 1781) can be read as providing the framework for, as well as interrogating and challenging, some of today's postmodern, Lacan-inspired paradigms. See Christoph F. E. Holzhey, "On the Emergence of Sexual Difference in the 18th Century: Economies of Pleasure in Herder's *Liebe und Selbstheit*," *The German Quarterly* 79 (2006): 1–25.

[53] For further discussion, see L. P. Wessell, Jr., "Alexander Baumgarten's Contribution to the Development of Aesthetics," *Journal of Aesthetics and Art Criticism* 30 (1972): 333–42; Nicholas Davey, "Baumgarten's Aesthetics: A Post-Gadamerian Reflection," *British Journal of Aesthetics* 29 (1989): 101–15; and R. A. Makkreel, "The Confluence of Aesthetics and Hermeneutics in Baumgarten, Meier and Kant," *The Journal of Aesthetics and Art Criticism* 54 (1996): 65–75.

[54] "Aesthetica (theoria liberalium artium, gnoseologia inferior, ars pulchre cogitandi, ars analogi rationis) est scientia cognitionis sensitivae" (*Aesthetics*, §1; cf. *Metaphysica*, §533) in Alexander Gottlieb Baumgarten, *Texte zur Grundlegung der Ästhetik*, trans. and ed. Hans Rudolf Schweizer (Hamburg: Felix Meiner, 1983), 79.

medicine, Goethe came to occupy a central position in the history of the unconscious in nineteenth-century German thought. Yet as the contribution to this volume by Angus Nicholls demonstrates, this central status is contested. While some argue, as Nicholls does in chapter 3, that Freud's frequent quotations from Goethe's works are often merely rhetorical and not representative of a deeper epistemological agreement between the poet and the psychoanalyst, in the remainder of this chapter I shall present a different, yet complementary, view, arguing that it is possible to read Freud's work – and psychoanalysis in general – as a kind of coming-to-terms with Goethe; in the case of Freud, a life-long, direct, and intimate preoccupation with various aspects of the *œuvre* and his life, that could well be described, as Ernst Cassirer's relation to Goethe has been, as a kind of "eavesdropping" on Goethe.[55] This preoccupation is reflected not least in Freud's numerous references to Goethe, the way in which his writing is saturated with echoes of Goethe's prose.[56]

Now where does Goethe's "On Nature" fit into the sense of the dynamic nature of the unconscious, which grows and develops in the period spanning from the Storm and Stress to Weimar classicism, as an important component of the historico-intellectual background to Freud's formulation of his psychoanalytic theories? True, "On Nature" may, as Franz

---

[55] Barbara Naumann, *Philosophie und Poetik des Symbols: Cassirer und Goethe* (Munich: Wilhelm Fink, 1998), 14. For a psychoanalytically informed discussion of Johann Peter Eckermann's accounts of his conversations with (and his dreams about) Goethe, see Avital Ronell, *Dictations: On Haunted Writing*, 2nd edn. (1986; Lincoln, NE: University of Nebraska Press, 1993).

[56] For a discussion of how, see Walter Schönau, *Sigmund Freuds Prosa: Literarische Elemente seines Stils* (Stuttgart: Metzler, 1968). For further discussion of the Goethe–Freud relationship, see Victor Lange, "Goethe in psychologischer und ästhetischer Sicht," *Psychologie in der Literaturwissenschaft: Viertes Amherster Kolloquium zur modernen deutschen Literatur, 1970*, ed. Wolfgang Paulsen (Heidelberg: Stiehm, 1971), 140–56; Horst Thomé, "Goethe-Stilisierung bei Sigmund Freud: Zur Funktion der enigmatischen Persönlichkeit in der psychoanalytischen Bewegung," *Klassik und Moderne: Die Weimarer Klassik als historisches Ereignis und Herausforderung im kulturgeschichtlichen Prozeß*, ed. Karl Richter and Jörg Schönert (Stuttgart: Metzler, 1983), 340–55; Bernd Nitzschke, "Goethe ist tot, es lebe die Kultur," *Über das Pathologische bei Goethe*, ed. P. J. Möbius (Munich: Matthes & Seitz, 1983), 9–75; Bernd Nitzschke, "Liebe – Verzicht und Versöhnung: Das Ethos der Entsagung im Werk des Goethepreisträgers Sigmund Freud," *Liebe und Gesellschaft: Das Geschlecht der Musen*, ed. Hans-Georg Pott (Munich: Fink, 1997), 139–53; and Robert C. Holub, "From the Pedestal to the Couch: Goethe, Freud and Jewish Assimilation," *Goethe in German-Jewish Culture*, ed. Klaus Berghahn and Jost Hermand (Rochester, NY: Camden House, 2001), 104–20. On Freud and the Goethe Prize, see Wolfgang Schivelbusch, "Der Goethe-Preis und Sigmund Freud," *Intellektuellendämmerung: Zur Lage der Frankfurter Intelligenz in den zwanziger Jahren* (Frankfurt: Insel, 1982), 77–93; Tomas Plänkers, "'Vom Himmel durch die Welt zur Hölle': Zur Goethe-Preisverleihung an Sigmund Freud im Jahre 1930," *Jahrbuch der Psychoanalyse* 30 (1993): 167–81; and S. S. Prawer, "A Change of Direction? Sigmund Freud between Goethe and Darwin," *Publications of the English Goethe Society* 76, no. 2 (2006): 103–17.

Wittels (1880–1950) surmised, have formed part of a kind of "screen memory" on Freud's part, designed to conceal his real motives for his choice of study.[57] And yet Goethe himself regarded the text as a reflection of his early (Storm and Stress) thinking on nature,[58] and Gay links the comments, made by Freud in his "Autobiographical Study," that he was moved to study medicine "by a sort of greed for knowledge" to his later view that "the sexual curiosity of youngsters" constitutes "the true source of scientific inquisitiveness."[59]

According to T. S. Eliot, it "may be true" to say that we cannot understand the nineteenth century "until we are able to understand Goethe."[60] By the same token, nor can we understand Freud – as well as, by extension, the concept of the unconscious in the nineteenth century – until we are able to understand his relation to Goethe, particularly in respect of what one might call "the dialectic of time and pleasure." So in relation to what German studies or *Germanistik* calls the "long" nineteenth century (reaching from the Storm and Stress beginnings of Romanticism in the last decades of the eighteenth century to the period of the twentieth leading up to the First World War), we need to explore further Freud's relationship to Goethe as a means to understanding the development of the concept of the unconscious.

Shortly after the outbreak of the First World War, the *Goethebund* in Berlin invited Freud to contribute to the anthology *Das Land Goethes 1914–1916* (1916), a wartime propaganda volume intended to raise money for libraries in Germany. In his contribution, entitled "On Transience" ("Vergänglichkeit," written in 1915; published in 1916), Freud recalled his visit in August 1913 to the Dolomites, part of the Italian Alps, and related how he had undertaken a walk in this beautiful Italian mountain

---

[57] Fritz Wittels, *Sigmund Freud, der Mann, die Lehre, die Schule* (Leipzig: Tal, 1924), 13–14. For Freud's notion here, see the early paper "Screen Memories" ("Über Deckerinnerungen," 1899); *SE*, III: 301–22; *GW*, I: 531–54. Peter Gay agrees with this judgment, and has suggested that Freud's account was a screen memory concealing "not prudential but emotional motives." Peter Gay, *Freud: A Life for Our Time* (New York and London: Norton, 1988), 24–5.

[58] The fragmentary essay appeared anonymously in the *Tiefurter Journal* (1782/1783); in 1828, Goethe explained to von Müller: "I cannot, in fact, remember having composed these remarks, but they reflect accurately the ideas to which my understanding had then attained"; [Daß ich diese Betrachtungen verfaßt, kann ich mich faktisch zwar nicht erinnern, allein sie stimmen mit den Vorstellungen wohl überein, zu denen sich mein Geist damals ausgebildet hatte]. Goethe, *Scientific Studies*, 6; *HA*, XIII: 48.

[59] Gay, *Freud*, 25.

[60] T. S. Eliot, "Introduction to Goethe," *The Nation and Athenaeum* 44 (January 12, 1929), 527, cited in Henry F. Fullenwider, "The Goethean Fragment 'Die Natur' in English Translation," *Comparative Literature Studies* 23, no. 2 (1986), 170–7, here 175. For further discussion, see Maurice Benn, "Goethe and T. S. Eliot," *German Life and Letters* 5, no. 3 (April 1952): 151–61; here 158.

landscape in the company of two people, "a taciturn friend" and "a young but already famous poet."[61] These two companions, with whom he enjoyed "a summer walk through a smiling countryside," are not named by Freud,[62] but in the recent book by Matthew von Unwerth, *Freud's Requiem*, it is suggested that the poet is Rainer Maria Rilke, and the friend is Lou Andreas-Salomé.[63] In fact, these identifications were first made by Herbert Lehmann in 1966,[64] and remain, for various reasons, improbable (not least because the friend, in Freud's text, is masculine).[65]

In his essay, Freud records the response of the poet to the beauty of the natural landscape around them:

> The poet admired the beauty of the scene around us but felt no joy in it. He was disturbed by the thought that all this beauty was fated to extinction, that it would vanish when winter came, like all human beauty and all the beauty and splendour that men have created or may create. All that he would otherwise have loved and admired seemed to him to be shorn of its worth by the transience which was its doom.[66]

---

[61] [ein schweigsamer Freund]; [ein junger, bereits rühmlich bekannter Dichter]. *SE*, XIV: 305; *GW*, X: 358. The setting of Freud's discussion in the mountains recalls another famous climb, Petrarch's *The Ascent of Mount Ventoux* (1336), although its conclusions are far removed from those of St. Augustine, to whose *Confessions* Petrarch turns for an appropriate expression of awe when confronted with the view from the top. And in a letter to Wilhelm Fliess of August 6, 1899 Freud laid out the plan for *The Interpretation of Dreams* (*Die Traumdeutung*) in terms of "an imaginary walk" ("eine Spaziergangsphantasie"). Sigmund Freud, *The Complete Letters of Sigmund Freud to Wilhelm Fliess 1887–1904*, trans. and ed. Jeffrey Moussaieff Masson (Cambridge, MA and London: The Belknap Press of Harvard University Press, 1985), 365; *Briefe an Wilhelm Fließ 1887–1904*, ed. Jeffrey Moussaieff Masson (Frankfurt am Main: S. Fischer, 1986), 400. A similar moment of surprise when entering a clearing occurs in Schiller's famous poem "Elegy" (*Elegie*) (1795), later called "The Walk" (*Der Spaziergang*). Schiller, *NA*, 2, I: 308–14. In other words, the mountain climb or the countryside walk constitutes a long-established literary *topos* of whose history Freud was clearly well aware.

[62] [einen Spaziergang durch eine blühende Sommerlandschaft]. *SE*, XIV: 305; *GW*, X: 358. For a similar example of Freud's failure to identify a figure to whom he refers, see "Some Character-Types met with in Psycho-Analytic Work" ("Einige Charaktertypen aus der psychoanalytischen Arbeit," 1916), *SE*, XIV: 333; *GW*, X: 391.

[63] Matthew von Unwerth, *Freud's Requiem: Mourning, Memory, and the Invisible History of a Summer Walk* (New York: Riverhead Books, 2005), 4. These identifications are accepted by Paul Roazen in his review of *Freud's Requiem*, in *The American Journal of Psychiatry* 163, no. 2 (February 2006): 333–4.

[64] Herbert Lehmann, "A Conversation between Freud and Rilke," *The Psychoanalytic Quarterly* 35 (1966): 423–7.

[65] Even though there is no evidence that the poet in question is Rilke, a poem entitled "Transitoriness" ("Vergänglichkeit"), written in February 1924, in some respects captures much of what Freud wished to say in his essay; see Rainer Maria Rilke, *Die Gedichte* (Frankfurt am Main: Insel, 1986), 945.

[66] [Der Dichter bewunderte die Schönheit der Natur um uns, aber ohne sich ihrer zu erfreuen. Ihn störte der Gedanke, daß all diese Schönheit dem Vergehen geweiht war, daß sie im Winter dahingeschwunden sein werde, aber ebenso jede menschliche Schönheit und alles Schöne und Edle, was Menschen geschaffen haben und schaffen könnten. Alles,

Like the opening line of Friedrich Schiller's elegiac poem "Nänie," Freud's poet laments the fact that "Even the beautiful must die!" (*Auch das Schöne muß sterben!*).[67] According to Freud, contemplation of the transitoriness of beauty and perfection can give rise to two responses.[68] First, there is the response that leads to "aching despondency," the response of the young poet; and second, there is the denial that natural and artificial forms of beauty are in fact transitory at all. For Freud, such a response – "the demand for eternity" – reflects the strength of our unconscious "life of desire," our *Wunschleben*.[69] As von Unwerth concedes, "the identities of his two companions, even whether the walk took place at all are ultimately unknowable," and he is right to say that the real question is "what made Freud memorialize or possibly invent a summer walk in an essay dedicated to Goethe."[70]

Time and pleasure

The answer, inasmuch as it reveals the connection with Goethe, lies in the way in which Freud's essay succinctly states one of the most important themes of Goethe's iconic work, *Faust*. In his earlier essay, "Leonardo da Vinci and a Memory of His Childhood" ("Eine Kindheitserinnerung des Leonardo da Vinci," 1910), Freud had compared the Italian artist and inventor to the quintessentially Goethean figure of Faust:

> Because of his insatiable and indefatigable thirst for knowledge Leonardo has been called the Italian Faust. But quite apart from doubts about a possible transformation of the instinct to investigate back into an enjoyment of life – a transformation which we must take as fundamental in the tragedy of Faust – the view may be hazarded that Leonardo's development approaches Spinoza's mode of thinking.[71]

In his description of the tragedy of *Faust* as the transformation of the instinct to investigate back into the enjoyment of life, Freud has articulated

---

was er sonst geliebt und bewundert hätte, schien ihm entwertet durch das Schicksal der Vergänglichkeit, zu dem es bestimmt war.] Freud, *SE*, XIV: 305; *GW*, X: 358.
[67] Schiller, *NA*, 2, I: 326.
[68] For Freud, the problem of transience relates ultimately to the intrapsychic process of the "work of mourning," a term he introduced in "Mourning and Melancholia" ("Trauer und Melancholie"), a paper published in the following year after his essay "On Transience" in 1917.
[69] [der schmerzliche Weltüberdruß]; [diese Ewigkeitsforderung]. *SE*, XIV: 305; *GW*, X: 358.
[70] Von Unwerth, *Freud's Requiem*, 211, 6.
[71] [Man hat Leonardo wegen seines unersättlichen und unermüdlichen Forscherdranges den italienischen Faust geheißen. Aber von allen Bedenken gegen die mögliche Rückverwandlung des Forschertriebes in Lebenslust abgesehen, möchte man die Bemerkung wagen, daß die Entwicklung Leonardos an spinozistische Denkweise streift.] *SE*, XI: 75; *GW*, VIII: 142.

nothing less than the premise of his later essay on transience, as well as one of the central themes of Goethe's *œuvre* and one of the great ambitions of psychoanalytic therapy. Out of *Faust* – a text itself arising from and containing elements of the Storm and Stress and Weimar classicism – is born the spirit of psychoanalysis. For intrinsic to the psychoanalytic conception of the unconscious is the notion of non-rational desire, which lies at the heart of *Faust*, Part One, the opening lines of which are concerned with the problem of knowledge and its existential relevance.

For the issue of transitoriness is expressed in the elderly academic's ironic challenge to the devil – "Show me the fruit that rots before it's plucked" *(Zeig mir die Frucht, die fault, eh' man sie bricht)* – and in the detail of the wager itself, in which he expresses the desire to halt time.[72] In Part Two, the problem of the transient nature of beauty is allegorized in the encounter between Faust and Helena in Act 3.[73] "And so the spirit looks neither forward nor back" *(Nun schaut der Geist nicht vorwärts, nicht zurück)*, Faust says to Helena, "The present alone" *(Die Gegenwart allein)* – and she completes the line – "is our joy" *(ist unser Glück)*.[74] (For a further discussion of the relevance of *Faust* to the concept of the unconscious as elaborated by Carl Gustav Carus, see chapter 6 of this volume, by Matthew Bell.)

Transitoriness is a motif present elsewhere in Goethe's works; indeed, as Nicholas Rennie has noted, the motif can be found in almost all genres of Goethe's work,[75] including his poetry. The poem entitled "The Godlike" *(Das Göttliche*, 1783) says of Man: "He can endow / The moment with permanence" *(Er kann dem Augenblick / Dauer verleihen)*.[76] The problem of pleasure in relation to time lies at the heart of Goethe's poem "Lasting Change" *(Dauer im Wechsel*, 1803), in which (just as in Freud's essay) the stanza moves rapidly from the enjoyment of nature to an awareness of – and a meditation on – its transitoriness:

> Oh, if only springtime's blessing
> Could be held for just one hour!

---

[72] *Faust I*, line 1686; Johann Wolfgang von Goethe, *Faust: Part One*, trans. David Luke (Oxford: Oxford University Press), 51; see also lines 1699–1706.

[73] For further discussion, see Matthijs Jolles, "Goethes Anschauung des Schönen," *Deutsche Beiträge zur geistigen Überlieferung* 3 (1957): 89–116 (especially 95–6, 106). Elsewhere, Goethe is equally insistent on the transient nature of beauty. In one of his distichs written with Schiller, Beauty itself asks Zeus why she is transient, and the god replies that only what is transient is beautiful: "'Warum bin ich vergänglich, o Zeus?' so fragte die Schönheit. / 'Macht' ich doch,' sagte der Gott, 'nur das Vergängliche schön,'" *HA*, I: 225. Indeed, for Goethe, beauty has to be transient, in order for beauty always to be something living and fruitful (Jolles, "Goethes Anschauung des Schönen," 106); the "immortality" of art is something we impart to it, not something inherent in it.

[74] *Faust II*, lines 9381–9382.

[75] Nicholas Rennie, *Speculating on the Moment: The Poetics of Time and Recurrence in Goethe, Leopardi, and Nietzsche* (Göttingen: Wallstein, 2005), 42.

[76] Goethe, *Selected Poems*, trans. John Whaley (London: Dent, 1998), 46–7.

> But the mild west wind is pressing
> And already blossoms shower.
> All this green, should I enjoy it,
> Grateful for its recent shade?
> Autumn's storms will soon destroy it
> Once it's rocked the leaves that fade.
>
> *Hielte diesen frühen Segen*
> *Ach, nur Eine Stunde fest!*
> *Aber vollen Blütenregen*
> *Schüttelt schon der laue West.*
> *Soll ich mich des Grünen freuen,*
> *Dem ich Schatten erst verdankt?*
> *Bald wird Sturm auch das zerstreuen,*
> *Wenn es falb im Herbst geschwankt.*[77]

The second stanza of the poem then goes on to echo the problematic of *Faust* –

> From the fruits your share ensuring
> Grasp them quickly as you need!
> These ones here begin maturing
> And already others seed;
>
> *Willst du nach den Früchten greifen,*
> *Eilig nimm dein Teil davon!*
> *Diese fangen an zu reifen,*
> *Und die andern keimen schon;*

– while hinting that the problem of time belongs to a tradition initiated by Heraclitus, who famously remarked that "it is not possible to step twice into the same river":[78]

> See your lovely valley quiver
> Altering instantly in rain;
> Oh, and in the self-same river
> You will never swim again.
>
> *Gleich mit jedem Regengusse*
> *Ändert sich dein holdes Tal,*
> *Ach, und in demselben Flusse*
> *Schwimmst du nicht zum zweitenmal.*

---

[77] Goethe, *Selected Poems*, 84–5. For further discussion of the psychological ideas in this text, see William Stephen Davis, "Subjectivity and Exteriority in Goethe's 'Dauer im Wechsel,'" *The German Quarterly*, 66 (1993): 451–66.

[78] Heraclitus, Diels-Kranz, 22 B 91; Jonathan Barnes, *Early Greek Philosophy* (Harmondsworth: Penguin, 1987), 177. By way of critique, Cratylus, the teacher of Plato, maintained that not only is it impossible to step twice into the same river, but "one could not do it even once," *Metaphysics*, Book 4, chapter 5, 1010 a 7; in Aristotle, *The Basic Works*, ed. Richard McKeon (New York: Random House, 1941), 746.

Furthermore, a later poem, "Testament" (*Vermächtnis*, 1829), concludes with the following lines: "The past's forever re-created, / The future here anticipated, / The moment is eternity" (*Dann ist Vergangenheit beständig, / Das Künftige voraus lebendig, / Der Augenblick ist Ewigkeit*).[79]

And so, in his essay "On Transience," Freud denies neither the transitoriness of all things nor the transitoriness of beauty, but he does reject the pessimism of the young poet, arguing that transitoriness is, in fact, part of the value of beauty. "Transience value" (*der Vergänglichkeitswert*) is, he proposes, "scarcity value in time" (*ein Seltenheitswert in der Zeit*), such that "limitation in the possibility of an enjoyment raises the value of the enjoyment."[80] To this statement, Freud adds, in tribute to Ronsard, Herrick, and the entire poetic tradition back to Horace's *carpe diem*, a typical twist: "A flower that blossoms only for a single night does not seem to us on that account less lovely."[81] As Pierre Hadot has rightly insisted, "Horace's *carpe diem* is not at all, as it is often presented, the advice of a sensual man," but rather, "quite the contrary, this is an invitation to a conversion, that is, to a coming to an awareness of the vanity of great and empty desires, a coming to an awareness also of the imminence of death, the uniqueness of life, the uniqueness of the instant."[82]

As far as Freud is concerned, this argument about the "scarcity value of time" applies to natural beauty (the seasons, the human body, a flower) and to cultural achievement (plastic and intellectual, and indeed civilization itself) alike. His position is thus closely allied to the one adopted by Goethe in one of his *Maxims and Reflections*:

I feel sorry for those people who make a lot of fuss about the transience of things and lose themselves in the contemplation of earthly vanity. After all, we are here precisely to make what is transitory eternal; but that can only happen, when one knows how to appreciate both.[83]

---

[79] Goethe, *Selected Poems*, 150–1. In the 1950s Hermann Schmitz placed Goethe's conception of the *Augenblick* in a major philosophical tradition stretching from Parmenides, Plato, and Aristotle to Augustine, Kierkegaard, and Klages. See Hermann Schmitz, *Goethes Altersdenken im problemgeschichtlichen Zusammenhang* (Bonn: Bouvier, 1959), 51.
[80] [Die Beschränkung in der Möglichkeit des Genusses erhöht dessen Kostbarkeit.] *SE*, XIV: 305; *GW*, X: 359.
[81] [Wenn es eine Blume gibt, welche nur eine einzige Nacht blüht, so erscheint uns ihre Blüte darum nicht minder prächtig.] *SE*, XIV: 306; *GW*, X: 359. See Pierre de Ronsard, *L'Amour de Cassandre*, no. 25; Robert Herrick, *Hesperides*, no. 208; Horace, *Odes*, book 1, no. 11.
[82] Pierre Hadot, "'The Present Alone is our Joy': The Meaning of the Present Instant in Goethe and in Ancient Philosophy," *Diogenes* 133 (1986): 60–82; here 69. For further discussion, see Pierre Hadot, *N'oublie pas de vivre: Goethe et la tradition des exercices spirituels* (Paris: Albin Michel, 2008), where Goethe's approach to time and the affirmation of existence is related to Nietzsche's (256–67).
[83] [Ich bedaure die Menschen, welche von der Vergänglichkeit der Dinge viel Wesens machen und sich in Betrachtung irdischer Nichtigkeiten verlieren. Sind wir ja eben deshalb

Likewise, the theme of the transience of beauty is considered by Ludwig Feuerbach (1804–72) in his late (and unfinished) essay, "Eudaemonism" (*Der Eudämonismus*, 1867–9). In his discussion of "the transitoriness of the beautiful" (*die Vergänglichkeit des Schönen*), Feuerbach criticizes those philosophers who, like Hegel with the "concept" (*Begriff*) or Kant with the "thing-in-itself" (*Ding an sich*), remain in hock to the old theological conception of a timeless, spaceless essence, and attribute time (and transitoriness) to the sensible human being alone, to an involuntarily fantastic version of what we really are, thereby robbing themselves – and us – of a true view of life and nature (*die wahre Lebens- und Naturanschauung*).[84]

In line with this tradition, Freud's essay insists on the dialectical relationship between time and pleasure. Moreover, in a conversation with the theologian Johannes Daniel Falk (1768–1826), Goethe coined the phrase "half-Stoic, half-Epicurean" (*halb Stoiker und halb Epikuräer*),[85] an expression which, as Hadot observes,[86] might well be applied to Goethe's own position – and, one could add, to Freud's as well. For the concept of the "Stoic-cum-Epicurean" captures the essence of both men's concerns about the dialectic of time and pleasure. On the Epicurean side of Freud, we have the importance he attaches to Eros, to the pleasure principle, to bodily needs, and to the satisfaction of the id which, if repressed, will merely return. During a discussion at the Viennese Psychoanalytic Society, Freud even advocated the return to an educational institution prominent in the age of antiquity – "the creation of a love academy, where the arts of love would be taught."[87] And on the Stoic side, there is Freud's recognition that happiness is necessarily limited (not least, because of the demands of the super-ego). As he put it in *Studies on Hysteria* (*Studien über Hysterie*, 1895), in response to the objection raised by a hypothetical patient that psychological illness is connected with circumstances and events of life that cannot be altered:

> no doubt fate would find it easier than I do to relieve you of your illness. But you will be able to convince yourself that much will be gained if we succeed in transforming your hysterical misery into common unhappiness.

da, um das Vergängliche unvergänglich zu machen; das kann ja nur dadurch geschehen, wenn man beides zu schätzen weiß.] Goethe, *Maxims and Reflections*, HA, XII: 512.

[84] Ludwig Feuerbach, *Sämtliche Werke*, ed. Wilhelm Bodin and Friedrich Jodl, 2nd edn., 10 vols. (Stuttgart: Frommann, 1960), vol. X, 253. Time, Feuerbach insists, is in fact no mere form of intuition [keine blosse Anschauungform], but rather "the essential form of life and condition of life" [wesentliche Lebensform und Lebensbedingung].

[85] Goethe, *Goethes Gespräche: Gesamtausgabe*, ed. Flodoard von Biedermann, 5 vols. (Leipzig: Biedermann, 1909–1911), vol. IV, 469.

[86] Hadot, "'The Present Alone is our Joy'," 76–7.

[87] [die Errichtung einer Liebesakademie, wo die ars amandi gelehrt würde]. Herman Nunberg and Ernst Federn, eds., *Protokolle der Wiener Psychoanalytischen Vereinigung*, 4 vols. (Frankfurt am Main: S. Fischer, 1976–1981), vol. I, 293. See also Gay, *Freud*, 162–4.

To this, Freud added the typical remark that, "with a mental life that has been restored to health, you will be better armed against that unhappiness."[88]

Likewise, the theme of work – its necessity, as well as (dare one say it?) its pleasures – is central to Goethe and Freud. Goethe's activist ethic is well summarized in *Wilhelm Meister's Journeyman Years* (*Wilhelm Meisters Wanderjahre*, 1821/1829), in which one of the characters of the novel – the educated aristocrat and major turned mineralogist and mining engineer, Jarno, now called Montan – insists on the reciprocity of "thinking" and "doing," delivering the celebrated maxim, "thought and action, action and thought, that is the sum of all wisdom" (*Denken und Tun, Tun und Denken, das ist die Summe aller Weisheit*).[89] The central tenet of this injunction is found in numerous reflections of Goethe, such as this one: "There is nothing more miserable than a decent man without work; the most beautiful of gifts becomes disgusting to him."[90] In his correspondence with Oskar Pfister, Freud had already remarked in his letter of March 6, 1910 that he was unable to contemplate with equanimity a life without work: "to fantasize and to work are the same thing for me, there is nothing else that I enjoy" (*Phantasieren und Arbeiten fällt für mich zusammen, ich amüsiere mich bei nichts anderem*).[91] And the American psychoanalyst Erik Erikson (1904–94) recalls Freud's answer when he was once asked what a normal person should be able to do. *Lieben und arbeiten*, "love and work," was Freud's answer – in Erikson's view, a "simple formula" which, however, "gets deeper as you think about it."[92]

Of course, this emphasis on work is not restricted to Goethe and Freud. Kant, for example, believed that "work is the best way of enjoying one's life" (*Arbeit … ist … die beste Art sein Leben zu genießen*),[93] and the

---

[88] [Ich zweifle ja nicht, daß es dem Schicksale leichter fallen müßte als mir, Ihr Leiden zu beheben: aber Sie werden sich überzeugen, daß viel damit gewonnen ist, wenn es uns gelingt, Ihr hysterisches Elend in gemeines Unglück zu verwandeln. Gegen das letztere werden Sie sich mit einem wiedergenesenen Seelenleben besser zur Wehre setzen können.] Freud, *SE*, II: 305; *GW*, I: 312.

[89] Johann Wolfgang von Goethe, *Conversations of German Refugees/Wilhelm Meister's Journeyman Years or The Renunciants*, ed. J. K. Brown, trans. J. van Heurck, K. Winston, *Goethe's Collected Works*, vol. X (New York: Suhrkamp, 1989), 280.

[90] [Elender ist nichts als der behagliche Mensch ohne Arbeit, das schönste der Gaben wird ihm eckel.] *Tagebuch*, January 13, 1779; Goethe, *WA*, 3, I: 77.

[91] Sigmund Freud and Oskar Pfister, *Briefe 1909–1939*, ed. Ernst L. Freud and Heinrich Meng (Frankfurt am Main: S. Fischer, 1963), 32.

[92] Erik H. Erikson, "Growth and Crises of the Healthy Personality" (1950), *Identity and the Life Cycle* (New York: Norton, 1980), 51–107; here: 102.

[93] Kant, *Anthropologie*, book 2, §260; *Anthropology*, trans. Gregor, 101; *Gesammelte Schriften*, vol. VII, 232; compare with Kant's advice to a young person: "get fond of work: deny yourself enjoyments, not to *renounce* them but to keep them, as much as possible, only in prospect"; [gewinne die Arbeit lieb; versage dir Vergnügen, nicht um ihnen zu entsagen,

emphasis on work constitutes part of the legacy of German idealism in psychoanalysis. Given his reputation, it might be surprising to learn that the psychoanalyst Wilhelm Reich (1897–1957) was attached to the idea of a "work democracy," believing that – in the words of his motto – "love, work, and knowledge are the wellspring of our life" (*Liebe, Arbeit und Wissen sind die Quellen unseres Lebens*), and so "they should also govern it" (*sie sollen es auch regieren*). Reich's message was, as one of his commentators has put it, one of "extraordinary simplicity":

> You don't have to do anything special or new. All you have to do is to continue what you are doing: plough your fields, wield your hammer, examine your patients, take your children to the school or to the playground, report on the events of the day, penetrate ever more deeply into the secrets of nature.[94]

Psychoanalysis: a vitalist materialism?

Underlying the "half-Stoic, half-Epicurean" ethics of Goethe and, in turn, of Freud is an important ontological question, determining the way in which each considers the problem of the relationship between time and pleasure. As we have seen, the dialectic of time and pleasure in both Goethe and Freud is deeply linked to the problem of conscious and unconscious desire: first and foremost, the desire to overcome the transience of all things beautiful and pleasurable. In both thinkers this desire and its unconscious elements arguably emerge from the same ontological basis, which amounts to nothing less than a "vitalist materialism." For Freud's Stoic-Epicurean principles are informed by his materialist outlook, and his subterranean connection with the Storm and Stress and, in turn, with Weimar classicism lies in his acceptance of similar materialist principles as those embraced by Goethe. Evidence of those materialist principles can be found in Goethe's "Ephemerides" of 1770, a kind of notebook-summary of his early philosophical-cum-scientific-cum-literary interests. The "Ephemerides" contains a text, written in Latin, which has been described as nothing less than Goethe's "credo,"[95] and which paraphrases a passage from the German philologist Johann Albert Fabricius (1668–1736) on the philosophy of Spinoza, stating:

---

sondern so viel als möglich immer nur im Prospect zu behalten!] (*Anthropologie*, book 2, §63, 105; *Gesammelte Schriften*, vol. VII, 237.

[94] Wilhelm Reich, *Listen, Little Man* (London: Souvenir Press, 1972), 116; cited in David Boadella, *Wilhelm Reich: The Evolution of his Work* (London: Arkana, 1985), 236.

[95] Rolf Christian Zimmermann, *Das Weltbild des jungen Goethe: Studien zur hermetischen Tradition des deutschen 18. Jahrhunderts*, 2 vols. (Munich: Fink, 1969–1979), vol. I, 48; cited in *Der junge Goethe in seiner Zeit*, vol. I, 632.

To speak separately of God and of nature is as difficult and as delicate as thinking of the body and the soul as separate entities. We know the soul only through the body; we know God only through nature.[96]

This phrase anticipates Goethe's later commentary to Chancellor von Müller on his (or Tobler's) aphoristic essay "On Nature":

> The missing capstone is the perception of the two great driving forces in all nature: the concepts of *polarity* and *intensification*, the former a property of matter insofar as we think of it as material, the latter insofar as we think of it as spiritual.[97]

Now something resembling these two great driving forces recurs again in Freud's later thinking, in the form of love or Eros, which seeks to bind more tightly together, and Thanatos (the death-drive or *Todestrieb*), which seeks to pull further apart.[98] And these drives are at work in all aspects of the human being – physiologically, inasmuch as we think of the human being as body; and psychologically, inasmuch as we think of the human being as psyche.

Indeed, Goethe's "Ephemerides" is, in important respects, comparable with Freud's "Project for a Scientific Psychology" (*Entwurf einer Psychologie*) of 1895.[99] Neither is a completed work, neither represents a mature outlook or system; and neither was ever published by its author. In the case of both texts, however, we have an early sketch that indicates the future directions of its author's thoughts, and which hence makes the underlying principles of that thought easier to discern. And in

---

[96] [Separatim de Deo, et natura rerum disserer difficile et periculosum est, eodem modo quam si de corpore et anima sejunctim cogitamus; animam non nisi mediante corpore, Deum non nisi perspecta natura cognoscimus.] Goethe, *WA*, I, XXXVII: 90–1; Joseph-François Angelloz, *Goethe*, trans. R. H. Blackley (New York: The Orion Press, 1958), 32.

[97] [Die Erfüllung aber, die ihm fehlt, ist die Anschauung der zwei großen Triebräder aller Natur: der Begriff von *Polarität* und von *Steigerung*, jene der Materie, insofern wir sie materiell, diese ihr dagegen, insofern wir sie geistig denken, angehörig]. Goethe, *Scientific Writings*, 6; *HA*, XII: 48. Compare with Knebel's remark that "the difference between *materialism* and *spiritualism* simply must be rescinded if one is to arrive at the truth. There is only One true being — or All is a dream" [Der Unterschied zwischen *Materialismus* und *Spiritualismus* muß schlechterdings aufgehoben werden, ehe man zur Wahrheit gelangen kann. Es gibt nur Ein wahres Wesen, oder es ist Alles Traum]; Karl Ludwig von Knebel, *Literarischer Nachlaß und Briefwechsel*, ed. K. A. Varnhagen von Ense und Theodor Mundt, 3 vols. (Leipzig: Reichenbach, 1836), vol. III, 489.

[98] See Freud, *Beyond the Pleasure Principle* (*Jenseits des Lustprinzips*, 1920), §5, *SE*, XVIII: 34–43; *GW*, XIII: 35–45.

[99] Freud, *The Origins of Psycho-Analysis: Letters to Wilhelm Fliess, Drafts and Notes, 1887–1902*, trans. Eric Mosbacher and James Strachey, ed. Marie Bonaparte, Anna Freud, and Ernst Kris (London: Imago Publishing Company, 1954), 355–445; *GW, Nachtragsband*, 375–486. For a discussion of the relevance of the "Project" for current research, see Marcel Kinsbourne, "Taking the *Project* Seriously: The Unconscious in Neuroscience Perspective," *Annals of the New York Academy of Sciences* 843 (May 1998): 111–15.

50   Paul Bishop

the "Project," Freud makes his materialist presuppositions unmistakably clear, stating that:

the intention of this project is to furnish us with a psychology which shall be a natural science: its aim, that is, is to represent psychical processes as quantitatively determined states of specifiable material particles and so to make them plain and void of contradictions.[100]

According to the editors of the German edition of the "Project," one of the two principles explored in it, "Q" (*Q*), is something material, which becomes "Q ēta" (*Qη*), that is, something which stands in relation to the nervous system and which, it is suggested, is related to the notion of "psychic energy" found in *The Interpretation of Dreams* (*Die Traumdeutung*, 1900). As the editors note, however, Freud's discussion remains essentially physiological,[101] and in this respect it inherits an important strand of eighteenth-century thought.

During his medical studies at Vienna at the end of the nineteenth century, Freud was strongly influenced by the leading theory of the day: materialism, and specifically, mechanism, as represented by his teacher in physiology, Ernst Brücke (1819–92), by the mechanist scientist, Hermann Helmholtz (1821–94), and by the German physiologist, Emil Du Bois-Reymond (1818–96). In a letter to his student friend Eduard Silberstein (1857–1925) of March 15, 1875, Freud gave an account of a visit he and Josef Paneth paid to Franz Brentano, in which he commented that Brentano knew perfectly well that they were materialists.[102] When Freud writes to Silberstein approvingly of Ludwig Feuerbach as "someone whom I revere and admire above all other philosophers," and pays tribute to "so steadfast a champion of 'our truths,'"[103] this phrase – *our truths* – should be understood, Wilhelm Hemecker has argued, as a reference to materialism.[104]

---

[100] [Absicht, eine naturwissenschaftliche Psychologie zu liefern, d.h. psychische Vorgänge darzustellen als quantitativ bestimmte Zustände aufzeigbarer materieller Teile [und sie] damit anschaulich und widerspruchsfrei zu machen.] Freud, "Project for a Scientific Psychology," in *The Origins of Psycho-Analysis*, 355; *GW, Nachtragsband*, 387.
[101] Freud, *GW, Nachtragsband*, "Entwurf einer Psychologie, Anhang B: Die Natur von Q," 480–6; especially 483–4.
[102] *The Letters of Sigmund Freud to Eduard Silberstein 1871–1881*, trans. Arnold J. Pomerans, ed. Walter Boehlich (Cambridge, MA: The Belknap Press of Harvard University Press, 1990), 102; Freud, *Jugendbriefe an Eduard Silberstein 1871–1881*, ed. Walter Boehlich (Frankfurt am Main: S. Fischer, 1989), 116.
[103] [den ich unter allen Philosophen am höchsten verehre und bewundere]; [eines so gesinnungstüchtigen Kämpfers für "unsere" Wahrheiten]. Freud, *Letters*, 96; *Jugendbriefe*, 111.
[104] Wilhelm H. Hemecker, *Vor Freud: Philosophiegeschichtliche Voraussetzungen der Psychoanalyse* (München: Philosophia Verlag, 1991), 53.

Unconscious from Storm and Stress to Weimar classicism 51

As Günter Gödde also points out in chapter 10 of this volume, Freud's earliest scientific work was into nerve cells, involving experiments on crayfish and crabs, and later eels. His psychoanalytic theory makes extensive use of mechanistic, hydraulic metaphors: repression, de-repression, libidinal flow, and so on.Yet these images of flux and flow begin to move Freud's materialism away from the mechanistic models of French eighteenth-century materialism (not to mention the Germanic tradition of Helmholtz, Du Bois-Reymond, and Brücke) and towards a more vitalist conception, such as the one embraced by Feuerbach, who wrote in his 1837 study of Leibniz:

Blocks of stone and logs are not true types of the concept of matter. The true essence of matter, its *idea*, *exists* in the animal, in the human being as sensuousness, drives, desire, passion, as the lack of freedom and as confusion.[105]

In addition to Carl Brühl, another mediating figure between Goethe and Freud may well have been Karl Grün (1817–87, the pseudonym of Ernst von der Haide), a left-wing Hegelian and socialist thinker, who had published Feuerbach's correspondence and *Nachlass* in 1843.[106] Grün also published an essay on the German political writer and satirist Ludwig Börne (1786–1837) that Freud much admired;[107] lectured to the *Leseverein der Deutschen Studenten* (German Students' Reading Union) at the University of Vienna on Darwin and Haeckel (a session that Freud attended); and, as it turns out, wrote a commentary on Goethe.[108] In a passage in *The Interpretation of Dreams*, in the context of his recollection of a discussion of the relation of philosophy to science at the student union, Freud pays discreet tribute to Karl Grün, as W. McGrath has suggested.[109] Increasingly throughout his career, Freud maintained his

---

[105] [Steinblöcke und Klötze sind nicht die wahren Typen zu dem Begriff der Materie. Das wahre Wesen der Materie, die *Idee* derselben, *existiert* im Tiere, im Menschen als Sinnlichkeit, Trieb, Begierde, Leidenschaft, als Unfreiheit und Verworrenheit.] Ludwig Feuerbach, *Gesammelte Werke*, ed. Werner Schuffenhauer, 22 vols.(Berlin: Akademie Verlag, 1967–), vol.III, 69.
[106] Karl Grün, ed., *Ludwig Feuerbach in seinem Briefwechsel und Nachlass sowie in seiner Philosophischen Charakterentwicklung dargestellt*, 2 vols. (Leipzig und Heidelberg: Winter, 1874). For further discussion of Freud's possible indebtedness to Feuerbach, see Hemecker, *Vor Freud*, 52–61.
[107] See Karl Grün, *Bausteine* (Darmstadt: Leske, 1844), 19.
[108] See Karl Grün, *Über Göthe vom menschlichen Standpunkte* (Darmstadt: Leske, 1846).
[109] Freud observed of himself: "I was a green youngster, full of materialistic theories, and thrust myself forward to give expression to an extremely one-sided point of view"; [Ich *grüner* Junge, der *materialistischen* Lehre voll, drängte mich vor, um einen höchst einseitgen Standpunkt zu vertreten]. *SE*, IV: 212; *GW*, II/III: 218. See also: William McGrath, *Freud's Discovery of Psychoanalysis: The Politics of Hysteria* (Ithaca: Cornell University Press, 1986), 105. For evidence of Freud's thoughtful approach to his materialism, see his letter to Silberstein of April 11, 1875, *Letters*, 109–110; *Jugendbriefe*, 124.

insistence on the vitalist-materialist aspect of psychoanalysis, writing, for example, in the posthumously published "An Outline of Psychoanalysis" ("Abriß der Psychoanalyse," 1940) that "the phenomena with which we were dealing do not belong to psychology alone; they have an organic and biological side as well."[110]

It is from this aspect of Freud's thought that the French psychoanalyst Jacques Lacan (1901–81) tried to move away, contending that "Freudian biology has nothing to do with biology,"[111] and replacing Freud's materialism with his own "materialism of the signifier."[112] But the materialism of Freud's outlook is hard to avoid. The stages of psycho-sexual development (oral, anal, phallic, genital) are, after all, organized around the body, while the physiological core of hysterical symptoms is likened to the piece of sand around which pearls of neurosis develop,[113] thereby anticipating the use of chemical intervention to effect psychological cures.[114] In one of his introductory lectures on psychoanalysis (1916), Freud commented that "the theoretical structure of psycho-analysis that we have created is in truth a superstructure, which will one day have to be set upon its organic foundation," adding: "But this foundation is still unknown to us."[115] Similarly, in another of his lectures, Freud emphasized that "the sexual function is not a purely psychical thing any more

---

[110] [die Phänomene, die wir bearbeiten, gehören nicht nur der Psychologie an, sie haben auch eine organisch-biologische Seite]. "An Outline of Psycho-Analysis" ("Abriss der Psychoanalyse," 1938), SE, XXIII: 195; GW, XVII: 125. "Accordingly," Freud added, "in the course of our efforts at building up psycho-analysis we have also made some important biological discoveries and have not been able to avoid framing new biological hypotheses" [dementsprechend haben wir in unseren Bemühungen um den Aufbau der Psychoanalyse auch bedeutsame biologische Funde gemacht und neue biologische Annahmen nicht vermeiden können]. Compare with the skepticism about a physiological conception of the psyche expressed in "The Unconscious" ("Das Unbewußte," 1913) and "The Claims of Psycho-Analysis to Scientific Interest" ("Das Interesse an der Psychoanalyse," 1913), GW, X: 266–7; VIII: 406.

[111] "Freud, Hegel, and the Machine," Jacques Lacan, *The Seminar*, book 2: *The Ego in Freud's Theory and in the Technique of Psychoanalysis 1954–1955*, trans. Sylvana Tomaselli, ed. Jacques-Alain Miller (NewYork: Norton, 1991), 75.

[112] "The Highway and the Signifier 'Being a Father,'" Jacques Lacan, *The Seminar*, book 3, *The Psychoses 1955–1956*, trans. Russell Grigg, ed. Jacques-Alain Miller (London: Routledge, 1993), 289.

[113] Somatic influences (whether normal or pathological), says Freud, play the part of the grain of sand which a mollusc coats with layers of mother-of-pearl [spielen die Rolle jenes Sandkorns, welches das Muscheltier mit den Schichten von Perlmuttersubstanz umhüllt hat]; *Introductory Lectures on Psycho-Analysis* (*Vorlesungen zur Einführung in die Psychoanalyse*, 1916–17), SE, XVI: 391; GW, XI: 406.

[114] "Outline of Psycho-Analysis," §6; SE, XXIII: 182; GW, XVII: 108.

[115] [Das Lehrgebäude der Psychoanalyse, das wir geschaffen haben, ist in Wirklichkeit ein Überbau, der irgend einmal auf sein organisches Fundament ausgesetzt werden soll; aber wir kennen dieses noch nicht.] *Introductory Lectures*, no. 24, SE, XVI: 389; GW, XI: 403.

than it is a purely somatic one," for "it influences bodily and mental life alike." He went on to conclude that

> if in the symptoms of the psychoneuroses ... we have become acquainted with manifestations of disturbances in the *psychical* operation of the sexual function, we shall not be surprised to find in the "actual" neuroses the direct *somatic* consequences of sexual disturbances.[116]

And likewise, the Viennese-born psychoanalyst Ernst Kris (1900–57) records that Freud

> repeatedly spoke of the connection between psychological and biochemical processes as a field awaiting explanation, and always emphasized that the terminology of psychoanalysis was provisional, valid only until it could be replaced by physiological terminology.[117]

Conclusion: psychoanalysis and nature

So one of the reasons why Freud found Goethe so compelling was because he saw in the fragment "On Nature" a vision of nature that is materialist, but not reductionist. What links them, and what underpins their view of the dialectic of time and pleasure, is this shared materialist outlook. Thus the notion of the unconscious that emerges from Goethe and Freud alike is one that is conceived as essentially desiring and pleasure-seeking, one might even say: as hedonist. To put it another way, in the aphoristic essay "On Nature" we also find an anticipation of Freud's concept of the unconscious as an account of our *inner* nature. This idea of "inner nature" is one explicitly foregrounded by Freud, who speaks in *Civilization and Its Discontents* (*Das Unbehagen in der Kultur*, 1930) about "a piece of unconquerable nature" (*ein Stück der unbesiegbaren Natur*) forming part of our psychic constitution.[118] Although the phrase is originally found in Jung – another psychoanalyst inspired by Goethe, and who wrote in his paper "Psychological Types" ("Psychologische Typen," 1923) that "the unconscious is the residue of unconquered nature in us, just as it is also

---

[116] [daß die Sexualfunktion nichts rein Seelisches ist, ebensowenig wie etwas bloß Somatisches. Sie beeinflußt das körperliche wie das seelische Leben. Haben wir in den Symptomen der Psychoneurosen die Äußerungen der Störung in ihren psychischen Wirkungen kennen gelernt, so werden wir nicht erstaunt sein, in den Aktualneurosen die direkten somatischen Folgen der Sexualstörungen zu finden.] *SE*, XVI: 387–8; *GW*, XI: 402.

[117] Ernst Kris, "Introduction," *The Origins of Psycho-Analysis*, 45. See also Kris, "The Nature of Psychoanalytic Propositions and Their Validation," *Freedom and Experience: Essays presented to Horace M. Kallen*, ed. Sidney Hook and Milton R. Konvitz (New York: Cooper Square Publishers, 1947), 239–59.

[118] Freud, *SE*, XXI: 86; *GW*, XIV: 445.

the matrix of our unborn future"[119] – it crops up time and again in the thinking of the first and second generations of the Frankfurt School, where it is always attributed to Freud.

In *Dialectic of Enlightenment* (*Dialektik der Aufklärung*, 1944), for example, T. W. Adorno (1903–69) and Max Horkheimer (1895–1973) speak of the "remembrance of nature in the subject" (*Eingedenken der Natur im Subjekt*) as the central point at which the Enlightenment is opposed to tyranny. "By virtue of this remembrance of nature in the subject," they write, "in whose fulfilment the unacknowledged truth of all culture lies hidden, enlightenment is universally opposed to domination."[120] In his *Theory of Communicative Action* (*Theorie des kommunikativen Handelns*, 1981), Jürgen Habermas (born 1929) also focuses on this key phrase. As part of *his* critique of Adorno's and Horkheimer's critique of instrumental reason, Habermas accuses his colleagues of following "the (largely effaced) path that leads back to the origins of instrumental reason, so as to *outdo* the concept of objective reason"; thus their theory of mimesis, Habermas argues, leads them to speak about it "only as they would about a piece of uncomprehended nature." Habermas' judgment on Adorno is particularly severe: "As opposed as the intentions behind their respective philosophies of history are, Adorno is in the end very similar to Heidegger as regards his position on the theoretical claims of objectivating thought and of reflection: the mindfulness [*Eingedenken*] of nature comes shockingly close to the recollection [*Andenken*] of being."[121]

---

[119] [das Unbewußte ist der Rest unbezwungener Urnatur in uns, so wie es auch der Mutterboden ungeschaffener Zukunft in uns ist.] C. G. Jung, *Collected Works*, ed. Sir Herbert Read, Michael Fordham, Gerhard Adler, and William McGuire, 20 vols. (London: Routledge and Kegan Paul, 1953–83), vol. VI, §907; Jung, *Gesammelte Werke*, ed. Lilly Jung-Merker, Elisabeth Ruf, and Leonie Zander, 20 vols. (Olten und Freiburg im Breisgau: Walter-Verlag, 1960–83), vol. VI, §971. Compare with his comment about "the fantasy-images of the unconscious which our rationalism has rejected" [die Phantasiebilder des Unbewußten ..., die der rationale Verstand ehedem verworfen hatte] as constituting "part of the nature *in us*" [*gehören zur* Natur in uns]; "Analytical Psychology and 'Weltanschauung'" ("Analytische Psychologie und Weltanschauung," 1927), *Collected Works/Gesammelte Werke*, vol. VIII, §739. For further discussion of Jung's awareness and development of major motifs of German classicism, see Paul Bishop, *Analytical Psychology and German Classical Aesthetics*, 2 vols. (London and New York: Routledge, 2008–9).

[120] [Durch solches Eingedenken der Natur im Subjekt, in dessen Vollzug die verkannte Wahrheit aller Kultur beschlossen liegt, ist Aufklärung der Herrschaft überhaupt entgegengesetzt.] Max Horkheimer and Theodor W. Adorno, *Dialectic of Enlightenment: Philosophical Fragments*, trans. John Cumming (New York: Continuum, 1996), 40; *Dialektik der Aufklärung: Philosophische Fragmente* (Frankfurt am Main: Fischer Verlag, 1969), 47.

[121] [Horkheimer und Adorno verfolgen vielmehr die weitgehend verwischte Spur, die zu den Ursprüngen der instrumentellen Vernunft zurückführt, um so den Begriff der objektiven Vernunft noch zu *überbieten*]; [wie über ein undurchschautes Stück Natur]; [So sehr die Intentionen ihrer jeweiligen Geschichtsphilosophien entgegengesetzt

Of course, the shared legacy with Heidegger could alternatively be seen as a strength, not a weakness, and as evidence of the global appeal and universal truth of this *topos*.[122] For the concept of the unconscious as our "inner nature," as something at once material or physiological as well as dynamic or vitalist, is one of the greatest legacies of the *Goethezeit* to the nineteenth century and to Freud.

In his essay "On Transience," Freud suggests that the cycle of the seasons recurs over the human life-span in a manner that could be called "eternal" – "as regards the beauty of Nature, each time it is destroyed by winter it comes again next year, so that in relation to the length of our lives it can in fact be regarded as eternal."[123] We might equally consider this insight to be Goethean, inasmuch as precisely this idea of circularity, or of recurrence, informs at a formal (or structural) level another one of Goethe's great texts about nature, the early poem "On the Lake" ("Auf dem See," 1775). The opening "Und" of the first line expresses this repetition, this infinite return, as well as the necessary destruction that forms of part of our own existence amid the nature in which we trust:

> And now I suck fresh food, new blood,
> From all the world with zest;
> Dear nature, how she's fair and good
> Who holds me to her breast!
>
> *Und frische Nahrung, neues Blut*
> *Saug ich aus freier Welt;*
> *Wie ist Natur so hold und gut,*
> *Die mich am Busen hält!*

---

sind, so sehr ähneln sich beide, Adorno am Ende seines Denkwegs, und Heidegger, in ihrer Stellung zum theoretischen Anspruch des objektivierenden Denkens und der Reflexion: das Eingedenken der Natur gerät in schockierende Nähe zum Andenken des Seins.] Jürgen Habermas, *The Theory of Communicative Action*, trans. Thomas McCarthy, 2 vols. (London: Heinemann, 1984; Cambridge: Polity Press, 1987), vol. I: *Reason and the Rationalization of Society*, 382 and 385; *Theorie des kommunikativen Handelns*, 2 vols. (Frankfurt am Main: Suhrkamp, 1987), vol. I: *Handlungsrationalität und gesellschaftliche Rationalisierung*, 511–12 and 516.

[122] For further discussion of the links between Freiburg and Frankfurt, see Fred R. Dallmayr, *Life-World, Modernity and Critique: Paths Between Heidegger and the Frankfurt School* (Cambridge: Polity Press, 1991). For further specific discussion of Habermas and Heidegger, see Jozef Keulartz, *Die verkehrte Welt des Jürgen Habermas*, trans. Inge van der Aart (1992; Hamburg: Junius, 1995); and of Adorno and Heidegger, see Hermann Mörchen: *Macht und Herrschaft im Denken von Heidegger und Adorno* (Stuttgart: Klett-Cotta, 1980), and *Adorno und Heidegger: Untersuchung einer philosophischen Kommunikationsverweigerung* (Stuttgart: Klett-Cotta, 1981).

[123] [Was die Schönheit der Natur betrifft, so kommt sie nach jeder Zerstörung durch den Winter im nächsten Jahre wieder, und diese Wiederkehr darf im Verhältnis zu unserer Lebensdauer als eine ewige bezeichnet werden.] Freud, *SE*, XIV: 305; *GW*, X: 359.

The final lines of the poem go on to draw the link between nature as external and nature as internal, referring to the process of development inherent in that "nature within us" that we call the self:

> Morning wind wings gently
> Round the shadow-filled bay,
> Ripening fruit contently
> Mirrors itself in the sway.
>
> *Morgenwind umflügelt*
> *Die beschattete Bucht,*
> *Und im See bespiegelt*
> *Sich die reifende Frucht.*[124]

According to Freud, psychoanalysis is a cure "effected by love";[125] and love, too, is the culmination of the vision in "On Nature":

Her crown is love. Only through love do we come to her. She opens chasms between all beings, and each seeks to devour the other. She has set all apart to draw all together. With a few draughts from the cup of love she makes good a life full of toil.[126]

One of Freud's biographers records Freud's sister recalling an early ambition on the part of her brother: "I want to help people who suffer," he is recorded as saying.[127] This essentially therapeutic ambition is thoroughly in keeping with the utilitarian philosophy of J. S. Mill, four of whose essays Freud translated into German.[128] Through promoting a materialist-vitalist understanding of the self, the concept of the unconscious-as-nature bequeathed to the nineteenth century by the Storm and Stress and Weimar classicism, preeminently in the person of Goethe – a concept which, as we have seen, is subsequently developed by Freud – has been one of the most important attempts in modern times to bring about healing.[129]

---

[124] Goethe, *Selected Poems*, 30–31.
[125] [Es ist eigentlich eine Heilung durch Liebe.] Freud to Jung, December 6, 1906, *The Freud/Jung Letters*, trans. Ralph Manheim and R.F.C. Hull, ed. William McGuire (Cambridge, MA: Harvard University Press, 1988), 12–13; Sigmund Freud/C. G. Jung, *Briefwechsel*, ed. William McGuire and Wolfgang Sauerländer (Frankfurt am Main: Fischer, 1974), 13.
[126] [Ihre Krone ist die Liebe. Nur durch sie kommt man ihr nahe. Sie macht Klüfte zwischen allen Wesen und alles will sich verschlingen. Sie hat alles isoliert um alles zusammenzuziehen. Durch ein paar Züge aus dem Becher der Liebe hält sie für ein Leben voll Mühe schadlos.] Goethe, *Scientific Studies*, 3–4; *HA*, XIII: 47.
[127] Anna Bernays-Freud, "My Brother, Sigmund Freud," *American Mercury*, vol. 51, no. 203 (November 1940): 335–42; here 338–40; cited in Ronald W. Clark, *Freud: The Man and the Cause* (London: Paladin, 1982), 37.
[128] See Ernest Jones, *The Life and Work of Sigmund Freud*, 3 vols. (New York: Basic Books, 1953–7), vol.I, 55–6.
[129] I should like to thank Angus Nicholls for his patience, care, and editorial assistance in adapting my original paper for inclusion as a chapter in this volume.

2 The philosophical significance of Schelling's conception of the unconscious

Andrew Bowie

Locating the unconscious

Philosophical investigations which trace the genesis of a concept from what preceded it, and then trace how the concept influenced what succeeded it, encounter a problem in relation to "the unconscious."[1] This problem might admittedly seem to arise in relation to any concept, because disagreements about the content of a concept inevitably result from the never finally delimitable contexts in which it is encountered. Philosophers don't even agree, for example, on whether "Water is H_2O" is "necessarily true in all possible worlds." In such a case we can at least refer to the familiar fluid that we are disagreeing about and describe some of its properties. With respect to the unconscious the problem is more fundamental because we don't *know* what we are talking about: if we did, it would not be unconscious. As we shall see, much will depend here on the sense of "know." Before getting to Friedrich Wilhelm Joseph Schelling (1770–1854), who has some claim to being the first person to use the term "unconscious" in the kind of ways which have been important in modern thought, we therefore need to explore some of the issues that make the unconscious a peculiarly recalcitrant topic. This should also enable us both to avoid the problem of just parroting what Schelling says when he employs the word "unconscious" and related terms, and to gauge whether his ideas are still philosophically significant.

The popular appeal of the idea of the unconscious, which leads to some questionable uses of the term, comes about because the unconscious is seen as explaining how it can be that when we do something we may not really know what we are doing. If the explanation is that something is making us do that which we cannot be aware of or cannot resist, we can get the kind of thrill provoked by Peter Lorre's murderer in *M*, who "Will nicht. Muss!" (Don't want to. Have to!), because he is

---

[1] The inverted commas indicate the problematic status of the idea that there is "an" or "the" unconscious, as opposed to the less questionable idea that motivations, desires, representations, etc., may be unconscious, perhaps because they have been repressed.

driven by a perverted "other of himself." The unconscious has in this respect to do with the notion of a "divided self." The idea that we may be driven by what our rational self cannot control supposedly frees us from responsibility for our actions by loosening the bonds of civilization. At the same time, this loosening can also be pathological: the link of the unconscious to madness is an enduring theme in modernity – though it is one which can also too easily be used as an excuse not to think about the social causes of pathologies. Thinking in terms of this link can, however, lead to a failure to appreciate the sense in which the unconscious, as the "other of oneself," cannot in fact be completely lacking in rationality. As Donald Davidson shows, if it were, we would just be talking about causally determined processes, which do not involve the interpretative elements involved in many issues associated with the unconscious.[2] In this essay I want to show that these issues go to the heart of the concerns of German idealism which are playing a major new role in contemporary philosophy.

The disputed borderline between nature and consciousness – which is the underlying source of the renewed debate about German idealism – is necessarily an issue in consideration of the unconscious.[3] In most construals of the notion, the unconscious has to do with impulses which have a basis in natural causality but must also involve intentionality, because what is at issue relates to the *meanings* of those impulses in relation to things like human sexuality. Philosophical attempts to reduce intentionality and meaning to causal explanations by regarding them as merely part of "folk psychology" are now looked at with justifiable suspicion in some quarters. This has led to reflections on the limits of natural scientific explanation which have wide-ranging social and political implications. Schelling remains significant because he not only challenges dominant ways of thinking about nature in modern philosophy in a manner that prefigures some contemporary objections to scientistic reductionism, but also offers alternatives to some of these objections on the basis of his consideration of the unconscious.

The basic problem in this context remains, though, that an unconscious which could be directly encountered would obviously not deserve the name. The most familiar strategy here is Freud's: he points to phenomena – "Freudian slips," and the like – from which it can be inferred

---

[2] D. Davidson, *Problems of Rationality* (Oxford: Clarendon Press, 2004).
[3] This debate has become central to contemporary analytical philosophy via John McDowell's influential *Mind and World* (Cambridge, MA: Harvard University Press, 1994). The title of Robert Pippin's critique of McDowell, "Leaving Nature Behind," *Reading McDowell's "Mind and World,"* ed. N. Smith (London: Routledge, 2002), suggests the tension which underlies the debate.

that what motivates an action is not the conscious intention of the performer of that action.[4] That's fine as far as it goes – and we shall encounter an analogous inferential approach in Schelling – because we do often do and say things for reasons not fully apparent to ourselves at the time that we do and say them. The question is what this allows us to infer about the unconscious. Does one, for example, need to substantivize it, meaning that we commit ourselves to the existence of something called "*the* unconscious"? But what sort of an entity is this, given that it is neither present to our awareness, nor an object in any determinable sense? If this is essentially a question about whether there is something to which the noise of the unconscious "corresponds," it is not necessarily clear that we really know what that means. Language as a whole cannot be understood in terms of words corresponding to things, and the notion of correspondence has so far proved impossible to explicate in a generally convincing manner. In these terms the question should be "can we use the locution 'the unconscious' in a way which I can justify to others?"

Certain basic issues concerning the meanings of the term "unconscious" should be addressed at this point. Most of what is "in our minds" is not "conscious," because we are, in one sense at least, only really conscious of what is immediately "present to our minds."[5] Much that we could attend to never reaches the level of reflective awareness, although when it does we realize that it was already "there" (though here one still needs to ask "where, exactly?"), and thus must have been in some sense conscious before we became aware of it. A version of this view, which is explored in detail in phenomenology, was already put forward by Leibniz, in his theory of *petites perceptions*, perceptions that were not "apperceived," in the sense of one being reflectively aware of having them (for a discussion of this idea, see the Introduction to this volume). Similarly, when we realize that our motivation was not what we thought it was, we gain access to something which was unconscious, but not wholly opaque – if it were, how would it cease to be opaque and how could it have motivated us with respect to our conscious relations to the world? Something similar may apply to undeveloped thoughts which later emerge in clearly articulated

---

[4] It may seem somewhat strange, given the mention of Freud, that I do not explicitly deal with the libidinal aspect associated with the unconscious in what follows. The brief reason for this is that the libidinal is only one form of the interface between nature and consciousness that is the basis of what I have to say concerning the unconscious. Once one accepts the notion of the divided self, the divisions can result from repression and sublimation of sexual impulses, but they can also result from repression and sublimation of other kinds of impulse.
[5] Like so many locutions in this area, this one is hard to give a clear sense to, because it suggests a duality between our minds and what is "present to" them, when such experience does not involve a duality.

form. What does it mean to say that these things previously belonged to whatever the unconscious is?

One problematic response to this question can lead to the model familiar from Schopenhauer's image (which was influenced by Schelling's reflections on the Will of the 1810s) of our being in a phenomenal, conscious boat sailing the dark, unfathomable, noumenal, unconscious sea of the Will, which contains countless hidden drives, etc., waiting for their chance to emerge. This sort of conception is summed up when Eduard von Hartmann quotes Jean Paul: "Our measurements of the wealth of lands of the I are much too small or narrow if we leave out the massive realm of the unconscious, this in every sense true inner Africa."[6] But how does one get to Africa? Africa may have been something inaccessible to fantasize about for Jean Paul, but we can get on a plane. As the mysteries of physical nature give way to causal explanations and to forms of technological control, doesn't something similar happen to the mysteries of the mind? In that case, shouldn't the idea of the unconscious be likely to lose its sense of mystery, as the causal mechanisms underlying the workings of the mind are discovered? In certain respects this may well be the case. However, even though the sciences increasingly dispel mysteries about some areas of mental functioning, if what is at issue cannot be reduced to causal terms, there may still be significant issues concerning the unconscious.

The sense of a limit to what causal explanation can achieve in this respect leads to a decisive point. A great deal turns on how "nature" is conceived here: is it just the system of necessary causal laws which Kant called nature in the "formal" sense, or is nature itself to be thought of as in some sense conscious, given that conscious beings are part of it? Moreover, if the unconscious has to do with the interface between nature and consciousness, and is not reducible to either, it would seem to have some relationship to what is not causal, and thus to whatever might be meant by "freedom." These issues will take us to the heart of Schelling's conception of philosophy, and to some of the central questions in the contemporary revaluation of German idealism, in which the relationship of subjectivity to nature and freedom is a decisive theme.

One influential way of thinking about the unconscious, which both avoids the "inner Africa" problem, and which cannot be reduced to a causal explanation, is in relation to language. In Jacques Lacan's terms

---

[6] [Wir machen von dem Länderreichthum des Ich viel zu kleine oder enge Messungen, wenn wir das ungeheure Reich des Unbewussten, dieses in jedem Sinne wahre innere Afrika, auslassen.] Eduard von Hartmann, *Philosophie des Unbewussten*, 10th edn., 3 vols. (Leipzig: Wilhelm Friedrich, 1890), vol. I, 22.

we are "inserted into" a preexisting language, so language cannot be wholly transparent to us. Language is itself not consciously produced, though once it is there it can be consciously manipulated, and seems to be located between nature and society: there is no society without it, so that in some sense it must precede society, even though it cannot develop without social intercourse. Schelling suggests how we might think about such a conception when he says of the ideas (*Vorstellungen*) of mythology, which, as anthropology shows, first constitute societies as societies, that they "are products of a necessary process, or of natural consciousness which is left to its own devices, on which there is no influence of any free cause [in the sense of a conscious decision to create something],"[7] and he links mythology to language: "One is almost tempted to say: language itself is only faded mythology, in it is preserved in only abstract and formal differences what mythology preserves in still living and concrete differences."[8] If we assume that language is part of what we are, it adds to the sense that we are more than we can ever know, and this is one of the potentially useful ways of thinking about the unconscious. As Herder had already observed, given how much we unreflectively assimilate from the cultures into which we are socialized, what we think and feel must be based on something which does not all come to the level of reflective evaluation while it is being acquired. This symbolic and other expressive material can subsequently become rigidified and abstract, losing its power when subjected to reflection, and so creating the need for something which can replace it. The question is then how far conscious reflection can actually exhaust what is generated by such processes, and responses to this question have important consequences for modern philosophy.[9]

Each culture necessarily involves exclusions and inclusions which entail various kinds of "repression," because the culture fails to do justice to needs and desires which are not articulable with the resources of that culture. These needs and desires provoke resistance and create

---

[7] [Erzeugnisse eines notwendigen Prozesses, oder natürlichen, sich selbst überlassenen Bewußtseins sind, auf welches keine freie Ursache einen Einfluß ausübte.] F. W. J. Schelling, *Philosophie der Offenbarung* (1841–2), ed. Manfred Frank (Frankfurt: Suhrkamp 1977), 250.
[8] [Beinahe ist man versucht zu sagen: die Sprache selbst sey nur die verblichene Mythologie, in ihr sey nur in abstracten und formellen Unterschieden bewahrt, was die Mythologie noch in lebendigen und concreten bewahre.] Friedrich Wilhelm Joseph Schelling, *Sämmtliche Werke*, ed. K. F. A. Schelling, 2 parts, 14 vols. (Stuttgart: Cotta, 1856–61), part 2, vol. I, 52 (hereafter cited as *SW*, followed by part, volume and page numbers).
[9] Hans-Georg Gadamer insists, in this vein, that we can never reach a completely external viewpoint on what we have become by entering into a language and a culture, even though reflection can highlight much that was previously unthematized.

tensions both within and between the subjects of the culture, and many of these tensions will not reach the level of reflective evaluation. They may, though, be dealt with via other symbolic and expressive resources, and this will be one of the reasons why the unconscious is often related to art, as the locus of what is not conveyed conceptually.[10]

The varying forms of expression which we acquire through different processes of acculturation and the differing degrees of reflective evaluation of these forms at various times therefore mean that the unconscious must have a history. It also cannot be wholly internal to the individual subject, as its content includes the effects of symbolic and other aspects of the world which the subject inhabits.[11] The historicity of the unconscious can remind us that, like the notion of "self-consciousness," the very notion of the unconscious is generally not thought of as such until sometime around the Enlightenment. Prior to this what we use the notion of the unconscious to address is more likely to be linked to fate and to the gods, thus to an external order of things – think of Oedipus in Sophocles, as opposed to Freud's Oedipus. Despite such changes, it is clear, however, that what is in question must, given the constitutive role of repression in every culture, be in some sense ubiquitous.

What changes in the modern period is therefore the relationship between the "internal" and the "external." Indeed, it might even be maintained that the now prevalent ideas of such a relationship are a result of the beginnings of modernity. The relationship becomes highlighted as a philosophical problem by Descartes' separation of thinking and extension, which is part of the modern concern with the relationship between mind and world. The separation of mind and world, which gives rise to modern philosophical epistemology, is arguably itself best regarded in historical terms. It is an expression of a change in the relationship between "inside" and "outside" occasioned by the beginnings of the scientific revolution, which put in question the sense of external certainty derived from the theological or metaphysical idea of a "ready-made," objective world. This separation, the overcoming of which is the aim of a great deal of modern philosophy, also leads to philosophical concern with the unconscious. The familiar problem here is that if subject (thinking) and object (extension) are separate it is not clear how they connect at all. Skeptical answers to this question can lead, as Descartes argued, in

---

[10] See A. Bowie, *Aesthetics and Subjectivity from Kant to Nietzsche* (Manchester: Manchester University Press, 2003), and *Music, Philosophy, and Modernity* (Cambridge: Cambridge University Press, 2007), and below.

[11] This conception in no way commits one to the highly questionable notion of a "collective unconscious," because the significance of collective resources differs for each individual.

the direction of the idea that our thinking could be controlled by an evil demon which blocks the transparency of our relationship to reality. It is a small step from this idea to the idea of the unconscious as what threatens the transparency of our relationship to reality, but there are many different ways in which this problem can be construed, as the divisions within German idealism will suggest.

Schelling and the sources of German idealism

In his 1833–4 Lectures, *On the History of Modern Philosophy* (*Über die Geschichte der neueren Philosophie*), Schelling contends that the question of the "I" has dominated modern philosophy.[12] Like the other German idealists, he assumes that the philosophical answer to the Cartesian problem of the separation of mind and body must be that they cannot be wholly distinct, and so must in some sense be "identical." This is intuitively obvious, but the claim can lead in very divergent directions, because the notion of identity is notoriously difficult to explicate. One can, for example, argue, as contemporary "eliminative materialism" does, that there is nothing but "matter," and that mental states are therefore to be thought of as in fact physiological states, the identity being resolved into the world side of the split. On the other hand, one can, as does an idealism that takes thoughts as the only certain forms of existence – *what* thoughts are of can always be mistaken, *that* one has thoughts cannot – argue that the world is only intelligible because of the operations of "mind."

German idealism is concerned to explicate the identity of mind and nature, even as it acknowledges aspects of Kant's transcendental philosophy which can make this explication a problem. One influence on Schelling's work is apparent when Leibniz distinguishes between degrees of consciousness in attempting to account for how bodily impulses (which are material, being manifest in causal processes) can become conscious aspects of thought. As Leibniz puts it: "For because the nature of things is uniform our own substance cannot be infinitely different from the other simple substances of which the whole universe consists."[13] We have already seen that Leibniz was led to one sense in which one can talk of what is unconscious: nature in these terms has degrees of

---

[12] His critique of Descartes in this text preempts both Nietzsche's and Heidegger's attacks on Cartesianism. Despite Schelling's reputation as an obscure thinker, it is a model of clarity. See Schelling, *On the History of Modern Philosophy*, ed. and trans. A. Bowie (Cambridge: Cambridge University Press, 1994).

[13] Gottfried Wilhelm Leibniz to Burcher de Volder, June 30, 1704, cited in M. Heidegger, *Wegmarken* (Frankfurt: Klostermann 1978), 90.

64   Andrew Bowie

"consciousness," from the minimal level involved in matter, to the "apperceptive" level of the reflective subject. By assuming only differences of degree within nature as a whole, this position seeks to avoid trying to cross a gap between two separate realms. The "unconscious" is simply a form of lesser consciousness, and this means that it is not something that is wholly causally determined. This conception is, however, not enough to set in train the specific modern forms of interest in the unconscious, even though aspects of it are relevant to those forms and do influence Schelling. The crucial other dimension has to do with the question of freedom, which, following Rousseau and Kant, comes to be seen in terms of the human capacity for self-determination which is independent of natural causality.

The issue of freedom in this sense might seem to take one away from the unconscious towards the rationalist side of modern philosophy which insists, as Kant does, that we "give the law" to nature in cognition, and to ourselves in moral action, on the basis of publicly justifiable criteria. However, the manner in which Kant explicates the relationship between thinking and freedom soon indicates how things are not so straightforward. The reason has to do with the nature of the subject's reflection on its own thinking, which is the core of Kant's approach. "Transcendental" philosophy looks at the "conditions of possibility" of the scientific knowledge that is exemplified by Newton's laws of motion. The question is how there could be a science of such conditions of possibility, if they are themselves the conditions of scientific knowledge: a regress of "conditions of conditions," of the kind that results when one tries to trace the sequence of causes of any phenomenon, threatens, which would render knowledge impossible. There seems therefore to be a constitutive blind-spot at the heart of the subject's self-awareness, and Kant's arguments do not necessarily dispel this worry.

Von Hartmann makes the link of this issue to the unconscious evident in his discussion of Kant's conception. In doing so he highlights the relationship between the "spontaneous" and the "receptive" aspects of cognition which is crucial to the renewed interest in Kant and German idealism in contemporary philosophy. This interest results from suspicion of models of cognition that rely on the idea that there is a source of direct evidence which furnishes epistemological reliability.[14] Kant sees the spontaneous and the receptive as wholly separate sources of cognition (so already posing the question as to how they connect):

According to Kant the pure concepts of the understanding (categories) seem as though they ought to belong to unconscious representations, insofar as they lie

---

[14] The idea that there is such a source is what Wilfrid Sellars and others refer to as the "myth of the given."

beyond cognition, which only becomes possible by the fact that a blind function of the soul spontaneously makes synthetic links between the given manifold of the perceived material of representation.[15]

In order to overcome the difference between the never identical, contingent perceptual material given in receptivity, and the stable forms of identity (such as causality) brought to bear on that material by the spontaneity of the understanding, Kant has to introduce an intermediary between the two, which he terms the "schema": this cannot itself be an object of knowledge, as it is part of what makes knowledge possible. The schema is required not just for the pure concepts, like causality and substance, but also for the application of empirical concepts: "This idea of a universal procedure of imagination to provide a concept with its image I call the schema to this concept. Indeed it is not images of the objects which underlie our purely sensuous concepts, but schemata."[16] Images will always differ, so there needs to be some form of apprehension which enables us to understand different images as identical in cognitive terms.

The idea of the schema plays an influential role in post-Kantian thinking: Heidegger makes it central to the whole conception of *Being and Time*, for example. Schleiermacher says a schema is a "shiftable image,"[17] which means that apparently very different cases of something can be connected by it, like a bonsai and a giant redwood as both being trees. Schelling suggests that "The schema ... is not an idea that is determined on all sides, but an intuition of the rule according to which a particular object can be produced,"[18] e.g. the rule for seeing a bonsai and a redwood as "trees." Were this not to be an intuition of a rule, it would have to be a rule for a rule, which is the source of the kind of regress we saw threaten Kant's conception above.[19] Schematism, for Kant, is – and here

---

[15] [Zu den unbewussten Vorstellungen scheinen nach Kant die reinen Verstandesbegriffe (Kategorien) gehören zu sollen, insofern sie jenseits der Erkenntniss liegen, welche erst dadurch möglich wird, dass eine blinde Function der Seele in spontaner Weise das gegebene Mannigfaltige des percipirten Vorstellungsmaterials synthetisch verknüpft.] Hartmann, *Philosophie des Unbewussten*, vol. I, 18.

[16] [Diese Vorstellung nun von einem allgemeinen Verfahren der Einbildungskraft, einem Begriff sein Bild zu verschaffen, nenne ich das Schema zu diesem Begriffe. In der Tat liegen unsern reinen sinnlichen Begriffen nicht Bilder der Gegenstände, sondern Schemate zum Grunde.] Kant, *Kritik der reinen Vernunft* (Frankfurt am Main: Suhrkamp, 1968), 140–1.

[17] Quoted in Manfred Frank, *Das Sagbare und das Unsagbare* (Frankfurt am Main: Suhrkamp, 1989), 28.

[18] [Das Schema ... ist nicht eine von allen Seiten bestimmte Vorstellung, sondern nur Anschauung einer Regel, nach welcher ein bestimmter Gegenstand hervorgebracht werden kann.] Schelling, *SW*, 1, III: 508.

[19] Schelling sees this as the basis of language's capacity to identify apparently different phenomena as the same.

the link to the idea of the unconscious becomes explicit – the "hidden art in the depths of the human soul" which connects the spontaneous and the receptive sides of cognition.[20] We cannot be conscious of schematism doing its work because in order for what we are aware of to be intelligible at all, schematism must always already be in play to organize the contingency of what we apprehend into something subsumable into the identity provided by concepts. Heidegger thinks this is the core of Kant's epistemology because it suggests that cognition depends on a prior intelligibility which cannot itself be explained, being itself the condition of the possibility of explanation.

Novalis sums up a key problem with regard to schematism's relationship to self-consciousness as follows: "Can I look for a schema for myself, if I am that which schematises?"[21] How do we describe the act of seeing the act of seeing? The very idea of doing so leads to a regress, but there is no doubt that we do "see" the world – in the sense that we "apprehend the world as intelligible." Schelling's use of the term "intuition" is the key here. *Anschauung* is the word Kant uses for the unconceptualized material of receptivity, which means that it is not knowledge, knowledge taking the form of judgments that "x" is the case, based on the identifying of intuitions by subsuming them under a rule. "Intuition" is, though, often employed at this time in the wider sense of a direct connection between mind and world. The crucial aspect of this sense of intuition is that the connection is not conceptual. It therefore does not come into the domain of knowledge, and so avoids the problems entailed by reflection on knowledge that we have just encountered. In many respects the differences within German idealism revolve around the status of what belongs to "intuition," rather than to knowledge, and ideas about the unconscious differ according to the status attributed to intuition.

Kant's reference to schematism as an "art" indicates a change in the understanding of some key issues in the later part of the eighteenth century. "Art" can, following from the Greek, simply mean *techné*, in the sense of an ability to do something, but it also begins at this time to take on the sense, later employed by Schleiermacher, of "production which is not governable by rules."[22] "Art" therefore has to do with what takes us beyond nature *qua* deterministic system to the question of the interface of nature and consciousness. Whereas material nature can be seen as governed by necessary laws, our ability to apprehend such laws, and our

---

[20] [eine verborgene Kunst in den Tiefen der menschlichen Seele]. Kant, *Kritik der reinen Vernunft*, 190.
[21] [Kann ich ein Schema für mich suchen, da ich das Schematisirende bin?] Novalis, *Das philosophisch-theoretische Werk* (Munich: Hanser 1978), 162.
[22] See Bowie, *Aesthetics and Subjectivity*, chapter 6.

ability to transcend causal impulses take us into the realm of freedom. This is precisely because knowledge requires "spontaneity," that which is "cause of itself," which makes possible the connections of intuitions in judgments. Were the operations of the understanding not spontaneous, they would be caused like everything else in nature. Explaining how we could *know* that this is the case would then be impossible. As we saw, the result would be the kind of regress that made the intelligibility which allows the understanding of a cause *as* a cause, rather than it just being reacted to in the way animals do when they respond to their environment, incomprehensible.[23] The problem which comes to haunt German idealism is that freedom for Kant is itself not an object of knowledge – that can only be what is given in perception and subsumed under a concept – and this will leave open the path to connecting the idea of freedom to the unconscious which is implicit in Hartmann's view of Kantian spontaneity. The core issue is how to conceive of nature if it is governed by determinism and yet produces self-determining beings who can both take their own stance on knowledge of the nature which has produced them and respond to their existence in expressive ways which cannot be reduced to a cognitive account of those ways.

In these terms what *produces* consciousness must itself initially be unconscious. How, then, is one to explain the move from nature understood as a deterministic system to it being the source of consciousness and freedom? Schelling sees this move in terms of nature "coming to itself," which means it has both to be "apart from itself" when it does not yet know itself, and yet still be "one," in that it comes to *itself*. This might appear as a move from total opacity to total transparency, but things are not that simple. It should be clear from the problems in conceiving of this move why the issues here are still alive. The reductionist strand of contemporary naturalist philosophy, which thinks that issues to do with consciousness will turn out to be questions of neuroscience, argues that there is no such move, and that what is at issue will be explicable in terms of the causal functioning of the brain. The problem of this approach lies in explaining how it is that we are aware of this issue at all: the objective states of affairs which reductive naturalist philosophers invoke can only be seen *as* objective in relation to the judgments of a subject which can take a stance on what belongs to objectivity. This stance cannot itself claim to be objective in the same sense, because the very idea of objectivity depends on it. One side of German idealism can be characterized

---

[23] The person who realized the danger of a conception based solely on things conditioning other things most clearly was F. H. Jacobi. See Bowie, *From Romanticism to Critical Theory* (London: Routledge 1997), and below.

by its claim that the prior aspect here is therefore the very possibility of taking a stance that involves responsibility for the commitments entailed by asserting one claim rather than another, including claims about the explanation of consciousness.[24] Whilst it is arguable that the contemporary employment of German idealist ideas can indeed show the implausibility of reductionist naturalism, the complexities of the issue of freedom in Schelling can suggest problems in some versions of those ideas.

German idealism and the unconscious

German idealism's unstable reputation, which led to it being rejected from the 1840s onwards by the "Young Hegelians" like Feuerbach and the early Marx, and ignored or dismissed by most analytical philosophers for most of the twentieth century, has a lot to do with the more extreme claims Fichte and Hegel in particular can be construed as making. Fichte, for example, takes the idea that the world would be simply opaque without the spontaneity of thought as a reason for regarding the spontaneity of the I as the ground of philosophy, so that "freedom" is the basis of the world's intelligibility. The obscurity of Fichte's presentation of his ideas means, though, that there is little agreement over what he actually meant. He seems to suggest that the "absolute I" produces the world, but saying what this means is hardly easy. Answers range from something close to a theological conception to an emphatic version of the Kantian idea that without the spontaneous activity of thought there is no intelligible world. For our purposes the interpretative issues are, however, not such a problem, as it matters more how Fichte was in fact construed and how this affected the development of the notion of the unconscious.

In his illuminating retrospective account of how he arrived at his own *System of Transcendental Idealism* (*System des transcendentalen Idealismus*) of 1800 (*STI*), Schelling suggests in 1833 how Fichte's conception that "Everything is only via the I and for the I" necessarily leads to a notion of the unconscious. If the world is really the free product of the I, why is it in so many respects not as we would wish it to be? As such "if he attributes a production of those ideas [of the necessities of the external world] to the I, then this must at least be a production that is blind and not grounded in the *will* but rather in the *nature* of the I."[25] This remark involves what

---

[24] See Robert Pippin, *The Persistence of Subjectivity* (Cambridge: Cambridge University Press, 2005).
[25] [wenn er dem Ich ein Produzieren jener Vorstellungen zuschreibt, so muß dieses wenigstens ein blindes, nicht in dem *Willen*, sondern in der *Natur* des Ich gegründetes Produzieren sein]. Schelling, *SW*, 1, X: 94.

seems to be an equivocation concerning the mind/nature relationship, but this is precisely congruent with our main theme.

Nature is opposed to the I, insofar as its necessities are felt by the I to be objective, to "stand against" its will (Schelling and others use the etymology of the German term for "object," *Gegen-stand*, to suggest this). At the same time the necessities are seen as being inherent in the I itself, as otherwise the connection of mind to the world is threatened. Schelling elucidates his relation to and difference from Fichte as follows:

> Here it was immediately evident, however, that the external world is admittedly only there *for* me insofar as I myself am there at the same time and am conscious of myself (this goes without saying), but it was also evident that, conversely, the *moment* I am *there* for myself, I am *conscious* of myself, with the statement "I am", I also find the world as already being – there, thus that the *already conscious* I cannot possibly produce the world. But nothing stopped a return with this I which is *now* conscious of itself in me to a moment when it was not yet conscious of itself – the assumption of a region beyond *now present* consciousness and an activity which no longer comes itself, but comes only via its result into consciousness.[26]

This conception involves the same strategy as in Freud, where the necessity of something not present to consciousness is inferred in order for key aspects of conscious life to be explicable. But what exactly is Schelling referring to?

Schelling's retrospective text is concerned with his proximity to and eventual distance from Fichte at the end of the eighteenth century, which means that the ideas are couched in terms of the relationship between the individual, empirical I, and the "absolute I." Schelling makes it clear that the latter notion is one which he now regards as indefensible, as he had sporadically already done in the 1790s. An I must be relative to a not-I (and so not absolute), because otherwise it loses the characteristic, that makes it an I, of being in a self-conscious relation to what it is not. The key for our theme, which takes the issue beyond the particular concern with Fichte, is the "activity" whose "result" comes into consciousness, but which itself does not.

---

[26] [Hier ergab sich nun aber sogleich, dass freilich die Aussenwelt *für* mich nur da ist, inwiefern ich zugleich selbst da und mir bewusst bin (dies versteht sich von selbst), aber dass auch umgekehrt, *sowie* ich für mich selbst *da*, ich mir *bewusst* bin, dass, mit dem ausgesprochenen Ich bin, ich auch die Welt als bereits da seiend finde, dass also auf keinen Fall das *schon bewusste* Ich die Welt produciren kann. Nichts verhinderte aber, mit diesem *jetzt* in mir sich-bewussten Ich auf einen Moment zurückzugehen, wo es seiner noch nicht bewusst war, eine Region jenseits des jetzt *vorhandenen* Bewusstseins anzunehmen, und eine Thätigkeit, die nicht mehr selbst, sondern nur durch ihr Resultat in das Bewusstsein kommt]. Schelling, *SW*, 1, X: 92–93.

The self-conscious I of every individual is dependent on something of which it is the result: this has in some sense to be "nature," but it cannot be nature in the Kantian sense of a system of necessary causal laws. The something from which the I results is an "activity," which is expressly directed against a deterministic view. At the same time, this activity cannot be the same as that involved in the taking of self-determined cognitive and ethical stances, because these involve "now present consciousness." Consequently, the division between nature and freedom cannot be regarded as between two mutually exclusive opposites. There has to be some kind of "identity" between them, based on the fact that the activity reaches the point where it becomes self-determining and is able to trace its own genesis from what is neither self-determining nor capable of reflecting on itself. The activity is unconscious, in the sense that it is the aspect of ourselves which makes reflective consciousness possible but cannot itself be thought of *either* as self-determined *or* as causally determined. If it were the former, it would already be "present consciousness"; if it were the latter, it could not become conscious because nothing would differentiate it from causal process. The activity no doubt depends on causal processes, but these are necessary, not sufficient, for self-consciousness and self-determination. If this all sounds rather implausible, the fact that something like such a process can be seen as taking place in becoming a social human being from being a baby suggests that avoiding a rigid opposition between self-determination and other "activity" can affect how we understand human action.

In the terms of the contemporary reinterpretations of German idealism by Robert Brandom and Robert Pippin and others, "conscious" in the sense at issue here includes being able to apprehend causes *as* causes by inferentially differentiating them from what is not causal, and thus being able to take self-determined normative stances on both cognitive and ethical issues. A key question is whether the move to self-determination can be as transparent as this implies, given that so many stances taken in real life are the result, for example, of internalized external pressure or of forms of self-deception, neither of which is self-consciously determined as such.[27] Schelling's position points to ways of thinking about the fact that, while we can come to the point of self-consciously acknowledging that we were affected by pressures of which we were not conscious, or that we were deceiving ourselves, there may be no point from which final certainty in such matters can be established. Such certainty becomes just a

---

[27] That, as Davidson and others argue, reasons can be causes, does not mean that there is no difference between being consciously caused to do something for a reason and being caused by natural prompting or unexamined social pressure.

regulative idea, and there is consequently always a potential unconscious element in thinking. Schelling suggests the importance of considering means of coming to terms with this situation which take one outside many dominant approaches to philosophy, and this is where his albeit quite short-lived concern with aesthetics and the unconscious in the *STI* is significant. The decisive point will be that what is thought of in terms of the unconscious can be both a source of the lack of insight or self-deception at issue here, *and* of creative possibilities, most evident in art, which are not best understood in terms of conscious self-determination and knowledge.

It is in this respect that the *STI*, as Schelling's probably most coherent (though also most schematic) piece of philosophy, has resonances which can still affect contemporary debate. At the turn of the century Schelling is seeking to reconcile what seem to be thoroughly contradictory alternatives, namely Fichte's idealism, and Spinoza's "realist" monism. He tries to negotiate a relationship between "transcendental philosophy," which is concerned with the spontaneity of the I as the principle of the world's intelligibility, and what he, from his work of the second half of the 1790s onwards, termed *Naturphilosophie*. The latter seeks to explain how the intelligibility made possible by the I emerges from a nature bound by deterministic laws, while ensuring that there is no Cartesian split of mind and nature: "one can push as many transitory materials as one wants, which become finer and finer, between mind and matter, but sometime the point must come where mind and matter are One, or where the great leap that we so long wished to avoid becomes inevitable."[28] His approach in the *STI* was suggested by the discussion of the idea of "activity" above: in the *Naturphilosophie* the "activity" of nature, via which it develops from inanimate matter into living self-conscious organisms, is in some sense identical with the activity of thought which apprehends an intelligible world rather than a mere chaos of sensations. There is, therefore, "nothing impossible in the thought that the same activity via which nature reproduces itself at every moment anew is reproductive in thought but via the medium of the organism."[29]

---

[28] [Man ... kann zwischen Geist und Materie so viel Zwischenmaterien schieben, die immer feiner und feiner werden, aber irgendeinmal muß doch ein Punkt kommen, wo der große Sprung, den wir so lange vermeiden wollten, unvermeidlich wird]. Schelling, *SW*, 1, I have detailed the way the tensions inherent in the relationship between transcendental philosophy and *Naturphilosophie* recur in Schelling in Bowie, *Schelling and Modern European Philosophy* (London: Routledge, 1993).

[29] [ist nichts Unmögliches in dem Gedanken, daß dieselbe Thätigkeit, durch welche die Natur in jedem Moment sich neu reproducirt, im Denken nur durch das Mittelglied des Organismus reproduktiv sei]. Schelling, *SW* 1, III: 274.

The conceptual problem here follows from the discussion above: what is this "activity"? It is not the same as causal process or as self-determined action, but cannot be separate from them either. That issues concerning the unconscious should be located in this space is unsurprising, given the combination of the natural and the intentional which we have seen as fundamental to the unconscious. One obvious way to think about this is via dreams, which are produced "naturally," via causal processes, but which have a level of intentional content, and which, although largely independent of one's will, can at times be affected by it. Schelling also refers to what he is concerned with as "productivity." The key to the conception is the following claim: "As the object [i.e. any natural phenomenon] is never absolute then something per se non-objective must be posited in nature; this absolutely non-objective postulate is precisely the original productivity of nature."[30] What counts in such a philosophical conception of nature, which is expressly not a form of explanatory natural science, is nature's capacity for change and development, rather than the laws governing the particular empirical manifestations of this capacity. If we are part of nature, nature must be more than can be conceived of in terms of its objective causal processes, which only give rise to "products," i.e. the things in material nature which we identify via their relations to other things. Jacobi saw the objective world in this sense as a world of regressing "conditioned conditions," and as therefore lacking a basis for those conditions being manifest *as* conditions. The sense that the world seen purely in terms of one thing conditioning another is meaningless leads to what Jacobi terms "nihilism." An understanding of the "unconditioned" that would overcome the problem of nihilism is what Schelling and the other German idealists are seeking, and this is part of what led Fichte to the idea of the "absolute," unconditioned, "I".

In the *STI* Schelling follows Fichte's route with respect to the unconditioned status of the I while seeking to incorporate a more emphatic sense of the status of the world of material nature into the account of the development of the I. This is, not surprisingly, a hard act to bring off, and the relationship between nature and the I is anything but transparent in Schelling's work around this time. The source of the connection of Schelling's account to the idea of the unconscious lies in the notion that the world is a result of the absolute or the absolute I, which lacks limits, limiting or "inhibiting" itself in order to become determinate: this can therefore be seen as a kind of "repression" of its original nature.

---

[30] [Da das Objekt nie unbedingt ist, so muß etwas schlechthin Nicht-Objektives in die Natur gesetzt werden, dieses absolut Nichtobjektive ist eben jene ursprüngliche Produktivität der Natur]. Schelling, *SW*, 1, II: 284.

The philosophical significance of Schelling's conception 73

The question is how there can be philosophical access to the "infinite"/ "absolute" / "unconditioned." Because we only have empirical access to "products," not to the "productivity," it is through our awareness of the limitation of the particular product that the philosophical need to articulate our sense of this limitation arises.[31] Transcendental philosophy depends on the ability of thought to reflect upon itself, and thus seeks to objectify the spontaneous activity of subjectivity.[32] The problem is that philosophy can only look at thought in "reflection," i.e. in terms of a subject-object structure, but in doing so it always already has to employ what it is looking at, namely the activity of thought. It therefore constitutively misses what it is seeking, because it cannot attain an external perspective on it.

The idea of the *STI* is that we can come to understand what thought cannot objectify in concepts via what appears in art, which exists in objective form, and so relates to the conscious mind, but whose significance does not derive from its ability to articulate things conceptually, which connects it to the unconscious. The basic structure of Schelling's contentions is apparent in the following: whereas "production in art directs itself outwards in order to reflect the unconscious through products, philosophical production directs itself immediately inwards, in order to reflect it in intellectual intuition."[33] "Intellectual intuition" would be the activity seeing itself as activity, rather than just seeing its results (i.e. the forms of thought of transcendental philosophy that result from philosophical reflection on the necessities in thinking). Apprehending the activity can, however, only happen by being engaged in it, so the activity can never be objectively manifest: by being engaged in it, one precludes stepping outside it.

The claim of the *STI* is that it is through the encounter with something objective which is not comprehensible in conceptual terms – the artwork – that we can infer how the unconscious workings of nature lead to the workings of mind and to human freedom. In order to comprehend an artwork we cannot just regard it in terms of what it has in common with other artworks, i.e. of what we establish through the spontaneity of conceptual judgment (which, as we saw, cannot itself be present to consciousness). There has to be an element which is grasped in

---

[31] This is the source of Hegel's arguments against Kant's thing in itself, which suggest that any limit on knowledge always entails being beyond that limit if we are to know it as a limit.
[32] See Schelling, *SW*, 1, III: 345.
[33] [die Produktion in der Kunst nach außen sich richtet, um das Unbewußte durch Produkte zu reflektieren, richtet sich die philosophische Produktion unmittelbar nach innen, um es in intellektueller Anschauung zu reflektieren]. Schelling, *SW*, 1, III: 35.

a non-conceptual manner. One way of trying to understand this is via the analogy to metaphors, which may take the form of conceptual judgments, but which cease to be living metaphors if they can be fully cashed out in conceptual terms. Schelling wishes to understand the "ground of identity between the absolutely subjective and the absolutely objective, the conscious and the unconscious, which, precisely in order to appear, separate themselves in free action."[34] In this ground, which Schelling terms "absolute identity," there is "no duality," and "because the condition of all consciousness is duality" it can "never arrive at consciousness," and so demands some form of indirect access which allows us to infer its nature.[35] It is therefore not just the aspects of objective nature which precede the development of consciousness which are "unconscious," but also the higher ground of unity which links conscious and unconscious productivity. Consciousness is located between two inaccessible unconscious domains: one is unconscious because it does not reach the level of consciousness, the other because it must transcend the limitations which consciousness inherently involves. Schelling refers to absolute identity as "This eternal unconscious, which, as it were the eternal sun in the realm of spirits, hides itself by its own unclouded light."[36] In the same way as it is only if there is darkness that light can manifest itself *as* light, human conceptual consciousness both makes possible a manifest objective world, and, precisely by making it manifest, makes inaccessible how it is that the world produces conceptual consciousness from itself.

The reason aesthetic activity is so important for the *STI*, then, is that it gives access to what conceptual determination obscures: "nature begins unconsciously and ends consciously [i.e. with the conscious subject], the production is not purposive, but the product is. In the activity which we are talking about here the I must begin with consciousness (subjectively) and end in the unconscious or *objectively*, the I is conscious according to the production, unconscious with regard to the product."[37] The artwork is manifest as an object in the way subjectivity cannot be, but it is only

---

[34] [Grund der Identität zwischen dem absolut Subjektiven und dem absolut Objektiven, dem Bewußten und dem Bewußtlosen, welche eben zum Behuf der Erscheinung im freien Handeln sich trennen.] Schelling, *SW*, 1, III: 600.
[35] [gar keine Duplizität … weil die Bedingung alles Bewußtseins Duplizität ist … nie zum Bewußtsein gelangen.] Schelling, *SW*, 1, III: 600.
[36] [Dieses ewig Unbewußte, was, gleichsam die ewige Sonne im Reich der Geister, durch sein eignes ungetrübtes Licht sich verbirgt]. Schelling, *SW*, 1, III: 600.
[37] [die Natur fängt bewußtlos an und endet bewußt, die Produktion ist nicht zweckmäßig, wohl aber das Produkt. Das Ich in der Tätigkeit, von welcher hier die Rede ist, muß mit Bewußtsein (subjektiv) anfangen, und im Bewußtlosen oder *objektiv* enden, das Ich ist bewußt der Produktion nach, bewußtlos in Ansehung des Produkts.] Schelling, *SW*, 1, III: 613.

art insofar as it manifests the freedom that is essential to subjectivity through its capacity to appear in new ways and never to be exhausted by its interpretations. The artwork is therefore not merely an object to be identified, it is rather something which shows what cannot be "said," in the sense of "conceptually articulated." What it shows is never finally determinable, as it changes with each new interpretation: it is therefore analogous to the productivity of nature, which never reaches a definitive product. Were it to do so, it would cease to be itself because the productivity would disappear into an inert product. Following Kant's idea – which encapsulates one way of seeing the unconscious's combination of the natural and the intentional – that nature "gives the law to art" through the genius, Schelling sees artistic production as being driven by something ultimately not in the artist's conscious control, and this is why it is linked to the idea of the unconscious. The fact that unconsciously driven activity results in something intelligible harmonizes freedom and nature. Art is "the only true and eternal organ and document of philosophy, which always and continuously documents what philosophy cannot represent externally,"[38] because it overcomes the split between subjective and objective, revealing how freedom can providentially be reconciled with the objective course of nature and history.

The logical structures of the *STI* are quite clear, and the metaphysics of the text pretty coherent, but can we make any contemporary philosophical sense of the implications of its account of the unconscious? The basic philosophical problem of the kind of metaphysics present in the *STI* has been suggested by Wolfram Hogrebe:

> However plausible it initially seems to be that the world which has produced a knowing being has to be thought in such a way that the producing forces are in the last analysis also capable of such a result, it is still problematic that these forces are supposed to be of the same kind as what they have produced.[39]

Schelling himself later suggests, in *On the Essence of Human Freedom* (*Über das Wesen der menschlichen Freiheit*, 1809), that if there is a harmony between subjective and objective of the kind proposed in the *STI*, freedom would ultimately be reduced to being part of the (teleologically conceived) mechanics of nature, rather than being, as the transcendental approach holds, what differentiates us from nature *qua* deterministic

---

[38] [das einzige wahre und ewige Organon zugleich und Document der Philosophie, welches immer und fortwährend aufs neue beurkundet, was die Philosophie äußerlich nicht darstellen kann.] Schelling, *SW*, 1, III: 627.
[39] Wolfram Hogrebe, *Prädikation und Genesis: Metaphysik als Fundamentalheuristik im Ausgang von Schellings „Die Weltalter"* (Frankfurt am Main: Suhrkamp, 1989), 54 (my translation).

system. Moreover, the elevated status attributed to art, as the locus of the resolution of the epistemological problems of the division between subject and object, now seems hard to defend in the light of the history of modern art, which is not best understood as manifesting a reconciliation of freedom and nature. However, even though the positive claims of the *STI* are evidently problematic, its approaches to certain issues may not be so indefensible, and they can help to question aspects of the contemporary revaluations of Hegelian idealism.

Hegelian objections

The core objection to Schelling on the part of Hegel and his successors is that he fails to make the absolute philosophically transparent. Schelling's reliance on "intuition" presupposes an initial unity of subject and object which remains conceptually inaccessible, hence the recourse to art as a way out of the impossibility of conceptualizing that which "hides itself by its own unclouded light." This is the kind of view associated with Hegel's famous critical phrase about the inadequacy of an absolute which is the "night in which all cows are black."[40] The philosophical debate on this issue is very extensive, and is unlikely to come to a rapid conclusion, so it would be presumptuous in the space available here to seek to settle the matter. Such fundamental conflicts can, though, be read as indications of instructive tensions in the motivations of modern philosophy, of the kind that are still apparent in some of the differences of focus between the analytical and European traditions.

Take Will Dudley's recent summary of Hegel's position, namely that by "Absolute Knowing" in the *Phenomenology of Mind* (*Phänomenologie des Geistes*, 1807) Hegel means "the subject ... articulating the rational structure of its own thought, which is at the same time the rational structure of being."[41] In the contemporary revivals of Hegel there are various ways of interpreting how Hegel, or anyone else, should go about doing this, but most would concur that something like this is indeed the aim of Hegelian rationality. What is clear is that the orientation is therefore predominantly epistemological – albeit from a perspective which seeks to obviate the very idea of a gap between subject and world, thus overcoming the difference between ontology and epistemology. The question I want to ask is whether Schelling's approach, despite being formulated in epistemological terms, can actually be used to question the primacy of the epistemological orientation in much modern philosophy. Hegel

---

[40] It is not clear that the remark is expressly directed at Schelling.
[41] W. Dudley, *Understanding German Idealism* (Stocksfield: Acumen, 2007), 157.

has become the new focus of analytical philosophers who think that the empiricist epistemological approach which has dominated analytical philosophy is untenable. This suggests, however, that there may be elements of his vision which are also subject to the limitations of a predominantly epistemological orientation: it is noticeable how little of the wider vision of Hegel plays a role in the work of McDowell and Brandom, for example.[42]

Dudley grants that it is not clear that Hegel achieves the intended philosophical elimination of doubts about how the structures of thought relate to those of being. One response to the concern that Hegel may not have achieved this aim is, as some Hegelians do, to attempt to improve the system (others just say it has not yet been interpreted correctly). But what if, in the light of the reliability of much modern science, one is not greatly troubled by the possible failure of this version of overcoming the epistemological divide? As Rorty puts it: "Time will tell; but epistemology won't." Does philosophy necessarily have to be focused on an answer to the epistemological skeptic, an answer which seems rather a long time coming? The notion of the unconscious is, as we have seen, often related to the subject's sense of being divided both from the world and from itself that is a central aspect of culture in modernity. Ways of responding to that sense need not, though, be predominantly linked to epistemology, because the sense of division is (except among certain kinds of philosopher) generally not based on skeptical concerns about the truth of scientific theories. Indeed, the sense of division may actually be intensified by what science tells us about ourselves and the world, as the attempts to come to terms with the contrast between the "manifest" and the "scientific image" (Sellars), or science and the "life-world" (Husserl) suggest. In this perspective the issue of the unconscious points to ways of responding to our sense of a divided nature that results from what we can know conflicting with other ways in which we relate to our being. Such responses, as Schelling suggests in the *STI*, are apparent in aesthetic activity.[43]

Hegel clearly had more in mind than a narrowly conceived epistemological project, and he says many very insightful things about the place of aesthetic issues in modernity. However, the decisive source of his systematic approach *is* the idea of overcoming skepticism by rethinking the implications of the failure of attempts to establish epistemological

---

[42] Pippin stands out for his preparedness to countenance a Hegelianism which engages with a broad range of cultural issues.

[43] Schleiermacher makes the vital additional move for a contemporary version of such an idea – that prevents it being based on a reification of the artwork – of locating aesthetic activity even in everyday practices: see Bowie, *Aesthetics and Subjectivity*, chapter 6.

foundations. That is the basis of his core notion of "determinate negation," where the refutation of a stance leads to a higher stance, but depends on what it refutes to be determinate. In the contemporary versions of the Hegelian position, this idea is encapsulated in the demand that any approach to philosophy must enter the game of giving reasons for the stance that one adopts with regard to the mind/world relationship, reasons only being able to be legitimated through the dialogical process of countering objections. Otherwise one is prey precisely to the objections to "intuition" suggested above: instead of, as Hegel does, seeking to provide a philosophical legitimation by working through and transcending the failure of foundational claims that generates skepticism, one makes dogmatic assumptions about the basis of our relation to the world. Now there is no doubt that reliance on "intuition" in epistemological matters is questionable, because it can preclude the critical questioning of "immediate" assumptions that is a motor of some of the major advances of modernity, in the natural sciences, law, etc., and can just be another version of the "myth of the given."[44] Furthermore, assertions based on the notion that all claims have their origin in an only intuitively accessible source can always be confronted with the following knock-down objection. Assertions about knowledge having its source, for instance, in unconscious drives must themselves have a source in unconscious drives, and so have no greater claim on our assent than any other assertions: they still have to be legitimated in the game of giving reasons.

However, despite the plausibility of these objections with respect to the epistemological questions, the idea of the unconscious as relating to the interface between nature and mind is not exhausted by the demand that claims about this interface be cashed out in a philosophical stance that avoids the objections just outlined. Making systematic philosophical claims about nature's "unconscious productivity" may indeed involve dogmatism, but we might still be responding inadequately to questions about nature and subjectivity if we restrict ourselves to claims that can be sustained by discursively articulated reasons. One way of construing aspects of the *STI* in a contemporary perspective is in terms of its search for non-cognitive connections between the subject's dividedness within itself – which is what leads to the idea of a tension and interaction between conscious and unconscious – and the division between the subject and nature.

These are not issues that can be obviated by the argument that such divisions are based on a failure to see how Hegel overcomes a skeptical

---

[44] See Bowie, "German Idealism's Contested Heritage," *German Idealism: Contemporary Perspectives*, ed. Espen Hammer (London: Routledge, 2007), 309–30.

approach to the subject–object relationship, and so shows that we should, as Pippin puts it, "leave nature behind" because it cannot be a source of normativity, normativity being inherently social. Forms of cultural expression of the kind at issue here change and develop not least because they involve resources for responding to shifting tensions between what we know and the other ways in which we relate to the world. These tensions involve aspects which can be thought of in relation to the unconscious, because they cannot be made fully accessible in cognitive terms, and so demand other forms of expression. It is not, of course, that cultural production is immune to normative assessment, but such assessment is secondary to what happens in that production. Hegel himself is clear about this: the "Owl of Minerva" of philosophy comes after whatever it has to understand. The question is whether the philosophical understanding can in principle articulate everything that happens.

If the conception I am trying to develop via a critical appropriation of Schelling's notion of the interaction of conscious and unconscious productivity appears problematic, the example of changes in the significance of music in modernity can perhaps make it more plausible. The revaluation of music's significance from the later eighteenth century onwards, from being an inferior art to being the art to whose "condition" all others "aspire" (Walter Pater), is not something that comes about predominantly via the practice of "giving reasons," even though the revaluation is also partly the result of philosophical arguments. More important is the production and reception of music itself as a non-conceptual form of expression that fulfills needs which conceptual articulation cannot. The changes in the understanding of language that accompany the revaluation of music are also not primarily the result of philosophical claims being definitively proven. They result rather from a sense that too much fails to become manifest when language is regarded as a means of representing objects, rather than as the fundamental human form of expression.[45] If something has previously not been manifest, it is in one sense unconscious, and it may have effects on culture which change when it becomes manifest via new forms of expression. The effects in question can be both creative and destructive. Beethoven and Wagner can, for example, be understood both as bringing about positive revelations of new affective possibilities and as having potentially disturbing cultural effects via their destabilizing of received conventions governing the

---

[45] See A. Bowie, *From Romanticism to Critical Theory*, and *Music, Philosophy, and Modernity*. A serious awareness of the history of philosophy makes it clear that philosophical claims seem never to be definitively proven: the practice of Anglo-American philosophy rarely explicitly reflects this. One of the strengths of the early Romantics is precisely that they build a sense of provisionality into the way they express their philosophy.

expression of affective life. The same applies, of course, to the cultural forms that they put in question, which both conceal possibilities and yet also enable other possibilities.

This interplay between the hidden and the manifest can suggest ways of rethinking the notion of nature in the light of Schelling and the unconscious. There are, it must be added, considerable difficulties here. One danger is of seeking to "reenchant" nature by regarding it as a positive source of meaning: this move can easily repeat the providential view of the *STI* that Schelling gives up in his later work, where the earlier sense of harmony gives way to the "veil of melancholy which is spread over the whole of nature" that results from the necessarily transient nature of everything particular. Attempts to reenchant nature can too easily lead to using it as an ideological counter to what is held to be wrong with modernity, when what one invokes may in fact only become manifest because of modernity. A further danger is apparent in Schopenhauer, who, by making nature the repository of the intuitively accessible, metaphysical principle of the Will (which he, of course, connects closely to music), obscures any sense in which nature can be more than an arbitrary series of warring quanta of power.

However, giving up any sense in which nature can be a resource for meaning in modern culture, either because it can lead to an illusory reenchantment, or because the brutality of nature means it is supposedly no more than the realm of eat or be eaten, seems to me mistaken. The tradition that goes from Schelling to Heidegger, Adorno, and contemporary ecological thinking, which warns of the danger of regarding nature solely in objective terms, would not have been possible if nature could really be "left behind" in the game of giving publicly justifiable reasons. Although we rely on the sciences to substantiate fears about the devastation of nature, the genesis of those fears is not just a result of scientific confirmation but also depends on other forms of connection to the non-human world, and these can play a vital role in the responses to that devastation.[46] The role of the concept of the unconscious in thinking about these issues lies in its both sustaining a difference between nature and mind – otherwise, as we saw, the unconscious would be either causally explicable and/or not unconscious at all – and yet connecting them in ways not central to many philosophical positions. Schelling has a manifestly ecological concern with the damage humankind can do to nature, which is most obvious in his critical responses to Fichte's insistence that nature is merely the object of practical reason, rather than also a part of ourselves as subjects.

---

[46] I am thinking, for example, of how Andrei Tarkovsky's film *Stalker* expressed such devastation in a form which was subsequently realized at Chernobyl.

It will, of course, be apparent here that what is meant by "nature" shifts in relation to its "other." Nature, as Adorno argues, has a history which depends on its interaction with the social. Once the relationship between nature and mind is put in question, it becomes dogmatic to claim exclusive legitimacy for any conception of nature. Modernity's most dominant conception, namely of nature as the system of necessary laws established by the sciences, can often justifiably be used to argue that other conceptions are merely sentimental, or indefensibly metaphysical. But if, as consideration of the idea of the unconscious suggests, the division between the cultural and the natural is not as straightforward as that between the self-determining and the causally determined, what is not articulated within scientific and philosophical views needs to be approached in other ways. These, as we have seen, are often associated with the aesthetic, but the aesthetic should not be construed in the narrow sense of a specialized domain of philosophy concerned with art and beauty. As Kant already suggested in the *Critique of Judgment* (*Kritik der Urteilskraft*, 1790), aesthetic questions can change how we approach epistemological and ethical matters. In the view of nature linked to the aesthetic tradition, as Charles Taylor puts it: "There is something more in nature between full spontaneity and mere mechanism," and this, as we have seen, is precisely the space of the unconscious.[47]

There are, I think, good reasons for maintaining that the Hegelian stance based on giving reasons, rather than relying on foundational epistemic guarantees, should be regarded as the most plausible stance in relation to the modern legitimation of claims to knowledge. However, it may not always be adequate for responding to questions about why we should invest in what we seek to know and do. Just saying that we "determine ourselves" to adopt a stance misses the ways in which the content in relation to which stances are adopted is bound up with processes which also involve what we have been considering via the unconscious. What produces motivation may be more accessible in expressive forms that embody our investment, from painting, to literature, to dance, to music, than via arguments. The modern dissemination of the awareness of nature as a value in itself, rather than as a manifestation of the divinity, for example, results from the ways in which a new investment in nature is expressed in romantic culture of all kinds. It is no coincidence, then, that Schelling's ideas about the unconscious are contemporaneous with this new investment.

One of the problems for "post-metaphysical" forms of modern philosophy is that questions of "meaning" are regarded with suspicion

---

[47] Charles Taylor, "Foundationalism and the Inner-Outer Distinction," *Reading McDowell's "Mind and World,"* 106–20, here 111.

because they seem to demand theological or dogmatic metaphysical responses. Meaning in the analytical tradition is largely a semantic issue, other senses of meaning often being regarded as too vague to be given philosophical dignity. The question of motivation and investment at issue here is, though, not a question about "meaning" in the semantic sense, nor need it be construed in theological terms. What is intended has to do with what is meant when we talk about life feeling "meaningless." Such a feeling may be alleviated by experiences in nature in ways that arguments that life does have meaning may not achieve.[48] In this respect "nature" can evidently "mean" more than is accounted for by establishing its laws, and what it means need not just be anthropomorphic projection or randomly subjective: such meanings can have objective effects on people's orientation in their lives. The metaphysical aspect of Schelling's idea that nature's unconscious productivity is identical with the productivity of thinking cannot be defended. However, the sense that the meanings nature can involve may become part of our relation to the world, and in ways which cannot be understood in terms of giving reasons, points to a dimension that some of the contemporary appropriation of Hegel seems to underplay. It is not that McDowell and others necessarily ignore the importance of the aesthetic, but they do not always pursue the implications of expressive responses to nature with regard to the epistemological agenda that dominates their perspective. The difficulty of what I am suggesting lies, though, in characterizing "nature" in the appropriate manner.

Conclusion

In order to outline a way in which one might do this, I shall conclude by briefly looking at a few remarks by Adorno in his unpublished Aesthetics lectures, on the relationship between beauty in nature and beauty in art. The reason for this is quite simple: the question as to why we see nature as beautiful at all is, as the *STI* suggests, closely connected to the idea of the unconscious as having to do with the interface of nature and consciousness. While we may sometimes be able to give reasons for why we find an aspect of nature beautiful in terms of the socially developed conventions

---

[48] The obvious objection here is that the line between nature and its other is a product of social developments. However, if it is already accepted that, like the mind/nature division, there is no definitive line between the two sides of the division, the idea of nature as a clearly delimitable realm is a myth anyway. That does not mean, though, that "nature" cannot be a resource in relation to socially generated feelings of meaninglessness: indeed, such feelings may actually be part of the genesis of certain conceptions of nature, as the Romantic fears about the effects of technology on nature indicate.

of beauty of an era, the fact that there is natural beauty at all cannot be given an explanation of the same kind. The beauty of nature relates instead to the domain of "unconscious production," because it involves a non-conceptual, and non-causal, connection of mind and nature. This conception does not, one should add, entail the idea that natural beauty is something perennial: central to the conception is the emergence of natural beauty as a response to historical developments in modernity, which is connected to the emergence of ideas about the unconscious.[49]

Adorno's concern is with what modern forms of technological rationality and the commodity form tend to repress and damage, and which he regards art as being able to express and articulate. This concern is decisively linked to the question of how we are to understand nature.[50] Art makes manifest what is otherwise hidden, not in conceptual form, but rather in the form of "mimesis" in Adorno's particular sense: examples of this are the affectively laden gestures of music, or the tone of a poem, or expressive moves in dance. Artworks are "appearances of society which are not conscious of themselves,"[51] and beauty in art "loses its substance" if the "experience of beauty as an immediate experience ... before the separation from the beauty of nature" does not play a role in it.[52] Adorno is generally, in Hegelian fashion, highly critical of invoking immediacy, but he realizes that without this moment of "unconscious" immediacy the investment in aesthetic beauty, that is based on its offering a sense of otherwise inaccessible meaning, is inexplicable. He therefore has no hesitation in talking of "the voice of nature," but this is not to be understood as a revival of pre-modern metaphysical and theological

---

[49] Explanations of natural beauty in terms of evolutionary psychology have to be solely causal, and are clearly irrelevant to the issues here. As Adorno suggests, paradigmatic romantic cases of natural beauty – sunsets, etc. – can become nothing but kitsch in some circumstances: the roles of the social and the natural in aesthetic matters cannot be separated in the manner required by an evolutionary explanation. The model which explains beauty as an evolutionary advantage just relies on the kind of circular argument so common when the cultural is invalidly subordinated to natural causality. This does not mean that beauty has nothing to do with evolution, but evolution is not a sufficient explanation of the complexity of the phenomenon, which, as we have seen, necessarily involves both the intentional and the causal.

[50] His view of technological rationality is in some respects, as Habermas has argued, indefensibly totalizing, but one does not need to accept the totalizing aspect in order to see the justification of the ideas I shall examine here. If we accept that the Holocaust was not possible without employment of the means of technological rationality, an adequate response to the issue of human control of nature becomes imperative, even if we find parts of Adorno's particular response problematic.

[51] [ihrer selbst unbewußte Erscheinungen der Gesellschaft]. Theodor W. Adorno, *Ästhetik Vorlesungen*, June 20, 1961, *Adorno-Archiv* (Berlin: Akademie der Künste, 1961), 6448.

[52] [verliert er ... seine Substanz]; [Erfahrung der Schönheit als eine unmittelbare ... vor der Lostrennung von dem Naturschönen]. Adorno, *Ästhetik Vorlesungen*, November 30, 1961, *Adorno-Archiv*, 6944.

ideas. Instead – and this claim is sometimes made in questionable ways that result from Adorno's too rigidly modernist aesthetic agenda – it is art in modernity which has the "task … of enabling mutilated nature, i.e. nature through its mediations, in the particular form in which it finds itself in a specific state of history, to speak."[53] What is defensible here, independently of Adorno's particular take on aesthetic modernism, is the notion that, because the capacity for conceptual determination and manipulation of nature grows so radically in modernity, the need for means of expressing what may be obscured or damaged by these approaches to nature increases as well.

Even experiences of natural beauty can become distorted by the effects of the culture industry (the kitsch sunset problem). The fact that art may express what nothing else can, might therefore sustain a sense of possibilities that are not dependent on the subject's conceptual control of nature. Adorno talks in this respect of art as the "spokesman of suffering that has … been repressed."[54] By giving a voice to the suffering occasioned by distortions in the development of civilization, art can "restore … the undivided, the unified state, for which one might use the word nature."[55] Elsewhere Adorno claims that "There is no other determination of the beauty of nature … than as the appearance of something as speaking … as expression which is not made by human beings," i.e. which is not a result of instrumental manipulation of nature for practical purposes.[56] The fact that until the emergence of the awareness of the ecological crisis such views would be most likely regarded as mere "romanticism" in the sentimental sense itself indicates how this view of the concept of nature can be legitimated. Rather than nature being formally defined, it results from the interface between the human and the non-human, in which each changes as the other changes, and it is here that reflection on the unconscious must be located.

Adorno goes on to maintain that "the deciphering of art depends on the deciphering of that relationship to nature, which, in whatever way, is

---

[53] [Aufgabe … die verstümmelte Natur, also die Natur jeweils in der Gestalt, in der sie auf einen bestimmten Stand der Geschichte durch ihre historischen Vermittlungen hindurch sich befindet, zum Sprechen zu bringen]. Adorno, *Ästhetik Vorlesungen*, December 9, 1958, *Adorno-Archiv*, 3582.
[54] [Sprecher des Leidens, das … verdrängt worden ist]. Adorno, *Ästhetik Vorlesungen*, January 29, 1959, *Adorno-Archiv*, 3716.
[55] [wiederherstellen … was eben nun einmal als der unzerrissene, als der einheitliche Zustand mit dem Wort Natur bezeichnet werden kann]. Adorno, *Ästhetik Vorlesungen*, July 13, 1961, *Adorno-Archiv*, 6537.
[56] [Es gibt keine andere Bestimmung des Naturschönen … als die Erscheinung eines nicht von Menschen Gemachten als sprechend … als Ausdruck.] Adorno, *Ästhetik Vorlesungen*, November 9, 1961, *Adorno-Archiv*, 6851.

unconscious of itself and latent."[57] The result of this deciphering cannot be a conceptual determination of the relationship, because that would abolish what matters most about the relationship, namely that it remains able to generate new involvement. It cannot be brought to explicit conceptual consciousness, and therefore constantly poses the challenge of how it can be expressed: that is a key source of the constant demand for aesthetic innovation in modernity that enables art to remain expressive. If there were a propositionally statable truth about the relationship, philosophy would transcend natural beauty and art, in the manner Hegel suggests it does, but the sense that meaning-creating resources play a relatively minor role in modern philosophy after Hegel seems to contradict a strong version of the Hegelian view.[58] While science legitimately replaces much of mythology, religion, and metaphysics, when it is divorced from a vision of human flourishing that does not irrevocably damage the natural world, it can also have catastrophic effects both on the natural and the human world. How we register and respond to these effects is not just a matter of theoretical claims, but of being able to express those effects in a manner which does justice to them by enabling people to connect to what they may mean.

Schelling's and Adorno's responses to the issue of the relations between nature and consciousness are able to offer more than just another contribution to the endless reworking of the epistemological problematic. They allow one to ask why it is that, even though modern science constantly confirms its efficacy in many domains, the question of the validation of knowledge still dominates much modern philosophy.[59] The danger in questioning the primacy of epistemology in this manner is that it can bring one into proximity with some less than defensible ideas. One of the reasons for the relative neglect of Schelling's and Adorno's conceptions is that the idea of the unconscious in modern German thought has sometimes taken disreputable forms.[60] The unconscious is too often assimilated to the "irrational," such that the "divided self" is predicated on a hidden power that supposedly either needs releasing from the bonds of rationality or is a lurking threat under the veneer of civilization. Schelling and Adorno, however, do not see the irrational

---

[57] [die Dechiffrierung der Kunst abhängt von der Dechiffrierung jenes wie immer auch sich selbst unbewußten oder latenten Verhältnisses zur Natur]. Adorno, *Ästhetik Vorlesungen*, November 14, 1961, *Adorno-Archiv*, 6855.
[58] See Bowie, *Aesthetics and Subjectivity* and *Music, Philosophy, and Modernity*.
[59] There are, of course, areas of science where there are deep theoretical divisions, but these are unlikely to be overcome just with the tools of epistemology.
[60] Schelling is, for example, cited by Georg Lukács as a representative of the "destruction of reason" in *Die Zerstörung der Vernunft: Der Weg des Irrationalismus von Schelling zu Hitler* (Berlin: Aufbau, 1955).

as an undialectical counter to conceptually articulated rationality. They rather reveal the limits of a too narrowly conceived rationality which has no place for what we have considered in relation to the shifting tensions in modernity between nature and mind, which demand new forms of expression. There are no easy answers here, but the choices highlight some key issues in contemporary philosophy. Pippin says that the core of his Hegelianism is the idea that "to live freely" is to lead a "life commonly and justifiably measured by some norm."[61] The question posed by Schelling and Adorno is whether this characterization is adequate to getting in touch with what makes such norms worth investing in at all. The unconscious can be a realm of dangerous fantasies, but it can also be the source of visions of hope.

[61] Robert Pippin, *Idealism as Modernism* (Cambridge: Cambridge University Press, 1997), 409.

3 The scientific unconscious: Goethe's post-Kantian epistemology

Angus Nicholls

Introduction: the unconscious in relation to the human and natural sciences

Perhaps the most important legacy of the various nineteenth-century German discourses on the unconscious is the cardinal status of this concept within what Freud understood to be the "science" of psychoanalysis. Despite the much-disputed scientific status of psychoanalysis, even as late as the second half of the twentieth century Michel Foucault saw the unconscious as an epistemological category which demarcates not only psychoanalysis or psychology, but also the field of the human sciences in general. "On the horizon of any human science," writes Foucault,

> there is the project of bringing man's consciousness back to its real conditions, of restoring it to the contents and forms that brought it into being, and elude us within it; this is why the problem of the unconscious – its possibility, status, mode of existence, the means of knowing it and of bringing it to light – is not simply a problem within the human sciences which they can be thought of as encountering by chance in their steps; it is a problem that is ultimately coextensive with their very existence.[1]

Foucault argues that what separates the human from the natural sciences is that in the former, the category of "the human" necessarily becomes both the subject and the object of any possible knowledge. Thus, while Descartes had assumed that the logical *cogito* may have the capacity to know the non-human world of extended substance through purely rational deduction, this situation changed radically during the nineteenth century, when "the human" came, in newly professionalized fields such as psychology and sociology, to be an empirical object of scientific investigation. Any researcher taking "the human" as its object would thus have to incorporate the self-reflexive awareness that he or she is also a part of the subject matter under consideration, and this self-awareness would

---

[1] Michel Foucault, *The Order of Things: An Archaeology of the Human Sciences* (1966; London: Routledge, 2002), 397.

also presumably require a recognition of how unconscious processes and affects may influence scientific research.[2]

Within the new fields of the human sciences – or the *Geisteswissenschaften*, as they came to be known in the German-speaking world during the second half of the nineteenth century – the question of the "scientific" character of knowledge took on an increased importance as the century drew to a close. The pressure placed upon the very concept of *Wissenschaft* is registered in how the function of this term changed in the second half of the nineteenth century, when academic disciplines underwent the processes of demarcation and professionalization that led to the establishment of modern research universities as we know them today.

In the early stages of the nineteenth century in Germany, *Wissenschaft* could refer to any body of knowledge that elaborated a systematic methodology and could be taught as an academic discipline, independently of any materialist or empirical basis.[3] This situation was in part attributable to Kant's insistence, in his *Metaphysical Foundations of Natural Science* (*Metaphysische Anfangsgründe der Naturwissenschaft*, 1786) that *Wissenschaft* is defined by its systematic character, and that knowledge can only be *wissenschaftlich* in the strictest sense of that term when it is true logically or apodictically rather than empirically.[4] While this maneuver effectively equated *Wissenschaft* with what Kant took to be the aims of philosophy, he was also at pains to draw clear limits concerning the types of knowledge claims that humans could conceivably make about external nature *an sich* or "in itself." In particular, Kant argued, in the second part of the *Critique of Judgment* (*Kritik der Urteilskraft*, 1790), that when humans perceive a teleology or design at work in natural organisms, such judgments are reflective (belonging to the structure and tendencies of human subjectivity) rather than determinate (belonging to empirical nature in itself). Yet despite Kant's attempt carefully to circumscribe the type and extent of such knowledge claims, especially those

---

[2] For a more recent discussion of these issues, see: Bruce Mazlish, *The Uncertain Sciences*, 2nd edn. (New Brunswick, NJ: Transaction, 2007), 10–36; Roger Smith, *Being Human: Historical Knowledge and the Creation of Human Nature* (New York: Columbia University Press, 2007), 79–82.

[3] On this subject, see H. Hühn, S. Meier-Oeser, and H. Pulte, "Wissenschaft," *Historisches Wörterbuch der Philosophie*, 12 vols., ed. Joachim Ritter et al. (Basel: Schwabe, 1971–2004), vol. XII, 902–47; here 915–16.

[4] Kant writes: "Eine jede Lehre, wenn sie ein System, d.i. ein nach Prinzipien geordnetes Ganze der Erkenntnis sein soll, heißt Wissenschaft ... Eigentliche Wissenschaft kann nur diejenige genannt werden, deren Gewißheit apodiktisch ist; Erkenntnis, die bloß empirische Gewißheit enthalten kann, ist ein nur uneigentlich so genanntes Wissen." Immanuel Kant, *Metaphysische Anfangsgründe der Naturwissenschaft* (1786), *Werke in sechs Bänden*, ed. Wilhelm Weischedel (Darmstadt: Wissenschaftliche Buchgesellschaft, 1983), vol. V, 12–13.

concerning a teleology or "mind" apparently at work in nature, his philosophical definition of *Wissenschaft* nevertheless gave rise to a whole series of speculative *Wissenschaften* propagated by his German idealist successors. Overstepping the limits of reason set out by Kant, these thinkers posited the existence of spiritual or mind-like structures that unfold in nature, running the gamut from Fichte's *Wissenschaftlehre* to the vitalist *Naturphilosophie* of Schelling and his successors like Carl Gustav Carus.[5]

By the second half of the nineteenth century, this situation was beginning to change, most notably in the attempts made by some natural scientists to differentiate their own field of enquiry – die *Naturwissenschaften* – from the human sciences or *Geisteswissenschaften*, as well as from the legacies of German idealism and vitalism in general.[6] A case in point is a public lecture delivered by the renowned German physicist and physiologist Hermann von Helmholtz (1821–94) at the University of Heidelberg in 1862, entitled "On the Relation of the Natural Sciences to Science in General" (*Über das Verhältniss der Naturwissenschaften zur Gesamtheit der Wissenschaft*). Helmholtz begins his lecture by declaring that the age of the Renaissance man – in which, for example, Johannes Kepler (1571–1630) could simultaneously hold professorships in mathematics and morals – is over. Due to the increased level of specialization and detail achieved in the various disciplines of both the natural and the human sciences, it is no longer possible, declared Helmholtz, to offer grand syntheses which would combine the human and natural sciences into a unified body of knowledge.[7]

The chief target in Helmholtz's sights was what he called the "Icarus flight of speculation" (*Icarus Flug der Spekulation*) to be found in German idealism – first and foremost in the thought of Georg Wilhelm Friedrich Hegel (1770–1831).[8] By arguing that both nature and human life are the

---

[5] See Robert J. Richards, *The Romantic Conception of Life: Science and Philosophy in the Age of Goethe* (Chicago: University of Chicago Press, 2002), 11, 67, 72–4, 137–39.

[6] See, in this connection, Alwin Diemer, "Die Begründung des Wissenschaftscharakters der Wissenschaft im 19. Jahrhundert," *Beiträge zur Entwicklung der Wissenschaftstheorie im 19. Jahrhundert*, ed. A. Diemer (Meisenheim am Glan: Verlag Anton Hain, 1968), 3–62; Alwin Diemer, "Die Differenzierung der Wissenschaften in die Natur- und die Geisteswissenschaften," *Beiträge zur Entwicklung der Wissenschaftstheorie im 19. Jahrhundert*, 174–221; H. Hühn, S. Meier-Oeser, and H. Pulte, "Wissenschaft," 916.

[7] Hermann von Helmholtz, "On the Relation of the Natural Sciences to Science in General," *Science and Culture: Popular and Philosophical Essays*, ed. David Cahan (Chicago: University of Chicago Press, 1995), 76–95; here 78. "Über das Verhältniss der Naturwissenschaften zur Gesamtheit der Wissenschaft," *Vorträge und Reden*, vol. I, 4th edn. (Braunschweig: Vieweg, 1896), 159–85; here 162.

[8] Helmholtz, "On the Relation of the Natural Sciences to Science in General," 80; "Über das Verhältniss der Naturwissenschaften zur Gesamtheit der Wissenschaft," 165 (translation altered).

result of a single creative spirit, Hegel had, thought Helmholtz, falsely assumed an identity between human thought and external nature that could allegedly be established without recourse to empirical experience. While Hegel's thesis concerning the identity of thought and external reality seemed to receive confirmation from *Geisteswissenschaften* such as history, theology, and law, the real test of his identity hypothesis lay not in these fields, but in what Helmholtz called the "facts of nature" (*Thatsachen der Natur*). Yet it was precisely natural scientists who, according to Helmholtz, regarded Hegel's identity hypothesis as "absolutely senseless" (*absolut sinnlos*) and who accordingly sought to free themselves from all philosophical influences and presuppositions, basing their claims purely on inductions that could be concretized into strict laws, and then tested against empirical reality. It was in this way that a sharply defined opposition (*scharfer Gegensatz*) between the natural and human sciences came into being, an opposition which, argued Helmholtz, often saw the human sciences being denied any scientific status at all.[9]

Helmholtz elaborates upon this opposition by ascribing different methodological procedures to the natural and human sciences. While the natural sciences are based upon rigorous processes of induction that emerge from the "conscious and logical activity of the mind" (*bewusste logische Tätigkeit unseres Geistes*), the human sciences are more inclined to rely on "judgments based upon psychological tact" (*Urtheilen nach psychologischem Tactgefühl*) and on processes of "artistic, not strictly logical induction" (*künstlerische, nicht eigentlich logische Induction*). This does not, however, rule out that possibility that, in some limited instances, discoveries in the natural sciences may rely on what Helmholtz refers to as the "instinctive intuition" (*instinktive Anschauung*) that characterizes the human sciences. It was, after all, an artist (*Künstler*) by the name of Johann Wolfgang von Goethe who had, according to Helmholtz, initiated the scientific discipline of comparative anatomy through his botanical and zoological researches.[10]

Helmholtz's reference to Goethe as someone who relied upon instinctive intuition rather than conscious logic belongs to a dominant tradition of writing about Goethe – beginning with Friedrich Schiller and continuing through figures such as Friedrich Nietzsche, Wilhelm Dilthey, and Georg Simmel, into the work of Freud – which sees him as the

---

[9] Helmholtz, "On the Relation of the Natural Sciences to Science in General," 79–80; "Über das Verhältniss der Naturwissenschaften zur Gesamtheit der Wissenschaft," 163–5 (translation altered).

[10] Helmholtz, "On the Relation of the Natural Sciences to Science in General,"176, 171–2, 175; "Das Verhältniss der Naturwissenschaften zur Gesamtheit der Wissenschaft," 88, 85–6, 88 (translation altered).

great German example of unconscious artistic productivity and intuitive aesthetic sense.[11] In fact, not unlike the category of the "human" in Foucault's analysis of the human sciences, Goethe has played a role as both subject and object in the history of nineteenth-century German science: as subject he is seen as the last of the Renaissance men, whose essentially artistic and intuitive theory of color was also a radically flawed attempt to supplant Newton's *Opticks*; while as object, he is the preternatural genius, whose creativity is not explicable in terms of the empirical natural sciences, thereby demonstrating their very limits.[12]

At the heart of this image of Goethe – as at the heart of the human sciences themselves, if we follow Foucault's analysis – stands the unconscious, and, to be more precise, Goethe's historical relation to psychoanalysis. This topic is most directly considered by Freud himself, in an address written on the occasion of his receiving the Goethe Prize in 1930. This address, in which Goethe once again appears as both subject and object of the scientific discipline in question, outlines Goethe's dual relation to psychoanalysis, in that Freud makes the following two important claims: first, Goethe is said to have used with his friends a talking cure that in some respects resembled psychoanalysis, or in other words, he is seen to have been a proto-psychoanalyst; and second, Goethe's personality and works are seen as providing an ideal object for psychoanalysis, making him an exemplary neurotic and therefore an ideal analysand.[13] As Paul Bishop also notes in his contribution to this volume, a third claim regarding Goethe is made by Freud in his "Autobiographical Study" ("Selbstdarstellung") of 1925. Here Goethe is said to have influenced the history of psychoanalysis, chiefly though the inspiration that Freud derived from the essay on "Die Natur" that he mistakenly

---

[11] See Nietzsche's discussion of Goethe in his *Götzen-Dämmerung*, §49, *Werke in drei Bänden*, ed. Karl Schlechta (Munich: Hanser, 1954), vol. II, 1024–25. See also Wilhelm Dilthey, *Das Erlebnis und die Dichtung*, 4th edn. (1906; Stuttgart: Teubner, 1957); Georg Simmel, *Goethe* (Leipzig: Klinkhardt und Biermann, 1916).

[12] In this connection, see Angus Nicholls, "The Subject-Object of *Wissenschaft*: On Wilhelm Dilthey's *Goethebilder*," *Colloquia Germanica* 39, no. 1 (2006): 69–86.

[13] Sigmund Freud, "Address Delivered in the Goethe House at Frankfurt," *The Standard Edition of the Complete Psychological Works of Sigmund Freud*, ed. and trans. James Strachey and Anna Freud *et al.*, 24 vols. (London: The Hogarth Press, 1953–74), vol. XXI, 208–2; (hereafter cited as *SE* followed by volume and page numbers). "Ansprache im Frankfurter Goethe-Haus," *Gesammelte Werke in achtzehn Bänden mit einem Nachtragsband*, ed. Anna Freud *et al.*, 18 vols. (Frankfurt am Main: S. Fischer, 1986–99), vol. XIV, 547–50; (hereafter cited as *GW* followed by volume and page numbers). On Freud's ideas regarding Goethe as an analysand, see also: Freud, "A Childhood Recollection from *Dichtung und Wahrheit*," *SE*, XVII, 147–56; "Eine Kindheitserinnerung aus *Dichtung und Wahrheit*," *GW*, XII, 15–26. Goethe's sparkling career as an analysand reached its heights in Kurt Eissler's monumental two-volume psychoanalysis of Goethe: *Goethe: A Psychoanalytic Study* (Detroit, MI: Wayne State University Press, 1963).

attributed to Goethe.[14] Continuing in a similar vein, a recent study has even announced that Goethe, especially in his first novel *Die Leiden des jungen Werthers* (*The Sorrows of Young Werther*, 1774) as well as in his great drama *Faust*, helped to create a "culture of the unconscious" by depicting the fates of narcissistic individuals within the context of modernity.[15] It is on the basis of such claims that Goethe has come to occupy a central position in what might polemically be called the "historical mythology" concerning the origins of psychoanalysis. This mythology still requires a thoroughgoing critique, to which this chapter might be seen as being a preliminary contribution, while also functioning as kind of supplement to Paul Bishop's contribution to this volume.

What I hope to show is that in terms of Goethe's relation to psychoanalysis and the history of the unconscious in nineteenth-century German thought, what Freud did not say about Goethe is in fact far more revealing and important than what he did say. When one compares the scientific methodologies of Goethe and Freud, it is often difficult to believe that only forty-five or so years separate the death of Goethe in 1832 from the beginnings of Freud's earliest activity as a scientist in the mid 1870s. It was during these years that the related group of epistemologies known as German idealism, *Naturphilosophie*, and vitalism were comprehensively displaced by the materialist positivism of Helmholtz, the German physiologist Emil Du Bois-Reymond (1818–96) and Freud's early instructor in the subject of physiology, Ernst Brücke (1819–92). A possible scientific "bridge" from Goethe to Freud may have been provided by the physiologist Johannes Müller (1801–58),[16] who had early in his career expressed sympathies with Goethe's approach to science as well as with Schelling's *Naturphilosophie*. But this link to Goethe was decisively severed by Helmholtz, Du Bois-Reymond and Brücke, all of whom were students of Müller, but who, especially in the wake of Darwin's *On the Origin of Species* (1859), made it their aim to remove all traces of vitalism and *Naturphilosophie* from the natural sciences. Thus, when Freud attended the public lecture given by Professor Carl Brühl

---

[14] Freud, "An Autobiographical Study," *SE*, XX, 8; "Selbstdarstellung," *GW*, XIV, 34. See also, in this connection, Joseph Margolis, "Goethe and Psychoanalysis," *Goethe and the Sciences: A Reappraisal*, ed. Frederick Amrine, Francis J. Zucker and Harvey Wheeler (Dodrecht: Kluwer, 1987), 83–100.

[15] Gerhard Oberlin, *Goethe, Schiller und das Unbewusste: Eine literaturpsychologische Studie* (Gießen: Psychosozial Verlag, 2007). Oberlin's study fluctuates between two approaches: underlining Goethe's significance in the history of psychology on the one hand, and interpreting certain works by Goethe through a psychoanalytic framework on the other. As such, it does not successfully demonstrate the existence of a clear line of influence from Goethe to Freud with respect to the *concept* of the unconscious.

[16] As is noted by Margolis, "Goethe and Psychoanalysis," 91.

The scientific unconscious 93

in August 1873 – in which the speaker read sections of the pantheistic fragment "Die Natur" written by the Swiss theologian Georg Christoph Tobler but mistakenly attributed to Goethe – he was in all likelihood witnessing one of the last death-throes of *Naturphilosophie* as a significant theoretical model in German science.[17]

Goethe's reputation as a natural scientist was, at least in the mind of the late nineteenth-century scientific public to which Freud belonged, attached to the collection of ideas known as *Naturphilosophie* by the two key figures of the so-called *Berliner physikalische Gesellschaft* who led the campaign against vitalism in German science: Helmholtz and Du Bois-Reymond. Significantly, both of these scientists saw Brücke, who was arguably Freud's most influential teacher in Vienna, as being their "ambassador in the east."[18] Both Helmholtz and Du Bois-Reymond gave important public lectures in which Goethe's scientific reputation was unequivocally and damningly associated with a pantheistic understanding of nature and a teleological theory of morphology, as well as with his purportedly failed critique of Newton in the *Theory of Color* (*Farbenlehre*, 1810). All of this meant that, when Freud was developing the theoretical basis of psychoanalysis in the 1880s and 1890s, Goethe's reputation as a natural scientist was at its very lowest ebb. At the same time, however, Goethe stood at the very core of theoretical justifications of the *Geisteswissenschaften* as they were elaborated by their chief late nineteenth century German proponent: Wilhelm Dilthey.[19] He was also, moreover, a key figure at the heart of Germanic cultural identity in general, following the growth of Goethe philology in the 1860s, and the establishment of the German nation in 1871.[20] It is perhaps for

---

[17] Goethe's fragment entitled "Die Natur" can be found in: Goethe, *Sämtliche Werke: Briefe, Tagebücher und Gespräche*, 2 parts, 40 vols., ed. Hendrik Birus et al. (Frankfurt am Main: Deutscher Klassiker Verlag, 1985–2003) part I, vol. XXV, 11–13. This edition of Goethe's *Sämtliche Werke*, otherwise known as the *Frankfurter Ausgabe*, will hereafter be cited with the letters *FA*, followed by part, volume and page numbers. For the context of this lecture, see Peter Gay, *Freud: A Life for Our Time* (New York: Norton, 1998), 24–5.

[18] Margolis, "Goethe and Psychoanalysis," 91.

[19] In his *Einleitung in die Geisteswissenschaften* (*Introduction to the Human Sciences*, 1883) Dilthey invokes Goethe as a scientific object which shows the limits of a purely empirical approach to the sciences. Goethe's creativity, he argues, can be reduced neither to "structure of his brain" (*Bau seines Gehirns*) nor to the "characteristics of his body" (*Eigenschaften seines Körpers*), and this demonstrates the necessity of an alternative form of science dealing not simply with physical bodies or forces, but rather with inner experience (*inneres Erlebnis*) or *Geist*. Wilhelm Dilthey, *Einleitung in die Geisteswissenschaften*, *Gesammelte Schriften*, 26 vols., ed. Karlfried Gründer et al. (Göttingen: Vandenhoek und Ruprecht, 1959–2005), vol. I, 8–9.

[20] See, on this subject, Karl Robert Mandelkow, "Die Anfänge der Goethe Philologie," in *Goethe in Deutschland: Rezeptionsgeschichte eines Klassikers*, 2 vols. (Munich: Beck, 1980–9) vol. I, 157–8. See also Mandelkow's discussion of Goethe as a cultural symbol for the new German nation, I, 201–4.

this reason that Freud sees Goethe as one of the "great men" (*großen Männer*) who often appear in people's dreams – including Freud's own, documented in the *Interpretation of Dreams* (*Die Traumdeutung*, 1900) – as father symbols.[21]

In his "Goethe Prize" address, Freud follows Helmholtz in arguing that Goethe allowed science and art to harmonize with one another.[22] Yet on the basis of Freud's quotations from Goethe's works, combined with the scientific and historical contexts in which Freud read Goethe, no such harmony between the two cultures exists in Freud's reception of Goethe. The Goethe invoked by Freud as a forerunner of psychoanalysis was the Goethe of *Faust*, rather than the Goethe who wrote the essays on scientific method that led to the *Theory of Color*. This has led Joseph Margolis correctly to conclude that Freud's allusions to Goethe "utterly fail to come to terms with his [i.e. Goethe's] conception of science."[23] What, then, are the implications of these factors for an examination of the concept of the unconscious in the works of Goethe? And, perhaps more importantly, *does* Goethe in fact elaborate a concept of the unconscious that is in any way similar to the various notions of the unconscious developed by Freud and his successors?

My attempt to answer these questions will be guided by the following hypothesis. Since Freud's attempt to develop a rigorously scientific psychology in the 1880s and 1890s was dominated by the materialist positivism of Brücke, Goethe's conception of science played little if any direct role in the development of Freud's early theoretical constructs. But once the rudiments of Freud's early theory were in place – say by 1900, after the composition of the "Project for a Scientific Psychology" (*Entwurf einer Psychologie*, 1895) and the publication of *The Interpretation of Dreams* – Goethe begins to be invoked by Freud as a *cultural* as opposed to a *scientific* authority. This means that, when Freud uses quotations from Goethe's poetic works in order to bolster his own theorization of the unconscious, he normally commits the cardinal sin of the history of ideas: projecting a contemporary theory back onto an earlier epoch in order to find an historical lineage that leads to one's own point of view.

My suspicion is that, if, indeed, Goethe does have a uniquely "scientific" theory of the unconscious that might be important for psychoanalysis, then it is, in all likelihood, not to be found in the poetic works quoted so frequently by Freud. As Rüdiger Görner shows in chapter 4

---

[21] See Freud, *SE*, V: 354; *GW*, II/III: 358–9. For Freud's dreams about Goethe, see: *SE*, IV: 326–7; *SE*, V: 354, 439–44, 448–9, 474, 662–5.
[22] See Freud, *SE*, XXI: 208; *GW*, XIV: 547.
[23] Margolis, "Goethe and Psychoanalysis," 85.

of this volume, literary examples alluding to unconscious processes were legion in early nineteenth-century German literature, and Goethe was by no means the only author who focused upon such themes. Rather, it is in his essays on scientific method that Goethe draws attention to issues which are relevant both to theories of the unconscious as they are elaborated in psychoanalysis, as well as to historical and contemporary discussions on the relations between the natural and human sciences. Here a clarification of what is meant by the term "scientific" is in order: it is not my claim that Goethe's conception of the unconscious is "scientific" in the sense of being empirically testable or objectively verifiable; rather, I will argue that Goethe draws to our attention unconscious *processes* or *affects* which may influence both the formulation of scientific hypotheses and the interpretation of the results arising from experiments.

In what follows, I shall first of all briefly consider the mid to late nineteenth-century scientific reception of Goethe offered by Helmholtz and Du Bois-Reymond, before turning to the influence of these theorists upon Freud's early model of the psyche: "The Project for a Scientific Psychology" of 1895. I will then examine some of Freud's Goethe quotations in the "Goethe Prize" address, in order to assess the extent to which Goethe's literary works may have served as a model for Freud's theory of the unconscious. Finally, I will turn back to Goethe's post-Kantian scientific epistemology, suggesting how this epistemology, rather than the literary sources, might be significant for the unconscious and for psychoanalysis.

The reception of Goethe by Helmholtz, Du Bois-Reymond, and the young Freud

In the "Goethe Prize" address, Freud offers the valuable if by now rather clichéd insight that Goethe was "not only a great revealer, but also … a careful concealer."[24] Freud may well have been aware that Goethe played, through his autobiographical writings like *Dichtung und Wahrheit* (*Poetry and Truth*, 1811–33) and especially in his published conversations with his assistant Johann Peter Eckermann,[25] a definitive role in shaping his own reception as a public figure and author during the second half of the nineteenth century. With regard to the reception of Goethe's scientific studies, perhaps the most important image of Goethe – an image

---

[24] Freud, *SE*, XXI: 212; [nicht nur … ein großer Bekenner … sondern auch … ein sorgsamer Verhüller], *GW*, XIV: 550.
[25] See Johann Peter Eckermann, *Gespräche mit Goethe in den letzten Jahren seines Lebens* (*Conversations with Goethe in the Last Years of his Life*, 1835), Goethe, *FA*, 2, XII.

propagated by Goethe himself, with some help from Schiller – was that of the poet as a visually-oriented individual or *Augenmensch*: the sensuous and intuitive natural philosopher with a special empathy for nature and a tendency to favor empirical experience over philosophical theorizing. Schiller first hit upon this formulation in his long letter to Goethe dated August 23, 1793,[26] and Goethe was later willing to confirm this interpretation when he observed of himself that he had no real inclination for philosophy, that Kant's works were entirely beyond his range of comprehension, and that when he did philosophize he did so with a certain unconscious naïveté (*unbewußte Naivetät*).[27]

Goethe's use of the term unconscious (*unbewußt*) in relation to his engagement with philosophy needs to be seen as belonging to the pantheistic aesthetics of genius that predominated in Germany during the late eighteenth and early nineteenth centuries.[28] As early as 1764, with Herder's *Fragments of a Treatise on the Ode* (*Fragmente einer Abhandlung über die Ode*), artistic production was associated with what Herder called *Affekt*:

Affect, which at the outset silently, encapsulated within, benumbed the entire body and surged as a dark feeling, gradually pervades all slight stirrings, until it finds expression in recognizable signs. It moves through the facial expressions and unarticulated sounds to the level of reason, where at last it seizes upon language, and here, too, through most subtle differentiation it loses itself at last in a clarity that gives it identity ... In affect one perceives the most comprehensive sensuous unity without being able to bring it into correspondence with the intellect.[29]

[26] See Schiller to Goethe, Jena, August 23, 1794, Goethe, *Sämtliche Werke nach Epochen seines Schaffens* (Münchner Ausgabe), ed. K. Richter, H. G. Göpfert, N. Miller and G. Sauder, 21 vols. in 31 (Munich: Carl Hanser, 1985–8), vol. VIII/1, 12–16. (The *Münchner Ausgabe* of Goethe's works will hereafter be cited in text with the letters *MA*, followed by volume and page numbers).

[27] See Goethe, "Einwirkung der neueren Philosophie," *FA* 1, XXIV: 442–6, here 443. Translated by Douglas Miller as "The Influence of Modern Philosophy," in Goethe, *Scientific Studies, Goethe's Collected Works,* vol. XII, ed. Douglas Miller (New York: Suhrkamp, 1988), 28–30.

[28] See Jochen Schmidt, *Die Geschichte des Genie-Gedankens in der deutschen Literatur, Philosophie und Politik, 1750–1945*, 2nd edn., 2 vols. (Darmstadt: Wissenschaftliche Buchgesellschaft, 2004), vol. I, 120–41.

[29] [Der Affekt, der im Anfange stumm, inwendig eingeschlossen, den ganzen Körper erstarrte, und in einem dunkeln Gefühl brauste, durchsteigt allmählig alle kleine Bewegungen, bis er sich in kennbaren Zeichen prediget. Er rollt durch die Mienen und unartikulierte Töne zu der Vernunft herab, wo er sich erst der Sprache bemächtigt: und auch hier durch die genausten Merkmale der Absteigerung sich endlich in eine Klarheit verliert, die ihm schon sein Selbstgefühl frei läßt ... In ihm [Affekt] empfindet man die sinnlich größte Einheit, ohne sie mit der Übereinstimmung des Verstandes vergleichen zu können.] Johann Gottfried Herder, *Fragments of a Treatise on the Ode*, in *Selected Early Works 1764–1787*, ed. Ernest A. Merze and Karl Merges, trans. Ernest A. Merze and Michael Palma (University Park, PA: The Pennsylvania State University Press,

Emerging from nature, the body and the lower emotional faculties, Herder proposes that *Affekt* surges through the individual before being refined by reason and expressed in language. The genius is the figure who is best able to mediate between the natural force of *Affekt* and the rational requirements of linguistic expression. As Goethe wrote to Schiller in 1801, this is achieved unconsciously rather than consciously, since Goethe believed that "everything that the genius does *as genius*, occurs unconsciously" (*alles was das Genie, als Genie, thut, unbewußt geschehe*).[30] This opinion is in line with the idea – found in both the early Goethe and in Herder, and inspired particularly by Herder's aesthetic interpretation of the Dutch philosopher Benedict de Spinoza (1632–77) – that nature herself is in fact the artist, with the genius functioning as a kind of medium who renders forces in nature intelligible.[31]

If, according to Spinoza in the *Ethics*, God is indistinguishable from extended substance, being the "immanent, and not the transitive cause of things,"[32] and if, in the view of Herder, this means that God exists "everywhere in the world ... complete and inseparable,"[33] then this would entail that the individual human being is part of a divinely-infused natural world in which divine forces may come to express themselves through human subjectivity. Something resembling this view can be found in Goethe's own consideration of Spinoza, his "Study after Spinoza" (*Studie nach Spinoza*) of 1785. Here Goethe argues that since every limited living being (*eingeschränktes lebendiges Wesen*) is bound up with the infinity (*Unendlichkeit*) which is God or Nature, then it also partakes of this infinity, and has something infinite (*etwas Unendliches*) within itself. The genius is he who is able to express this sense of infinity located within the self, which Goethe associates with the term "sublime" (*erhaben*). Yet since this sense of infinity cannot be an object of our conscious thoughts (*kann von uns nicht gedacht werden*) then it follows that it remains to some degree unconscious.[34]

1992), 43–4; Herder, *Fragmente einer Abhandlung über die Ode, Werke*, ed. G. Arnold, M. Bollacher, *et al.*, 10 vols. in 11 (Frankfurt am Main: Deutscher Klassiker Verlag, 1985–2000), vol. I, 88–90.

[30] Goethe to Schiller, Oberoßla, April 3 or 4, 1801, *MA*, VIII/1: 854. My emphasis in the English.

[31] See, for example, the sixty-third letter in Herder's *Briefe zu Beförderung der Humanität*, in Herder, *Werke*, vol. VII, 363–4.

[32] Benedict de Spinoza, *Ethics*, ed. and trans. Edwin Curley (Harmondsworth: Penguin, 1996), 16.

[33] [überall in der Welt ... ganz u. untheilbar]. Johann Gottfried Herder to Friedrich Heinrich Jacobi, February 6, 1784, Johann Gottfried Herder: *Briefe, Gesamtausgabe 1763–1803*, vol. V, ed. Wilhelm Dobbek and Günter Arnold (Weimar: Hermann Böhlhaus Nachfolger, 1979), 29.

[34] Goethe, "Studie nach Spinoza," *FA*, I, 25: 14–17; here 15.

It is more or less this notion of genius that Schiller saw embodied in Goethe, and in *Poetry and Truth*, Goethe retrospectively applies the aesthetics of *Affekt* to the composition of his early epistolary novel concerning the obsessive unrequited love and eventual suicide of a young man: *The Sorrows of Young Werther*. Here he uses the term *unbewußt* in order to describe the state in which he composed *Werther*, comparing the process of writing to sleepwalking, and to a general confession that enabled him to overcome a youthful and stormy element in his own personality. Marveling at his own unconscious artistic powers, Goethe observes that

> Since I had written this little work rather unconsciously, like a somnambulist, I was amazed myself when I looked through it to make changes and improvements.[35]

The influence of this account upon Freud can be found in notes accompanying a letter to Fliess dated May 31, 1897, in which Freud proposes a relation between poetic composition and hysterical fantasies, arguing that the process of writing *Werther* enabled Goethe to overcome his own suicidal tendencies.[36]

It is also the image of the non-theoretical and intuitive genius that prevails in the mid to late nineteenth-century assessments of Goethe's scientific studies to which Freud would in all likelihood have been exposed: namely, the important public lectures delivered by Hermann von Helmholtz (in 1853 and 1892) and Emil Du Bois-Reymond (in 1882) on Goethe and science. Helmholtz's lecture of 1853, entitled "On Goethe's Scientific Studies" (*Über Goethes naturwissenschaftliche Arbeiten*), and Du Bois-Reymond's lecture of 1882, entitled "Goethe and No End" (*Goethe und kein Ende*), offer more or less the same thesis regarding Goethe's work as a natural scientist. Goethe's critique of Newton in the *Theory of Color* is seen, in the words of Helmholtz, as the tendentious and emotional attempt of an artist to "rescue the unmediated truth of sensuous impressions from the attacks of science."[37] Goethe's polemic against Newton was, according to this argument, couched in aesthetic rather than scientific terms, in that he sought to protect the "pure" phenomena of light and color from the intrusions of Newton's technical and

---

[35] [Da ich dieses Werklein ziemlich unbewußt, einem Nachtwandler ähnlich, geschrieben hatte, so verwunderte ich mich selbst darüber, als ich es nun durchging, um daran etwas zu ändern und zu bessern.] Goethe, *Dichtung und Wahrheit*, FA 1, XIV:639.

[36] See Freud, *SE*, I:256.

[37] [die unmittelbare Wahrheit des sinnlichen Eindrucks gegen die Angriffe der Naturwissenschaft zu retten.] Hermann von Helmholtz, "Über Goethes wissenschaftliche Arbeiten (1853)," *Vorträge und Reden*, 4th edn., 2 vols. (Braunschweig: Vieweg, 1896), vol. I, 23–47; here 42.

conceptual apparatus. Accordingly, Helmholtz proposed that Newton's step into the realm of conceptual physics and the corpuscular theory of light "scared the poet [i.e. Goethe] away."[38] Du Bois-Reymond's assessment was rather less charitable: since, he argued, Goethe's *Theory of Color* "completely departed from the concept of mechanical causality," it amounted to little more than the "stillborn fiddling of an autodidactic dilettante."[39]

At the same time, however, both of these scientists thought that Goethe was more successful in the fields of morphology and comparative anatomy, but only because these types of empirical research enabled him to use techniques of observation – referred to as "unmediated intellectual intuition" (*unmittelbare geistige Anschauung*) by Helmholtz, and as "artistic intuition" (*künstlerische Anschauung*) by Du Bois-Reymond – that are also found in artistic practice.[40] But on the level of scientific epistemology, Goethe is unequivocally condemned: Helmholtz alleges that Goethe either misunderstood or had insufficient patience for the ideas of Kant as they were allegedly mediated to him by Schiller, and associates Goethe's epistemology with the philosophical systems of Schelling and Hegel, both of whom he sees as having falsely assumed that intellectual concepts are realized either in the organic developments of nature (Schelling), or in the progress of history (Hegel).[41] As was his tendency, Du Bois-Reymond took this condemnation a step further, arguing that Goethe promoted the "delirium-potion" (*Taumeltrank*) of *Naturphilosophie*, which saw German science fall into an "aesthetic dreaminess" (*ästhetische Träumerei*) that hindered its development for decades. Nevertheless, this last and most trenchant of criticisms does not prevent Du Bois-Reymond from identifying the fate of Goethe (the poet, not the scientist!) with the heroic life-trajectory (*Lebensgang*) of the recently unified German nation, leading him dramatically to proclaim that "Deutschland ist Goethe."[42]

The second essay by Helmholtz, "Goethe's Anticipations of Coming Scientific Ideas" (*Goethes Vorahnungen kommender wissenschaftlicher Ideen*, 1892), delivered almost forty years after the first, is rather more positive about Goethe's achievements in the natural sciences. The central dualism of Helmholtz's earlier essay, in which Goethe's "artistic intuition"

---

[38] [Schritt in das Reich der Begriffe … schreckt den Dichter zurück]. Ibid, 40.
[39] [Der Begriff der mechanischen Kausalität war es, der Goethe gänzlich abging … totgeborene Spielerei eines autodidaktischen Dilettanten]. Emil Du Bois-Reymond, "Goethe und kein Ende (1882)," *Reden von Emil Du Bois-Reymond in zwei Bänden*, 2nd edn., ed. Estelle Du Bois-Reymond (Leipzig: Veit, 1912), 157–83; here 172–3.
[40] Helmholtz, "Über Goethes naturwissenschaftliche Arbeiten (1853)," 34; Du Bois-Reymond, "Goethe und kein Ende (1882)," 173.
[41] Helmholtz, "Über Goethes naturwissenschaftliche Arbeiten (1853)," 35.
[42] Du Bois-Reymond, "Goethe und kein Ende (1882)," 175, 163.

(*künstlerische Anschauung*) is confronted by the logical and conscious "thinking" (*Denken*) of scientific method, is still maintained.[43] But there is a new assessment of Goethe's relation to two giants of British science: Newton and Darwin. In terms of Goethe's critique of Newton, Helmholtz at least partially revises his earlier view: although Goethe's own theory of color is still seen as having been hopelessly incorrect, his methodological criticisms of Newton are seen as having shown "certain gaps" (*gewisse Lücken*) in Newtonian physics.[44] Goethe was right, argues Helmholtz, in his allegation that Newton designed the prism experiments in such a way as to confirm his pre-conceived corpuscular theory of light, which caused Newton to confuse abstract concepts with actual natural phenomena.[45] In relation to Darwin, who had published his *Origin of Species* (1859) in the years intervening between Helmholtz's first and second essays on Goethe and science, Goethe's work on morphology and comparative anatomy is seen by Helmholtz to have anticipated certain aspects of Darwinian biology.[46] It was artistic intuition (*Anschauung*), according to Helmholtz, which allowed Goethe to identify common morphological types or structures that suggested developmental relations between species. But since intuition is not the same as the mechanistic explanations required by the modern natural sciences, it took Darwin to give these ideas a proper scientific framework in his theory of natural selection. Thus, whereas Goethe's method is still seen as being based purely on observation, description and intuition, only Darwin's theory gives a logically compelling account of mechanistic causes resident in nature.[47]

How influential would these views of Goethe have been upon the young Freud? When, in 1873, Freud listened to Carl Brühl's invocation of the fragment on nature attributed to Goethe, Helmholtz's first trenchant criticism of Goethe's science had been in the air for some twenty years. As both Wilhelm W. Hemecker and Günter Gödde have observed, the year 1873 saw the continuation of a process begun by Helmholtz

---

[43] Hermann von Helmholtz, "Goethes Vorahnungen kommender wissenschaftlicher Ideen," *Vorträge und Reden*, vol. II, 336–61; here 341.
[44] Ibid., 354.
[45] Ibid., 351, 354.
[46] Recent scholarship has also examined the question of Goethe's possible influence on Darwin. See Timothy Lenoir, "The Eternal Laws of Form: Morphotypes and the Conditions of Existence in Goethe's Biological Thought," *Goethe and the Sciences: A Reappraisal*, ed. F. Amrine, F. J. Zucker and H. Wheeler (Dordrecht: D. Reidel, 1987), 17–28; Richards, *The Romantic Conception of Life*, 511–52; Angus Nicholls, "On Science and Subjectivity," *History of the Human Sciences* 18, no. 1 (2005): 143–58.
[47] Helmholtz, "Goethes Vorahnungen kommender wissenschaftlicher Ideen," 342, 345, 349. See also, Jeffrey Barnouw, "Goethe and Helmholtz," *Goethe and the Sciences*, 45–82.

and later intensified by the publication of Darwin's *On the Origin of Species* in 1859: namely, the transition from the world-picture of pantheistic *Naturphilosophie* adopted by the likes of Schelling and Carus, to the positivist world-view championed by Helmholtz and Du Bois-Reymond. The nature fragment attributed to Goethe was, for precisely this reason, almost completely at odds with the dominant scientific tendencies of Freud's student years: positivism and Darwinian evolutionism.[48]

Emerging from Tobler's discussions with Goethe during his stay in Weimar in 1780 and 1781, the fragment on nature offers, according to Goethe's recollection in 1828, a reasonably accurate account of his pantheistic, Spinoza-inspired view of nature.[49] Humanity is seen as being conditioned by nature, but at the same time not privy to her deepest secrets. Nature is the All: she is both a mother and an artist who brings objects into being without any sign of effort, and who speaks through the tongues and hearts of her creatures.[50] The task of the natural scientist is, we presume, to attempt to understand the secrets of nature, while at the same time recognizing that, since nature is one's origin and mother, exhaustive and complete knowledge of her intentions is by definition impossible. Of course, the fact that "Goethe" (or Tobler) saw nature as having goals and intentions at all made the fragment extremely problematic from a Darwinian point of view. Since, however, both Ernst Haeckel and Friedrich Strauss had, in 1868 and 1871 respectively, tried to reconcile Goethe's morphology with Darwin's theory of natural selection and the methods of the positivist natural sciences, and since the lecture itself was delivered by a renowned Darwinian in Carl Brühl, Freud probably viewed the fragment in relation to Darwin rather than in terms of its affinities with Romantic *Naturphilosophie*.[51] Yet in a letter to Fliess, as well as in the *Interpretation of Dreams*, Freud referred to Goethe as a scientist who relied upon unconscious intuition rather than rigorous method, which suggests that he had been influenced by the views of both

---

[48] Wilhelm W. Hemecker, *Vor Freud: Philosophiegeschichtliche Voraussetzungen der Psychoanalyse* (Munich: Philosophia, 1991), 14, 94; Günter Gödde, *Traditionslinien des Unbewussten: Schopenhauer, Nietzsche, Freud* (Tübingen: edition diskord, 1999), 88.

[49] Goethe's own comments on this fragment can be found in *FA*, 1, XXV: 81–2. Here Goethe writes that although he cannot remember having written the fragment, it nonetheless represents the pantheistic sentiments regarding nature which were part of his world-view during the 1770s and 1780s. The text, written by G. C. Tobler, was published in late 1782 or early 1783 (see *FA*, 1, XXV: 859–60). For a broader discussion of debates concerning the authorship of this fragment, see Hemecker, *Vor Freud*, 96–98.

[50] Goethe, "Die Natur," *FA*, 1, XXV:12–13

[51] Gödde, *Traditionslinien des Unbewussten*, 87–8. Hemecker notes that Haeckel included the nature fragment at the beginning of his Darwinian work *Natürliche Schöpfungsgeschichte* (1868), and that Freud's reference to the fragment in his "Selbstdarstellung" follows shortly after a positive reference to Darwin. See Hemecker, *Vor Freud*, 78–9.

Helmholtz and Du Bois-Reymond, seeing Goethe as having a less than rational scientific orientation that aligned him with *Naturphilosophie*.[52] Such an impression of Goethe may also in part have emerged from Freud's philosophy teacher Franz Brentano (1878–1917), who had engaged in an active campaign against *Naturphilosophie* in general as well as against "Goethe's" fragment on nature in particular.[53]

Perhaps the logical conclusion to Freud's turn away from *Naturphilosophie* and vitalism is his so-called "psychology for the neurologist" (*Psychologie für den Neurologen*): the "Project for a Scientific Psychology." Written in 1895, the intention of the "Project" was to establish a natural-scientific psychology which would "represent psychical processes as quantitatively determined states of specifiable material particles."[54] This "economics of nerve forces" (*Ökonomik der Nervenkraft*) as Freud called it in a letter to Fliess,[55] was based upon an epistemological world-view that favored empiricism over German idealism, and which proffered a mechanistic model of the mind in which material particles known as "neurones" form a network that allows for the distribution of energy or quantity throughout the psychic system. This theoretical construct was clearly a product of the materialist positivism of Brücke's laboratory, and Freud was relatively quick to see its rather pronounced limitations.

The working model of the "Project" was clearly theoretical and abstract, yet since Freud alluded to what he called "specifiable material particles," he at least initially seems to have thought that there could be a direct correspondence between his theory and the actual anatomy of the brain.[56] A possible reason for Freud's confusion regarding the "Project" can be found in a letter dated September 9, 1875, in which he applauds British empiricist philosophers. These thinkers were correct, he proposes, in arguing against Kant's theory of synthetic a priori judgments, and for maintaining that

---

[52] In a letter to Fliess dated October 4, 1897, Freud refers to the moment of scientific illumination that led to Goethe's vertebral theory of the skull. The letter reveals that Fliess reported this event from Goethe's life to Freud two years earlier, as an example of scientific inspiration. See *The Complete Letters of Sigmund Freud to Wilhelm Fliess, 1807–1904*, ed. and trans. J. Moussaieff Masson (Cambridge, MA: Harvard University Press, 1985), 269. In the *Interpretation of Dreams*, Freud uses Goethe an example of someone whose intellectual discoveries were achieved unconsciously rather than consciously (*SE*, V: 613; *GW*, II/III: 618).

[53] Hemecker, *Vor Freud*, 14.

[54] Freud, "Project for a Scientific Psychology," *SE*, I: 295; [psychische Vorgänge darzustellen als quantitativ bestimmte Zustände aufzeigbarer materieller Teile]. Freud, "Entwurf einer Psychologie," *GW*, *Nachtragsband*, 387–477; here 387.

[55] Freud to Fliess, 25 May 1895, in *The Complete Letters of Sigmund Freud to Wilhelm Fliess*, 129; Sigmund Freud, *Aus den Anfängen der Psychoanalyse: Briefe an Wilhelm Fliess, Abhandlungen und Notizen aus den Jahren 1887–1902* (London: Imago, 1950), 129.

[56] On this subject, see Richard Wollheim, *Freud*, 2nd edn. (London: Fontana, 1991), 44.

all knowledge not only begins, but also emerges, from empirical experience. Such insights allowed them to establish what Freud called a "very great and scientific school" of thought.[57] If Freud maintained such a view during the period in which he formulated the "Project," then this would explain why he completely failed to recognize that there would necessarily be a yawning gulf between his theoretical model of mental functioning and what Kant would have called anatomical reality "in itself."

Yet Freud, probably without realizing it, came around fairly quickly to what might, in a very broad sense, be called a "Kantian" point of view. As early as November 29, 1895 he informed Fliess that he had given up on his ambition of uniting anatomy and psychology, and that he could no longer relate to the mental state in which the "Project" was formulated.[58] Notwithstanding Freud's disclaimers, the "Project" enjoyed, as many Freud scholars have observed, a second life as the heuristic and methodological basis of key elements in Freud's later metapsychology.[59] When, in his "Autobiographical Study" of 1925, Freud called his metapsychology a "speculative superstructure" (*spekulativer Überbau*) the elements of which could be abandoned or changed once proven inadequate,[60] he was, in the terminology of Kant's *Critique of Judgment*, proposing a psychology *als ob* or *as if* – a heuristic model of mental functioning that did not necessarily correspond with external reality. One method of refining this model was to revise it in light of further clinical experience. Another way of strengthening and defending this model – albeit in cultural rather than in strictly scientific terms – was to list worthy precursors who had purportedly anticipated some of its precepts. And, in the German-speaking world of 1930 (the year of Freud's "Goethe Prize" address), there was probably no greater cultural authority upon which one could draw than Goethe.

Freud's Goethe quotations in the "Goethe Prize" address

It would of course be impossible, in a chapter of this length, to draw upon all of Freud's many Goethe quotations.[61] For the sake of brevity,

---

[57] [ganz große und wissenschaftliche Schule]. Cited in Gödde, *Traditionslinien des Unbewussten*, 89.
[58] Freud to Fliess, November 29, 1895, in *The Complete Letters of Sigmund Freud to Wilhelm Fliess*, 152.
[59] On this subject, see Frank J. Sulloway, *Freud, Biologist of the Mind* (New York: Basic Books, 1979), 118–31; Alfred Grünbaum, *The Foundations of Psychoanalysis: A Philosophical Critique* (Berkeley, CA: University of California Press, 1984), 3; Wollheim, *Freud*, 63; Gay, *Freud: A Life for Our Time*, 78.
[60] Freud, *SE*, XX: 32–3; *GW*, XIV: 58.
[61] For a more detailed account of Freud's references to Goethe, see Uwe Henrik Peters' essay "Goethe und Freud," *Goethe Jahrbuch* (1986): 86–105.

I will confine myself here to a brief analysis of the two main Goethe quotations that Freud uses in his "Goethe Prize" address, as these quotations are used by Freud in order to demonstrate what he regards as Goethe's anticipation of key elements in psychoanalysis. The first of these is taken from the dedication (*Zuneigung*) in the first part of *Faust*:

> Again ye come, ye hovering forms! I find ye,
> As early to my clouded sight ye shone!
> Shall I attempt, this once, to seize and bind ye?[62]
>
> *Ihr naht euch wieder, schwankende Gestalten!*
> *Die früh sich einst dem trüben Blick gezeigt.*
> *Versuch' ich wohl euch diesmal fest zu halten?*

Freud argues that these lines could be repeated "for each of our analyses," in that they demonstrate Goethe's familiarity with what he calls the "incomparable strength of the first affective ties of human creatures."[63] In this sense, one assumes that Freud associates the *schwankende Gestalten* with memories of early childhood and perhaps with childhood sexual experiences or fantasies that remain in the unconscious. Goethe's use of the verb *festhalten* (to hold fast or to capture) is thus presumably interpreted by Freud in a scientific or epistemological sense, in that psychoanalysis attempts to understand the patient's history through the interpretation of the forms or images (manifested in dreams, free associations, slips of the tongue, and so on) that relate to one's "first affective ties."

This is, to say the least, a highly motivated and tendentious interpretation of the passage. In the commentaries of the two most recent and comprehensive editions of Goethe's works, the Munich and Frankfurt Editions, this passage, probably written in June 1797, is interpreted in relation to Goethe's contemporaneous work on morphology.[64] During the early 1790s and in the wake of Kant's *Critique of Judgment* (1790), Goethe became preoccupied with developing a post-Kantian scientific methodology, the central issue of which was the question as to whether diverse natural organisms could be organized according to ideal types or forms. It was this methodological problem which led Goethe to posit the existence of an *Urpflanze* or "Primal Plant" which might function as

---

[62] Freud, *SE*, XXI: 209; *GW*, XIV: 548. I have, for reasons of historical accuracy, used the translation which appears in the *Standard Edition* of Freud's works, which also quotes Goethe's German in the original. A more modern translation exists in the version of Stuart Atkins: "Once more you hover close, elusive shapes / my eyes but dimly glimpsed when I was young. / Shall I now try to hold you captive?" Goethe, *Faust I & II*, ed. and trans. Stuart Atkins, *Goethe's Collected Works* (1984), vol. II, 1.

[63] Freud, *SE*, XXI: 209; [die wir für jede unserer Analysen wiederholen könnten]; [die unvergleichliche Stärke der ersten affektiven Bindungen], *GW*, XIV: 547–8.

[64] For these interpretations, see *FA* 1, VII/2: 149–53, and *MA*, 6, I: 994–5.

a developmental archetype for all forms of plant life.[65] Likewise, in the field of zoology, Goethe was attempting to formulate ideal morphological types against which different animal species might be examined.[66]

The method involved in the formulation of such ideal types was essentially inductive: they were to be arrived at by synthesizing disparate observations of individual phenomena into heuristic general models of organic development. Thus, while Goethe's idea of induction was essentially derived from the example of Francis Bacon,[67] his understanding of heuristic teleological ideas was influenced by Kant, and especially by the second part of the third *Critique*: the *Kritik der teleologischen Urteilskraft* (Critique of Teleological Judgment).[68] In light of his extensive intellectual engagement with the works of Kant, an engagement that was also mediated through his correspondence with Friedrich Schiller during the 1790s, Goethe eventually came to realize that such ideal types were merely abstract ideas which could never correspond with the protean forces at work in sensuous nature. Thus, writing in January 1798 (about six months after composing the "Dedication" to part one of *Faust*), Goethe observes that while the scientist may wish to establish what he calls a "pure constant phenomenon" (*reines konstantes Phänomen*), such an ideal type can only ever be achieved by passing over or eliding the "many empirical fractions" (*viele empirische Brüche*) which make up the minute particularities of actual individual organisms.[69] Likewise, in a much later piece entitled "Intuitive Judgment" (*Anschauende Urteilskraft*, 1817), Goethe referred to teleological reflections on organic development as adventures of reason rather than as scientific facts that correspond directly with the physical world.[70]

In light of these methodological questions, the "hovering forms" (*schwankende Gestalten*) referred to by Goethe at the beginning of *Faust* are normally associated with organic forms that are subject to continual

---

[65] See Goethe, *Versuch die Metamorphose der Pflanzen zu erklären* (1790), *FA*, 1, XXIV: 109–51.
[66] See Goethe, "Erster Entwurf einer allgemeinen Einleitung in die vergleichende Anatomie, ausgehend von der Osteologie" (written in 1795–6), *FA*, 1, XXIV: 225–81.
[67] On Goethe's relation to Bacon, see H. B. Nisbet, *Goethe and the Scientific Tradition* (London: Institute of Germanic Studies, 1972), 23–47.
[68] See, in this connection: Richards, *The Romantic Conception of Life*, 427–30; Daniel Steuer, "In Defence of Experience: Goethe's Natural Investigations and Scientific Culture," *The Cambridge Companion to Goethe*, ed. Lesley Sharpe (Cambridge: Cambridge University Press, 2002), 160–178; here 171.
[69] Goethe, "Erfahrung und Wissenschaft," *FA*, 1, XXV: 125–7; here 125. Translated by Douglas Miller as "Empirical Observation and Science," in Goethe, *Scientific Studies*, 24–5.
[70] See Goethe, "Anschauende Urteilskraft," *FA*, 1, XXIV: 448. Translated by Douglas Miller as "Judgment Through Intuitive Perception," in Goethe, *Scientific Studies*, 31–2.

transformation, and are not susceptible of being represented as fixed or static. This interpretation resonates with Faust's own vocation as a scientist or natural philosopher, in that he attempts to understand the secrets of nature without, at least initially, realizing that nature itself is protean and resistant to the strictures of scientific method. As we shall see later in this chapter, such an interpretation also accords with Goethe's post-Kantian scientific method in the *Theory of Color*, which insists that scientific representations of natural objects can only be figurative, heuristic and subject to the inaccuracies of language. Hermeneutically speaking, Freud's interpretation of this passage is highly subjective and selective, in that he makes no attempt to understand Goethe's lines in terms of their historical context or their function within Goethe's thought as a totality.

The second main quotation used by Freud comes from the last stanza of the poem "An den Mond" (To the Moon), initially written in 1777 or 1778 and then substantially revised in 1789.[71] Freud claims that the following lines from the second version of the poem paraphrase what he calls "the content of dream life" (*Inhalt des Traumlebens*):

> Something not known by men,
> Or not considered,
> Which, through the labyrinth of the breast,
> Wanders in the night.[72]
>
> *Was von Menschen nicht gewußt,*
> *Oder nicht bedacht,*
> *Durch das Labyrinth der Brust*
> *Wandelt in der Nacht.*

Although I do not wish to go into a long exegesis of Goethe's poem here,[73] it is fair to say that Freud's reading of this last stanza is only slightly less problematic than his interpretation of the passage from *Faust*. Of interest here is the first version of the poem, not quoted by Freud, the first line of which uses the term *unbewußt* (unconscious or non-conscious) rather than "nicht gewußt," and which therefore resonates more directly with the terminology of psychoanalysis than does the later version. The poem is normally interpreted as being primarily about the desire to possess a love-object, and secondarily about the relationship between human

---

[71] See the most recent commentary on this poem in Goethe, *FA*, 1, I: 964–8. The first version of the poem can be found in *FA*, 1, I: 234–5, the second in *FA*, 1, I: 301–2.
[72] Goethe, "An den Mond," *FA* 1, I: 302. Quoted in Freud, *SE*, XXI: 209; *GW*, XIV: 548. I have replaced the translation that appears in the *Standard Edition* with my own rendering.
[73] For an account of the poem's reception history, see Helmut Arntzen, "An den Mond," *Goethe Handbuch*, ed. B. Witte *et al.*, vol. I/1 (Stuttgart: Metzler, 1996), 180–7.

consciousness and nature. The last stanza in particular focuses upon the extent to which there is a connection between human subjectivity and nature of which the human subject itself is not fully aware. The *Brust* (breast) is a labyrinth in the sense that the ties between human desires and what might be called the natural or cosmic order (symbolized by the moon) are so deep and elemental that they exceed conscious reflection: they are, in short, neither "gewußt" (known) nor "bedacht" (considered). Thus, insofar as Goethe's stanza addresses aspects of human subjectivity that are not open to conscious deliberation, it may be fair to interpret it in relation to the unconscious, and such an interpretation is certainly supported by Goethe's use of the term *unbewußt* in the first version of the poem. Yet apart from Goethe's reference to "night," there is nothing at all to suggest that the poem is about what Freud calls "the content of dream-life," and Goethe's late eighteenth-century understanding of the term *unbewußt* was surely quite different to Freud's. As we have seen in Goethe's reflections on the composition of *Werther*, and as further examples will also demonstrate, when Goethe uses the term *unbewußt* in relation to individual subjectivity, it is normally associated not only with desire, but also with unknown sources of artistic creativity or inspiration; rarely if ever is it in any way explicitly related to the repression of unpalatable mental contents or the etiology of neuroses.

It could, with some justification, be protested here that I am analyzing in rather too much detail a text that the elderly Freud wrote in some haste in order to make some fitting and appropriate remarks upon his receipt of the Goethe Prize.[74] Indeed, as Paul Bishop shows in chapter 1 of this volume, the broad cultural influence exerted upon Freud by the *literary* Goethe (and especially the Goethe of *Faust*) is profound and multifaceted. At the same time, however, this influence arguably belongs not to the *epistemology*, but rather to the *rhetoric* of psychoanalysis. Seen in this light, Freud's Goethe quotations in the "Goethe Prize" speech demonstrate in a general sense the way in which Freud invoked Goethe in order to lend cultural legitimacy to the project of psychoanalysis. These passages are removed completely from their context in Goethe's works and Goethe's position within the history of ideas, and are used in order to lend cultural weight to Freud's own hypotheses. Apart from Freud's paper on Goethe's *Dichtung und Wahrheit*, which in any case treats Goethe as an analysand rather than as a theoretician of the unconscious,[75] there is no extended and systematic analysis of Goethe's works in Freud's writings.

---

[74] Here it should be noted that Freud could not attend the award ceremony in Frankfurt due to illness. The "Goethe Prize" address was delivered by his daughter, Anna.
[75] Here I am referring to Freud's analysis of an event in Goethe's childhood: "A Childhood Recollection from *Dichtung und Wahrheit*," *SE*, XVII: 147–56; *GW*, XII: 15–26.

What, then, are the implications of this for Goethe's alleged role in the development of the concept of the unconscious? And how might one accurately describe Goethe's relation to psychoanalysis? Answers to the first question have been offered by a number of scholars, including Ludwig Klages, Lancelot Law Whyte, Henri F. Ellenberger, and (more recently) three contributors to this volume: Paul Bishop, Matthew Bell, and Günter Gödde.[76] All of these authorities generally agree that there is in Goethe's works, and especially in *Faust*, a notion of the unconscious that emerges from the relationship between human subjectivity and nature – with "nature" being understood in the broadly pantheistic terms propagated by Herder and Goethe in their reception of Spinoza. Goethe gives expression to this notion when he says to Riemer in 1805 that "the human cannot remain in a conscious state or in consciousness for long; he must flee once again into unconsciousness, as therein live his roots."[77] The unconscious is in this sense often seen by Goethe as playing a positive role in human creativity, in that there is an apparent order in nature that comes to expression in works of art. It is for this reason that in a poetic piece composed in the year of his death (1832), Goethe wrote the following:

> The philosopher, in whom I trust so readily,
> Teaches, if not against all, then against the majority
> That we always achieve the best results unconsciously[78]
>
> *Der Philosoph, dem ich so gern vertraue,*
> *Lehrt, wo nicht gegen alle, doch die meisten,*
> *Daß unbewußt wir stets das Beste leisten*

The philosopher to whom Goethe refers in these lines is, not surprisingly, normally taken to be Spinoza.[79] These lines were quoted by the philosopher Ludwig Klages in 1932, in a chapter entitled "Goethe as

---

[76] In this connection see: Ludwig Klages, *Goethe als Seelenforscher*, 3rd edn. (Zürich: Hirzel,1949), 36–46; Lancelot Law Whyte, *The Unconscious before Freud* (London: Friedmann, 1978), 126–9; Henri F. Ellenberger, *The Discovery of the Unconscious: The History and Evolution of Dynamic Psychiatry* (New York: Basic Books, 1970), 203–4; Paul Bishop, "Goethe on the Couch: Freud's Reception of Goethe," *Goethe at 250: London Symposium/Goethe mit 250: Londoner Symposion*, ed. T. J. Reed, Martin Swales, and Jeremy Adler (Munich: Iudicium, 2000), 156–68; Gödde, *Traditionslinien des Unbewussten*, 27, 37–9; Matthew Bell, *The German Tradition of Psychology in Literature and Thought, 1700–1840* (Cambridge: Cambridge University Press, 2005), 208.
[77] [Der Mensch kann nicht lange im bewußten Zustande oder im Bewußtsein verharren; er muß sich wieder in's Unbewußtsein flüchten, denn darin lebt seine Wurzel.] Goethe to Riemer, August 5, 1810 in *Goethes Gespräche*, ed. Woldemar Freiherr von Biedermann, 9 vols. (Leipzig: Biedermann, 1889–91), vol. II, 324.
[78] Goethe, "Zahme Xenien, Nachlese, 1800–1832," *FA*, 1, II: 727.
[79] See the commentary in *FA*, 1, II:1238.

Discoverer of the Unconscious" (*Goethe als Entdecker des Unbewussten*).[80] This demonstrates that, since the first half of the twentieth century, scholars have traced what Günter Gödde has called a tradition-line of the vitalist unconscious, beginning with Herder's reception of Spinoza and developing concurrently in Goethe and the early works of Schelling, before continuing (as Matthew Bell shows in chapter 6 of this volume) in the writings of Carus.[81] As we have seen, Goethe often portrays this notion of the unconscious in a positive light, as enabling artistic production, and in this sense it was closely related to his conception of genius. A slightly darker unconscious element, also related to Goethe's discourse on genius, is his notion of *das Dämonische* (the daemonic).[82] This concept – derived from the classical notion of the daemon, seen by Plato and other classical authors as an intermediary between the human and divine worlds – is rendered immanent in Goethe's aesthetics of genius, most notably in *Dichtung und Wahrheit* and in the conversations with Eckermann. The daemonic individual is thus seen as a preternaturally creative figure who is a mediator of pantheistic nature. In the case of daemonic individuals like Shakespeare, Mozart, or Byron, Goethe argues that this mediation produces artistic works; but in the case of Napoleon, who for Goethe was the daemonic individual *par excellence*, this unconscious productivity can also lead to political acts, some of which may be less than rational and of a dubious moral status.[83]

In terms of our second question – that regarding Goethe's relation to Freud and to psychoanalysis – it seems quite unlikely that Goethe's broadly pantheistic or vitalist notion of the unconscious could have exerted a direct scientific influence upon Freud. Or, to put this in another way, one might argue that Goethe's scientific (as opposed to cultural) influence on Freud is rather more latent or subterranean than it is manifest. As we have seen, when Freud began to develop his theory of the unconscious, the vitalist and pantheistic metaphysics that underlay Goethe's understanding of the unconscious had been surmounted by the positivist materialism of Helmholtz and Du Bois-Reymond. Goethe's authority at this time was as a cultural figure and definitely not as a philosopher of science. Freud would no doubt have been aware of the vitalist tradition-line of the unconscious to which Goethe belonged – indeed he

---

[80] See Klages, *Goethe als Seelenforscher*, 36–46.
[81] Gödde, *Traditionslinien des Unbewußten*, 27.
[82] On this subject, see Angus Nicholls, *Goethe's Concept of the Daemonic: After the Ancients* (Rochester, NY: Camden House, 2006).
[83] See, for example, part 4 (book 20) of *Dichtung und Wahrheit*, FA, 1, XIV: 839–42; and Eckermann's conversations with Goethe dated March 11, 1828 (*FA*, 2, XII: 652–60) and December 6, 1829 (*FA*, 2, XII: 364).

was exposed to elements of it when he heard the fragment on nature – but its metaphysical underpinnings would have been, at least on the level of epistemology, wholly unacceptable to him and his scientific milieu. Instead, it is likely that Freud retrospectively invoked isolated instances of Goethe's understanding of the unconscious after the basic theory of psychoanalysis was already in place, and these invocations relate to Goethe's authority as a cultural phenomenon rather than as a scientist.

Yet here one cannot necessarily assume that such an abstract opposition between the natural sciences on the one hand and literary-philosophical culture on the other actually existed in the late nineteenth century. As Paul Bishop's contribution to this volume clearly demonstrates, Freud belonged to an epoch in which literary and philosophical ideas often intermingled with scientific discourses, even if natural scientists of the period (like Freud) tended officially to play down the influence of such ideas upon their scientific work. Likewise, as Bruce Mazlish has recently argued, the division between the natural sciences on the one hand and the humanities or human sciences on the other is not an absolute one: the natural sciences, insofar as they are developed by historically and culturally situated human agents, are not "inhuman," any more than the human sciences, in emerging from the ideas of human beings situated in nature, are "unnatural."[84] Perhaps a useful solution to the question of how Goethe's literary works may have influenced Freud's understanding of the unconscious is to replace the word "influence," which is suggestive of a direct causative link, with two ideas found in philosophical hermeneutics: *facticity* and *horizon*. If a person's facticity refers to the concrete historical situation in they find themselves, and which precedes any form of theoretical reflection, then we can say that Goethe's literary works were part of Freud's facticity: the highly educated German-speaking cultural tradition or horizon to which he ineluctably belonged.[85] At the same time, however, any trace of Goethe's science in the officially elaborated scientific methodology of Freudian psychoanalysis is very hard to find indeed.

Goethe's post-Kantian scientific epistemology

In the "Goethe Prize" address, Freud speculates about how Goethe may have reacted to the science of psychoanalysis, making the claim that

---

[84] Mazlish, *The Uncertain Sciences*, 11.
[85] On the questions of facticity and horizon, see: Martin Heidegger, *Ontology: The Hermeneutics of Facticity*, trans. John van Buren (Bloomington, IN: Indiana University Press, 1999), based upon Heidegger's lectures on this subject delivered in 1923; Hans-Georg Gadamer, *Truth and Method*, 2nd revised English edn., trans. Joel Weinsheimer and Donald G. Marshall (London: Continuum, 2004), 265–307.

"Goethe would not have rejected psycho-analysis in an unfriendly spirit, as so many of our contemporaries have done."[86] As we have seen, Freud substantiates this claim on the basis of some rather dubiously deployed quotations from Goethe's literary works, while at the same time scrupulously avoiding any theoretical use of Goethe's actual scientific studies. Freud's tendency to avoid invoking Goethe's scientific work takes on a greater importance when we keep in mind the following facts: that he owned a thirteen-volume edition of Goethe's scientific publications;[87] that Wilhelm Fliess at one point suggested to Freud that he read some of Goethe's scientific theories;[88] and that an isolated reference to Goethe's work on morphology in the *Interpretation of Dreams* shows that Freud was at least to a limited extent aware of Goethe's scientific research.[89]

Freud was in this regard typical of his age, in that his reception of Goethe was dominated by the image of Goethe as genius: the author of *Faust* who had explored the depths of the human soul and survived to tell the tale. In fact, Goethe managed, mainly through *Poetry and Truth* and the conversations with Johann Peter Eckermann, to interpret his own life and works in terms of the theory of the unconscious that emerged during the Storm and Stress period, and was later refined in the era of Weimar classicism. The young Goethe is accordingly seen as the poet who is almost overwhelmed by the force of his own subjectivity, but who later manages to bring these unconscious elements under some control through the use of formal aesthetic elements derived from the cultures of classical Greece and Rome, and by undertaking sensuous research into objective nature. As we have seen, Freud himself subscribes to this narrative regarding Goethe's life in his letter to Fliess dated May 31, 1897.

The popular myth about Goethe's involvement with philosophy is that he completely misunderstood Kant until a philosophical discussion with Schiller in 1794 set him on the right path.[90] In this way, Goethe and Schiller are seen as the twin forces of Weimar classicism: on the one hand, Goethe's intuitive genius, unconscious productivity, and empathy for nature made him the ideal lyric poet who approximated the achievements of the ancients; while on the other hand Schiller was, through his superior knowledge of Kant's critical philosophy, able to understand Goethe's creativity in philosophical terms. In Goethe and Schiller

---

[86] Freud, *SE*, XXI: 208; [Goethe hätte nicht, wie so viele unserer Zeitgenossen, die Psychoanalyse unfreundlichen Sinnes abgelehnt], *GW*, XIV: 547.
[87] As is noted by Peters in "Goethe und Freud," 95.
[88] See Bishop, "Goethe on the Couch," 159.
[89] Freud refers to Goethe's vertebral theory of the skull in the *Interpretation of Dreams*, *SE*, V: 664; *GW*, II/3: 678.
[90] See Goethe's account of this conversation in "Glückliches Ereignis," *FA*, 1, XXIV: 434–8.

unconscious intuition and philosophical reflection were thus combined, and the movement in modern German literature known as Weimar classicism was born.[91] Unfortunately, this neat dialectical narrative has not stood the test of time. We now know that Goethe intensively studied Kant's first and third *Critiques* some three years prior to the discussion with Schiller about Kant in 1794.[92] In fact, Goethe developed his own philosophy of science, which conforms neither with Schiller's relatively orthodox Kantian idealism, nor with Schelling's *Naturphilosophie*. I suspect, moreover, that if the mature Freud had been aware of this philosophy of science, he would have had more persuasive grounds for invoking Goethe as his intellectual forebear.

Goethe's mature scientific epistemology was essentially a skeptical form of Kantianism.[93] As we have seen, during the late 1780s and the 1790s, Goethe's botanical and anatomical research was concerned with how one might develop a general natural philosophy based upon minute observations of natural objects. His concern was to unite the concrete particulars of individual objects on the one hand, with a general theory of nature on the other. Empirical observations were seen as being of primary importance, but they should nevertheless lead to general synthetic archetypes that might at least heuristically reveal something about nature as a totality. An example of such an archetype was Goethe's *Urpflanze* or "primal plant," which he thought might serve as a universal model of botanical development. When Schiller was presented with this model in 1794, he viewed it as a transcendental idea rather than as an object of experience, and it is this discussion, reported by Goethe in the text known as "Glückliches Ereignis" ("Fortunate Encounter"), which has led to the view that Goethe had no real understanding of Kant until 1794.[94]

Yet when one reads Goethe's essay written in April 1792 and entitled "The Experiment as Mediator between Object and Subject" (*Der Versuch als Vermittler von Objekt und Subjekt*), the extent to which he was already developing a scientific methodology under the influence of Kant becomes clear. This essay is, according to John Neubauer, Goethe's "first polemical reaction to Newton's scientific method and its emphasis on the *experimentum crucis* [crucial or decisive experiment] in color theory."[95]

---

[91] See, for example, the account of the Goethe–Schiller correspondence offered by T. J. Reed: "Weimar Classicism: Goethe's Alliance with Schiller," *The Cambridge Companion to Goethe*, 101–15.
[92] On this subject, see Geza von Molnár, *Goethes Kantstudien* (Weimar: Hermann Böhlhaus Nachfolger, 1994).
[93] See Steuer, "In Defence of Experience," 171.
[94] See Goethe, "Glückliches Ereignis," *FA*, 1, XXIV: 437.
[95] John Neubauer, "Goethe and the Language of Science," *The Third Culture: Literature and Science*, ed. Elinor S. Schaffer (Berlin: De Gruyter, 1998), 51–65; here 56.

It begins by arguing that humans normally view natural objects in a highly subjective and non-reflective fashion, perceiving them in relation to their emotions, likes and dislikes. It is this subjective and emotional approach to nature which, according to Goethe, leads us into a thousand errors (*tausend Irrtürmer*). A more difficult and rewarding task, says Goethe, is that of attempting to view natural objects "in themselves" (*an sich selbst*); that is, independently of the projections that flow from our desires and wishes.[96] Like Kant, Goethe is aware that such objectivity is impossible, but he nevertheless demands that stringent self-reflection be the scientist's goal. This is particularly the case with regard to the formulation of scientific experiments, as the conditions of an experiment may unconsciously be designed in order to achieve results that the researcher already has in mind. Accordingly, the scientist must always remember that his concepts are merely the heuristic constructions of his own subjectivity rather than aspects of nature "in itself."

This argument would later comprise the essence of Goethe's critique of Newton in the polemical part (*polemischer Teil*) of the *Theory of Color*. Newton had theorized that white light is corpuscular, being comprised of different "rays" that are refrangible to differing degrees, and which (when passed through prisms configured in a particular way) produce a geometrically calculable spectrum of colors. As early as 1800, Goethe had argued that these rays (*Lichtstrahlen*) were, in the Kantian sense, only hypothetical or heuristic phenomena (*hypothetische Wesen*)[97] It could not be proven, as Newton had assumed, that they exist in actual nature "in itself"; rather, nature would have to be manipulated through an artificial experimental situation in order to achieve the desired results, which would then be interpreted using only the "ray" concept, to the exclusion of other hypotheses. In this way, Goethe argued that Newton already had a corpuscular or ray-oriented theory of light in mind when he formulated the prism experiments, and that these experiments simply served to confirm this pre-conceived theory.[98] Goethe's critique of Newton was therefore not, as Helmholtz had thought in his first essay on Goethe's science, an attempt to refute Newton's experimental *results*; rather, it was a Kantian critique of Newton's entire scientific method, which Goethe saw as manipulating nature in order to make it conform to an abstract

---

[96] Goethe, "Der Versuch als Vermittler von Objekt und Subjekt," *FA*, 1, XXV: 26–36; here 26. Translated by Douglas Miller as "The Experiment as Mediator between Object and Subject," in Goethe, *Scientific Studies*, 11–17.
[97] Goethe, "Anfänge der Farbenlehre," *Die Schriften zur Naturwissenschaft* (Leopoldina Ausgabe), ed. Dorothea Kuhn *et al.*, 21 vols. (Weimar: Hermann Böhlhaus Nachfolger, 1947–), 1, III: 300.
[98] See Goethe, *Zur Farbenlehre*, *MA*, X: 278.

hypothesis, and as "dogmatically" assuming the objective existence of a concept (that of the "ray") which was merely heuristic.[99] It was this critique which the elderly Helmholtz, in his second essay on Goethe's science, saw as having demonstrated gaps in Newton's methodology, in that Goethe showed that Newton's corpuscular theory is characterized by an "artificial presupposition" (*künstlerische Voraussetzung*),[100] a view that has, in the meantime, become more or less the standard line in recent scholarship on Goethe's critique of Newton.[101]

The danger that Goethe highlights in his critique of Newton is that of viewing nature or external objects in an instrumental fashion, in terms of our projects, desires and goals. Arguing that humans take more pleasure "in the idea than in the thing" (*an der Vorstellung als an der Sache*), Goethe continually emphasized the discontinuity between human ideas about nature and nature "in itself."[102] Unlike the early Schelling, Goethe did not think that there could be a parallelism between human ideas about the natural world and external nature;[103] and unlike Kant, Goethe did not think that reason coincided with freedom from sensuous nature.

If we keep these features of Goethe's scientific epistemology in mind, the answer to Freud's speculation as to what Goethe would have thought of psychoanalysis might be as follows: first, Goethe would probably have rejected Freud's "Project for a Scientific Psychology" on the same grounds that Freud eventually did – namely, because there was a lack of empirical evidence that could confirm its conceptual content, and because it claimed to refer to reality "in itself" rather than to reality cognized according to an heuristic conceptual scheme; second, Goethe might have approved of Freud's later distinction between a provisional

---

[99] In relation to Newton's corpuscular theory, Goethe writes: "Solche bisher nur gelegentlich gleichnissweise gebrauchte Ausdrücke macht endlich Neuton dogmatisch indem er die Farben als integrirende Theile des Lichts darzustellen unternimmt" [such expressions, which have up until now only been used occasionally and by way of analogy, are finally made dogmatic by Newton, in that he undertakes to represent colors as the integrated parts of light.] Goethe, *Zur Farbenlehre, historischer Teil, Ergänzungen und Erläuterungen, Die Schriften zur Naturwissenschaft*, II/6: 75.

[100] Helmholtz, "Goethes Vorahnungen kommender wissenschaftlicher Ideen," 352.

[101] See, for example: Roger Stephenson, *Goethe's Conception of Knowledge and Science* (Edinburgh: Edinburgh University Press, 1995), 25; Dennis L. Sepper, *Goethe contra Newton: Polemics and the Project for a New Science of Colour* (Cambridge: Cambridge University Press, 1998), 147; Daniel Steuer, *Die stillen Grenzen der Theorie. Übergänge zwischen Sprache und Erfahrung bei Goethe und Wittgenstein* (Cologne: Böhlau, 1999), 209–15.

[102] Goethe, "Der Versuch als Vermittler," *FA*, 1, XXV: 31.

[103] See in this connection, Goethe's criticisms of Schelling in his correspondence with Schiller: Goethe to Schiller, January 6, 1798 (*MA* 8, I: 489); and Goethe to Schiller, February 21 and 25, 1798 (*MA* 8, I: 536). On Goethe's skepticism regarding Schelling's *Naturphilosophie*, see Jeremy Adler, "Science, Philosophy and Poetry in the Dialogue between Goethe and Schelling," *The Third Culture*, 66–102; here 71.

and heuristic metapsychology on the one hand, and clinical experience on the other, although Freud probably did not always maintain this distinction as Goethe might have liked. Goethe believed that synthetic, theoretical ideas were necessary for science, but he also thought that they must continually be corrected and revised through the careful, diligent, and even pedantic accumulation of empirical research.[104] And when we use experimental results to bear out a certain hypothesis that is particularly dear to us, our powers of self-reflection and self-awareness must be at their keenest. This is because, as Goethe writes,

> We can never be too careful in our efforts to avoid drawing hasty conclusions from experiments. For here at this pass, this transition from empirical evidence to judgment, cognition to application, all the inner enemies of man lie in wait: imagination; impatience; haste; self-satisfaction; rigidity; formalistic thought; prejudice; ease; frivolity; fickleness – this whole throng and its retinue. Here they lie in ambush, and surprise not only the active observer but also the contemplative one who appears safe from all passion.[105]

It could be argued that what Goethe approaches here is a conception of the *experimental or scientific unconscious*; namely, the tendency of the scientist to find his own wishes and projections confirmed in the phenomena created by his conceptual apparatus and experiments. Yet, as H. B. Nisbet has helpfully pointed out, Goethe's words of caution in "The Experiment as Mediator" were, in 1792, hardly new to the philosophy of science; in fact, Goethe was well aware of their most obvious precedent: Francis Bacon's discussion, in his *New Organon* (1620), of the "idols" or "false dogmas" of science.[106] These idols are, according to Bacon, "inherent in the nature of the intellect itself, which is found to be much more prone to error than the senses," and the only solution to them is to "fix and establish for ever the truth that the intellect can make no judgment except by induction in its legitimate form."[107]

---

[104] Goethe, "Der Versuch als Vermittler," *FA*, 1, XXV: 35.
[105] [Mann kann sich daher nicht genug in acht nehmen, aus Versuchen nicht zu geschwind zu folgern: denn beim Übergang von der Erfahrung zum Urteil, von der Erkenntnis zur Anwendung ist es, wo dem Menschen gleichsam wie an einem Passe alle seine inneren Feinde auflauren, Einbildungskraft, Ungeduld, Vorschnellichkeit, Selbstzufriedenheit, Steifheit, Gedankenform, vorgefaßte Meinung, Bequemlichkeit, Leichtsinn, Veränderlichkeit, und wie die ganze Schar mit ihrem Gefolge heißen mag, alle liegen hier im Hinterhalte und überwältigen unversehens sowohl den handelnden Weltmann als auch den stillen vor allen Leidenschaften gesichert scheinenden Beobachter.] Goethe, *FA*, 1, XXV: 30.
[106] See Nisbet, *Goethe and the Scientific Tradition*, 23–7. Nisbet notes (pages 24–5) that Goethe expressed his explicit approval of Bacon's treatment of the "idols" in a conversation with Sulpiz Boisserée held in 1815.
[107] Francis Bacon, *The New Organon*, ed. Lisa Jardine and Michael Silverthorne (Cambridge: Cambridge University Press, 2000), 18–19.

The main problem with Bacon's recourse to "pure" or legitimate induction can be found in Kant's famous statement to the effect that intuitions without concepts are blind; that is, in order to carry out scientific research at all, one must, on some level, have conceptualized or anticipated what one is seeking to discover. Kant makes this point in his *Anthropology from a Pragmatic Point of View (Anthropologie in pragmatischer Hinsicht,* 1798) when he explicitly criticizes Bacon, arguing that in science one cannot avoid beginning with a hypothesis (*von einer Hypothese anfangen*).[108] This is also the essence of Karl Popper's critique of Bacon in both the *Logic of Scientific Discovery* and in *Conjectures and Refutations*, where he argues that all science is based open initial anticipations, conjectures or hypotheses which must subsequently be tested (and either corroborated or falsified) through experiments. Seen in this light, the "purging of our minds of all anticipations or conjectures" demanded by Bacon represents, according to Popper, an impossible task that has very little to do with the methodology of modern science.[109]

As H. B. Nisbet has noted, Goethe's own critique of Baconian induction displays significant similarities with that of Popper.[110] Nisbet points out that although Goethe's emphasis on induction originally emerged from his reception of Bacon, when it came to the theoretical background to the *Theory of Color*, Goethe took the view that it is impossible to undertake inductions without hypotheses. This insight is given its classical formulation in the opening section of the *Theory of Color*:

An extremely odd demand is often set forth but never met, even by those who make it: i.e. that empirical data should be presented without any theoretical context ... because it is useless simply to look at something. Every act of looking turns into observation, every act of observation into reflection, every act of reflection into the making of associations; thus it is evident that we theorize with every attentive look into the world.[111]

---

[108] Kant, *Anthropologie in pragmatischer Hinsicht, Werke in sechs Bänden*, ed. Wilhelm Weischedel, 6 vols. (Darmstadt: Wissenschaftliche Buchgesellschaft, 1960), vol. VI, 542.

[109] See Karl Popper, *The Logic of Scientific Discovery* (London: Routledge, 2002), 1–10; *Conjectures and Refutations: The Growth of Scientific Knowledge* (London: Routledge and Kegan Paul, 1963), 13–15. Popper's general assessment of Bacon's relevance to modern science has more recently been reiterated by Michel Malherbe in his essay "Bacon's Method of Science," *The Cambridge Companion to Bacon* (Cambridge: Cambridge University Press, 1996), 75–98; here 75. These judgments of Bacon are, however, the subject of some debate. For the view that Bacon remains relevant to modern scientific method and also offers an anticipation of Popper's theory of falsification, see: Peter Urbach, "Francis Bacon as a Precursor to Popper," *British Journal for the Philosophy of Science* 33 (1982):113–32. For a general critique of Popper's view of Bacon, see Paolo Rossi, "Bacon's Idea of Science," *The Cambridge Companion to Bacon*, 25–46; here 43–6.

[110] Nisbet, *Goethe and the Scientific Tradition*, 29.

[111] Goethe, *Theory of Color*, trans. Douglas Miller, *Scientific Studies*, 159 (translation altered). [Ist es doch eine höchst wunderliche Forderung, die wohl manchmal gemacht, aber auch

The scientific unconscious

Goethe goes on to argue that, although "pure" or non-theoretical induction is not possible, a degree of objectivity may be attained if one proceeds with what he calls "awareness," "self-knowledge," "freedom," and even "irony."[112]

In short: what differentiates Goethe's approach to scientific induction from that of Bacon is the influence of Kant. Through his reading of Kant, Goethe became aware that all scientific induction is ineluctably conceptual and thus to a certain degree subjective; as he puts it in a letter to Christoph Ludwig Schultz: "I am grateful to the critical and idealist philosophy for the fact that it made me aware of myself, which is an enormous advantage."[113] Yet the "freedom" to which Goethe alludes above is tempered by the fact that all theorizing is dependent upon language, which is in turn part of a scientific tradition of which the researcher may not be fully aware.[114] In the "Didactic Part" (*Didaktischer Teil*) of the *Theory of Color*, Goethe sees one of the major pitfalls of science as being the tendency to elide the radical discontinuity between the linguistic sign (*Zeichen*) and the actual thing or object (*Sache*) which it attempts to describe.[115] This danger arises when certain accepted modes of description become embedded within the vernacular of scientific disciplines, leading us to forget that accepted scientific terminology is only ever an approximation (and therefore a distortion) of the natural phenomena which it describes. "The conflict of the individual with unmediated experience and mediated tradition," writes Goethe in the historical part (*Historischer Teil*) of the *Theory of Color*, "is actually the history of science."[116] Every scientist stands within a tradition of inherited terms and concepts, the influence of which he must strive to be aware; and if, as is highly likely, he fails to become fully conscious of this tradition and its effects on his approach to nature, "it will encounter him unconsciously" (*so wird es ihm unbewußt begegnen*).[117]

---

selbst von denen, die sie machen, nicht erfüllt wird: Erfahrungen solle man ohne irgend ein theoretisches Band vortragen ... Denn das bloße Anblicken einer Sache kann uns nicht fördern. Jedes Ansehen geht über in ein Betrachten, jedes Betrachten in ein Sinnen, jedes Sinnen in ein Verknüpfen, und so kann man sagen, daß wir schon bei jedem aufmerksamen Blick in die Welt theoretisieren.] Goethe, *Zur Farbenlehre, MA*, X: 11.

[112] [mit Bewußtsein, mit Selbstkenntnis, mit Freiheit, und ... mit Ironie]. Ibid.

[113] [Ich danke der kritischen und idealistischen Philosophie, daß sie mich auf mich selbst aufmerksam gemacht hat, das ist ein ungeheuer Gewinn.] Goethe to Ludwig Schultz, September 18, 1831, *FA*, 2, XI: 466.

[114] On this issue, see: Neubauer, "Goethe and the Language of Science"; Angus Nicholls, "The Hermeneutics of Scientific Language in Goethe's Critique of Newton," *Sprachkunst* 36, no. 2 (2005): 203–26.

[115] Goethe, *Zur Farbenlehre*, §754, *MA*, X: 227.

[116] [Der Konflikt des Individuums mit der unmittelbaren Erfahrung und der mittelbaren Überlieferung, ist eigentlich die Geschichte der Wissenschaften.] Ibid., 570.

[117] Ibid., 561.

In the language of the recent and contemporary philosophy of science, Goethe's *Theory of Color* is concerned with issues relating to something called "reflexivity." Roger Smith sees reflexivity as "the examination of the unfounded assumptions in any body of knowledge ... and the process whereby knowledge of what is human changes what it is to be human."[118] According to this definition, reflexivity is necessarily a characteristic of all the sciences, but plays a particularly key role in the human sciences, in which the category under investigation – the human – is not merely an empirical object, but also a mode of consciousness with protean capacities for self-representation. It is for this reason that Foucault associates reflexivity predominantly with the human sciences, in which "the human" is at once subject and object, "researcher" and "researched." The human sciences, he writes, treat "as their object what is in fact the condition of their possibility," and for this reason "they never cease to exercise a critical examination of themselves."[119]

Yet contemporary philosophers of science have questioned the special status that Foucault affords the human sciences in relation to reflexivity. Bruce Mazlish has argued that all science is in a certain sense "human" (and therefore exposed to reflexivity), in that it emerges from human subjectivities, concepts, and procedures,[120] while Roger Smith has also contended that reflexivity is not a feature that differentiates the human sciences from the natural sciences, since in both fields there are no "transcendental grounds for asserting empirical knowledge."[121] Certainly Goethe seems to have been keenly aware that self-reflexivity and self-knowledge are key issues in the natural sciences, a view which aligns his position with those of Mazlish and Smith.

With respect to psychoanalysis and the history of the unconscious, it is important to note that Foucault regards psychoanalysis as the key to the human sciences, since, in its analysis of the human subject and the unconscious, it addresses "what makes all knowledge in general possible in the field of the human sciences."[122] Although the scientific status of Freudian psychoanalysis has been a heated subject of debate at least since Karl Popper's critique of Freud,[123] for Foucault psychoanalysis is a "science" precisely by virtue of its attempt to theorize reflexivity as part of its methodology.[124] How, then, did Freud attempt to incorporate reflexivity into the practice of psychoanalysis; or, to put the question another

---

[118] Smith, *Being Human*, 62.
[119] Foucault, *The Order of Things*, 397.
[120] Mazlish, *The Uncertain Sciences*, 11.
[121] Roger Smith, "Does Reflexivity Separate the Human Sciences from the Natural Sciences?" *History of the Human Sciences* 18, no. 4 (2005): 1–25; here 19.
[122] Foucault, *The Order of Things*, 410.
[123] See Popper, *Conjectures and Refutations*, 33–7.
[124] Foucault, *The Order of Things*, 407–21.

way, how did he recognize what I have called, with reference to Goethe's scientific studies, the "scientific unconscious"? Freud addressed reflexivity – the ways in which desires, wishes, and projections of the analyst may influence his treatment of the patient – in his theory of the "counter-transference" (*Gegenübertragung*):

> We have become aware of the "counter-transference," which arises in him [the analyst] as a result of the patient's influence on his unconscious feelings, and we are almost inclined to insist that he shall recognise this counter-transference in himself and overcome it. Now that a considerable number of people are practising psychoanalysis and exchanging their observations with one another, we have noticed that no psycho-analyst goes further than his own complexes and internal resistances permit; and we consequently require that he shall begin his activity with a self-analysis and continually carry it deeper while he is making his own observations on his patients. Anyone who fails to produce results in a self-analysis of this kind may at once give up any idea of being able to treat patients by analysis.[125]

In the mythology of psychoanalysis, Freud's own alleged "self-analysis" (documented in the *Interpretation of Dreams*) is regarded as a kind of founding act, which gave birth to a new science. Since, however, not all analysts are endowed with Freud's apparently extraordinary capacity for self-analysis, Freud introduced the training analysis (the requirement that all analysts should themselves undergo analysis before practicing) as an attempt to incorporate reflexivity into the procedures of psychoanalysis. Should an analyst fail to undergo such a "psycho-analytic purification" (*psychoanalytische Purifizierung*) before practicing, he would, according to Freud, "easily fall into the temptation of projecting outwards some of the peculiarities of his own personality, which he has dimly perceived, into the field of science."[126]

Here the similarities between Freud's idea of the counter-transference and Goethe's highlighting of the "inner enemies" (*innere Feinde*) that

---

[125] Freud, SE, XI: 144–5; [Wir sind auf die "Gegenübertragung" aufmerksam geworden, die sich beim Arzt durch den Einfluß des Patienten auf das unbewußte Fühlen des Arztes einstellt, und sind nicht weit davon, die Forderung zu erheben, daß der Arzt diese Gegenübertragung in sich erkennen und bewältigen müsse. Wir haben, seitdem eine größere Anzahl von Personen die Psychoanalyse üben und ihre Erfahrungen untereinander austauschen, bemerkt, daß jeder Psychoanalytiker nur so weit kommt, als seine eigenen Komplexe und inneren Widerstände es gestatten, und verlangen daher, daß er seine Tätigkeit mit einer Selbstanalyse beginne, und diese, während er seine Erfahrungen an Kranken macht, fortlaufend vertiefe. Wer in einer solchen Selbstanalyse nichts zustande bringt, mag sich die Fähigkeit, Kranke analytisch zu behandeln, ohne weiteres absprechen.] *GW*, VII: 108.

[126] Freud, "Recommendations to Physicians Practising Psychoanalysis," SE, XII: 111–20; here 116–17. [Er wird leicht in die Versuchung geraten, was er in dumpfer Selbstwahrnehmung von den Eigentümlichkeiten seiner eigenen Person erkennt, als allgemeingültige Theorie in die Wissenschaft hinaus zu projizieren.] *GW*, VII: 382–3.

attend scientific research and cognition are clear. Yet it is extremely improbable that Freud derived his awareness of issues relating to self-reflection and reflexivity through any encounter with Goethe's writings on scientific method. Nevertheless, from the perspective of scientific method it is arguably Goethe's post-Kantian scientific epistemology, rather than his poetic works, which has the greatest and most enduring relevance for psychoanalysis.

Conclusion

Goethe's role in the history of the unconscious in nineteenth-century German thought is at once central and ambiguous. There is no doubt that Goethe elaborated, albeit in a non-systematic way, a notion of the unconscious that is both redolent of Spinoza's pantheism and deeply related to the concept of genius, according to which the unconscious forces of nature are seen as being expressed through works of art. It was, moreover, this understanding of the unconscious which influenced Goethe's status as the central genius of modern German literature: the preternaturally gifted poet who allegedly relied on intuition and unconscious inspiration as opposed to the conscious Kantian theorizing of Schiller. Indeed, Goethe himself readily contributed to this self-image in his autobiographical works and conversations.

It is also this image of Goethe that is given a mythic status in one of the founding narratives of psychoanalysis, according to which Freud was inspired to become a scientist upon hearing the dithyrambic essay "Die Natur." At the same time, however, when it came to the theoretical elaboration of psychoanalysis, Goethe was an entirely unacceptable precursor for the establishment of a new "science" in the age of Darwin and Helmholtz. Accordingly, Goethe became a figure to be selectively and often tendentiously invoked by Freud as a cultural (as opposed to scientific) precursor. Goethe, according to Freud, was intuitively and poetically aware of truths about human nature which had, prior to the birth of psychoanalysis, lacked an appropriate scientific formulation. In this way Goethe was afforded an exemplary status in the psychoanalytic canon and therefore also in the history of the unconscious: being variously depicted as mythic origin, proto-psychoanalyst and intriguing analysand. Yet as I have argued in this chapter, once the myths about Goethe's genial powers of intuition and his alleged dislike for philosophy are stripped away, and once his real and independent engagement with Kant's critical philosophy is properly examined, he is revealed to be an important theorist of science who offers valuable insights as to how unconscious affects may influence scientific research.

4 The hidden agent of the self: towards an aesthetic theory of the non-conscious in German romanticism

Rüdiger Görner

The novels and poems come unwatched out of one's pen.[1]
D. H. Lawrence

The phenomenology of introspection

One significant part of the romantics' legacy was their awareness of layers beneath human consciousness and the desire to explore them. Studying the ways in which many romantics approached this counterfoil to consciousness, or "night side of science" as one of their key proponents called it,[2] amounts to describing the emergence of a theory. Yet the usage of the word "theory" requires some qualification, for all the tentative or emphatic references to the sub-conscious in romanticism resembled an attempted mapping out of unknown territory, consisting of assumed inner landscapes of boundless expansiveness but necessarily without much empirical data to support this undertaking. The fact that the romantics insisted on exploring this sphere by means of what were deemed dubiously pseudo-scientific methods has given critics sufficient grounds for questioning what they saw as the blunt expression of irrationality by mostly poetically minded intellectuals.

What those critics did not appreciate was the romantics' main presupposition: namely, that there is a non-rational area of human existence with its own logic and pronounced forms of, at times erratic, expression. The romantic project of exploring the non-conscious or sub-conscious stretched, incidentally, from some notes by the poet-philosopher Friedrich von Hardenberg (otherwise known as Novalis, 1772–1801) on

[1] D. H. Lawrence, *Fantasia of the Unconscious and Psychoanalysis and the Unconscious* (Harmondsworth: Penguin, 1983), 15.
[2] Gotthilf Heinrich von Schubert, *Ansichten von der Nachtseite der Naturwissenschaft* (1808; Darmstadt: Wissenschaftliche Buchgesellschaft, 1967); Schubert, *Die Symbolik des Traumes* (1814; Heidelberg: Lambert Schneider Verlag, 1968).

psychological phenomena, to Marie von Ebner-Eschenbach's (1830–1916) late romantic novella in the shape of correspondence cards, *Die Poesie des Unbewussten* 1883 (*The Poetry of the Non-conscious*), which, ironically, refuses to differentiate between consciousness and non-consciousness.[3]

The appropriate rendering of "das *Un*bewusste" in English poses a problem; for "unconscious" can also mean that one has lost one's consciousness whereby non-conscious only suggests a specific state of being. Therefore, in the following, the latter concept is preferred. "Sub-conscious" is used with specific reference to "das *Unter*bewusste." In German and English the subtle semantic difference between the two concepts is often overlooked and both are used almost synonymously. Semantically, the French concept "inconscience" can include the meaning "pre-conscious," too. Freud's point was that "das Unbewusste" contained contents that would not be capable of becoming conscious (*bewusstseinsfähig*).

One main difficulty for an intellectually satisfying approach to the sub- and non-conscious in romanticism was the realization that it would be impossible to ascribe a specifically historical development to that sphere; in other words, one could not do for the sub- or non-conscious what Hegel did with his *Phenomenology of the Mind* (*Phänomenologie des Geistes*, 1806), namely to write, in effect, a history, or even phenomenology, of the sub-conscious nor indeed the non-conscious. It would make sense, however – and the history-conscious romantics from Novalis to the German poet and medical writer Justinus Kerner (1786–1862) were aware of this – to work on a history that showed the ways in which particularly the sub-conscious expressed itself and was treated. Animal magnetism, hypnosis, reflections on dreams and their impact on (artistic) creativity, emotions and intuitions but also mental disorders, were treated in different ways at different times, yet mostly in relation to a state "beneath" or outside reason. The major contribution of the romantics to thinking about these phenomena was first of all their readiness to take them seriously. Beginning as objects of speculation and hypothesis, they soon turned into objects of more systematic analysis, the results of which were often presented as narratives, most notably by Justinus Kerner, whose contribution to research on the sub-conscious remains a recognized landmark in its history.[4]

---

[3] Marie von Ebner-Eschenbach, *Erzählungen*, vol. III, ed. Edgar Groß (Munich: Nymphenburger Verlagsanstalt, 1961), 192–208.

[4] See Justinus Kerner, *Die Seherin von Prevorst*, 8th edn. (Stuttgart: Steinkopf Verlag, 1999); Friedrich Pfäfflin *et al.*, eds., *Justinus Kerner, Dichter und Arzt 1786–1862*, 2nd edn. (Marbach am Neckar: Deutsche Schillergesellschaft, 1990); Jürgen Klatte, Hans Göbbel and Heinz Schott, eds., *Justinus Kerner, Medizin und Romantik: Kerner als Arzt und Seelenforscher* (Weinsberg: Stadt Weinsberg, 1990).

The hidden agent of the self 123

In view of what has just been said about the inner landscape of the sub-conscious and, to some extent, the non-conscious, it is no surprise to find that the most eminent representative of an analytical approach to it – Carl Gustav Carus, who is discussed at length by Matthew Bell in chapter 6 of this volume – also excelled in writing about landscape painting and was himself a painter (see the cover to this volume). His "Nine Letters" on that subject (1831) sought to establish a connection between the perception of the "real" landscape and its artistic renderings on the one hand and its effect on the emotional state of the viewer on the other. He implied that there was a visual and resounding correspondence between the landscape of nature and the soul as expressed by the various moods that a certain view arouses. Carus envisaged a detailed depiction of the "soul-scape," so to speak, that would take account of the development of consciousness from the sub-conscious, too. Writing on Carus, Ricarda Huch, in her major re-examination of the significance of romanticism (1951), which still compares well to other such assessments, argues that Carus assumed the existence of a non-conscious "idea" that would gain visible shape and progress towards consciousness. But the "light of consciousness" could only illuminate a mere fraction of the dark rivers than run beneath the ground of discourses informed by reason.[5] According to what can be called the first traces of neurophysiology in romanticism, medical researchers like Johann Christian Reil (1759–1813), arguably the founding father of integrative psychiatry and psychotherapy, proposed that there was an identifiable location of sub-conscious streams (in a pre-Freudian sense of the word), namely the ganglia of the nervous system. He regarded any signs of madness or som-nambulism as a sudden emergence of so-called ganglia-currents gaining temporary predominance over rational behavior patterns.[6]

Introspection and with it the discovery of the rich worlds within human-ity provided an intellectual experience with pertinent poetic consequences, as first displayed in Goethe's *The Sorrows of Young Werther* (*Die Leiden des jungen Werthers*, 1774). It was Johann Gottfried Herder (1744–1803), however, who in a diary report of his sea voyage in May 1769, first gave expression to this feeling in a conceptually illuminating manner. Facing the sheer vastness of the sea, he remarks that nature stands on an abyss of infinity without knowing it; and it is due to this very "felicitous ignorance"

---

[5] Carl Gustav Carus, *Neun Briefe über Landschaftsmalerei*, in Friedmar Apel, ed., *Romantische Kunstlehre: Poesie und Poetik des Blicks in der deutschen Romantik* (Frankfurt am Main: Deutscher KlassikerVerlag, 1992), 203–79; Carus, *Psyche: Zur Entwicklungsgeschichte der Seele* (Pforzheim, 1846); Carus, *Vergleichende Psychologie oder Geschichte der Seele in der Reihenfolge der Tierwelt* (Vienna, 1866); Ricarda Huch, *Romantik. Blütezeit. Ausbreitung. Verfall* (Tübingen: Rainer Wunderlich Verlag, 1951), 434.
[6] Johann Christian Reil, *Rhapsodieen über die Anwendung der psychischen Curmethode auf Geisteszerruettungen* (Halle: Curtsche Buchhandlung, 1803).

that she stands firmly and assuredly.[7] Herder, who found himself caught between the Enlightenment and its romantic transformation, if not dissolution, refers to what lies beneath the "clarity of consciousness" as something potentially menacing that knows of no limitations. The word "infinity" or *Unendlichkeit* turned into both a keyword and a central poetic theme of the soul-searching prose in early romanticism. Its mathematical symbol (∞), for example, features prominently in the notes of Novalis, suggesting that there is an implicit link between spiritual, psychological, and algebraic "infinities." The inner-depths of humanity and the mathematical repetend were to Novalis intimately connected. Whilst the natural "happy" state of being depended, according to Herder, on the human capacity to forget, or rather the inability to retain everything in consciousness, Novalis and other early romantics, like the young author and dramatist Heinrich von Kleist (1777–1811), claimed that the state of happiness would rest with the full exploration of the senses, knowing that any stage in one's education involved the restraining of sensual pleasures and demanded the ability to come to terms with the "darker sides" of the soul that often unearth themselves unexpectedly.[8]

If it can be assumed that, according to Hegel, there is "infelicitous" and, according to Adorno, even "false" consciousness then, surely, the same does not apply to the sphere of the non-conscious. This is not to say, however, that we are altogether unaccountable for what emerges from this sphere. Freud famously argued that the realm of the non-conscious consisted of former experiences or (frustrated) aspirations that resurface under particular circumstances, often causing a false impression of surprise in us; for we need to be aware that what we are and enact can only be fathomed against the backdrop of things past.[9] But no matter how advanced psychoanalysis has become, this inner sphere of humanity cannot but remain a construction. It is a sphere that is by and large void of empirical data. One cannot measure the infinity of the soul nor its

---

[7] [Die mütterliche Natur ... steht auf einem Abgrunde von Unendlichkeit und weiß nicht, daß sie darauf steht; durch diese glückliche Unwissenheit steht sie fest und sicher.] Johann Gottfried Herder, *Journal meiner Reise im Jahr 1769*, *Werke*, vol. I, ed. Wolfgang Pross (Munich: Hanser, 1984), 361.
[8] Heinrich von Kleist, "Aufsatz, den sichern Weg des Glücks zu finden, und ungestört, auch unter den größten Drangsalen des Lebens, ihn zu genießen!" *Werke und Briefe*, ed. Peter Goldammer *et al.*, 4. vols. (Berlin and Weimar: Aufbau Verlag, 1978), vol. III, 433–49. See also: Mark-Georg Dehrmann, "Die problematische Bestimmung des Menschen: Kleists Auseinandersetzung mit einer Denkfigur der Aufklärung im 'Aufsatz, den sichern Weg des Glücks zu finden', im 'Michael Kohlhaas' und in der 'Herrmannsschlacht'," *Deutsche Vierteljahrsschrift für Literaturwissenschaft und Geistesgeschichte* 81, no. 2 (2007): 193–227.
[9] See Cord Friebe, *Theorie des Unbewußten: Eine Deutung der Metapsychologie Freuds aus transzendental-philosophischer Perspektive* (Würzburg: Königshausen & Neumann, 2005).

aspiration to ultimately "break through the narrow bonds of individuality" and attain universality.[10]

Drawing heavily on neo-Romantic notions, Stefan Zweig (1881–1942) in his essay *The Secret of Artistic Creation* (*Das Geheimnis des künstlerischen Schaffens*, 1938), echoes his conception of the daemonic as developed with reference to Hölderlin, Kleist, and Nietzsche in his earlier and widely read collection of essays *Struggling with Demons* (*Der Kampf mit dem Dämon*, 1925), which did much – for better or worse – to perpetuate the (early and neo-) romantic notion of the artist driven by his sub- *and* non-conscious.[11] Zweig suggested that the artist was a hypnotized medium of a higher will; and the basis of what he could produce in this state would amount to a "continuous struggle between non-consciousness and consciousness."[12]

Arguably, these positions that, by and large, disregard socio-cultural influences upon the creative process are rooted in decidedly romantic images of the non-conscious and its contribution to art. But, as recent research has shown, and as Andrew Bowie outlines in chapter 2 of this volume, this discourse on the non-conscious was at least latently and sometimes manifestly present in the philosophy of German idealism, whereby Schelling provided a link between the two by suggesting that the absolute was the "eternal non-conscious."[13] Any attempt to comprehend the significance of the non-conscious as the underscoring element in romantic aesthetics presupposes some notion of how its influence can be perceived in the artefact itself. By stressing the need to clarify the intellectual force of consciousness and self-awareness, Hegel, in the opening sections of his *Phenomenology of the Mind*, seems to suppress the

---

[10] Isaiah Berlin, *The Roots of Romanticism*, ed. Henry Hardy (London: Pimlico, 1999), 15.
[11] In Stefan Zweig, *Gesammelte Werke in Einzelbänden*, ed. Knut Beck (Frankfurt am Main: S. Fischer, 1984), 384. See also Rüdiger Görner, "Dialog mit den Nerven: Stefan Zweig und die Kunst des Dämonischen," *Stefan Zweig und das Dämonische*, ed. Matjaž Birk and Thomas Eicher (Würzburg: Königshausen & Neumann, 2008), 36–44. For further contextualizing reference see Angus Nicholls, *Goethe's Concept of the Daemonic: After the Ancients* (Rochester, NY: Camden House, 2006), 32–76.
[12] [beständiges Ringen zwischen Unbewußtheit und Bewußtheit]; Stefan Zweig, *Das Geheimnis des künstlerischen Schaffens: Essays*, ed. Knut Beck (Frankfurt am Main: S. Fischer, 1984), 17. Similarly, Arthur Koestler, and after him George Steiner, but without referring to either Koestler or Steiner, implied that artistic expression means to enliven one particular aspect of the incommensurable of which the non-conscious is one crucial component. Arthur Koestler, *The Act of Creation* (London: Penguin, 1964); George Steiner, *Grammars of Creation* (London: Faber and Faber, 1991).
[13] See the ground-breaking study by Elke Völmicke, *Das Unbewusste im Deutschen Idealismus* (Würzburg: Königshausen & Neumann, 2005). See also: Hans-Georg Bensch, *Perspektiven des Bewußtseins: Hegels Anfang der Phänomenologie des Geistes* (Würzburg: Königshausen & Neumann, 2005). Bensch emphasizes the critical dimension of Hegel's conception of consciousness and refers to the non-conscious more by implication.

notion that the world of the non-conscious might have an impact both on how the "I" perceives the world at large in its state of self-awareness, and how it apprehends individual aspects and turns them into objects of its own creation. Only rarely does Hegel offer glimpses of the pitfalls of consciousness, for instance, when he concedes that "consciousness lost its senses in the dialectics of sensual certainties."[14] This is a distinctly ironic statement on Hegel's part; for it implies that the contradictions within the perception of the world through the senses expose our consciousness to the dangers of bewilderment and of actually losing those very senses.

In his *Prolegomena on Aesthetics* (*Vorschule der Ästhetik*, 1803), this most "romantic" and ironic of aesthetic theories, Jean Paul Friedrich Richter (1763–1825) introduces the notion of the "instinct of the non-conscious" as a moral corrective and aesthetic agent that appears to perform miracles in the hands of the artistic genius.[15] As with next to everything else in his *Prolegomena*, Jean Paul's extended references to this instinct seem to have been written with tongue in cheek, especially when he argues that this instinct, or drive, will be the sense of the future.[16] This faculty only makes collective sense if applied by the genius, whom Jean Paul portrays as the liberator of life who can beautify even death.

Jean Paul was working on what amounted, at least partly, to a parody of aesthetic theory when Schelling gave his lectures in Jena on the philosophy of art (1802/3). In one of his most significant passages, Schelling stated that art would rest on the identity of conscious and non-conscious activity.[17] Art refers us back to what Schelling called primordial images (*Urbilder*). He even defines art as a representation, or reworking, of such *Urbilder*, whose archetypal qualities bring us into close touch with divinity and primordial conceptions of the imagination. As such, *Urbilder* result from an initial transposition into consciousness of a non-conscious state of being.

The philosopher Johann Gottlieb Fichte (1762–1814) assumed the existence of a force juxtaposed with consciousness which could only be sensed, or divined, but not recognized. Interestingly, it is this point that was of the utmost importance for one of Fichte's initially most devout students, Novalis, and his extensive reflections on consciousness.

---

[14] [Bewußtsein ist in der Dialektik der sinnlichen Gewißheit das Hören und Sehen vergangen.] Georg Wilhelm Friedrich Hegel, *Phänomenologie des Geistes*, ed. Gerhard Göhler, 2nd edn. (Frankfurt am Main, Berlin and Vienna: Ullstein Verlag 1973), 84.

[15] [Instinkt des Unbewußten]. Jean Paul Richter, *Vorschule der Ästhetik*, ed. Wolfhart Henckmann, 4th edn. (Hamburg: Felix Meiner, 1980), 59.

[16] Ibid., 60.

[17] Friedrich Wilhelm Joseph Schelling, *Philosophie der Kunst* (Darmstadt: Wissenschaftliche Buchgesellschaft 1976), 28.

The hidden agent of the self

"Consciousness is an image of the Being in Being," notes Novalis in his studies on Fichte.[18] What intrigues him is the ontological status of consciousness. In this definition, "consciousness" is denied any form of immediacy but is connected with knowledge, reflection, and a representational function; for it is the "image" of Being within Being.

Fichte connected the notion of "infinity" with "imagination," claiming that there was a sub-conscious imaginative power (*Einbildungskraft*) that precedes any form of conscious self-awareness of the I or *Ich*. He refused, though, to subscribe to Herder's notion of history and memory being the main agents of consciousness. Instead, Fichte saw humanity as being open to all of the possibilities made available by time. According to Fichte, the human subject remembers the past and expects the future on basically equal terms and as but one expression of its sense of time; he did not, however, share with his fellow romantics the view that the main point of intellectual pursuits should be the discovery of a primordial world, deep down in the past or sub-conscious. Fichte entertained the idea that the present mediates between the past and the future, but he clearly saw the subject as orientating itself more to the potential of the unexplored future, which, in a sense, matches the unexplored pre-conscious states of the mind and the soul.[19] At the same time, he knew that both, the "Ich" and its consciousness, need memory and a sense of origin, the latter having, from Fichte's point of view, no transcendental quality.

But soon Novalis was to take issue with this Fichtean approach. In his collection of reflections, which he called *Pollen* (*Blüthenstaub*, 1797/98), he claims that it was one of the most arbitrary prejudices to assume that humans could not consciously transcend their senses. On the contrary, Novalis suggests, "Man is capable of being a trans-sensual being at any moment."[20] This ability to transcend oneself is masterminded by consciousness, self-awareness and poetry. Part and parcel of this process is the "romanticization" of the world that Novalis understood to be his most essential task. He did not necessarily strive back towards a primordial state of non-conscious Being or *Seyn*; his perspective was that of a poet and thinker who hoped always to expand his own consciousness in order eventually to transcend it. His was not so much an *aesthetics* of consciousness but an *aisthesis*, the perception of the function of consciousness and

---

[18] [Das Bewußtseyn ist ... ein Bild des Seyns im Seyn.] Novalis, *Werke, Tagebücher und Briefe*, ed. Hans-Joachim Mähl and Richard Samuel, 3 vols. (Darmstadt: Wissenschaftliche Buchgesellschaft, 1999), vol. II, 10.
[19] See Rüdiger Safranski, *Romantik: Eine deutsche Affäre* (Munich: Hanser Verlag, 2007), 70–88.
[20] [Der Mensch vermag in jedem Augenblick ein übersinnliches Wesen zu seyn.] Novalis, *Werke, Tagebücher und Briefe*, vol. II, 234.

the senses, with the view to go beyond them in acts of ever-intensified reflection. In that sense Novalis subscribed to the conception of intensity (*Intensität*) as the prime purpose of reflection and expression.[21] What "expression" meant in the context of his own poetry and, in particular, in his poetic prose, becomes apparent at the beginning of *The Apprentices of Sais* (*Lehrlinge zu Sais*, 1798/9) as well as in the first part of his fragmentary novel *Heinrich von Ofterdingen* (written in 1800, published in 1802). The narrator refers to the hieroglyphic signs in nature that one needs to decipher in order to enrich one's vocabulary. Once we have learnt more such words from nature, we can truly comprehend what we see and give better expression to what we say. For the time being, music will be the main source of reference when it comes to the expression of our innermost feelings. What applies to the hieroglyphs in nature is also true for sounds: they already exist and wait to be discovered: "The sounds are already in the strings and what is required is the ability to move them in order to awaken these sounds in an appealing sequence."[22]

Novalis did not suggest relying on our sub-conscious when discovering those sounds or tonal sequences; it is rather an intensified usage and expansion of our consciousness that will enable us to reach out to these hieroglyphs and sounds for the purpose of enhancing the quality of our self-expression. The level of self-expression, though, Novalis seemed to suggest, will depend on the nature of our self-awareness. This approach resounded even in self-appointed critics of romanticism, like Nietzsche, who in *The Birth of Tragedy* (*Geburt der Tragödie*, 1872) argues that those who have a mother-child relationship with music invariably entertain a sub-conscious musical relation to external objects, too.[23]

Becoming aware of the sub-conscious

Few writers were more torn between the universal claims of the Enlightenment, idealism and classicism on the one hand, and on the

---

[21] See Erich Kleinschmidt, *Die Entdeckung der Intensität: Geschichte einer Denkfigur im 18. Jahrhundert* (Göttingen: Wallstein, 2004). Kleinschmidt identifies Novalis as one of the main agents of *Intensität* who exemplified, and reflected upon, this category around 1800.

[22] [Die Töne liegen schon in den Saiten, und es gehört nur eine Fertigkeit dazu, diese zu bewegen um jene in einer reitzenden Folge aufzuwecken.] Novalis, *Werke, Tagebücher und Briefe*, vol. I, 255.

[23] [nur an diejenigen habe ich mich zu wenden, die, unmittelbar verwandt mit der Musik, in ihr gleichsam ihren Mutterschooss haben und mit den Dingen fast nur durch unbewusste Musikrelationen in Verbindung stehen]. Friedrich Nietzsche, *Die Geburt der Tragödie*, in *Sämtliche Werke: Kritische Studienausgabe*, 15 Vols., ed. Giorgio Colli and Mazzino Montinari (Berlin: Walter de Gruyter; Munich: Deutscher Taschenbuch Verlag, 1980), vol I, 135.

other, the unleashing of romantic emotion and inner conflict, than Heinrich von Kleist. It is fair to say, though, that Kleist needed to achieve a high degree of intellectual consciousness, partly informed by his reading of Kant's first *Critique* and his studies of mathematics, to discover the attraction of the pathologically sub-conscious. His novella *The Marquise of O –* (1808) approaches not only the question as to "whether such a thing as an unwitting conception was possible"; it also addresses the nature of the sub-conscious with all its potentially embarrassing but also fertile implications.[24] Yet it is in Kleist's last play, *Prinz Friedrich von Homburg* (1810), where the sub-conscious turns into the main protagonist. This Prussian prince is portrayed as a somnambulist who is not only perceived as such by the others but *knows* of his condition. His awareness of his non-conscious state puts him into a precarious position: as a military commander of the highest rank he cannot help but drift away into the land of dreams when vital orders are given. Homburg appears like a string puppet at the mercy of his own sub-conscious being. If he is brought to his senses he can succeed, but only partially. Complete victory (against the Swedes), as is expected from him by his master, the Elector, can never be within his reach because as an acting officer he has to deny his most vital force: the sub-conscious within him. Instead of accepting marching orders, he is seen sleepwalking, dreaming of his glory with the moonlight "winding the wreath" of honor around him. When he is called by his fellow officer he admits not to know "where he is" except that he remembers having been in a state of non-consciousness.[25] Homburg, literally speaking, cannot help himself. His condition makes him incapable of acting responsibly, and also leads to existential consequences. Homburg faces the death penalty for his blunders but also challenges in the others "poetic" sentiments that will save him. Seeing the Prince in this condition triggers metaphoric speech in those who are normally used to speaking in military terms. In this, his final drama, Kleist empowers the sub-conscious and makes it into a governing force.

Romantic prose, too, roughly until 1810, tended to refer to dreams and fantasies and alluded to the non-conscious. Friedrich Schlegel's novella *Lucinde* (1799) is somewhat of an exceptional case in that it seems to be driven by an unrestrained playing of the senses with each other. Similarly, the

---

[24] [Und ob die Möglichkeit einer unwissentlichen Empfängnis sei.] Kleist, *Werke und Briefe* vol. III, 135; Heinrich von Kleist, *The Marquise of O – and Other Stories*, trans. with an introduction by David Luke and Nigel Reeves (Harmondsworth: Penguin, 1987), 91.

[25] [Mir unbewußt / Im Mondschein bin ich wieder umgewandelt!] Kleist, *Werke und Briefe*, vol. II, 359. The double meaning of the word "umgewandelt" is revealing: it is short for "umhergewandelt", meaning "to roam," but the shortened version also implies a state of transformation.

narrative in Clemens Brentano's (1778–1842) *Godwi* (1802) is based on self-perpetuating associations and a playful use of analogies. E. T. A. Hoffmann (1776–1822), by contrast, delivered an intriguing interplay of meticulously calculated narrative structures and the emergence of the unexpected, or uncanny, or even the sinister. Novellas that draw on historical topics – for example *The Guardians of the Crown* (*Die Kronenwächter*, 1817) and *The Mad Invalid at the Fort of Ratonneau* (*Der tolle Invalide auf dem Fort Ratonneau*, 1818) by Achim von Arnim (1781–1831) – could rarely employ the non-conscious as a narrative theme or compositional device. The same is true for those texts, particularly by Jean Paul, but also Ludwig Börne (1786–1837, *The Sulfur Baths near Montmorency* (*Die Schwefelbäder bei Montmorency*, 1823), and Karl Immermann (1796–1840, *Drei Tage in Ems*, translated as *Three Days in Ems Spa*, 1830), in which irony features as the main mode of expression, since the use of irony signals, after all, a highly developed form of consciousness.

If a shadow can be interpreted as an image, or, as in Nietzsche's *Zarathustra*, as a visual echo of the sub-conscious, then Adelbert von Chamisso's (1781–1838) novella *Peter Schlemihl's Miraculous Story* (*Peter Schlemihls wundersame Geschichte*, 1812) would need to be considered in this context, too. This troubling fantasy of a man who sells his shadow for a fortune that will bring him unhappiness epitomizes a state of detachedness in which no intuition or mind-focusing memory can provide meaningful direction. Schlemihl's sub-conscious seems to have disappeared with his shadow. He cannot even hope for involuntary memories that would provide access to his sub-conscious. It is his "shadowlessness" that haunts him from place to place and from one disappointment to the next.

Figures of memory-related speech do not always, however, necessarily cancel allusions to the non-conscious. In some of the above-mentioned prose-works this is particularly the case at narrative moments in which a protagonist breaks out into song and, in effect, performs a poem. Such poems either represent an object of memory or an instantaneous creation. In some cases it is not clear what conditions such poetic outbursts. In Brentano's *Godwi* (1802) to mention but one example, the source of inspiration is distinctly idiosyncratic, but quintessentially "romantic": "Quietly, like a song of thanksgiving, Eusebio's voice was struck like a matchstick by the moon."[26] This image of moon-struck inspiration accomplishes what the narrator had referred to before as a visible transition from one state of being to another.

---

[26] [Leise, wie ein Lied des Danks, zündete sich Eusebios Stimme am Monde an.] Clemens Brentano, *Godwi oder das steinerne Bild der Mutter: Ein verwilderter Roman*, ed. Ernst Behler (Stuttgart: Reclam Verlag 1995), 131.

The hidden agent of the self 131

More prominent still is the connection between poetic expression, involuntary memory and the state of non-consciousness, or rather, the absence of reflection, in the prose of Joseph Freiherr von Eichendorff (1788–1857). The following example stands for many an occasion where the junction between narration and poetry provides the location for the *mémoire involontaire* to flourish. The transition from explanatory narrative to soul-exposing poetry creates a space for seemingly sub-conscious images to emerge. The protagonist in Eichendorff's novella *A Sea Voyage* (*Eine Meerfahrt*, 1835–6) experiences such a moment at the beginning of his fateful voyage:

> I see from the edge of the ship
> Deep into the floods:
> Mountains and green lands,
> My ancient garden,
> The home upon the seabed,
> As I often imagined it in dreams,
> All of this dawns down below
> As if in a glorious night.

> *Ich seh' von des Schiffes Rande*
> *Tief in die Fluten hinein:*
> *Gebirge und grüne Lande,*
> *Der alte Garten mein,*
> *Die Heimat im Meeresgrunde,*
> *Wie ich's oft im Traum mir gedacht,*
> *Das dämmert alles da drunten*
> *Als wie eine prächtige Nacht.*[27]

The sea turns into a looking-glass for dreams and things past. The seafarer's eye penetrates into the impenetrable. It reaches the bottom of the sea and, in so doing, the bottom of memory and consciousness. But it also brings to light images of the sub-conscious or of what lies beneath the water's surface. The sheer richness of the sub-conscious imagery contrasts sharply with the stillness and emptiness that surrounds the ship. In aesthetic terms, Eichendorff's approach to the sub-conscious is of general interest, for it attributes a specific form to the rendering of what escapes mere reason. A song or poem is required to give expression to this dimension of otherwise unaccountable mental activity. Prose by itself is deemed inadequate by the narrator to perform this task of giving shape to the inner world. In a sense the song has a toxic effect; or rather it is a substitute for toxic potions that were thought at the time to aid the

---

[27] Joseph von Eichendorff, *Werke in sechs Bänden*, ed. Wolfgang Frühwald *et al.*, 6 vols. (Frankfurt am Main: Deutscher Klassiker Verlag. 1993), vol. III, 358.

individual in his attempts to discover the other side of reason. Famously, the English author Thomas de Quincey (1785–1859) had described the effects of opium in terms of its unleashing powers. He spoke of the "creative state of the eye" and the arising "sympathy between the waking and the dreaming states of the brain"; equally, he knew of "phantoms of the eye" that developed in artificially induced darkness. But in order to illustrate the opulent imagery that the opium initially helped him to access, de Quincey's self-analysis referred to Wordsworth's epic poem *The Excursion* (1814), and particularly to the section in which it speaks of "a wondrous depth" into which the mind sinks without end.[28]

De Quincey's *Confessions of an English Opium Eater* (1822) is void of any noteworthy aural perceptions. Sounds or musical modes inform, however, reflections of the sub- or non-conscious among German romantics.[29] But the most powerful musical expression of the sub-conscious in the 1820s and 1830s can be found in the work of a French composer: Hector Berlioz's (1803–69) *Symphonie fantastique* (1830), which he called an "Episode in the Life of an Artist." Its five movements seem to denominate five stages of opium-affected interplay between the sub-conscious and reflection, dream and self-awareness. The German composer and critic Robert Schumann (1810–56), in his far-sighted appreciation of Berlioz's symphony (1835), was the first to have shown just how much conscious compositional effort is necessary to conjure up musical representations of the sub-conscious.[30] This was, in fact, quite in line with the German philosopher and theologian Friedrich Schleiermacher's (1768–1834) concept of *Gefühlsbewußtsein* (consciousness of feeling) which saw in feelings a mediator between the sub-conscious and consciousness. Furthermore, Schleiermacher believed feelings to have a catalytic effect towards unifying these two separate spheres. He spoke of aesthetic feelings, which he believed to interact between the intellect and desire, emphasizing their creative potential.[31]

---

[28] Thomas de Quincey, *Confessions of an English Opium Eater*, ed. Alethea Hayter (London: Penguin, 1986), 103, 106.

[29] The discourse on the significance of the sub-conscious in musical composition begins with Guiseppe Tartini's so-called "devil's thrill" sonata. Tartini is reported to have dreamt of a pact with the devil to inspire the most sublime piece of music. In his dream he then heard a melody that he afterwards noted down and turned into the sonata. In 1713 when this story was spread by J. J. Lalande, this episode was seen as a prime example for the presence of the "demonic" in the creative process. Later, the Russian musicologist Lev Ginsburg connected Tartini's experience with I. P. Pawlow's discovery of the "waking point" in sleep, a phase of intensified mental activity during one's sleep in which the sub-conscious and consciousness interact. See Lev Ginsburg, *Giuseppe Tartini*, trans. from Russian into German by Albert Palm (Zürich: Eulenburg, 1976), 103–6.

[30] Robert Schumann, *Schriften über Musik und Musiker*, ed. Josef Häusler (Stuttgart: Reclam, 1982), 34–53.

[31] Friedrich Schleiermacher, *Dialektik* (1822): *Aus dem handschriftlichen Nachlaß*, ed. L. Jonas, *Sämtliche Werke*, part 3, vol. IV/2 (Berlin, 1839), 231 (§276).

The hidden agent of the self 133

Given the increasing prominence of what no longer only featured in Gotthilf Heinrich Schubert's (1780–1860) terminology as the "night side" of consciousness and its most pronounced form, science, but also as the fertile backdrop to the imagination, it is perhaps less surprising to find a thoroughly positive assessment of the sub-conscious at the threshold between romanticism and modernism, first and foremost in music. The most elaborate appreciation of the sub-conscious and its constructive contribution to modern art can be found in Richard Wagner's notes on *The Artistry of the Future* (*Das Künstlertum der Zukunft*, 1849). True to form, Wagner (1813–83), ever the revolutionary, claimed in this fragment, which informed most of his pamphlets and essays written around that time, that "the sub-conscious is the activity of nature" and the very origin of any revolutionary force. The artist, Wagner continued, derives all of his creative strength as well as his desire to produce something innovative, from the sub-conscious. Furthermore,

the sub-conscious is, after all, the involuntary, the necessary and the creative – and only once a general need has, out of this involuntary necessity, contented itself, can consciousness then join it, and that which has been satisfied and has elapsed turn into an object of conscious treatment through (artistic) representation.[32]

This passage is significant for any definition of the "aesthetics of the sub-conscious", for Wagner claims that any creative act requires the existence of a sub-conscious "preparatory" stage. In terms of Wagner's own artistic development, this emphasis on the essentiality of the sub-conscious is of great importance; for it can be argued that in his last opera (*Parsifal*, 1882), Wagner focuses on the dramatization of the sub-conscious. The interplay of leitmotifs throughout indicates the sub-conscious confusion that characterizes so much of this opera, with the character of Kundry being the main agent of the sub-conscious world. For good reason, *Parsifal* has been called Wagner's most psychoanalytical work *avant la lettre*.[33] But it was in a decidedly non-Wagnerian context that the aesthetics of the sub-conscious became an object of narration. It can be found in Eduard Mörike's (1804–75) novella *Mozart on his Journey to Prague* (*Mozart auf der Reise nach Prag*, 1855).

---

[32] [das Unbewußte ist die Tätigkeit der Natur]; [das Unbewußte ist eben das Unwillkürliche, Notwendige und Schöpferische, – erst wenn ein allgemeines Bedürfnis aus dieser unwillkürlichen Notwendigkeit heraus sich befriedigt hat, tritt das Bewußtsein hinzu, und das Befriedigte, Vergangene kann Gegenstand bewußter Behandlung durch Darstellung sein.] Richard Wagner, *Dichtungen und Schriften: Jubiläumsausgabe in zehn Bänden*, ed. Dieter Borchmeyer, vol. V (Frankfurt am Main: Insel, 1983), 244.

[33] Tilmann Moser, "Parsifals Weg vom Es zum Ich: Wagners Bühnenweihfestspiel aus psychoanalytischer Sicht," *Frankfurter Allgemeine Zeitung*, November 23, 1985.

Musical interludes

The year is 1787 and the scene an *Orangerie* in a fictive Italian-style estate in Bohemia to which Mozart is magically drawn during a short period of rest on his journey to Prague, where he is to premiere his opera *Don Giovanni*. Near a fountain, Mozart sits down and listens contentedly to the plashing. His eyes rest on an orange-tree and with a pensive smile he reaches out to the nearest orange, feels its sensual shape and succulent coolness in the hollow of his hand. It is this sensual experience that triggers memories of a scene from his youth and, in particular, a "long-forgotten musical memory, and for a while his reverie followed its uncertain trace."[34] These interwoven experiences at the blurred borderline between the sub-conscious and actual memory lead Mörike's Mozart to actually grasp the orange. "He saw this happen and yet did not see it." Eventually, he slowly cuts through the yellow globe of the orange from top to bottom: "He had perhaps been moved by an obscure impulse of thirst, yet his excited senses were content merely to breathe in the fruit's exquisite fragrance."[35] The sensual perception seems self-sufficient; a sense of utter contentment prevails. Any expression of consciousness is entirely obliterated from the narrative, so much so that the reader is to forget that this episode, too, is the result of a highly conscious narrative composition. This is achieved through the diversion of the mind towards the subtle sensuality or sensual subtlety of the imagery. Mozart appears absent-minded and yet his intuition and the sub-conscious are working in a way that seems to symbolize a particular form of the creative process: "For some moments he gazed at its two inner surfaces, then joined them gently, very gently together, parted them and reunited them again."[36] This seemingly non-conscious interplay of parting and reuniting is interrupted by the estate's gardener and Mozart is startled into sudden awareness "of where he was and what he had done."[37]

Mozart, in his letter of apology to the mistress of the estate, pleads innocence but links this incident with Genesis, saying that he cannot

[34] Eduard Mörike, *Mozart's Journey to Prague and a Selection of Poems*, trans. David Luke (London: Libris and Penguin, 2003), 17; [eine längst verwischte musikalische Reminiszenz, auf deren unbestimmter Spur er sich ein Weilchen träumerisch erging]. Eduard Mörike, *Sämtliche Werke*, ed. Helmut Koopmann, 6th edn., vol. I. (Darmstadt: Wissenschaftliche Buchgesellschaft 1997), 579.

[35] [Er sieht und sieht es nicht. ... Es mochte ihn dabei entfernt ein dunkles Durstgefühl geleitet haben, jedoch begnügten sich die angeregten Sinne mit Einatmung des köstlichen Geruchs.] Ibid., 580.

[36] [Er starrt minutenlang die beiden inneren Flächen an, fügt sie sachte wieder zusammen, ganz sachte, trennt und vereinigt sie wieder.] Ibid., 580.

[37] [und das Bewußtsein, wo er ist, was er getan, stellt sich urplötzlich bei ihm ein]. Ibid., 580.

even blame "a good Eve" (*eine gute Eva*) for having tempted him. But, in fact, his "Eve" at this moment was the interplay of the sub-conscious with dreamlike memory. Later in the narrative, the reader learns from Mörike's Mozart just how accurate his memory was when he gives a detailed, and by now very conscious, account of an episode that took place near Naples in 1770.

In the royal gardens of the Villa Reale some Sicilian actors perform a bucolic comedy of passions with overtly erotic connotations. For the young Mozart this explicit pastoral is both a rite of passage and an initiation into advanced artistic, or compositional, processes. What he sees is a parable of creation; and the way in which he describes it some twenty years later is so evocative that his audience has reason to believe that they have listened to the verbal transposition of a symphonic composition. Mozart depicts his memories as a triumph of sensuality, a comedy of the senses in which the game or play is the main protagonist. It is playfulness per se that engages in a sequence of self-representations. Playing for playing's sake is the real theme of this performance in the most alluring of settings, with Vesuvius in the background and the gentle curve of a lovely shimmering coastline.[38]

But the most important aspect of his recollection, and of the interplay of consciousness and sub-consciousness, is that it inspires Mozart, at least as far as Mörike's novella is concerned, to compose a missing duet for his opera *Don Giovanni* (Zerlina's "Giovinette, che fatte all'amore, che fatte all'amore"). The character of this interlude-like duet suggests that it is itself positioned between Zerlina's consciousness and her playful innocence. That is to say, this episode brings us closer to what can be referred to as the aesthetics of the non-conscious in late romanticism. Mörike suggests, or so it seems, that creations of disarming immediacy like Zerlina's duet, as opposed to, say, Leporello's distinctly reflected, if not calculated, so-called register-aria, derive directly from non- or semi-conscious experiences. But the point in question is that Mozart first needed to talk about his sensually mediated recollection before it could mature into an actual composition. The orange in his hand reminded him of the oranges with which the "figli di Nettuno" were playing in this animating pastoral.

The significance of this episode relates to the question as to whether phases or moments of "inconscience," as experienced by Mörike's Mozart, trigger modes of creation that come close to *écriture automatique* or automatic writing, meaning an almost involuntary way of writing as

---

[38] [Gerade vor sich hat man den Vesuv, links schimmert sanft geschwungen eine reizende Küste herein.] Ibid., 588.

explained by Pierre Janet in his seminal study on *Psychological Automatism* (*L'Automatisme psychologique*, 1889). Or is it that such modes of being bring to the fore that which presses to be connected with new meaning and artistic expression? Based on the way in which he makes Mozart present his case, Mörike seemed to have favored the latter formulation.

Paradoxically speaking, the sub-conscious expresses itself in a moment of sudden realization. The romantics emphasized that point by suggesting that the actual moment of creation lies on the threshold between the "sub-conscious" and "consciousness," implying the transitory nature of this occurrence. But they also knew of sudden eruptions of sub-consciously accumulated experience, fantasies, and dreams and their breaking out into the pre-coded modes of expression and recollection (for example, the song in Eichendorff's *A Sea Voyage*, mentioned above). The aesthetics of the sub-conscious can acquire symbolic expression in narrative terms through the composition of prefaces indicating, or reflecting, the stages of pre-consciousness in the creative process. Exemplary cases are Jean Paul's and E. T. A. Hoffmann's various prefaces to one particular narrative. The various editorial prefaces to Hoffmann's *The Life and Opinions of Kater Murr* (*Lebens-Ansichten des Katers Murr*, part 1: 1819; part 2: 1821) provide reflections on various stages of a type of literary composition that apparently owes more to accident than to intention, thus revealing the innermost desire of the editor, namely, to present a narrative *mixtum compositum* that represents the true state of his confused mind. The editor's claim is that Murr, the writing tom cat, scribbled much of his reflections on life on pages he had torn out of the memoirs of the composer Kreisler. The printer had then mixed it all up and published both: the cat's manuscript and sections of the composer's biography. Due to his negligence the editor had failed to notice the chaotic state of this manuscript before it went to print.

The editor of Murr's papers then claims "that authors often owe their most daring thoughts and extraordinary phrases to the type setters who aid the upsurge of their thoughts through misprints."[39] In other words, the misprint turns into a midwife for extraordinary thoughts. This comment is not only the pinnacle of romantic irony applied to philology and editorial processes; it also seems to regard the misprint as a sign, or chiffre, for sub-conscious, and therefore unaccountable, mechanisms. In his essay "The Uncommon Reader" George Steiner quotes one such

---

[39] [daß Autoren ihre kühnsten Gedanken, die außerordentlichsten Wendungen, oft ihren gütigen Setzern verdanken, die dem Aufschwunge der Ideen nachhelfen durch sogenannte Druckfehler]. E. T. A. Hoffmann, *Die Elexiere des Teufels: Lebens-Ansichten des Katers Murr: Zwei Romane*, ed. Carl Georg von Maassen and Georg Ellinger with an afterword by Walter Müller-Seidel, 2nd edn. (Munich: Artemis & Winkler, 1978), 298.

example of a Freudian or printer's slip that is so ingenious that any application of editorial correctness to this mistake must be seen as highly questionable, for it would disturb the sub-consciously generated beauty of a poetic phrase created by an anonymous printer: "The twentieth-century textual editor who has substituted 'brightness fell from her hair' for Thomas Nashe's 'brightness falls from the air' may be correct, but he is, surely, of the damned."[40]

The point is that the "aesthetics of the sub-conscious" indicate an element of the unexpected within the creative process. When, in the late 1830s, Honoré de Balzac (1799–1850) stated in his novella *Louis Lambert* (1832) that the sub-conscious, or *inconscience*, represented an entirely new field of science,[41] he simply reiterated what the Romantics had already discovered as their mainstream concern in both literature and music. In Berlioz's *Symphonie fantastique*, and in Schumann's reception of this piece of Berlioz, we find what is arguably the most direct connection between musical composition and the world of dreams, between supposed self-abandonment and the non-conscious.

What these examples show is that reflections on any expression of sub-conscious states of being can only be approximations. Likewise, we can hardly presume the existence of an actual *aesthetics* of the sub-conscious; the more appropriate concept is the *aisthesis* of the sub-conscious; that is, art-related forms of perceiving the impenetrable sub-layer of consciousness, which provide glimpses of what conditions the fallibility of our motivations and actions.

Hidden agents of the self

If the creative process as considered by literary and theoretical discourses in the romantic period entails the sub-conscious gaining artistic shape by blending voluntary efforts and involuntary occurrences, then we cannot but describe this case of aesthetic transformation in terms of borderline experiences. Along this thin line between states of mind and perception run persistent attempts to define the indefinable. In the case of one *Künstlernovelle* the attempts have a protagonist who is in search of his own identity *between* consciousness and sub- or non-consciousness. He is the agent of a life between nature and civilization, orientation and alienation, recollection, indifference, and concern and self-abandonment. This agent is the main character in Georg Büchner's (1813–37) *Lenz*

---

[40] George Steiner, *No Passion Spent: Essays 1978–1996* (London: Faber and Faber, 1997), 7.
[41] Honoré de Balzac, *Louis Lambert*, in *Oeuvres Complètes*, vol. XXXI (Paris: Louis Conard, 1927).

(1835). Emptiness, nothingness, and madness are the denominators of Lenz's split identity: "he appeared to himself like a dream" we read, and "what he did he did so with consciousness and yet felt forced by an inner instinct."[42] This state of mind is reflected in the way he speaks: "In conversation he often faltered, an indescribable anguish attacked him for he had lost the end of his sentence; then he thought he had to retain the last word spoken and had therefore to speak compulsively and it was only with greatest effort that he suppressed these desires."[43] This fear of losing the end of his sentences and his attempt to counteract moments of aphasia are actual demarcations of a borderline situation in linguistic terms. The ends of Lenz's sentences would relapse into states of non-conscious nothingness or emptiness, which he tries to overcome by attempting to speak in the first place. Büchner's Lenz hopes to break through his isolation and, at the same time, uses this isolation as an invisible shield to protect himself from the demands of others upon him.

Büchner's narrator frequently refers to the menacing sounds of nature that surround Lenz and to which he wants to surrender himself. These sounds are powerful (*gewaltig*), dreadful (*entsetzlich*), and wild, so much so that Lenz feels that he will dissolve in them.[44] He is obsessed by a particular *idée fixe*, namely the image of a dead girl of whom he had heard. That is to say, a mere sound or rumor can provide material for Lenz to transform into one of his inner images that then keep haunting him – in this particular case until he actually finds this dead young body, the sight of which profoundly disturbs and unsettles him, for he associates it with the recollection of his former beloved.

It is noteworthy that Büchner's novella presents us with an almost uncanny analogy to the aforementioned *Symphonie fantastique* by Berlioz, composed only a few years before Büchner might have started work on his *Lenz*, and probably at the same time as when Schumann published his eulogy of this startling symphonic masterpiece. The analogy between Berlioz's symphonic protagonist and Büchner's Lenz exists in the *idée fixe*: the trance-like application of sound to the haunting image of the dead female. Yet Büchner's novella is anything but a purely romantic text. It anticipates psychological realism by vehemently attacking life-denying idealist conceptions of Being. In the novella, idealism is reproached by

---

[42] [er war sich selbst ein Traum]; [Was er tat, tat er mit Bewußtsein und doch zwang ihn ein innerlicher Instinkt.] Georg Büchner, *Werke und Briefe*, ed. Franz Josef Görtz, with an afterword by Friedrich Dürrenmatt (Zürich: Diogenes Verlag, 1988), 120, 143.

[43] [Im Gespräch stockte er oft, eine unbeschreibliche Angst befiel ihn, er hatte das Ende seines Satzes verloren; dann meinte er, er müsse das zuletzt gesprochene Wort behalten und immer sprechen, nur mit großer Anstrengung unterdrückte er diese Gelüste.] Ibid., 143.

[44] [er verging fast unter den Tönen]. Ibid., 135.

Lenz for its disregard for human nature. In most other respects, however, Lenz comes across as undecided. His various attempts to commit suicide, for example, are described as half-hearted efforts to take his life (*halbe Versuche zum Entleiben*) suggesting that he was in no way a Werther. In fact, he "drowned in the non-conscious," to use Ricarda Huch's words.[45]

Like the original writer on whose life Büchner's novella is based – Jakob Michael Reinhold Lenz (1751–92), who was to suffer from an acute Goethe-complex – Büchner's protagonist is a borderline figure who experiences the crossovers between reflection and insanity. This narrative rendering of Lenz plays with what is in fact known about the historical figure and with what can only be inferred from the documents about his state of mind. In artistic terms this constellation creates an intriguing structure. Büchner's novella operates with two double-layers: first, the historical persona with his consciousness as far as it is documented by the imagined or fictive Lenz; second, the latter's predominantly subconscious or instinct-driven impulses and his seemingly conscious suffering from what he perceives. Both levels constantly engage with each other, informing a multi-layered discourse on Lenz's schizophrenic identity, which involves the narrator, Lenz, as well as the voices around and within him.

The romantic aesthetics of the non-conscious in the German context can be situated somewhere between Mörike's novella on Mozart and Büchner's on Lenz, between Jean Paul and Richard Wagner. It amounts to the engagement of all senses and impulses, mysteries, and imaginations, sounds and silences in a virtual project called the uprooting of certainties, the dislocation of shadows and the discovery of darkness as an appropriate illumination for the soul. The Romantic ironic twist to all this comes when one realizes, somewhat incredulously, that clearly so many of the writers (not intellectuals though!) involved in this "project" were seemingly unaware of what they were doing.

[45] [im Unbewußten ertrinken]. Ricarda Huch, *Romantik*, 455.

5 The real essence of human beings: Schopenhauer and the unconscious will

Christopher Janaway

In *The World as Will and Representation* (*Die Welt als Wille und Vorstellung*, 1819 and 1844) Arthur Schopenhauer aims at a global metaphysics, a theory of the essence of the world as it is in itself. He calls this essence *will* (*Wille*), which, to put it briefly, he understands as a blind striving for existence, life, and reproduction. Human beings have the same essence as all other manifestations of will in the world, and this has several consequences for Schopenhauer's conception of humanity. Neither rationality, nor intentional action, nor consciousness is primary or foundational in human beings. The true core of the personality is not the self-conscious "I" or subject of knowledge, but rather the will, which is fundamentally blind and without knowledge, but which interacts with the intellect almost as an agent distinct from it. As we shall see, Schopenhauer makes a number of psychological observations about the interplay of intellect and will. These include the omnipresence of sexual desire in or beneath our experience; the persistence of desires and affects unknown to the self-conscious intellect; the will's capacity to prohibit representations in the intellect that are liable to arouse certain emotions; and the occurrence of madness when memories painful to the will are shielded from the intellect and arbitrary representations are substituted. In this paper I propose to elucidate and interrogate Schopenhauer's notion of will and its relation to ideas about the unconscious, with the aim of addressing its significance as an exercise in philosophical psychology.

Schopenhauer in the history of the unconscious

This paper will be more exegetical than historical in any comparative or genealogical sense. Schopenhauer rather encourages an ahistorical appreciation of his work. He tends to say that all previous thinkers have failed to solve that "riddle of the world" which he answers by saying that the world is will; and that all previous thinkers have failed to see will as having primacy in human beings, instead making willing secondary to knowing, or to something called reason, soul, or intellect. He infamously portrays most of what has happened in philosophy since the publication of Kant's *Critiques* as dishonest, worthless, and irrelevant – though we should not always take this at face value. Schopenhauer is much less of a Kantian than he implies; he is without doubt more of his immediate time than his rantings against the German idealists and university professors of the day would have us believe; and he is extremely well read, constantly citing a wide range of historical and contemporary authors in philosophy, literature, and the sciences.

In the case of Goethe, Schopenhauer knew him personally in the decade 1810–20 through his mother's literary set in Weimar. He quotes Goethe's verse liberally in *The World as Will and Representation*, but more to the point in an offhand remark he does acknowledge some continuity between Goethe and his own central doctrine of the will. He says of Goethe's novel *The Elective Affinities* (*Die Wahlverwandtschaften*, 1809) that: "as its title indicates, though Goethe was unaware of this, [it] has as its foundation the idea that the will, which constitutes the basis of our inner being, is the same will that manifests itself in the lowest, inorganic phenomena."[1]

Schopenhauer's surviving notebooks attest that he had spent some time studying Schelling's works of the early 1800s, including the *System of Transcendental Idealism* (*System des Transzendentalen Idealismus*, 1800).[2] It has been suggested that Schopenhauer appropriates some of Schelling's central notions: Andrew Bowie has written that "Schopenhauer avoids the term 'the absolute', but his notion of the Will has the same function as the absolute in the structure of [his] argument,"[3] and that Schopenhauer's position "echoes what is intended by [Schelling's] notion of 'intellectual intuition'" – this despite the fact that Schopenhauer not only avoids, but on numerous occasions elaborately deplores, the whole notion of "intellectual intuition," and is generally quite rude about Schelling. Sebastian Gardner has recently questioned the extent to which Schopenhauer's theory of will parallels anything in Schelling, on the grounds that

---

[1] Arthur Schopenhauer, *The World as Will and Representation*, trans. E. F. J. Payne (New York: Dover, 1969), vol. II, 297. [liegt, wie schon der Titel andeutet, wenn gleich ihm unbewußt, der Gedanke zum Grunde, daß der Wille, der die Basis unsers eigenen Wesens ausmacht, der selbe ist, welcher sich schon in den niedrigsten, unorganischen Erscheinungen kund giebt]. Schopenhauer, *Sämtliche Werke*, ed. Arthur Hübscher (Mannheim: F. A. Brockhaus, 1988), vol. III, 336–7. Schopenhauer goes on to comment that the spirit of Goethe's approach to the natural sciences coincided with his own theorizing, although he (i.e. Schopenhauer) was not conscious of this influence. See Schopenhauer, *World as Will*, vol. II, 298; *Sämtliche Werke*, vol. III, 338.
[2] See Arthur Schopenhauer, *Manuscript Remains*, ed. Arthur Hübscher, trans. E. F. J. Payne, (Oxford: Berg, 1988), vol. III, 339–91.
[3] Andrew Bowie, *Aesthetics and Subjectivity from Kant to Nietzsche* (Manchester: Manchester University Press 2003), 263.

Schopenhauer's philosophy is not genuinely a form of transcendental philosophy, and in particular is not concerned to offer an account of the world from within the conditions of self-consciousness, instead propounding a form of naturalism underlain by what is ultimately a fully realist metaphysics.[4] To debate this issue further would take us too far afield for present purposes – which is not to deny that it is a worthwhile and promising debate to pursue.

If we look for influences forward in time, Schopenhauer is well established as a staple in the history of the unconscious.[5] In their different ways Eduard von Hartmann and Friedrich Nietzsche are indebted to Schopenhauer in an explicit and thematic manner. Both Freud and Jung were also very much aware of his work, though the nature and medium of Schopenhauer's influence on the development of psychoanalysis is often seen as less clear cut. There is a body of literature on the Schopenhauer–Freud connection (effectively reviewed by Gardner in the piece mentioned above),[6] which reveals that Schopenhauer's anticipations of Freud are indeed remarkable – something the latter famously but guardedly acknowledged, saying, for example in 1916–17, that "There are famous philosophers who may be cited as forerunners – above all the great thinker Schopenhauer, whose unconscious 'will' is equivalent to the mental instincts of psycho-analysis."[7] Earlier (in 1905) he had remarked that

---

[4] Sebastian Gardner, "Schopenhauer, Will, and the Unconscious," *The Cambridge Companion to Schopenhauer*, ed. Christopher Janaway (Cambridge: Cambridge University Press, 1999), 391–8.

[5] As mentioned in Lancelot Law Whyte, *The Unconscious Before Freud* (London: Julien Friedman, 1979); Henri Ellenberger, *The Discovery of the Unconscious: The History and Evolution of Dynamic Psychiatry* (New York: Basic Books, 1970); Michel Henry, *The Genealogy of Psychoanalysis*, trans. Douglas Brick (Stanford: Stanford University Press, 1993).

[6] For comments see Gardner, "Schopenhauer, Will, and the Unconscious," and W. Bischler, "Schopenhauer and Freud: a Comparison," *Psychoanalytic Quarterly* 8 (1939): 88–97; Ernst Cassirer, *The Myth of the State* (Oxford: Oxford University Press, 1946), 31–2; Thomas Mann, "Freud and the Future," *Essays of Three Decades*, trans. H. T. Lowe-Porter (London: Secker and Warburg, 1947), 411–28; Nancy Proctor-Gregg, "Schopenhauer and Freud," *Psychoanalytic Quarterly* 25 (1956): 197–214; Paul-Laurent Assoun, *Freud: La Philosophie et les philosophes* (Paris: Presses Universitaires, 1976), part II; R.K. Gupta, "Freud and Schopenhauer," *Schopenhauer: His Philosophical Achievement*, ed. Michael Fox (Sussex: Harvester, 1980), 226–35; Christopher Young and Andrew Brook, "Schopenhauer and Freud," *International Journal of Psychoanalysis* 75 (1994): 101–18. See also Bryan Magee, *The Philosophy of Schopenhauer*, 2nd edn. (Oxford: Oxford University Press 1998); Günther Gödde, *Traditionslinien des "Unbewussten": Schopenhauer, Nietzsche, Freud* (Tübingen: edition diskord, 1999); Marcel R. Zentner, *Die Flucht ins Vergessen: Die Anfänge der Psychoanalyse Freuds bei Schopenhauer* (Wissenchaftiche Buchgesellschaft, 1995).

[7] Sigmund Freud, "A Difficulty in the Path of Psycho-Analysis," *The Standard Edition of the Complete Psychological Works of Sigmund Freud*, ed. and trans. James Strachey and Anna Freud et al., 24 vols. (London: The Hogarth Press, 1953–74), vol. XVII, 143–4 (hereafter cited as *SE* followed by volume and page numbers); [Es sind namhafte

"Arthur Schopenhauer, the philosopher, showed mankind the extent to which their activities are determined by sexual impulses – in the ordinary sense of the word,"[8] and (in 1914) that "what [Schopenhauer] says … about the struggle against accepting a distressing piece of reality coincides with my conception of repression so completely that once again I owe the chance of making a discovery to my not being well read."[9] Finally, in his *Autobiographical Study* of 1925 Freud says:

> The large extent to which psycho-analysis coincides with the philosophy of Schopenhauer – not only did he assert the dominance of the emotions and the supreme importance of sexuality but he was even aware of the mechanism of repression – is not to be traced to my acquaintance with his teaching. I read Schopenhauer very late in life.[10]

One may wish to dig around to show that Freud must have had more direct acquaintance with Schopenhauer's doctrines than he claims here. But even if we take Freud's remarks at face value, it is safe to say that Schopenhauer's immense influence on many areas of intellectual and cultural life in the latter half of the nineteenth century provided a seedbed in which the specific theoretical claims of psychoanalysis could easily grow. In this sense, if in no other, one can proclaim Schopenhauer "the true philosophical father of psychoanalysis."[11] However, in the relatively short space remaining here I shall not be pursuing any of these links back or forward, but shall restrict myself to an internal investigation of Schopenhauer's notion of will and what is distinctive about it.

Philosophen als Vorgänger anzuführen, vor allem der große Denker Schopenhauer, dessen unbewusster "Wille" den seelischen Trieben der Psychoanalyse gleichzusetzen sei.] Freud, "Eine Schwierigkeit der Psychoanalyse," *Gesammelte Werke in achtzehn Bänden mit einem Nachtragsband*, ed. Anna Freud et al., 18 vols. (Frankfurt am Main: S. Fischer, 1986–99), vol XII, 12 (hereafter cited as *GW* followed by volume and page numbers).

[8] Sigmund Freud, *Three Essays on the Theory of Sexuality*, SE, VII: 134. [Der Philosoph Arthur Schopenhauer hat bereits vor geraumer Zeit den Menschen vorgehalten, in welchem Maß ihr Tun und Trachten durch sexuelle Strebungen – im gewohnten Sinne des Wortes – bestimmt wird.] Freud, *Drei Abhandlungen zur Sexualtheorie*, *GW*, V: 32.

[9] Sigmund Freud, "On the History of the Psycho-analytic Movement," SE, XIV: 15. [Was dort [in Schopenhauer] über das Sträuben gegen die Annahme eines peinlichen Stückes der Wirklichkeit gesagt ist, deckt sich so vollkommen mit dem Inhalt meines Verdrängungsbegriffes, daß ich wieder einmal meiner Unbelesenheit für die Ermöglichung einer Entdeckung verpflichtet sein durfte.] Freud, "Zur Geschichte der psychoanalytischen Bewegung," *GW*, X: 53.

[10] Sigmund Freud, "An Autobiographical Study," SE, XX: 59. [Die weitgehenden Übereinstimmungen der Psychoanalyse mit der Philosophie Schopenhauers – er hat nicht nur den Primat der Affektivität und die überragende Bedeutung der Sexualität vertreten, sondern selbst den Mechanismus der Verdrängung gekannt – lassen sich nicht auf meine Bekanntschaft mit seiner Lehre zurückführen. Ich habe Schopenhauer sehr spät im Leben gelesen.] Freud, "Selbstdarstellung," *GW*, XIV: 86.

[11] Gardner, "Schopenhauer, Will, and the Unconscious," 379. On Jung, I merely comment that the index to his complete works lists around ninety references to Schopenhauer.

144   Christopher Janaway

Awakened out of unconsciousness

Let me start with two resounding passages of Schopenhauerian prose, which remain impressive even in translation. Both are from the second volume of *The World as Will and Representation*, first published in 1844.

Unconsciousness [*Bewußtlosigkeit*] is the original and natural condition of all things, and therefore is also the basis from which, in particular species of beings, consciousness appears as their highest efflorescence; and for this reason, even then unconsciousness still predominates. Accordingly, most beings are without consciousness; but yet they act according to the laws of their nature, in other words of their will. Plants have at most an extremely feeble analogue of consciousness, the lowest animals merely a faint gleam of it. But even after it has ascended through the whole series of animals up to man and his faculty of reason, the unconsciousness of the plant, from which it started, still always remains the foundation, and this is to be observed in the necessity for sleep as well as in all the essential and great imperfections ... of every intellect produced through physiological functions. And of any other intellect we have no conception.[12]

Awakened to life out of the night of unconsciousness [*Bewußtlosigkeit*], the will finds itself as an individual in an endless and boundless world, among innumerable individuals, all striving, suffering, and erring; and, as if in a troubled dream, it hurries back to the old unconsciousness. Yet till then its [the will's] desires are unlimited, its claims inexhaustible, and every satisfied desire gives birth to a new one. No possible satisfaction in the world could suffice to still its craving, set a final goal to its demands, and fill the bottomless pit of its heart. ... Everything in life proclaims that earthly happiness is destined to be frustrated, or recognized as an illusion. The grounds for this lie deep in the very nature of things.[13]

---

[12] Schopenhauer, *World as Will*, vol. II, 142. [Bewußtlosigkeit ist der ursprüngliche und natürliche Zustand aller Dinge, mithin auch die Basis, aus welcher, in einzelnen Arten der Wesen, das Bewußtseyn, als die höchste Efflorescenz derselben, hervorgeht, weshalb auch dann jene immer noch vorwaltet. Demgemäß sind die meisten Wesen ohne Bewußtseyn: sie wirken dennoch nach den Gesetzen ihrer Natur, d. h. ihres Willens. Die Pflanzen haben höchstens ein ganz schwaches Analogon von Bewußtseyn, die untersten Thiere bloß eine Dämmerung desselben. Aber auch nachdem es sich, durch die ganze Thierreihe, bis zum Menschen und seiner Vernunft gesteigert hat, bleibt die Bewußtlosigkeit der Pflanze, von der es ausgieng, noch immer die Grundlage, und ist zu spüren in der Nothwendigkeit des Schlafes, wie eben auch in allen ... wesentlichen und großen Unvollkommenheiten jedes durch physiologische Funktionen hervorgebrachten Intellekts: von einem andern aber haben wir keinen Begriff.] *Sämtliche Werke*, vol. III, 156.

[13] Schopenhauer, *World as Will*, vol. II, 573. [Aus der Nacht der Bewußtlosigkeit zum Leben erwacht findet der Wille sich als Individuum, in einer end- und gränzenlosen Welt, unter zahllosen Individuen, alle strebend, leidend, irrend; und wie durch einen bangen Traum eilt er zurück zur alten Bewußtlosigkeit. – Bis dahin jedoch sind seine Wünsche gränzenlos, seine Ansprüche unerschöpflich, und jeder befriedigte Wunsch gebiert einen neuen. Keine auf der Welt mögliche Befriedigung könnte hinreichen, sein Verlangen zu stillen, seinem Begehren ein endliches Ziel zu setzen und den bodenlosen Abgrund seines Herzens auszufüllen ... Alles im Leben giebt kund, daß das irdische

Let me highlight three themes apparent here: first, the continuity of the human essence with that of nature as a whole; next, the secondary and superficial nature of the human intellect, which is in complex interaction with the more fundamental part of us that is the will; and finally, the unhappiness, worthlessness, or nothingness (*Nichtigkeit*) of the life we lead as manifestations of this will, and the consequent need, in Schopenhauer's eyes, for a redemption from this existence.

Will as real essence

We must be careful with the concept *will*. Schopenhauer asks us not to think of wanting, desiring, or intentionally acting as constitutive of will in his sense, but to stretch the concept much more widely. So we must think away its traditional associations with rationality and consciousness, and indeed with mentality as such. Will has some manifestations that are mental, conscious and rational, some that are mental and conscious but not rational, some that are mental but neither conscious nor rational, and some that are none of these.

Human beings manifest acts of will (*Willensakte*), which are conscious mental states which may well be rational, in that the motives causing someone's actions may be rationally formed beliefs that give them a reason to act. However, Schopenhauer gives a fundamentally anti-dualist account of action, insisting that the act of will is not a *purely* mental volition that causes physical effects; rather, it is identical with bodily action. So the physical movements I make in the course of intentionally doing something are a case of willing. In fact, Schopenhauer starts his argument for the world as will from this very place. The will in this first sense is immediately known to each subject, in a unique way not captured by the Kantian conception of nature as the realm of objects in space and time and subordinate to causal laws. As the subject of willing, I do not, indeed cannot, understand my body in those objective terms. There is an immediate and inner knowledge of the self as conjointly subject and body, and this, for Schopenhauer, is the key that unlocks the internal essence (*inneres Wesen*) of all those things distinct from us which present themselves to our outer knowledge as empirical objects. They are all objective manifestations of the same essence, they are all the objectivation or objecthood (*Objektivation, Objektivität*) of will, or appearance of the will (*Willenserscheinung*).

The initial argument for this is somewhat as follows: I *know* myself and I *am* myself, but in the case of everything else, I can only know it and not

Glück bestimmt ist, vereitelt oder als eine Illusion erkannt zu werden. Hiezu liegen tief im Wesen der Dinge die Anlagen.] *Sämtliche Werke*, vol. III, 657.

be it. But if I were to regard other things only to the extent that they are known or knowable, I would be denying them any real being (*Wesen*) at all. They would remain: "mere representation, i.e. mere phantoms" (*bloße Vorstellung, d.h. bloße Phantome*).[14] External things would then be, if you like, mere knowable outsides with no true core within. If we can know our own inner essence directly, we face a choice: either we can regard ourselves as divorced from the rest of the world by virtue of our uniquely having this essence, or we can infer that, as belonging to the world, we must share its essence. A suppressed premise here is that whatever is my essence must be the essence of everything in the world – or of everything that indeed has any essence. So there is a deep-seated naturalism in Schopenhauer's treatment of human beings, which from the start is metaphysical in character; though at the empirical level of description he is amenable to a more scientific naturalism – as we saw in his remark that we have no conception of any form of intellect that is not produced through physiological functions. Schopenhauer also believes that all empirical explanations given in science, though perfectly in order in their own right, must eventually peter out into something inexplicable, and that they need completion by a unifying metaphysical account of the nature of reality as a whole.

Having established the intimate connection of body and will in intentional action, Schopenhauer finds other instances of that connection:

every impression on the body is also at once and directly an impression on the will. As such it is called pain when it is contrary to the will or pleasure when it is in accordance with the will. ...The identity of the body and the will further shows itself ...in the fact that every vehement and excessive movement of the will, in other words, every emotion, agitates the body and its inner workings directly and immediately, and disturbs the course of its vital functions.[15]

Schopenhauer embraces as movements of the will:

all desiring, striving, wishing, longing, yearning, hoping, rejoicing, exulting and the like, as well as the feeling of unwillingness or repugnance, detesting, fleeing, fearing, being angry, hating, mourning, suffering, in short, all affects and passions. For these are only movements more or less weak or strong, stirrings at one moment violent and stormy, at another mild and faint, of our own will that is either checked or given its way, satisfied or unsatisfied.[16]

[14] Schopenhauer, *World as Will*, vol. I, 104; *Sämtliche Werke*, vol. II, 124.
[15] Schopenhauer, *World as Will*, vol. I, 101. [jede Einwirkung auf den Leib [ist] sofort und unmittelbar auch Einwirkung auf den Willen: sie heißt als solche Schmerz, wenn sie dem Willen zuwider; Wohlbehagen, Wollust, wenn sie ihm gemäß ist. ... Ferner zeigt sich die Identität des Leibes und Willens ... auch darin, daß jede heftige und übermäßige Bewegung des Willens, d.h. jeder Affekt, ganz unmittelbar den Leib und dessen inneres Getriebe erschüttert und den Gang seiner vitalen Funktionen stört.] *Sämtliche Werke*, vol. II, 120–1.
[16] Arthur Schopenhauer, *Prize Essay on the Freedom of the Will*, ed. Günter Zöller, trans. E. F. J. Payne (Cambridge: Cambridge University Press, 1999), 10. [alles Begehren,

Though they cannot be classified as *acts* of the will, such affects and passions are (or at least often are) states of mind of which a subject is conscious. What unites them with bodily acts of will is their dynamic nature: they are partially constituted by a condition of desiring or striving in the individual who undergoes them. Schopenhauer is also clear that affects and passions can be present unconsciously:

> For years we can have a desire without admitting it to ourselves or letting it come to clear consciousness, because the intellect is not to know anything about it. ... but if the wish is fulfilled, we get to know from our joy, not without a feeling of shame, that this is what we desired; for example, the death of a near relation whose heir we are.[17]

Schopenhauer gives many such examples, to which I shall return below when discussing the relation of will to intellect.

From the close association of the above mental states with the body Schopenhauer makes the claim that the body itself, which is the condition of willing in the narrower sense, must also be an objectivation of will. The motives which cause me to act in a certain way do not explain my willing: the foundation of my willing in these particular conscious ways must lie elsewhere than in the causes of my acts of will or of my affects. Schopenhauer concludes that my "whole body must be nothing but my will become visible";[18] the body is "objectivation of the will" (*Objektivation des Willens*). This is a prime case of will's "blind activity" (*blinde Thätigkeit*), or of its being "without knowledge" (*erkenntnißlos*),[19] as he frequently puts it, and here will is neither rational, nor conscious, nor mental. The very organized structure and normal functioning of my body, its growth, and all the processes of it which presuppose neither consciousness nor even mindedness are manifestations of what Schopenhauer now calls will to life (*Wille zum Leben*). The inner nature

---

Streben, Wünschen, Verlangen, Sehnen, Hoffen, Lieben, Freuen, Jubeln, u. dgl., nicht weniger, als Nichtwollen oder Widerstreben, als Verabscheuen, Fliehen, Fürchten, Zürnen, Hassen, Trauern, Schmerzleiden, kurz alle Affekte und Leidenschaften ... da diese Affekte und Leidenschaften nur mehr oder minder schwache oder starke, bald heftige und stürmische, bald sanfte und leise Bewegungen des entweder gehemmten, oder losgelassenen, befriedigten, oder unbefriedigten eigenen Willens sind]. *Sämtliche Werke*, vol. IV, 11.

[17] Schopenhauer, *World as Will*, vol. II, 209–10. [Wir können Jahre lang einen Wunsch hegen, ohne ihn uns einzugestehen, oder auch nur zum klaren Bewußtseyn kommen zu lassen; weil der Intellekt nichts davon erfahren soll; ... wird er aber erfüllt, so erfahren wir an unserer Freude, nicht ohne Beschämung, daß wir Dies gewünscht haben: z. B. den Tod eines nahen Anverwandten, den wir beerben.] *Sämtliche Werke*, vol. III, 234–5.

[18] Schopenhauer, *World as Will*, vol. I, 107; [Also muß der ganze Leib nichts Anderes seyn, als mein sichtbar gewordener Wille.] Schopenhauer, *Sämtliche Werke* vol. II, 128.

[19] See Schopenhauer, *World as Will*, vol. I, 114 and vol. II, 293–304; *Sämtliche Werke*, vol. II, 136; and vol. III, 331–46.

of the human being is that it tends towards maintaining and propagating life, and this same inner nature is common to every inhabitant of the organic world. A tiger, a sunflower, or a single-celled organism have the same inner nature or essence. Schopenhauer even argues that at the most fundamental level the same inner nature must be that of the whole phenomenal world, not only in the organic but also in the inorganic realm where it underlies the processes of gravitation, magnetism, and crystal formation:

> Everything presses and pushes towards *existence*, if possible towards *organic existence*, i.e., *life*, and then to the highest possible degree thereof. In animal nature, it then becomes obvious that *will to life* (*Wille zum Leben*) is the keynote of its being, its only unchangeable and unconditioned quality.[20]

But my essence is the same as that of every other thing in the world. The boundary between human willing and other processes of organic end-directedness is not one between metaphysical kinds. I as agent have an "inner nature" in virtue of which I tend towards local ends and the overarching end of life – being alive and reproducing life. And since throughout nature the striving for existence is "blind," not essentially mediated by consciousness, this must apply also to my essence. So what I essentially am is a thing that blindly tends towards living existence. It is crucial to Schopenhauer that I tend by nature not only to preserve my own existence, but to propagate the existence of more living things. For him, reproductive sexuality is as basic to the nature of the human individual as the drive towards continuing his or her own existence. The genitals, he comments, are "the real focus of the will."[21] The whole body, including the brain, is objecthood of the will, but the organs of reproduction are where the will to life is seen most plainly for what it is.

So what seemed distinctive of human beings, their capacity for intentional action, is just another instance of the will manifesting itself in nature.[22] Indeed, "the real self is the will to life": in other words, the real self is the principle of blind striving for existence and reproduction that manifests itself as organic body, as me, the bodily individual, while not pertaining to me alone.[23] And human willing is one among a multitude

---

[20] Schopenhauer, *World as Will*, vol. II, 350: [Alles drängt und treibt zum Daseyn, wo möglich zum organischen, d.i. zum Leben, und danach zur möglichsten Steigerung desselben: an der thierischen Natur wird es dann augenscheinlich, daß Wille zum Leben der Grundton ihres Wesens, die einzige unwandelbare und unbedingte Eigenschaft desselben ist.] *Sämtliche Werke*, vol. III, 399–400.

[21] Schopenhauer, *World as Will*, vol. I, 330. [der eigentliche Brennpunkt des Willens]. *Sämtliche Werke* vol. II, 390.

[22] Schopenhauer, *World as Will*, vol. I, 327.

[23] Ibid., vol. II, 606; [das eigentliche Selbst ist der Wille zum Leben]. *Sämtliche Werke* vol. III, 695.

of ways in which organisms tend towards a *telos*, distinguished from other organic processes merely by the kind of causal antecedents which deflect the organism's course.

Once we regard humanity in this way, we have to attribute to ourselves some of the characteristics of the world at large. The will (the world) is itself groundless and has no exterior purpose. It merely, as a brute fact, manifests itself endlessly as individuals which endlessly strive. Nothing in the world strives or tends as it does for any ultimate reason. It is not to fulfill any *rational purpose*, or because there is a *good* end-state to be attained, that plants or crystals grow, or that objects gravitate towards the earth. And so it is with humanity. We each exist as an individual organism that blindly and for no good reason "gravitates" towards survival and sexual reproduction. Hence, although rational thought and choice are characteristics of human beings, they are not at the core of the human psyche, and are, Schopenhauer believes, explicable as mere instruments of the more fundamental will to life. Even consciousness, let alone the self-consciousness which was earlier proclaimed the true starting-point for philosophy, must be underlain by a nature that is more fundamental than it.

Schopenhauer casts his theory of will from the start in Kantian terms. The world of representation is governed by the laws of space, time and causality, but beyond it lies the realm of the thing in itself, which Kant had left as a riddle. Schopenhauer offers a solution to the riddle: the thing in itself is will. The notion that the will is beyond the realm of the subject's representation of objects licences the idea that the will is beyond the principle of individuation. Hence Schopenhauer can regard it as an undifferentiated whole, not split up into plural individuals at all – though strictly speaking it must be beyond the whole question of plurality and unity. The will is also not causally related to anything, does not exist in time, and is not subject to change.

Forcing his doctrine into this Kantian framework might in retrospect be regarded as one of Schopenhauer's most unfortunate moves – it certainly gives rise to numerous problems of consistency and intelligibility. I could not begin to rehearse them all here, but a couple of consequences are worth noting. First, it is hard for Schopenhauer consistently to separate the notion of the thing in itself considered as the world *apart from all knowability* on the one hand, and the notion of will as the most general form under which the world *is knowable* to us. In the latter sense will is the thing in itself, while in the former it is not.[24] Secondly, it is hard for Schopenhauer to distinguish the undifferentiated will of which everything in nature is the objective appearance, from the will which is my

---

[24] See Schopenhauer, *World as Will*, vol. II, 198.

individual essence or real nature – what I am in myself. Schopenhauer borrows Kant's term "intelligible character" (*intelligibler Charakter*) for this: the intelligible character is an innate and unchanging disposition of will quite specific to the human individual. Working only with a notion of the thing in itself which places it outside time and space, and thus outside of individuation, makes the notion of the "in itself" aspect of the individual hard to negotiate, yet Schopenhauer's psychology requires a timeless and unchanging will to underlie all of the individual's conscious states and actions, and to be a character peculiar to that individual.

Will and intellect

Many of Schopenhauer's most interesting psychological insights occur in a chapter of the second volume of *The World as Will and Representation* entitled "The Primacy of the Will in Self-Consciousness" (*Vom Primat des Willens im Selbstbewußtseyn*), where he catalogues different ways in which the relationship between primary will and secondary intellect shows up in self-conscious experience. The will is a more primitive, indeed simple and childish part of the psyche. Schopenhauer notes how infants are full of will at a time when their intellect is hardly developed at all:

> through uncontrollable, aimless storming and screaming, they show the pressure of will with which they are full to overflowing, whereas their willing as yet has no object, in other words, they will without knowing what they will.[25]

In adult life, as soon as the developed intellect represents anything in thought or imagination, this same will, unchanged, responds:

> If, for example, we are alone, and think over our personal affairs, and then vividly picture to ourselves, say, the menace of an actually present danger, and the possibility of an unfortunate outcome, anxiety at once compresses the heart and the blood ceases to flow. But if the intellect then passes to the possibility of the opposite outcome, and allows the imagination to picture the happiness long hoped-for as thereby attained, all the pulses at once quicken with joy, and the heart feels as light as a feather, until the intellect wakes up from its dream.[26]

And so on through numerous examples, in which

> the intellect strikes up the tune and the will must dance to it; in fact, the intellect causes the will to play the part of a child whom its nurse at her pleasure

---

[25] Ibid., vol. II, 211. [durch unbändiges, zweckloses Toben und Schreien zeigen sie den Willensdrang, von dem sie strotzen, während ihr Wollen noch kein Objekt hat, d.h. sie wollen, ohne zu wissen was sie wollen.] *Sämtliche Werke*, vol. III, 236.

[26] Schopenhauer, *World as Will*, vol. II, 207–8. [Wenn wir z.B., mit uns selbst allein, unsere persönlichen Angelegenheiten überdenken und nun etwan das Drohende einer wirklich vorhandenen Gefahr und die Möglichkeit eines unglücklichen Ausganges

puts into the most different moods by chatter and tales alternating between pleasant and melancholy things.[27]

However, though the will is simpler than the intellect, it reasserts its true hegemony in the following manner:

by prohibiting the intellect from having certain representations, by absolutely preventing certain trains of thought from arising, because it knows, or in other words experiences from the self-same intellect, that they would arouse in it any one of the emotions previously described. It then curbs and restrains the intellect, and forces it to turn to other things.[28]

Note that the more primitive will has the power of absolutely preventing certain trains of thought from arising in the intellect. That is to say, although such thoughts are in some sense present as ours, we never consciously entertain them. The process of prevention must therefore be an unconscious one. And it is a process that the conscious intellect is powerless to resist:

it is bound to succeed the moment the will is in earnest about it; for the resistance then comes not from the intellect, which always remains indifferent, but from the will itself; and the will has an inclination in one respect for a representation it abhors in another. Thus the representation is in itself interesting to the will, just because it excites it. At the same time, however, abstract knowledge tells the will that this representation will cause it a shock of painful and unworthy emotion to no purpose.[29]

---

uns lebhaft vergegenwärtigen; so preßt alsbald Angst das Herz zusammen und das Blut stockt in den Adern. Geht dann aber der Intellekt zur Möglichkeit des entgegengesetzten Ausganges über und läßt die Phantasie das lang erhoffte, dadurch erreichte Glück ausmalen; so gerathen alsbald alle Pulse in freudige Bewegung und das Herz fühlt sich federleicht; bis der Intellekt aus seinem Traum erwacht.] *Sämtliche Werke*, vol. III, 232.

[27] Schopenhauer, *World as Will*, vol. II, 207–8. [der Intellekt spielt auf und der Wille muß dann dazu tanzen; ja, jener läßt ihn die Rolle eines Kindes spielen, welches von seiner Wärterin, durch Vorschwätzen und Erzählen abwechselnd erfreulicher und trauriger Dinge, beliebig in die verschiedensten Stimmungen versetzt wird]. *Sämtliche Werke*, vol. III, 232–3.

[28] Schopenhauer, *World as Will*, vol. II, 208. [indem er ihm gewisse Vorstellungen verbietet, gewisse Gedankenreihen gar nicht aufkommen läßt, weil er weiß, d.h. von eben dem selben Intellekt erfährt, daß sie ihn in irgend eine der oben dargestellten Bewegungen versetzen würden: er zügelt jetzt den Intellekt und zwingt ihn sich auf andere Dinge zu richten]. *Sämtliche Werke*, vol. III, 233.

[29] Schopenhauer, *World as Will*, vol. II, 208; [muß es doch gelingen, sobald es dem Willen Ernst damit ist; denn das Widerstreben dabei geht nicht vom Intellekt aus, als welcher stets gleichgültig bleibt; sondern vom Willen selbst, der zu einer Vorstellung, die er in einer Hinsicht verabscheut, in anderer Hinsicht eine Neigung hat. Sie ist ihm nämlich an sich interessant, eben weil sie ihn bewegt; aber zugleich sagt ihm die abstrakte Erkenntniß, daß sie ihn zwecklos in quaalvolle, oder unwürdige Erschütterung versetzen wird.] *Sämtliche Werke*, vol. III, 233.

An extension of the will's repression of thoughts – for that is what we have here – allows Schopenhauer to account for madness (*Wahnsinn*), which for him is a kind of defect of memory. He says,

> if, in a particular case, the resistance and opposition of the will to the assimilation of some knowledge reaches such a degree that that operation is not clearly carried through; accordingly, if certain events or circumstances are wholly suppressed for the intellect, because the will cannot bear the sight of them; and then, if the resultant gaps are arbitrarily filled up for the sake of the necessary connexion; we then have madness.[30]

Schopenhauer gives other examples from everyday life – the sort of thing that "anyone who is attentive can observe in himself"[31] – in which the will makes decisions or plans as it were "in secret," decisions from which the intellect remains excluded and "can only get to know them, like those of a stranger, by spying out and taking unawares; and it must surprise the will in the act of expressing itself, in order merely to discover its real intentions."[32] Consequently, I do not really know how attached I am to a certain obligation or course of action: Schopenhauer narrates examples where a conscious judgment as to the desirability or undesirability of acting thus-and-so is swept away "to my own astonishment" (*zu meinem eigenen Erstaunen*) by a "jubilant, irresistible gladness" (*eine jubelnde, unaufhaltsame Freudigkeit*) that reveals the true orientation of my underlying will.[33] Many of these eloquent passages are frequently quoted in the literature and constitute Schopenhauer's most visible contributions to the history of thought about the unconscious. The will, as he puts it, has a "direct, unconscious, and disadvantageous influence on knowledge"[34] – and the disadvantage of our natural condition is something we shall see emphasized more as we proceed.

---

[30] Schopenhauer, *World as Will*, vol. II, 400; [Erreicht hingegen, in einem einzelnen Fall, das Widerstreben und Sträuben des Willens wider die Aufnahme einer Erkenntniß den Grad, daß jene Operation nicht rein durchgeführt wird; werden demnach dem Intellekt gewisse Vorfälle oder Umstände völlig unterschlagen, weil der Wille ihren Anblick nicht ertragen kann; wird alsdann, des nothwendigen Zusammenhanges wegen, die dadurch entstandene Lücke beliebig ausgefüllt; – so ist der Wahnsinn da.] *Sämtliche Werke*, vol. III, 458.
[31] Schopenhauer, *World as Will*, vol. II, 210. [jeder Aufmerksame ... an sich beobachten kann]. *Sämtliche Werke*, vol. III, 235.
[32] Schopenhauer, *World as Will*, vol. II, 209. [daß er sie bisweilen, wie die eines fremden, nur durch Belauschen und Ueberraschen erfahren kann, und ihn auf der That seiner Aeußerungen ertappen muß, um nur hinter seine wahren Absichten zu kommen]. *Sämtliche Werke*, vol. III, 234.
[33] Schopenhauer, *World as Will*, vol. II, 209; *Sämtliche Werke*, vol. III, 234.
[34] Schopenhauer, *World as Will*, vol. II, 219. [unmittelbarer und unbewußter nachtheiliger Einfluß auf die Erkenntniß]. *Sämtliche Werke*, vol. III, 245.

Sexual will

One of Schopenhauer's major themes is that the will in nature is greater than the individual living being, and has the individual at its mercy. A prime illustration occurs in his discussion of human sexuality.[35] We saw above how the sexual functioning of the body is the primary expression of the will to life in human beings. The sex-drive or sexual impulse (*Geschlechtstrieb*) is the "kernel of the will-to-life ... the concentration of all willing":[36]

> it may be said that the human being is concrete sexual impulse, for his origin is an act of copulation, and the desire of his desires is an act of copulation, and this impulse alone perpetuates and holds together the whole of his phenomenal appearance. It is true that the will to life manifests itself primarily as an effort to maintain the individual; yet this is only a stage towards the effort to maintain the species ... The sex-drive is therefore the most complete manifestation of the will to life.[37]

It is not surprising, then, if sexual love (*Geschlechtsliebe*) directed towards another individual is a powerful force in human life:

> It is the ultimate goal of almost all human effort; it has an unfavourable influence on the most important affairs, interrupts every hour the most serious occupations, and sometimes perplexes for a while even the greatest minds. It does not hesitate to intrude with its trash, and to interfere with negotiations of statesmen and the investigations of the learned. It knows how to slip its love-notes and ringlets even into ministerial portfolios and philosophical manuscripts ... it appears on the whole as a malevolent demon, striving to pervert, to confuse, and to overthrow everything.[38]

---

[35] See especially his essay "The Metaphysics of Sexual Love," Schopenhauer, *World as Will*, vol. II, 531–67; "Metaphysik der Geschlechtsliebe," *Sämtliche Werke*, vol. III, 607–51.
[36] Schopenhauer, *World as Will*, vol. II, 514. [der Kern des Willens zum Leben ... die Koncentration alles Wollens]. *Sämtliche Werke*, vol. III, 588.
[37] Schopenhauer, *World as Will*, vol. II, 513–4. [man kann sagen, der Mensch sei konkreter Geschlechtstrieb; da seine Entstehung ein Kopulationsakt und der Wunsch seiner Wünsche ein Kopulationsakt ist, und dieser Trieb allein seine ganze Erscheinung perpetuirt und zusammenhält. Der Wille zum Leben äußert sich zwar zunächst als Streben zur Erhaltung des Individuums; jedoch ist dies nur die Stufe zum Streben nach Erhaltung der Gattung ... Daher ist der Geschlechtstrieb die vollkommenste Aeußerung des Willens zum Leben.] *Sämtliche Werke*, vol. III, 588.
[38] Schopenhauer, *World as Will*, vol.II, 533–4. [wo sie ... das letzte Ziel fast jedes menschlichen Bestrebens ist, auf die wichtigsten Angelenheiten nachtheiligen Einfluß erlangt, die ernsthaftesten Beschäftigungen zu jeder Stunde unterbricht, bisweilen selbst die größten Köpfe auf eine Weile in Verwirrung setzt, sich nicht scheut, zwischen die Verhandlungen der Staatsmänner und die Forschungen der Gelehrten, störend, mit ihrem Plunder einzutreten, ihre Liebesbriefchen und Haarlöckchen sogar in ministerielle Portefeuilles und philosophische Manuskripte einzuschieben versteht ... demnach im Ganzen auftritt als ein feindsäliger Dämon, der Alles zu verkehren, zu verwirren und umzuwerfen bemüht ist]. *Sämtliche Werke*, vol. III, 610–11.

"It" is clearly being conceived here as some agency or purpose which is not fully subject to the individual's conscious control – though Schopenhauer appears to wish it were. Sexuality is not only ubiquitous for him, but tormenting.[39]

His account of sexual love operates on two levels: at the level of individual consciousness, the other is singled out as the object of desire and idealized. He or she is, apparently, beloved for qualities of value he or she uniquely possesses; and satisfaction of the desire by another interchangeable object is ruled out. Thus it seems to the individual lover. But all this is an illusion, according to Schopenhauer. The individual is merely being used. For at a deeper level, all (heterosexual) sexual desire can be explained functionally as enabling reproduction:

The sex-drive ... knows how to assume very skillfully the mask of an objective admiration, and thus to deceive consciousness; for nature requires this stratagem in order to attain her ends. But in every case of being in love, however objective and touched with the sublime that admiration may appear to be, what alone is aimed at is the generation of an individual of a definite disposition.[40]

Schopenhauer maintains that the "will of the species" (*Wille der Gattung*)[41] directs the behavior of individuals whilst deluding them that they pursue by choice their own individual preferences and purposes, such as seeking their own pleasure. Since the will as thing in itself is beyond individuation, it lives on in future generations: thus "the kernel of our nature" (*Kern unseres Wesens*) is indestructible and shared with our whole species.[42] He even says it is the will to life of the as yet unconceived child that draws a man and a woman to love one another.[43] In general, the unique intensity of the passions that attend sexual behaviour and the (sometimes absurd and ruinous) seriousness with which it is pursued confirm Schopenhauer in his view that it expresses the very core of human inner nature which is the will to life.

Escaping the will

Human happiness is frustrated or rendered impossible by the situation as Schopenhauer describes it. The will intrudes upon, and interferes with,

---

[39] As Nietzsche realized; see the well-known passage in *Zur Genealogie der Moral* (*On the Genealogy of Morality*), vol. III, §6.
[40] Schopenhauer, *World as Will*, vol. II, 535: [nun weiß der Geschlechtstrieb ... sehr geschickt die Maske einer objektiven Bewunderung anzunehmen und so das Bewußtseyn zu täuschen: denn die Natur bedarf dieses Stratagems zu ihren Zwecken ... so objektiv und von erhabenem Anstrich jene Bewunderung auch erscheinen mag, bei jedem Verliebtseyn [ist] doch allein abgesehn auf die Erzeugung eines Individuums von bestimmter Beschaffenheit]. *Sämtliche Werke*, vol. III, 612.
[41] Schopenhauer, *World as Will*, vol. II, 554–5; *Sämtliche Werke*, vol. III, 636.
[42] Schopenhauer, *World as Will*, vol. II, 559; *Sämtliche Werke*, vol. III, 642.
[43] See Schopenhauer, *World as Will*, vol. II, 536.

our conscious life. For us there can only be perspectival knowing, in that affects, passions, and hidden drives, inclinations, and aversions invariably "twist, colour, and distort" our judgment and perception.[44] The will calls the tune, never leaving us in peace. The sexual drive dominates and torments us. The will is timeless and can never be satisfied, so that fulfillment of any desire brings only a momentary release from pain which yields instantly to more unfulfilled desiring. The will is our essence, but it is our essence that blights our existence. To be an individual expression of will is a condition of purposelessness and suffering – to the extent that, for Schopenhauer, if we really understood the nature of things fully, we should much prefer non-existence. Schopenhauer describes death as the "great opportunity no longer to be I."[45] Lapsing back into the unconscious will of nature is a release from individuality and pain.

Schopenhauer's philosophy as a whole unfolds a series of states which redeem what he sees as the absence of positive value in life. Aesthetic experience, in which consciousness is disinterested and temporarily freed of the will, is at one end of the spectrum, extinction of the individual at the other. Value can be retrieved to the extent that the individual embodiment of will abates. One wills less and less, and locates significance less and less in the individual living manifestation of will one happens to be. In aesthetic experience willing abates totally but temporarily, and one ceases to be aware of oneself as individual. But similar notions of selfless objectivity apply in Schopenhauer's ethics and philosophy of religion. In describing those who have undergone the ultimate redemption which he calls the denial of the will, Schopenhauer asks us to recall his characterization of aesthetic experience as that of a "pure, will-less, painless, timeless" subject (*reines, willenloses, schmerzloses, zeitloses Subjekt*) and imagine such a state prolonged indefinitely.[46] Aesthetic objectivity prefigures the disintegration of one's ability to place value in the striving, material individual one is – that disintegration which is for Schopenhauer the sole hope of cheating life of its emptiness of genuine, positive worth. It is sometimes asked whether Schopenhauer's philosophy deserves the title "pessimism": that it probably does is borne out by his consistent central thought that the very essence of each human being, of humanity, and of the world as a whole causes only grief and is something to escape from, if possible, at all costs.

---

[44] Schopenhauer, *World as Will*, vol. I, 373: [jeder Affekt oder Leidenschaft, die Erkenntniß trübt, ja, jede Neigung oder Abneigung, nicht etwan bloß das Urtheil. Nein, schon die ursprüngliche Anschauung der Dinge entstellt, färbt, verzerrt]. *Sämtliche Werke*, vol. III, 426.
[45] Schopenhauer, *World as Will*, vol. II, 507. [die große Gelegenheit, nicht mehr Ich zu seyn]. *Sämtliche Werke*, vol. III, 582.
[46] See Schopenhauer, *World as Will*, vol. I, 179, 390; *Sämtliche Werke*, vol. II, 210–11, 461–2.

6 Carl Gustav Carus and the science of the unconscious

Matthew Bell

Carus' place in intellectual history

"The key to understanding the conscious life of the soul lies in the realm of the unconscious."[1] In its explicitness, straightforwardness, perhaps even bravery, this sentence demands our attention. It was published in 1846, the opening sentence of a book, *Psyche: On the Developmental History of the Soul* (*Psyche: Zur Entwicklungsgeschichte der Seele*), whose author, Carl Gustav Carus (1789–1869), has a strong claim to be considered the first proper theorist of the unconscious. Carus' achievement was to present an explicit and systematic theory of the unconscious and to make this theory the foundation and the centerpiece of his theory of mind. Earlier philosophers developed theories of the unconscious: Plato and Aristotle perhaps, certainly Plotinus (204/5–270 CE), and in the modern period Marsilio Ficino (1433–99), Ralph Cudworth (1617–88), Gottfried Wilhelm Leibniz (1646–1716), Christian Wolff (1679–1754), Friedrich Schelling (1775–1854), and Arthur Schopenhauer (1788–1860). Yet these theories were only ever adjuncts or by-products of more general theories of mind. No one before Carus makes the unconscious central to a theory of mind. Historically then, and as far as the range of this volume is concerned, with Carus we reach a tipping point. From this point onwards the unconscious becomes an unavoidable issue in German psychological theory.

Yet it is tempting to say that Carus is the forgotten man of the history of German psychological theory. Carus' psychology is seldom read today. Germany's equivalent of the *Dictionary of National Biography*, in a long article on Carus' life, does not even mention his psychological writings.[2] Carus is remembered for other achievements. The university hospital of the Technische Universität Dresden bears his name: besides being court

---

[1] [Der Schlüssel zur Erkenntnis vom bewußten Seelenleben liegt in der Region des Unbewußtseins.] Carl Gustav Carus, *Psyche: Zur Entwicklungsgeschichte der Seele* (Pforzheim: Flammer und Hoffmann, 1846), 1.
[2] *Allgemeine Deutsche Biographie*, vol. IV (Leipzig: Duncker & Humblot, 1875–1912), 37–8.

physician to the King of Saxony, Carus was a pioneer of gynecology, of which he published a groundbreaking study in 1820.[3] As a zoologist, Carus made two important discoveries in comparative anatomy. He formulated an early version of the vertebrate archetype – an ideal model of which all vertebrate skeletons could be considered variations – which was subsequently developed by Richard Owen and Charles Darwin.[4] He is also remembered by historians of entomology. In 1826 he published the first exact study of the circulatory system of insects, which was hailed by the great French biologist Georges Cuvier, resulting in Carus being awarded the Montyon Prize for experimental physiology of the Institut de France. He is also not entirely unknown to German art-lovers. His paintings, largely derivative of his friend and mentor Caspar David Friedrich, hang in several major German art galleries (and on the cover of this volume). Carus was indeed a polymath, like his friend Goethe, with Carus arguably the better scientist and artist, though unarguably the worse writer. (Eduard von Hartmann wrote, perhaps a little unkindly, of Carus' "senile long-windedness and verbosity.")[5] His documentary remains include four volumes of memoirs, eight monographs on comparative anatomy, eleven books and articles on physiognomy and cranioscopy, a theory of nature in the manner of Schelling, three books on aesthetics and art,[6] numerous travel writings, and three studies of Goethe.

If Carus' other achievements have tended to overshadow his psychology, the latter has not been entirely forgotten. It was undeniably important and was read in its day. Carus records in his autobiography, in a tone of warm self-congratulation, that *Psyche* had been much acclaimed and he had received many letters of praise from readers.[7] Goethe's diary records that he was reading Carus' *Lectures on Psychology* (*Vorlesungen über Psychologie*, 1831) in March 1832, two weeks before he died. Only later in the century did a reaction set in. As we have seen, Eduard von Hartmann attacked Carus, and not just on account of his verbosity: he also criticized Carus' "lack of logical precision, cogency and incisiveness."[8] The attitude of the later nineteenth-century scientific

---

[3] Carus, *Lehrbuch der Gynäkologie* (Leipzig: Gerhard Fleischer, 1820).
[4] Nicolaas A. Rupke, "Richard Owen's Vertebrate Archetype," *Isis* 84 (1993): 231.
[5] [greisenhafte Weitschweifigkeit und Redseligkeit]. Eduard von Hartmann, *Philosophie des Unbewußten: Speculative Resultate nach inductiv-naturwissenschaftlicher Methode*, 12th edn. (Leipzig: Kröner, 1923), vol. III, 496.
[6] One of these was published recently in English translation: *Nine Letters on Landscape Painting Written in the Years 1815–1824, with a Letter from Goethe by Way of Introduction*, trans. David Britt (Oxford: Oxford University Press, 2002).
[7] Quoted in Friedrich Arnold, "Foreword," Carl Gustav Carus, *Psyche: Zur Entwicklungsgeschichte der Seele* (Darmstadt: Wissenschaftliche Buchgesellschaft, 1975), vii.
[8] [der Mangel logischer Präcision und beweiskräftiger Schneidigkeit]. Hartmann, *Philosophie des Unbewußten*, vol. III, 496.

community was one of polite condescension towards Carus' unempirical and idealizing approach.[9] A more recent historian of science is less equivocal: "There are islands of visionary insight in his book, surrounded by an ocean of vague and confused generalization."[10] Carus' influence seems to have been strongest at the margins of science, among ethically, religiously, or holistically inclined thinkers. Dostoevsky was impressed by *Psyche* and considered translating it into Russian in 1854.[11] Carus was a favorite author of Friedrich Froebel, founder of the kindergarten movement.[12] He influenced Georg Groddeck, a pioneer of psychosomatic medicine, whom Freud credited with first using the term "the id" (*das Es*).[13] He is repeatedly referred to by the great biocentric philosopher and self-publicist Ludwig Klages, who claimed to have rediscovered him in 1910.[14] Jung also names Carus on several occasions.[15]

Any account of Carus' psychology must attempt to explain this very mixed reception. Although his project as a whole is innovative, Carus' theory of the unconscious is excessively abstract and, in large parts, derivative. Carus drew heavily on psychological writings reaching back from Schelling to Aristotle, as his critics have been quick to point out. Nor is there anything scandalous or disturbing in the character of Carus' vision of the unconscious: it is in fact rather demure and serene. This is despite his predecessors having preempted Freud in showing that the unconscious and conscious minds could be at cross-purposes. Eighteenth-century philosophers were familiar with the idea that the unconscious could cause embarrassment to our conscious intentions, and (as Christopher Janaway points out in chapter 5 of this volume)

---

[9] [C[arus] war eine geistvolle, künstlerisch angelegte Natur, welche die natürlichen Erscheinungen, wol mit zu geringer Anerkennung der Tatsachen, in einem harmonisch abgerundeten, ästhetisch wohlthuenden Gesammtbilde zu vereinigen suchte.] *Allgemeine Deutsche Biographie*, vol. IV, 38.

[10] Franz Alexander, "The Development of Psychosomatic Medicine," *Psychosomatic Medicine* 24 (1962): 18.

[11] Robert C. Williams, "The Russian Soul: A Study in European Thought and Non-European Nationalism," *Journal of the History of Ideas* 31 (1970): 583.

[12] Kevin J. Brehony, *The Origins of Nursery Education: Friedrich Froebel and the English System* (London: Routledge, 2001), vol. II, 287.

[13] Karl M. Grossman and Sylvia Grossman, *The Wild Analyst: The Life and Work of Georg Groddeck* (New York: George Braziller, 1965), 105–16. See also Sigmund Freud, *The Standard Edition of the Complete Psychological Works of Sigmund Freud*, 24 vols. ed. James Strachey and Anna Freud (London: Hogarth Press, 1953–74), vol. XIX, 13 (hereafter cited as *SE* followed by volume and page numbers).

[14] Ludwig Klages, *Prinzipien der Charakterologie* (Leipzig: Barth, 1910), 9.

[15] C. G. Jung, *The Collected Works of C. G. Jung*, trans. R. F. C. Hull, ed. H. Read, M. Fordham, and G. Adler, 20 vols. (Princeton: Princeton University Press, 1953–79), vol. IV, 748; vol. V, 258; vol. VIII, 212, 355, 358, 359, 361; vol. IX/1, 1, 259; vol. IX/2, 11; vol. XI, 141, 375; vol. XIV, 791; vol. XV, 84, 157, 158; vol. XVI, 204, 294; vol. XVIII, 1070, 1223, 1295, 1732, 1739.

the conflict between conscious and unconscious minds is a persistent feature of Schopenhauer's psychology.[16] Carus was either unaware of or uninterested in the dramatic potential of such ideas. His unconscious is a form of biological information-processing system. His historical significance is as a systematizer of the unconscious. In this respect Carus resembles Christian Wolff in the eighteenth century. Wolff's *Empirical Psychology* (1732) made psychology a respectable subject in Germany and made Germany the leader in psychological theory, even though his psychological theory was largely derived from Aristotle, Descartes, and Leibniz.[17] Carus did something similar for the unconscious. He created a space for the psychology of the unconscious, established a more-or-less viable framework, and pointed to some of the areas which would be of interest later in the century.

Moreover, again like Wolff, Carus reached his groundbreaking statement that "the key to understanding the conscious life of the soul lies in the realm of the unconscious" not because he had anything of great significance to say about the unconscious, but because he inherited a problem in German philosophy which required its existence. This problem dated back to Leibniz and resonated on through the psychological thinking of Kant, Goethe, Schopenhauer, and others. In order to assimilate the new philosophy of Descartes and later Hume, Leibniz and the German idealists needed to postulate an unknown (and unknowable) area of mental activity that guaranteed the wholeness of mind. The problem has been analyzed brilliantly by Panayotis Kondylis in his study of the philosophy of the European Enlightenment.[18] Kondylis shows how a focus on psychology was needed to arm German philosophy against the potentially dangerous consequences of French and English rationalist thought, and how this psychological focus created the conditions for the emergence of the German idealist tradition. Kondylis' view can be supplemented with Odo Marquard's argument that the philosophical terminology developed by the German idealists provided some of the basic concepts of Freud's theory of the unconscious. Key concepts of psychoanalysis, such as the ego (*das Ich*), were in origin philosophical concepts, developed by the early nineteenth-century German idealists in the wake of Kant.[19] Together Kondylis and Marquard form an overarching

---

[16] See Matthew Bell, *The German Tradition of Psychology in Literature and Thought, 1700–1840* (Cambridge: Cambridge University Press, 2005), 32.
[17] Christian Wolff, *Psychologia empirica* (Frankfurt am Main and Leipzig: Renger, 1732).
[18] Panayotis Kondylis, *Die Aufklärung im Rahmen des neuzeitlichen Rationalismus* (Stuttgart: Klett-Cotta, 1981).
[19] Odo Marquard, *Transzendentaler Idealismus, Romantische Naturphilosophie, Psychoanalyse* (Cologne: Dinter, 1987).

argument that maps the emergence of German depth psychology out of earlier philosophy. Carus is a typical case of this process: whilst he created the space in which the scientific study of the unconscious could occur, his own psychology is more a product of philosophical developments than of the science of mind.

The great Germanic tradition of psychological theory is at once innovative, far ahead of developments in England and France, and at the same time conservative, for it remains fundamentally a neo-Aristotelian project, in an age when Aristotle was otherwise in terminal decline. The German tradition originated from a problem in Descartes. In fending off skepticism, Descartes conferred a special status upon consciousness. Even if we were to deny the validity of all knowledge that we might plausibly doubt, we would still have to admit the truth of the statement "I am," for the very act of doubting requires that there be a subject able to doubt. For this reason, consciousness – the condition in which we are aware of ourselves as thinking subjects – acquires a new significance: it guarantees certainty in the skeptical Descartes' very uncertain world. We can be certain about truths that are grounded in consciousness, even if we cannot be certain about anything a posteriori. This dualistic epistemology corresponds to a dualistic ontology. The world consists of thinking matter or souls (*res cogitans*), and physical matter (*res extensa*). The former operates according to rational laws, the latter according to mechanical ones which ultimately resolve down to quantities.

From this position, Descartes is able to mount his greatest coup, replacing the Aristotelian theory of physical qualities with a modern, progressive quantitative science. But it was the consequences of Descartes' dualistic ontology that caused difficulties for Germans. Descartes considered human and animal bodies to be simply machines. At the same time he equated mind with consciousness, which appeared to undermine traditional notions of the soul as a constantly active and immortal principle: if mind ended where consciousness ended, then how could the persistence of mind after death be proved? The *cogito* only counters the skeptic's denial that I can be certain of my existence at this moment in time. It does not assure me that I will still exist when I am no longer conscious. It does not therefore prove adequately that my soul is immortal. In these two ways – in having mechanical bodies and souls that do not outlive consciousness – humans seemed to have a large part of their being in a realm apart from God's grace.[20] Hence Leibniz could accept Descartes' theory of knowledge, but not his equation of soul with consciousness or the scandalous view that bodies were simply machines.

---

[20] Kondylis, *Die Aufklärung*, 537–649, especially 591–5.

This is why for eighteenth-century German rationalism consciousness no longer enjoys the special status accorded to it by Descartes. And Leibniz's theory of the monadic soul – a simple constantly active substance that is not affected by changes outside it and contains the principle of its own growth – is designed to guarantee that the mental activity that underlies consciousness, or if you like unconscious mental activity, is continuous and unceasing. Leibniz argued, perhaps adopting an argument of Plotinus, that the mind's activity is incessant.[21] Leibnizian continuous, unconscious mental activity rescues the Cartesian model of mind from materialism and atheism.

Repeatedly German philosophers of the eighteenth and nineteenth centuries will make a similar move: they will resort to psychological arguments to protect the wholeness and inviolability of the soul. It has been said many times that philosophy in the idealist era is concerned with the relation of subject to object; it might be said with more justice that it is concerned with the relation of consciousness to its unconscious other. For Kant, our empirical consciousness is affected by sense impressions; empirical consciousness is therefore passive. Kant must, however, retain an inviolable space for the active will. The chief problem that Kant seeks to address in the *Critique of Pure Reason* (*Kritik der reinen Vernunft*, 1781/1787) is how the activity of will and the passivity of empirical consciousness can be reconciled. For Leibniz, Wolff, Kant, and the idealists, the idea that there existed an unconscious (or unknown or unknowable) part of the mind preserved a wholeness that was felt to be threatened by materialism and empiricism. In arguing that the mind is never inactive and that Descartes was wrong to equate mind with consciousness, Leibniz was therefore responsible for the founding act of the German tradition of psychology, giving to German thought its distinctive psychological coloring. In the 1720s and 1730s, Wolff cemented Leibniz's argument and elevated psychology to a position alongside ontology and logic, when in Britain and France the term psychology was not even in common philosophical use. Kant, though ill disposed towards Wolff's Rational Psychology, was nonetheless dependent on Wolff's theory of mind. One might even say that the *Critique of Pure Reason* had a Wolffian argument at its core. Kant posited an unknowable but necessarily existent subjectivity – the Transcendental Unity of Apperception – in order to secure the unity of self and refute Hume's dangerous skepticism. The postulated unknown mind preserved the integrity of the known mind. Schopenhauer made a similar move, though in the opposite direction, for

---

[21] Phillip Merlan, *Monopsychism, Mysticism, Metaconsciousness: Problems of the Soul in the Neoaristotelian and Neoplatonic Tradition* (The Hague: Martinus Nijhoff, 1963), 57.

he used the unconscious, or will, as he termed it, to ground a return to Berkeleian idealism. For Schopenhauer, as Christopher Janaway points out in his contribution to this volume, will is the ultimate reality that is masked by illusion.

Before we move on to Carus, we should take note of one further example (in this case from literature) that was of supreme relevance to Carus. In the "Prologue in Heaven" that initiates the action of Goethe's *Faust* on a metaphysical level, the Lord and Mephistopheles agree on the broad principles of a plan to test humanity. The extent of their agreement is startling. Mephistopheles launches an attack on human reason, which he says is destructive. The Lord agrees, to the extent that he admits that human striving is erratic, "for man will err as long as he can strive."[22] That is to say, challenged by Mephistopheles, the Lord agrees that their conscious purposes do not lead humans to goodness or happiness. On the other hand, there is an unconscious force in humans that is more promising. It is striking again how much agreement there is on this. It is Mephistopheles who first suggests the organic metaphor ("his fevered mind is in a constant ferment")[23] which the Lord then adapts to his own positive purposes: like a plant, Faust will reach his fulfillment, even if at times this seems unlikely, for whereas his conscious purposes are erratic, a "dark impulse" (*dunkler Drang*) gives him direction. (In passing it should be noted that *dunkel* was the word used by the Wolffians to describe the unclear, unconscious ideas that populate the human imagination; it was generally agreed in the Late Enlightenment that humans are motivated to a large extent by such dark ideas.) In other words, according to the Lord, the unconscious mind makes good the metaphysical deficit of the conscious, gives meaning and direction to meaningless, directionless empirical consciousness. We shall return to *Faust* later.

Carus' philosophical commitments

For Carus as for Leibniz, the unconscious is in the first instance an antidote to Descartes' mechanical view of the body. Around 1800, the specific form of the problem concerned Kant's perceived failure to give an account of the genesis of the subject that could transcend the subject's empirical existence as a piece of conditioned nature. Carus is not directly concerned with these philosophical issues. His approach is determined by his prior commitment to Schelling's *Naturphilosophie*, which to his mind had satisfactorily reconfigured the relationship between spirit and matter:

---

[22] Johann Wolfgang von Goethe, *Faust: The First Part of the Tragedy*, trans. John Williams (Ware: Wordsworth, 1999), 12. [es irrt der Mensch so lang er strebt]. Line 317.

[23] Goethe, *Faust: First Part*, trans. Williams, 11. [Ihn treibt die Gährung in die Ferne.] Line 302.

Carl Gustav Carus and the science of the unconscious 163

That the movement of the stellar bodies, the orbit of the planets and comets and moons, was in just the same measure an annunciation of life itself as were the metamorphoses of plants and the circulation of the blood corpuscles in the animal spirits – in this insight I had experienced the liberation of my spirit from the dark cramped ideas of a dead mechanism, and the desire to proclaim the triumph of this knowledge and bring it to the attention of the world motivated me above all other things.[24]

The role of evangelist of Schellingian *Naturphilosophie* suited Carus. Following Schelling, he occupied a series of philosophical positions opposed to Cartesianism. He rejected the division between organic and inorganic matter, viewed the universe as an organism, not a mechanism, and treated the philosophy of nature and philosophy of mind as complementary parts of one system. The essence of nature is that it produces the subjectivity which enables it to understand itself. In this sense, psychology's job is to trace the emergence of subjective consciousness out of nature, and the medium for this is the unconscious. For Carus, then, as for Schelling, the unconscious is "not yet conscious self" (*noch nicht bewußtes Ich*).[25] In psychology, Carus' aim would be to discover the unknown, unconscious productivity behind all consciousness.

It is important to recognize that this project is intended to replace the Faculty Psychology of Wolff. All of the idealists, from Kant onwards, looked for a replacement for this hated discipline, with its predilection for analytical dissection and its multiplicity of mental faculties and capacities.[26] In place of the analytical approach, Carus offers a genetic one. The advantage of the genetic approach is that it promises to show how the many of consciousness could evolve from a primal unity. It would thus undermine the rationale of the analytical method:

Should we not reach a clear and beautiful insight into the mental [*geistig*] nature of man by trying here to follow, step by step, the path of development, if – instead of beginning by analyzing and splitting the fully developed mental [*geistig*] organism in its infinite multiplicity and mutability – we were to set

---

[24] [Daß die Bewegung der Weltkörper, der Umschwung der Planeten und Kometen und Monde, in eben dem Maße eine Verkündigung eigenthümlichen Lebens sei, wie die Verwandlungen der Pflanzen und das Umkreisen der Blutkörperchen in den Säften der Thiere – in dieser Erkenntniß hatte ich eben besondere Befreiung meines Geistes aus dunklen beengenden Vorstellungen eines todten Mechanismus empfunden, und den Triumph dieser Erkenntniß öffentlich auszusprechen und zur Anerkennung zu bringen, drängte es mich denn vor allen Dingen.] Carus, *Mnemosyne: Blätter aus Gedenk- und Tagebüchern* (Pforzheim: Flammer und Hoffmann, 1848), 442.

[25] Werner Felber and Otto Bach, "Carl Gustav Carus und das Unbewußte: Ein philosophisch-psychologisches Entwicklungskonzept im 19. Jahrhundert," *Carl Gustav Carus: Opera et efficacitas: Beiträge des wissenschaftlichen Symposiums zu Werk und Vermächtnis von Carl Gustav Carus am 22. September 1989*, ed. Günter Heidel (Dresden: Carus-Akademie, 1990), 120.

[26] Bell, *The German Tradition of Psychology*, 162–4.

ourselves the task of beginning at the very beginning, by first investigating the first dark, dim, vague stirrings of the mental world [*Geisterwelt*] within us?[27]

In tracing the emergence of the finished product, consciousness, the most important idea is that of "becoming" (*Werden*). Here Carus combines the ideas of a number of thinkers, preeminently Aristotle, Leibniz, Herder, and Goethe. Carus claims to have developed his genetic approach to psychology from Herder and Goethe.[28]

The distinctions that Carus makes between the different stages of development of the unconscious and conscious psyche derive partly from Aristotle's biologistic model of the five souls and partly from Leibniz's cognitive model. For Aristotle, each of the five different types of soul has different capacities (*dynameis*). The most basic, vegetable soul has the powers of nutrition and growth.[29] The second type of soul has these powers plus sensation.[30] The third type has all of the above plus desire. The fourth has the above plus movement. And the fifth species has all of the others plus "intellect and the reflective capacity" (*nous kai hē theorētikē dynamis*).[31] In each case the higher soul comprises the lower. As well as describing different classes of organism – vegetables, immobile animals, lower mobile animals, higher mobile animals, and humans – the model of five souls describes the process of development through which each human being passes, from an original vegetable state up towards full consciousness. Leibniz has a similar scheme. According to this model, inorganic matter has no consciousness, plants have appetition, animals have empirical consciousness, and humans have reason.

For Carus, too, the psyche proceeds through a number of different forms of biological existence, with each stage subsuming the prior stages, much like the five species of souls in Aristotle's *De anima*. The successive phases of individual development are thus the same as the evolutionary phases of the species' development. In this sense Carus will argue, following Aristotle and prior to the theory's explicit formulation by biologists Karl Ernst von Baer and Ernst Haeckel, that ontogeny recapitulates

---

[27] [Sollte es aber wirklich nicht zu einer klaren und schönen Einsicht in die geistige Natur des Menschen führen, wenn wir auch hier versuchten, recht Schritt vor Schritt dem Entwicklungsgange zu folgen, wenn wir, anstatt mit Betrachtung und Spaltung des völlig entwickelten geistigen Organismus in seiner unendlichen Vielgestaltigkeit und Veränderlichkeit zu beginnen, uns zur Aufgabe nähmen, den Anfang wirklich am Anfang zu machen, zuerst die ersten dunklen, dumpfen, unbestimmten Regungen der Geisterwelt in unserem Inneren aufzusuchen?] Carus, *Vorlesungen über Psychologie, gehalten im Winter 1829–30 zu Dresden* (Leipzig: Verlag von Gerhard Fleisher, 1831), 23.
[28] Ibid., xi.
[29] Aristotle, *De anima*, 413a, 21–34.
[30] Ibid., 413b, 1–10.
[31] Ibid., 413b, 24.

phylogeny: each individual in its development passes through the stages through which the human race has evolved.[32] It is worth emphasizing in this connection that the theory of recapitulation would continue to exercise influence in nineteenth-century psychology. Following Haeckel, psychological recapitulation was espoused by Henry Maudsley and by Granville Stanley Hall, founder of the American Psychological Association and a pioneer of childhood developmental psychology. And Freud and Jung were both strongly committed to recapitulation.[33] Freud's *Totem and Taboo* is subtitled: *Resemblances Between the Mental Lives of Savages and Neurotics* (*Einige Übereinstimmungen im Seelenleben der Wilden und der Neurotiker*) and argues that social organization of tribal cultures resembles stages of infant development.[34] Stephen Jay Gould has argued for the central importance of recapitulation in Freud's theory of the unconscious.[35] Similar arguments concerning the "chthonic" parts of mind can be found in Jung's "Mind and Earth" ("Seele und Erde").[36]

The structure of the unconscious according to Carus

While none of this can be attributed to Carus' influence, it reinforces the general sense that orginally Aristotelian theories continued to exert a hold on the German psychological tradition. Having said this, Carus' model of the psyche is considerably more complex than Aristotle's, and it is to this model that we turn now. Carus' system is set out most fully and schematically in the *Lectures on Psychology* (*Vorlesungen über Psychologie*, 1831). By way of clarification of the following summary, the structure is set out in table 6.1.

The first important structural distinction is between the unconscious and conscious parts of the psyche. Each of these is further subdivided, the conscious psyche into consciousness of world (*Weltbewußtsein*) and the more developed consciousness of self (*Selbstbewußtsein*), and the unconscious into a "relative unconscious" (*relativ Unbewußtes*) and an "absolute unconscious" (*absolut Unbewußtes*), with the latter further subdivided

---

[32] Carus, *Vorlesungen*, 118–36; Carus, *Lehrbuch der Zootomie* (Leipzig: Fleischer, 1818), 667; Carus, *Versuch einer Darstellung des Nervensystems und insbesondre des Gehirns nach ihrer Bedeutung, Entwickelung und Vollendung im thierischen Organismus* (Leipzig: Breitkopf & Härtel, 1814), 2.

[33] See Peter T. Hoffer, "The Legacy of Phylogenetic Inheritance in Freud and Jung," *Journal of the American Psychoanalytic Association* 40 (1992): 517–30.

[34] Freud, *SE*, XIII: vii–162. See also: *Introductory Lectures on Psychoanalysis*, *SE*, XVI: 199, and *Three Essays on the Theory of Sexuality*, *SE*, VII: xvi.

[35] Stephen Jay Gould, *Ontogeny and Phylogeny* (Cambridge, MA: Belknap Press, 1977), 161.

[36] Jung, *Collected Works*, vol. X, 29–49.

Table 6.1: *The structure of the psyche in Carus's Vorlesungen über Psychologie, 41–157*

Structure of psyche			Powers, functions, qualities		
Unconscious	Absolute unconscious	General absolute unconscious	Non-sentient biological being	No sense of present; strong sense of past and future	Unindividuated
		Partial absolute unconscious	Interior senses		
	Relative unconscious		Sleep; "buffer"		Partly individuated
Consciousness	*Weltbewußtsein* (empirical consciousness)		Six senses; pleasure and pain	Strong sense of present; weak sense of past and future	
	Selbstbewußtsein (self-consciousness)		Reflection		Individuated

into a "general absolute unconscious" (*allgemeines absolut Unbewußtes*) and a "partial absolute unconscious" (*partielles absolut Unbewußtes*). Like Aristotle, Carus assumes that the psyche is basically biological.[37] The absolute unconscious is the biological basis of mind: it comprises the psychic activity that is generated by our biological being, whether that activity is non-sentient (in the general absolute unconscious) or sentient (in the partial absolute unconscious). By a non-sentient unconscious, what Carus has in mind is something like Aristotle's first species of psyche, which controls the functions of nutrition and growth: "the fundamental function of life is always and only that of organic growth."[38] This is the form of psyche of a human embryo. And like Leibniz, Carus insists that the unconscious psyche is constantly active: "it is, to a certain extent, continuous, it is constantly re-forming, always destroying and renewing."[39] The sentient unconscious is the part of the psyche created

---

[37] Carus, *Psyche*, 4.
[38] [die wesentliche Lebensfunction ist immer nur noch die organisch bildende]. Carus, *Vorlesungen*, 41.
[39] [sie ist in gewissem Maße andauernd, sie ist umgestaltend, immer zerstörend und neu bildend]. Carus, *Psyche*, 24.

by the internal nervous system: not by sensation, but by what romantic medics and psychologists like Johann Christian Reil were wont to call the ganglious system. This equates roughly to what we now term the autonomic nervous system, which carries out physiological maintenance activities, without conscious control or sensation, such as the maintenance of heart and respiration rates, digestive functions, and salivation.

The most important part of the psyche for Carus is the relative unconscious. This is where most mental activity takes place. Carus calls it the *relative* unconscious because it is not properly and entirely unconscious. Most of its content is conscious experience that has been forgotten. All conscious experience returns to the relative unconscious once it leaves consciousness. Interestingly, Carus seems to believe that nothing is ever truly forgotten or obliterated from the psychic record; all thought is preserved in one form or another.[40] One can see how this might derive from his Aristotelian idea that the higher souls comprise the lower: developed consciousness thus never frees itself from its biological basis. The relative unconscious is, among other things, the place where experience is preserved. This is, in common parlance, our memory. But one must distinguish Carus' conception of memory from our common usage of the term. For Carus there are two forms of memory: the conscious and the unconscious. This is analogous to a distinction in Wolff's psychology between the imagination (*Einbildungskraft*) and the faculty of recognitional memory (*recordatio* or *Gedächtnis*). *Recordatio* is a cognitive faculty: the ability to recognize that what is presented to us is indeed a recollection of an impression we have already experienced.[41] The imagination, on the other hand, is what makes us re-experience memories, and that is an automatic process beyond our control. Thus, on the one hand we have a conscious memory that consists in our recognizing past experiences as our own, and on the other hand an enormous mass of past experiences that are constantly and uncontrollably being forced up into consciousness. In principle, then, we are subject to the recurrence of undesired memories. The conscious mind is subordinate to the unconscious. However, Carus' unconscious is entirely harmless. For Carus, memory is a dynamic biological system. A further power of the relative unconscious is to produce dreams. Dreams are composed of two kinds of material: the biological substrate that floats up into the relative unconscious from the absolute unconscious, and residues of experience drifting down into the relative unconscious from consciousness. Finally, the relative unconscious acts

---

[40] Ibid., 101–2. See also Reinhard Abeln, *Unbewußtes und Unterbewußtes bei C. G. Carus und Aristoteles* (Meisenheim am Glan: Anton Hain, 1970), 34.
[41] Christian Wolff, *Gesammelte Werke*, ed. Jean École *et al.*, part 2, vol. V (Hildesheim and New York: Olms, 1965), 164–5.

as a buffer, where material is loaded before being processed up into the conscious psyche.

The conscious psyche in Carus' system is structured broadly along the lines of the traditional German Leibniz-Wolffian model, but there are some notable differences that derive in part from Carus' Schellingian *Naturphilosophie* and in part from Carus' biologism. In consciousness Carus distinguishes between consciousness of world and consciousness of self, just as Leibniz distinguishes between empirical consciousness and reason.[42] The formation of a consciousness of world requires four prerequisites, and here Carus' biologism is powerfully evident. By consciousness of world, Carus means our sensory faculties. These comprise the traditional five plus a sense of warmth.[43] At the same time, consciousness of world is continuously affected by the unconscious:

Like the unconscious proper, all feelings and experiences that have already attained consciousness, but then have unconsciously slept in the psyche, have an effect on the conscious psychic life, just as they affect what we have named the absolute unconscious.[44]

The first prerequisite of consciousness of world is a nervous system which can "concentrate" (*concentriren*) the stirrings (*Regungen*) of the non-nervous parts of the body.[45] Consciousness of world always begins as, and is underpinned by, "the vague feeling of the condition of one's own organization," which is experienced either as pleasure or pain.[46] The second prerequisite of consciousness is the availability of external stimuli. The third is a mass of memories, which Carus glosses as "the epimethean fixing of all stimuli (*Anregungen*) of the psychic life."[47] The fourth is a critical mass of representations (*Vorstellungen*) corresponding to a particular mass of gray matter.[48]

Whereas traditionally German philosophers, following Descartes and Leibniz, had distinguished between empirical consciousness and reason, Carus replaces reason with consciousness of self. In this respect he follows his master, Schelling. Human consciousness is nature becoming

---

[42] Carus, *Vorlesungen*, 48.
[43] Ibid., 114.
[44] [Gleich dem durchaus Unbewußten wirken ... alle bereits früher einmal zum Bewußtsein gelangten, dann aber wieder unbewußt in der Seele schlummernden Gefühle und Erkentnisse immerfort auf das bewußte Seelenleben, wie auf das was wir das absolut unbewußte Seelenleben genannt haben, ein.] Carus, *Psyche*, 76.
[45] Ibid., 103.
[46] [das unbestimmte Gefühl des Zustandes der eignen Organisation]. Carus, *Vorlesungen*, 111.
[47] [das epimetheïsche Festgehaltensein aller Anregungen des Seelenlebens, d.h. ... die Erinnerung]. Ibid., 104–5.
[48] Ibid., 108.

aware of itself; human reason, therefore, is a reflection of nature's awareness of itself, and thus a doubly reflexive consciousness. This follows Schelling's scheme of powers (*Potenzen*), an application to the natural world of a mathematical metaphor. As we move up the ladder of consciousness, we find consciousness progressively raised to higher powers. Mind, therefore, is not essentially different from nature; it is nature raised to a higher power: "mind [*Geist*] is not something apart from nature, it is only nature's purest creation and therefore its symbol, its language."[49]

Carus' views on individuation follow a similar pattern. As unconscious beings we are unindividuated. Indeed, Carus believes that fundamentally all souls are one, and that the unconscious psyche belongs to the genus, not to the individual.[50] (This is one of the reasons why Jung was attracted to Carus.)[51] It is self-consciousness that causes the impression of individuation: humans become aware that they are different from other humans. Animals, by contrast, which do not have self-consciousness, think that they are the same as all other animals of their species, since animal consciousness is not fully individuated. Individuation proper sets in in humans in the relative unconscious: this is where (individual) consciousness returns for storage. At this level, the psyche works according to the laws of association established by eighteenth-century thinkers such as Hume and David Hartley (1705–57). Ideas are connected to one another in the relative unconscious because of their similarity or proximity in time.[52]

Note, finally, that as we move from the absolute unconscious through the relative unconscious to consciousness, we appear to be set on a ramifying path. The psyche becomes increasingly individuated and differentiated, above all by one's sex. This is a fundamental ontological principle for Carus. All change is from the simple to the complex.[53] The tragic fate of self-consciousness is that it can never return to the wholeness of its unconscious state. One can see how for the pioneering gynecologist Carus the sense that women's fate as child-bearers – through which they contribute so much to the progress of the species, but which causes them such pain as individuals – might seem tragic. However, Carus believes that the ultimate fate of consciousness resides not in the individual, but in the species. For instance, whilst our sex makes us irreversibly individual, the regulation of a roughly equal proportion of males to females in

[49] [der Geist [ist] nichts von der Natur Verschiedenes, nur ihre reinste Ausgeburt und daher ihr Symbol, ihre Sprache]. Carus, *Vorlesungen*, 39–40.
[50] Carus, *Vorlesungen*, 19, 42–3.
[51] Jung, *Collected Works*, vol. V, 258.
[52] Carus, *Vorlesungen*, 137–57.
[53] Ibid., 14.

the human population is, says Carus, a function of our species psyche.[54] For a woman, bearing children represents the triumph of the species soul over the individual soul. We only become truly human in as much as we act as a whole species: humanity as a whole represents the true nature of human beings.

Related to this is Carus' account of our consciousness of time, which he considers to be the fundamental feature of self-consciousness. Kant argued in the *Critique of Pure Reason* that our internal sense is conditioned by our experience of the passage of time. Accordingly, for Carus consciousness lives in the present. Inasmuch as we attend to an idea, that idea is present to us. Whereas to the conscious psyche the present is strong, the past and future are relatively weak.[55] This is because, as we have already noted, conscious memory is a weak faculty compared to the memory of the relative unconscious. The unconscious psyche by contrast has no sense of the present and is instead dominated by the past and the future. Past and future stand in an organic relation to one another.[56] What Carus means by this is that the unconscious is in a process of organic development, which he illustrates by analogy with plants. Plants contain within them their own future and past, for instance in their seeds. Carus thinks there is an unconscious psychic analogy to this, which he defines as Promethean and Epimethean tendencies. In using these terms, Carus alludes to Goethe's drama *Pandora* of 1807.[57] The characters Prometheus and Epimetheus are each doomed to a different though equally partial temporal consciousness: Prometheus is doomed to push unreflectively into the future, Epimetheus to live always in the shadow of the past. So for Carus the unconscious consists at the same time of those ideas that have fallen from consciousness back into the unconscious, and those ideas that are destined to rise from the unconscious back into consciousness.

Carus' Goethean unconscious

Although most heavily indebted to Aristotle and Schelling for its psychological argument, Carus' psychology quotes Goethe more than it does any other writer, and *Faust* more than any other text by Goethe. Perhaps Carus' theory of the unconscious is ultimately as Goethean, or even

---

[54] Ibid., 85. Compare Ludwig Feuerbach's conception of "species being" (*Gattungswesen*): *The Essence of Christianity*, trans. Marian Evans (London: John Chapman, 1854), 1–5.
[55] Carus, *Psyche*, 26.
[56] Ibid., 25.
[57] Johann Wolfgang Goethe, *Pandora: Ein Festspiel*, in *Werke*, ed. Erich Schmidt *et al.*, part 1, vol. L (Weimar: Böhlau, 1900), 295–344.

Faustian, as it is Aristotelian or Schellingian. For Carus, Faust represents the unconscious. As the Lord says to Mephistopheles in the "Prologue in Heaven," Faust will eventually find his way to representing the goodness of the human race. Like a plant that grows without any consciousness of the fruit that it will bear, Faust is driven by a "dark impulse" (*dunkler Drang*), which will ultimately, so the Lord thinks, bear the fruit of humanity.[58] Faust also offers a model for Carus' conception of time. As a symbol of the unconscious Faust has no sense of the present. Famously, in the wager with Mephistopheles, Faust denies that the present has any rights over him:

> If I should bid the moment stay, or try
> To hold its fleeting beauty, then you may
> Cast me in chains and carry me away,
> For in that instant I will gladly die.[59]

Thus Faust's own words confirm him as "dark impulse," unconscious of the present moment, tumbling out of the past and lurching into the future.

Carus is fond of illustrating his argument with quotations from Goethe.[60] In this regard he is no different from Freud and Jung, who constantly appeal to Goethe for cultural legitimation (on Freud's appeals to Goethe, see chapters 1 and 3 of this volume). Carus, however, appeals to Goethe for scientific legitimation too, and this might be considered one indicator of the weakness of his theory of the unconscious. Carus is easy to criticize for the fuzzy, schematic, biologistic, and holistic character of his thought. On some counts – the tedious prose is one – Carus cannot be defended. But to say that Carus' psychology is schematic and biologistic is not necessarily to discredit it, once its place in the development of German psychological theory is properly understood. Freud was no stranger to biologism. As far as its being schematic is concerned, Carus' psychology was more philosophical, within the terms of Schellingian idealism, than it was properly psychological. Jung had it more or less right when he observed that "[Freud] demonstrated empirically the presence of an unconscious psyche which had hitherto existed only as a philosophical postulate, in particular in the philosophies of C. G. Carus and Eduard von Hartmann."[61] Still, there are aspects of

---

[58] Goethe, *Faust: First Part*, 12, line 328.
[59] Ibid., 52: [Werd' ich zum Augenblicke sagen: / Verweile doch! du bist so schön! / Dann magst du mich in Fesseln schlagen, / Dann will ich gern zugrunde gehn!] Lines 1699–1702.
[60] For instance, Carus, *Vorlesungen*, 11, 23, 48; and *Psyche*, 24, 75.
[61] Quoted in Stephen Segaller and Merrill Berger, *The Wisdom of the Dream: The World of C. G. Jung* (London: Weidenfeld & Nicolson, 1989), 169. Compare the verdict of Franz

Carus' model that do preempt important theoretical developments of the late nineteenth and early twentieth centuries, such as the recapitulation of phylogeny by ontogeny; the relative weight given to conscious and unconscious memory; the possibly conflicting functions of dreams; and the biological information-processing approach. As for Carus' holism, this appealed to some later thinkers on or beyond the margins of mainstream science and philosophy. The positive image of Carus that was sometimes presented by such figures as Klages and Jung was no doubt exaggerated for tactical reasons, such as when Jung claimed that Carus and not Freud discovered the unconscious.[62] Even when providing Jung with a stick with which to beat Freud, Carus' primacy in the field of the unconscious was acknowledged.

Alexander: "Carus sets the problem correctly, but pitifully fails to advance any methodological tools to achieve the goal which he stated with admirable clairvoyance." Franz Alexander, "The Development of Psychosomatic Medicine," *Psychosomatic Medicine* 24 (1962): 18.

[62] Jung, *Collected Works*, vol. XVIII, 1070.

7 Eduard von Hartmann's *Philosophy of the Unconscious*

Sebastian Gardner

In the second volume of Baldwin's *Dictionary of Philosophy and Psychology*, published in 1902, the following is given as the entry for the concept "unconscious":

Unconscious (**the**, philosophy of): Ger. *Philosophie des Unbewussten*. The metaphysical system of E. v. Hartmann, by whom the absolute principle is called "the Unconscious."
"According to v. Hartmann (*Philos. d. Unbewussten*, 3) the unconscious is the absolute principle, active in all things, the force which is operative in the inorganic, organic, and mental alike, yet not revealed in consciousness (ibid., 365). It is the unity of unconscious presentation and will (ibid., 380) of the logical (idea) and the alogical (will). The unconscious exists independently of space, time, and individual existence, timeless before the being of the world (ibid., 376). For us it is unconscious, in itself it is superconscious (überbewusst)" (Eisler, *Wörterb. d. philos. Begriffe*, "Unbewusst").[1]

This is both a succinct summary of Eduard von Hartmann's leading ideas, and an index of his remarkable historical success – the relevant volume of the *Dictionary* was published thirty-four years after the appearance of the first edition of the *Philosophy of the Unconscious* (*Philosophie des Unbewussten*) in 1868,[2] and at a time when unconscious ideas and

---

[1] James Mark Baldwin, *Dictionary of Philosophy and Psychology*, 3 vols. (New York: Macmillan, 1901–5), vol. II, 724–5.
[2] The full title of the work is *Philosophie des Unbewussten: Speculative Resultate nach inductiv-naturwissenschaftlicher Methode* (original sub-title, in 1st edn. [Berlin: Carl Duncker, 1869]: *Versuch einer Weltanschauung*). A second and enlarged edition appeared in 1870, and many further editions appeared in response to public demand for several decades; the 11th edition of 1904 was the last published in Hartmann's lifetime. References to *Philosophy of the Unconscious* (hereafter *PU*) are to the single-volume Kegan Paul (London) edition of 1931 (with a preface by C. K. Ogden), which is based on the three-volume authorized English translation of 1884 by William Chatterton Coupland (from the 9th German edition of 1882). A more recent edition, in 3 volumes and repaginated, is available from Living Time Press (Shrewsbury, 2001–2). References take the form, e.g. "*PU* I (B), 220," referring to volume-division I, part (B), page 220. References in square brackets are to the (12th) German edition, *Philosophie des Unbewussten: Speculative Resultate nach inductiv-naturwissenschaftlicher Methode*, 3 vols. (Leipzig: Kröner, 1923), and take the form, e.g. "[I (B), 190]": volume I, part (B), page 190.

173

inferences had a well-established place in psychology, yet Baldwin allows the concept of the unconscious to be identified exclusively with Hartmann's conception of it.[3]

Hartmann's *Philosophy of the Unconscious* is helpfully regarded as being composed of three parts, which Hartmann presents as forming a systematic whole, but which need to be distinguished if we are to determine accurately what is historically original in Hartmann's conception of the unconscious. The first part of Hartmann's system consists in a *teleological metaphysics of nature*, a view of nature (and reality in its entirety) as grounded in a manifold of acts of will or events of willing, unified ultimately under the single act of will or process of willing which he calls the (All-One) Unconscious. The second part is Hartmann's interpretation of this metaphysics as revealing an original *synthesis of logical idea and alogical will*. Here we find Hartmann claiming a far-reaching philosophical significance for his "Philosophy of the Unconscious": it comprises, he claims, an overcoming of the great antinomy formed by Hegel and Schopenhauer which constitutes, in his view, the horizon of contemporary philosophical thought. The third part, based on the second, and which I will refer to as Hartmann's *world-view*, comprehends everything in Hartmann's system that falls outside metaphysics: his philosophical pessimism, conception of world history, and theory of cosmic salvation, his ethical system and religious doctrines, characterization of the quality of human life, aesthetic theory, and miscellaneous other elements, including much reflection on contemporary public matters and cultural questions. I will take the parts in turn, but spend most time on the first and second.

Hartmann's teleological metaphysics of nature

One of the most striking features of Hartmann's endeavor – one of the respects in which his system appears alien to us, though to his contemporary readers it was in this regard a more familiar kind of enterprise[4] – is his combination of a metaphysics of absolute idealism with a philosophical *methodology* which denies anything more than auxiliary value to a priori reflection,[5] and according to which derivation from *experience*

---

[3] Sonu Shamdasani has pointed out that Baldwin's own antipathy to the concept of the unconscious is likely to have played a role, Baldwin's intention being to damn by association.
[4] In Rudolf Hermann Lotze, too, natural science and metaphysics are brought close together, and an absolute idealism is advanced on a regressive, non-deductive basis. Eugen Dühring and Hans Vaihinger also combine naturalism with metaphysics.
[5] Hartmann has no single justification for his rejection of the a priori but instead argues on a case-by-case basis; see, e.g., *Schellings philosophisches System* (Leipzig: H. Haacke, 1897), ch. 2.

is the proper source of metaphysical cognition: scientifically processed experience is held to be sufficient to support the most robust metaphysical conclusions, not with complete certainty, yet with a very high degree of confidence. Hartmann calls his method "inductive," although his understanding of this concept is broad, and can be glossed as simply a commitment to theorizing about the data of experience on the basis of principles of scientific methodology and inference to the best explanation. The importance Hartmann attaches to this methodological innovation is signalled by his sub-title for *Philosophy of the Unconscious – Speculative Results According to the Inductive Method of Physical Science*.[6]

In terms of his methodology, then, Hartmann is a naturalist, and his further peculiarity lies in his supposition that reflection on the results of the natural sciences is sufficient to warrant conclusions about the ultimate nature of reality which are thoroughly *anti*-materialist, indeed, which take us all the way to Platonic Ideas. Hartmann regards it as a mistake to attach naturalism to materialism: a naturalism that "*takes full account of all the results of the natural sciences*" will, he says, oppose itself to materialism.[7]

Hartmann's alliance of natural science and metaphysics

How is this co-option of natural science to traditional metaphysical ends to be achieved? Hartmann's strategy has two stages. The first consists in the application to the organic and psychological realms of a basic and essentially simple argument schema, which he sets out and defends at the beginning of *Philosophy of the Unconscious*. The starting point is provided by direct observations of teleological phenomena and by instances of scientific explanation that have teleological form, i.e. that explain some feature of X by attributing to X purposiveness or end-directedness.[8] The basic question for Hartmann, as for Kant in the section of the *Critique of the Power of Judgment* (*Kritik der Urteilskraft*, 1790) entitled the "Critique of Teleological Judgment" (*Kritik der teleologischen Urteilskraft*), is what provides for the *truth* of such statements, and Hartmann supposes that there is only one possibility: namely that X contains and is determined by an immanent *will*, which has as its *content* the representation (or idea) of the end to be achieved.[9]

---

[6] [Speculative Resultate nach inductiv-naturwissenschaftlicher Methode]. Hartmann's "Motto"; *PU* I, 13 [I, 11].
[7] [welche allen Resultaten der Naturwissenschaften volle Rechnung trägt]. *PU* II (C), 63 [II, 17].
[8] See *PU* I, 43–5 [I, 36–7].
[9] See esp. *PU* I (A), 98 [I (A), 84] and 113–14 [I (A), 112–13], and *PU* II (C), ch. VIII.

Hartmann claims that there is no other way of making the observed relation of fit between means and ends intelligible: an explanation that refers only to mechanism and that leaves the relation miraculous, a case of naked coincidence, while any explanation that instead posits a *remote* intelligent cause for the mechanism – in deist fashion, on the analogy with a watch designed by a watchmaker – is refuted, according to Hartmann, by the intelligent plasticity of function, the indefinitely fine attunement of appropriate means to projected ends that, Hartmann claims, we can observe in the relevant cases. In terms of the watch analogy, it is as if the watch *redesigned itself* and its mode of functioning as required by changing circumstance, in order to be able to continue to discharge the function of keeping time. So, Hartmann is arguing, the agent of the watch's design, the watchmaker, must be *within* the watch, not outside and temporally behind it. The cases most amenable to application of this argument schema are of course phenomena in organic nature such as instinctive behavior, reflex responses, the functioning of internal organs, and reparative processes (for example, worms cut in half regenerating), and these are the sorts of phenomena on which Hartmann focuses in Part (A) of *Philosophy of the Unconscious*.

Hartmann does not, however, simply return to a pre-modern conception of teleology as a causality whose operation can be considered independently of any material medium. He assumes – he takes it as a fact established by science – that every instance of teleological causality, including all conscious mental activity, must be *realized* in efficient material causality.[10] So, wherever there is teleology, there is a corresponding mechanical physiological process, and this latter process is an instance of the *unconscious willing* of the end which the process serves.[11] Hartmann also gives a striking application of his argument designed to show that we must admit explanation in terms of unconscious will even in the context where we would least expect it to be needed.[12] Our own consciously intended actions involve, Hartmann points out, a causal chain running from brain events via nerve fibers to our muscles, and all this neuro-electrical and cellular level causality must, he claims, be conceived on the teleological,

---

[10] Hartmann is in *this* (limited) sense a materialist, insofar as he accepts the principle that all conscious mental activity can come to pass only by the normal functioning of the brain (*PU* II (C), 64 [II (C), 18]), and "cerebral vibrations, more generally material movement" [Gehirnschwingungen, allgemeiner die materielle Bewegung] as conditions of consciousness (*PU* II (C), 80 [II (C), 31]; see also *PU* II (C), ch. II). Hartmann's metaphysics of the mind–body relation involves therefore three levels: (1) conscious mental activity, which reduces to (2) brain function, which reduces in turn to (3) unconscious will.

[11] E.g. *PU* I (A), 123–4 [I (A), 106]: when the ganglionic will wills to contract the cardiac muscle, it must possess the idea of this contraction, "for otherwise God only knows what could be contracted, but not the cardiac muscle" [denn sonst könnte weiss Gott was contrahirt werden, nur nicht der Herzmuskel]. See also *PU* I (A), 69–70 [I (A), 59–60].

[12] The argument is summarized at *PU* I (A), 77 [I (A), 66–7].

X-as-a-means-to-Y pattern. So, although it is of course no part of my self-conscious intention, when I raise my hand to wave to you, that *this* nerve should send *that* signal to *that* tendon, the execution of my intention does require that such intentions exist, and these are to be ascribed to sub-centers of my nervous system. Hartmann is thus not an epiphenomenalist, still less an eliminativist, about self-conscious agency:[13] his claim is rather that, in terms of the famous distinction drawn by Daniel Dennett, explanation of "personal"-level agency forces us to "sub-personal" postulation, and that the postulated sub-personal shares the same (on Hartmann's view) *irreducibly* intentional structure as the personal.

Tracing out in detail the teleological structure of organic and human nature according to this model occupies many pages of *Philosophy of the Unconscious*. Thus in Part (B), "The Unconscious in the Human Mind,"[14] Hartmann applies the concept of unconscious will to the spheres of sexuality and love, ethics, language, art, human history, mystical experience, psychology, epistemology, and so on. In the department of psychology and epistemology, Hartmann argues that mental activity, since it always has a teleological character – acts of memory are strivings to retrieve the past, thought and inference are attempts to formulate true representations, even making associations involves determining the likeness of the terms associated – requires analysis into sub-tasks, just as does bodily action.[15] Similarly, the (Kantian) conditions of knowledge, categories such as causality and space as the form of intuition, cannot be taken as transcendental givens: according to Hartmann, they involve representational elements which need to be first *manufactured*, referring us again to purposive unconscious action.[16]

It seems fair to assume that this richness of empirical detail must have been partly responsible for the work's enormous popular appeal – like Fontenelle in the Early Enlightenment and popular Darwinian writers in our own times, Hartmann provided a gratifying synoptic overview and integration of natural and human science. (There is more to be said on the topic of Hartmann's popularity, which I will return to at the end.)

Hartmann's theory of teleology: between Kant and Darwin

Hartmann is in agreement with Kant that there are *objectively valid* teleological judgments of nature – true statements to the effect that such and such is the function of a natural object X, or that an organism

---
[13] See *PU* I (A), 138 [I (A), 118].
[14] [Das Unbewusste im menschlichen Geiste].
[15] See *PU* I (B), 301ff. [I (B), 261ff.].
[16] See *PU* I (B), 304ff. [I (B), 264ff.], and *PU* I (B), ch. VIII.

being or acting thus and not otherwise is explained by its having a certain purpose Y. Where Hartmann differs from Kant is in his fully realistic understanding of these judgments. Hartmann spends no time on the Kantian "critical" possibility that the objective validity of teleological judgments derives from a subjective necessity of our reason, and that when we consider nature in terms of means and ends we are employing an *analogy* with our own practical agency, which forbids our taking teleological judgments realistically and obliges us to understand them, in Kant's terminology, as merely regulative. In Kant's terms,[17] Hartmann is a *transcendental realist* regarding teleology in nature (and therefore, in Kant's eyes, "dogmatic").

Second, Hartmann's approach to teleology differs in a fundamental respect from that of Schelling, despite their shared non-Kantian understanding of teleology as not merely regulative of scientific enquiry but constitutive of its object. Schelling's claims regarding the teleological structure of nature are made against a supporting a priori background: Schelling gives a (transcendental) argument that nature and natural phenomena are *conceivable* only as manifestations of activity and that nature as a whole can be conceived only as a single organism. Hartmann however abjures this a priori reasoning, believing that Schelling's organic, *naturphilosophisch* conception can be supported wholly a posteriori, and only in that way.

The third contrast to be drawn is with Darwin, whose mechanistic account of teleology in the organic world Hartmann paid much critical attention to – understandably, since the Darwinian explanation is the opposite of Hartmann's.[18] Whereas Hartmann subsumes mechanistic under teleological explanation, grounding instances of mechanical causality in the organic realm on teleological causality, Darwin has teleological description supervening on (a particular kind of) mechanical causality (and where there is no relevant mechanism to which to reduce teleology, there can *be* no teleology, only an illusion of such). As regards his criticism of Darwin, one of the main points on which Hartmann convicts Darwinism of inadequacy is its lack of explanation for morphological

---

[17] And in his own terms: see *PU* I, Addenda, 323–6 [I, Nachträge, 490–2], where Hartmann claims that the objects of natural science qualify as things in themselves, and *PU* I (B), 329–30 [I (B), 285], on the transcendental reality of empirical objects. See also Hartmann's *Kritische Grundlegung des transcendentalen Realismus* (Berlin: Carl Duncker, 1875). For an exposition and criticism of Hartmann's epistemology, see W. Caldwell, "The Epistemology of Ed. v. Hartmann," *Mind* 2 (1893): 188–207.
[18] See *PU* I (B), 287–8 [I (B), 248–9], and, at greater length, Hartmann's *Wahrheit und Irrtum im Darwinismus: Eine Kritische Darstellung der organischen Entwicklungstheorie* (Berlin: Carl Duncker, 1875). Parts I–II translated as "The True and the False in Darwinism: A Critical Representation of the Theory of Organic Development," *Journal of Speculative Philosophy* 11 (1877–8): 244–51 and 392–9.

structure and change, the *relations of likeness* that define species and that exist between different organic types, allowing nature to be apprehended as a systematic set of variations on underlying themes.[19]

Hartmann's conception of teleology is thus situated between, on the one hand, the a priori and subjectivist conception of Kant, and the a posteriori and realist, but mechanistic, conception of Darwin: in his own eyes, Hartmann is defining a Golden Mean between two one-sided positions (and, with regard to Schelling, he takes himself to be improving on a view which is substantially correct but inappropriately supported).

In our eyes, however, it appears rather that Hartmann is attempting to tread a very thin line. His criticism of Darwin is, we can see, extremely weak, for he merely assumes that nature's comprising a *chain of being*, a rationally patterned taxonomy, is an unquestionable empirical datum and has the status of a primary explanandum. Darwinians of course reject this as a mere appearance that supervenes on a messy mechanistic reality, an example of how our essentializing "folk" biology gets things wrong. This is one of many points where Hartmann appears to lean on and assume the natural-scientific plausibility of metaphysical conceptions and world-images whose origins are remote from modern science, conceptions that the German idealists by contrast regarded as capable of surviving into modernity only if equipped with a transcendental, non-a posteriori foundation. The same point can be made with respect to Hartmann's openly declared commitment to the principle, explicit in Schelling, Schopenhauer, and most of German romanticism, that nature's intelligibility is secured by the justified assumption that external nature is essentially akin to us and that we may take ourselves, more exactly our *inner* experience, to provide the right model for understanding it.[20] Hartmann appears not to see that adherence to this venerable romantic principle is highly questionable so long as philosophical warrants are required to derive from the sorts of natural scientific a posteriori sources to which he (officially) confines philosophical enquiry.[21]

---

[19] See *Wahrheit und Irrtum*, 8–9 ["The True and the False in Darwinism", 248–9], and *PU* II (C), ch. X, esp. 306–7 [II (C), 229–30]. At *PU* I (B), 287–8 [I (B), 248–9], Darwin is said to explain the transmission of features (capacities), but not their existence (their "*essence*" [*Wesen*] and "*first origination*" [*erste Entstehung*]), a criticism which implies rejection of the theory of random mutation. Hartmann does accept however Darwin's theory of natural selection in the struggle for existence, as a teleology-subordinated mechanism devised by the unconscious (*PU* II (C), 314ff. [II (C), 236ff.] and 330 [II (C), 250]).

[20] *PU* III (C), 143–4 [II (C), 412–13]. On the ancestry of this idea, see Alexander Godevon Aesch, *Natural Science in German Romanticism* (New York: Columbia University Press, 1941), ch. 6.

[21] Showing how discreditable this assumption could appear by Hartmann's time, see Lange, *Geschichte des Materialismus: Und Kritik Seiner Bedeutung in der Gegenwart* (1865;

More generally, Hartmann is clearly open to criticism from mechanistic quarters, insofar as he attempts to establish the necessity of teleological explanation by appealing to the insufficiency of efficient material causes. Thus Friedrich Albert Lange objects that Hartmann is no more entitled to infer a limit to physical explanation from the fact of its current unavailability, than the Australian savage is entitled to infer that the spark in a Leyden jar is the work of the devil, and that explanation in terms of the unconscious exhibits the same lack of intellectual sophistication as primitive animism.[22] Similarly Franz Brentano indicates the weakness of the premise in Hartmann's argument that our mental performances entail unconscious will, pointing out that only if our knowledge of physiological processes is complete, which we know it not to be, can we infer that physiological processes underpinning mental life have no mechanistic explanation.[23]

Hartmann's theory of inorganic nature

With the idea of immanent unconscious unities of will and representation established as the explanatory ground of the organic and human realms, we come to the second part of Hartmann's strategy, his attempt to account for the non-organic in the same metaphysical terms. This can be summarized much more briefly. The transition from organic to non-organic is effected in two simple steps. First Hartmann adopts the position (which has a long and honorable history, going back to Leibniz and Kant) that the explanatory basis of the material realm lies in the postulation not of extended substance or mass but of *force* – matter is properly analyzed into atomic points of force, according to Hartmann's "Atomistic Dynamism" (*atomistischer Dynamismus*).[24] Second, Hartmann advances a teleological interpretation of the concept of force as a (simple and immaterial) *striving* to either attract or repel, and this according to Hartmann

Leipzig: Baedeker, 1896), book 2, 279–81 [*The History of Materialism, and Criticism of its Present Importance*, 3rd edn., trans. Ernest Chester Thomas (London: Routledge and Kegan Paul, 1950), book 2, sect. 2, ch. 4, 74–5].

[22] *Geschichte des Materialismus*, book 2, 278 [*History of Materialism*, book 2, sect. 2, ch. 4, 72]. Lange criticizes the formal argument from probability (*Geschichte des Materialismus*, book 2, 281–3 [*History of Materialism*, book 2, sect. 2, ch. 4, 75–9]) that Hartmann presents in *PU* I, 45–51 [I, 38–46]. Lange is typical of Hartmann's contemporaries in dismissing his claim to scientificity: see *Geschichte des Materialismus*, book 2, 80 n. 87 [*History of Materialism*, book 2, sect. 2, ch. 4, 80 n. 87].

[23] *Psychologie vom empirischen Standpunkt*, vol. I, ed. Oskar Kraus (Leipzig: Meiner, 1924), 162 [*Psychology from an Empirical Standpoint*, ed. Oskar Kraus, trans. Antos C. Rancurello, Dailey Burnham Terrell, and Linda L. McAlister (London: Routledge and Kegan Paul, 1973), 116].

[24] *PU* II (C), 175 [II (C), 114]. See the analysis of matter in *PU* II (C), ch. V.

is conceptually equivalent to an end-directed will.[25] The real constitution of non-organic nature thus comprises once again an unconscious unity of will and representation.

In the non-organic realm, Hartmann cannot apply the argument schema described earlier, since there is no hint of intelligence in the way that gravity "operates," but he is nonetheless able to employ as a premise the result which he has arrived at in his consideration of organic nature: his argument is that, since we *know already* that what appears to be mere material mechanism is really (in the organic world) the operation of will, and since we know also that non-organic material phenomena are to be explained in terms of force, the general demand for theoretical economy and uniformity of explanatory principles entails that we should carry across the *same*, volitional, conception of the essence of natural force to the non-organic sphere.

Hartmann's monism

One more element needs to be added before we arrive at Hartmann's full concept of the unconscious, namely Hartmann's *monism*. The ideas just described are compatible with a pluralistic ontology, an irreducible and underived *manifold* of distinct unities of will and representation. Hartmann rules out this possibility on the grounds that we, as a matter of fact, find in the natural and human order chains of teleological connection that converge on a single point (to wit: the creation of conscious life in its maximally developed form, that is, human civilization at the extreme height of its possible development).[26] So again we have an a posteriori argument for a conclusion traditionally derived in a priori fashion.[27] With all of this in position, we have arrived at Hartmann's concept of the unconscious – which he calls the All-One Unconscious, as distinct from the plurality of individuated unconsciousnesses that we discover within individual beings (people, ganglions, etc.).[28] The All-One Unconscious is quite simply that ultimate unity of will and representation which grounds the totality of the phenomena given to us a posteriori as composing the empirical world.

---

[25] *PU* II (C), 178–80 [II (C), 117–19].
[26] See *PU* II (C), ch. VII and *PU* III (C), ch. XIV, esp. 124–5 [II (C), 395–6].
[27] Which leaves a gap in Hartmann's reasoning (common also to physico-theological arguments for monotheism): Hartmann talks of the All-One Unconscious in a way that suggests its *necessary* unity, a claim which cannot be sustained on a finite a posteriori basis. For this reason Hartmann turns in *PU* II (C), ch. VII, to other grounds for monism.
[28] Hartmann makes this distinction clear at *PU* I, 4–5 [I, 3–4]; see also "Vorwort zur 12en. Auflage" [I, xxxviii]. Hartmann's distinction does not correspond to Carus' distinction of "absolute" and "relative" unconsciousnesses, which is closer to Freud's distinction, in

182   Sebastian Gardner

The conceptual character of Hartmann's conception of the unconscious

Some comments on Hartmann's conception of the unconscious. In the first place, Hartmann has clearly *nominalized* the concept – it refers to an individual, a substance, indeed, the *only* individual and substance (hereafter capitalized: the Unconscious). Previous Romantics, with the exception of Carus,[29] had not *consistently* employed the concept of the Unconscious, in place of other concepts such as *Leben* (life) or the Absolute, to indicate the One-and-All.

As regards his differences from Carus, there is at least the difference that Carus does not appeal to the same extensive body of natural scientific evidence as Hartmann.[30] Hartmann's innovation was therefore to recruit a mass of scientific material which would appear to be the rightful property of mechanistic materialists in the mould of Hermann von Helmholtz, in support of ideas associated with *naturphilosophisch* thinkers like Schelling and Carus. Depending on which angle one considers it from, this development is either a case of making *Naturphilosophie* properly "scientific" (Hartmann's own view), or a misappropriation that betrays a culpably erroneous understanding of the nature of science (the view of Hartmann's many contemporary critics), or a travesty of *Naturphilosophie* that cuts it off from its true sources (the view of Hartmann from an orthodox *naturphilosophisch* standpoint).

In any case, to this extent Hartmann's conception of the Unconscious is certainly original. But it is notable that Hartmann does not have an innovative conception of the *nature* or *constitution* of what he calls the Unconscious: his whole emphasis is, on the contrary, on its *continuity*, on the identity of its constitution, with the two fundamental classes of phenomena grasped in ordinary consciousness, namely will and representation.[31] What Hartmann has to say *conceptually* about the intrinsic nature of the Unconscious draws from ordinary thought, and he does not claim that with its discovery we enter a new and *unfamiliar* kind of territory: certainly we come upon new ground, but the landscape is of the sort that is

---

individual psychology, of *Ucs.* and *Pcs.* or of levels within the *Es*; see Carl Gustav Carus, *Psyche: Zur Entwicklungsgeschichte der Seele* (Pforzheim: Flammer und Hoffmann, 1846), 66ff. [Extracts from Part I translated as *Psyche: On the Development of the Soul* (Dallas: Spring, 1989), 52ff.]. On Carus, see also the previous chapter in this volume, by Matthew Bell.

[29] See *PU* I, 38 [I, 32–3].

[30] Though some overlap is to be noted: see, e.g., Carus' comments on the body's self-healing, *Psyche*, 92–5 [*Psyche* (Eng.), 70–2]. On the evidential basis of Carus' philosophy, see Mathew Bell's contribution to this volume.

[31] Clear statements are found at *PU* I, 44 [I, 37]; *PU* I (B), 291–2 [I (B), 252]; *PU* I (A), 126 [I (A), 108]; and *PU* II (C), 81 [II (C), 32].

before our eyes all the time – it does not display a new set of laws, has no oneiric aspect, and certainly does not amount to an irrational or unintelligible realm beyond the reach of discursive thought.[32] On the contrary, what strikes us most, Hartmann insists, is its display of "*rational intelligence*" (*vernünftige Intelligenz*).[33] In this sense Hartmann's conception is *conservative*, not innovative.[34]

Matters are admittedly a bit more complicated, for, although what I have just said applies straightforwardly to the unconscious as multiply individuated, the unconscious as described in Parts (A) and (B) of *Philosophy of the Unconscious*, it does not apply so straightforwardly to the All-One "absolute" Unconscious of Part (C). Thus Part (C) opens with an account of how the Unconscious differs from consciousness. The chief differences stated by Hartmann concern (i) the form of representation: conscious representation is sensory, representation in the Unconscious is non-sensory or intellectual-intuitive;[35] (ii) temporality: the form of existence of conscious mental activity is temporal, that of the Unconscious is non-temporal; and (iii) the relation of will and representation: will and representation "*are united in inseparable unity*" (*in untrennbarer Einheit verbunden*) in the Unconscious,[36] whereas consciousness is able to entertain representations without willing their realization.[37]

These differences are certainly metaphysically deep. But two points need emphasis. First, the differences cited leave untouched the basic identity of the *mode of functioning* of consciousness with that of unconsciousness, namely *the means-end principle of practical reason*. Second, what motivates Hartmann to ascribe these differentiating characteristics to the Unconscious are exclusively *philosophical* considerations deriving from Hartmann's interest in raising the Unconscious, as it emerges from his "inductive" reflections on nature, up to the status of the Absolute as

---

[32] To be sure, Hartmann associates the Philosophy of the Unconscious with mysticism, but in a way that implies the latter's deflation: see *PU* I (B), ch. IX, which concedes nothing to mysticism that a Hegelian would not be happy to allow it.

[33] *PU* II (C), 247 [II (C), 177]. Hartmann reasserts Carus' idea that that which is unconscious *for us* is "*super*-conscious" [*über*bewusste] *for itself* (*PU* II (C), 247 [II (C), 177] and 258 [II (C), 186]), but this entails no new form of rationality.

[34] Brentano claims exactly the contrary (*Psychologie*, 150 [*Psychology*, 107]). To the extent that Brentano has Hartmann's "relative" unconscious in mind, this is a mistake, which appears to result from Brentano's confusion (see *Psychologie*, 151–2 [*Psychology*, 108]) either of the question of homogeneity/heterogeneity with that of psychological/metaphysical status, or of the relative with the absolute Unconscious.

[35] See *PU* II (C), 338 [II (C), 257], and "Vorwort zur 12en. Auflage" [I, xlv].

[36] *PU* II (C), 55 [II (C), 10].

[37] *PU* II (C), ch. I, differentiates the absolute Unconscious from consciousness; *PU* I (B), ch. XI, differentiates the relative unconscious from consciousness.

conceived in monistic objective idealism, in preparation for the worldview that Hartmann will then base on this metaphysics.

This point can be sharpened by considering Hartmann in the light of a well-known conceptual point made by Freud in his metapsychological writings. Every introduction of a concept of the unconscious in a theoretical context, whether psychological or philosophical, stands in need of justification, and this must of course have to do with gains of explanation, whether transcendental (as in Schelling) or empirical-psychological (as in Freud). But the designation "unconscious" does not *of itself* identify a property which turns any explanatory wheels: it merely creates a space for the postulation of something that will do explanatory work, by lifting the epistemological barrier to its postulation set by the item's non-existence in consciousness. Thus Freud insists that the interest of psychoanalysis lies not in its employment of unconsciousness in a merely *descriptive* sense – which, he notes, is old hat – but in its novel *systematic* conception of the formation, content, and causality of the unconscious. And it is often observed that in Freud's metapsychological writings the property of unconsciousness, and appeals to mental processes defined in terms thereof, such as repression, become over time less important for psychoanalytic explanation, and that other concepts, defined with indifference to their conscious/unconscious status, such as phantasy, assume more of the explanatory burden.

There is a further point to be made concerning the contrast between Hartmann and Freud. One of the most philosophically interesting features of psychoanalytic theory concerns its conception of the (metaphysical, non-epistemological) relation of the unconscious to the "I" of self-consciousness and to the person as opposed to the mere human organism. The question is this: Granted that I have no direct knowledge of the contents of my unconscious, can these contents nevertheless be thought to be *mine*, a *part* of me, to *belong* to me, with all that this apparently entails?[38] Whatever the right answer to this question may be,[39] it seems to me beyond doubt that psychoanalysis, correctly understood, *precludes* our thinking of unconscious contents as straightforwardly extra-personal (in the way that my vital organs are external to my personality). Hartmann however *does* claim exactly this extra-personal status for instances of the Unconscious in us: he writes, I may be proud of the work

---

[38] This point is connected with the fact that, whereas for Freud the unconscious is aligned explanatorily with cases of irrationality and abnormality, the opposite is true for Hartmann: the unconscious is tailored to explain the normal case. See Hartmann's remarks on the mental diseases, *PU* I (A), 164–5 [I (A), 141–2].

[39] See my "Psychoanalysis and the Personal/Sub-Personal Distinction," *Philosophical Explorations* 3 (2000): 96–119.

of consciousness, as *my own* deed, but "the fruit of the Unconscious is as it were a gift of the gods, and man only its favoured messenger."[40] Hartmann is not alive to the deep and difficult issue concerning the borders of selfhood with which psychoanalysis is engaged on both its theoretical and practical-therapeutic fronts.

Do these various points reveal a *limitation* of von Hartmann's philosophy? They might well be regarded as such, if Hartmann's philosophy were pretending to offer *original* conceptual materials with which to understand ourselves and the world, or if our measure of the progressiveness of a conception of the unconscious were the degree to which it anticipates the Freudian conception. But neither of these provides the right understanding of Hartmann, whose concerns are in no way proto-Freudian,[41] and who makes no claim for his own fundamental originality – Hartmann's emphasis is always on the way that the materials that he is using have already been worked out and lie ready to hand,[42] his own role being that of a re-organizer of previously tried-and-tested elements.[43] Where he locates his own original philosophical achievement is (in addition to his methodological combination of science with philosophy) in his synthesis of Hegel and Schopenhauer, to which I now turn.

---

[40] [die Leistung des Unbewussten ist gleichsam ein Geschenk der Götter, und der Mensch nur ihr begünstigter Bote]. *PU* I (B), 40 [I (B), 357]. The marked tendency of the *Philosophy of the Unconscious* is to rub out the line separating the personal from the sub-personal and to identify the "I" or person with, as he puts it on *PU* I (A), 78 [I (A), 67], an "indivisible spiritual-corporeal organism" [einheitlichen geistig-leiblichen Organismus], within which the conscious/unconscious distinction is not of ultimate importance. G. Stanley Hall, *Founders of Modern Psychology* (NewYork: D. Appleton and Co., 1924), 186, excogitating Hartmann, writes: "We will, e.g., to move the foot and it is as correct to say it is moved *for* us as that it is moved *by* us. It is done, we know not how, or by what agency." Hartmann's derogation of the "I" and self-consciousness is explicit at *PU* II (C), 78–9 [II (C), 29–30] and 108–13 [II (C), 56–60]. See Hartmann's neurological reduction of the unity of consciousness, *PU* II (C), 113–18 [II (C), 60–4], and rejection of free will, *PU* II (B), 1–2 [I (B), 322]. Carus by contrast is a (Leibnizian) realist about the individual self-conscious self and its freedom: see *Psyche*, part I, 71ff. [*Psyche* (Eng.), 55ff.], and part II.

[41] This point is brought out if Hartmann is contrasted with the later, Freud-influenced figure of Georg Groddeck, whose *Das Buch vom Es: Psychoanalytische Briefe an eine Freundin* (Leipzig: Internationaler Psychoanalytischer Verlag, 1923) revolves around the very same conceptual figure as Hartmann – viz. the idea of our being inhabited and penetrated by an impersonal, trans-individual agency – but who connects this agency tightly with the specific explanation of irrational phenomena in human life.

[42] Hartmann offers detailed accounts of his relations to his predecessors, *PU* I, 16–42 [I, 13–35] and *PU* III (C), 147–59 [II (C), 416–26].

[43] Hartmann says that the principle of the Unconscious has been arrived at by a gradual historical process and that *PU* has only asserted plainly and shown the significance of this principle, and by no means aired it as "a brand-new discovery" [funkelnagelneue Entdeckung]. *PU* I, Addenda, 295–6 [I, Nachträge, 444].

Hartmann's theory of an original synthesis of idea (Hegel) and will (Schopenhauer)

The notion of a synthesis of Hegel and Schopenhauer sounds at first blush bizarre and unpromising, but it is important to recognize that, in the light of Hartmann's guiding preoccupations, it has sound motivation. Hartmann shared with certain other late nineteenth-century German philosophers – among whom may be included Eugen Dühring, Julius Bahnsen, Julius Frauenstädt, and Johannes Volkelt – a broad approach to philosophical enquiry which set them apart from the dominant schools of neo-Kantianism, and which typically involved taking not Kant but rather Hegel, Schelling, and (especially) Schopenhauer as primary historical points of reference. On this basis they pursued what can only be described as the *unfinished business* of German idealism – the argument of Schelling with Hegel, and the (to some extent parallel) argument of Schopenhauer with Fichte, Schelling and Hegel. Their motive for picking up the threads from the first half of the nineteenth century – the reason why those who belonged to the same philosophical tendency as Hartmann directed their concern to earlier idealist thinkers whose reputation, it must be remembered, was far from high post-1850 – lay in the way that, so it seemed, the central metaphysical issues in German idealism allowed nebulous questions of *Weltanschauung* and post-Christian life-orientation, of optimism and pessimism, to be pursued fruitfully. Hartmann's Hegel-Schopenhauer synthesis was calculated, therefore, not primarily to resolve problems of metaphysics, but rather to facilitate a fully comprehensive view of human life, specifically, a *unity* of optimism and pessimism.[44]

The primordial duality and erroneous synthesis of idea and will

What does Hartmann's metaphysical synthesis consist in?[45] If we took Hartmann's teleological metaphysics of nature – the part of his system considered so far – in isolation and asked what it shows regarding the ultimate nature of reality, what we should then expect him to say, is that Will and Idea (representation), although conceptually distinct, form a

---

[44] *PU* III (C), 134 [II (C), 403–4].
[45] The Hegel-Schopenhauer synthesis is referred to repeatedly: see *PU* I, 4–5 [I, 4–5]; *PU* I, 27ff. [I, 23ff.]; *PU* I (A), 117–25 [I (A), 100–7]; *PU* II (C), 55–61 [II (C), 10–15]; *PU* II (C), 181 [II (C), 119–20]; *PU* II (C), 333–4 [II (C), 253–4]; *PU* III (C), 126 [II (C), 396–7]; *PU* III (C), 147 [II (C), 416]; *PU* III (C), 150ff. [II (C), 418ff.]; *PU* III (C), 165 [II (C), 431–2].

primordial unity: in other words, that with respect to the ultimate ground of reality, viz. the absolute Unconscious, the will/representation distinction is a rational or modal but not a *real* distinction. Hartmann's view would then be that what is ontologically basic is a primitive and undecomposable *purposive-striving*, from which the concepts of "will" and "understanding" are abstractions. Hartmann, since he eschewed transcendental reflection, could not have followed Fichte and Schelling in taking it that "activity" – intentional, goal-directed activity – is a *conceptual* primitive in philosophical thought, but he could still have treated it as an *ontological* primitive, and his insistence on so many pages of *Philosophy of the Unconscious* that will and idea are inseparably united seems to demand exactly this view.

Had Hartmann followed this pattern, then his system would have been little more than an attempted restatement on a posteriori grounds of Schelling's *Naturphilosophie*. But this is not his view. Instead, Hartmann declares that Will and Idea (representation) are *in themselves* and at the most fundamental ontological level – meaning: not *in* the world, but in the *pre*-mundane grounds *of* the world – absolutely distinct, absolutely independent, and absolutely heterogeneous. In addition, influenced heavily by the later Schelling, Hartmann associates each of Will and Idea with the two basic and primordially distinct dimensions of all things: Will corresponds to the "Daß" (that) of things, the dimension of sheer existence, and Idea to the "Was" or "Wie" (what or how) of things, the dimension of essence.[46]

This primordial dualism must be overcome, of course, in order for the existence of the world and the Unconscious which is its ground to be possible, but this need for supplementary explanation is for Hartmann not a problem, for it allows him to introduce an explanation for the world's coming-to-be from which it follows (so he claims) that the world *ought not to be*. On this basis Hartmann can then present the soteriological doctrine with which his *Philosophy of the Unconscious* is famously associated: his idea that the existence of the world is a *mistake*, and that the final purpose of natural and human history is its rectification, through the development of a collective human consciousness which, upon achieving insight that the world ought not to be, brings itself and the world to an end, thereby liberating the Idea from the Will, and returning reality to its initial state.[47] The world is thus only a device for cancelling the original synthesis of Will and Idea.

In this way, Hegel and Schopenhauer are synthesized, and shown to have each grasped one side (but only one side) of the truth: Hegel is

---

[46] See *PU* III (C), 125–6 [II (C), 396–7], and (C), ch. XII.
[47] Until, presumably, the process repeats itself: see *PU* III (C), 171–3 [II (C), 437–9].

right that the world and its history is the realization of the Concept, and Schopenhauer is right that the world as representation is a manifestation of Will which, regarded for what it is intrinsically, is purposeless. Hegelian "optimism" regarding the world is squared with Schopenhauerian pessimism: ours is the best of all possible worlds *and yet* its very existence is the worst of all metaphysical possibilities (as is the existence of *any* world, since all worlds presuppose the fusion of Idea and Will). And Hartmann's collective version of Schopenhauer's individualist denial of will can be identified with the consummation of rationality in collective human existence which marks the Hegelian end of history.

Problems of Hartmann's theory of synthesis

From a systematic philosophical point of view, the interesting question is whether Hartmann's synthetic proposal is successful by his own lights: since, if Hartmann is right that the pressure of the opposition of Hegel and Schopenhauer forces us to embrace its rational resolution in the *Philosophy of the Unconscious*, then Hartmann's system must be considered the consummation and true culmination of German idealism.

The decisive issue concerns the story that Hartmann tells about how the original metaphysical mistake, the original "fall" of will and idea which forms the Unconscious and creates the world, takes place. His account, he acknowledges, draws extensively on the late Schelling, whom he considers to have come closer than anyone to the correct synthetic view (but to have failed to bring his insights to a consistent final form, on account of his a priorism and his inability to shake off his attachment to pre-scientific, especially Christian, forms of thought).[48]

Hartmann describes Idea as something that is properly *pre-ontological*,[49] and Will as a potentiality-for-willing[50] which, on account of its character as pure object-less striving, experiences its existence as pain, from which it attempts to free itself by uniting itself with Idea – as if through taking on conceptual structure, the Will could gain for itself a determinate goal, which it could then realize, thereby making the transition from painful longing to pain-free fulfillment. The upshot, however, is only that the eternal bliss of the Idea – the "eternal peace of its being-for-itself"

---

[48] See *PU* III (C), 156 [II (C), 423], and *Schellings Positive Philosophie als Einheit von Hegel und Schopenhauer* (Berlin: Otto Loewenstein, 1869), e.g. 4.

[49] See *PU* III (C), 165 [II (C), 431] and 182 [II (C), 446]. This late Schellingian form of explanation is in Carus too, with the difference that Carus, in neo-Platonic fashion, attributes to the Idea an immediate "desire for existence" [*Werdelust*]: *Psyche*, 52–6 [*Psyche* (Eng.), 43–5].

[50] *PU* III (C), 161ff. [II (C), 428ff.].

[*ewigen Ruhe ihres Fürsichseins*][51] – is destroyed. In Hartmann's figurative or mythological presentation of the philosophical story, the seizing of the female Idea by the male Will is pictured as a sexual act, which issues in the birth of the Unconscious. This child produces the world and determines its history, however, with no other aim than that of undoing the mistake of its own original conception.[52]

Without going further into the detail of Hartmann's synthetic story, it is possible to see why his speculation, for all that it exhibits ingenuity and indisputable metaphysical originality, must be regarded as unsuccessful. First, there is the matter of epistemology. On what basis can we *know* (or even just hold it to be probable) that behind the Unconscious lies an original dis-unity of Will and Idea? Our empirically grounded knowledge appears to stop at the fact of their necessary unity – this fact constitutes "the apex of the pyramid of inductive knowledge"[53] – and Hartmann eschews a supra-empirical method of intellectual intuition. So the teleological metaphysics of nature does not motivate the theory of an original synthesis of Will and Idea.

Hartmann's answer is that there is *indirect* empirical evidence of original dis-unity. This has an unusual source: it stems, according to Hartmann, from our experience of dissatisfaction with our own place in and relation to the world. Hartmann supposes that it is a necessary part of the experience of *being conscious*, that the world is experienced as failing to *measure up*, and that this serves us as a metaphysical clue: if the world is not "as it should be," then there must be some idea in the light of which it is so judged.

It seems Hartmann is right that, if the datum that the world "falls short" were established firmly, then there would be some ground for inferring backwards, for going behind the back of the empirically given and comprehended world, to the original disharmony and hence distinction of Will and Idea which he hypothesizes. The problem, however, is that Hartmann's account of the world's "failure" by the light of conscious experience is shallower and considerably less impressive than that of, say, Kant, who can appeal to our knowledge of the transcendence of Nature by Reason in various spheres (of theoretical reason, morality, the sublime and so on) as grounds for thinking that the empirical world lacks full reality and that a noumenal realm must be posited in addition. Hartmann by contrast appeals exclusively to *hedonic* considerations – the

---

[51] *PU* III (C), 154 [II (C), 422], translation altered.
[52] Hartmann's exposition of the synthesis story is mainly in *PU* II (C), ch. VIII, and *PU* III (C), chs. XIV–XV [II (C), chs. XIV–XV]. There is a hint in Carus too of Hartmann's sexualization: see *Psyche*, 62 [*Psyche* (Eng.), 49].
[53] [die Spitze der Pyramide der inductiven Erkenntniss]. *PU* III (C), 146 [II (C), 415].

empirically discovered preponderance of pain over pleasure in human life – and this, surely, is something for which plain, non-speculative, naturalistic (e.g. evolutionary) explanations are easily available.[54] So a compelling epistemological basis for Hartmann's synthetic theory is lacking.

The *metaphysical* difficulties begin with Hartmann's dualism of fundamental principles. In Descartes' metaphysics – which, it may be noted, Hartmann himself criticizes for its dualistic character[55] – mind and matter both fall under the concept of "created substance." With Hartmann's Will and Idea, by contrast, there is no higher category under which both can be brought, not even that of "existences": Will and Idea are regarded as alien to one another in all thinkable respects. Nor can the relation into which they are brought through their synthesis be rationalized in the way that Spinoza identifies mind and body as double attributes of a single substance, or in the way that Schelling's identity philosophy conceives subjectivity and objectivity, ideality and reality, as different powers of a single indifference point. Nor, again, are Will and Idea contrasted by Hartmann, as they are in Schopenhauer, as reality and appearance. Hartmann's dualism thus goes all the way up,[56] and in consequence there is an aporia concerning how it is possible for anything whatever, let alone a third thing in which Will and Idea are inseparably united, to derive from the original dualism.[57]

Even if this difficulty is held aside, and the sheer possibility of an ontological fusion of absolutely heterogeneous elements is allowed, the synthesis of Will and Idea envisaged by Hartmann encounters a further problem, on account of the specific character of the elements synthesized (a problem of content, as opposed to the previous, purely formal problem). Hartmann insists that the philosophical principles expressed by Will and Idea are, respectively, the *logical* or *rational*, and the *alogical* or anti-logical or *irrational*.[58] This characterization, note, is essential for Hartmann's claim to have united Hegel and Schopenhauer: the contrast of Will and Idea

---

[54] Exposited at great length in *PU* III (C), ch. XIII. See also *PU* III (C), 124–5 [II (C), 395], where the normative repugnance of Will in the eyes of Idea is flatly reduced to a hedonic matter. Hartmann's commitment to hedonistic consequentialism is explicit at *PU* II (C), 364–5 [II (C), 280–1].

[55] *PU* II (C), 86 [II (C), 36].

[56] In *PU* III (C), 187–97 [II (C), 451–60]), Hartmann makes a very late attempt to recast his dualism in monistic form, affirming that his model is Spinoza, and that Will and Idea are distinct attributes of a single substantial whole. This, however, fails to convince, if only because of the difficulty of understanding what meaningful conceptions of "substance" and "attribute" could be in play here.

[57] Hartmann himself states the problem, in one of its several possible formulations, at *PU* III (C), 165 [II (C), 431–2]; his solution is to posit a condition intermediate between potentiality and act.

[58] See e.g. *PU* III (C), 124–5 [II (C), 396–7].

cannot be *merely* of Existence and Reason, for this would take Hartmann only as far as the late Schelling, and Hartmann denies that Schelling's late philosophy provides an *Aufhebung* or sublation of the Hegel-Schopenhauer antinomy.[59] But this immediately suggests a paradox. Under what concept are we to bring (how are we to think) the synthetic unification of Will and Idea? Hartmann wants us to think of it as a *mistake* – as something that *ought not* to have happened (or "been done").[60] But to say this is evidently to situate the event within the space of reasons and so to *give priority* to reason, the Idea, over Will.[61] In fact, the details of Hartmann's synthesis story imply this directly: he suggests that Will commits an *error of judgment* in incarnating itself, which implies that Will is engaged in practical reasoning, which means in turn either that Will and Idea are *not* primordially independent, or that Idea (reason) is prior to Will.[62] If, however, Hartmann were to withdraw his description of the event as a mistake, or even just set this description in inverted commas, then the grounds for pessimism – for thinking of the world as something that ought not to be, the product of an event that ought not to have occurred – would disappear. (And at this point it should be remembered that, as indicated above, pessimism is a necessary epistemological premise of the synthetic theory: the badness of the world is the only reason we have for thinking that Will and Idea are originally disunited.) More generally, it seems that whatever concept we employ to conceive the unification of Will and Idea must belong to and derive from either the sphere of Idea *or* that of Will. If the former, then we are back to a kind of Hegelianism. If the latter, then we have a victory for Schopenhauer over Hegel, and therefore still nothing that bears out Hartmann's claim to have provided a synthesis of the two systems, and furthermore nothing that shows the world to be something that ought not to exist, since if Will's unification with Idea has *no* description in the language of Reason, then it is *just* something that happens – an absolute contingency, with regard to which all normative assessment is out of place.

---

[59] As Hartmann puts it, on his conception Will is Reason's "negative of itself" [das Negative ihrer selbst] (*PU* III (C), 151 [II (C), 419]). Hartmann's pessimism requires this strong construal of the distinction.
[60] See the talk at *PU* III (C), 124–5 [II (C), 396–7], of "mischief done by the irrational Will" [was der unvernünftige Wille schlecht gemacht hat], which is "guilty of the 'That' of the world" [schuld ist an dem "Dass" der Welt].
[61] As Wilhelm Windelband observes, in Hartmann "Hegel has triumphed over Schopenhauer" [hat Hegel über Schopenhauer gesiegt], *Lehrbuch der Geschichte der Philosophie*, 3rd edn. (Tübingen and Leipzig: J. C. B. Mohr, 1903), §46, 547 [*A History of Philosophy*, trans. James H. Tufts (New York: Harper and Row, 1958), vol. II, 674].
[62] *Contra* Hartmann's assertion that the existence of the world was decided by "the act of a *blind* will illuminated by no ray of rational intelligence" [durch den Act eines blinden, von keinem Lichtstrahl der vernünftigen Intelligenz erhellten Willens] (*PU* II (C), 273 [II (C), 200]).

The problem, in other words, is that, although Hartmann denies that there is any higher unity of Will and Idea, and affirms only their lower, derivative unity in the Unconscious, we are required to position ourselves in philosophical reflection *beyond* the original dualism, and to think that duality *as* a unity, insofar as we attempt to grasp the story that Hartmann tells of how Idea and Will are originally confounded; and in thinking *this* unity, it is necessary, moreover, for *either* Will *or* Idea to predominate. (Schelling himself, it may be noted, does not come to grief in this way: the claim of Schelling's identity philosophy of 1802–3 is precisely that final dualities cannot be co-thought in terms other than those of absolute indifference/identity; and in the accounts that Schelling gives later, from the *Freiheitsschrift* of 1809 onwards, Will has priority over Idea or what Schelling calls Reason, *Vernunft*.)

This paradox – an indication that Hegel and Schopenhauer are, after all, not contraries but rather contradictories – represents, I suggest, the fundamental incoherence in the *Philosophy of the Unconscious*, but it is reflected at many other points further down the line where Hartmann can be charged with failing to achieve coherence. For instance: Hartmann maintains that the "proper motive and main purpose" (*eigentlicher Kernpunct und nächster Zweck*) of the creation of consciousness is the independence that it permits of Idea from Will (which is essential for the world's salvation).[63] This is one of the deep points of differentiation allowed by Hartmann of the conscious from the Unconscious: consciousness can entertain representations without also willing them, the Unconscious cannot. The purpose of creating consciousness, Hartmann notes, "would be absurd" (*wäre aber widersinnig*) – consciousness would be "superfluous" (*überflüssig*) – if the Unconscious as such already contained the possibility of the emancipation of Idea from Will.[64] But it appears that exactly this possibility *must* be contained in some form in the Unconscious, in order for the idea of the intellect's independence from the will to figure as a content of the Unconscious's intention. If Idea and Will are, as Hartmann wrote, *"united in inseparable unity"* (*in untrennbarer Einheit verbunden*) in the Unconscious, then it is impossible to explain how the Unconscious can form or even entertain as coherent the possibility of either existing independently of the other:[65] to do so would require the Unconscious to think about itself in counterfactual terms, and possession of this capacity would entail the independence of intellect from will which, according to Hartmann, only consciousness possesses.

---

[63] *PU* II (C), 59 [II (C), 13].
[64] *PU* II (C), 58–9 [II (C), 13].
[65] Hartmann comes closest to discussing this problem at *PU* II (C), 257 [II (C), 185].

Many other points at which it is reasonable to allege incoherence in Hartmann's synthesis story were pointed out by his contemporaries,[66] but I will here end the discussion of its metaphysical difficulties.

Hartmann's criticisms of Schelling, Hegel, and Schopenhauer

Finally, some comment is due on Hartmann's attempt to situate his *Philosophy of the Unconscious* historically, since this forms an important part of his argument. The motivation for Hartmann's theory of synthesis, according to his presentation of it, depends to a considerable degree on the inadequacy of the alternatives as Hartmann sees them, namely, the philosophical systems of early Schelling, Hegel, Schopenhauer, and late Schelling.

A review of everything that Hartmann has to say about these philosophers would take a good deal of space,[67] so I will restrict myself to two observations. First, Hartmann needs to proceed with considerable care in his criticism of his predecessors, since if the strength of his objection rises above a certain level, then it will seem that the right conclusion to draw – and that *had* been drawn, of course, by the overwhelming majority of Hartmann's contemporaries – is that the whole project of idealistic system-building is ill conceived, and that philosophy must follow some other (neo-Kantian, materialist, or whatever) path. Given the severity of Hartmann's misgivings about the design and foundations of his predecessors' systems, it is not at all clear that this condition is met. The particular danger, of course, is that, in endorsing Hegelian criticisms of Schopenhauer, and Schopenhauerian criticisms of Hegel, Hartmann will merely succeed in showing how each cancels the other out, leaving nothing behind to build upon.

Second, insofar as we agree with Hartmann that the salient historical legacy is the Hegel–Schopenhauer antinomy, and that its resolution defines the present task of philosophy, the direction in which we are pointed is no doubt, as Hartmann says, late Schelling. A lot hangs therefore on Hartmann's criticisms of Schelling's late, "positive," philosophy.

---

[66] See, e.g., N. Kurt, *Wahrheit und Dichtung in den Hauptlehren Eduard von Hartmanns* (Leipzig: Friedrich Fleischer, 1894), 24ff., and Julius Bahnsen, *Der Widerspruch im Wissen und Wesen der Welt: Princip und Einzelbewährung der Realdialektik*, 2 vols. (Berlin: Theobald Grieben, 1880), vol. II, 209.

[67] For a selection of Hartmann's criticisms of Schelling, see *PU* I, 24–6 [I, 20–3]; *PU* II (C), 333 [II (C), 253]; *PU* III (C), 156–9 [II (C), 423–6]. Of Hegel: *PU* I, 27–9 [I, 23–4]; *PU* II (C), 333–4 [II (C), 253–4]; *PU* III (C), 150–5 [II (C), 418–23]. Of Schopenhauer: *PU* I, 29–31 [I, 24–6]; *PU* I (A), 117–19 [I (A), 101–2]; *PU* II (C), 339–43 [II (C), 258–61]; *PU* III (C), 149–51 [II (C), 418–19].

If Hartmann's alternative to late Schelling proves incoherent, then Schelling's position is vindicated as representing the furthest that one can (or need) go in the direction of accommodating the reality of the extra-logical from an absolute idealist standpoint.

Hartmann's relations to idealism, naturalism, and critical philosophy

I have argued that Hartmann's system divides, on the one hand, into a monistic teleological metaphysics of nature – which has some degree of originality and which, whatever its weaknesses, at least hangs together coherently – and on the other, a dualistic synthetic theory, which is highly original but unsuccessful. For this last reason, Hartmann is not usually numbered among the great absolute idealists: philosophers who are interested from a systematic point of view in post-Hegelian developments in absolute idealism typically turn to the British and American idealists, without stopping to look at Hartmann. The third part of Hartmann's system, the world-view, collapses along with the synthetic theory.

We may now ask what has gone wrong at bottom in Hartmann's philosophical endeavor. It is natural for us, in view of our present-day philosophical outlook, to suppose that the root problem with Hartmann must lie in his attempt to yoke together the contradictory positions of naturalism on the one hand and idealism on the other; and it is generally true that the interaction of naturalistic and non-naturalistic – idealist, transcendentalist – elements is responsible for much in, and can explain many of the distinctive features of, late nineteenth-century German philosophy.

This assessment of Hartmann is, however, not straightforwardly correct. As regards the naturalism/anti-naturalism opposition, Hartmann is quite clear where he stands: he is on the side of idealism, and he is furthermore right to think that absolute idealism is capable of supporting an image of reality that integrates the results of natural science with metaphysics and that coincides on some points with naturalism, as it does in Schelling and Hegel. And while it is true, or so I suggested, that Hartmann's naturalistic methodology renders his position weak as regards its *justification*, it does not render it *incoherent*. The "naturalism *vs.* idealism" opposition is not, therefore, the proximate source of Hartmann's problems.

Instead, one might seek to lay the blame for the infelicity of Hartmann's system on the *non-critical* character of his realism – his rejection of, or indifference to, the whole transcendental idea that metaphysical speculation needs to be conditioned by reflection on the conditions under which metaphysical knowledge is possible, and that speculation which is not shaped in that way puts itself at the mercy of transcendental illusion and thus tends to incoherence. On this account, Hartmann's problem is his imperfect, epistemologically naïve appropriation of the idealist legacy.[68]

This would be a standard Kantian or German idealist critical take on Hartmann. However, and aside from the fact that this explanation will seem correct only to those who have faith in the original idealist project, it seems unlikely that this is the whole story, for we should still want to know *why* Hartmann decided against taking up the transcendentalist orthodoxy, his departure from which cannot be reduced to a mere misunderstanding. In the next section I will suggest that, when we reflect on the reception of Hartmann's ideas, another and more interesting diagnostic possibility comes into view.

Hartmann's world-view and its positive reception

Hartmann's extraordinary popular success was recognized as puzzling (and deplored) by his neo-Kantian contemporaries. Lange writes:

[I]t remains a remarkable fact that so soon after the campaign of our Materialists against the whole of philosophy, a [i.e. Hartmann's] system could find so much acceptance, which opposes itself more decidedly to the positive sciences than any of the earlier systems, and which in this respect repeats all the errors of Schelling and Hegel in a much coarser and more palpable shape.[69]

Windelband too describes the Hartmann phenomenon, with a hint of exasperation, as "remarkable and dubious" (*verwunderlich und bedenklich*). More precisely, Windelband suggests that, whereas the historically earlier positive reception of Schopenhauer's pessimism can be attributed to social and political circumstance – the disappointment of expectations of liberal reform – the wave of philosophical pessimism which followed in Hartmann's wake in the 1870s has no such excuse, and he goes on

---

[68] Hartmann claims to be critical, but appears to confound this with being fallibilistic and probabilistic: see *Neukantianismus, Schopenhauerianismus und Hegelianismus in ihrer Stellung zu den philosophischen Aufgaben der Gegenwart* (Berlin: Carl Duncker, 1877), 28. Hartmann rejects self-consciousness as a principle of philosophical explanation: see, e.g. his objection to Lotze's putting "Fürsichsein" in place of "Wille," in *Lotzes Philosophie* (Leipzig: Wilhelm Friedrich, 1888), 156ff. Heinz Heinrichs, in *Die Theorie des Unbewußten in der Psychologie von Eduard von Hartmann* (Bonn: Verein Studentenwohl, 1933), 28ff., diagnoses Hartmann's errors as stemming from his inadequate conception of the "Ich."

[69] [bleibt es bemerkenswerth, dass schon so bald nach dem Feldzuge unsrer Materialisten gegen die gesammte Philosophie ein System bedeutenden Anklang finden konnte, welches sich zu den positiven Wissenschaften in einen schrofferen Gegensatz stellt als irgend eines der früheren, und welches in dieser Beziehung alle Fehler eines Schelling und Hegel in weit gröberer und handgreiflicherer Form wiederholt]. Lange, *Geschichte des Materialismus*, 283–4 [*History of Materialism*, book II, sect. 2, ch. 4, 79–80].

to describe the manner in which Hartmann's "brilliant but misleading" (*blendende und verblendende*) *Philosophy of the Unconscious* achieved domination of popular philosophical literature, as "a manifestation of relaxation and surfeit" (*eine Erschlaffungs- und Uebersättigungserscheinung*) at the present stage of civilization.[70] Windelband's suggestion of decadence surrounding the *Philosophy of the Unconscious* certainly has the ring of truth, but if we are to regard it as anything more than an extrinsic matter, pertaining to the circumstances of Hartmann's reception but not to the content of his thought, then we need to nail down more precisely what it is in virtue of which his philosophy might be considered an expression of cultural decay.

Now one of the most striking dimensions of Hartmann's *Philosophy of the Unconscious* – which I have left until last – concerns its purported practical, ethical and religious upshot. I said earlier that the late nineteenth-century tendency to which Hartmann belongs was guided by a concern with "life orientations,"[71] and Hartmann expressed confidence that the *Philosophy of the Unconscious* would answer to man's religious needs, which he regarded as abiding, legitimate, and neglected by the philosophies of his contemporaries, even entertaining the hope that the *Philosophy of the Unconscious* would help to elicit the formation of a new religion.[72] However, I think it is clear to all readers of Hartmann that the *Philosophy of the Unconscious* fails utterly in this respect. It simply has no existential grip. In stark contrast to his idealist predecessors, Hartmann's metaphysics fail to give articulate form to anything deep in the human situation.

In support of this judgment, consider first the way in which Hartmann's practical philosophy demands a *total* self-transcendence for which no intelligible motivational root is (or can be) provided. Hartmann requires us to take up directly the point of view of the universe – indeed, a point of view *before* the metaphysical beginning of the universe – and to identify, as constituting the Good for us, the welfare of an "object," the Idea, to which

---

[70] Windelband, *Lehrbuch*, §46, 546 [*A History of Philosophy*, vol. 2, 673]. Windelband was not exaggerating Hartmann's success: studies devoted to Hartmann, in English and German, appeared regularly from the 1870s right into the early twentieth century; according to one source, their number in 1892 stood at "over 1000"; see Hartmann, *The Sexes Compared and other Essays*, trans. A. Kenner (London: Swan Sonnenschein, 1895), Translator's Preface, iii.

[71] Hartmann describes the solution of ethical problems as the "most important test for the verifying" of philosophical systems, *PU* I, Preface to 8th edn., xxx.

[72] See Hartmann, *Die Religion des Geistes* (Berlin: Carl Duncker, 1882) [*The Religion of the Future*, trans. Ernest Dare (London: W. Stewart & Co. 1886)]. Hartmann describes himself as synthesizing the Christian and Indian religions (*PU* I, Preface to 9th edn., xxxvii), and his philosophy as the philosophical "purification" (*Begriffsläuterung*) of theism (*PU* II (C), 271 [II (C), 198]).

not even existence can be attributed.[73] Hartmann's argument for this conception of the Good proceeds by elimination, but what he seems to fail to recognize is that, if the elimination of all other candidates for the final purpose of mankind leaves nothing but the beatitude of the Idea, then the more plausible conclusion to be drawn is that human beings are in fact without any purpose whatever: we may as well accept the instruction to concern ourselves with, or be reassured to learn that our lives ultimately contribute to, the happiness of the system of natural numbers, as affirm that human history will achieve its inherent end when it has allowed conceptuality to withdraw from nature. Hartmann simply does not see how remote his proposal lies from the comparatively more intelligible, reflexively contentful, and existentially engaged forms of self-transcendence urged by Spinoza, Schelling, and Schopenhauer.

Nietzsche's assessment of Hartmann in *Beyond Good and Evil* (*Jenseits von Gut und Böse*, 1886) draws the contrast between the type of philosopher found among the ancients – a Heraclitus, Plato, or Empedocles – and contemporary representatives of philosophy such as the "*Amalgamist*" Hartmann, who find themselves, "thanks to fashion, as much on top as they are really at the bottom."[74] The latter, Nietzsche says, are

all losers who have been *brought back* under the hegemony of science, after having desired *more* of themselves at some time without having had the right to this "more" and its responsibilities – and who now represent, in word and deed, honorably, resentfully, and vengefully, the *unbelief* in the masterly task and masterfulness of philosophy.[75]

---

[73] See *PU* III (C), 123–4 [II (C), 394–5], where Hartmann identifies the Good strictly with a state of happiness. Hartmann's claim that what really matters most to us is the beatitude of the super-human Idea reflects his repudiation of the first-person standpoint; this Hartmann tends to identify with egoism, and so supposes it to be overcome through the rejection of egoism: see *PU* III (C), 133–4 [II (C), 402–3]. For a summary of Hartmann's ethical and political argument, see W. Caldwell, "Von Hartmann's Moral and Social Philosophy I – The Positive Ethic," and "Von Hartmann's Moral and Social Philosophy II – The Metaphysic," *Philosophical Review* 8 (1899): 589–603 and 465–83; see esp. 594, regarding Hartmann's claim that I should identify myself with God for the sake of God's happiness.

[74] Friedrich Nietzsche, *Beyond Good and Evil: Prelude to a Philosophy of the Future*, trans. Walter Kaufmann (New York: Vintage, 1966), 123. [Dank der Mode ebenso oben-auf als unten-durch sind]. *Jenseits von Gut und Böse: Vorspiel einer Philosophie der Zukunft*, §204, *Werke: Kritische Gesamtausgabe*, ed. Giorgio Colli *et al.* (Berlin and New York: De Gruyter, 1967-), part 6, vol. II, 135.

[75] Nietzsche, *Beyond Good and Evil*, 123. [das sind ja allesammt Überwundene und unter die Botmässigkeit der Wissenschaft *Zurückgebrachte*, welche irgendwann einmal mehr von sich gewollt haben, ohne ein Recht zu diesem "mehr" und seiner Verantwortlichkeit zu haben – und die jetzt, ehrsam, ingrimmig, rachsüchtig, den *Unglauben* an die Herren-Aufgabe und Herrschaftlichkeit der Philosophie mit Wort und That repräsentiren]. *Werke*, part 6, vol. II, 135.

The late nineteenth-century, post-Schopenhauerian optimism/pessimism debate, with which Hartmann is so deeply preoccupied, Nietzsche dismisses elsewhere as a "priestly squabble" (*Pfaffenstreit*).[76]

Though Nietzsche's standards for a genuine philosophical spirit are higher than most and his conception of the task of philosophy is far from orthodox, Nietzsche's estimates are persuasive: while certainly the *echo* can be heard in Hartmann of a truly deep and demanding philosophical task, the way that Hartmann has tried to execute it shows it to have been drained of genuine import. The existential roots of the optimism/pessimism debate lie in the antinomial experience which we have of the distinctness and irreconcilability of, as Wittgenstein put it, the worlds of the happy man and the unhappy man, and in the *practical* necessity of life in the face of suffering, to which corresponds the *practically motivated* philosophical task of answering the objection that suffering puts, or appears to put, to life. Whereas Nietzsche devoted his philosophical endeavors to defining a standpoint which could claim to have genuinely transcended the antinomy and answered the objection, Hartmann handles the issue of optimism *vs.* pessimism in merely *wissenschaftlich* terms, as if it were merely an opposition within *theoretical* reason that simply poses a formal problem for the construction of a systematic, "scientific" conception of reality – a conflict of two rival natural-scientific or metaphysical hypotheses concerning the nature of the world.

And yet, Hartmann's *Philosophy of the Unconscious*, instead of falling stillborn from the press, captured Europe's imagination.[77] Why did this happen?

Pursuing Nietzsche's suggestion, it may be supposed that Hartmann's pessimistic world-view had its appeal not in spite of but *because of* its failure to turn any genuine motivational wheels in its readership: it answered to a state of deep dissatisfaction in European high culture by furnishing a representation, a *Weltbild*, to which that diffuse negative affect could attach itself, and in which it could be felt to have received expression, but it did so without bringing to light, and it even served to deflect insight into, the real causes or grounds of the malaise. The practical and existential nullity of Hartmann's ethics and "religion," the fact that in reality it demands nothing from us, reflects his philosophy's function of passively certifying, without interrogating or genuinely putting to the test,

---

[76] Nietzsche, *Philosophy and Truth: Selections from Nietzsche's Notebooks of the Early 1870s*, ed. and trans. Daniel Breazeale (Atlantic Highlands, NJ: Humanities Press, 1979), 101. From *Nachlaß* (1873), *Werke*, part 3, vol. II, 331.

[77] As Hartmann himself put it: his work fed "a *fierce philosophical hunger* on the part of the public at large, concealed beneath the extreme apathy in regard to philosophical enquiries" (*PU* I, Preface to 7th edn., xx).

the discontent of European high culture. In this way it is appropriate to regard the *Philosophy of the Unconscious* as a *symptom* in the Nietzschean-Freudian sense.

It seems fair to conclude that, contrary to Hartmann's order of presentation of his ideas, what fundamentally determines the structure of his thinking is his world-view, and that his appropriation of absolute idealist metaphysics to the end of promulgating a *Weltanschauung* which in fact repudiates, even more thoroughly than Schopenhauer, all of the basic and inspirational elements of German idealism – its commitment to freedom, autonomy, subjectivity, self-consciousness – is what is ultimately responsible for the skewed character of the *Philosophy of the Unconscious*. In this more subtle sense, there is arguably some truth in the idea that Hartmann manifests the unresolved contradiction, which runs through nineteenth-century German philosophy, of naturalism and anti-naturalistic idealism.

Be that as it may, as regards the history of the concept of the unconscious, the by-product of Hartmann's endeavor was a conception of the unconscious more sober, more systematically elaborated, and considerably closer than its ancestors in *Romantik* and *Naturphilosophie* to modern materialistic-mechanistic science. In this way, though quite independently of his intentions, Hartmann indisputably helped to prepare the way for Freud.[78]

---

[78] I am grateful to Angus Nicholls for helpful editorial suggestions, and to the Arts and Humanities Research Council and the Philosophy Department of University College London for research leave that allowed me to complete this paper.

8 Gustav Theodor Fechner and the unconscious

Michael Heidelberger[1]
Translated by Simon Thomas

In his 1873 review of Eduard von Hartmann's *Philosophy of the Unconscious* (*Philosophie des Unbewussten*, 1868), Rudolf Haym attributed to the idea of the unconscious a contribution to the emergence of German idealism equal to that made by the philosophy of Kant. "Out of the stimulating contact between the intellectual views and intuitions of Jacobi, Goethe and Herder [in relation to the unconscious] and the Kantian philosophy as it was refined by Fichte," he wrote, "there grew the thoroughly idealistic systems of Schelling and Hegel."[2] According to Haym, the idea of the unconscious, which was most explicitly discernible among the aforementioned figures, surfaced in the second half of the eighteenth century "under the influence of the sensualist views of the English and the French" and then as now demanded that the "rights of the emotions as opposed to those of the understanding, of natural talent as opposed to acquired skill, of the original powers of the mind as opposed to those of statutes and rules" once again be recognized. The idea of the unconscious, Haym argued, directed itself "against the one-sided arrogance of rationality [and] against the over-valuation of that which is conscious, contrived, and reflected."[3] For Haym, the major contrast between his own

---

[1] All quotations are from the first cited edition of any particular work. In the case of some original sources which are not easily available, I have also given bibliographical details of reprint editions and/or translations.
[2] [Aus der befruchtenden Berührung der geistvollen Gesichtspunkte und Anschauungen von Jacobi, Goethe und Herder [in Bezug auf das Unbewusste], mit der von Fichte zugespitzten Kant'schen Philosophie erwuchsen die durch und durch idealistischen Systeme Schellings und Hegels.] Rudolf Haym, "Die Hartmann'sche Philosophie des Unbewußten." *Preußische Jahrbücher* 31: 1–3 (1873): (1): 41–80; (2): 109–39, (3): 257–311; here 1: 42.
[3] [unter dem Einfluss der sensualistischen Ansichten der Engländer und Franzosen]; [Rechte des Gefühls gegen die des Verstandes, der natürlichen Begabung gegen die erworbene Fertigkeit, ursprünglicher Geistesmacht gegen die der Satzung und der Regel]; [gegen einseitigen Verstandeshochmuth, gegen die Ueberschätzung des Bewussten, Gemachten, Reflektirten]. Ibid., 43, 42.

period (that of the 1870s) and the time of Jacobi, Goethe, and Herder lay precisely in relation to German idealism: while German idealism still lay in front of the early thinkers of the unconscious like Jacobi, Goethe, and Herder, its contemporary representatives had it behind them and therefore had to acknowledge its weaknesses, especially in the light of empirical science. "In fact," he observed,

the shadows of Schelling's and Hegel's systems loom everywhere in the new conception of the world unrolling before our eyes, but they proved themselves to be powerless to provide protection against the approaching undertow of materialism.[4]

Hartmann and German philosophy in the 1870s

In order to be able to assess what a philosophy of the unconscious meant for the last third of the nineteenth century, one must grasp the course of development taken by philosophy in Germany since what Hans Vaihinger termed the "great crisis of Hegelian philosophy."[5] Not only did the systems of Hegel and Schelling "collapse," as the *topos* goes, time and again, but there began a period of complete contempt for philosophy which found its expression in the materialism of the middle of the century. Philosophy was thus often equated *per definitionem* with anti-materialism, as the great critic of idealism, Haym, puts it in the previous quotation. The rebirth of philosophy in the late 1860s and 1870s is, to a considerable extent, to be seen as an attempt to develop a *new* idealism, one that might avoid the mistakes of the old. But there were also efforts to develop an intellectually sophisticated philosophy through collaboration with the empirical sciences and/or with historiography, a philosophy which would be compatible with the sciences without at the same time falling into the dogmatic materialism of the age. The attempts made by Hermann von Helmholtz and Friedrich Albert Lange to understand the physiological theory of perception as a philosophical epistemology is perhaps the best known move in this direction, which ultimately led to the "scientific philosophy" of the time.

Hartmann's *Philosophy of the Unconscious* offered the following innovations: first, and for the first time since German idealism, it recreated a

---

[4] [Ueberall zwar ragen ihre Schatten [d.h. der Systeme Schellings und Hegels] in das neue vor unseren Augen sich aufrollende Weltbild hinein, aber sie erweisen sich ohnmächtig, vor dem niederziehenden Geist des Materialismus zu schützen.] Ibid., 45.
[5] Hans Vaihinger, *Hartmann, Dühring und Lange: Zur Geschichte der deutschen Philosophie im XIX. Jahrhundert: Ein kritischer Essay* (Iserlohn: J. Baedeker, 1876). See also Klaus Christian Köhnke, *Entstehung und Aufstieg des Neukantianismus: Die deutsche Universitätsphilosophie zwischen Idealismus und Positivismus* (Frankfurt am Main: Suhrkamp, 1986). Trans. R. J. Hollingdale as *The Rise of Neo-Kantianism: German Academic Philosophy between Idealism and Positivism* (Cambridge: Cambridge University Press, 1991).

philosophical "system" with an ideological character, in which the absolute spirit of Hegel and the unconscious were united. Second, it elaborated a philosophy which claimed for itself compatibility with modern natural science, as the sub-title of his principal work already announces: "Speculative Results According to the Inductive Method of Natural Science" (*Spekulative Resultate nach inductiv-naturwissenschaftlicher Methode*). Third, it offered a philosophy which rendered materialism harmless, "while acknowledging it within certain limits and contractually employing it in its service," as Haym put it. And finally, it provided a theoretical standpoint which, with the region of the unconscious, provided "a counterweight to the exclusive appreciation of conscious reason."[6]

As publicly well received as Hartmann's philosophy was, it also aroused little approval among academic philosophers. For Haym, Hartmann's philosophy of the unconscious was "nothing other than *a mythology in disguise*, a materialism or Spinozism that turns back to the mythological," and which takes natural appearances to be "mental powers" (*geistige Mächte*) "that are somehow or other perceived to be analogous to the mind of the viewer." Although he conceded that this system stood with one foot "completely on the ground of modern science," he saw the other foot as resting "on the ground of mystical-scholastic speculation, on the ground of the most abstruse, medieval realism."[7] Friedrich Albert Lange, who, through his "History of Materialism" (*Geschichte des Materialismus*, 1873–5), contributed much, and perhaps even decisively, to the popularity of philosophy, and especially of Neo-Kantianism, reacted more harshly: like an Australian Aborigine (*Australneger*), according to Lange, Hartmann attributed everything that he could not explain to "devil-devil" (the name of a native god), in other words: to the "unconscious." Lange continues in his sarcastic tone:

Yet the Australian Aborigine and the philosopher stop where their powers of natural explanation break off, and attribute everything which remains to a new principle, through which everything is explained, in a highly satisfying manner, by a single word.[8]

---

[6] [indem sie ihn in bestimmten Grenzen anerkenne und contractlich in Dienst und Pflicht nehme]; [ausschließlichen Schätzung der bewußten Vernunft ein Gegengewicht]. Haym, "Die Hartmann'sche Philosophie des Unbewußten," 44.

[7] [nichts Anderes als eine *verschämte Mythologie*, ein in's Mythologische zurückgewendeter Materialismus oder Spinozismus]; [geistige Mächtige ... die irgendwie nach den Analogie des eignen Geistes vorgestellt werden]; [ganz und gar auf dem Boden der modernen Naturwissenschaft]; [auf dem Boden mystisch-scholastischer Speculation, auf dem Boden des abstrusesten mittelalterlichen Realismus]. Ibid., 45, 120.

[8] [Der Australneger aber und der Philosoph machen da halt, wo ihr Vermögen natürlicher Erklärung aufhört und schieben den ganzen Rest auf ein neues Prinzip, mit welchem alles durch ein einziges Wort höchst befriedigend erklärt ist.] Friedrich Albert Lange,

The critiques of Haym and Lange were combined with that of the Strasbourg Darwinist Oscar Schmidt, who with cool objectivity picked Hartmann's theory to pieces from the standpoint of natural science.[9] At the same time, the Berlin philosopher Eugen Dühring called Hartmann's work a "sideshow of American spiritualism" (*Seitenstück des Amerikanischen Spiritismus*), alluding to the American Henry Slade, who at that time was arranging sensational séances in Germany. Dühring did not mince his words: "sham mysticism" (*Schwindelmystik*), "spiritualistic belief in ghosts" (*spiritistischer Gespensterglaube*), "rubbish-heap of the weakest waste-products of Schopenhauerian idiocies" (*Abort der schwächsten Abfälle der Schopenhauerschen Idiotismen*), "high nonsense" (*höherer Blödsinn*) and "metaphysical humbug" (*metaphysischer Humbug*) represent just a selection of the strong language he directed against Hartmann's work.[10]

Under these circumstances, whoever within academic philosophy or natural science seriously wanted to hold onto the concept of the unconscious had to seek out other approaches. The two alternatives to Hartmann that entered the equation were offered by Arthur Schopenhauer (1788–1860) and Gustav Theodor Fechner (1801–87). Although Schopenhauer's philosophy in fact commended itself as an original and comparatively moderate starting point for Hartmann's philosophy, one that was free of Hegelian speculation, it presented no real alternative. In 1876, the energetic young philosopher Hans Vaihinger (1852–1933) led contemporary German philosophy – along with its most significant representatives Hartmann, Dühring, and Lange – back to its Schopenhauerian roots. Like others, Vaihinger opted to side against Hartmann, in whom (as in the case of Eugen Dühring) he viewed Schopenhauer's philosophy as having turned into dogmatism. Vaihinger thus declared his support not for Hartmann, but for Albert Lange, whom he saw as refraining from all systematic philosophy, and as establishing, through his considered critique of materialism, a standpoint which could be adopted by natural scientists. According to Vaihinger, another distinguishing characteristic of Lange was the way in which he dismissed Schopenhauer's pessimism and his teachings on the will.

Apart from Lange, it was thus really only Fechner who still remained. As with Fechner's work overall, his conception of the unconscious was

---

Geschichte des Materialismus und Kritik seiner Bedeutung in der Gegenwart, 2nd edn., 2 vols. (Iserlohn: Baedeker,1873–5). Cited according to reprint in 2 vols., ed. Alfred Schmidt (Frankfurt am Main: Suhrkamp, 1974), vol. II, 772.

[9] Oscar Schmidt, *Die naturwissenschaftlichen Grundlagen der Philosophie des Unbewussten* (Leipzig: F. A. Brockhaus, 1877).

[10] Eugen Dühring, *Kritische Geschichte der Philosophie von ihren Anfängen bis zur Gegenwart*, 3rd edn. (Leipzig: Fues, 1878), 523–7.

Janus-faced: it played a role in both his scientific psychophysics and in his speculative philosophy.[11] It made possible a serious scientific research program, as well as the continuation of a comparatively speculative philosophy. The Janus-faced character of Fechner's work led, and is moreover still leading today, to two fundamentally different interpretations. On the one hand, one saw and still sees his philosophy (as Fechner did himself) as a speculative extension of a serious scientific point of departure, one free from philosophical assumptions. From this perspective, one can then reject Fechner's philosophical continuation of his empirical starting-point as being too speculative, without having to give up his scientific theories. On the other hand, one could infer his work in natural sciences from his speculative philosophy, and also view with suspicion the psychophysical works as well as the philosophy of science connected with it. I have tried to show elsewhere that Fechner's work does in fact contain a rational core which is scientifically tenable, and which can be justified independently of the wilder, more speculative strands of his metaphysics. As will become clear, when it came to the foundations of his science (i.e. that of psychophysics), Fechner was even more critical of metaphysics than were his contemporaries.[12]

At first glance, it was difficult for many of Fechner's contemporaries to differentiate between his theory and the respective theories of von Hartmann, Schopenhauer and others. Those who made the effort, however, to immerse themselves in Fechner's work could see that Fechner's point of departure was scientifically serious, or at least far less metaphysically suspicious and compromising than those of von Hartmann and Schopenhauer. This is not to deny that the rational core of Fechner's philosophy of nature, as he himself stated, also originally emerged (at least in part) out of his fantasies regarding the world-soul. But just as the emergence of Newton's concept of force out of (among other things) alchemico-theological speculation does not speak against its fruitful deployment in mechanics (and the history of science readily admits of many similar cases), so too is Fechner's panpsychism neither an argument against the scientific status of his psychophysics (i.e. his mind-body theory), nor against his concept of the unconscious.

---

[11] See Mai Wegener, "Das psychophysische Unbewusste – Gustav Theodor Fechner und der Mond," *Das Unbewusste*, ed. Michael B. Buchholz and Günter Gödde, vol. I: *Macht und Dynamik des Unbewussten. Auseinandersetzungen in Philosophie, Medizin und Psychoanalyse* (Gießen: Psychosozial Verlag, 2005), 240–61.

[12] See Michael Heidelberger, *Nature from Within: Gustav Theodor Fechner's Psychophysical Worldview*, trans. Cynthia Klohr (Pittsburgh, PA: University of Pittsburgh Press, 2004), ch. 6. Translation of *Die innere Seite der Natur: Gustav Theodor Fechners wissenschaftlich-philosophische Weltauffassung* (Frankfurt am Main: Klostermann, 1993).

Fechner's "psychophysical parallelism"

Before we can present Fechner's treatment of the unconscious and its historical background, an excursus into his "psychophysical parallelism" – that is, into his solution to the mind-body problem, which characterizes his entire work – is necessary.[13] The expression "psychophysical parallelism" did not, incidentally, originate with Fechner, but later gained widespread acceptance in the German-speaking world, probably via the work of Wilhelm Wundt (1832–1920). As an alternative to the Cartesian dualism between thinking and extended substance, psychophysical parallelism forms the premise for Fechner's conception of the unconscious, even for his entire thought.[14] There are three different versions of psychophysical parallelism, seldom differentiated from one another,[15] which must be distinguished according to the strength of their philosophical content. From the 1860s, a first version of psychophysical parallelism, which was free of philosophical speculation, very quickly adapted itself to the prevailing bases of all those sciences which in one form or another dealt with the psychical field. As such, it represented an important point of reference not only for Fechner's work, but for all relevant nineteenth-century science in general. The second and third versions of psychophysical parallelism are concerned with providing the most philosophically rational and empirically plausible *completion* of the initial version; the second version with reference to the mind-body problem; the third version with regard to the philosophy of nature.

Fechner assumes that progress in philosophy and in all of the empirical sciences dealing with the psychical realm depends on a solution to the mind-body problem, or, as Fechner prefers to put it, to the connection between psychical and physical appearances. However, this solution may not, from the beginning, be taken for granted in the sciences, but must over the course of time arise from empirical findings. In order to have a possible solution at all, a basic methodological consensus must be provided that is both free of metaphysics and can be accepted by all participating scientific parties. Without such a consensus, there exists the danger that an approach is established from the start which is incompatible with

---

[13] For further details on this question see Heidelberger, "The Mind-Body Problem in the Origin of Logical Empiricism: Herbert Feigl and Psychophysical Parallelism," *Logical Empiricism: Historical and Contemporary Perspectives*, ed. Paolo Parrini and Wesley Salmon (Pittsburgh, PA: University of Pittsburgh Press, 2003), 233–62.
[14] For the benefit of Anglophone readers, it should be stressed that the expression "parallelism" as used here has nothing historically to do with occasionalism or with Leibniz's teachings concerning pre-established harmony.
[15] This tripartite division is not itself explicit in Fechner's thought, but is nevertheless helpful in keeping the different strands of Fechner's thought separate from one another.

other approaches, and which consequently makes impossible any agreement obtained through the facts. But when a common empirical basis is available to all the sciences concerned with the psychical realm, then a rational decision concerning the question of the mind-body problem can gradually, through collective endeavor, be reached.

Fechner believed he had found just such a point of departure in the first version of psychophysical parallelism. In this context, Fechner argues as follows: in order to reach the stated goal of a solution to the mind-body problem, two different issues must be clarified. First, it must be clear as to what can count as empirical knowledge in the psychical sphere. Second, an expression for the facts, as well as for the laws concerning the relationships between them, must be found; an expression which, in regard to the connection between mind and body, avoids any metaphysical interpretation which might exceed the bounds of empirical knowledge. It was precisely the lack of such a commonly accepted expression which had hitherto led to divisions within the field.

With reference to the first requirement, Fechner, like many others, takes the objects of inner perception to be the basis of psychology. He refers to these objects as "inner" or "psychical appearances." In the German context this means, on the one hand, the rejection of the eighteenth-century faculty psychology of Christian Wolff; and on the other hand, the refusal to admit the existence of the soul as substance. In his rejection of faculty psychology, Fechner follows the philosopher Johann Friedrich Herbart (1776–1841), who, as Wundt put it, counted "the critical destruction of the doctrine of the faculties as being among his greatest accomplishments."[16] Herbart rejected as arbitrary and lacking in explanatory power the a priori assumption of the soul faculties in psychology. According to Herbart, the hypothesis that the faculties exert effects upon one another suggests a war between all of the faculties, and makes a mockery of any rational approach to theory. Instead, one would have to discover a psychical mechanism which could, already on the basis of the interaction between representations, make plausible as secondary phenomena both the emergence and the number of the faculties. For Herbart, the "facts of consciousness, as well as the inner perception that they provide,"[17] form the point of departure for psychology. In this

---

[16] [der die kritische Vernichtung der Vermögenslehre zu seinen besten Ruhmestaten zählt]. Wilhelm Wundt, "Die Psychologie im Beginn des zwanzigsten Jahrhunderts," *Die Philosophie im Beginn des zwanzigsten Jahrhunderts: Festschrift für Kuno Fischer*, ed. Wilhelm Windelband (Heidelberg, 1904), 184.

[17] [Thatsachen des Bewusstseins, so wie die innere Wahrnehmung sie darbietet]. Johann Friedrich Herbart, *Psychologie als Wissenschaft: Neu gegründet auf Erfahrung, Metaphysik und Mathematik: Erster, synthetischer Theil* (Königsberg: Unzer, 1824), 8. Reprinted in

respect, according to Herbart, "psychology has an immeasurable claim upon the manifold facts of consciousness ... which general metaphysics leaves untouched."[18]

Psychology might in fact prefer to leave the bare facts alone, but it still has to make assumptions, in Herbart's view, which follow from what he calls "general metaphysical dogmas." Since the facts of consciousness bear with them two characteristics, "they unfailingly fall back into the main problems of general metaphysics." They evoke, on the one hand, the problem of substance; that is, how a variety of qualities can be attributed to a single entity which is independent of external being; and on the other hand, the problem of change, since this individual being can adopt variable states without becoming dependent on the outside.[19] With reference to John Locke, Herbart makes the assumption that the human being has a "soul" (*Seele*) in the form of a "simple substance" (*einfache Substanz*) or a "simple essence" (*einfaches Wesen*) with a simple but unique quality.[20] In order to preserve this singularity "against multifarious disturbances by other natures," it develops "representations" (*Vorstellungen*) and "sensations" (*Empfindungen*) as "self-preservations" (*Selbsterhaltungen*).[21] It is only through encountering "opposing representations" that the psychical faculties subsequently develop.[22] In this way, Herbart concludes that "all laws of thinking, willing and feeling simply arise from the unity of the soul, and the oppositions in the midst of its self-preservations."[23] Fechner had, for his part, already expressed the conjecture that Herbart's explanation of the soul as a "simple essence" is to be regarded as an unworthy

---

Herbart, *Sämtliche Werke*, ed. Karl Kehrbach and Otto Flügel, 19 vols. (Aalen: Scientia 1989), vol. V, 189. (Hereafter *SW*, followed by volume and page number.)

[18] [die Psychologie [hat] an den mannigfaltigen Thatsachen des Bewusstseins [...] ein unermessliches Eigenthum, welches die allgemeine Metaphysik unangetastet lässt]. Herbart, *Psychologie als Wissenschaft*, 39; Herbart, *SW*, V: 209.

[19] [allgemeinen metaphysischen Lehrsätzen]; [sie unfehlbar in die allgemein metaphysischen Haupt-Probleme zurückfallen]. Ibid. See also Heidelberger, *Nature from Within*, 31–5.

[20] Herbart, *Lehrbuch zur Psychologie* (Königsberg: Unzer, 1816), §109; *SW*, IV: 363. Trans. M. K. Smith as *A Text-Book in Psychology: An Attempt to Found the Science of Psychology in Experience, Metaphysics, and Mathematics* (New York: Appleton, 1891). See also, Herbart, *Psychologie als Wissenschaft*, 112; *SW*, V: 253 and Herbart, *Lehrbuch zur Einleitung in die Philosophie* (Königsberg: Unzer, 1813), §156ff.; *SW*, IV: 232ff.

[21] [gegen mannigfaltige Störungen durch andre Wesen]. Herbart, *Lehrbuch zur Psychologie*, §113; *SW*, IV: 364. See also: Herbart, *Psychologie als Wissenschaft: Neu gegründet auf Erfahrung, Metaphysik und Mathematik: Zweyter, analytischer Theil* (Königsberg: Unzer, 1825), 295; *SW*, VI: 190f.

[22] [entgegenstehender Vorstellungen]. Herbart, *Lehrbuch zur Psychologie*, §124; *SW*, IV: 369ff.

[23] [Alle Gesetze des Denkens, Wollens, und Fühlens entspringen lediglich aus der Einheit der Seele, und den Gegensätzen unter ihren Selbsterhaltungen.] Herbart, *Lehrbuch zur Einleitung in die Philosophie*, §131; *SW*, IV: 221.

attempt to save its immortality,[24] while also turning against Herbart's theory in other ways.

Herbart, incidentally, makes a thoroughgoing distinction between the "soul" and the "I" or "self-consciousness," furnishing a separate genetic explanation for the latter. The formation of the I, according to Herbart, presupposes a consciousness of material objects that is developed, for its part, out of the "mobility" (*Beweglichkeit*) of things and thereby from their separability from surroundings, but also from the significance of things for the satisfaction of one's needs. "The observation of a moved object," he writes, "implies a continual alternation of aroused and satisfied desire."[25] Through the observation that there are objects which direct themselves towards other objects, without necessarily coming into contact with them, and which (in contemporary parlance) we would describe as having intentional states, the human being learns "that there are things whose representations are inherent to them."[26] Once the individual has come this far, then it has gained the "representation of the 'I' in general." In order that it become a *"representation of* Me, i.e. *of* my I," the representation of space must be developed and the human being must discover him- or herself as the

moving centre of things, from which not only the distances but also the difficulties related to reaching the desired object grow, and towards which the attained object always moves through the satisfaction of desires. In this way, egoism is not the *reason* for the desires, but it is a *type of representation that is attributed to these desires*.[27]

Out of these reflections, Herbart developed a fundamental critique of Johann Gottlieb Fichte and of German idealism in general; a critique which anticipates contemporary cognitivist insights, according to which

---

[24] Gustav Thedor Fechner, "Kurze Darlegung eines Princips mathematischer Psychologie," *Zend-Avesta oder über die Dinge des Himmels und des Jenseits: Vom Standpunkt der Naturbetrachtung*, 3 vols. (Leipzig: Leopold Voß, 1851), vol. II, 341; reprint edition (Eschborn: Klotz 1998), vol. II, 373–86; part translated by Eckart Scheerer as "Outline of a New Principle of Mathematical Psychology," *Psychological Research* 49 (1987): 203–7.

[25] [Die Beobachtung eines Bewegten ist ein unaufhörlicher Wechsel aufgeregter und befriedigter Begierde.] Herbart, *Lehrbuch zur Psychologie*, §197; *SW*, IV: 401.

[26] [dass es Dinge giebt, denen Vorstellungen inwohnen]. Herbart, *Lehrbuch zur Psychologie* §199; *SW*, IV: 402. See also: Herbart, *Psychologie als Wissenschaft, Zweyter, analytischer Theil*, 264; *SW*, VI: 172.

[27] [*Vorstellung von* irgend einem Ich]; [*Vorstellung von* Mir, d.h. *von* meinem Ich]; [beweglicher Mittelpunct der Dinge, von wo aus nicht bloss die Entfernungen, sondern auch die Schwierigkeiten wachsen, das Begehrte zu erreichen, und zu welchem hin sich allemal das Erreichte bewegt, indem es die Begierden befriedigt. So ist der Egoismus nicht der Grund der Begierden, sondern er ist eine *Vorstellungsart, die zu denselben hinzugedacht wird.*] Herbart, *Lehrbuch zur Psychologie*, §201; *SW*, IV: 404.

children at around the age of four develop a "theory of mind."[28] "It was," according to Herbart,

a violently engendered and just as violently maintained error of Idealism, that the I should have created a *Non-I* to which it opposes itself – as if all things were originally characterized by the negations of the *I*. In this way, a You and a He would never arise – another personality, other than one's own, would never be acknowledged. Rather, what was inwardly felt is, wherever possible, transferred to the outside. Thus the You is formed at the same time as the I, and the *We* almost simultaneously with both – which latter Idealism forgot and had to forget if it did not want to be woken from its dreams.[29]

For Fechner, the metaphysical assumption of the soul upon which Herbart's psychology rests is a priori in nature, and thus useless as a point of departure for a philosophically neutral scientific treatment of the mind-body problem. A metaphysical premise such as the assumption of the existence of an unknowable "soul," according to Fechner, must not be added to the empirically given in inner and outer experience. For Fechner,

all discussions and investigations of psychophysics merely refer to the appearances of the physical and mental world, to that which either appears immediately through inner or outer perception, or can be inferred from the apparent object; in short: to the physical realm as it is understood by physics and chemistry and to the psychical realm along the lines of empirical psychology [*Erfahrungsseelenlehro*], without referring back either to the essence of the body, or to the soul as it is understood by metaphysics.[30]

---

[28] The "theory of mind" describes the ability of human beings (and, with qualifications, non-human primates) to understand as intentional agents those other natures whose behavior is guided by intentional states such as believing and wishing.

[29] [Es war ein gewaltsam erzeugter, und eben so gewaltsam festgehaltener Irrthum des Idealismus, das Ich setze *sich* ein *Nicht-Ich* entgegen, – als ob die Dinge ursprünglich mit der Negation des *Ich* behaftet wären. Auf die Weise würde nimmer ein Du und ein Er entstehn, – nimmer eine andre Persönlichkeit, ausser der eignen, anerkannt werden. Vielmehr, was innerlich empfunden war, das wird, wo irgend möglich, auf das Aeussere übertragen. Daher bildet sich mit dem Ich zugleich das Du; und fast gleichzeitig mit beyden das *Wir*, welches der Idealismus vergass, und vergessen musste, wenn er nicht aus seinen Träumen geweckt seyn wollte.] Herbart, *Lehrbuch zur Psychologie* (supplement to 2nd edn. of 1834), §198; *SW*, IV:402.

[30] [Alle Erörterungen und Untersuchungen der Psychophysik beziehen sich überhaupt blos auf die Erscheinungsseite der körperlichen und geistigen Welt, auf das, was entweder unmittelbar durch innere oder äussere Wahrnehmung erscheint, oder aus dem Erscheinlichen erschliessbar ... ist; kurz auf das Physische im Sinne der Physik und Chemie, auf das Psychische im Sinne der Erfahrungsseelenlehre, ohne dass auf das Wesen des Körpers, der Seele hinter der Erscheinungswelt im Sinne der Metaphysik irgendwie zurückgegangen wird.] Fechner, *Elemente der Psychophysik*, 2 vols. (Leipzig: Breitkopf & Härtel, 1860), vol. I, 8. Reprint editions (Amsterdam: Bonset, 1964 Bristol: Thoemmes, 1998). Vol. 1 translated by Helmut E. Adler as *Elements of Psychophysics*, ed. Davis H. Howes and Edwin G. Boring, introd. Edwin G. Boring (New York: Holt, Rinehart & Winston, 1966).

Concerning the second aforementioned point regarding the non-metaphysical interpretation of the mind-body relation, Fechner intended this correlation to be known through the compound "functional dependency" (*funktionelle Abhängigkeit*), that is, as the type of dependency akin to that found in a mathematical function. The reason for this, according to Fechner, lies in the way that a mathematical function only maintains the dependence of the y-value on the x-value, without thereby necessarily including a cause and effect connection from x to y or vice-versa (or any other metaphysical component). With every *causal* interpretation of the mind-body correlation, an additional philosophical component comes into play with this mathematical dependency, one which does not (directly) rest upon experience and is thus of a metaphysical nature. A claim of functional dependency is thus always weaker than a causal assertion. In order to create a point of departure which would be free of metaphysics, and which would therefore suit a science concerned with the natural laws connecting the physical and the psychical realms, one must, in psychophysics, refrain from any statements concerning the causal nature of the body-soul relation, whether they be positive or negative statements. In addition, one must confine oneself only to appearances and assume nothing about the nature of the objects belonging to appearances. Otherwise, psychophysics would go beyond the relations given in experience, and, as is the case with Herbart, make metaphysical assumptions. Instead, the verdict concerning such assumptions is to be left to the future, when, on the basis of a wider range of experience, an inductive conjecture about both the nature of the underlying causal relations and the type of appearing objects will be possible. The avoidance of metaphysics with regard to the mind-body relation thus means: restriction to the phenomenal realm and neutrality with regard to causality, and, accordingly, restriction to "functional dependency."

There is another reason why Fechner was not favorably disposed towards Herbart's psychology. Since the beginning of the development of his psychophysics, he had already been convinced that a method of measuring sensation (*Empfindungsmaß*) could only be developed in accordance with the material phenomena upon which sensation is functionally dependent. Herbart attempted to develop his mathematical psychology purely by means of psychical magnitudes, which cannot, according to Fechner's conviction, lead to any unit of measurement.[31] An important

---

[31] On this question, see Fechner, "Kurze Darlegung eines Princips mathematischer Psychologie," 169; Lange, *Die Grundlegung der mathematischen Psychologie: Ein Versuch zur Nachweisung des fundamentalen Fehlers bei Herbart und Drobisch* (Duisburg: Falk & Volmer, 1865).

third reason, which for Fechner spoke against Herbart, was Herbart's (and Hermann Lotze's) "monadology": the view that the soul displays a "simple nature." Against this, Fechner supported the standpoint of "synechology" – or, in modern language, the systems-theoretical view that psychical qualities are always bound to a physical manifold, and are thus of a systemic nature.

What, then, does the first version of psychophysical parallelism actually argue? It maintains that all psychical appearances are functionally dependent upon *physical* appearances, and thus arise in law-like dependence upon physical appearances. In other words, there is no psychical change without it being accompanied by a functional physical counterpart.[32] That is why, in 1860, Fechner defined his new science of psychophysics as "an exact theory about the functional connections, or the connections of dependency, between body and soul, or, in more general terms, between the corporeal and mental, the physical and psychical worlds."[33] In order to be really precise, this doctrine must strive to supply mathematical expressions for the functional dependence between body and soul. To achieve this aim, psychophysics must be divided into two branches: *outer* psychophysics, which investigates the functional relations between the stimuli in the external world and the psychic appearances that are caused by these stimuli, and *inner* psychophysics, which explores the interdependence of the neuro-physiological conditions of psychic appearances and these appearances themselves. Fechner describes as "psychophysical" (*psychophysisch*) the parts of the brain which have a direct functional dependence on psychic appearances, while referring to their process of change as "psychophysical activity" (*psychophysische Aktivität*).[34]

In other words, to make the expression "parallelism" more intelligible, according to psychophysical parallelism in its first form, there is a physical

---

[32] The law-like dependency here is of an asymmetrical nature; the reverse may not be true for the brains of living human beings, in which two different psychophysical activities may be mentally indistinguishable.

[33] [eine exacte Lehre von den functionellen oder Abhängigkeitsbeziehungen zwischen Körper und Seele, allgemeiner zwischen körperlicher und geistiger, physischer und psychischer, Welt]. Fechner, *Elemente der Psychophysik*, vol. I, 8.

[34] Ibid., vol. I, 10. See also: Heidelberger, "Fechner's (Wider) Conception of Psychophysics – Then and Now," *Fechner Day 2004: Proceedings of the Twentieth Annual Meeting of The International Society for Psychophysics*, ed. Armando M. Oliveira, Marta Teixeira, Graciete F. Borges and Maria J. Ferro (Coimbra: International Society for Psychophysics and Institute of Cognitive Science of the University of Coimbra, 2004), 18–25; Walter H. Ehrenstein and Addie Ehrenstein, "Psychophysical Methods," *Modern Techniques in Neuroscience Research*, ed. U.Windhorst and H. Johansson (Berlin: Springer, 1999), 1211–41; here 1211; and Eckart Scheerer, "The Unknown Fechner," *Psychological Research* 49 (1987): 197–202; here 200–2.

parallel for every psychical appearance, which means that every mental event has a physiological correlate, and every mental event is physically conditioned. In the case of outer psychophysics, it is the physical stimulus which runs in parallel with the sensation; for inner psychophysics, it is the psychophysical activity inside the brain of human beings (that is, a physiological process) which runs alongside the psychical process, and which, as Fechner also puts it, represents the material *vehicle* of the psychical process, and realizes it physically. All of these ways of speaking should in fact express a strict correspondence between psychical and physical appearances, but leave open the question as to which element is dependent on the other.

When two types of hitherto unknown appearances are lawfully correlated in this way, the role of causality must still be discovered through a methodical procedure. Barometric variations and changes of weather are actually correlated with each other, but neither phenomenon gives rise to the other nor vice-versa; instead both are evoked by a common cause, the air pressure. Or, to take another example of a similarly non-causal connection which can underlie an empirical parallelism: the kinetic energy of molecules in a gas is correlated with the heat of the gas, but not because the one gives rise to the other, and also not because a common cause stands behind them, but because heat and kinetic energy are identical. To interpret causally a functional dependence between X and Y does not mean that in every case X gives rise to Y or vice-versa. It can, as both examples show, also mean that X and Y have a common cause or that X and Y are identical with one another.

How does Fechner justify the claims made in the first version of his psychophysical parallelism? In his opinion, it is already universally confirmed by experience: whenever psychical changes arise, they run in parallel with physiological changes, or we have good experiential grounds to assume that they do. In this form, parallelism is so well confirmed that it not only expresses an empirical fact, but can be taken to be a maxim of research, a methodological guiding principle of neuro-scientific investigation, or, as Wilhelm Wundt would later put it, an "empirical postulate" of science. Fechner saw a second reason for the validity of psychophysical parallelism's first form in the theorem of the conservation of energy – or, as it was referred to in German at this time, the *Prinzip von der Erhaltung der Kraft* (principle of the conservation of force).[35] Were one to seek to grasp the causal efficiency of psychic phenomena and processes without regard to their physical side, one would be denying the self-sufficiency of physical causality, thereby contravening the energy principle. Fechner

---

[35] Fechner, *Elemente der Psychophysik*, vol. I, ch. 5, esp. 34–45.

was thus "the first to have based the theory of the relations between the mental and the corporeal on the consequences arising from the principle of the conservation of energy."[36]

Almost all physiologists, psychologists and also many philosophers after the 1870s could enter into agreement with psychophysical parallelism in this form. This "empirical parallelism," as William James called it, might perhaps seem trivial to us today, but it had first to secure its own ground and is today the common property of all empirical sciences applicable to these phenomena. After 1847, biophysics eliminated from physiology the concept of the "life force" (*Lebenskraft*) as lacking any physical basis. In the middle of the 1870s, any substantial "soul" independent of a physical substrate had also disappeared from physiology and psychology, so that Friedrich Albert Lange could characterize scientific psychology (in an affirmative sense) as "psychology without soul" (*Psychologie ohne Seele*).[37] The widely held formulation in today's research literature – "neural correlate of X" or "neural basis of X," whereby X stands for a psychic phenomenon such as, for example, consciousness – supplies eloquent testimony as to how alive and well psychophysical parallelism (as an empirical postulate) remains today.[38]

Considering all relevant empirical knowledge, the *second form* of psychophysical parallelism now provides the most probable hypothesis concerning the precise way in which the connection between body and soul should, from a causal point of view, be interpreted – a research question which the first version of psychophysical parallelism had left unresolved. This hypothesis also contains implications concerning the nature of mind and body. In relation to the underlying causal relations concerning

---

[36] [der erste, der die Theorie vom Verhältnisse zwischen dem Seelischen und Körperlichen auf den Konsequenzen des Satzes von der Erhaltung der Energie aufbaute]. Harald Höffding, *Psychologie in Umrissen auf Grundlage der Erfahrung*, translated from the Danish by F. Bendixen, 2nd German edn. according to the 3rd Danish edn. (Leipzig: Reisland, 1893), 92. Translated into English by Mary E. Lowndes as *Outlines of Psychology* (London: Macmillan, 1893).

[37] Lange, *Geschichte des Materialismus*, 823.

[38] One could consider, for example, the entry in the English *Wikipedia* under "neural correlate": "A neural correlate of a content of experience is any bodily component, such as an electro-neuro-biological state or the state assumed by some biophysical subsystem of the brain, whose presence necessarily and regularly correlates with such a specific content of experience." Christoph Koch writes, in this connection, that "there must be an explicit correspondence between any mental event and its neuronal correlates. Another way of stating this is that any change in a subjective state must be associated with a change in a neuronal state." Koch, *The Quest for Consciousness: A Neurobiological Approach* (Englewood, CT: Roberts & Co., 2004), 16. On the search for the "neural correlate of consciousness," a critical account is provided by Alva Noë and Evan Thompson, "Are There Neural Correlates of Consciousness?" *Journal of Consciousness Studies* 11, no. 1 (2004): 3–28.

the mind-body connection, neutrality is thus surrendered and an *explanation* for, or *interpretation* of, the functional dependency is sought. In an analogous way to the examples given concerning empirical correlations, we can also distinguish various causal explanatory hypotheses, which are logically possible in relation to the mind-body relation: (1) The hypothesis which claims a reciprocal causal influence of mind and body or which describes one as being caused by the other; (2) the hypothesis which states that a common cause influences both; and (3) the hypothesis which takes mind and body to be distinguishable modes of appearance of one and the same object, or which, in the words of Fechner, sees them as being "identical" with one another.

The first hypothesis, that mind and body exert a reciprocal causal influence upon one another, is of course represented by substance dualism *à la* Descartes and also closely resembles our everyday experiences. Variations on it are materialism or idealism, both of which level off the differences between mind and body. The second hypothesis corresponds with occasionalism or the pre-established harmony of Leibniz. The third hypothesis, that inner and outer appearances are qualities of one and the same object, is referred to by Fechner (undoubtedly following Friedrich Schelling's *Identitätsphilosophie* or identity-philosophy) as the "identity view" (*Identitätsansicht*). This third possible hypothesis concerning an "interpretation" or "fundamental view" of the functional dependency between mind and body corresponds precisely with the second form of psychophysical parallelism.[39]

At first glance, it may appear strange that the identity theory does away with neutrality in relation to the underlying causal relations between mind and body. The identity theory certainly rejects *all* causal hypotheses concerning the relation between mind and body, and maintains that the correlation between mind and body comes about neither through a causal effect of the mind upon the body or vice-versa, nor through the causal effect of a third agent upon both. But this rejection is certainly a *negation* of the existence of a *causal connection* with regard to the mind-body relation, and thus an *offence* against neutrality and a retraction of the skepticism of the first form of psychophysical parallelism in regard to causality. Through a decision in favor of the identity theory, a closer determination of the nature of the functional dependency of mind and

---

[39] I have shown that Herbert Feigl's "identity theory" developed historically out of Fechner's "identity theory," mainly through the mediation of Alois Riehl, though without the two versions being identical with one another. See Heidelberger, "The Mind-Body Problem in the Origin of Logical Empiricism: Herbert Feigl and Psychophysical Parallelism," *Logical Empiricism: Historical and Contemporary Perspectives*, ed. Paolo Parrini and Wesley Salmon (Pittsburgh, PA: University of Pittsburgh Press, 2003), 233–62.

body is thus provided, a determination which *explains* the existence of that functional dependency. Fechner takes the view that the identity theory represents, for explanatory purposes, a supplementation of the (then currently known) facts, a supplementation which actually goes beyond the bare stating of the facts and the functional dependency between them. At the same time, this supplementation is the most economical move that can be made in order to maintain an explanation of the mind-body relation. All other explanations of the mind-body relation supplement direct experience to a *far greater extent* than does the identity theory.

But how then can mind and body be identical? Translated into Fechner's terminology concerning "outer" and "inner" appearances, this is to say that such appearances are aspects or "modes of appearance" (*Erscheinungsweisen*) of one and the same object or "fundamental essence" (*Grundwesen*). In contemporary philosophy of mind we would say that Fechner posited a property dualism: the psychical realm is not an independent essence existing alongside physical bodies; rather, it is a sort of property which can (under certain circumstances still to be explained) belong to physical bodies alongside their physical qualities. A human being is thus not composed of two distinct kinds of substance, as Descartes wanted to say; rather, there is a certain part of the body (namely, the brain) which, alongside its physical properties, also possesses psychical properties. These psychical properties are distinguishable from the physical properties, as well as being causally related to and functionally dependent on them.

An appearance thus means for Fechner a psychic or "inner" appearance if it is given solely to the subject who experiences it: this subject is itself the same entity which appears, either as a whole or in part, to itself alone. Therefore, Fechner also calls the psychic appearances "self-appearances" (*Selbsterscheinungen*). In contradistinction to Herbart, this "self" (*Selbst*) is no longer postulated as a metaphysical unity, rather, it only comes to expression, according to Fechner, in the self-reference which is grounded in psychical appearances. By comparison, physical appearances are outer or "alien appearances" (*Fremderscheinungen*); that is, appearances which are accessible not only to the one who has them, but also to other people through their own perceptions. Again, in contemporary parlance, the states that someone "has" are of an inner kind if they cannot be directly perceived by others, but are attributed to the subject with the help of the "theory of mind" that human beings make use of in social life. The states are external if they (at least potentially) can be directly perceived by everyone, not only by those who have them.[40]

---

[40] See Fechner, *Elemente der Psychophysik*, vol. I, 4–6.

One sees that some conceptual effort is needed to draw out and understand the difference between the first and second versions of psychophysical parallelism. Fechner himself struggled at length with this differentiation, until he was reasonably satisfied with his formulations. It is no wonder that many of the empirical scientists of his time considered this second version to be either too subtle, too methodically obscure, or else, in comparison with his first position, completely unnecessary. The view was widely disseminated that the first version had been entirely adequate for the purposes of empirical research, and that the philosophical subtleties could be left to the specialists in this area. But there were also other intellectual contemporaries who, like Albert Einstein for example, would pose the question as to how psychical and physical realities were related to each other, and who found a thoroughly satisfying answer to this question in the second version of Fechner's psychophysical parallelism. In 1922, on the occasion of a discussion of the Theory of Relativity, Einstein wrote in a letter to a Swiss magazine: "To avoid a collision between the different sorts of 'reality' dealt with by physics and psychology, Spinoza and Fechner invented the theory of psychophysical parallelism, which, to be quite frank, completely satisfies me."[41]

While the first version of parallelism still manages to be compatible with a reductionist materialism, so that the possibility of an equally valid replacement of all psychological explanations by purely neurophysiological descriptions is left open, Fechner's second version of psychophysical parallelism, in taking psychical autonomy into consideration, is thus of a non-reductive nature, without however separating the mind from its physiological correlate, as is the case in Cartesian dualism. It has been, however, and certainly remains to the present day, notoriously unclear as to whether this version can be distinguished from epiphenomenalism. This view in fact implies, as is claimed in the first version, that the psychical is correlated with the physical realm, but that the causal effects which the brain exerts as a psychophysical unity are only exerted by virtue of its *physical* properties – so that the mental realm is a secondary effect, which is not in itself a primary cause.

Finally, one should mention Fechner's *third form* of psychophysical parallelism, in which a conjecture is entertained concerning the

---

[41] [Zur Vermeidung einer Kollision der verschiedenen Sorten von 'Realitäten', von denen Physik und Psychologie handeln, hat Spinoza bezw. Fechner die Lehre des psychophysischen Parallelismus erfunden, welche mich offen gestanden völlig befriedigt.] Quoted in E. Bovet, "Die Physiker Einstein und Weyl: Antworten auf eine metaphysische Frage," *Wissen und Leben* 15, no. 19 (1922): 901–6, here 902. On the reception of Fechner's parallelism, especially in the German-speaking world, see Heidelberger, "The Mind-Body Problem in the Origin of Logical Empiricism."

dissemination of inner appearances in the external world. In the first and second forms, it was really only a matter of the connection between the physical and psychical realms *among human beings* (or other higher mammals) and an *asymmetry* between both sides was maintained in both the first and second versions. Expressed in simple terms: there is no psychical world without a physical vehicle on which it is functionally dependent (first version), or whose inner-side it represents (second version). The reversal of this functional dependency, that no physical world exists without a psychical correlate, was not asserted or claimed. It was precisely this thesis that Fechner thought himself able to take up only in the speculative third version of psychophysical parallelism. In reversing the first version, it says the following: there is no physical change in the world without a psychical change, and there can be no physical reality without a mind to which it appears internally.

In fact, Fechner is, to the present day, notorious for the permissive way in which he referred to minds or "souls": according to Fechner, not only are plants and animals "en-souled" because of certain structural or systemic qualities, but also the earth, the planets, and even the whole universe possess inner-sides, which are given as self-appearance, alongside their physical outer-sides. It is also notable that this panpsychism does not purport simply to be an arbitrary assumption, but claims to represent the most probable supplementation of the known psychophysical facts. This is not a plea for the very speculative "atomic en-soulment" (*Atombeseelung*) as Fechner's contemporaries – the biologist Ernest Haeckel and the astrophysicist Karl Friedrich Zöllner – represented it, but the beginning of a systems theory and of a functionalistic view of the psychical world.

Of course, to this day Fechner's panpsychism lends itself to amusement, mockery and contempt. Here, however, it is necessary to distinguish between two questions: firstly, is panpsychism logically possible; and secondly: is it, as Fechner claimed, empirically probable? The revolutionary element in Fechner's view remains the fact that – more than a hundred years before the advent of functionalism in the philosophy of mind – he understood the mind to be a *functional* state of a material system, independently of its (that is, the mind's) material basis. The rejection of a soul-substance in Herbart's sense of that term allows the mind to be understood, in contemporary terms, as "software" which can also "run" on other material systems than human "wetware" alone. Only such a functionalistic view makes it *logically* possible to impute a mind to a robot, to a computer, or any other system. The Turing Test starts from the premise that a machine might possess or be animated by a mind if it had the same functional structure as a human being – independently of its material characteristics.[42] Whoever accepts the Turing Test as being logically possible must also, however, acknowledge the *logical possibility* of Fechner's panpsychism.

So far nothing has yet been said in answer to the second question as to whether there are such systems in our world at all, whether they could exist according to the laws of nature, and whether plants and less intelligent animals do in fact possess the material-functional structure attributed to mind-endowed beings. In short: whether this possibility is also in fact realized in our world. In his affirmative answer to this question, Fechner might have overshot the mark by some distance. His proofs are, in this connection, too meager and his enthusiasm turns into endless speculation – or perhaps into an esoteric irony which mocks the reader.[43] At any rate, it must be emphasized that, according to Fechner's understanding, the world-soul as the soul of God (like every soul in general) cannot exist without a physical correlate, namely the universe. It can also be stated, in Fechner's defence, that his panpsychism reveals something which, in many other solutions to the mind-body problem, is often either unintentionally or intentionally concealed as an undesirable implication.[44]

When we now finally take into consideration all three versions of psychophysical parallelism, the question arises as to the relations between them. It ought to have become clear that, when viewed logically, they build upon one another and progressively increase in their hypothetical content as well as in the intensity of their philosophical speculation. Whoever accepts the third form of psychophysical parallelism must also accept the second, and whoever acknowledges the second must also endorse the first. The reverse, however, does not hold. Whoever approves psychophysical parallelism as a regulative methodological maxim for research does not have to subscribe to the identity theory. And whoever subscribes to the identity theory is not necessarily thereby a panpsychist or a pantheist.

Finally, something further must be said concerning the first version of psychophysical parallelism, since, as a methodological maxim, it can be understood according to different degrees and in different forms. In its strong version, it demands that only those psychical phenomena for

---

[42] The Turing Test, developed in 1950 by the British logician and mathematician Alan Mathison Turing, was designed to answer the question as to whether machines can think, and led to the notion of "artificial intelligence."

[43] This may not be the first time that Fechner allows scientific seriousness to veer into satire, so that it becomes unclear exactly where for him the boundary between science and satire lies.

[44] This is how Thomas Nagel in fact stands by the panpsychical implications of his body-soul theory, but, in the anomalous monism disseminated by Donald Davidson, for example, it is far from clear whether he was not also an unwitting representative of panpsychism.

which there is a physiological correlate and for which working mechanisms can concretely be indicated or are already known, can be admitted as having explanatory power. The weaker position, by contrast, also admits explanatory power to theoretical psychical entities for which no concrete physiological correlate is given.

In the nineteenth century, these differentiated levels of strength in the first version of psychophysical parallelism became especially influential in the physiological theory of perception, and led, for example, to a vehement exchange between the physiologists Hermann von Helmholtz and Ewald Hering concerning the perception of space.[45] Hering, whose own position was close to that of Fechner, was of the conviction that every psychical event is "carried and conditioned" (*getragen und bedingt*) by organic processes in the nervous system. The processes of and the connections between the phenomena of consciousness would, according to Hering, need to be explained through the course of physiological processes, which would have to be concretely furnished. The reasons for Hering's view are exclusively methodological in character. Were one to start out from the existence of psychical processes, to which no physiological process corresponds (or, even if a corresponding physiological process could be found, but only in a provisional way), then, according to Hering "any further physiological investigation [would be] pointless."[46] The assumption of psychical processes in research, without the provision of physiological correlates for them, would amount to an admission that physiological research could be dispensed with in the future. Hering even accuses Helmholtz of reintroducing, through the assumption of psychic activities without the provision of corresponding physiological correlates, something like the notion of a life-force (*Lebenskraft*):

> As we once explained everything that we could not or did not want to investigate physiologically through a life force, so there appears now on every third page of a physiological optics the "soul" or the "mind," the "judgment," or the "inference" as a *deus ex machina*, in order to help us over every difficulty.[47]

---

[45] On this question see Heidelberger, "Räumliches Sehen bei Helmholtz und Hering," *Philosophia Naturalis* 30, no. 1 (1993): 1–28; Heidelberger, "Beziehungen zwischen Sinnesphysiologie und Philosophie im 19. Jahrhundert," *Philosophie und Wissenschaften. Formen und Prozesse ihrer Interaktion*, ed. Hans Jörg Sandkühler (Frankfurt am Main: Peter Lang, 1997), 37–58.

[46] [jede weitere physiologische Untersuchung zwecklos]. Ewald Hering, *Zur Lehre vom Lichtsinne: Sechs Mittheilungen an die Kaiserl. Akademie der Wissenschaften in Wien*, 2nd edn. (Vienna: Carl Gerold, 1878), 71; see also 76, 106, 2. Trans. Leo M. Hurvich and Dorothea Jameson as *Outlines of a Theory of the Light Sense* (Cambridge, MA: Harvard University Press, 1964).

[47] [Wie man einst alles was man nicht physiologisch untersuchen konnte oder wollte, aus einer Lebenskraft erklärte, so erscheint jetzt auf jedem dritten Blatte einer physiologischen Optik die "Seele" oder der "Geist," das "Urtheil," oder der "Schluss" als *deus*

This reproach must have hit Helmholtz especially hard, above all when one considers that he had been the leading light of the bio-physicalist movement since 1847, which had made the cause of eradicating the concept of the life-force from physiology a central element of its platform. In fact Helmholtz had, in his work of 1867 entitled "Physiological Optics" (*Physiologische Optik*), characterized the perception of space, in agreement with George Berkeley, as the result of a "mental inference" (*geistiger Schlussvorgang*), which in ontogenetic development is so merged with flesh and blood that it ultimately becomes unconscious. Instead, Hering also attempted from the very beginning to explain the perception of space through physiological processes without the insertion of mental processes. Ernst Mach, who was Hering's colleague in Prague for twenty-five years, shared Hering's view when he wrote: "All of the details of the psychical realm correspond with the details of the physical."[48] Yet Mach had only understood this psychophysical parallelism to be an heuristic principle, while Hering insisted it was rather the *conditio sine qua non* of any psychophysical and physiological research.[49] Incidentally, Helmholtz did not waste a single word in his work on the localization theories of his age (for example those of Eduard Hitzig and Gustav Theodor Fritsch), which were flourishing in Berlin, a city in which Helmholtz had lived from 1871 onwards. The reason for this is to be sought in the way in which Helmholtz saw the material localization of mental functioning in the brain as being too tightly bound up with *Identitätsphilosophie* along the lines of Schelling.

It is to be emphasized once again that psychophysical parallelism, in spite of its compatibility with the most diverse philosophical meanings, or, as Fechner says, "fundamental views" (*Grundansichten*), already takes up in its first version a clear position, one which marks the emergence of the new experimental psychology. First of all, the "soul," in the sense of a substance as it had been for Descartes but also for Herbart and other psychologists of the time, is abolished as a metaphysical premise

---

ex machina, um über alle Schwierigkeiten hinweg zu helfen.] Hering, *Zur Lehre vom Lichtsinne*, 2.

[48] [Allen Details des Psychischen correspondiren Details des Physischen.] Ernst Mach, "Über die Wirkung der räumlichen Vertheilung des Lichtreizes auf die Netzhaut," *Sitzungsberichte der Kaiserlichen Akademie der Wissenschaften (Wien)*, math-naturw. Klasse II. Abtheilung 52 (1865):303–322; here: 320.

[49] Hering, *Zur Lehre vom Lichtsinne*, 76. On Hering's psychophysical parallelism, see his: "Über das Gedächtnis als eine allgemeine Funktion der organisirten Materie" (Vortrag gehalten in der feierlichen Sitzung der Kaiserlichen Akademie der Wissenschaften in Wien am 30. Mai 1870), *Fünf Reden von Ewald Hering*, ed. H. E. Hering (Leipzig: Engelmann 1921), 5–31. Trans. Samuel Butler as "Professor Ewald Hering 'On Memory'," *Unconscious Memory*, ed. Samuel Butler (London: A. C. Fifield, 1880). Also trans. Paul Carus as *On Memory and the Specific Energies of the Nervous*

Gustav Theodor Fechner and the unconscious

for psychology; secondly, the centrality of physiology for psychology and the notion that it functions as the "corporeal foundation" (*körperliche Unterlage*) of the psychical realm, as Fechner called it, became firmly established and thereby also extended beyond the works of Herbart and many others.

The "threshold" and the unconscious in Fechner's psychophysics

The unconscious did not initially stand at the centre of Fechner's psychophysics; rather, it was almost a chance by-product of his theories. At the end of his *Elements of Psychophysics* (*Elemente der Psychophysik*),[50] Fechner describes how, in the drafting of his *Zend-Avesta*,[51] he set himself the task "of finding a functional relation between both [i.e. the psychical and physical] modes of appearance." Finally, the idea came to him to assume no *proportional* correlation between them, but rather "to make the proportional increase of the living corporeal force [that is, the stimulus energy] ... a measure of the *increase* of the accompanying mental intensity."[52] Out of this, he derived the so-called "fundamental formula" (*Fundamentalformel*), which states that a noticeable increase $d\gamma$ of a sensation γ with the intensification of a physical stimulus β thus depends on the *corresponding* raising of the stimulus, that is, $d\beta/\beta$. This formula, advanced by Ernst Heinrich Weber as "Weber's law," takes into account such empirical knowledge as provided by the following example: the difference in the playing of two violins together in comparison with only one is easily audible; whereas, in a full orchestra, more and more violins must be added, increasing in proportion with the original size of the orchestra, in order to make an audible difference. In the same way, the weight which one must add to an existing weight, in order to achieve a noticeable difference, must be heavier the greater the size of the original weight.

After the integration of the fundamental formula Fechner produced the so-called "formula of measurement" (*Maßformel*) $\gamma = k (\log \beta - \log b)$, in which the empirical significance of b first remained mysterious to him:[53]

System (Chicago: Open Court, 1897). On Fechner's relation to Mach, see: Heidelberger, *Nature from Within*, chs. 4–6.

[50] Fechner, *Elemente der Psychophysik*, vol. II, 533–60.
[51] See Fechner, *Zend-Avesta oder über die Dinge des Himmels und des Jenseits*.
[52] [ein functionelles Verhältnis zwischen beiden [d.h. den psychischen und physischen] Erscheinungsweisen zu finden]; [verhältnissmässigen Zuwachs der körperlichen lebendigen Kraft [also der Reizenergie] ... zum Masse des Zuwachses der zugehörigen geistigen Intensität zu machen]. Fechner, *Elemente der Psychophysik*, vol. II, 553.
[53] On the development of the psychophysical law in Fechner, see Heidelberger, *Nature from Within*, ch. 6; David Murray, "A Perspective for Viewing the History of Psychophysics," *Behavioral and Brain Sciences* 16, no.1 (1993): 115–86; here 116.

At first, it gave me trouble to establish that, according to the formula of measurement, the sensation γ disappears rather than the living force [i.e. the intensity of the physical stimulus] on which it depends, until I found this circumstance represented in the phenomena of sleep and unconscious sensation, and with this a new and striking confirmation of the formula, which significantly strengthened my conviction about the cogency and fruitfulness of the same.[54]

He thus emphasized that the constant b lends itself to being understood as a "threshold," i.e. as that (physical) magnitude which the stimulus must reach for the sensation to become perceptible and thus conscious.

Fechner interpreted this to mean that the "psychophysical activity" or "movement" (that is, the physical occurrences in the brain, understood as "neural correlates") are directly correlated with psychical appearances, in accordance with psychophysical parallelism. For this reason, it must acquire an external physical stimulus, transmitted with a certain strength, for the correlative psychical appearances to be made conscious at all. In this way, the stimulus must overcome an *inner* threshold between psychophysical activity and sensation. He had thereby quite unintentionally discovered that

> the relations between the conscious and unconscious life of representations, sleeping and waking, general and particular phenomena of consciousness, in short the most general relations of the life of the soul, allow a very simple and satisfying psychophysical representation [i.e. modeling] owing to the premise that the threshold concept is transferable onto the psychophysical movement.[55]

The concept of the inner threshold thus became for him a "central concept" (*Zentralbegriff*) of his inner psychophysics:

> For all this, the concept of the psychophysical threshold already has the most important significance in that it provides a firm basis for the concept of the unconscious in general. Psychology cannot abstract from unconscious sensations and from representations.[56]

---

[54] [Anfangs machte mir der Umstand zu schaffen, dass nach der Massformel die Empfindung γ schon eher verschwindet, als die lebendige Kraft [d.h. die Intensität des physischen Reizes], wovon sie abhängt, bis ich in den Phänomenen des Schlafes und der unbewussten Empfindungen diesen Umstand repräsentirt und hiemit eine neue auffallende Bestätigung der Formel fand, welche meine Ueberzeugung von der Triftigkeit und Fruchtbarkeit derselben erheblich verstärkte.] Fechner, *Elemente der Psychophysik*, vol. II, 554ff.

[55] [die Verhältnisse zwischen bewusstem und unbewusstem Vorstellungsleben, Schlaf und Wachen, allgemeinen und besonderen Bewusstseinsphänomenen, kurz die allgemeinsten Verhältnisse des Seelenlebens eine sehr einfache und befriedigende psychophysische Repräsentation [d.h. Modellierung] auf Grund der Voraussetzung, dass der Schwellenbegriff auf die psychophysische Bewegung übertragbar sei, zulassen]. Ibid., vol. II, 435.

[56] [Über das Alles hat der Begriff der psychophysischen Schwelle die wichtigste Bedeutung schon dadurch, dass er für den Begriff des Unbewusstseins überhaupt ein festes

Already since around 1868, and especially in the late 1870s, Fechner's transference of the threshold concept from outer to inner psychophysics (that is, onto the psychophysical correlate) was being challenged through the works of the Göttingen psychologist Georg Elias Müller.[57] In opposition to Fechner's "psychophysical interpretation" of the elementary law of psychophysics, the so-called "physiological interpretation" was posited, which transfers the threshold onto the neural periphery. According to this view, a weak sound, for example, will remain unheard because the stimulus is too weak to transmit the excitation in the auditory nerve to the psychophysical activity in the brain. This is not, according to Müller, because the psychophysical activity *in the brain* must first exceed a certain threshold, as Fechner had intended. The physiological interpretation thus saw in Fechner's law an expression for the "friction in the neural machine," as William James once dramatically put it,[58] while Fechner interpreted it as a threshold phenomenon in the transition between psychophysical activity and psychical appearance. Still in 1882 Fechner maintained, in opposition to the physiological view, that it could not offer any "representation of unconscious mental life." Fechner argued that "insofar as, according to the physiological view, there is no inner threshold, the representation of unconscious life also ceases to exist."[59] The transferability of the law of the threshold onto inner psychophysics is, according to Fechner, the decisive question for his psychophysics, even for the possibility of psychophysics at all, and is the pivotal point on which all other aspects of psychophysics depend. Without the law of the threshold, psychophysics would, alongside psychology and physics, only play a modest supporting role as the connecting link between the two, while modifications to or the demise of all other laws of psychophysics, including Weber's law, would be easier to cope with.[60]

The concept of the threshold stems from Herbart, with whom it appears for the first time in 1816, and from whom Fechner adopted it.[61]

Fundament giebt. Die Psychologie kann von unbewussten Empfindungen, Vorstellungen nicht abstrahiren.] Ibid., vol. II, 438.

[57] See Heidelberger, *Nature from Within*, 212–17.
[58] William James, *The Principles of Psychology*, 2 vols. (New York: Holt, 1890), vol. I, 548.
[59] [Repräsentation des unbewussten geistigen Lebens]; [Sofern es nach der physiologischen Ansicht keine innere Schwelle giebt, fällt auch für sie diese Repräsentation des unbewussten Lebens weg.] Fechner, *Revision der Hauptpuncte der Psychophysik* (Leipzig: Breitkopf & Härtel, 1882), 219.
[60] [nur eine bescheidene Nebenrolle neben Psychologie und Physik als Verbindungsglied beider spielen]. Ibid., 226; see also 235ff. Also relevant is Fechner, *In Sachen der Psychophysik* (Leipzig: Breitkopf & Härtel, 1877), reprint (Amsterdam: Bonset, 1968), 71, and in general 70–106.
[61] Herbart refers to a "Schwelle des Bewusstseyns." Herbart, *Lehrbuch zur Psychologie*, §130; *SW*, IV: 372; compare also Herbart, *Psychologie als Wissenschaft*, 175; *SW*, V: 292f.

As is already explained above, Herbart understands the soul to be a simple substance of unknown quality which is to be postulated metaphysically as a substance that distinguishes itself from other substances:

> It originally has neither representations, nor feelings, nor desires; it knows nothing of itself and nothing of other things; moreover, there lie within it no forms of intuition and thinking, no laws of willing and acting; also not even the remotest preparations for any of these.[62]

If several substances come together – be they souls or material substances – then each will attempt to resist the other and to preserve its original individual qualities against the external disturbance. An inner resistance (*Gegendruck*) thus emerges and as a result of these "self-preservations" (*Selbsterhaltungen*) representations arise which are qualitatively dependent on the other substances. Herbart thus attempts to explain all psychical appearances as the result of the pressure and counter-pressure of simple substances.

However, with the great number of other substances to which the soul is permanently exposed, an inner dynamic of representations now arises. These representations reciprocally attract or repel, connect or separate, inhibit or stimulate each other, according to their constitution and intensity. Through this, a new, weaker representation can thereby also suppress an older, stronger one below the threshold of consciousness, without this latter representation wholly disappearing:

> But thereupon its striving [i.e. the striving of the older representation to assert itself] is not to be regarded as ineffectual ... rather it works with all its powers against the representations located within consciousness. It thus brings about a state of consciousness, the object of which is, at the same time, not represented. If many representations exist in the aforementioned state at the same time, then objectless feelings of anxiety may arise, which are mostly (at the same time) affects, since, with such a wide deviation from the static point [i.e. the threshold], the mood must be very changeable. Physiological conditions can be linked to these underlying circumstances, but can also produce similar effects independently of them.[63]

---

[62] [Sie hat ursprünglich weder Vorstellungen, noch Gefühle, noch Begierden; sie weiss nichts von sich selbst und nichts von andern Dingen; es liegen auch in ihr keine Formen des Anschauens und Denkens, keine Gesetze des Wollens und Handelns; auch keinerley, wie immer entfernte, Vorbereitungen zu dem allen.] Herbart, *Lehrbuch zur Psychologie*, §111; *SW*, IV: 364.

[63] [Alsdann aber ist ihr Streben [d.h. das Streben der älteren Vorstellung, sich zu behaupten] nicht als unwirksam zu betrachten ..., sondern es arbeitet mit ganzer Macht wider die im Bewusstseyn befindlichen Vorstellungen. Sie bewirkt also einen Zustand des Bewusstseyns, während ihr Object keinesweges wirklich vorgestellt wird. Sind viele Vorstellungen zugleich in der nämlichen Lage, so entstehn daraus die objectlosen Gefühle der Beklemmung, die meistens zugleich Affecte sind, weil bei so weiter Abweichung vom statischen Puncte [d.h. der Schwelle] die Gemüthslage sehr veränderlich sein muss.

Herbart thus makes an explicit differentiation between conscious and unconscious representations, without, however, using the latter concept. "The expression: *a representation is in consciousness* must be distinguished from: *I am conscious of my representation.* To the latter belongs inner perception, but not to the former."[64] Were all of those representations which lie below the threshold – like, for example, those stored in memory – to become conscious or suddenly to impact upon consciousness, we would, according to Herbart, "find ourselves in an incessant state of the most unbearable apprehension; or rather, the human body would become subject to a tension which would cause death in only a few moments."[65]

In Fechner's adoption of the concept of the threshold from Herbart's psychology, the whole metaphysical model of a substantial soul and its self-preservation falls away and the concept of the threshold becomes primarily applied to sensations (*Sinnesempfindungen*). Fechner distinguishes the "stimulus threshold" (*Reizschwelle*, also referred to simply as the "threshold") from the "threshold of difference" (*Unterschiedsschwelle*). Pressure upon the skin must reach a certain intensity – that of the "stimulus threshold" – before we notice it. When this pressure is further increased, the difference in pressure must reach a certain intensity in relation to the initial stimulus (*Ausgangsreiz*) for it to be able to be felt: the "threshold of difference." Fechner grasped the relation of the perceptible increase of the stimulus to the original stimulus itself, which we encountered above in the fundamental formula, as a unit of measurement for sensitivity, and established, through countless experiments, thresholds of difference for the different sensory regions (*Sinnesgebiete*). In this connection, he used three methods in order to determine the measurement of sensation (*Empfindlichkeitsmaßes*), which have become milestones in experimental psychology, and which focused for the first time upon the genuine statistical constitution of psychical reality.[66]

The closer consideration of the unconscious which is to be found in Fechner's psychophysics emerges from the phenomena of attention.

Physiologische Umstände können sich damit verbinden, auch etwas ähnliches allein hervorbringen.] Herbart, *Lehrbuch zur Psychologie*, §133; *SW*, IV: 373.

[64] [Der Ausdruck: *eine Vorstellung ist im Bewusstseyn*, muss unterschieden werden von dem: *ich bin mir meiner Vorstellung bewusst*. Zu dem letztern gehört innere Wahrnehmung, zum erstern nicht.] Herbart, *Lehrbuch zur Psychologie*, §130; *SW*, IV: 372.

[65] [so würden wir uns unaufhörlich in dem Zustande der unerträglichsten Beklemmung befinden; oder vielmehr, der menschliche Leib würde in eine Spannung gerathen, die in wenigen Augenblicken tödten müsste]. Herbart, *Lehrbuch zur Psychologie*, §133; *SW*, IV: 373.

[66] Fechner, *Elemente der Psychophysik*, vol. I, ch. 8 (69–134); see also Murray, "A Perspective for Viewing the History of Psychophysics," 128–31, and Ehrenstein, "Psychophysical Methods," 1214–17.

When we are "all eyes" or "all ears," and thus concentrating on the seeing of an object or the hearing of a sound, we can, as it is sometimes said, become "oblivious to the world" around us. The threshold of awareness for the eye or the ear sinks, but is raised for the remaining senses, so that sensations produced under the latter conditions can remain unconscious. Fechner depicts an especially striking example of this in his *Elements of Psychophysics*: it may be the case that one lies there with open eyes, reflecting intensely upon something without noticing one's surroundings. In this situation there may arise the after-image of a visual impression (*Seheindruck*) that one completely fails to notice, but which becomes conscious as soon as one shuts one's eyes. "The physical impression was thus made in such a form that the visual sensation (*Gesichtsempfindung*) could emerge, but so long as the attention was distracted, it remained unconscious but could still enter into consciousness at a later stage."[67]

The question as to what precisely is to be understood by unconscious sensations had, since the 1870s, strongly determined the reception of psychophysics while also entangling Fechner in many arguments with his critics. One peculiarity of Fechner's treatment of unconscious sensations is also that, with the further development of the measurement formula, its values of measurement became negative values. This caused especially strong irritation among Fechner's critics, because we hold negative sensations to be meaningless. Fechner was, however, able to counter this argument. When reading his psychophysical treatment of the unconscious, one can sense clearly the effort to avoid any speculation.[68] Even in his final essay, he wrote with resignation: "It might be indisputably desirable that the controversy over negative sensation values might finally come to an end; but based upon my experiences up until now, even my shadow will not be left in peace by this controversy."[69]

---

[67] [Der physische Eindruck war also in solcher Form gemacht, dass die Gesichtsempfindung entstehen konnte, aber er war, so lange die Aufmerksamkeit abgelenkt war, unbewusst geblieben, und konnte doch nachmals noch in das Bewusstsein treten.] Fechner, *Elemente der Psychophysik*, vol. II, 432.

[68] Especially instructive in this connection, and in relation to the issue of negative sensation values, is the correspondence, first published in 1890, that Fechner pursued between 1874 and 1883 with the Jena professor of physiology William Thierry Preyer (1841–97). See also footnote 76 below.

[69] [Es wäre unstreitig erwünscht, wenn die Kontroverse über die negativen Empfindungswerte endlich einmal ein Ende fände; aber nach meinen bisherigen Erfahrungen wird wohl noch mein Schatten davor keine Ruhe haben.] Fechner, "Ueber die psychischen Massprincipien und das Weber'sche Gesetz: Discussion mit Elsas und Köhler," *Philosophische Studien* 4 (1887): 161–230; here 224. An excerpt (178–98) of this paper is translated by Eckart Scheerer as "My Own Viewpoint on Mental Measurement," *Psychological Research* 49 (1987): 213–19.

As a further refinement of the issue raised in the above quotation – that concerning the notion that psychology cannot dispense with unconscious sensations – Fechner formulates the following questions:

But how can "what is not" have an effect; or by what means is an unconscious sensation, representation, to be distinguished from one which we do not have at all? The differentiation must be made, but how it is to be made clearly? And where is the clarity concerning this question to be found since its inception?[70]

Fechner held these questions to have been resolved by his psychophysics: "I considered it, in fact, to be one of the most beautiful outcomes of our theory that it provides this clarity."[71] True to the first version of psychophysical parallelism, he defines unconscious sensations in a purely operational way. An unconscious sensation is for him the psychical side of that physical activity of the organism which, under other conditions (namely, when the physical activity is stronger), is directly correlated with a psychical or conscious side (and is thus psychophysical) and which has causal effects on the conscious side:

Sensations and representations have, in the unconscious state, certainly ceased to exist as real sensations and representations, insofar as one grasps them abstractly and as separated from their foundation. But something goes on in us, the psychophysical activity, of which the sensations and representations are a function, and on which the possibility of their re-emergence depends, in accordance with the oscillation of life [i.e. natural spontaneous fluctuations], or with specific inner or outer causes, which raise this movement over the threshold; and this movement can also intervene in the play of the conscious psychophysical movements, which belong to other phenomena of consciousness, and call forth alterations within them, the reasons of which remain for us in the unconscious.[72]

At first glance, it might seem as though what Fechner calls unconscious activity is not really unconscious, but a purely physical activity. If unconscious

---

[70] [Aber wie kann wirken, was nicht ist; oder wodurch unterscheidet sich eine unbewusste Empfindung, Vorstellung von einer solchen, die wir gar nicht haben? Der Unterschied muss gemacht werden, aber wie ist er klar zu machen? Und wo ist seither eine Klarheit darüber zu finden?] Fechner, *Elemente der Psychophysik*, vol. II, 439.

[71] [Ich betrachte es in der That als eins der schönsten Ergebnisse unserer Theorie, dass sie diese Klarheit giebt.] Ibid., vol. II, 439.

[72] [Empfindungen, Vorstellungen haben freilich im Zustande des Unbewusstseins aufgehört, als wirkliche zu existiren, sofern man sie abstract von ihrer Unterlage fasst, aber es geht etwas in uns fort, die psychophysische Tätigkeit, deren Function sie sind, und woran die Möglichkeit des Wiederhervortrittes der Empfindung hängt, nach Massgabe als die Oscillation des Lebens [d.h. natürliche spontane Schwankungen] oder besondere innere oder äussere Anlässe die Bewegung wieder über die Schwelle heben; und diese Bewegung kann auch in das Spiel der bewussten psychophysischen Bewegungen, welche zu anderen Bewusstseinsphänomenen gehören, eingreifen und Abänderungen darin hervorrufen, deren Grund für uns im Unbewusstsein bleibt.] Ibid.

sensations below the threshold are not "real," as he expresses it, they would also not be able to have any effect and only the physical realm would remain effectual. Where then does the "mental" (*das Geistige*) reside in the unconscious? One was thus inclined to conclude that Fechner offered a so-called "dispositional understanding" of the unconscious, for which, in fact, the states in question possess a disposition toward mental (*per definitionem* conscious) states, but which are not really mental (*geistig*).[73] This is, however, incorrect. Here we must first distinguish between outer and inner psychophysics. According to outer psychophysics, only the functional dependency between the external stimulus and the inner-side is maintained. The negative sensation values inform us as to how much the stimulus must be raised for the sensation to cross the threshold of consciousness. Whatever in these values is, in addition, "sensation-like" (*empfindungsmässig*) is a question which does not apply to outer psychophysics. Apart from this, Fechner clearly states that unconscious processes have an effect on consciousness:

If, in the state of sleep, our [psychophysical] process should fall below this [threshold-] value [i.e. become unconscious], it still contributes to the elevation of general consciousness and its psychical value is not then nothing; rather *our* consciousness merely has no sense of it any more, in fact its psychical value, as determined by the distance from the point at which it becomes *real* for us, is negative.[74]

Finally, Fechner also makes an explicit distinction between the terms "unconscious" (*unbewusst*) and "conscious-less" (*bewusstlos*). Consciousless processes have no influence on the life of the soul, whereas unconscious processes do:

---

[73] This is the position of Franz Brentano in his *Psychologie vom empirischen Standpuncte*, 2 vols. in 1 (Leipzig: Duncker & Humblot, 1874), vol. I, 168. Translated by Benito Müller as *Descriptive Psychology* (London: Routledge, 1995). More recently, David Livingstone Smith has also argued that "The group of thinkers (among them Fechner) whom I called the *dispositionalists* ... preserved the Cartesian framework by denying that apparently unconscious mental states were genuinely mental, and claimed that they are actually neurophysiological dispositions for (by definition, conscious) mental states." See Smith, "'Some Unimaginable Substratum': A Contemporary Introduction to Freud's Philosophy of Mind," *Psychoanalytic Knowledge*, ed. Man Cheung Chung and Colin Feltham (Houndmills, Basingstoke: Palgrave Macmillan, 2003), 54–75; here 60. Furthermore, Mai Wegener also falsely claims that "Fechner's unconscious is unambiguously physical" [Fechners Unbewusstsein ist unzweideutig ein physisches]. See Wegener, "Das psychische Unbewusste," 253. The unconscious is, of course, both for Fechner: physical *and* psychical!

[74] [Fällt nun unser [psychophysischer] Prozess im Schlafe unter diesen [Schwellen]Wert [d.h. wird er unbewusst], so trägt er immer noch zur Erhebung des Allgemeinbewusstseins bei, sein psychischer Wert ist also nicht Nichts; nur dass *unser* Bewusstsein nichts mehr davon hat, ja für uns ist der psychische Wert als Abstand von dem Punkte, wo er *wirklich* für uns wird, ein negativer.] Fechner, *Die Tagesansicht gegenüber der Nachtansicht* (Leipzig: Breitkopf & Härtel, 1879), 245; reprint (Eschborn: Klotz, 1994).

Gustav Theodor Fechner and the unconscious

What we call unconscious or sleeping for consciousness is not, on this account, without influence upon consciousness, and is not to be confused with being conscious-less; in the former state, nothing is distinguishable for consciousness, but rather comes together in a general influence. Whoever goes walking in beautiful surroundings and reflects deeply does not know what sort of birds are singing around him, what sort of trees he encounters; the sun warms and shines; he thinks nothing of it; but yet his soul is otherwise tuned than when he sits in a cold dark room and similarly reflects; the surroundings themselves will certainly have an influence on the form and liveliness of his train of thought; thus all of those unconscious elements are not without influence on his consciousness, they are only termed unconscious because they do not distinguish themselves for consciousness according to particular characteristics.[75]

Fechner did not, however, closely investigate the type of effect exerted by the unconscious on the psychical level, but left this to psychology, which he strictly distinguished from psychophysics.

The concept of a negative sensation must not, by the way, be confused with the concept of the opposing quality of a sensation, as was done by some of Fechner's contemporaries: a negative sensation of heat is not a sensation of cold, but the degree (*Ausmass*) of psychophysical activity which is still lacking that would make the (unconscious) sensation of heat become perceptible – or, as Fechner puts it in the above quotation, "real" (*wirklich*) – that is, raising it to consciousness. Negative sensations are not even synonymous with weak sensations, as was likewise assumed. Sensations aroused through strong stimuli can also remain unconscious.

Considered from the perspective of inner psychophysics, the reproach that unconscious activity is purely physical and not mental is likewise to be rejected. Such a reproach would fall back into a Cartesian mode of thinking and overlook the fact that for Fechner the psychical is always coupled with a psychophysical activity, which, in principle, also appears physically. Fechner expressly states that unconscious sensations and representations do not really exist only "insofar as one grasps them

---

[75] [Was wir unbewusst oder für das Bewusstsein schlafend nennen, ist darum nicht ohne Einfluss auf das Bewusstsein, nicht mit bewusstlos zu verwechseln; es scheidet sich nur nichts darin für das Bewusstsein, sondern geht in einen allgemeinen Einfluss zusammen. Wer in schöner Gegend spazieren geht und tief nachdenkt, weiß nicht, was für Vögel um ihn singen, was für Bäumen er begegnet; die Sonne wärmt und scheint; er denkt nicht daran; aber doch ist seine Seele anders gestimmt, als wenn er im finstern kalten Zimmer säße und dasselbe bedächte; ja die Umgebungen werden selbst einen Einfluss auf die Form und Lebendigkeit seines Gedankenganges haben; also ist alles jenes Unbewusste doch nicht ohne Einfluss in seinem Bewusstsein, heißt nur darum unbewusst, weil es sich für das Bewusstsein nicht nach besonderen Bestimmungen scheidet.] Fechner, *Zend-Avesta oder über die Dinge des Himmels und des Jenseits*, vol. III, 204, and also chs. 5 and 7. On this issue, see also Fechner, *Elemente der Psychophysik*, vol. II, 241; Fechner, *Einige Ideen zur Schöpfungs- und Entwickelungsgeschichte der Organismen* (Leipzig: Breitkopf & Härtel, 1873), ch. 2, fn. 2, reprint (Tübingen: edition diskord, 1985).

abstractly and as separated from their foundation" (*sofern man sie abstract von ihrer Unterlage fasst*) – meaning, when one disregards their physical correlates. If one does *not* disregard these correlates, and this is certainly expressly demanded by psychophysical parallelism, then the same physical process which in the conscious case is the vehicle of the psychical certainly remains present in unconscious sensations, if only with an attenuated physical intensity. It must thus have a psychical side, only with the difference that this side is not internally given; meaning that it is not conscious. In addition, a measurement for the "depths of the unconscious" (*Tiefe des Unbewusstseins*) is provided through the negative sensation values, a measurement which once again establishes a functional connection between the physical and the psychical.[76] For the recognition of the reality of the unconscious, the decisive thing is not whether, according to whatever philosophical interpretation, its psychical nature is guaranteed, but whether processes which were formerly conscious can, through whichever mechanism, also exert an effect on present psychical processes. Precisely this is provided by Fechner: the psychophysical activity, which once was conscious, is still capable of exerting observable effects even when it is no longer correlated with any psychical side.

One might then think, and the cited examples also suggest this, that for Fechner unconscious mental states are only ever preconscious, and are thus principally in fact those which are capable of becoming conscious (*bewusstseinsfähig*). According to this view, unconscious mental states are not available to consciousness at a certain point in time, but can easily be moved into consciousness through a focusing of the attention. In the *Vorschule der Aesthetik*, Fechner deals, for example, with the "creative role of fantasy" (*schöpferische Rolle der Phantasie*) and notes that the source of fantasy, whether it develops from inner or outer causes, is always the same; namely, consciousness:

It is everywhere the echo, sunk into and blended with unconsciousness, of that which was once in consciousness, and which, through this or that outer or inner cause, in this or that combination, can enter consciousness again. Every associated impression is an already complete particular combination, called into consciousness by an external cause ... According to this, we are right to search within the unconscious for the source from which fantasy creates, only not in an *Ur-unconscious*, it is rather a source which first had to fill

---

[76] Fechner, *Elemente der Psychophysik*, vol. II, 39; Fechner, *Wissenschaftliche Briefe von Gustav Theodor Fechner und W. Preyer: Nebst einem Briefwechsel zwischen K. von Vierordt und Fechner und 9 Beilagen*, ed. William Thierry Preyer (Hamburg and Leipzig: Leopold Voß, 1890), 20.

itself with contents from consciousness and only through conscious activity can it be emptied again.[77]

An *Ur-unconscious* (Fechner uses this expression only in this connection) might then be an unconscious that did not originally emerge from consciousness. Three things are to be noted here. First, under the influence of Schelling and his followers, Fechner assumes in his philosophy of nature (as, incidentally, does Charles Sanders Peirce) a conscious "cosmorganic" (*kosmorganischer*) originary state of nature (*Urzustand*), out of which organic as well as inorganic nature have developed as products of crystallization (*Kristallisationsprodukte*) and as the opposing results of a differentiation.[78] Secondly, Fechner did not support the view that everything that is unconscious for the *single individual* originates in states of mind that have at one time been conscious to *him or her*. Rather, he holds it to be probable that

the whole purposeful formation of the embryo today is only the inherited legacy of the first consciously created constitution of the human, which was elaborated through a long series of conscious generations. The born human being can therefore only elaborate upon the finer details of this constitution, because he or she received, at birth, the main mental structures as the inheritance of former consciously made acquisitions.[79]

The view that everything unconscious arises out of consciousness may thus, when viewed ontogenetically, not necessarily apply. Third, the door to speculation *à la* Hartmann or that of the German idealists would be opened under the following conditions: namely, if one is permitted to

---

[77] [Es ist überall der ins Unbewusstsein gesunkene, darin verschmolzene, Nachklang dessen, was je im Bewusstsein war, und durch diese oder jene, äußere oder innere, Anlässe, in dieser oder jener Kombination, wieder ins Bewusstsein treten kann. Jeder assoziierte Eindruck ist eine, durch einen äußern Anlass ins Bewusstsein gerufene, schon fertige besondere Kombination. ... Man hat hiernach Recht, den Quell, aus dem die Phantasie schöpft, im Unbewusstsein zu suchen, nur nicht in einem Ur-Unbewusstsein, vielmehr ist es ein Quell, der sich erst aus dem Bewusstsein füllen musste und nur durch bewusste Tätigkeit wieder ausgeschöpft werden kann.] Fechner, *Vorschule der Aesthetik*, 2 vols. (Leipzig: Breitkopf & Härtel, 1876), vol. I, 113; reprint (Hildesheim: Olms 1978). Part of the *Vorschule der Aesthetik* (vol. I, ch. 14), entitled "Verschiedene Versuche, eine Grundform der Schönheit aufzustellen: Experimentale Ästhetik: Goldner Schnitt und Quadrat," is translated by Monika Niemann, Julia Quehl and Holger Höge as "Various Attempts to Establish a Basic Form of Beauty: Experimental Aesthetics, Golden Section, and Square," *Empirical Studies of the Arts* 15, no. 2 (1997): 115–30.
[78] See Heidelberger, *Nature from Within*, 255–71.
[79] [die ganze heutige zweckmäßige Bildung des Embryo nur die vererbte Hinterlassenschaft der durch eine lange Reihe von bewussten Generationen geschehenen Ausarbeitung der ersten, ihrerseits bewusst zu Stande gebrachten Anlage des Menschen sei, die der geborene Mensch eben deshalb nur noch in feinere Bestimmungen ausarbeiten kann, weil er die ganze Hauptanlage als Erbe früheren bewussten Erwerbes bei der Geburt fertig mitbekommen]. Fechner, *Einige Ideen zur Schöpfungs- und Entwickelungsgeschichte der Organismen*, 102.

regard physical processes as carrying unconscious states, even when we know nothing (and can therefore not first form a rational scientific supposition) about what is happening on those occasions when the intensity of the psychophysical activity inherent in the material vehicle of the unconscious oversteps the threshold of consciousness. We can, in other words, only grant an unconscious to that system which is fundamentally capable of consciousness. Accordingly, Fechner argues that Hartmann's conception of the unconscious violates this fundamental rule.[80]

The "psychophysical structural levels of the world" and their dynamics

Fechner believed that he was able to derive clues from psychophysics for his views concerning the philosophy of nature, as well as for his religious vision of nature – perspectives which for him had once been the point of departure for his psychophysical reflections. Especially important for Fechner are the philosophical elaborations that follow from a generalization of his concept of the threshold. Fechner derives from this concept a hypothesis regarding the dynamics of the unconscious. He did not regard his theories of the unconscious to be scientifically proven or corroborated, but thought that they were at least suggested by science and in that sense compatible with it. Later on, this type of theoretical formation – which takes findings from the natural sciences as clues for philosophical conjectures – would be referred to as "inductive metaphysics."

In the conscious activity of the senses, the activities of all sensory organs are bound together with one another in an overarching consciousness. Fechner adds that the "upper waves" or harmonics of each of the activities of the senses (*Sinnestätigkeiten*) belong together with one another in a "main wave" (*Hauptwelle*). The main wave of the total consciousness (*Gesamtbewusstsein*) must cross a certain level, that of the "main threshold" (*Hauptschwelle*), in order that the central consciousness (*Zentralbewusstsein*) be conscious. The upper waves represent the attention, which fluctuates according to time and to particular settings. The individual senses can cross beneath their own thresholds, without the total consciousness ceasing to be conscious:

What [constitutes] separation of consciousness between neighboring levels is only differentiation in consciousness of a higher level … The sensory areas of our eyes and ears are separated, insofar as neither of them shares their sensations

---

[80] On Fechner's critique of Hartmann, see ibid., 15, 101; Fechner, *Vorschule der Aesthetik*, vol. I, chs. 9 and 12. Fechner's late philosophical work of 1879, *Die Tagesansicht gegenüber der Nachtansicht*, originally emerged from a polemic against Hartmann. On the history of this work see Heidelberger, *Nature from Within*, 62.

Gustav Theodor Fechner and the unconscious   233

with the other. But the consciousness of the whole human being grasps both as being differentiated; and according to the perspective of human beings the individual intuiting points of the senses are still separated, yet the entire intuition of the human being grasps them as a unity which is differentiated.[81]

Should the main wave now sink – for example, in sleep – beneath the main threshold, then there is no main consciousness any more, but individual upper waves can cross the main threshold. An example of this would be found in dreams, where consciousness exists for separate parts of the psychophysical activity, without these being enclosed (as is the case in the waking state) by the overarching central consciousness of the sleeper. Dreams therefore have a different "scene" (*Schauplatz*) of appearance, as Fechner puts it.[82] It is as if, through something lacking in the central consciousness, "the psychophysical activity were moving from the brain of a rational person into that of a madman" or, better, into that "of a child or a savage." What is lacking here is namely that "organization formulated by upbringing."[83] Fechner's argumentation is represented in the diagrams from *Elements of Psychophysics* shown in Figure 8.1.

In these diagrams, A B is the main threshold, a, b, c, etc. ... are the upper waves, and A' B' the threshold of the upper waves. The upper waves join together above the main threshold through a main consciousness but can be distinguished from one another, since they lie discontinuously over their thresholds. The illustrations can be interpreted for a single individual, whereby: a, b, c, etc. represent the activity of the individual senses; A' B' represents the affiliated thresholds below which unconscious sensory activity can take place; and A B portrays the threshold for the main consciousness, under which unconscious processes can take place for the main consciousness. But they can also be interpreted as the inclusion of the individual consciousnesses of separate human beings in a more collective consciousness. In this case a, b, c, etc. represent the activity of these individual consciousnesses of different human beings, which are conscious insofar as they exist above A' B',

---

[81] [Was Scheidung des Bewusstseins zwischen Nachbarstufen, ist nur Unterscheidung im Bewusstsein einer höhern Stufe ... Die Sinneskreise unserer Augen und Ohren sind geschieden, sofern keiner seine Empfindungen mit dem andern teilt, das Bewusstsein des ganzen Menschen aber greift, beide unterscheidend, beide in sich; und im Auge des Menschen sind noch die einzelnen anschauenden Punkte geschieden, doch der ganze Anschauungskreis des Menschen greift, beide unterscheidend, beide in sich.] Fechner, *Die Tagesansicht gegenüber der Nachtansicht*, 30.

[82] Fechner, *Elemente der Psychophysik*, vol. II, 520; this expression is also used on pages 450 and 523.

[83] [die psychophysische Thätigkeit aus dem Gehirne eines Vernünftigen in das eines Narren übersiedelte]; [eines Kindes oder eines Wilden]; [durch Erziehung ausgearbeitete Organisation]. Ibid., vol. II, 522.

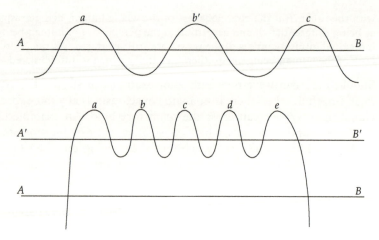

Figure 8.1 Illustrations by Fechner, *Elements of Psychophysics* (*Elemente der Psychophysik*), vol. II, 529 and 540.[84]

but which are individually unconscious, yet conscious for the overarching consciousness, insofar as the activity falls beneath A B.

This image of the relation of sensory consciousness (*Sinnesbewusstsein*) to total consciousness (*Gesamtbewusstsein*) can now also be applied to the relation of the individual human consciousness to an overarching consciousness. Although each sense organ has its own "consciousness," which shares its perception with no other sense, these separate regions of consciousness (*Bewusstseinsbereiche*) are at the same time held together through the overarching consciousness of the perceiving person. In a similar way, the individual "consciousnesses" of human beings find their unity in an overarching consciousness without the individual consciousness knowing anything about it. The main threshold of this overarching consciousness lies deeper than that of any individual consciousness, so that the unconscious of the single individual corresponds to a conscious psychical correlation in the higher system that embraces it. It is important to recognize that every overarching consciousness must, true to psychophysical parallelism, possess a physical vehicle which encloses the bodies of separate individuals, just as our body surely also represents a corporeal system which encloses all of the senses.

[84] The first illustration is also found in a work by William James in his translation of Fechner's *Elements of Psychophysics* (vol. II, 526–30), wherein he declares his support for Fechner's considerations. See William James, *Human Immortality: Two Supposed Objections to the Doctrine* (Boston/New York: Houghton, Mifflin & Co, 1898), 92. Cited according to reprint in *The Works of William James*, vol. IX: *Essays in Religion and Morality* (Cambridge, MA: Harvard University Press, 1982), 75–101.

The separating out (*Ausdifferenzierung*) of the universe into organic-conscious and inorganic realms, of which we spoke above, operates for Fechner according to a general developmental law (*Entwicklungsgesetz*), the "principle of the tendency toward stability" (*Princip der Tendenz zur Stabilität*). He established this law in 1873 with the publication of his book entitled *Some Ideas Concerning the Creative and Developmental History of Organisms* (*Einige Ideen zur Schöpfungs- und Entwickelungsgeschichte der Organismen*).[85] Neither the causal law, nor the principle of the conservation of energy, tell us anything about the general direction in which the consequences that they are referring to might lead. The causal law says something about the behavior of the individual parts of a system and the principle of the conservation of energy, as well as something about the total energy of the system (*Gesamtenergie*) during its development, but this does not suffice to explain the frequency of the occurrence of individual conditions in the total system. Only through a supplementary law does any information emerge about how the individual effects are exerted with regard to the state of the system as a whole. Such a law possesses a finalistic character, without the goal of development being assumed as given from the outset. (In modern parlance, in the terminology of the evolutionary biologist Ernst Mayr, Fechner's developmental law might be considered as "teleonomic," but not as "teleological," in the same way that the second law of thermodynamics also possesses the property of striving for a goal without being teleological.)[86] Only by combining all of the stated laws within such a developmental law does there emerge for Fechner a *general* concept of the "lawfulness" (*Gesetzlichkeit*) of a system; only in this way can such knowledge about the total development of a system be gained by referring back to the behavior of the individual parts.

The borderline cases for the behavior of a system are constituted by complete stability, when no part is moving within it, and complete instability, when the parts lawlessly scatter themselves into infinity without reference to one another. Between these extremes there lies a spectrum of different levels of stability: a system becomes more stable when its particles (*Teilchen*) periodically return to the same state, or into something approximating this state. Thus, there must be a tendency toward full or approximate stability within this intermediate realm (*Zwischenbereich*). On closer inspection it emerges that world events as a whole as well as individually are indeed governed by a tendency toward approximate stability. The movements of the planets in the solar system possess approximate

---

[85] See Heidelberger, *Nature from Within*, ch. 7.
[86] See Ernst Mayr, "Teleological and Teleonomic: A New Analysis," *Methodological and Historical Essays in the Natural and Social Sciences*, ed. Robert S. Cohen and Marx W. Wartofsky (Dordrecht: Kluwer, 1974), 91–117.

stability, since a full stability in their periodic rotations around the sun is hindered by their reciprocal influence on one another. In a similar way, a pendulum would, in the absence of friction, also be fully stable. Furthermore, every organism displays a condition of approximate stability in its functions. The principle of the tendency toward stability, which is subject to all of these experiences, expresses in abstract form the idea that every system that is left to itself under the same external conditions will, over the course of time, approach a condition of approximate or full stability. Strictly speaking, the principle holds only for the world as a whole (*Weltganze*), because this is the only system that succumbs to no external influences; it holds for parts of the whole only in a modified way.

Fechner took these considerations much further still, but we cannot explore these developments here. Of interest to us here, however, are the consequences of these considerations for the unconscious. If, as Fechner's third version of psychophysical parallelism implies, every physical happening also has a psychical side, then the principle of stability must also possess a psychical significance. The most general form of consciousness is feeling, which shows itself as pleasure or as unpleasure. A pleasurable event is always accompanied by the striving for the preservation of the state of pleasure, while an event generating unpleasure possesses the opposite: striving for the avoidance and elimination of the state of unpleasure. If an unpleasurable state is voluntarily assumed, this is only because it is accompanied by the expectation of a later and longer-lasting pleasurable condition. The more a system develops in this way, the more it comes – analogously to the psychical process of heightened attention – to a concentration of the acts of consciousness in stable individual aggregates, in which consciousness is refined, improved, and increased, and in which the consciousness of those more stable parts that are subordinate to the aggregates sinks below the threshold of consciousness. In this way consciousness is freed for the development of higher functions. Activities which, to begin with, still called for consciousness, thus become unconscious:

Operations in the service of conscious life, which we describe as being purposeful, be they outer or inner, require in every aspect for their *first* emergence the special direction of conscious activity towards their purpose. But once they have emerged, they require, in order to be repeated, only a general co-activation of consciousness, in which a traceable connection to this purpose has more or less receded. In short: *the special form of consciousness which is necessary for the initial emergence of effective operations is no longer required for their repetition.*[87]

[87] [Einrichtungen zum Dienste bewussten Lebens, die wir als solche zweckmäßig nennen, seien es äußere oder innere, bedürfen zu ihrer *erstmaligen* Entstehung überall der spezialen Richtung bewusster Tätigkeit auf ihren Zweck, einmal entstanden aber zu ihrer Wiederholung nur noch einer allgemeinen Mitbetätigung des Bewusstseins, bei

Gustav Theodor Fechner and the unconscious

When we now go back from the cosmic significance of the principle of stability to its significance for human beings, we ascertain from Fechner that those psychophysical movements lying above the threshold are felt to be pleasurable when they tend towards a stable state and unpleasurable when the state loses its stability. Therefore, the objection cannot even be raised that the condition of absolute peace (or the full stability of inorganic bodies) would have to yield the greatest pleasure, when in the long term it in fact produces only boredom and thus unpleasure. Such a condition is situated below the threshold of consciousness and tends, in the case of boredom, to come closer to this threshold. Fechner speaks of a qualitative threshold pertaining to both pleasure and unpleasure, which in the case of pleasure lies higher and in the case of unpleasure lies lower than the main threshold, which he also in this connection describes as a quantitative threshold.[88] Between both thresholds – that is, the qualitative threshold and the main or quantitative threshold – there is situated a zone of indifference (*Indifferenzzone*), in which consciousness is in fact present, but neither pleasure nor unpleasure, because in the approach towards stability the qualitative threshold of pleasure and unpleasure has not yet been crossed. According to circumstances, states of pleasure or unpleasure can also be of an unconscious nature. As Fechner observes:

Psychophysical states, in which the qualitative threshold of pleasure is exceeded, are called, according to the use already introduced earlier, *harmonious*, those in which that of unpleasure is exceeded, *dissonant*, those falling between the two, *indifferent*. Harmonious and dissonant states alike can, however, just as well be conscious as unconscious according to whether the quantitative threshold is crossed or not. And so pleasure and unpleasure alike can thereby recede, through the psychophysical activity or its determination, which is able to carry pleasure or unpleasure along with it, sinking below the quantitative threshold, as well as through sinking below the qualitative threshold; and the intensity of the aesthetic feeling depends at the same time and in compound relations on the crossing of the quantitative and qualitative thresholds.[89]

---

welcher eine verfolgbare Beziehung zum Zweck mehr oder weniger geschwunden ist. Kurz: *Das zur ersten Hervorbringung zweckmäßiger Einrichtungen nötige Spezialbewusstsein wird bei deren Wiederholung mehr oder weniger erspart.*] Fechner, *Die Tagesansicht gegenüber der Nachtansicht*, 116.

[88] Ibid., 217; *Einige Ideen zur Schöpfungs- und Entwickelungsgeschichte der Organismen*, 94ff.
[89] [Psychophysische Zustände, in welchen die qualitative Schwelle der Lust überstiegen wird, heißen uns, nach schon früher eingeführtem Gebrauch, *harmonische*, solche, in welchen die der Unlust überstiegen wird, *disharmonische*, zwischen beide fallende *indifferente*. Harmonische wie disharmonische Zustände können aber ebensowohl bewusst als unbewusst sein, jenachdem die quantitative Schwelle dabei überschritten wird oder nicht. Und es kann also Lust wie Unlust überhaupt ebensowohl dadurch schwinden, dass die psychophysische Tätigkeit oder Bestimmung derselben, welche Lust oder Unlust mitzuführen vermag, unter die quantitative Schwelle sinkt, als dass sie unter die qualitative Schwelle sinkt; und hängt die Stärke des ästhetischen Gefühls überhaupt

Fechner also made these reflections into the basis of his aesthetics, in which he deals not only with the crossing of thresholds as pleasure-heightening and thereby more aesthetically appealing, but still with other conditions such as, for example, the unified integration of the manifold. In any case, the human being strives throughout his or her entire life for pleasure and thereby fulfills a tendency which belongs to the whole universe. In this case, the unconscious stands in service of the further and higher development of consciousness. For Fechner, this gives rise to a *eudaimonistic* ethics, the principle of which he had already expressed in 1846: "The human being should, so much as he can, in general seek to bring the greatest pleasure and the greatest happiness into the world; to seek to bring them into the totality of time and space."[90]

Fechner finally connected a peculiar conception of death to his theories of natural philosophy. As a living or dead being, the human being is for him part of a living whole. Individual human consciousnesses are bound up with the all-consciousness (*Allbewusstsein*) and merge into it. During our conscious life we are unconscious of the all-consciousness and only in individual consciousness does it cross the threshold. In death we in fact lose the ability as individuals to have conscious experiences, but the experiences acquired during our life persist after the decline of our body, since they are bound up with the material consequences which certainly go on existing after death and which possess a psychical side. Every human being is thus, during his life, creating his future life: "the life beyond of our spirits relates to this life as though it were a living memory of the intuited life from which it grew."[91] After our lifetime, we continue to exist as memories and representations of the earth, even of the whole universe. And the stronger our connection to other human beings was during our life, the stronger is our memory of them, and the more intensely will we remember them again after our death. Fechner elaborates on these speculations in the following passages:

> When I finally close my eyes in death, and my sensory life of intuitions is extinguished, will a life of recollection not then also be able to awaken in its place in the higher spirit? And when, in the life of intuition, it [i.e. the higher spirit]

---

zugleich und in zusammengesetztem Verhältnisse vom Übersteigen der quantitativen und der qualitativen Schwelle ab.] Fechner, *Die Tagesansicht gegenüber der Nachtansicht*, 217ff.

[90] [Der Mensch soll, soviel an ihm ist, die größte Lust, das größte Glück in die Welt überhaupt zu bringen suchen; ins Ganze der Zeit und des Raumes zu bringen suchen.] Fechner, *Ueber das höchste Gut* (Leipzig: Breitkopf & Härtel, 1846), 10; reprint (Frankfurt am Main: Diesterweg, 1925).

[91] [Das jenseitige Leben unserer Geister verhält sich zu dem diesseitigen ähnlich wie ein Erinnerungsleben zu dem Anschauungsleben, aus dem es erwachsen ist.] Fechner, *Zend-Avesta oder über die Dinge des Himmels und des Jenseits*, vol. III, 8.

saw everything brightly and intensely through me, yet only ever just what was there and how it actually pushed itself forth, will now the recollection of all that which belonged to my life of intuitions not, through its own strength – individually less brightly, as a totality livelier and richer – begin to live and to weave, and in relation to and in interaction with the spheres of memory, which the higher spirit gained through the death of others? As truly as my life of intuitions has been the life of an autonomous, self-aware and self-differentiating being within the higher spirit, so too will this also have to be the case in my life of memory.[92]

We do not ... assume that *after* death we will first sleep for a time in order then to awaken, rather we are spared this sleep, since our future body is already sleeping during this life, in order to awake through death into the future life. We might regard this as a kind of resurrection, in which everything that had become unconscious during our lives and which had sunk into sleep recovers in death the ability to enter into consciousness again or to gain an influence upon consciousness. In the same way that something of our effects extends beyond us, all that which is unconscious sinks into the sleeping body and awakens to consciousness only in death.[93]

We can still recognize even here the influence of Herbart, who adopted from John Locke the concept of the "narrowness of consciousness" – the view that memories reciprocally displace one another, and thus cannot step into consciousness all at once, but only do so successively.[94] In the consciousness of the "All-mind" (*Allgeistes*), however, which is far wider than that of an individual human being, the memories of all human beings are in consciousness at one and the same time, just as the perceptions of the different senses can also exist in our narrow human consciousness at the same time.[95]

---

[92] [Wenn ich nun das Auge im Tode schließe, und mein sinnliches Anschauungsleben erlischt, wird dann nicht auch statt seiner ein Erinnerungsleben im höhern Geist dafür erwachen können? Und wenn er durch mich im Anschauungsleben alles hell und stark sah, doch immer nur, was eben da war, und wie sich's eben aufdrang, wird nicht jetzt auch die Erinnerung alles dessen, was mein Anschauungsleben umfasste, im Einzelnen wohl weniger hell, im ganzen lebendiger und reicher, selbstkräftig anfangen zu leben und zu weben, und in Beziehung und Verkehr zu treten mit den Erinnerungskreisen, die er durch den Tod andrer Menschen gewonnen? So wahr aber mein Anschauungsleben das eines selbständig in ihm sich fühlenden und unterscheidenden Wesens war, so wahr wird es auch noch das Erinnerungsleben sein müssen.] Ibid., vol. III, 8.
[93] [Wir nehmen ... nicht an, dass wir *nach* dem Tode erst eine Zeit lang schlafen werden, um dann zu erwachen, sondern dass uns dieser Schlaf dadurch erspart sei, dass unser zukünftiger Leib schon während des Jetztlebens schläft, um mit dem Tode ins künftige Leben zu erwachen. Ja wir können es als eine Art Auferstehung betrachten, dass all das im Laufe unsers Lebens Unbewusstgewordene, in Schlaf Versenkte, mit dem Tode die Fähigkeit wiedererhält, ins Bewusstsein zu treten oder auf dasselbe Einfluss zu gewinnen. So wie etwas von unseren Wirkungen jetzt über uns hinaus ist, versinkt es in den schlafenden Leib, der erst im Tode für das Bewusstsein erwacht.] Ibid., vol. III, 8.
[94] Herbart, *Psychologie als Wissenschaft*, 48, 178; *SW*, V: 214, 294.
[95] Fechner, *Zend-Avesta oder über die Dinge des Himmels und des Jenseits*, vol. III, ch. 21.

Conclusion

As much as Fechner took a pronounced critical stance against the philosophy of German idealism, and although he vehemently rejected all of the scientifically unproven attempts to keep alive the idea of the unconscious in the age of natural science, he can also not in the end deny that he and his entire philosophy originally stems from the lineage of Schelling.[96] In comparison, however, with all of the other attempts to secure the unconscious as an element of German idealism and yet also to align it with natural science, Fechner made the greatest progress. His efforts are, however, ultimately not apologetic and conservative in nature – otherwise they would justifiably, like those of Eduard von Hartmann, have sunk into oblivion. They are efforts which brought new and fruitful ways of thinking into the world, which inspired many of his contemporaries and even today do not seem to have been fully exhausted. They perhaps turn out to be not powerful enough "to provide protection against the spiritual undertow of materialism," as its author definitely intended, and as was expressed in the quotation from Haym in the introduction to this chapter. But they have turned out to be (and are still turning out to be) fruitful for getting to know new dimensions of human existence.

[96] Fechner, *Ueber die physikalische und philosophische Atomenlehre* (Leipzig: Hermann Mendelssohn, 1855), iiiv.

9 Friedrich Nietzsche's perspectives on the unconscious

Martin Liebscher

Shortly before his mental breakdown at the beginning of January 1889, Friedrich Nietzsche wrote in *Ecce Homo* (1888) that "out of my writings there speaks a *psychologist* who has not his equal, that is perhaps the first thing a good reader will notice."[1] Since then, posterity has subscribed to his verdict. Today his opus is regarded as an essential contribution to a psychology of the unconscious and he himself is supposed to have been a precursor to psychoanalysis. This is rather surprising, as Nietzsche's philosophy contains no explicit theory of the unconscious; in other words, the concept of the unconscious is not at the center of his thinking. Instead one can – especially in the early writings – detect an understanding of the unconscious which aligns Nietzsche with a tradition of thought from early Romanticism to Schopenhauer, a concept with which he assumed his learned audience would be familiar. But at the same time he began – in his unpublished observations, and under the influence of contemporary scientific and linguistic theories – to bestow his own meaning upon this conception of the unconscious. This stream of thought led, in connection with his theory of the drives, to a somatic understanding of the unconscious in his middle period. As I will argue, Nietzsche's middle-period writings already pointed towards the dissolution of the concept of the unconscious, a process that was finally completed in Nietzsche's late writings on the will to power.

The attempt to elucidate Nietzsche's understanding of the unconscious has to deal with a twofold problem: first, Nietzsche refers to other theories without giving any references; second, his concept undergoes a constant development and therefore evades any fixed definition. Thus,

---

[1] Friedrich Nietzsche, *Ecce Homo*, trans. R. J. Hollingdale (Harmondsworth: Penguin, 1979), 75. [Dass aus meinen Schriften ein *Psychologe* redet, der nicht seines Gleichen hat, das ist vielleicht die erste Einsicht, zu der ein guter Leser gelangt.] Nietzsche, *Sämtliche Werke: Kritische Studienausgabe*, 15 vols., ed. Giorgio Colli and Mazzino Montinari (Berlin: Walter de Gruyter; Munich: Deutscher Taschenbuch Verlag, 1980), vol. VI, 305 (this edition will hereafter be cited with the letters *KSA*, followed by volume and page numbers).

one is confronted with some basic questions of Nietzsche philology, which have to be clarified in advance of my undertaking.

At the outset, one needs to ask whether there is a unity to be found in the various phases of Nietzsche's thought. From the beginnings of Nietzsche research, commentators have tried to divide Nietzsche's works into different phases in order to bridge obvious contradictions.[2] Nietzsche's attempt in 1886 to write forewords to his previous works seems to be an indication of his awareness of the alleged inconsistencies. In opposition to Nietzsche scholarship which tried to find in Nietzsche's writings a consistent process of development, Karl Jaspers was the first to declare the breaks and discrepancies to be a crucial characteristic of Nietzsche's philosophy,[3] something which was later also taken on board by French poststructuralist thinkers interpreting Nietzsche's style as an expression of perspectivism.[4] With regard to Nietzsche's conceptualizations of the unconscious, this means taking into consideration the conflicting features of this concept within his work, which undergoes a series of transformations, beginning with the early writings – *The Birth of Tragedy* (*Die Geburt der Tragödie*, 1872) and *Untimely Meditations* (*Unzeitgemässe Betrachtungen*, 1873–6) – through the middle period (with its emphasis on the body), and ending with Nietzsche's late reflections on the will to power. A philologically sound approach therefore necessitates revealing the underlying connections between these distinct conceptions, by examining the influences exerted by Nietzsche's reading and by his engagement with questions in philosophy and science that were prevalent during his lifetime.

It is indeed vital to notice that Nietzsche's reflections – and this is of special importance for those on the unconscious – did not come out of the blue, but were grounded in the philosophical, scientific and historical contexts of his time. The mystical emphasis on Nietzsche's independent uniqueness along the lines of a "cult of genius" – one might think of the Stefan George circle here[5] – was rejected by the detailed study

---

[2] See Lou Andreas-Salomé's classical classification of Nietzsche's writings in *Friedrich Nietzsche in seinen Werken*, ed. Thomas Pfeifer (Frankfurt am Main: Insel, 2000).

[3] Jaspers observes: "Through interpretation one might see, in this heap of rubble, the intellectual and experienced dialectical movements in which every position – really every position – was incorporated and thus overcome," my translation; [Durch Interpretation vermag man in dem Trümmerhaufen die gedanklichen und erfahrenen dialektischen Bewegungen zu sehen, in die jede Position, aber auch schlechthin jede, hineingenommen und damit überwunden wurde.] Karl Jaspers, "Zu Nietzsches Bedeutung in der Geschichte der Philosophie," *Aneignung und Polemik: Gesammelte Reden und Aufsätze*, ed. H. Saner (Munich: Piper, 1968), 389–401, here 391.

[4] Jacques Derrida, *Spurs: Nietzsche's Styles*, trans. Barbara Harlow (Chicago: University of Chicago Press, 1979); Sarah Kofman, *Nietzsche and Metaphor*, trans. Duncan Large (Stanford, CA: Stanford University Press, 1993).

[5] For the enthusiastic reception of Nietzsche among members of the Stefan George circle see: Raymond Furness, *Zarathustra's Children: A Study of a Lost Generation of German Writers* (Rochester, NY: Camden House, 2000).

of Nietzsche's sources, initiated by the editors of the critical edition, Giorgio Colli and Mazzino Montinari. Only on the basis of these results can Nietzsche's philosophy adequately be investigated.[6]

Last but not least, this undertaking must also assess the significance of Nietzsche's unpublished writings (the *Nachlass*) for his thinking, especially as one finds a different conception of the unconscious in these sources. This is especially the case for Nietzsche's late period, where the unconscious was to be understood against the background of the theory of the will to power. Here, one has to consider very carefully to what extent these fragments offer a valid basis for an interpretation. Heidegger's approach, according to which the *Nachlass* represents Nietzsche's actual philosophy, is far too superficial.[7] On the other hand, the restriction of the *Nachlass* to the role of being a mere supplement to the published writings – as Maudemarie Clarke contends – is equally one-sided.[8] According to this principle, *On Truth and Lies in an Extra-Moral Sense* (*Ueber Wahrheit und Lüge im aussermoralischen Sinne*, 1873) would be insignificant as it obviously contradicts Nietzsche's other published writings at this time. Nietzsche retrospectively stated that he had refrained from publishing the text in 1873 because of its radical nature. But, as we shall see, this small unpublished text contains some remarkable insights into Nietzsche's understanding of the unconscious.

The *Nachlass* will therefore be used to clarify the contents of the published writings, but if a *Nachlass* text stands alone without corresponding to the published material, it must also be taken into consideration. It is, however, quite often impossible to assess whether a fragment is an abandoned experiment of thought or a vital clue that would supplement one's understanding of a key text. As such a judgment concerning the significance of any given fragment from the *Nachlass* can only be made upon the basis of a hermeneutical prejudice, a fact which therefore demands a high level of vigilance when dealing with the *Nachlass*.

---

[6] Mazzino Montinari demands a historical-philological reading of Nietzsche's works as the foundation for any philosophical engagement with Nietzsche's philosophy. See Mazzino Montinari, *Reading Nietzsche*, trans. Greg Whitlock (Illinois: University of Illinois Press, 2003), 5.

[7] Heidegger writes: "What Nietzsche himself published during his creative life was always foreground. That is also true for his treatise, *The Birth of Tragedy Out of the Spirit of Music* (1872). His philosophy proper was left behind as posthumous, unpublished work." Martin Heidegger, *Nietzsche*, vol. I: *The Will to Power as Art*, trans. David Farrell Krell (San Francisco, CA: Harper Collins, 1991), 9. [Was Nietzsche seit seines Schaffens selbst veröffentlicht hat, ist immer im Vordergrund. Dies gilt auch von der ersten Schrift *Die Geburt der Tragödie aus dem Geist der Musik* (1872). Die eigentliche Philosophie bleibt als *Nachlaß* zurück.] Heidegger, *Nietzsche*, vol. I: *Der Wille zur Macht als Kunst* (Stuttgart: Neske, 1961), 6.

[8] Maudemarie Clark, *Nietzsche on Truth and Philosophy* (Cambridge: Cambridge University Press, 1990).

In the following I will attempt to read Nietzsche's different conceptions of the unconscious against the backdrop of his perspectivism, which means giving no privilege to any of them, regardless of their place within Nietzsche's philosophical development. Of course, this does not absolve me of the obligation to examine the links between those different understandings or interpretations, but it is in accordance with Nietzsche's theory of the will to power, which – as we shall see – not only relativizes the concept of the unconscious, but actually dissolves it.

The unconscious between anti-Socratism and *Artistenmetaphysik*

In his early published writings, *The Birth of Tragedy* and *Untimely Meditations*, Nietzsche's usage of the concept of the unconscious is strongly influenced by Schopenhauer's philosophy and his close ties with Wagner. Here, the concept appears mainly in the context of his critique of Socratism.[9] In *The Birth of Tragedy*, Nietzsche characterizes Euripides as the poetic mouthpiece of Socrates and holds him responsible for the death of Attic tragedy. Euripides' tragedies bear the traces of the attempt to abandon the Dionysian aspect of tragedy and to create a pure Apollonian work, that is: a dramatized epos. He is thereby guided by the principle that everything must be conscious to be beautiful, which is equivalent to the Socratic insight that everything must be conscious in order to be good. Nietzsche concludes that the opposing tendencies of early classical tragedy, the Apollonian and the Dionysian, are transformed into a new opposition between the Dionysian and the Socratic principles, the latter of which leads to the decline of the work of art.[10]

As Socrates and Euripides made consciousness the basis of philosophy and tragedy, Dionysus was excluded from the realm of thought and poetry. According to Nietzsche, the unconscious had still been the central feature of the creative process of artists like Aeschylus and Sophocles,

---

[9] Nietzsche uses the adjective "unconscious" for the first time in 1862. See Nietzsche, *Werke. Historisch-kritische Gesamtausgabe*, ed. H. J. Mette, Carl Koch, Karl Schlechta, 5 vols. (Munich: C. H. Beck, 1933–1940), vol. II, 60 (this edition will hereafter be cited with the letters *BAW*, followed by volume and page numbers). The noun appears in his writings during his reception of Hartmann's philosophy in 1869, see *KSA*, VII: 21. See Federico Gerratana, "Der Wahn jenseits des Menschen: Zur frühen Eduard von Hartmann-Rezeption Nietzsches (1869–1874)," *Nietzsche-Studien* 17 (1988), 421; Günter Gödde: "Dionysisches – Triebe und Leib – 'Wille zur Macht': Nietzsches Annäherungen an das 'Unbewusste'," *Das Unbewusste*, 3 vols., ed. Michael Buchholz and Günter Gödde (Gießen: Psychosozial Verlag, 2005), vol. I: *Macht und Dynamik des Unbewussten: Auseinandersetzungen in Philosophie, Medizin und Psychoanalyse*, 203–34; here 205.

[10] Nietzsche, *The Birth of Tragedy and Other Writings*, ed. R. Geuss and R. Speirs, trans. R. Speirs (Cambridge: Cambridge University Press, 1999), 60; *KSA*, I: 83.

but Plato could only express his contempt for them, ironically calling those poets *bewusstlos* (without consciousness), meaning that reason no longer dwells within them and that they have no understanding of how their works are composed. But, Nietzsche continues, the artistic creative human being relies upon the Dionysian, as Socrates himself seems to have proven by referring to his *daimonion* every time his mind could not find a decisive answer to a problem:

> In this utterly abnormal nature the wisdom of instinct only manifests itself in order to *block* conscious understanding from time to time. Whereas in the case of all productive people instinct is precisely the creative-affirmative force and consciousness makes critical and warning gestures, in the case of Socrates, by contrast, instinct becomes the critic and consciousness the creator – a true monstrosity *per defectum*![11]

Two years prior to *The Birth of Tragedy* Nietzsche had given a paper in Basel, entitled "Socrates and Tragedy," which in adapted form became part of his book on tragedy. The above quotation can be found in the Basel text, but in this new version Nietzsche replaced the term "unconscious wisdom" (*unbewusste Weisheit*) with the expression "instinctive wisdom" (*instinctive Weisheit*).

Günter Gödde has interpreted this substitution as an expression of Nietzsche's increasing alienation from Eduard von Hartmann's philosophy at this time.[12] Nietzsche read the *Philosophy of the Unconscious* in 1869, one year before his Basel paper.[13] Although this was not Nietzsche's first encounter with a theory of the unconscious – in 1867 he had come across Julius Bahnsen's *Contributions to Characterology* (*Beiträge zur Charakterologie*, 1867) – Hartmann's philosophy was of special significance for him in the context of his engagement with Schopenhauer's thinking, since, as in Wagner's text on Beethoven (1870), he found an appreciation and creative revision of Schopenhauer's philosophy in Hartmann's book. One can draw this conclusion from a letter written by Cosima Wagner to Nietzsche, which suggests that the latter had recommended Hartmann to her as the successor of Schopenhauer.[14]

---

[11] Nietzsche, *The Birth of Tragedy*, 66. [Die instinctive Weisheit zeigt sich bei dieser gänzlich abnormen Natur nur, um dem bewussten Erkennen hier und da *hindernd* entgegenzutreten. Während doch bei allen productiven Menschen der Instinct gerade die schöpferisch-affirmative Kraft ist, und das Bewusstsein kritisch und abmahnend sich gebärdet: wird bei Sokrates der Instinct zum Kritiker, das Bewusstsein zum Schöpfer – eine wahre Monstrosität per defectum!] *KSA*, I: 90.
[12] Gödde, "Dionysisches – Triebe und Leib," 206.
[13] See Gerratana, "Der Wahn jenseits des Menschen"; Jörg Salaquarda: "Studien zur Zweiten Unzeitgemäßen Betrachtung," *Nietzsche-Studien* 13 (1984): 1–45.
[14] Cosima Wagner to Friedrich Nietzsche, November 30, 1869. Nietzsche, *Briefwechsel: Kritische Gesamtausgabe*, ed. Giorgio Colli, Mazzino Montinari *et al.*, 3 parts, 24 vols.

But as Federico Gerratana argues, although traces of Nietzsche's reading of Hartmann can be found in the *Birth of Tragedy* (for example, in Nietzsche's concept of the primal-one or "Ur-Eine," or in his rejection of Schopenhauer's world denial),[15] there is not a single moment in which Nietzsche's reception of Hartmann's motives can be separated from his thoroughgoing critique of Hartmann.[16] The direction of Nietzsche's critique is mainly pointed at the telic principle of world redemption, which, as Sebastian Gardner demonstrates in chapter 7 of this volume, lies at the center of Hartmann's philosophy. Nietzsche shows utter contempt for Hartmann's system of thought as an attempt to plunder Schopenhauer's originality – this criticism being most famously articulated at the end of the second *Untimely Meditation*, where Hartmann's philosophy is described as a form of unconscious irony.[17] To that extent one has to agree with Gerratana's conclusion that the influence of Hartmann can be maintained neither for Nietzsche's later concept of the unconscious, nor for his objection to Socratic optimism. At the very most, it can be stated that the Schopenhauerian element in Nietzsche was strengthened by his reading of Hartmann.[18]

This is most obviously apparent where Nietzsche addresses Schopenhauer's metaphysics of the will, and it is also here where we find another aspect of Nietzsche's understanding of the unconscious in his early writings. In the *Birth of Tragedy*, Nietzsche places the concept of the "Ur-Eine" at the centre of his "artists' metaphysics" (*Artistenmetaphysik*). At first glance his understanding corresponds with Schopenhauer's concept of the will to life, where the world of representation is an objectification of the will in its different forms: it is also a primal entity and a metaphysical whole, from which the world of representation is derived. But Nietzsche also goes further than Schopenhauer. The creation of the reality of the world is, for Nietzsche, the same as the primal imagination and dream (*Ur-Vorstellung*) of the "Ur-Eine." Thus, there is a twofold concept of appearance in Nietzsche's thought, in which the conscious representation of the individual is opposed to the *Ur-Vorstellung*.[19]

Nietzsche criticizes the Kantian-Schopenhauerian theory of representation (*Vorstellung*) for its failure to recognize that the *principium*

(Berlin, New York: Walter de Gruyter, 1975–2004), part 2, vol. II, 84 (this edition will hereafter be cited with the letters *KGB*, followed by part, volume, and page numbers). See also Gerratana, "Der Wahn jenseits des Menschen," 402.

[15] For a discussion of the non-Schopenhauerian elements of Nietzsche's Dionysian concept, see: Hans Matthias Wolff, *Friedrich Nietzsche. Der Weg zum Nichts* (Bern: Francke, 1956).

[16] See Wolff, *Friedrich Nietzsche*.

[17] See Nietzsche, *KSA*, I: 314.

[18] Gerratana, "Der Wahn jenseits des Menschen," 421.

[19] Ibid., 413.

individuationis is not part of our conscious knowledge (*Erkennen*), but rather of the primal intellect (*Ur-Intellekt*):

> I shy away from deriving space, time and causality from the pitiful human consciousness: they all belong to the will. They are conditions for every symbolism of appearances: now, the human being itself is such a symbolism, the state as well, the earth too. Now, this symbolism is absolutely not present for the individual human being alone –.[20]

As the individual consciousness is opposed to the *Ur-Vorstellung* it becomes evident that Nietzsche identifies the unconscious with the *Ur-Eine* or will. The obscure consequence of this is that the world itself is an imagination or dream of the unconscious.

The unconscious in relation to Nietzsche's *Sprachskeptizismus*

If we turn to Nietzsche's unpublished writings of the early 1870s, we find the concept of the unconscious less related to Hartmann, but more in the context of *Sprachskepsis* (language skepticism), which finds its most articulate expression in the text *On Truth and Lies in an Extra-Moral Sense* of 1873. There has been immense speculation about the significance of this short text as it seems so obviously to contradict the metaphysical contents of *The Birth of Tragedy*. Nietzsche mentions this text in the preface to the second part of *Human, All too Human* (*Menschliches, Allzumenschliches*, 1886), explaining that he had kept it secret as it contradicted or undermined everything which he had expressed publicly. At this time he had ceased to believe in anything, even in Schopenhauer.[21]

In recent years, research has demonstrated that *On Truth and Lies* had emerged from Nietzsche's critical reception of philosophical theories of language and can only be understood within this context.[22] This

---

[20] My translation. [Ich scheue mich Raum, Zeit und Kausalität aus dem erbärmlichen menschlichen Bewusstsein abzuleiten: sie sind dem Willen zu eigen. Es sind Voraussetzungen für alle Symbolik der Erscheinungen: nun ist der Mensch selbst eine solche Symbolik, der Staat wiederum, die Erde auch. Nun ist diese Symbolik unbedingt nicht für den Einzelmenschen allein dar;] *Fragment September 1870–January 1871* in Nietzsche, *Nachgelassene Fragmente 1869–1874, KSA*, VII: 114.

[21] Nietzsche, *KSA*, II: 370.

[22] See Gerald Hödl, *Nietzsches frühe Sprachkritik: Lektüren zu "Über Wahrheit und Lüge im außermoralischen Sinne"* (Vienna: Wiener Universitätsverlag, 1997); Andrea Orsucci: "Unbewusste Schlüsse, Anticipationen, Übertragungen: Über Nietzsches Verhältnis zu Karl Friedrich Zöllner und Gustav Gerber," *Centauren-Geburten: Wissenschaft, Kunst und Sprache beim frühen Nietzsche*, ed. T. Borsche, F. Gerratana, and A. Venturelli, *Texte und Monographien zur Nietzsche-Forschung* 27 (Berlin, New York: Walter de Gruyter 1994); Anthonie Meijers, "Gustav Gerber und Friedrich Nietzsche: zum historischen Hintergrund der sprachphilosophischen Auffassungen des frühen Nietzsche," *Nietzsche-*

is also valid for Nietzsche's concept of the unconscious, which, in *On Truth and Lies*, he relates to his theory of truth. The latter is based upon the assumption that the intellect is a mere tool for self-preservation and cannot access true knowledge at all, remaining always on the level of appearance. "What do human beings really know about themselves!" exclaims Nietzsche, before undertaking an analysis of reason that seeks to explain the existence of an urge for truth under specific historical circumstances.[23]

According to Nietzsche, this urge for truth originated in the attempt to find valid and binding terms for things in order to avoid the harshest "war of all against all" (*bellum omnium contra omnes*) amongst human beings. Thus, by letting the unreal appear to be real, the creation of language led to the first laws of truth. Language, for Nietzsche, does not have any access to a "thing in itself"; it merely depicts human relations to things. The progenitors of language used metaphors to transfer nervous stimuli into images and images into tones. This consideration leads to Nietzsche's famous definition of truth as a

> mobile army of metaphors, metonymies, anthropomorphisms, in short a sum of human relations which have been subjected to poetic and rhetorical intensification, translation, and decoration, and which, after they have been in use for a long time, strike a people as firmly established, canonical, and binding; truths are illusions of which we have forgotten that they are illusions, metaphors which have become worn by frequent use and have lost all sensuous vigor.[24]

With regard to the theme of the unconscious, the aspect of forgetting alluded to by Nietzsche is of great importance, since Nietzsche concludes that through his forgetting, the human being becomes an unconscious liar. The unconscious is therefore the condition which underlies our belief in truth.

Studien 17 (1988): 369–90; Anthonie Meijers and Martin Stingelin, "Konkordanz zu den wörtlichen Abschriften und Übernahmen von Beispielen und Zitaten aus Gustav Gerber: Die Sprache als Kunst (Bromberg 1871) in Nietzsches Rhetorik-Vorlesung und in 'Über Wahrheit und Lüge im außermoralischen Sinne'," *Nietzsche-Studien* 17 (1988): 350–68; Sören Reuter: "Reiz – Bild – Unbewusste Anschauung: Nietzsches Auseinandersetzung mit Hermann Helmholtz' Theorie der unbewussten Schlüsse in Über Wahrheit und Lüge im außermoralischen Sinne," *Nietzsche-Studien* 33 (2004): 351–72.

[23] Nietzsche, "On Truth and Lies in an Extra-Moral Sense," *The Birth of Tragedy*, 873–90, here 142: [Was weiss der Mensch eigentlich von sich selbst!] *KSA*, I: 877.

[24] Nietzsche, "On Truth and Lies," 146. [ein bewegliches Heer von Metaphern, Metonymien, Anthropomorphismen, kurz eine Summe von menschlichen Relationen, die, poetisch und rhetorisch gesteigert, übertragen, geschmückt wurden, und die nach langem Gebrauche einem Volk fest, kanonisch und verbindlich dünken: die Wahrheiten sind Illusionen, von denen man vergessen hat, dass sie welche sind, Metaphern, die abgenutzt und sinnlich kraftlos geworden sind]. *KSA*, I: 880.

As a number of scholars have shown convincingly, the language-philosophical contents of Nietzsche's *On Truth and Lies* are derived from his study of Gustav Gerber's *Language as Art* (*Die Sprache als Kunst*, 1871).[25] Occasionally, Nietzsche even repeats phrases and whole sentences from Gerber's book. But the engagement with Gerber's language theory is only a part of Nietzsche's general interest in philosophical considerations of language at this time. The appeal of Gerber's concept of metaphorical transference for Nietzsche can be explained by his lively interest in the theory of "unconscious inferences," which was widely discussed in those years. In particular two scientists caught Nietzsche's attention: the astrophysicist Karl Friedrich Zöllner (1834–82) and the physiologist Hermann von Helmholtz (1821–94).[26]

Nietzsche had his first encounter with the theory of unconscious inferences through Schopenhauer's *On the Fourfold Root of the Principle of Sufficient Reason* (*Über die vierfache Wurzel des Satzes vom zureichenden Grunde*, 1813), where the function of the understanding (*Verstand*) is described as an unconscious inference from a sensation (as effect) to its cause (the material object). Although Helmholtz fiercely rejected any similarities with Schopenhauer's thinking, Nietzsche could have understood this concept of sensual perception as an equivalent to Schopenhauer's theory when he first came across it, presumably via the neo-Kantian Friedrich Albert Lange's *History of Materialism* (*Geschichte des Materialismus*, 1866).[27] His assumption was then affirmed when he read Johann Nepomuk Czermak's lecture on Schopenhauer's theory of color, which argued that the research of Helmholtz, following the argument of Thomas Young, had only reproduced Schopenhauerian thoughts in an empirical manner.[28] In 1872, a book was published which emphasized the same similarities, provoking a controversy with Helmholtz and his supporters: Zöllner's *On the Nature of Comets: Contributions to the History and Theory of Knowledge* (*Über die Natur der Cometen. Beiträge zur Geschichte und Theorie der Erkenntnis*). In his preface, Zöllner defended

---

[25] See Meijers and Stingelin, "Konkordanz zu den wörtlichen Abschriften"; Hödl, *Nietzsches frühe Sprachkritik*.
[26] Hartmann also refers to both scientists in his *Philosophie des Unbewussten*.
[27] Reuter, "Reiz – Bild – Unbewusste Anschauung," 352; Claudia Crawford: *The Beginnings of Nietzsche's Theory of Language* (Berlin and New York: Walter de Gruyter, 1988).
[28] Johann Nepomuk Czermak, "Über Schopenhauers Theorie der Farben," *Sitzungsberichte der mathematisch-naturwissenschaftlichen Classe der Kaiserlichen Akademie der Wissenschaften (Wien)*, vol. LXII, part 2, folders 6–10 (1870). In a letter to Carl von Gersdorff from December 12, 1870, Nietzsche referred to this text as a great triumph; Nietzsche, *Sämtliche Briefe: Kritische Studienausgabe*, 8 vols, ed. Giorgio Colli and Mazzino Montinari (Berlin and Munich: Walter de Gruyter and Deutscher Taschenbuch Verlag, 1986), vol. III, 161 (this edition will hereafter be cited with the letters *KSB*, followed by volume and page numbers). See Orsucci, "Unbewusste Schlüsse," 193.

Wilhelm Weber's electrodynamics against the attacks of William Thomson and Peter Tait, whose *Treatise on Natural Philosophy* had been translated by Helmholtz.[29] He also attempted to ground an a priori physics based upon Weber's electrodynamics, opposing it to Helmholtz's theory of energy. The latter responded with a fierce reply:

> Judging from what he [i.e. Zöllner] aims at his ultimate object, it comes to the same thing as Schopenhauer's metaphysics. The stars are to love and hate one another, feel pleasure and displeasure, and to try to move in a way corresponding to these feelings. Indeed, in blurred imitation of the Principle of Least Action, Schopenhauer's pessimism, which declares this world to be indeed the best of possible worlds, but worse than none at all, is formulated as an ostensibly generally applicable principle of the smallest amount of discomfort, and this is proclaimed as the highest law of the world, living as well as lifeless.[30]

Despite Helmholtz's critique, it was precisely the Schopenhauerian aspect of Zöllner's theory that seems to have attracted Nietzsche at this time. He borrowed Zöllner's *Cometen* from the Basel library a number of times between November 1872 and April 1874, and in the second *Untimely Meditation* he referred to its author as the "noble Zöllner" who is attacked by Helmholtz because of his close ties with Schopenhauer.[31] In particular, Zöllner's claim that the unconscious need for causality forms the basis of our moral behavior attracted Nietzsche's interest. As a fragment written between summer 1872 and the beginning of 1873 shows, Nietzsche adopted this thought from his reading of Zöllner. Here, Nietzsche places a special emphasis on Zöllner's attempt to link emotional sensation (*Lustempfindung*) and causality, as this approach gave him the chance to associate the motivation for gaining knowledge (*Antrieb der Erkenntnis*) with the fulfillment of positive or negative sensations (*Lust- oder Unlustempfindung*).[32]

Nietzsche's epistemological considerations in the years before *On Truth and Lies* are shaped by his reception of the theory of unconscious inferences. But this theory was gradually replaced by Gerber's theory concerning the transference of images: "Unconscious *inferences* arouse my suspicion: it is probably more a case of the transition from image

---

[29] On the controversy between Helmholtz and Zöllner see Jed Z. Buchwald, "Electrodynamics in Context: Object States, Laboratory Practice and Anti-Romanticism," *Hermann von Helmholtz and the Foundations of Nineteenth-Century Science*, ed. David Cahan (Berkeley, CA: University of California Press, 1993), 363–73.

[30] Hermann von Helmholtz, "On the Use and Abuse of the Deductive Method in Physical Science," *Nature* 11 (December 24, 1874): 149–151, here 150.

[31] *KSA*, I: 292.

[32] *KSA*, VII: 19; see also Orsucci, "Unbewusste Schlüsse," 198.

to image."[33] There are different opinions about the decisiveness of this substitution.[34] Fragment 19 seems to suggest that Nietzsche completely abandoned Zöllner's concept:

> Our sensory perceptions are based on tropes, not on unconscious inferences. Identifying similar thing with similar thing – discovering some similarity or other in one thing or another thing is the primordial procedure. *Memory* thrives on this activity and constantly practices it. *Misapprehension* is the primordial phenomenon.[35]

This is the background against which Nietzsche's published writings emerge. Nietzsche himself gives an indication as to how the *Nachlass* of this time should be evaluated when he tells us that *On Truth and Lies* had already anticipated the enlightened and critical spirit of *Human, All Too Human*. But the *Nachlass* and the published writings seem to have at least a common theoretical horizon that links the language critique with the anti-Socratic thoughts of *The Birth of Tragedy*. One of those aspects is his understanding of the unconscious. In an unpublished fragment, written between September 1870 and January 1871, Nietzsche writes:

> Any expansion of our knowledge evolves out of making the unconscious conscious. Now one wonders which sign-language we have for this purpose. Some knowledge is only present for some people and other knowledge can, in an appropriately prepared mood, be recognized.[36]

Yet Nietzsche does not relate knowledge to the human liberation from the forces of nature or moral purification, but sees it as aiming at the destruction of the world. This is his argument against Socratic optimism. In another fragment, he opposes the belief in knowledge with his hopes in relation to the unconscious, which, in this context, correspond with his notion of the Dionysian: "The destruction of the world through

---

[33] Nietzsche, *Unpublished Writings from the Period of Unfashionable Observations*, trans. R. T. Gray (Stanford, CA: Stanford University Press, 1995), 37. [Die unbewussten *Schlüsse* erregen mein Bedenken: es wird wohl jenes Übergehen von Bild zu Bild sein.] *KSA*, VII: 19.

[34] Crawford calls it a turn, whereas Orsucci speaks of a mixture against the background of a common horizon of philosophical problems. See Crawford, *The Beginnings of Nietzsche's Theory of Language*, 210ff.; Orsucci, "Unbewusste Schlüsse," 201.

[35] Nietzsche, *Unpublished Writings from the Period of Unfashionable Observations*, 68. [Tropen sind's, nicht unbewusste Schlüsse, auf denen unsere Sinneswahrnehmungen beruhen. Ähnliches mit Ähnlichem identificiren – irgend welche Ähnlichkeit an einem und einem anderen Ding ausfindig machen ist der Urproceß. Das *Gedächtnis* lebt von dieser Thätigkeit .... Die Verwechslung ist das Urphänomen]; *KSA*, VII: 19.

[36] My translation. [Alle Erweiterung unsrer Erkenntniss entsteht aus dem Bewusstmachen des Unbewußten. Nun fragt es sich, welche Zeichensprache wir dazu haben. Manche Erkenntnisse sind nur für Einige da und Anderes will in der günstigsten vorbereiteten Stimmung erkannt sein.] *KSA*, VII: 116.

knowledge! Recreation through strengthening of the unconscious!"[37] Thus the question of which sign-language we possess to transfer the unconscious into consciousness is the main concern of Nietzsche's language-skeptical (*sprachskeptische*) reflections in the *Nachlass* up to *On Truth and Lies*, where he describes the metaphorical character of language as the basis of illusory truth. According to this, knowledge is not only destructive, but also impossible, which is something that the unconscious liar has forgotten.

Nietzsche's early philosophical thoughts are permeated by his engagement with the question of the unconscious, but his active reception of other theories of the unconscious tends to prevail over any single or original conception developed by Nietzsche himself. This conclusion is valid for his published writings as well as for the *Nachlass*, although the respective thinkers discussed in each of these formats differ. We have to look at Nietzsche's writings of the early 1880s to find his own original and self-contained concept of the unconscious.

The somatic unconscious

On 30 March 1881, Nietzsche wrote to Heinrich Köselitz about his approach to his earlier texts:

There is no help using my memory, e.g. I have almost forgotten the contents of my previous writings and I find this most comfortable. At least it is better than to have all these thoughts constantly in front of me and to engage with them. If there is any kind of engagement of this kind in me, it will happen "unconsciously" like the digestion of a healthy human being.[38]

This rather humorous comparison between the unconscious and the human digestive system is indeed an expression of Nietzsche's philosophical understanding of the unconscious as it is elaborated in his aphoristic volumes *Daybreak* (*Morgenröthe*, 1881) and *The Gay Science* (*Die fröhliche Wissenschaft*, 1882). This view is based on the priority of unconscious physical processes over the realm of consciousness, for which Nietzsche, in *Thus Spoke Zarathustra* (*Also sprach Zarathustra*, 1883–5), coins the phrase that "the body is a great intelligence" (*Der Leib ist eine*

---

[37] My translation. [Weltvernichtung durch Erkenntnis! Neuschaffung durch Stärkung des Unbewussten!]; *KSA*, VII: 75.

[38] My translation. [Denn mit dem Gedächtniss ist es nichts, ich habe z.B. den Inhalt meiner frühern Schriften fast vergessen, und finde dies sehr angenehm, viel besser jedenfalls als wenn man alles Gedachte immer vor sich hätte und sich mit ihm auseinandersetzen müsste. Giebt es vielleicht doch eine solche Auseinandersetzung in mir, nun, so geht sie im "Unbewußten" vor sich, wie die Verdauung bei einem gesunden Menschen!] *KSB*, VI: 77.

grosse Vernunft).³⁹ As each instinct seeks its expression, there is a struggle going on within the body. The conscious mind does not know about these processes and only notices their final consequences, which are concrete acts. The actual motives that condition particular actions remain hidden in the unconscious.⁴⁰

In aphorism 119 from *Daybreak*, entitled "Experience and Invention" (*Erleben und Erdichten*), one finds a connection with Nietzsche's earlier reflections on the unconscious in *On Truth and Lies*. Here he argues that consciousness is incapable of attaining a general overview of all the drives: their number and strength, their highs and lows, their play and counter-play, and especially the laws of their nutrition will always be unknown to the conscious mind.⁴¹ The dream is a compensation for the missing fulfillment of the drives, its contents are "interpretations of nervous stimuli we receive while we are asleep, *very free*, very arbitrary interpretations of the motions of the blood and intestines."⁴² The creative reason fantasizes about causes for these nervous stimuli, which are the results of the different drives seeking discharge. According to Nietzsche, this poetic creation of images is not only the *modus operandi* of the dreaming consciousness, but also of the waking state. The so-called conscious mind is a "more or less fantastic commentary on an unknown, perhaps unknowable, but felt text."⁴³ Nietzsche's argument that the struggle between contradictory drives in the body is the unknown cause of our actions is not restricted to the discharge of basic drives such as those pertaining to nourishment or sexuality. He also employs it in the realm of morality – where he sees moral judgments and values as being conscious

---

³⁹ Nietzsche, *Thus Spoke Zarathustra*, trans. R. J. Hollingdale (Harmondsworth: Penguin, 1961), 61; *KSA*, IV: 39.
⁴⁰ Nietzsche writes: "in short, there come into play motives in part unknown to us, in part known very ill, which we can never take account of beforehand. Probably a struggle takes place between these as well, a battling to and for, a rising and falling of the scales – and this would be the actual 'conflict of motives': something quite invisible to us of which we would be quite unconscious." Nietzsche, *Daybreak*, trans. R. J. Hollingdale (Cambridge: Cambridge University Press, 1982), 129; [kurz, es wirken Motive, die wir zum Theil gar nicht, zum Theil sehr schlecht kennen und die wir *nie vorher* gegen einander in Rechnung setzen könnten. Wahrscheinlich, dass auch unter ihnen ein Kampf Statt findet, ein Hin- und Wegtreiben, ein Aufwiegen und Niederdrücken von Gewichttheilen, – und diess wäre der eigentliche "Kampf der Motive": – etwas für uns völlig Unsichtbares und Unbewusstes.] *KSA*, III: 119.
⁴¹ Nietzsche, *Daybreak*, 74; *KSA*, III: 111.
⁴² Nietzsche, *Daybreak*, 76. [Interpretationen unserer Nervenreize während des Schlafes, *sehr freie*, sehr willkürliche Interpretationen von Bewegungen des Blutes und der Eingeweide]. *KSA*, III: 111.
⁴³ Nietzsche, *Daybreak*, 76. [mehr oder weniger phantastischer Commentar über einen ungewussten, vielleicht unwissbaren, aber gefühlten Text]. *KSA*, III: 111. One is reminded here of Nietzsche's thoughts on metaphorical transference into nervous stimuli, which he formulated along the lines of Gerber in 1873.

images and fantasies that emerge from unknown physiological processes[44] – and in relation to the human belief in logic:

> The cause of logical ideas and inferences in our brain today corresponds to a process and a struggle among impulses that are, taken singly, very illogical and unjust. We generally experience only the result of this struggle because this primeval mechanism now runs its course so quickly and is so well concealed.[45]

Here one also thinks of Nietzsche's famous statement from the Preface to *The Gay Science*, according to which philosophy has never been anything other than an interpretation of the body and a misunderstanding of the body.[46]

Nietzsche calls consciousness the last and latest development to emerge from the organic. Accordingly, it is deficient, untested and therefore dangerous to mankind. Only the remaining alliances of the instincts allow the human being to avoid the innumerable mistakes of the conscious mind.[47] This topic had been an interest of Nietzsche's dating back to his student days, when he declared self-observation to be a developmental disease, arguing that only the unconscious instincts provide a secure guide for every deed.[48] Nietzsche later linked this critique of consciousness and the ego with his language skepticism: language, as an attempt to make the inner processes of the subject conscious, is thereby regarded as the main obstacle to knowing them at all. Reason, which is always expressed in words, can only ever simplify in an unacceptable way the most extreme forms and conditions of the drives: "We are none of us that which we appear to be in accordance with the states for which alone we have consciousness and words, and consequently praise and blame."[49] When the human being constructs an opinion of himself via this wholly inadequate mediation of inner processes, he creates the ego.

---

[44] Nietzsche, *Daybreak*, 76; *KSA*, III: 111.
[45] Nietzsche, *The Gay Science*, trans. Walter Kaufmann (New York: Random House, 1974), 172. [Der Verlauf logischer Gedanken und Schlüsse in unserem jetzigen Gehirne entspricht einem Processe und Kampfe von Trieben, die an sich einzeln alle sehr unlogisch und ungerecht sind; wir erfahren gewöhnlich nur das Resultat des Kampfes: so schnell und so versteckt spielt sich jetzt dieser uralte Mechanismus ab.] *KSA*, III: 472.
[46] Nietzsche, *The Gay Science* (New York 1974) 34; *KSA*, III: 348.
[47] Nietzsche, *Die fröhliche Wissenschaft*; *KSA*, III: 382.
[48] Nietzsche, *Fragment Frühjahr bis Herbst 1868*, *BAW*, IV: 126. See also Gödde, "Dionysisches – Triebe und Leib," 209. In *Esquisse d'une morale sans obligation, ni sanction* Jean-Marie Guyau states that every instinct tends to abandon itself once it becomes conscious. Nietzsche noted "NB." in his copy of the text. See Hans Erich Lampl, ed., *Zweistimmigkeit – Einstimmigkeit: Friedrich Nietzsche und Jean-Marie Guyau* (Cuxhaven: Junghans, 1990).
[49] Nietzsche, *Daybreak*, 71. [Wir sind alle nicht Das, als was wir nach den Zuständen erscheinen, für die wir allein Bewusstsein und Worte – und folglich Lob und Tadel – haben]. *KSA*, III: 107.

The question then arises as to why human beings have developed consciousness at all, if its imperfect and illusory character seems to threaten their existence. Nietzsche explains this by the pressure of the need for expression. The ability to communicate one's needs has become an important tool for surviving. Inner processes become conscious via language. But owing to the categorizing and metaphorical character of language, our conscious world "is only a surface- and sign world, a world that is made common and meaner."[50]

These considerations lead to Nietzsche's philosophical thoughts of the late 1880s, in which he calls the differentiation between a "true" and a "false" world a "suggestion of decadence," and refuses to accept the assumption of a "true" world behind the apparent one. The role played by the concept of the unconscious in regard to these thoughts will be examined below.

Unconscious processes of power

From the beginning, Nietzsche did not try to understand the unconscious *ex negativo* as a lack of consciousness, as the philosophers of the Enlightenment had suggested it to be. Instead he tried to reverse this understanding of Western thought: according to Nietzsche, consciousness is an inadequate adaptation to the environment which is derived from organic processes that were originally unconscious:

Behind your thoughts and feelings, my brother, stands a mighty commander, an unknown sage – he is called self. He lives in your body, he is your body. There is more reason in your body than in your best wisdom. And who knows for what purpose your body requires precisely your best wisdom.[51]

In the context of his theory of the will to power, Nietzsche maintained the conviction that consciousness is a secondary phenomenon. According to Nietzsche the world is nothing other than will to power,[52] from which it follows that the actual agents of life are unconscious processes of power. Drives can give us a partial impression of these processes of power, but of course this information is incomplete, metaphorical, and simplified: "the whole of the human being has all those qualities of

---

[50] Nietzsche, *The Gay Science*, 299. [Oberflächen- und Zeichenwelt, eine verallgemeinerte, eine vergemeinerte Welt]. *KSA*, III: 593.
[51] Nietzsche, *Thus Spoke Zarathustra*, 62. [Hinter deinen Gedanken und Gefühlen, mein Bruder, steht ein mächtiger Gebieter, ein unbekannter Weiser – der heisst Selbst. In deinem Leib wohnt er, dein Leib ist er. Es ist mehr Vernunft in deinem Leibe, als in deiner besten Weisheit. Und wer weiss denn, wozu dein Leib gerade deine beste Weisheit nöthig hat?] *KSA*, IV: 40.
[52] Nietzsche, *KSA*, XI: 611.

the organic, which partially remain unconscious, partially become conscious in the form of *drives*."[53]

Undergoing constant change, the will to power is by no means a universal metaphysical concept, but a plurality of power quanta, struggling for an increase of power.[54] To achieve this aim, these entities merge to form more successful units of power. This is how Nietzsche explains the creation of consciousness, which results from the attempt to occupy a dominant perspective in order to gain protection from the outside. Here it is important to note that this accumulation of power quanta can only be sustained as long as it allows for the possibility of preserving the status quo or increasing power. In that sense Nietzsche understands the conscious ego as a transitory expression of the unconscious struggles between power quanta.

The struggle for power is also a struggle for the supreme interpretation. According to Nietzsche interpretation provides a way of gaining mastery over something.[55] To that extent, Nietzsche's concept of the will to power can be read in accordance with philosophical hermeneutics, as Figl or Hofmann have done.[56] The longing for power expresses the desire for a constant overcoming of other interpretations; each interpretation emerges from a particular perspective which, through its reading of other perspectives, attempts to achieve power. The ascendant perspective would thus assume the status of commanding over less successful interpretations, which are accordingly forced into a position of obedience. Thus, when Nietzsche is confronted by the question as to who is the interpreter, his answer is that this interpreter should not be understood as an individual human subject; for Nietzsche both the interpreter and the interpreted are equally manifestations of will to power.[57]

This anti-subjective turn in Nietzsche's thought does not allow any role for a concept of consciousness, since the conscious subject is no longer

---

[53] My translation. [die Gesammtheit des Menschen hat alle jene Eigenschaften des Organischen, die uns zum Theil unbewusst bleiben (zum Theil) in der Gestalt von *Trieben* bewusst werden]. Nietzsche, *Nachgelassene Fragmente: Frühjahr bis Herbst 1884*, Sommer-Herbst 1884, Nietzsche, *Werke: Kritische Gesamtausgabe*, 9 parts, 40 vols, ed. Giorgio Colli, Mazzino Montinari et al. (Berlin and New York: Walter de Gruyter, 1967-), part 7, vol. II, 282 (this edition of Nietzsche's works will hereafter be referred to with the letters *KGW* followed by part, volume and page numbers).

[54] See Müller-Lauter's critique of Heidegger. Wolfgang Müller-Lauter, *Heidegger und Nietzsche* (Berlin, New York: Walter de Gruyter, 2000).

[55] Nietzsche, *KGW*, 8, I: 138.

[56] Johann Figl, *Interpretation als philosophisches Prinzip: Friedrich Nietzsches universale Theorie der Auslegung im späten Nachlaß* (Berlin, New York: Walter de Gruyter 1982); Johann Nepomuk Hofmann, *Wahrheit, Perspektive, Interpretation: Nietzsche und die philosophische Hermeneutik* (Berlin, New York: Walter de Gruyter, 1994).

[57] Nietzsche writes: "It is the will to power that interprets: the creation of an organ is an interpretation; it separates, and defines ranks and differences of power" (my translation). [Der Wille zur Macht *interpretirt*: bei der Bildung eines Organs handelt es sich um eine Interpretation; er grenzt ab, bestimmt Grade, Machtverschiedenheiten.] *KGW*, 7, I: 137.

included in the process of interpretation.[58] It has to be doubted that the concept of the unconscious (as opposed to consciousness) can still be used in an accurate way, when consciousness itself is suspended. The latter has been described as a temporary and transitory effect of the will to power, which will be maintained as long as it achieves an increase in its own power. If the world is a struggle between the interpretations of power quanta, and the conscious subject only its temporary expression, it follows that the concept of human consciousness (as opposed to the unconscious) is an inadequate and unnecessary introduction of a dualistic principle, a deficient linguistic expression based upon metaphysical prejudices. A transcendental dualism of this kind is precisely what Nietzsche's theory of the will to power tries to argue against. Seen in this light, the concept of the unconscious becomes an abbreviation and a metaphorical reformulation achieved through language. It is itself an interpretation, an expression of the will to power as its highest form: the attempt to impose being, stasis, and theoretical structure upon processes of transition and becoming.

Nietzsche's arguments concerning the will to power lead to a severe problem. If the world is will to power and nothing else, and if the will to power dissolves all dualisms such as conscious/unconscious, ego/non-ego, and subject/object, then there can be no scale upon which to measure the increase of power any more. Consequently, it becomes impossible to grasp the will to power within this stream of becoming at all, at least not on the basis of our conscious understanding.

With regard to the history of the unconscious it is important to note that Nietzsche's late concept of the world as a plurality of will to power quanta, which he uses first and foremost to attack metaphysics, extinguishes the concept of the unconscious. Any later theorist who would call upon Nietzsche to substantiate his or her concept of the unconscious could therefore only invoke Nietzsche's thoughts of the early and middle periods, since to invoke the late Nietzsche would be to risk endangering the concept of the unconscious altogether.

The collective aspect of the unconscious in Nietzsche

My final section is dedicated to a significant question regarding the influence of Nietzsche's concept of the unconscious for the beginnings of psychoanalysis and its later schismatic development. To what extent do Nietzsche's understandings of the unconscious support the notion of a collective aspect of the unconscious as identified by Carl Gustav Jung?

---

[58] Erwin Schlimgen, *Nietzsches Theorie des Bewußtseins* (Berlin and New York: Walter de Gruyter 1999), 196.

Freud's remarks concerning his aversion to reading Nietzsche, because of Nietzsche's apparent anticipations of Freud's own theories, are well known.[59] The partially rhetorical character of those remarks has been examined by recent research, and is discussed by Günter Gödde in chapter 10 of this volume. Freud, however, never explicitly addressed the question as to whether his concept of the unconscious is derivative of Nietzsche's philosophy. Jung, by contrast, emphasized the importance of Nietzsche's insights for his concept of a collective unconscious, while also stressing the philosophical ignorance of Freud.[60] In the following, I want to examine whether Nietzsche can be seen as a precursor of the theory of the collective unconscious, or if one has to restrict his influence to individualistic theories of the subject.

Let us go back to Nietzsche's description of the Dionysian in *The Birth of Tragedy*, where he characterizes this state as corresponding with the disappearance of the subject into complete self-forgetting.[61] Through this process, the ties between human beings are strengthened and nature celebrates the reunion with its lost son:

Now hearing this gospel of universal harmony, each person feels himself to be not simply united, reconciled or merged with his neighbor, but quite literally one with them, as if the veil of maya had been torn apart, so that mere shreds of it flutter before the mysterious primordial unity. Singing and dancing, man expresses his sense of belonging to a higher community.[62]

---

[59] *Protokolle der Wiener Psychoanalytischen Vereinigung*, 2 vols., ed. H. Nunberg and P. Federn, vol. I: *1906–1908* (Frankfurt am Main: Fischer, 1976), 338 (April 1, 1908); vol. II: *1908–1910* (Frankfurt am Main: Fischer, 1977), 28 (October 28, 1908).

[60] In this connection, Jung writes: "I thought according to these concepts long before my encounter with Freud. 'The unconscious' is an *epistemological* concept that was coined by von Hartmann. Freud was not so much of a philosopher, in fact he was a medical doctor" (my translation). [Ich dachte schon lange vor meiner Begegnung mit Freud in diesen Begriffen. "Das Unbewusste" ist ein *epistemologischer* Begriff, den von Hartmann geprägt hatte. Freud war nicht so sehr ein Philosoph, er war eigentlich Mediziner.] Carl Gustav Jung, "Sigmund Freud," *Gesammelte Werke*, ed. Lily Jung-Merker, Elisabeth Rüf et al., 20 vols. (Zürich, Stuttgart, Olten, and Freiburg im Breisgau: Walter Verlag, 1958–94), vol. XV, 53–62; "Allgemeines zur Komplextheorie," *Gesammelte Werke*, vol. VIII, 108–20; *Ein großer Psychologe im Gespräch. Interviews. Reden. Begegnungen*, ed. Robert Hinshaw (Freiburg im Breisgau: Herder 1994), 64; Graham Parkes, "Nietzsche and Jung: Ambivalent Appreciation," *Nietzsche and Depth Psychology*, ed. J. Golomb et al. (Albany, NY: State University of New York Press, 1999), 212. Parkes writes: "This is the extent more or less of Jung's estimation of Nietzsche's contribution to depth psychology: he excels in the description of autonomous phenomena of the unconscious such as inspiration; he realizes the extent to which dreams can take us back to archaic phases of human development; and his openness to archetypal imagery allows him to convey a vivid sense of 'bygone spiritual worlds.'"

[61] Nietzsche, *Birth of Tragedy*, 18; *KSA*, I: 29.

[62] Nietzsche, *Birth of Tragedy*, 18. [Jetzt, bei dem Evangelium der Weltenharmonie, fühlt sich Jeder mit seinem Nächsten nicht nur vereinigt, versöhnt, verschmolzen, sondern eins, als ob der Schleier der Maja zerrissen wäre und nur noch in Fetzen vor dem

The redemption from individuality, from the *principium individuationis*, leads to a common primal oneness "Ur-Eine." The Apollonian, conscious ego has been abandoned; the boundaries separating individuals have ceased to exist. In this way, it could be said that the return to the primal one is also the descent into the unconscious. In *The Birth of Tragedy* the unconscious is first and foremost defined by the collective aspect which is opposed to the Apollonian *principium individuationis*. This is where Nietzsche is still dependent on Schopenhauer's metaphysical concept of will to life and Wagner's aesthetic interpretation of this concept.

By the time of *The Gay Science*, Nietzsche had already abandoned the theory of Apollonian appearance and Dionysian primal origin (*Urgrund*). Here, he approached the problem of the accessibility of reality with a certain kind of intellectual refinement, by reducing the possible knowledge of reality in an almost phenomenological manner to the consciousness of appearance:

> How wonderful and new and yet how gruesome and ironic I find my position vis-à-vis the whole of existence in the light of my insight! I have discovered for myself that the human and animal past, indeed the whole primal age and past of all sentient being continues in me to invent, to love, to hate, and to infer. I suddenly woke up in the midst of this dream, but only to the consciousness that I am dreaming and that I must go on dreaming lest I perish – as a somnambulist must go on dreaming lest he fall: What is "appearance" for me now?[63]

Consciousness is depicted as a necessary appearance because of its life-preserving character. At the same time, Nietzsche links this thought to questions concerning the possibility of knowledge. Nietzsche's discussion of the dreamer is a critique of Parmenides' conception of Being as the ground of truth. For Nietzsche, even when the dreamer awakens from his dream, he does not arrive at a stable position comparable to "truth"; rather, he gains an awareness of the fact that he is part of a dream. Despite Nietzsche's rejection of any faculty of "true" knowledge, he maintains the necessity of the dream for survival. The dream, for Nietzsche, is an expression of the interconnectedness of all knowledge, upon which subjects must agree in order for life to be possible; it is the common intelligibility of the dream amongst a variety of dreamers

geheimnisvollen Ur-Einen herumflattere. Singend und tanzend äussert sich der Mensch als Mitglied einer höheren Gemeinsamkeit.] *KSA*, I: 29.

[63] Nietzsche, *The Gay Science*, 54. [Wie wundervoll und neu und zugleich wie schauerlich und ironisch fühle ich mich mit meiner Erkenntnis zum gesammten Dasein gestellt! Ich habe für mich *entdeckt*, dass die alte Mensch- und Thierheit, ja die gesammte Urzeit und Vergangenheit alles empfindende Sein in mir fortdichtet, fortliebt, forthasst, fortschliesst, – ich bin plötzlich in diesem Traum erwacht, aber nur zum Bewusstsein, dass ich eben träume und dass ich weiterträumen muss, um nicht zugrunde zu gehen ... Was ist mir jetzt "Schein"! Wahrlich nicht der Gegensatz irgendeines Wesens.] *KSA*, III: 416.

that enables the dream to continue.[64] Whereas in *The Birth of Tragedy* the unity of mankind and the reconciliation with nature had been understood as a result of Dionysian ecstasy, the explanation of this process of unification has now been shifted into the – to use the language of *The Birth of Tragedy* – Apollonian realm of knowledge. In this way, reason as the metaphysical idea of the primal one becomes mere appearance for Nietzsche.

At the end of Nietzsche's philosophical development, the moment of collectivity – initially based on a metaphysical concept in *The Birth of Tragedy*, and then described by the "middle period" Nietzsche as a necessary illusion – is finally undermined by the plurality of the will to power. The "apparent" world is the only one; the "true" world, moreover, has been a deception, says Nietzsche in *Twilight of the Idols* (*Götzen-Dämmerung*, 1889).[65] He understands the world as a realm of constant becoming, as a continuous power struggle between different perspectives. As a fragmented form of the will to power, the Dionysian does not know a general basic collectivity, only a plurality of power quanta that increase, compete with one another, or fall apart. Thus, in the context of the late Nietzsche, both the differentiation between conscious and unconscious, as well as Nietzsche's early understanding of the unconscious as a collective entity, dissolve against the background of the will to power.

To summarize: Jung was not wrong to claim that the Nietzsche who wrote *The Birth of Tragedy* and the *Untimely Meditations* is the forefather of the theory of a collective unconscious. But, as has been shown (and this is equally valid for any concept of the unconscious that would call upon Nietzsche as a witness), Nietzsche's late understanding of the world as a plurality of competing power quanta, a notion which he uses to attack the very foundations of Western metaphysics, also undermines all theoretical conceptions of the unconscious.

---

[64] Nietzsche, *The Gay Science*, 54; *KSA*, III: 416.
[65] Nietzsche, "Twilight of the Idols," *The Portable Nietzsche*, ed. and trans. Walter Kaufmann (New York: Viking Press, 1976), 484; *KSA*, VI: 75.

10 Freud and nineteenth-century philosophical sources on the unconscious

Günter Gödde

Introduction

In *The Interpretation of Dreams* (*Die Traumdeutung*, 1900) Freud introduced what he called "the unconscious" (*das Unbewusste*) as the fundamental term of psychoanalysis. From this time onwards, Freud continually emphasized that his teachings were essentially a form of psychology which takes this "object" (i.e. the unconscious) to be its primary subject matter. As is well known, Freud then began to research the dynamics of the unconscious in the clinical context by researching and interpreting hysteria and dreams. Of key importance was the discovery that in internal psychic conflicts, embarrassing, distateful and unpleasurable mental contents are repelled (*abgewehrt*) and repressed (*verdrängt*). Under unfavorable circumstances, according to Freud, those repressed elements of the subject that are not integrated within the ego increasingly slip away from conscious control and can potentially develop into causes of mental disturbance. By contrast, the uncovering of repressions would, argued Freud, have a liberating and curing effect. As Freud later remarked, he arrived at the term "unconscious" through his teachings on repression: "the repressed is the prototype of the unconscious for us."[1]

In order to establish the scientific nature of his new path for psychology, Freud went beyond clinical psychology and began to focus on a more general theory of the psyche. He refers to this general theory as a *metapsychology*, a definition designed clearly to differentiate this form of psychology from metaphysics. As an empirical researcher, Freud credited himself with having found new methodological and clinical

---

[1] Freud, "The Ego and the Id," *The Standard Edition of the Complete Psychological Works of Sigmund Freud*, ed. and trans. James Strachey and Anna Freud *et al.*, 24 vols. (London: The Hogarth Press, 1953–74), vol. XIX, 15 (hereafter cited as *SE* followed by volume and page numbers). [Das Verdrängte ist uns das Vorbild des Unbewussten.] Freud, "Das Ich und das Es," *Gesammelte Werke in achtzehn Bänden mit einem Nachtragsband*, ed. Anna Freud *et al.*, 18 vols. (Frankfurt am Main: S. Fischer, 1986–99), vol. XIII, 241 (hereafter cited as *GW* followed by volume and page numbers).

ways of studying the unconscious via psycho-therapeutic experiences. Yet the notion that metapsychology was not created *ex nihilo*, and that important aspects of the philosophical tradition of the unconscious contributed to it, was for a long time hidden discreetly in the background of psychoanalysis. This was mainly due to a generally accepted belief, characteristic of Freud's age, in a thoroughgoing separation between the natural sciences and philosophy, and furthermore to the strict adherence to the empirical standards of the positivist natural sciences.

With regard to Freud's conception of the unconscious, it seems anything but easy to gain a clear picture of the origins and transformations of this term, let alone its implications for Freud's work as a whole. To enable a better orientation towards this problem, I investigated the philosophical prehistory of the concept of the unconscious in my book *Tradition-Lines of the "Unconscious": Schopenhauer, Nietzsche, Freud* (*Traditionslinien des "Unbewussten": Schopenhauer, Nietzsche, Freud*, 1999). This book made it clear that, if one is adequately to classify Freud's metapsychology, an account of the eighteenth- and nineteenth-century philosophical discourses on the unconscious is indispensable. With this aim in mind, I distinguished three main historico-philosophical tradition-lines of the unconscious,[2] which are outlined (for the first time in English) below.

The first of these is the tradition-line of the *cognitive* unconscious, which stems from the era of the Enlightenment. It appears for the first time in relation to Gottfried Wilhelm Leibniz's (1646–1716) notion of *petites perceptions*. These perceptions are seen as being too small or weak to be perceived in isolation, but when combined with others they have the ability to enter consciousness, as is shown by Leibniz's famous examples with regard to ocean waves and human voices.[3] This tradition-line was greatly influenced by Johann Friedrich Herbart's (1776–1841) notion of the "law of the threshold" (*Schwellengesetz*), according to which certain mental contents are repressed below the threshold of consciousness but can return into consciousness, and remains today a feature of the highly differentiated psychology of cognition. Examples of nineteenth-century proponents of this particular tradition-line include: Gustav Theodor Fechner (1801–87, analyzed at length by Michael Heidelberger in chapter

---

[2] Günter Gödde, *Traditionslinien des "Unbewussten": Schopenhauer, Nietzsche, Freud* (Tübingen: edition diskord, 1999; 2nd edn. Gießen: Psychosozial Verlag, 2009), 23–68; See also: Gödde, "Das Unbewußte als Zentralbegriff der Freudschen Metapsychologie und seine philosophischen Wurzeln," *Traum, Logik, Geld: Freud, Husserl und Simmel zum Denken der Moderne*, ed. U. Kadi, B. Keintzel and H. Vetter (Tübingen: edition diskord, 2001), 33–60.

[3] See Gottfried Wilhelm Leibniz, "Vorrede," *Neue Abhandlungen über den menschlichen Verstand* (1765) (Stuttgart: Reclam, 1993), 25.

8 of this volume),[4] along with Hermann von Helmholtz (1821–94), and Theodor Lipps (1851–1914).

A second (Romantic) tradition-line arose from the fear that the Enlightenment would stagnate into a flat and lifeless rationalism if the emotional, natural, biological, fantastic, and irrational dimensions of human experience were not taken into account. As Paul Bishop and Angus Nicholls discuss in chapters 1 and 3 of this volume, this countercurrent within the European Enlightenment was initiated by the German philosophers Johann Georg Hamann (1730–88) and Johann Gottfried Herder (1744–1803), as well as by the young Johann Wolfgang von Goethe (1749–1832), and experienced its peak in the Romantic philosophies of nature and medicine to be found in Germany around the beginning and middle of the nineteenth century. The school that developed out of the *Naturphilosophie* (philosophy of nature) of Friedrich Wilhelm Joseph Schelling (1775–1854, see chapter 2 of this volume, by Andrew Bowie) primarily invoked the unconscious in order to refer to the "dark sides" of the nature and the soul. As Matthew Bell shows in chapter 6 of this volume, the first systematization of this Romantic or vitalist understanding of the unconscious can be found in Carl Gustav Carus' book *Psyche: On the Developmental History of the Soul* (*Psyche. Zur Entwicklungsgeschichte der Seele*, 1846).

Finally, a third tradition-line developed in opposition to the two main streams of post-Kantian German idealism: on the one hand, the idealistic philosophy of reason associated with Johann Gottlieb Fichte (1762–1814) and Georg Wilhelm Friedrich Hegel (1770–1831), and on the other hand, Schelling's philosophy of nature (*Naturphilosophie*). This tradition-line emerged from Schelling's redefinition of the will as impulse (*Drang*), drive (*Trieb*), and desire (*Begierde*), and led to the recognition of potentially dangerous and destructive urges within human nature. One can speak, in this context, of the "drive-related irrational" (*triebhaft-irrationale*) tradition-line of the unconscious. This tradition-line includes Arthur Schopenhauer's metaphysics of the will to life (*Wille zum Leben*, discussed by Christopher Janaway in chapter 5 of this volume), Eduard von Hartmann's metaphysics of the unconscious (examined by Sebastian Gardner in chapter 7), and Friedrich Nietzsche's anti-metaphysical notion of the "will to power" (addressed by Martin Liebscher in chapter 9).

In what follows, three periods of Freud's theoretical development will be examined in relation to the three general tradition-lines of the

---

[4] See also, Michael Heidelberger, *Nature from Within: Gustav Theodor Fechner's Psychophysical Worldview*, trans. Cynthia Klohr (Pittsburgh, PA: University of Pittsburgh Press, 2004).

unconscious elaborated above: first, Freud's student years of the 1870s, in which he first encountered the subject matter of the unconscious and in particular those philosophers who were dedicated to its study; second, the 1890s, when Freud developed his own psychology of the unconscious, which led to the establishment of psychoanalysis; and finally the 1920s, when Freud radically modified and reformulated his earlier conceptions of the unconscious.

Freud's first encounters with the philosophy of the unconscious during the 1870s

Freud's first encounters with philosophy, psychology and the subject matter of the unconscious occurred in the 1870s. During the final two years of his secondary schooling at the Leopoldstädter Realgymnasium (1871–3) he took part in a philosophical *propaedeuticum* on the subjects of logic and psychology. Two textbooks written by the Herbartian philosopher of psychology Gustav Adolf Lindner (1828–77) formed the basis of this philosophical *propaedeuticum*. Thus, in the first instance, Freud's encounter with philosophy and psychology was influenced by Herbartianism, which was the mainstream psychology in Austria during the late nineteenth century. The dynamics between the conscious and subconscious contents of the psyche are dealt with in Lindner's *Textbook of Empirical Psychology as an Inductive Science* (*Lehrbuch der empirischen Psychologie als inductiver Wissenschaft*, 3rd edn. of 1872). Lindner argues that the majority of mental contents remain in the dark due to the fact that they are pressed below the threshold of consciousness. Such inhibited, obscured, or suppressed contents can only return to consciousness by overcoming what Lindner terms a "resistance" (*Widerstand*).[5] Yet despite the fact that sources such as Lindner appear to anticipate some of the ideas of psychoanalysis, the question as to how Herbartianism influenced the mind of the young Freud remains unclear.

By contrast, and as both Paul Bishop and Angus Nicholls have pointed out in earlier chapters of this volume (see chapters 1 and 3), Freud addressed the influence of Goethe explicitly by stating that in his final school year of 1873 he attended a public lecture which invoked the fragment "Die Natur" (On Nature), often attributed to Goethe but actually written by the Swiss theologian Georg Christoph Tobler (1757–1812). Freud was apparently so deeply moved by this lecture that he decided to study medicine. Tobler's hymn to nature begins with an invocation of

---

[5] Gustav Adolf Lindner, *Lehrbuch der empirischen Psychologie als inductive Wissenschaft*, 3rd edn., (Vienna: Carl Gerold's Sohn, 1873), 137.

the natural world in which humans are situated, and by which we are surrounded and entwined, and ends with a swan song which suggests that we should trustingly submit ourselves to the primacy of nature. If nature develops into an idealized image in order to replace the previously longed-for idea of God, then the natural scientist can feel like an apostle of a secular Gospel (*Apostel eines weltlichen Evangeliums*) in terms of his commitment to nature.[6]

During the first years of his medical studies (1873–81), and like many other natural scientists of the late nineteenth century, Freud implemented a shift from a philosophy of nature to a materialistic world-view. The basis for Freud's materialist orientation was provided by the new discoveries of biological evolution and physiology, which he assimilated during the first years of his medical degree. In 1876 Freud joined the physiological laboratory overseen by Ernst Brücke, dedicating some years there to histological research into fish and crayfish. According to the precepts of the Helmholtz School of scientific research, Brücke attempted to prove that

there are no other active forces in the organism than general physical-chemical ones, and that, where explanations of this kind are insufficient, either similar methods of the physical and mathematical sciences must be deployed in order to investigate organic activity in concrete cases, or new active forces must be posited which are of a similar order to those of the physical-chemical variety, which are inherent in the material being investigated, and which can always be traced back to attracting or repelling components.[7]

This decidedly anti-vitalist attitude contributed significantly to the dethronement of the philosophy of nature of Goethe, Schelling, and Carus, who believed the universe to be one grand organism. Freud, who researched at Brücke's physiological laboratory for six years (1876–82), was one of the most dedicated followers of this biophysical movement.[8]

Freud supplemented his materialist world-view under the influence of his philosophy teacher Franz Brentano (1838–1917). It was Brentano who

---

[6] Quoted in Wilhelm W. Hemecker, *Vor Freud: Philosophiegeschichtliche Voraussetzungen der Psychoanalyse* (Munich: Philosophia Verlag, 1991), 75.
[7] [im Organismus keine anderen Kräfte wirksam sind, als die gemeinen physikalisch-chemischen; dass, wo diese bislang nicht zur Erklärung ausreichen, mittels der physikalisch-mathematischen Methode entweder nach ihrer Art und Weise der Wirksamkeit im konkreten Falle gesucht werden muss, oder dass neue Kräfte angenommen werden müssen, welche, von gleicher Dignität mit den physikalisch-chemischen, der Materie inhärent, stets auf nur abstoßende oder anziehende Componenten zurückzuführen sind]. Quoted in Siegfried Bernfeld, "Freuds früheste Theorien und die Helmholtz-Schule," *Bausteine der Freud-Biographik*, ed. Siegfried Bernfeld and Suzanne Cassirer Bernfeld (Frankfurt am Main: Suhrkamp 1981), 54–77; here 62, my translation.
[8] See, in this connection, Peter Gay, *Freud: A Life for Our Time* (New York: Norton, 1998), 33–7.

familiarized Freud with problems relating to the psychology of religion, the theory of cognition, ethics and logic. Freud took part in Brentano's seminars from the winter semester of 1874 to the summer semester 1876. In a discussion held with the young Freud and his friend Josef Paneth in 1875, Brentano, according to Freud, criticized Herbart's

> a prioristic constructions in psychology and thought it inexcusable that he [i.e. Herbart] had never considered taking into account experience or the results of experiments ... [Brentano] told us of several strange observations that illustrated the weakness of Herbart's speculations. Rather than attempting to encompass the whole of philosophy, it would be more important, said Brentano, to thoroughly examine specific questions in order to gather a few correct results, because philosophy and psychology are still relatively new sciences and cannot rely on any support from physiology.[9]

In the coming decades, Brentano would initiate a second main school of psychology in Austria, which was based on the programmatic foundation reflected in his critique of Herbart.

As a student, Freud took part for five years (1873–8) in the activities of the *Leseverein der deutschen Studenten Wiens* (Reading Group of the German Students in Vienna), a society which had as its central purpose the stimulation of a strong sense of German nationalism.[10] It was arguably in this forum that Freud first encountered the ideas of Schopenhauer, Wagner, and Nietzsche, whose philosophies were based on the presumption of a drive-related and irrational will. The *Leseverein*'s great interest in these giants of late nineteenth-century Germanic culture can be associated with the at that time still prevalent crisis of liberalism in Austrian society. Schopenhauer's metaphysics of the "will to life" represented a philosophical turning point for Freud's generation, which was in search of philosophical role models and cultural ideals. This was due to the fact that Schopenhauer reduced the optimism and faith in progress shared by his predecessors to a form of absurdity. For Freud and his counterparts in the *Leseverein*, Wagner was the "highest representative of their ideal

---

[9] [aprioristische Konstruktionen in der Psychologie, hielt es für unverzeihlich, dass es ihm nie eingefallen sei, die Erfahrung oder das Experiment zu Rate zu ziehn ... [Brentano] erzählte uns einige merkwürdige psychologische Beobachtungen, die die Haltlosigkeit der Herbart'schen Spekulationen zeigen. Es tue mehr not, über einzelne Fragen gründliche Untersuchungen anzustellen, um zu einzelnen sicheren Resultaten zu gelangen, als das Ganze der Philosophie umfassen zu wollen, weil die Philosophie und Psychologie eine noch ganz junge Wissenschaft sei und besonders von der Physiologie keinerlei Unterstützung erwarten könne.] Freud to Silberstein, March 15, 1875, *Jugendbriefe an Eduard Silberstein 1871–1881*, ed. Walter B. Boehlich, (Frankfurt am Main: Fischer, 1989), 116, my translation.

[10] See William J. McGrath, *Freud's Discovery of Psychoanalysis: The Politics of Hysteria* (Ithaca, NY: Cornell University Press, 1986), 97; Günter Gödde, "Freuds philosophische Diskussionskreise in der Studentenzeit," *Jahrbuch der Psychoanalyse* 27 (1991): 73–113.

of a German cultural rebirth," while Nietzsche must have seemed to be "the heroically framed soul, who announces with prophetical words the possibility of a new culture." [11]

Another spokesperson of the *Leseverein* was Johannes Volkelt (1848–1930), who published several studies concerned with the unconscious and its related epistemological and methodological problems between the years of 1873 and 1876.[12] The main source of inspiration for Volkelt was Eduard von Hartmann's *Philosophy of the Unconscious* (*Philosophie des Unbewussten*, 1868) and the debates which it inspired during the 1870s. As Sebastian Gardner shows in chapter 7 of this volume, Hartmann's understanding of the unconscious attempted to synthesize Hegel's logic and Schopenhauer's illogical will, leading to what might be termed an "unconscious logic." According to this view, will and representation are the two inseparable parts of one and the same action. Volkelt's adherence to this notion of "unconscious logic" did not, however, prevent him from "deconstructing Hartmann's metaphysics in an Hegelian manner and triumphantly presenting Hegel as the philosopher in whose system all contradictions are resolved into a deep and all-inclusive unity."[13]

It is noteworthy that Brentano also elaborated a critique of Eduard von Hartmann's *Philosophy of the Unconscious*. According to Brentano, if one is to attribute a fact that is present in consciousness to the effects of unconscious psychological phenomena, then this initial (causal) fact would itself have to be rigorously established. It would also, moreover, be necessary to expose and empirically secure the precise laws of the posited unconscious phenomena. Brentano argued that instead of fulfilling these demands, Hartmann always invoked an "eternal unconscious" (*ewig Unbewusstes*) when mechanistic explanations did not provide the desired conclusions. "Everyone who is, even to a limited extent, an exact thinker," wrote Brentano, "will reject such a hypothetical absurdity as

---

[11] [höchster Vertreter der von der Gruppe verfolgten Ideale einer kulturellen deutschen Widergeburt]; [als die "heroisch-gefaßte Seele" erscheinen, die mit "profetischen Worten ... die Möglichkeit einer neuen Kultur anzeigte"]. Aldo Venturelli, "Nietzsche in der Berggasse 19: Über die erste Nietzsche-Rezeption in Wien," *Nietzsche-Studien* 13 (1984): 448–80; here 454.
[12] See, for example, the following publications by Volkelt: *Das Unbewußte und der Pessimismus* (Berlin: Frommann, 1873); *Die Traumphantasie* (Stuttgart: Meyer and Zeller, 1875), reprinted in *Traumarbeit vor Freud. Quellentexte zur Traumpsychologie im späten 19. Jahrhundert*, ed. Stefan Goldmann (Gießen: Psychosozial Verlag, 2005), 99–240; *Der Symbolbegriff in der neuesten Ästhetik* (Jena: Dufft, 1876).
[13] [die Metaphysik Hartmanns auf gut hegelisch zu zersetzen und Hegel als den Philosophen triumphierend hervorgehen zu lassen, in dessen System sich alle Widersprüche zur tief- und weitumspannenden Einheit aufheben]. Volkelt, "Mein philosophischer Entwicklungsgang," *Die Deutsche Philosophie der Gegenwart in Selbstdarstellungen*, ed. R. Schmidt (Leipzig: Meiner, 1921), 201–28; here 204.

being invalid."[14] Brentano ultimately came to the conclusion that every psychical act is accompanied by a consciousness to which it directly corresponds. In addition, he proclaimed that alongside the consciousness of material objects, there exists a second consciousness of self that is accessible to "inner apperception" (*innere Wahrnehmung*).[15]

The fact that, in the 1870s, the topic of the unconscious was widely discussed in the wake of Hartmann's *Philosophy of the Unconscious* is in part attributable to Nietzsche's considerations of the unconscious in his *Untimely Meditations* (*Unzeitgemässe Betrachtungen*) of 1874.[16] Although questions concerning the scientific study of the unconscious affected the discipline of philosophy for the entire second half of the nineteenth century, it was particularly during the 1870s that these debates became critical. In and around that decade the dream – as a phenomenon of the unconscious – was a highly debated philosophical topic, as is evident when one considers the publication dates of important dream researchers.[17] From all of this it becomes clear that Freud had already begun to come across various exponents of the philosophy of the unconscious in his years of study during the 1870s. However, the subject matter of the unconscious was at this time still far from being his most passionately engaging research question.

Freud's foundations for a psychology of the unconscious in the 1890s

It was predominantly his clinical practice of the 1890s that led Freud to posit the existence of a psychical unconscious. Confronted with the task of treating neurotic disturbances such as hysteria, neurasthenia, anxiety, and compulsion neuroses (among others), Freud, in close cooperation with his friend and mentor Josef Breuer (1842–1925),

---

[14] [Ein solches hypothetisches Unding wird jeder ... wenn er nur einigermaßen ein exakter Denker ist, als unzulässig verwerfen]. Franz Brentano, *Psychologie vom empirischen Standpunkt* (Hamburg: Meiner, 1874), 152.
[15] Ibid.
[16] Friedrich Nietzsche, *Unzeitgemässe Betrachtungen II: Vom Nutzen und Nachtheil der Historie für das Leben*, Werke: Kritische Gesamtausgabe, ed. Giorgio Colli, Mazzino Montinari et al., 9 parts, 40 vols. (Berlin: Walter de Gruyter, 1967–) vol. I, 243–334; here 311–24.
[17] Karl Albrecht Scherner, *Das Leben des Traums* (Berlin: Heinrich Schindler, 1861); Alfred Maury, *Le Sommeil et les rêves* (Paris: Didier, 1861) with a revised and expanded edition published in 1878; Ludwig Strümpell, *Die Natur und Entstehung der Träume* (Leipzig: Veit, 1874); Volkelt, *Die Traumphantasie*; and Friedrich Wilhelm Hildebrandt, *Der Traum und seine Verwerthung für's Leben* (Leipzig, 1875). The texts by Volkelt and Hildebrandt can be found in: Stefan Goldmann, ed., *Traumarbeit vor Freud: Quellentexte zur Traumpsychologie im späten 19. Jahrhundert* (Gießen: Psychosozial Verlag, 2005). See also Stefan Goldmann, *Via regia zum Unbewußten: Freud und die Traumforschung im 19. Jahrhundert* (Gießen: Psychosozial Verlag, 2003).

turned to the clinical project of elaborating a general theory of neurosis. Contemporaneous with this undertaking was his attempt, begun in 1895, to theorize a "Psychology for the Neurologist" (*Psychologie für den Neurologen*) which he hoped would build a bridge between physiology and psychology. He soon referred to this project as a *metapsychology* – a "psychology that would lead behind consciousness" (*hinter das Bewusstsein führende Psychologie*).[18] Still in the same year he composed the so-called *Project for a Scientific Psychology* (*Entwurf einer Psychologie*) for his Berlin friend and mentor Wilhelm Fliess (1858–1928), although this manuscript was not to be published until after Freud's death. In this materialist context, the mind-body problem became a key issue, since it was Freud's intention to "represent psychical processes as quantitatively determinate states of specifiable material particles."[19] Comparative research examining Herbart's and Freud's basic concepts of a psychical mechanism, after the manner of a physically structured machine or apparatus, has revealed significant similarities between the respective approaches of both theorists.[20] It has also, moreover, been shown that Fechner's psychophysical principles of stability and desire/aversion (*Lust/Unlust*) formed the basis of Freud's economical ideas concerning the principle of constancy and the pleasure principle.[21] The *Project for a Scientific Psychology* also anticipated important aspects of the later metapsychology, such as the primary and secondary processes, as well as the unconscious and preconscious elements of psychical activity. In this way, the *Project* exerted what Frank J. Sulloway has called a "considerable heuristic effect on Freud's thinking."[22]

Although Freud was, in November 1895, already distancing himself from the *Project for a Scientific Psychology*, this does not necessarily lead to the conclusion that he had completely given up on the plan (jointly conceived and worked upon by Freud and Fliess) of making a secure

---

[18] Freud, *The Complete Letters of Sigmund Freud to Wilhelm Fliess, 1887–1904*, ed. and trans. Jeffrey Moussaieff Masson (Cambridge, MA and London: The Belknap Press of Harvard University Press, 1985), 301–302; *Briefe an Wilhelm Fliess 1887–1904*, ed. Jeffrey Moussaieff Masson (Frankfurt am Main: Fischer, 1986), 329.

[19] Freud, "Project for a Scientific Psychology," *SE*, I: 295–343; here 295; [psychische Vorgänge darzustellen als quantitativ bestimmte Zustände aufzeigbarer materieller Teile]. Freud, "Entwurf einer Psychologie," *GW, Nachtragsband*: 387–477; here 387.

[20] See M. Dorer, *Historische Grundlagen der Psychoanalyse* (Leipzig: Meiner, 1932), 103; Hemecker, *Vor Freud: Philosophiegeschichtliche Voraussetzungen der Psychoanalyse*, 108–127.

[21] Mai Wegener, "Das psychophysische Unbewusste – Gustav Theodor Fechner und der Mond," *Das Unbewusste*, ed. Michael B. Buchholz and Günter Gödde, vol I: *Macht und Dynamik des Unbewussten: Auseinandersetzungen in Philosophie, Medizin und Psychoanalyse* (Gießen: Psychosozial Verlag, 2005), 240–61.

[22] Frank J. Sulloway, *Freud: Biologist of the Mind* (New York: Basic Books, 1979), 130.

connection between physiology and psychology. It is more appropriate to argue that, in light of his increasing doubts about the cogency of the *Project*, Freud was once again faced with the task of deciding which theoretical viewpoint he should deploy in order to establish his new psychology. Several options were considered, such as the Herbartian psychology, Brentano's approach, as well as a third direction including several philosophers and psychologists who, to paraphrase the words of Augustinus Karl Wucherer-Huldenfeld, tried to understand consciousness through its hidden and subterranean energies, affects, and drives; a direction that had, during the last third of the nineteenth century, gained widespread popularity under the ambiguous title of a philosophy of the unconscious.[23] In this context it was inevitable that Freud should concern himself with the traditional philosophical question as to whether it is possible for an unconscious psyche to exist at all. In order to clarify and attempt to resolve this question, Freud was required to deal with the two significant Austrian schools of philosophy at the time: those of Herbart and Brentano.

Herbart had already identified the dynamics of mental contents which are, as a result of their competition with other mental representations, repressed (*verdrängt*) below the threshold of consciousness, and which only return into consciousness once they have overcome the resistance (*Widerstand*) exerted by their competitors.[24] Since Herbart's theories concerning repression and resistance emerged in the context of a rationalistic philosophy, Freud referred to them as the "common psychological abstractions" (*gebräuchliche psychologische Abstraktionen*),[25] which he used as stepping-stones in order to convert his own observations concerning neuroses and dreams into his first theoretical formulations. Freud's innovation lay in bringing to life the theories of repression and resistance in the context of his own clinical practice, thus bringing them closer to the theory of alienation.[26]

At the same time, Freud also distanced himself from Brentano's theories concerning cognition, since the latter was fundamentally opposed to the assumption of an unconscious realm of psychical activity. Brentano

---

[23] Augustinus Karl von Wucherer-Huldenfeld, "Freuds Umsetzung der Philosophie in Metapsychologie," *Ursprüngliche Erfahrung und personales Sein: Ausgewählte philosophische Studien I* (Vienna: Böhlau 1994), 179–95; here 185.

[24] Johann Friedrich Herbart, *Lehrbuch zur Psychologie* (1816/1834), reproduction of the 2nd edn. (Amsterdam: Bonset, 1965); Herbart, *Psychologie als Wissenschaft neugegründet auf Erfahrung, Metaphysik und Mathematik: Erster synthetischer Theil* in *Sämmtliche Werke*, vol. V (Hamburg and Leipzig: Voss, 1886), 191–514.

[25] Odo Marquard, *Transzendentaler Idealismus, Romantische Naturphilosophie, Psychoanalyse* (Cologne: Dinter, 1987), 229; Gödde, *Traditionslinien des "Unbewussten,"* 172.

[26] Ibid., 175.

argued for a form of inner self-consciousness that exists alongside the consciousness of external objects, and which is accessible to the inner perception (*innere Wahrnehmung*). The judgments of the inner perception have, according to Brentano, "immediate and unmistakable evidence" (*unmittelbare untrügliche Evidenz*), which is not available to any other mode of cognition.[27] Freud's criticism of Brentano can be seen in a letter to Fliess dated May 25, 1895, in which he refers to the Vienna-based philosopher Wilhelm Jerusalem (1854–1923) and his book *The Function of Judgment* (*Die Urteilsfunktion*, 1895). This book, according to Freud, confirms his main objections to Brentano's philosophy of consciousness, by stating that assertions about internal perception cannot "claim to be evidence."[28]

Brentano had initially made a very strong impression on Jerusalem, but when it came to Brentano's claims regarding the "immediate and unmistakable evidence" of inner perception, Jerusalem felt it necessary to object in the most decisive way. It is often more appropriate, argued Jerusalem, to use the expression "it thinks inside me" (*es denkt in mir*) rather than the usual "I think" (*ich denke*). It is well known, he remarked, that

> self-deceptions are not at all rare, due to the fact that unconscious psychical processes comprise a significant factor of our inner life; their effects, however, can often only be recognized retrospectively.[29]

In particular, the reappearance of apparently vanished mental representations is said by Jerusalem to favor the assumption that an unconscious sphere of mental activity exists. Such reappearances can, he submits, only be explained through the "unconscious continued existence" (*unbewusstes Fortleben*) of certain mental representations. "We must," concluded Jerusalem,

> think of the unconscious as a persistent occurrence that continually influences the conscious life of the soul. In fact, we are continually under the influence of unconscious processes, which comprise the main part of our mental personality. We cannot get by without assuming the existence of the unconscious.[30]

---

[27] Brentano, *Psychologie vom empirischen Standpunkt*, 128.
[28] Freud, *The Complete Letters of Sigmund Freud to Wilhelm Fliess*, 129: [die innere Wahrnehmung nicht auf Evidenz Anspruch erheben kann]. Freud, *Briefe an Wilhelm Fliess 1887–1904*, 131.
[29] [Selbsttäuschungen gar nicht selten, schon deshalb, weil ja vielfach unbewusste psychische Vorgänge einen wesentlichen Faktor unseres Seelenlebens bilden, der sich der unmittelbaren Beobachtung entzieht, dessen Wirkungen aber auch mir selbst nachträglich erkannt werden können]. Wilhelm Jerusalem, *Die Urteilsfunktion: Eine psychologische und erkenntniskritische Untersuchung* (Wien: Braumüller, 1895), 194.
[30] [Wir haben uns dieses Unbewusste ... als ein fortwährendes Geschehen zu denken, welches auf das bewusste Seelenleben ständig einwirkt. In der Tat stehen wir fortwährend unter der Einwirkung unbewusster Vorgänge, und gerade diese bilden den

The question of the unconscious attained a particular relevance in 1898, when Freud began the preliminary work on the last chapter of *The Interpretation of Dreams*, which was variously conceived as both a philosophical and a psychological chapter. During this time, he oriented himself towards authors who argued not only for the effects of unconscious psychical contents, but who also saw the unconscious as being the primary determinant of psychical reality. Among various names, two in particular stand out in Freud's letters to Fliess and also in *The Interpretation of Dreams*.

The first is Gustav Theodor Fechner, whom Freud praises in his letter to Fliess dated February 9, 1898. Fechner's supposition that dream processes play themselves out on a different psychical terrain to that of consciousness was, wrote Freud to Fliess, the only sensible thought that he had encountered in his background reading on psychology.[31] Although Fechner initially developed his theories in the tradition of Herbart, he also critically distanced himself from Herbart on several occasions (see Michael Heidelberger's discussion in chapter 8 of this volume). One must, argued Fechner, strictly abide by what is given, and not make unquestioned metaphysical assumptions. As soon as one introduces metaphysics into science, he wrote, one inevitably alienates it from life.[32] In contrast to Herbart, Fechner argued for a radical empiricism that allows conclusions to be drawn only on the basis of experience. For Freud, Fechner embodied the new empirical paradigm of the nineteenth century; in trying to make the conception of the unconscious widely acceptable to the scientific world, Fechner had, thought Freud, gone one step further than Herbart.[33]

Hauptbestandteil unserer geistigen Persönlichkeit ... Wir können schlechterdings nicht auskommen ohne das Unbewusste.] Ibid., 12.

[31] See Freud to Fliess, February 9, 1898, *The Complete Letters of Sigmund Freud to Wilhelm Fliess*, 299; *Briefe an Wilhelm Fliess*, 325. Similar sentiments can be found in the *Interpretation of Dreams*: Fechner, according to Freud, proposes that the "scene of action of dreams is different from that of waking life" [der Schauplatz der Träume ein anderer sei als der des wachen Vorstellungslebens], and that only this assumption allows one to grasp the characteristics of dream-life. See Freud, *The Interpretation of Dreams*, SE, V: 536; *Die Traumdeutung*, GW, II/3: 541. Freud continued to invoke the ideas of Fechner in later works; for example, in his "Selbstdarstellung" of 1925, where he writes that he "was always open to the ideas of G. T. Fechner, and have followed that thinker upon many important points," Freud, "An Autobiographical Study," SE, XX: 59. [Ich war immer für die Ideen G. Th. Fechners zugänglich und habe mich in wichtigen Punkten an diesen Denker angelehnt.] Freud, "Selbstdarstellung," GW, XIV: 86.

[32] Gustav Theodor Fechner, "Zur Kritik der Grundlagen von Herbart's *Metaphysik*," *Zeitschrift für Philosophie und philosophische Kritik* 25 (1853): 70–102; here 70.

[33] Franz Buggle and P. Wirtgen, "Gustav Theodor Fechner und die psychoanalytischen Modellvorstellungen Sigmund Freuds," *Archiv für die Geschichte der Psychologie* 121 (1969): 148–201; here 168.

Despite Fechner's criticism of Herbart, it was arguably Herbart's notion of the *Schwellengesetz* (law of the threshold), and his notion of unconscious sensations, which enabled a scientific notion of the unconscious to develop. Following Herbart, Fechner argued that so long as sensations remain below the psychophysical threshold, they also remain unconscious, but nonetheless effective. This is why, according to Fechner,

> the concept of the psychophysical threshold has the most important meaning, in that it provides a stable foundation for the concept of the unconscious. Psychology cannot distance itself from unconscious sensations and representations ... Sensations and perceptions have admittedly ceased to exist as such in the condition of unconsciousness, insofar as we understand them abstractly and in terms of their basis, but something nevertheless goes on inside us, the psychophysical activity, of which these unconscious sensations are a function, and upon which the possibility of these sensations re-emerging into consciousness depends.[34]

It is precisely Fechner's consideration of the irrational on the one hand, and his strictly empirical-rational methodology on the other, that made his approach so appealing to Freud.

The second key author for Freud around 1898 was Theodor Lipps, who, alongside Wilhelm Wundt (1832–1920) and Brentano, was one of the leading figures in academic psychology at the time. It was particularly convenient for Freud that he found in Lipps a supporting witness for the scientific nature of a psychology of the unconscious. Lipps is first mentioned in Freud's letter to Fliess dated August 26, 1898, in which he states:

> I have set myself the task of building a bridge between my germinating metapsychology and that contained in the literature and have therefore immersed myself in the study of Lipps, who I suspect has the clearest mind among present-day philosophical writers.[35]

---

[34] [der Begriff der psychophysischen Schwelle hat die wichtigste Bedeutung schon dadurch, dass er für den Begriff des Unbewusstseins überhaupt ein festes Fundament gibt. Die Psychologie kann von unbewussten Empfindungen, Vorstellungen nicht abstrahieren ...Empfindungen, Vorstellungen haben freilich im Zustand des Unbewusstseins aufgehört, als wirkliche zu existieren, sofern man sie abstrakt von ihrer Unterlage fasst, aber es geht etwas in uns fort, die psychophysische Tätigkeit, deren Funktion sie sind, und woran die Möglichkeit des Wiedereintritts der Empfindung hängt.] Fechner, *Elemente der Psychophysik*, 2nd edn. (Leipzig: Breitkopf & Härtel, 1889), 438ff. On relations between the respective theorizations of the unconscious offered by Fechner and Freud, see also: Dorer, *Historische Grundlagen der Psychoanalyse*, 110.

[35] Freud to Fliess, August 26, 1898, *The Complete Letters of Sigmund Freud to Wilhelm Fliess*, 324. [Ich habe mir die Aufgabe gestellt, zwischen meiner keimenden Metapsychologie und der in Büchern enthaltenen die Brücke herzustellen und mich darum in das Studium von Lipps versenkt, in dem ich den klarsten Kopf unter den heutigen philosophischen Schriftstellern ahne.] Freud, *Briefe an Wilhelm Fliess 1887–1904*, 354.

And in a subsequent letter to Fliess, Freud admits that he

> found the substance of my insights stated quite clearly in Lipps, perhaps rather more so than I would like. "The seeker often finds more than he wished to find!" Consciousness is only a sense organ; all psychic content is only a representation; all psychic processes are unconscious. The correspondence [of our ideas] is close in details as well; perhaps the bifurcation from which my own new ideas can branch off will come later.[36]

Freud went on to mention that he studied Lipps' *Fundamental Facts of the Inner Life* (*Grundtatsachen des Seelenlebens*, 1883). A further reference can also be found in *The Interpretation of Dreams*, where Freud refers to a lecture given by Lipps on August 7, 1896 at the Third International Congress for Psychology in Munich, and entitled "The Concept of the Unconscious in Psychology" ("Der Begriff des Unbewussten in der Psychologie"). In this lecture, Lipps states his thesis that the question of the unconscious is "not so much a psychological question but rather *the question* of psychology."[37] Freud, needless to say, enthusiastically approved. In one of his last studies, he once again reminds us that Lipps was the first to adequately use the term unconscious in the scientific sense, while also endowing it with new content.[38]

The conception of the unconscious which was established in *The Interpretation of Dreams* stood in the framework of the theory of repression. On the clinical level, Freud referred to the repressed as dynamically unconscious, by arguing that repressed wishes, passions and fantasies return to consciousness by themselves. Another development in the *Interpretation of Dreams* is the notion of a *psychical* rather than just a

---

[36] Freud to Fliess, August 31, 1898, *The Complete Letters of Sigmund Freud to Wilhelm Fliess*, 325. [die Grundzüge meiner Einsicht ganz klar wiedergefunden, vielleicht etwas mehr, als mir recht ist. "Der Sucher fand oft mehr, als er zu suchen wünschte!" Das Bewußtsein ist nur Sinnesorgan, aller psychische Inhalt nur Vorstellung, die seelischen Vorgänge sämtlich Unbewusst. Auch in den Einzelheiten ist die Übereinstimmung groß, vielleicht kommt später die Gabelung, von der aus mein Neues ansetzen kann]. Freud, *Briefe an Wilhelm Fliess 1887–1904*, 356.

[37] [weniger eine psychologische Frage als die Frage der Psychologie]. My emphasis in the English. Quoted in L. Lütkehaus, ed., *Dieses wahre innere Afrika: Texte zur Entdeckung des Unbewußten vor Freud* (Frankfurt am Main: Fischer, 1989), 235. For Freud's reference to this lecture see Freud, *SE*, V: 611–12; *GW*, II/3: 616. M. Kanzer sees Freud's repeated appeals to the authority of Lipps as enabling Freud to free himself from his close relation with Fliess. M. Kanzer, "Freud, Theodor Lipps and Scientific Psychology," *Psychoanalytic Quarterly* 50 (1981): 383–410; here 401.

[38] See Freud, "Some Elementary Lessons in Psycho-Analysis." In relation to Lipps, Freud writes: "A German philosopher, Theodor Lipps, asserted with the greatest explicitness that the psychical is in itself unconscious and that the unconscious is truly psychical," *SE*, XXIII: 286; [Ein deutscher Philosoph, Theodor Lipps, hat mit aller Schärfe verkündet, das Psychische sei an sich unbewusst, das Unbewusste sei das eigentlich Psychische.] *GW*, XVII: 147.

strictly physiological apparatus of the nervous system. Freud accordingly began to speak of psychical instead of physiological energies, and of a psychical constancy principle. He also introduced the concept of *psychical topography*:

> I shall remain upon psychological ground, and I propose simply to follow the suggestion that we should picture the instrument which carries out our mental functions as resembling a compound microscope or a photographic apparatus, or something of the kind. On that basis, psychical locality will correspond to a point inside the apparatus at which one of the preliminary stages of an image comes into being. In the microscope and telescope, as we know, these occur in part at ideal points, regions in which no tangible component of the apparatus is situated.[39]

In line with this topographical model, Freud distinguished the essential unconscious from the systems of the preconscious (*das Vorbewusste*) and the conscious (*das Bewusste, Bewusstsein*) through the notion of a "censorship-barrier" (*Zensurschranke*):

> Let us therefore compare the system of the unconscious to a large entrance hall, in which the mental impulses jostle one another like separate individuals. Adjoining this entrance hall there is a second, narrower, room – a kind of drawing-room – in which consciousness, too, resides. But on the threshold between these two rooms a watchman performs his function: he examines the different mental impulses, acts as a censor, and will not admit them into the drawing-room if they displease him.[40]

Freud attributed to the system of the unconscious particular characteristics and functions: they proceed according to a primary process which displays the tendencies of condensation (*Verdichtung*) and displacement (*Verschiebung*); they are not controlled according to time; they are subject to the pleasure principle; and they demonstrate the attributes of

---

[39] Freud, *The Interpretation of Dreams*, SE, V: 536. [Wir bleiben auf psychologischem Boden und gedenken nur der Aufforderung zu folgen, dass wir uns das Instrument, welches den Seelenleistungen dient, vorstellen wie etwa ein zusammengesetztes Mikroskop, einen photographischen Apparat u. dgl. Die psychische Lokalität entspricht dann einem Orte innerhalb eines Apparats, an dem eine der Vorstufen des Bildes zustande kommt. Beim Mikroskop und Fernrohr sind dies bekanntlich zum Teil ideelle Örtlichkeiten, Gegenden, in denen kein greifbarer Bestandteil des Apparats gelegen ist.] Freud, *Die Traumdeutung*, GW, II/3: 541.

[40] Freud, "Resistance and Repression," *Introductory Lectures on Psychoanalysis*, SE, XVI: 295; [Wir setzen also das System des Unbewußten einem großen Vorraum gleich, in dem sich die seelischen Regungen wie Einzelwesen tummeln. An diesen Vorraum schließe sich ein zweiter, engerer, ein Art Salon, in welchem auch das Bewußtsein verweilt. Aber an der Schwelle zwischen beiden Räumlichkeiten waltet ein Wächter seines Amtes, der die einzelnen Seelenregungen mustert, zensuriert und sie nicht in den Salon einlässt, wenn sie sein Mißfallen erregen.] Freud, "Widerstand und Verdrängung," *Vorlesungen zur Einführung in die Psychoanalyse*, GW, XI: 305.

indestructibility and obliviousness to logical contradictions. On the one hand, these characteristics and functions illustrate the reconstruction of the fundament of Freud's clinical experiences "in searching for what lay beneath the surface communications and behaviour of his patients."[41] On the other hand, however, they display several important parallels with philosophical notions of *Lebenskraft* (life-force or vital power) to be found in prior sources: in the work of eighteenth-century German medical writers such as Friedrich Casimir Medicus (1736–1808) and Christoph Wilhelm Hufeland (1762–1836);[42] in Schopenhauer's notion of the will to life (*Wille zum Leben*); and in the conceptions of the unconscious elaborated by Carl Gustav Carus and Eduard von Hartmann. In relation to the preconscious, Freud assumes that, unlike the unconscious, it works predominantly according to the secondary process and the reality principle, and therefore shows attributes such as a sense of time, a general conformity to logic and the intolerance of inconsistencies or contradictions.

To recapitulate, it can be said that Freud's metapsychology was formed at the point of intersection between two philosophical traditions: on the one hand, the tradition of philosophers like Jerusalem, Fechner, and Lipps, who attributed the unconscious to the psyche; and on the other hand, the materialistic tradition of thought outlined by Brücke, Helmholtz, the neurologist Theodor Meynert (1833–92) and others, who tried to arrange the psyche according to the model of a mechanistic apparatus. In relation to this latter tradition, Freud's innovation lay in his *dynamic* conception of the unconscious, and in his introduction of a tripartite model of the self, consisting of unconscious, preconscious, and conscious components.[43] The possible influence of metaphysicians and speculative theorists of the unconscious such as Schopenhauer, Eduard von Hartmann, and Nietzsche during the 1890s is not positively verifiable and must therefore be presumed to be of only peripheral significance.

In relation to his tripartite model of conscious, preconscious, and unconscious, Freud's attention was directed towards the effectiveness and scientific verifiability of the psychical unconscious. In this context, the already existing tradition-line of the *cognitive unconscious* was of uppermost importance. But Freud's main focus, and his real innovation and discovery, was the *dynamic unconscious*. This is why, in contradistinction

---

[41] Joseph Sandler, Alex Holder, Christopher Dare, and Anna Ursula Dreher, *Freud's Models of the Mind: An Introduction* (London: Karnac, 1997), 81.
[42] See Stefan Goldmann, "Von der 'Lebenskraft' zum Unbewussten: Stationen eines Konzeptwandels der Anthropologie," *Macht und Dynamik des Unbewussten: Auseinandersetzungen in Philosophie, Medizin und Psychoanalyse*, ed. M. B. Buchholz and G. Gödde (Gießen: Psychosozial Verlag, 2005), 125–52.
[43] See Albrecht Hirschmüller, *Freuds Begegnung mit der Psychiatrie: Von der Hirnmythologie zur Neurosenlehre* (Tübingen: Edition Diskord, 1991).

to the cognitive tradition-line of Leibniz and his successors, he argued that the principle of continuity is not applicable to the unconscious, since a purely cognitive model of the unconscious would continually be exposed to the possibility of a rationalization, of seeking only examples of rational cognition, which would in turn fail to take the often irrational forces of repression and resistance into account.

Freud also drew a strong line of demarcation between himself and Lipps, by making the following programmatic statement:

> It is not without intention that I speak of "our" unconscious. For what I describe is not the same as the unconscious of the philosophers or even the unconscious of Lipps. By them [i.e., the philosophers] the term is used merely to indicate a contrast with the conscious ... Lipps carries things further with his assertion that the whole of what is psychical exists unconsciously and that a part of it also exists consciously. But it is not in order to establish *this* thesis that we have summoned up the phenomena of dreams and the formation of hysterical symptoms; the observation of normal waking life would by itself suffice to prove it beyond any doubt. The new discovery that we have been taught by the analysis of psycho-pathological structures ... lies in the fact that the unconscious (that is, the psychical) is found as a function of two separate systems and that this is the case in normal as well as in pathological life.[44]

Here Freud argues that his real innovation, which developed from the psychoanalytic investigation of neurosis as well as from the interpretation of dreams, was to present the unconscious not simply as the "other" of consciousness, but rather as a *differentiated* phenomenon, which is to be seen as a function of the "two separate systems" referred to above: the unconscious and the preconscious. This theoretical standpoint would, however, undergo a significant transformation during the 1920s.

The late Freud's treatment of the philosophy of the unconscious during the 1920s

In his *Three Essays on the Theory of Sexuality* (*Drei Abhandlungen zur Sexualtheorie*, 1905) Freud introduced the expression *Trieb* (drive) as

---

[44] Freud, *The Interpretation of Dreams*, SE, V: 614; [Ich sage nicht ohne Absicht, *in unserem Unbewußten*, denn was wir so heißen, deckt sich nicht mit dem Unbewußten der Philosophen, auch nicht mit dem Unbewußten bei Lipps. Dort soll es bloß den Gegensatz zu dem Bewußten bezeichnen ... Bei Lipps hören wir von dem weiter reichenden Satz, daß alles Psychische als unbewußt vorhanden ist, einiges davon dann auch als bewußt. Aber nicht zum Erweis für *diesen* Satz haben wir die Phänomene des Traums und der hysterischen Symptombildung herangezogen; die Beobachtung des normalen Tageslebens reicht allein hin, ihn über jeden Zweifel festzustellen. Das Neue, was uns die Analyse der psychopathischen Bildungen ... gelehrt, besteht darin, daß das Unbewußte – also das Psychische – als Funktion zweier gesonderter Systeme vorkommt und schon im normalen Seelenleben so vorkommt.] Freud, *Die Traumdeutung*, GW, II/3: 619.

a boundary term linking the somatic with the psychic, while also taking the genetic aspect of early childhood drive-destinies (*Triebschicksale*) into consideration. Since the core of the unconscious was now extended beyond the field of repression, in that it came to be seen as both drive-related and genetic, one can speak here of an important elaboration of, and even a shift within, Freud's understanding of the unconscious. Freud was, moreover, increasingly confronted by the limitations of the topographic model of the unconscious, which seemingly failed to answer the following questions: Where should one localize the powers of repression? Where should one locate the unconscious sense of guilt, which is closely linked with the individual's conscience, ideals, and values? How could one explain the phenomenon of unconscious fear? And perhaps most importantly, how might one account for the significant problem of aggression?

During the 1920s, and in answer to the above questions, the topographic model of the unconscious was transformed into a structural one. The new metapsychology was on the one hand characterized by the dualism involving Eros and the death-drive (*Todestrieb*), and on the other hand by the dynamic relationships between the ego (*Ich*), the id (*Es*), and the super-ego (*Über-Ich*). Freud introduced his theories relating to Eros and the death-drive in *Beyond the Pleasure Principle* (*Jenseits des Lustprinzips*, 1920). Here Freud proposes that the function of *Eros* is to link the subject's physical and mental natures through a wide range of human activities: in the relations between men and women; in the life of the family; in the formation of groups; and (in particular) in the highest forms of cultural achievement. At the same time, Freud described *Eros* as a *Störenfried* (trouble-maker), since it continually gives rise to tensions. Quoting the famous lines from Part One of Goethe's *Faust*, Freud proposes that Eros "presses ever forward, unsubdued" (*ungebändigt immer vorwärts dringt*).[45] At the same time, the death-drive opposes the tensions, transformations, and higher developments associated with *Eros*. In terms of Freud's theory of the unconscious, the death-drive hypothesis requires that both the emergence and the repression of aggressive and destructive mental contents be taken into account.

In his paper entitled "Something about the Unconscious" (*Etwas vom Unbewußten*), given on September 26, 1922 at the Seventh Psychoanalytic Congress in Berlin, Freud presented two pieces of evidence – namely, resistance in analysis initiated by the ego and the unconscious sense of guilt – both of which he thought demonstrated that "even in the ego

---

[45] Freud, *Beyond the Pleasure Principle*, SE, XVIII: 42; *Jenseits des Lustprinzips*, GW, XIII: 45.

there is an unconscious, which behaves dynamically like the repressed unconscious."[46] In order to elaborate on the new material presented in "Something About the Unconscious," Freud then examined, in a new essay entitled "The Ego and the Id" (*Das Ich und das Es*, 1923), what implications the discoveries outlined in the former essay would have for his conception of the unconscious.

In Freud's new structural model, the id is interpreted as the origin of libidinal as well as aggressive and destructive drives. This dark part of our personality, which Freud describes as being both barely accessible and almost impossible to control, is compared to a chaotic realm, "a cauldron full of seething excitations" (*Kessel voll brodelnder Erregung*), which has, according to Freud, "no organization, produces no collective will, but only a striving to bring about the satisfaction of the instinctual needs subject to the observance of the pleasure principle."[47] During the period in which the subject develops, a part of the id is modified, in order to become the ego, which serves the purposes of self-preservation and the preservation of material living conditions. The ego has the function of postponing and controlling drive-discharge through a number of mechanisms, including those which Freud describes as mechanisms of defence. The super-ego operates as the mouthpiece of the conscience, and as the mediator of parental and cultural values and ideals.

In psychoanalytic terms, the crucial aspect of this shift in Freud's understanding of the unconscious was the realization that acts of repression and resistance which emerge from the ego are not enabled to become conscious, since a conscious awareness of them would endanger the very success of repression. Accordingly, Freud concluded in "The Ego and the Id" that

A part of the ego, too – and Heaven knows how important a part – may be *Ucs.* [Unconscious], undoubtedly is *Ucs.* And this *Ucs.* belonging to the ego is not latent like the *Pcs.* [Preconscious]; for if it were, it could not be activated without becoming *Cs.* [Conscious], and the process of making it conscious would not encounter such great difficulties.[48]

---

[46] My translation: [es auch im Ich ein Unbewußtes gibt, das sich dynamisch wie das verdrängte Unbewusste benimmt]. Freud, "Etwas vom Unbewußten," *GW, Nachtragsband: Texte aus den Jahren 1885 bis 1938*, 752.

[47] Freud, "Dissection of the Personality," *New Introductory Lectures on Psychoanalysis, SE*, XXII: 73. [keine Organisation, bringt keinen Gesamtwillen auf, nur das Bestreben, den Triebbedürfnissen unter Einhaltung des Lustprinzips Befriedigung zu verschaffen]. Freud, "Die Zerlegung der psychischen Persönlichkeit," *Neue Folge der Vorlesungen zur Einführung in die Psychoanalyse, GW*, XV: 80.

[48] Freud, "The Ego and the Id," *SE*, XIX: 18; [Auch ein Teil des Ichs, ein Gott weiß wie wichtiger Teil des Ichs, kann *ubw* sein, ist sicherlich *ubw*. Und dies *Ubw* des Ichs ist nicht latent im Sinne des *Vbw*, sonst dürfte es nicht aktiviert werden, ohne *bw* zu werden, und

If the ego is related to the unconscious, is it incorrect to describe it as merely rational and superficial, and not subject to irrational forces and drives? Freud offers a decisive answer to this question, when he states that

> Pathological research has directed our interest too exclusively to the repressed. We should like to learn more about the ego, now that we know that it, too, can be unconscious in the proper sense of the word.[49]

Likewise, the super-ego, described by Freud as "a special agency in the ego ... which represents demands of a restrictive and rejecting character"[50] is also seen by the late Freud as containing unconscious components. Among these are the "unconscious sense of guilt,"[51] and in particular, "super-ego resistance"[52] and the "negative therapeutic reaction."[53]

How important is the transformation of the concept of the unconscious outlined by Freud in "The Ego and the Id"? Freud's new model no longer places psycho-sexuality, life instincts, or *Eros* at the center of the unconscious. In fact, the late Freud saw the dynamics of the unconscious as being much more dominated by irrational and destructive drives than he had previously assumed. From this point onwards, Freud advocates an organic or organism-related concept of the unconscious, arguing explicitly that the id is "open towards somatic influences" (*gegen das Somatische hin offen*).[54] Consequently, psychic experience does not just emerge out of bodily needs; it is itself a bodily experience. Several years prior to this Freud had also written to Groddeck, stating that the unconscious is the long-sought-after "missing link" between the physical and the psychic.[55]

---

seine Bewußtmachung dürfte nicht so große Schwierigkeiten bereiten.] Freud, "Das Ich und das Es," *GW*, XIII: 244.

[49] Freud, "The Ego and the Id," *SE*, XIX: 19; [Die pathologische Forschung hat unser Interesse allzu ausschließlich auf das Verdrängte gerichtet. Wir möchten mehr vom Ich erfahren, seitdem wir wissen, dass auch das Ich unbewusst im eigentlichen Sinne sein kann]. Freud, "Das Ich und das Es," *GW*, XIII: 246.

[50] Freud, "Dissection of the Personality," *New Introductory Lectures on Psychoanalysis*, *SE*, XXII: 69. [eine besondere Instanz im Ich ... die die einschränkenden und abweisenden Forderungen vertritt]. Freud, "Die Zerlegung der psychischen Persönlichkeit," *Neue Folge der Vorlesungen zur Einführung in die Psychoanalyse*, *GW*, XV: 75.

[51] Freud, "Das Ich und das Es," *GW*, XIII: 237–89; here 254.

[52] Freud, "Hemmung, Symptom und Angst," *GW*, XIV: 111–205; here 193.

[53] Freud, "Das Ich und das Es," *GW*, XIII: 278.

[54] Freud, "Dissection of the Personality," *New Introductory Lectures on Psychoanalysis*, *SE*, XXII: 73 (translation altered); Freud, "Die Zerlegung der psychischen Persönlichkeit," *Neue Folge der Vorlesungen zur Einführung in die Psychoanalyse*, *GW*, XV: 80.

[55] [Gewiss ist das Ubw die richtige Vermittlung zwischen dem Körperlichen und dem Seelischen, vielleicht das lang entbehrte "missing link."] Freud and Georg Groddeck, *Briefe über das Es* (Frankfurt am Main: Fischer, 1988), 15.

Even if he finally gave up on the idea of *the unconscious* (grammatically denoted by a noun), Freud nevertheless held fast to the topographical model of the unconscious. In "The Ego and the Id," this late structural model is referred to as the "second topographical model" (*zweite Topik*). Freud stressed, however, that "the three qualities of the characteristic of consciousness and the three provinces of the mental apparatus do not fall together into three peaceable couples,"[56] while also adding the following warning:

> In thinking of this division of the personality into an ego, a super-ego and an id, you will not, of course, have pictured sharp frontiers like the artificial ones drawn in political geography. We cannot do justice to the characteristics of the mind by linear outlines like those in a drawing or in primitive painting, but rather by areas of color melting into one another as they are presented by modern artists. After making the separation we must allow what we have separated to merge together once more.[57]

Freud's shift to ego-psychology led to a new conception of the ego as lacking in autonomy and freedom of will; this was a decisive revaluation that had a lasting impact on the development of psychoanalysis. In this context, Freud's late structural model can be seen to exist within a philosophical tradition, the central problem of which is the relationship between reason and drive-destiny.[58] According to Freud "reason and good sense" (*Vernunft und Besonnenheit*) represent the ego-pole within the psyche, with the "untamed passions" (*ungezähmte Leidenschaften*) functioning as the opposing id-pole.[59] As can be seen in chapter 5 of this volume, Schopenhauer had already offered a similar dualism of the subject, when he ascribed reason to the intellect, and passions or affects to the will.

---

[56] Freud, "Dissection of the Personality," *New Introductory Lectures on Psychoanalysis*, SE, XX: 72. [die drei Qualitäten der Bewusstheit und die drei Provinzen des seelischen Apparats sich nicht zu drei friedlichen Paaren zusammengefunden]. Freud, "Die Zerlegung der psychischen Persönlichkeit," *Neue Folge der Vorlesungen zur Einführung in die Psychoanalyse*, GW, XV: 79.

[57] Freud, "Dissection of the Personality," *New Introductory Lectures on Psychoanalysis*, SE, XXI: 79; [Sie denken bei dieser Sonderung der Persönlichkeit in Ich, Über-Ich und Es gewiss nicht an scharfe Grenzen, wie sie künstlich in der politischen Geographie gezogen worden sind. Der Eigenart des Psychischen können wir nicht durch lineare Konturen gerecht werden wie in der Zeichnung oder in der primitiven Malerei, eher durch verschwimmende Farbenfelder wie bei den modernen Malern. Nachdem wir gesondert haben, müssen wir das Gesonderte wieder zusammenfließen lassen.] Freud, "Die Zerlegung der psychischen Persönlichkeit," *Neue Folge der Vorlesungen zur Einführung in die Psychoanalyse*, GW, XV: 85.

[58] Walter Schulz, *Philosophie in der veränderten Welt* (Pfullingen: Neske, 1972), 673.

[59] Freud, "Dissection of the Personality," *New Introductory Lectures on Psychoanalysis*, SE, XXII: 76; Freud, "Die Zerlegung der psychischen Persönlichkeit," *Neue Folge der Vorlesungen zur Einführung in die Psychoanalyse*, GW, XV: 83.

When Freud introduced the term "id" (*Es*) in 1923, he brought it into explicit connection with Nietzsche, who, according to Freud, "habitually used this grammatical term for whatever in our nature is impersonal and, so to speak, subject to natural law."[60] And when Freud argues that "the ego is in the habit of transforming the id's will into action as if it were its own,"[61] this formulation points explicitly to the tradition according to which the will is the driving force behind the world of psychic representations. In relation to the supposition that unconscious psychic processes exist within the subject, Freud himself had referred to Schopenhauer a few years earlier, "whose unconscious 'will' is equivalent to the mental instincts of psycho-analysis."[62] Further to the connections made by Freud between himself and Schopenhauer, Max Horkheimer has also emphasized the basic congruence between Schopenhauer's metaphysics and Freud's metapsychology; arguing that Schopenhauer's notion of the will is susceptible of a psychological interpretation along the lines of Freud, while Freud's notion of the unconscious is in turn open to a philosophical interpretation that would link it with the metaphysics of Schopenhauer.[63]

A further comparison between Schopenhauer and Freud, undertaken by Marcel R. Zentner, concludes that Schopenhauer's metaphysical model of the personality and the meta-psychological model of Freud do not coincide merely according to their ideas, but even in terms of the actual terminology used by each thinker.[64] In relation to the structural characteristics of Schopenhauer's notion of the will and Freud's conception of the id, the literal coincidences referred to by Zentner are obvious. According to Schopenhauer the will is that which is deeper (*das Tiefere*), the inside (*das Innere*), the basis (*die Basis*), the primary and the substantial (*das Primäre und Substantiale*), while also being "everywhere the ultimate mover and creator, hence the condition of the entire organism" (*überall das eigentlich Bewegende und Bildende, mithin das Bedingende des ganzen Organismus*) as well as the "core of our being" (*Kern unseres*

---

[60] Freud, "The Ego and the Id," *SE*, XIX: 23, n. 3; [bei dem dieser grammatikalische Ausdruck für das Unpersönliche und sozusagen Naturnotwendige in unserem Wesen durchaus gebräuchlich ist]. Freud, "Das Ich und das Es," *GW*, XIII: 251, n. 2.

[61] Freud, "The Ego and the Id," *SE*, XIX: 25; [pflegt ... das Ich den Willen des Es in Handlung umzusetzen, als ob es der eigene wäre]. Freud, "Das Ich und das Es," *GW*, XIII: 253.

[62] Freud, "A Difficulty in the Path of Psycho-Analysis," *SE*, XVII: 143–4. [dessen unbewußter "Wille" den seelischen Trieben der Psychoanalyse gleichzusetzen sei]. Freud, "Eine Schwierigkeit der Psychoanalyse," *GW*, XII: 12.

[63] Max Horkheimer, "Das Schlimme erwarten und doch das Gute tun (Gespräch mit Gerhard Rein)," *Gesammelte Schriften* (Frankfurt am Main: Fischer, 1976), vol. VII: 442–65; here 454.

[64] Marcel R. Zentner, *Die Flucht ins Vergessen: Die Anfänge der Psychoanalyse Freuds bei Schopenhauer* (Darmstadt: Wissenschaftliche Buchgesellschaft, 1995), 86.

Wesens).⁶⁵ Similarly, Freud refers to the id in the following ways: as that which is deeper (*das Tiefere*); as the inner world (*Innenwelt*); as that which is original (*das Ursprüngliche*); as the primary process (*Primärvorgang*); and finally, in an expression which echoes Schopenhauer's description of the will directly, as the "core of our being" (*Kern unseres Wesens*) through which the organic drives act and strive for satisfaction.⁶⁶

With regard to the dynamic aspect of the unconscious, both Schopenhauer and Freud proceed on the assumption of an unremitting drive-work that is induced to action not just by the drive for self-preservation but also by the sex-drive. Closely linked with these fundamental drives are the qualitative and content-related characteristics of the unconscious, such as the striving for satisfaction associated with the pleasure principle. Yet despite all of the clear points of connection between Schopenhauer and Freud, we must keep in mind that Schopenhauer's notion of the will is at all times *metaphysical*, while Freud located the id within a continuum between the physical and the psychic.

It is also possible to make cogent and extensive comparisons between Freud's understanding of the ego and Schopenhauer's conception of the intellect: both are understood as something secondary, added, or derived; both do not exist and act *ex sua sponte*, but are weak in dynamic terms; finally, both belong to the outside, the periphery, or the surface layer of the personality, and are distant from its dynamic centre. In both cases, the main function of the intellect (Schopenhauer) and the ego (Freud) is to enable the subject to communicate with outer reality. While Schopenhauer named the intellect as the "ministry of foreign affairs" (*Ministerium des Aeußern*),⁶⁷ Freud describes the ego's job as that of representing the outside world to the id, since the id "could not escape destruction if, in its blind efforts for the satisfaction of its instincts, it disregarded that supreme external power."⁶⁸ By means of reality-testing, according to Freud, the ego can supplement the pleasure principle, which dominates the processes in the id, with the principle of reality.⁶⁹

---

⁶⁵ See Arthur Schopenhauer, *Die Welt als Wille und Vorstellung* (1844 edn.), *Werke in zehn Bänden* (Zürich: Diogenes, 1977–81), vol. III/4: 157, 238, 262, 279, 316.
⁶⁶ Freud, "An Outline of Psycho-Analysis," *SE*, XXIII: 162–3; 197–8; "Abriss der Psychoanalyse," *GW*, XVII: 85, 128.
⁶⁷ Schopenhauer, *Die Welt als Wille und Vorstellung*, 282.
⁶⁸ Freud, "The Dissection of the Personality," *New Introductory Lectures on Psychoanalysis*, *SE*, XXII: 75; [ohne Rücksicht auf diese übergewaltige Außenmacht im blinden Streben nach Triebbefriedigung der Vernichtung nicht entgehen würde]. Freud, "Die Zerlegung der psychischen Persönlichkeit," *Neue Folge der Vorlesungen zur Einführung in die Psychoanalyse*, *GW*, XV: 82.
⁶⁹ Freud, "The Dissection of the Personality," *New Introductory Lectures on Psychoanalysis*, *SE*, XXII: 75; Freud, "Die Zerlegung der psychischen Persönlichkeit," *Neue Folge der Vorlesungen zur Einführung in die Psychoanalyse*, *GW*, XV: 82.

As we have seen, a number of texts written by Freud suggest that, from 1919 onwards, he used various ideas from Schopenhauer for the conception of his late work. At the same time, however, Freud disapproved of Schopenhauer's monistic concept of the will, arguing that in significant respects it does not coincide with his (that is, Freud's) notion of the id. Freud pointed out that the id is more limited in its capabilities than is Schopenhauer's metaphysical conception of the will: the id, he wrote, "cannot say what it wants," has "no unified will" and is in a constant battle with "Eros and the death instinct."[70] At a later stage Freud further elaborated his self-differentiation from Schopenhauer, writing that

what we are saying is not even genuine Schopenhauer. We are not asserting that death is the only aim of life; we are not overlooking the fact that there is life as well as death. We recognize two basic instincts and give each of them its own aim.[71]

Freud also considered Nietzsche to be a philosopher "whose guesses and intuitions often agree in the most astonishing way with the laborious findings of psycho-analysis."[72] Freud's letters on Nietzsche, even those written after the immense rupture of the First World War, do not provide a genuine insight into the question of reception.[73] Instead, any analysis of Nietzsche's possible influence upon Freud must turn to structural comparisons between the works of both thinkers. These comparisons indicate some basic congruencies between Nietzsche's works and Freud's metapsychological writings of the 1920s, as well as those on cultural theory, most strikingly in the case of parallels between Nietzsche's *Genealogy of Morals* (*Genealogie der Moral*, 1887) and Freud's *Civilization and its Discontents* (*Unbehagen in der Kultur*, 1930).[74]

[70] Freud, "The Ego and the Id," *SE*, XIX: 59. [nicht sagen, was es will; es hat keinen einheitlichen Willen zustande gebracht. Eros und Todestrieb kämpfen in ihm.] Freud, "Das Ich und das Es," *GW*, XIII: 289.

[71] Freud, "Anxiety and Instinctual Life," *New Introductory Lectures on Psychoanalysis, SE*, XXII: 107. [Was wir sagen, ist nicht einmal richtiger Schopenhauer. Wir behaupten nicht, der Tod sei das einzige Ziel des Lebens; wir übersehen nicht neben dem Tod das Leben. Wir anerkennen zwei Grundtriebe und lassen jedem sein eigenes Ziel.] Freud, "Angst und Trieblehre," *Neue Folge der Vorlesungen zur Einführung in die Psychoanalyse*, *GW*, XV: 115; see also Wucherer-Huldenfeld, *Ursprüngliche Erfahrung und personales Sein*, 192.

[72] Freud, "An Autobiographical Study," *SE*, XX: 60. [dessen Ahnungen und Einsichten sich oft in der erstaunlichsten Weise mit den mühsamen Ergebnissen der Psychoanalyse decken]. Freud, "Selbstdarstellung," *GW*, XIV: 86.

[73] See Freud to Thomas Mann, November 23, 1929, in Thomas Mann, *Freud und die Psychoanalyse: Reden, Briefe, Notizen, Betrachtungen* (Frankfurt am Main: S. Fischer, 1991), 115; Freud to Lothar Bickel, June 28, 1931, quoted in Gay, *Freud*, 46 n.

[74] See: Wucherer-Huldenfeld, "Freuds Umsetzung der Philosophie in Metapsychologie," *Ursprüngliche Erfahrung und personales Sein*, 179–95; Reinhard Gasser, *Nietzsche und Freud* (Berlin: Walter de Gruyter, 1997); Gödde, *Traditionslinien des "Unbewußten"*, 524, 533.

It is noteworthy that Schopenhauer, Nietzsche, and Freud used similar metaphors in order to characterize the balance of power between will and intellect (in the case of Schopenhauer and Nietzsche) and id and ego (in the case of Freud). In a similar way to Schopenhauer and Nietzsche, Freud used the prominent metaphor of the rider and the horse. The ego resembles

a man on horse-back, who has to hold in check the superior strength of the horse; with this difference, that the rider tries to do so with his own strength while the ego uses borrowed forces. The analogy may be carried a little further. Often a rider, if he is not to be parted from his horse, is obliged to guide it where it wants to go; so in the same way the ego is in the habit of transforming the id's will into action as if it were its own.[75]

According to Freud the relation between id and ego is invariably a matter of a master–servant relation. When seen in this light, the ego is

not only a helper to the id; it is also a submissive slave who courts his master's love. Whenever possible, it tries to remain on good terms with the id; it clothes the id's *Ucs.* [unconscious] commands with its *Pcs.* [preconscious] rationalizations; it pretends that the id is showing obedience to the admonitions of reality, even when in fact it is remaining obstinate and unyielding; it disguises the id's conflicts with reality and, if possible, its conflicts with the super-ego too. In its position midway between the id and reality, it only too often yields to the temptation to become sycophantic, opportunist and lying, like a politician who sees the truth but wants to keep his place in popular favor.[76]

Conclusion

By now it should be clear that an understanding of "how the unconscious has been thought" – to paraphrase the title of this volume – can contribute a great deal to the classification of Freud's conception of the

---

[75] Freud, "The Ego and the Id," *SE*, XIX: 25. [im Verhältnis zum Es dem Reiter, der die überlegene Kraft des Pferdes zügeln soll, mit dem Unterschied, dass der Reiter dies mit eigenen Kräften versucht, das Ich mit geborgten … Wie dem Reiter, will er sich nicht vom Pferd trennen, oft nichts anderes übrigbleibt, als es dahin zu führen, wohin es gehen will, so pflegt auch das Ich den Willen des Es in Handlung umzusetzen, als ob es der eigene wäre.] Freud, "Das Ich und das Es," *GW*, XIII: 253.

[76] Freud, "The Ego and the Id," *SE*, XIX: 56. [nicht nur der Helfer des Es, auch sein unterwürfiger Knecht, der um die Liebe seines Herrn wirbt. Es sucht, wo möglich, im Einvernehmen mit dem Es zu bleiben, überzieht dessen *ubw* Gebote mit seinen *vbw* Rationalisierungen, spiegelt den Gehorsam des Es gegen die Mahnungen der Realität vor, auch wo das Es starr und unnachgiebig geblieben ist, vertuscht die Konflikte des Es mit der Realität und wo möglich auch die mit dem Über-Ich. In seiner Mittelstellung zwischen Es und Realität unterliegt es nur zu oft der Versuchung, liebedienerisch, opportunistisch und lügnerisch zu werden, etwa wie ein Staatsmann, der bei guter Einsicht sich doch in der Gunst der öffentlichen Meinung behaupten will.] Freud, "Das Ich und das Es," *GW*, XIII: 286.

unconscious in the history of philosophy and science. Freud certainly stands within, and also contributes to, the philosophical tradition of thinking about the unconscious. In particular, the late Freud belongs to a tradition – including both Schopenhauer and Nietzsche – that reflects upon the metaphysics of the will.

Yet the continuities and differences between the respective approaches of Nietzsche and Freud have not yet been sufficiently investigated by scholarly research. A number of questions arise from today's point of view: Is there a bridge over the gap between Freud's and Nietzsche's critical psychology of morals? What consequences might arise out of a closer alignment between psychoanalytic thinking and Nietzsche's anthropology of the will? How might psychoanalysis and depth psychology accord with Nietzsche's critiques of cognition and of science? It seems likely that many years after Freud's attempts to distance psychoanalysis from philosophy, and especially in light of new scholarly work on the relation between these two fields,[77] psychoanalysis can now turn to the intellectual correspondences between Freud and Nietzsche with much less hesitation and prejudice than was formerly the case. A new dialogue undertaken in a spirit of mutual respect could initiate a fruitful and forward-looking discourse, both for Nietzsche research as well as for psychoanalysis.

[77] See: Reinhard Gasser, *Nietzsche und Freud* (Berlin: Walter de Gruyter, 1997); Paul Laurent Assoun, *Freud and Nietzsche*, trans. Richard L. Collier (London: Continuum, 2000); Günter Gödde, "Die Öffnung zur Denkwelt Nietzsches – eine Aufgabe für Psychoanalyse und Psychotherapie," *Psychoanalyse: Texte zur Sozialforschung* 4, no. 7, (2000): 91–100; Günter Gödde, "Nietzsches Perspektivierung des Unbewussten," *Nietzsche-Studien* 31 (2002): 154–94; Günter Gödde, "Freuds 'Entdeckung' des Unbewussten und die Wandlungen in seiner Auffassung," *Macht und Dynamik des Unbewussten*, 325–60.

Epilogue: the "optional" unconscious

Sonu Shamdasani

In the course of the nineteenth century, concepts of consciousness underwent a transformation as competing concepts of unconscious mental functioning were developed in philosophy, physiology, biology, and psychology and psychical research in Europe and the United States. The papers in this volume have mainly traced trajectories of concepts of the unconscious in nineteenth-century German philosophical and literary thought. Alongside these philosophical developments, concepts of the unconscious were developed in other disciplines. For example, in nineteenth-century British physiology, this took place through an expansion of the concept of reflex action. Under the rubric of "unconscious cerebration," William Carpenter (1813–85) maintained that a large proportion of mental activity takes place automatically, which is to say unconsciously. At the same time, notions of organic memory arose in German biology, based on Jean-Baptiste Lamarck's (1744–1829) theory of the inheritance of acquired characteristics and Ernst Haeckel's (1834–1919) biogenetic law that ontogeny recapitulated phylogeny. Through figures such as the German physiologist Ewald Hering (1834–1918), trans-individual and collective concepts of the unconscious were developed, wherein the unconscious was seen to contain and transmit the history of the race. However, the most lasting legacy of these developments lay in the dynamic psychologies and psychotherapies of the twentieth century. As the basis for an explanation of psychopathology, the term was taken up for a while in twentieth-century psychiatry, and more widely within psychotherapy, where it became a means of explaining human behavior in general and a new source for self-knowledge, which increasingly came to signify knowledge of what was unconscious, in some shape or form, to the self. The unconscious demonstrates the manner in which psychological concepts, despite their disputed status, have been taken on by large sectors of contemporary Western societies and entered the vernacular. Elsewhere, I have reconstructed the history of these multiple formations, and some of their complex intersections.

Drawing upon these works, I intend here to reflect upon the status of these concepts.[1]

Any consideration of the history of the unconscious is indebted to Henri Ellenberger's monumental *Discovery of the Unconscious* (1970).[2] Ellenberger's text marked the constitution and delineation of a new field of enquiry. His central assumption is embedded in the title of his work. As Mark Micale aptly notes, for Ellenberger, "the unconscious mind was not invented, or formulated, it was 'discovered.'"[3] For Ellenberger, the reality and existence of the unconscious as a natural object was unquestioned, with different conceptions of the unconscious figuring as competing maps of a preexisting and ontologically secure terrain. A singular reality was supposed to underlie the multiple depictions. However, to grasp the historical constitution of the unconscious, such naturalism needs to be set aside. Without this suspension, the modes in which the unconscious came to be conceived of as a natural object, whose existence could simply be taken for granted, cannot be grasped.

At the end of the nineteenth century, many figures in the West sought to establish a scientific psychology that would be independent of philosophy, theology, biology, anthropology, literature, medicine, and neurology, whilst taking over their traditional subject matters. The very possibility of psychology rested upon the successful negotiation of these disciplinary crossings. The larger share of the questions that psychologists took up had already been posed and elaborated in these prior disciplines. They had to prise their subjects from the preserves of other specialists. Through becoming a science, it was hoped that psychology would be able to solve questions that had vexed thinkers for centuries, and to replace superstition, folk wisdom, and metaphysical speculation with the rule of universal law. The result would amount to nothing less than the completion and culmination of the scientific revolution.

A critical mutation occurred in the last quarter of the nineteenth century, during which conceptions of the unconscious became the basis for dynamic psychologies. Psychologists and philosophers were concerned with the questions that were posed by hypnosis, dreams, glossolalia,

---

[1] Sonu Shamdasani, *Jung and the Making of Modern Psychology: The Dream of a Science* (Cambridge: Cambridge University Press, 2003); "Encountering Hélène: Théodore Flournoy and the Genesis of Subliminal Psychology," *From India to the Planet Mars: A Case of Multiple Personality with Imaginary Languages* by Théodore Flournoy (Princeton, NJ: Princeton University Press, 1994); "Automatic Writing and the Discovery of the Unconscious," *Spring: A Journal of Archetype and Culture* 54 (1993): 100–31.

[2] Henri Ellenberger, *The Discovery of the Unconscious: The History and Evolution of Dynamic Psychiatry* (New York: Basic Books, 1970).

[3] Mark Micale, *Beyond the Unconscious: Essays of H. F. Ellenberger in the History of Psychiatry*, ed. Mark Micale (Princeton, NJ: Princeton University Press, 1993), 127.

Epilogue: the "optional" unconscious 289

fugues, automatic writing, maladies of memory, hallucinations, telepathy and other alterations of the personality that seemed to pose formidable problems for the philosophy and psychology of consciousness. In 1890, whilst reflecting on the future of science, the French philosopher Ernst Renan (1823–92) stated:

In studying the psychology of the individual, sleep, madness, delirium, somnambulism, hallucination offer a far more favourable field of experience than the normal state. Phenomena, which in the normal state are almost effaced because of their tenuousness, appear more palpable in extraordinary crises because they are exaggerated ... human psychology will have to be constructed by studying the madness of mankind.[4]

A general reordering of the relations between the normal and the pathological, the regular and the irregular took place at this time, which was constitutive of modern psychology. For the dynamic psychologies that flourished, the term that was most frequently used to conceptualize such states was the unconscious. In 1890, Eduard von Hartmann wrote of its advent that:

it was in the air and prepared from all sides; furthermore, it was also a requirement of the progress of the self-consciousness and self-understanding of mankind, and only because it was all this could it find such a quick and favourable acceptance with the public, so that one can now almost hear the sparrows chirping about it from the rooftops.[5]

That same year, with characteristic prescience, William James (1842–1910) noted what was to bedevil the use of the term. He wrote of the distinction between the conscious and the unconscious, that "it is the sovereign means for believing what one likes in psychology, and of turning what might become a science into a tumbling ground for whimsies."[6]

[4] [Le sommeil, la folie, le délire, le somnambulisme, l'hallucination offrent à la psychologie individuelle un champ d'expérience bien plus avantageux que l'état régulier. Car les phénomènes qui, dans cet état, sont comme effacés par leur ténuité, apparaissent dans les crises extraordinaires d'une manière plus sensible par leur exagération. ... la psychologie de l'humanité devra s'édifier surtout par l'étude des folies de l'humanité.] Ernst Renan, L'Avenir de la science: Pensées de 1848 (Paris: Calmann-Lévy, 1923), 184. Cited in Georges Canguilhem, The Normal and the Pathological, trans. C. Fawcett (New York: Zone Books, 1989), 44–5.
[5] [denn dasselbe lag in der Luft und war von allen Seiten vorbereitet; es war aber zugleich auch eine Forderung des Fortschritts in der Selbstbesinnung und dem Selbstverständniss der Menschheit, und nur weil es dies alles war, konnte es eine so schnelle und willige Aufnahme im Publicum finden, dass man es jetzt schon beinahe die Spatzen von den Dächern rufen hört]. Eduard von Hartmann, Philosophie des Unbewussten: Speculative Resultate nach inductiv-naturwissenschaftlicher Methode, 12th edn., vol. 3 (Leipzig: Alfred KrönerVerlag, 1923), 298. Cited in D. Darnoi, The Unconscious and Eduard von Hartmann (The Hague: Martinus Nijhoff, 1967), 75.
[6] William James, Principles of Psychology, 2 vols. (London: Macmillan, 1918), vol. I, 163.

For the dynamic psychologies, the concept of the unconscious was intended to carry the aspirations of their "will to science," and the attempt to form a unitary discipline of psychology. In this regard, the unconscious presented an ideal term. It was a site where new universal laws could be discovered and where periodic tables could be established. It enabled them to delineate their own domain of the mind and people it with a plethora of objects, mechanisms, and special modes of functioning, described in a language modeled after the technical languages of the natural sciences. There was little that could not be explained via the unconscious: dreams, delusions, passions, inspirations, and even religious experience. The unconscious of the psychologists had to be differentiated from that of the philosophers, to enable it to be presented as a scientific concept. In most cases, this was simply accomplished through a denial of filiation. Consequently, Hartmann's philosophy of the unconscious came in for extended criticism from psychologists. Physiologists were also at pains to differentiate their conceptions of the unconscious from Hartmann's. A case in point is the German psychologist Hermann Ebbinghaus (1850–1909), whose 1885 work *On Memory* (*Über das Gedächtnis*) was critical in establishing the experimental investigation of memory, and who wrote his 1873 dissertation as a critique of Hartmann's work. Ebbinghaus contended that what was true in Hartmann's book was not new, what was new in it was not true. Everything essential in it went back to Schopenhauer.[7]

In 1889, the American psychologist James Mark Baldwin (1861–1934) subjected the concept of the unconscious to a critique in his *Handbook of Psychology: Sense and Intellect*.[8] Von Hartmann's views were simply dismissed for being metaphysical. Baldwin concluded:

Phenomena called "unconscious mental states" may be accounted for partly from the physical side, as excitations inadequate to a mental effect, and partly from the mental side, as states of least consciousness. Where, in the progressive subsistence of consciousness, these two classes of fact come together we have no means of knowing ... As Binet says, if there be unconscious mental phenomena, "we know absolutely nothing about them."[9]

Oswald Külpe (1862–1915), a former student of Wilhelm Wundt who played a key role in establishing the experimental study of thought, gave an extended account of von Hartmann's work in his *The Philosophy of the Present in Germany* (*Die Philosophie der Gegenwart in Deutschland*, 1902)

---

[7] Hermann Ebbinghaus, *Über die Hartmannsche Philosophie des Unbewussten* (Düsseldorf, 1873), 67. See also Ebbinghaus, *Über das Gedächtnis: Untersuchungen zur experimentellen Psychologie* (Darmstadt: Wissenschaftliche Buchgesellschaft, 1992).

[8] James Mark Baldwin, *Handbook of Psychology: Sense and Intellect* (London: Macmillan, 1890), 45–58.

[9] Ibid., 58.

that indicates its contemporary significance. Külpe saw Hartmann's system as being, like that of Schopenhauer, "more a mythologically-colored speculation, like the myths of Plato, rather than an extension and completion of scientific knowledge."[10]

In 1890, William James devoted an extended section of his *Principles of Psychology* to a critique of the concept of the unconscious. In his chapter on the "mind-stuff" theory, James dealt with the existence of unconscious mental states. He set out ten supposed proofs of the unconscious, which were "most systematically urged" by von Hartmann, and then subjected them to a detailed point by point refutation.[11] What was significant in James' approach was that in each case, while recognizing the existence of the particular phenomenon in question, he demonstrated that they were amenable to other forms of explanation, which were in turn quite distinct from one another. In place of the monistic appeal to the unconscious, what was required was a pluralistic account of diverse phenomena. James dismissed von Hartmann's work, arguing that

Hartmann fairly boxes the compass of the universe with the principle of unconscious thought. For him there is no nameable thing that does not exemplify it ... the same is true of Schopenhauer.[12]

Likewise, there were critiques of psychological conceptions of the unconscious.

Hippolyte Bernheim (1840–1919), who had played a central role in instigating the modern hypnotic and psychotherapeutic movements, critiqued the "hypnotic unconscious," or the utilization of the unconscious to explain the hypnotic state. According to Bernheim, "this false idea of the unconscious has been the source of all the errors which have been committed. The subject is conscious ... The hypnotic unconscious ... does not exist."[13] Bernheim argued that the presumption of hypnotic

---

[10] [eher ... eine halb mythologisch gefärbte Spekulation, den platonischen Mythen vergleichbar, als eine Erweiterung und Vollendung der einzelwissenschaftlichen Erkenntnis zu nennen]. Oswald Külpe, *Philosophie der Gegenwart in Deutschland* (Leipzig: Teubner, 1902), 84.
[11] For a detailed consideration of James' arguments against the existence of unconscious mental states in the *Principles*, see Dennis Klein, *The Unconscious: Invention or Discovery? A Historico-Critical Inquiry* (Santa Monica, CA: Goodyear, 1977), 38–64.
[12] James, *Principles of Psychology*, vol. I, 169. In 1901, von Hartmann described recent psychology in uncomplimentary terms as constituting a "self-castration," a representative of the materialism and mechanical world view which he denounced (118). He argued that as a self-standing science, psychology would be a psychology of the unconscious, a science of the relations between the conscious and unconscious psyche, but that such a science did not yet exist (30). *Die Moderne Psychologie: Eine kritische Geschichte der Deutschen Psychologie in der Zweiten Haelfte des Neunzehnten Jahrhunderts* (Leipzig: Haacke, 1901).
[13] [Cette fausse idée d'inconscience ... a été la source de toutes les erreurs qui ont été commis. Le sujet est conscient ... L'inconscience hypnotique ... n'existe pas.] Bernheim, *Hypnotisme, suggestion, psychothérapie: Études nouvelles* (Paris: Alcan, 1891), 100.

amnesia was a mistake. Far from being unaware of their surroundings, hypnotized individuals were acutely aware of their surroundings, and responsive to cues:

> When memories of the somnambulistic state seem completely erased and when the subject cannot retrieve them spontaneously, it is sufficient to say to him, "You are going to remember everything that has happened." If the subject doesn't recover everything quickly, I put my hand on his forehead and say, "You are going to remember." After a certain time, the subject concentrates, recalls everything, and reports accurately everything that has happened. This proves that awareness is not abolished, that the somnambulist never acts like an unconscious robot, that he sees, hears, and knows what he is doing. He is dominated by images, ideas, suggested impressions, heightened credulity, and a tendency to obedience which is unrestrained [...] This is not unconsciousness – it is another state of consciousness.[14]

As we may recall, post-hypnotic suggestion was precisely what Bernheim's translator Sigmund Freud appealed to as demonstrating the proof of the unconscious. In 1915, he wrote: "Incidentally, even before the time of psycho-analysis, hypnotic experiments, and especially post-hypnotic suggestion, had tangibly demonstrated the existence and mode of operation of the mental unconscious."[15]

There was little that joined William James to Wilhelm Wundt, but one point in common was the critique of the concept of the unconscious. In his *Lectures on Human and Animal Psychology* (*Vorlesungen ueber die Menschen- und Thierseele*, 1863) Wundt argued that the interest in the unconscious arose from the false assumption that consciousness was a mental condition, a kind of stage upon which our representations

---

[14] Bernheim, *New Studies in Hypnotism*, trans. R. Sandor (New York: International Universities Press, 1980), 99. [Quand les souvenirs de l'état somnambulique paraissent complètement effacés et que le sujet ne peut les retrouver spontanément, il suffit de lui dire: "vous allez vous rappeler tout ce qui s'est passé." Si le sujet ne trouve pas toute de suite, je mets la main sur son front et je dis: "vous allez vous souvenir." Au bout d'un certain temps le sujet, s'étant concentré en lui-même, se rappelle tout et raconte avec une précision parfaite tout, absolument tout ce qui s'est passé. Preuve que la conscience n'était pas abolie, que la somnambule n'agit jamais comme un automate inconscient, qu'il voit, qu'il entend, qu'il sait ce qu'il fait; il est dominé par des images, par des idées et impressions suggérés, par une crédulité exaltée, par une tendance à l'obéissance non refrénée ... Ce n'est pas une inconscience; c'est un autre état de conscience.] Bernheim, *Hypnotisme, suggestion, psychothérapie*, 133–4.

[15] Freud, "The Unconscious," *The Standard Edition of the Complete Psychological Works of Sigmund Freud*, 24 vols., ed. James Strachey and Anna Freud (London: Hogarth Press, 1953–74), vol. XIV, 167. [Übrigens haben die hypnotischen Experimente, besonders die posthypnotische Suggestion, Existenz und Wirkungsweise des seelisch Unbewußten bereits vor der Zeit der Psychoanalyse sinnfällig demonstriert.] Freud, *Gesammelte Werke in achtzehn Bänden mit einem Nachtragsband*, 19 vols., ed. Anna Freud *et al.* (Frankfurt am Main: S. Fischer, 1988–99), vol. X, 267.

appeared like actors. This view led to the interest in what took place behind the scenes, i.e. in the unconscious. By contrast, Wundt argued that consciousness, unlike the stage, did not remain when the processes we are conscious of passed away, and that we knew nothing of a representation when it had disappeared from consciousness:

> There is scarcely any view which has been a greater source of error in psychology than that which regards representations as imperishable objects which may rise and sink ... but which, once they exist, are only distinguished by their changing distribution of consciousness and unconsciousness.[16]

Wundt contended that representations, like other mental experiences, were processes and occurrences, as opposed to objects.

Throughout the twentieth century, concepts of the unconscious continued to have a contested status. On the one hand, they have figured as the corner-stone for the plethora of psychoanalyses and dynamic psychotherapies, where, regardless of their status, they were operationalized as the theoretical basis for therapeutic interventions. Within this domain, there was further strife between different versions of the unconscious: Freudian, Jungian, and otherwise. On the other hand, they have had little place in mainstream experimental and social psychologies, where they were largely dismissed. However, protagonists and critics of the unconscious have in the main both tended to share commitments to realist ontologies and a correspondence theory of truth: either the unconscious exists, or it does not (or the unconscious of one particular school exists, and the unconscious of all the others does not). In other words, either people have unconsciouses, or they don't. Such positions fail to do adequate justice to the mode in which psychologies have functioned.

In a quasi-Wittgensteinian manner, I use the term "concept" here in a wide sense, as encompassing the ensemble of practices gathered under a term, what it enables one to do, and the uses to which it is put. Such breadth of consideration is necessary because, in the twentieth century, the unconscious became institutionalized, spawning a vast network of associations, guilds, and training societies, as well as becoming an influential societal idiom or idiolect.

Concerning the functioning of psychological concepts, I take my cue from William James' discussion in *The Principles of Psychology* concerning

---

[16] [Kaum gibt es darum eine Anschauung, die in der Psychologie eine grössere Verwirrung angerichtet hat, wie, dass die Vorstellungen unvergängliche Objekte seien, welche aufsteigen und sinken, die aber, einmal existirend, in nichts als in ihrer wechselnden Vertheilung über Bewusstsein und Unbewusstheit ... sich unterscheiden.] Wilhelm Wundt, *Vorlesungen ueber die Menschen- und Thierseele*, 2nd edn. (Hamburg: Verlag von Leopold Voss, 1892), 253.

Hegel, Georg Wilhelm Friedrich. *Phänomenologie des Geistes*. Ed. Gerhard Göhler, 2nd edn. Frankfurt am Main, Berlin, and Vienna: Ullstein Verlag, 1973.
Heidegger, Martin. *Nietzsche*. Vol. I. *The Will to Power as Art*. Trans. David Farrell Krell. San Francisco, CA: Harper Collins, 1991. [*Nietzsche*. Vol. I: *Der Wille zur Macht als Kunst*. Stuttgart: Neske, 1961].
Ontology: The Hermeneutics of Facticity. Trans. John van Buren. Bloomington, IN: Indiana University Press, 1999.
Wegmarken. Frankfurt am Main: Klostermann 1978.
Helmholtz, Hermann von. "Helmholtz on the Use and Abuse of the Deductive Method in Physical Science." In *Nature* 11 (December 24, 1874): 149–51.
Science and Culture: Popular and Philosophical Essays. Ed. David Cahan. Chicago: University of Chicago Press, 1995.
Vorträge und Reden. 4th edn. 2 vols. Braunschweig: Vieweg, 1896.
Herbart, Johann Friedrich. *Lehrbuch zur Einleitung in die Philosophie*. Königsberg: Unzer, 1813.
Lehrbuch zur Psychologie. Königsberg: Unzer, 1816. [*A Text-Book in Psychology: An Attempt to Found the Science of Psychology in Experience, Metaphysics, and Mathematics*. Trans. M. K. Smith. New York: Appleton, 1891].
Psychologie als Wissenschaft: Neu gegründet auf Erfahrung, Metaphysik und Mathematik: Erster, synthetischer Theil. Königsberg: Unzer, 1824.
Psychologie als Wissenschaft: Neu gegründet auf Erfahrung, Metaphysik und Mathematik: Erster, synthetischer Theil. In *Sämmtliche Werke*. Vol. V. Hamburg and Leipzig: Voss, 1886.
Psychologie als Wissenschaft: Neu gegründet auf Erfahrung, Metaphysik und Mathematik: Zweyter, analytischer Theil. Königsberg: Unzer, 1825.
Sämtliche Werke. 19 vols. Ed. Karl Kehrbach and Otto Flügel. Aalen: Scientia 1989.
Herder, Johann Gottfried. *Briefe, Gesamtausgabe 1763–1803*. Ed. Wilhelm Dobbek and Günter Arnold. Weimar: Hermann Böhlhaus Nachfolger, 1979.
Journal meiner Reise im Jahr 1769. In *Werke*. Vol I. Ed. Wolfgang Pross. Munich: Hanser, 1984.
Sculpture: Some Observations on Shape and Form from Pygmalion's Creative Dream. Trans. and ed. Jason Geiger. Chicago: University of Chicago Press, 2002.
Selected Early Works 1764–1787. Ed. Ernest A. Menze and Karl Menges. Trans. Ernest A. Menze and Michael Palma. University Park, PA: The Pennsylvania State University Press, 1992.
Werke. Ed. Günter Arnold, Martin Bollacher, *et al.* 10 vols. in 11. Frankfurt am Main: Deutscher Klassiker Verlag, 1985–2000.
Hering, Ewald. "Über das Gedächtnis als eine allgemeine Funktion der organisierten Materie" (Vortrag gehalten in der feierlichen Sitzung der Kaiserlichen Akademie der Wissenschaften in Wien am 30. Mai 1870). In *Fünf Reden von Ewald Hering*. Ed. H. E. Hering (Leipzig: Engelmann 1921), 5–31. [Translated as "Professor Ewald Hering 'On Memory.'" Trans. Samuel Butler. In *Unconscious Memory*. London: A. C. Fifield, 1880].
Zur Lehre vom Lichtsinne: Sechs Mittheilungen an die Kaiserl. Akademie der Wissenschaften in Wien. 2nd edn. Vienna: Carl Gerold, 1878. [*Outlines of a*

conceptions of hypnosis. James discussed the conflicts between the late nineteenth-century hypnotic schools. Concerning differing theories of the trance state, he wrote:

> The three states of Charcot, the strange reflexes of Heidenheim, and all the other bodily phenomena which have been called direct consequences of the trance-state itself, are not such. They are products of suggestion, the trance-state having no particular outward symptoms of its own; but without the trance-state there, those particular suggestions could never have been successfully made.[17]

Whilst conceived in a realist mode, psychological theories actually created new forms of experience, due to the impressionability of the trance state. This enabled any theory to be "realized." James' discussions of theories of trance are not solely concerned with one phenomenon, but with the malleability of experience to conceptual reframing in general, and how concepts become real. From this perspective, the context of clinical investigation does not uncover pure phenomena as such, as the phenomenon in question takes on the characteristics of the theory and parades it. From this perspective, theories of the unconscious functioned in a productive manner: far from being perpetually rediscovered and uncovered in a positivistic manner, the psychological unconscious was an artefact produced in the clinic. The theories in question do not function in a descriptive manner, but are more akin to theatrical scripts or stage directions.

However, this is by no means to say that the unconscious produced by such operations is illusory, unreal, or merely fictitious. Psychologies and psychotherapies have generated a plethora of optional ontologies through which individuals have come to rescript their lives. One of the most prominent among these has been that of the unconscious, which became one of the most powerful artefacts of modern psychology. From this perspective, one may raise the question as to what type of objects such unconsciouses are, and what uses they have been put to.

In this regard, concepts of the unconscious clearly had significant epistemological and professional utilities, which were interconnected. The unconscious was conceived as a natural object, which was trans-historical and cross-cultural. For psychoanalysts, everyone who had ever been alive must have had an unconscious, and furthermore, one whose laws had been discovered and laid down by Freud.[18] There was no place for

---

[17] James, *Principles of Psychology*, 2 vols. (Cambridge, MA: Harvard University Press, 1981), vol. II, 1201.
[18] On this issue, see Mikkel Borch-Jacobsen and Sonu Shamdasani, *The Freud Report: An Inquiry into the History of Psychoanalysis* (Cambridge: Cambridge University Press, forthcoming).

cultural variation, or the possibility of accepting that other peoples might have equally compelling alternative ontological conceptions and effective narratives of sickness and healing with no need for an unconscious. Consequently, historical and cross-cultural variations were nullified. With the unconscious, psychologists had their own epistemological object, with its particular laws, processes, and modes of functioning, just like other natural sciences, with compendious grammars of interpretive rules, which required special modes of training and instruction to be initiated into. This gave the sense that the disciplinary separation of psychology from other disciplines has been successfully negotiated, and indeed, that psychology could be considered to be a real entity that existed.

Within psychotherapy (at a theoretical level, as opposed to what occurred in practice) the unconscious led to the notion that the task of the psychotherapist lay in uncovering partially recessed unconscious representations which were concealed to the subject themselves but visible to the psychotherapist, whose task was one of transcribing behavior into the theoretical language of the unconscious. As such, the unconscious became a manner of rescripting the narrative description of a life, and a mode of hermeneutics for giving it significance.[19]

This language clearly did not remain a professional preserve, and was taken on by large social groupings, for whom it became a compelling form of self-description. In this perspective, posing the question as to whether the unconscious exists or not is generally unhelpful, as whatever one's views on this may be, we are faced today with a situation where a large body of people consider that they (and others) have an unconscious, and a still larger body of people consider that they (and others) don't. Geographically speaking, it would be possible in an approximate sense to chart this on a map upon which one would in all likelihood see the greatest density of individuals "with an unconscious" conglomerated around the European and American metropolises, with a minimal density in the so-called developing regions, such as Africa, China, and the Indian subcontinent. Given this situation, it would be useful to imagine how an anthropology of psychology might envisage such questions.[20] For instance, one might ask, how does one come to acquire an unconscious? Is there greater susceptibility among particular age groups? Are there

---

[19] This has functioned in a manner akin to the "illness narratives" described by the medical anthropologist Arthur Kleinman, *The Illness Narratives: Suffering, Healing, and the Human Condition* (New York: Basic Books, 1988).

[20] Such a study might take its cue from work in medical anthropology, such as Bryon Good, *Medicine, Rationality, and Experience: An Anthropological Perspective* (New York: Cambridge University Press, 1994), and Marc Augé's recent anthropology of modernity, *Pour une anthropologie des mondes contemporains* (Paris: Flammarion, 1994).

typical conversion experiences which give rise to the conviction of the reality of a particular unconscious? Why do people choose a particular type of unconscious? How do people try out different unconsciouses? What leads one to lose an unconscious? What effects, beneficial or otherwise, has living with an unconscious had on people's lives, in their own estimation? How does the unconscious compare with other optional ontologies? Furthermore, such investigations may be timely. If we live in an era marked by the increasing ascendancy of "brainhood," to use Fernando Vidal's excellent expression for the manner in which identity has come to be located in the brain, the psychological unconscious may well be on the wane.[21]

[21] Fernando Vidal, "Le Sujet cérébral: Une esquisse historique et conceptuelle," *PSN: Revue de Psychiatrie, Sciences humaines et Neurosciences* 3, no. 11 (2005): 37–48.

Works cited

PRIMARY SOURCES

Adelung, Johann Christoph. *Versuch eines vollständigen grammatisch-kritischen Wörterbuches der hochdeutschen Mundart, mit beständiger Vergleichung der übrigen Mundarten, besonders aber der oberdeutsche. Vierter Teil, von Sche–V.* Leipzig: Breitkopf, 1780.

Adorno, Theodor W. *Ästhetik Vorlesungen.* In *Adorno-Archiv.* Berlin: Akademie der Künste, 1961.

Allgemeine Deutsche Biographie. 56 vols. Leipzig: Duncker & Humblot, 1875–1912.

Aristotle. *The Basic Works.* Ed. Richard McKeon. New York: Random House, 1941.

De Anima (On the Soul). Trans. Hugh Lawson-Tancred. Harmondsworth: Penguin, 1986.

Arnold, Friedrich. "Foreword." In Carl Gustav Carus, *Psyche: Zur Entwicklungsgeschichte der Seele.* Darmstadt: Wissenschaftliche Buchgesellschaft, 1975.

Augustine. *De doctrina christiana; De vera religione.* Ed. Josef Martin and Klaus-D. Daur. Turnholti: Brepols, 1962.

De trinitate. Ed. W. J. Mountain. Turnholti: Brepols, 1968.

On the Trinity: Books 8–15. Ed. Gareth B. Matthews. Trans. Stephen McKenna. Cambridge: Cambridge University Press, 2002.

Bacon, Francis. *The New Organon.* Ed. Lisa Jardine and Michael Silverthorne. Cambridge: Cambridge University Press, 2000.

Bahnsen, Julius. *Beiträge zur Charakterologie.* Leipzig: J. A. Barth, 1867.

Der Widerspruch im Wissen und Wesen der Welt: Princip und Einzelbewährung der Realdialektik. 2 vols. Berlin: Theobald Grieben, 1880.

Baldwin, James Mark. *Dictionary of Philosophy and Psychology.* 11 vols. New York: Macmillan, 1901–5.

Handbook of Psychology: Sense and Intellect. London: Macmillan, 1890.

Balzac, Honoré de. *Louis Lambert.* In *Oeuvres Complètes.* Vol. XXI. Paris: Louis Conard, 1927.

Barnes, Jonathan, ed. *Early Greek Philosophy.* Harmondsworth: Penguin, 1987.

Baumgarten, Alexander Gottlieb. *Texte zur Grundlegung der Ästhetik.* Ed. and trans. Hans Rudolf Schweizer. Hamburg: Felix Meiner, 1983.

Bernheim, Hippolyte. *Hypnotisme, suggestion, psychothérapie: Études nouvelles.* Paris: Alcan, 1891.

298 Works cited

New Studies in Hypnotism. Trans. R. Sandor. New York: International Universities Press, 1980.

Brentano, Clemens. *Godwi oder das steinerne Bild der Mutter: Ein verwilderter Roman.* Ed. Ernst Behler. Stuttgart: Reclam, 1995.

Psychologie vom empirischen Standpunkt. Hamburg: Meiner, 1874.

Psychologie vom empirischen Standpuncte. 2 vols. in 1. Leipzig: Duncker & Humblot, 1874. [*Descriptive Psychology.* Trans. Benito Müller. London: Routledge, 1995].

Psychologie vom empirischen Standpunkt. Ed. Oskar Kraus. Leipzig: Meiner, 1924. [*Psychology from an Empirical Standpoint.* Ed. Oskar Kraus. Trans. Antos C. Rancurello, Dailey Burnham Terrell, and Linda L. McAlister. London: Routledge and Kegan Paul, 1973].

Büchner, Georg. *Werke und Briefe.* Ed. Franz Josef Görtz, with an afterword by Friedrich Dürrenmatt. Zürich: Diogenes Verlag, 1988.

Carus, Carl Gustav. *Lehrbuch der Gynäkologie.* Leipzig: Gerhard Fleischer, 1820.

Lehrbuch der Zootomie. Leipzig: Fleischer, 1818.

Mnemosyne: Blätter aus Gedenk- und Tagebüchern. Pforzheim: Flammer und Hoffmann, 1848.

Neun Briefe über Landschaftsmalerei. In *Romantische Kunstlehre: Poesie und Poetik des Blicks in der deutschen Romantik.* Ed. Friedmar Apel. Bibliothek Deutscher Klassiker, vol. 79. Frankfurt am Main: Deutscher Klassiker Verlag 1992, 203–79.

Nine Letters on Landscape Painting Written in the Years 1815–1824, with a Letter from Goethe by Way of Introduction. Trans. David Britt. Oxford: Oxford University Press, 2002.

Psyche: Zur Entwicklungsgeschichte der Seele. Pforzheim: Flammer und Hoffmann, 1846.

Vergleichende Psychologie oder Geschichte der Seele in der Reihenfolge der Tierwelt. Vienna, 1866.

Versuch einer Darstellung des Nervensystems und insbesondre des Gehirns nach ihrer Bedeutung, Entwickelung und Vollendung im thierischen Organismus. Leipzig: Breitkopf & Härtel, 1814.

Vorlesungen über Psychologie, gehalten im Winter 1829–30 zu Dresden. Leipzig: Verlag von Gerhard Fleisher, 1831.

Cassirer, Ernst. *The Myth of the State.* Oxford: Oxford University Press, 1946.

Czermak, Johann Nepomuk. "Über Schopenhauers Theorie der Farben." In *Sitzungsberichte der mathematisch-naturwissenschaftlichen Classe der Kaiserlichen Akademie der Wissenschaften (Wien).* Vol. LXII. Section 2. II. Folders 6–10. Vienna, 1870.

De Quincey, Thomas. *Confessions of an English Opium Eater.* Ed. with an introduction by Alethea Hayter. London: Penguin, 1986.

Derrida, Jacques. *Spurs: Nietzsche's Styles. Éperons. Les Styles de Nietzsche.* Chicago: University of Chicago Press, 1979.

Descartes, René. *A Discourse on Method; Meditations on the First Philosophy; Principles of Philosophy.* Trans. John Veitch. London: Dent; New York: Dutton, 1969.

Meditations on First Philosophy. Ed. and trans. John Cottingham. Cambridge: Cambridge University Press, 1996.

Œuvres. 12 vols. Ed. Charles Adam and Paul Tannery. Paris: Cerf, 1897–1913.
Diels, Hermann, and Walther Kranz, eds. *Die Fragmente der Vorsokratiker: Griechisch und Deutsch*. Hildesheim: Weidmann, 1951.
Dilthey, Wilhelm. *Das Erlebnis und die Dichtung*. 4th edn. Stuttgart: Teubner, 1957.
  Einleitung in die Geisteswissenschaften. In *Gesammelte Schriften*. 26 vols. Ed. Karlfried Gründer *et al*. Vol. I. Göttingen: Vandenhoek und Ruprecht, 1959–2005.
Du Bois-Reymond, Emil. "Goethe und kein Ende." *Reden von Emil Du Bois-Reymond in zwei Bänden*. Ed. Estelle Du Bois-Reymond. 2nd edn. Leipzig: Veit, 1912, 157–83.
Dühring, Eugen. *Kritische Geschichte der Philosophie von ihren Anfängen bis zur Gegenwart*. 3rd edn. Leipzig: Fues, 1878.
Ebbinghaus, Hermann. *Über das Gedächtnis: Untersuchungen zur experimentellen Psychologie*. Darmstadt: Wissenschaftliche Buchgesellschaft, 1992.
  Über die Hartmannsche Philosophie des Unbewussten. Düsseldorf, 1873.
Ebner-Eschenbach, Marie von. *Erzählungen*. Ed. Edgar Groß. Munich: Nymphenburger Verlagsanstalt, 1961.
Eckermann, Johann Peter. *Gespräche mit Goethe in den letzten Jahren seines Lebens*. In Johann Wolfgang von Goethe, *Sämtliche Werke: Briefe, Tagebücher und Gespräche*. 2 parts, 40 vols. Ed. Hendrik Birus *et al*. Part 2, vol. XII. Frankfurt am Main: Deutscher Klassiker Verlag, 1985–2003.
Eichendorff, Joseph von. *Werke in sechs Bänden*. Ed. Wolfgang Frühwald *et al*. Frankfurt am Main: Deutscher Klassiker Verlag, 1993.
Eliot, Thomas Stearns. "Introduction to Goethe." In *The Nation and Athenaeum* 44 (1929): 527.
Fechner, Gustav Theodor. *Die Tagesansicht gegenüber der Nachtansicht*. Leipzig: Breitkopf & Härtel, 1879. Reprint: Eschborn: Klotz, 1994.
  Einige Ideen zur Schöpfungs- und Entwickelungsgeschichte der Organismen. Leipzig: Breitkopf & Härtel, 1873. Reprint: Tübingen: edition diskord, 1985.
  Elemente der Psychophysik. 2 vols. Leipzig: Breitkopf & Härtel, 1860. Reprint editions: Leipzig: Breitkopf & Härtel, 1889; Amsterdam: Bonset, 1964; Bristol: Thoemmes, 1998. [*Elements of Psychophysics*. Vol. 1. Trans. Helmut E. Adler. Ed. Davis H. Howes and Edwin G. Boring. Introd. Edwin G. Boring. New York: Holt, Rinehart & Winston, 1966].
  In Sachen der Psychophysik. Leipzig: Breitkopf & Härtel, 1877. Reprint: Amsterdam: Bonset, 1968.
  "Kurze Darlegung eines Princips mathematischer Psychologie." In *Zend-Avesta oder über die Dinge des Himmels und des Jenseits: Vom Standpunkt der Naturbetrachtung*. 3 vols. Leipzig: Leopold Voß, 1851. Reprint edition, vol. II: Eschborn: Klotz 1998. [Part translated as "Outline of a New Principle of Mathematical Psychology." Trans. Eckart Scheerer, *Psychological Research* 49 (1987): 203–7].
  Revision der Hauptpuncte der Psychophysik. Leipzig: Breitkopf & Härtel, 1882.

Ueber das höchste Gut. Leipzig: Breitkopf & Härtel, 1846. Reprint: Frankfurt am Main: Diesterweg, 1925.
Ueber die physikalische und philosophische Atomenlehre. Leipzig: Hermann Mendelssohn, 1855.
"Ueber die psychischen Massprincipien und das Weber'sche Gesetz. Discussion mit Elsas und Köhler." In *Philosophische Studien* 4 (1887): 161–230. ["My Own Viewpoint on Mental Measurement." Trans. Eckart Scheerer, *Psychological Research* 49 (1987): 213–19].
Vorschule der Aesthetik. 2 vols. Leipzig: Breitkopf & Härtel, 1876. Reprint: Hildesheim: Olms 1978. [Part of the *Vorschule der Aesthetik* (vol. I, chapter 14), entitled "Verschiedene Versuche, eine Grundform der Schönheit aufzustellen: Experimentale Ästhetik: Goldner Schnitt und Quadrat," is translated by Monika Niemann, Julia Quehl, and Holger Höge as "Various Attempts to Establish a Basic Form of Beauty: Experimental Aesthetics, Golden Section, and Square." In *Empirical Studies of the Arts* 15, no. 2 (1997): 115–30].
Wissenschaftliche Briefe von Gustav Theodor Fechner und W. Preyer: Nebst einem Briefwechsel zwischen K. von Vierordt und Fechner und 9 Beilagen. Ed. William Thierry Preyer. Hamburg and Leipzig: Leopold Voß, 1860.
Zend-Avesta oder über die Dinge des Himmels und des Jenseits: Vom Standpunkt der Naturbetrachtung. 3 vols. Leipzig: Leopold Voß, 1851.
"Zur Kritik der Grundlagen von Herbarts *Metaphysik*." In *Zeitschrift für Philosophie und philosophische Kritik* 25 (1853): 70–102.
Feuerbach, Ludwig. *Gesammelte Werke*. Ed. Werner Schuffenhauer. 22 vols. Berlin: Akademie Verlag, 1967.
Sämtliche Werke. 10 vols. Ed. Wilhelm Bodin and Friedrich Jodl. Stuttgart: Frommann, 1960.
The Essence of Christianity. Trans. Marian Evans. London: John Chapman, 1854.
Fichte, Johann Gottlieb. *Introductions to the "Wissenschaftslehre" and Other Writings (1797–1800)*. Ed. and trans. Daniel Breazeale. Indianapolis, IN, and Cambridge: Hackett, 1994.
Foucault, Michel. *The Order of Things: An Archaeology of the Human Sciences*. London: Routledge, 2002.
Freud, Sigmund. *Briefe an Wilhelm Fließ 1887–1904*. Ed. Jeffrey Moussaieff Masson. Frankfurt am Main: S. Fischer, 1986. [*The Complete Letters of Sigmund Freud to Wilhelm Fliess 1887–1904*. Ed. and trans. Jeffrey Moussaieff Masson. Cambridge, MA and London: The Belknap Press of Harvard University Press, 1985.
Gesammelte Werke in achtzehn Bänden mit einem Nachtragsband. 19 vols. Ed. Anna Freud *et al.* Frankfurt am Main: Fischer, 1952–87.
Gesammelte Werke in achtzehn Bänden mit einem Nachtragsband, 19 vols. Ed. Anna Freud *et al.* Frankfurt am Main: S. Fischer, 1986–99.
Jugendbriefe an Eduard Silberstein 1871–1881. Ed. Walter Boehlich. Frankfurt am Main: S. Fischer, 1989. [*The Letters of Sigmund Freud to Eduard Silberstein 1871–1881*. Ed. Walter Boehlich. Trans. Arnold J. Pomerans. Cambridge, MA: The Belknap Press of Harvard University Press, 1990].

Sigmund Freud and Oskar Pfister. Briefe 1909–1939. Ed. Ernst L. Freud and Heinrich Meng. Frankfurt am Main: S. Fischer, 1963.
The Origins of Psycho-Analysis: Letters to Wilhelm Fliess, Drafts and Notes, 1887–1902. Ed. Marie Bonaparte, Anna Freud, and Ernst Kris. Trans. Eric Mosbacher and James Strachey. London: Imago Publishing Company, 1954.
The Standard Edition of the Complete Psychological Works of Sigmund Freud. 24 vols. Ed. James Strachey and Anna Freud. London: Hogarth Press, 1953–74.
Freud, Sigmund, and G. Groddeck. *Briefe über das Es.* Frankfurt an Main: Fischer, 1988.
Freud, Sigmund, and C. G. Jung. *Briefwechsel.* Ed. William McGuire and Wolfgang Sauerländer. Frankfurt am Main: Fischer, 1974. [*The Freud/Jung Letters.* Ed. William McGuire. Trans. Ralph Manheim and R.F.C. Hull. Cambridge, MA: Harvard University Press, 1988].
Fullenwider, Henry F. "The Goethean Fragment 'Die Natur' in English Translation." In *Comparative Literature Studies* 23 (1986), 170–7.
Gadamer, Hans-Georg. *Truth and Method.* 2nd revised English edn. Trans. Joel Weinsheimer and Donald G. Marshall. London: Continuum, 2004.
Goethe, Johann Wolfgang von. *Conversations of German Refugees/Wilhelm Meister's Journeyman Years or The Renunciants.* Ed. Jane K. Brown. Trans. J. van Heurck, K. Winston. New York: Suhrkamp Publishers, 1989.
Die Schriften zur Naturwissenschaft (Leopoldina Ausgabe). 21 vols. Ed. Dorothea Kuhn *et al.* Weimar: Hermann Böhlhaus Nachfolger, 1947.
Faust: The First Part of the Tragedy. Trans. John Williams. Ware: Wordsworth, 1999.
Faust: Part One. Trans. David Luke. Oxford and New York: Oxford University Press, 1987.
Goethe's Collected Works. 12 vols. Ed. Victor Lange, Eric A. Blackall, Cyrus Hamlin, *et al.* New York: Suhrkamp, 1983–9.
Goethes Gespräche. 9 vols. Ed. Woldemar Freiherr von Biedermann. Leipzig: Biedermann, 1889–91.
Goethes Gespräche: Gesamtausgabe. 5 vols. Ed. Flodoard von Biedermann. Leipzig: Biedermann, 1909–11.
Sämtliche Werke: Briefe, Tagebücher und Gespräche. 2 parts, 40 vols. Ed. Hendrik Birus *et al.* Frankfurt am Main: Deutscher Klassiker Verlag, 1985–2003.
Sämtliche Werke nach Epochen seines Schaffens (Münchner Ausgabe). Ed. Karl Richter, Herbert G. Göpfert, Norbert Miller, and Gerhard Sauder. 21 vols. in 31. Munich: Carl Hanser, 1985–98.
Selected Poems. Trans. John Whaley. London: Dent, 1998.
Werke: Hamburger Ausgabe. 14 vols. Ed. Erich Trunz. Hamburg: Wegener, 1948–60.
Werke: Weimarer Ausgabe. Ed. Johann Ludwig Gustav von Loeper, Erich Schmidt, and Paul Raabe. 4 parts, 133 vols. in 143. Weimar: Böhlau, 1887–1919.

Groddeck, Georg. *Das Buch vom Es: Psychoanalytische Briefe an eine Freundin.* Leipzig: Internationaler Psychoanalytischer Verlag, 1923.
Grün, Karl. *Bausteine.* Darmstadt: Leske, 1844.
Über Göthe vom menschlichen Standpunkte. Darmstadt: Leske, 1846.
ed. *Ludwig Feuerbach in seinem Briefwechsel und Nachlass sowie in seiner philosophischen Charakterentwicklung dargestellt.* 2 vols. Leipzig and Heidelberg: Winter, 1874.
Habermas, Jürgen. *Theorie des kommunikativen Handelns.* 2 vols. Frankfurt am Main: Suhrkamp, 1987. [*The Theory of Communicative Action.* 2 vols. Trans. Thomas McCarthy. London: Heinemann, 1984; Cambridge: Polity Press, 1987].
Hall, G. Stanley. *Founders of Modern Psychology.* New York: D. Appleton and Co., 1924.
Haller, Albrecht von. *Elementa physiologiae corporis humani.* 8 vols. Lausanne: Marci-Michael Bousquet & Sociorum, 1757–66.
Hamilton, William. *Lectures on Metaphysics and Logic.* 2 vols. Edinburgh: Blackwood, 1859.
Hartmann, Eduard von. *Die moderne Psychologie: Eine kritische Geschichte der Deutschen Psychologie in der zweiten Haelfte des neunzehnten Jahrhunderts.* Leipzig: Haacke, 1901.
Die Religion des Geistes. Berlin: Carl Duncker, 1882. [*The Religion of the Future.* Trans. Ernest Dare. London: W. Stewart & Co., 1886].
Kritische Grundlegung des transcendentalen Realismus. Berlin: Carl Duncker, 1875.
Lotzes Philosophie. Leipzig: Wilhelm Friedrich, 1888.
Neukantianismus, Schopenhauerianismus und Hegelianismus in ihrer Stellung zu den philosophischen Aufgaben der Gegenwart. Berlin: Carl Duncker, 1877.
Philosophie des Unbewussten. 10th edn. 3 vols. Leipzig: Wilhelm Friedrich, 1890.
Philosophie des Unbewußten: Speculative Resultate nach inductiv-naturwissenschaftlicher Methode. 12th edn. 3 vols. Leipzig: Kröner, 1923.
Philosophie des Unbewussten: Versuch einer Weltanschauung. Berlin: Carl Duncker, 1869.
Philosophy of the Unconscious. 3 vols. Shrewsbury: Living Time Press, 2001–2.
Philosophy of the Unconscious. 3 vols. Trans. William Chatterton Coupland. London: Kegan Paul, 1884.
Philosophy of the Unconscious. London: Kegan Paul, 1931
Schellings philosophisches System. Leipzig: H. Haacke, 1897.
Schellings positive Philosophie als Einheit von Hegel und Schopenhauer. Berlin: Otto Loewenstein, 1869.
The Sexes Compared and Other Essays. Trans. A. Kenner. London: Swan Sonnenschein, 1895.
Wahrheit und Irrtum im Darwinismus: Eine Kritische Darstellung der organischen Entwicklungstheorie. Berlin: Carl Duncker, 1875. [Parts I–II translated as "The True and the False in Darwinism: A Critical Representation of the Theory of Organic Development." In *Journal of Speculative Philosophy* 11 (1877–8): 244–51 and 392–9].
Haym, Rudolf. "Die Hartmann'sche Philosophie des Unbewußten." In *Preußische Jahrbücher* 31: 1–3 (1873): 41–80, 109–139, 257–311.

Theory of the Light Sense. Trans. Leo M. Hurvich and Dorothea Jameson. Cambridge, MA: Harvard University Press, 1964].

Hildebrandt, Friedrich Wilhelm. *Der Traum und seine Verwerthung für's Leben.* Leipzig, 1875.

Höffding, Harald. *Psychologie in Umrissen auf Grundlage der Erfahrung.* 2nd edn. Trans. F. Bendixen. Leipzig: Reisland, 1893. [*Outlines of Psychology.* Trans. Mary E. Lowndes. London: Macmillan 1893].

Hoffmann, Ernst Theodor Amadeus. *Die Elexiere des Teufels: Lebens-Ansichten des Katers Murr: Zwei Romane.* 2nd edn. Ed. Carl Georg von Maassen and Georg Ellinger with an afterword by Walter Müller-Seidel. Munich: Artemis & Winkler, 1978.

Horkheimer, Max. "Das Schlimme erwarten und doch das Gute tun (Gespräch mit Gerhard Rein)." In *Gesammelte Schriften.* Vol. VII. Frankfurt am Main: Fischer, 1976, 442–65.

Horkheimer, Max and Theodor Adorno. *Dialektik der Aufklärung: Philosophische Fragmente.* Frankfurt am Main: Fischer Verlag, 1969. [*Dialectic of Enlightenment: Philosophical Fragments.* Trans. John Cumming. New York: Continuum, 1996].

Huch, Ricarda. *Romantik. Blütezeit. Ausbreitung. Verfall.* Tübingen: Rainer Wunderlich Verlag, 1951.

Hume, David. *A Treatise of Human Nature.* Ed. David Fate Norton and Mary J. Norton. Oxford: Oxford University Press, 2000.

James, William. *Human Immortality: Two Supposed Objections to the Doctrine.* Boston and New York: Houghton, Mifflin & Co., 1898.

The Principles of Psychology. 2 vols. New York: Holt, 1890.

Principles of Psychology. 2 vols. London: Macmillan, 1918.

Principles of Psychology. 2 vols. Cambridge, MA: Harvard University Press, 1981.

The Works of Williams James. Vol. IX: *Essays in Religion and Morality.* Cambridge, MA: Harvard University Press, 1982.

Jaspers, Karl. "Zu Nietzsches Bedeutung in der Geschichte der Philosophie." *Aneignung und Polemik: Gesammelte Reden und Aufsätze.* Ed. H. Saner. Munich: Piper, 1968, 389–401.

Jerusalem, Wilhelm. *Die Urteilsfunktion: Eine psychologische und erkenntniskritische Untersuchung.* Vienna: Braumüller, 1895.

Jung, Carl Gustav. *Collected Works.* 20 vols. Ed. Sir Herbert Read, Michael Fordham, Gerhard Adler, and William McGuire. London: Routledge and Kegan Paul, 1953–83.

Ein großer Psychologe im Gespräch. Interviews. Reden. Begegnungen. Ed. Robert Hinshaw. Freiburg im Breisgau: Herder, 1994.

Gesammelte Werke. 20 vols. Ed. Lilly Jung-Merker, Elisabeth Ruf, *et al.* Zürich, Stuttgart, Olten, and Freiburg im Breisgau: Walter Verlag, 1960–83.

The Collected Works of C. G. Jung. Trans. R. F. C. Hull. Ed. H. Read, M. Fordham, and G. Adler. 20 vols. Princeton, NJ: Princeton University Press, 1953–79.

Kant, Immanuel. *Anthropology from a Pragmatic Point of View.* Trans. Mary J. Gregor. The Hague: Martinus Nijhoff, 1974.

Anthropology from a Pragmatic Point of View. Trans. Robert B. Louden. Cambridge: Cambridge University Press, 2006.
Critique of the Power of Judgment. Ed. and trans. Paul Guyer and Eric Matthews. *The Cambridge Edition of the Works of Immanuel Kant.* Cambridge: Cambridge University Press, 2000.
Critique of Pure Reason. Ed. and trans. Paul Guyer and Allen W. Wood. *The Cambridge Edition of the Works of Immanuel Kant.* Cambridge: Cambridge University Press, 1998.
Gesammelte Schriften (Prussian Academy Edition). 29 vols. Berlin: Reimer; Walter de Gruyter, 1902–80.
Kritik der reinen Vernunft. Frankfurt am Main: Suhrkamp, 1968.
Lectures on Metaphysics. Ed. and trans. Karl Ameriks and Steve Naragon. *The Cambridge Edition of the Works of Immanuel Kant.* Cambridge: Cambridge University Press, 1997.
Practical Philosophy. Ed. Mary J. Gregor. *The Cambridge Edition of the Works of Immanuel Kant.* Cambridge: Cambridge University Press, 1997.
Theoretical Philosophy, 1755–1770. Trans. David Walford and Ralf Meerbore. *The Cambridge Edition of the Works of Immanuel Kant.* Cambridge: Cambridge University Press, 1992.
Werke in sechs Bänden. 6 vols. Ed. Wilhelm Weischedel. Darmstadt: Wissenschaftliche Buchgesellschaft, 1960.
Kerner, Justinus. *Die Seherin von Prevorst.* 8th edn. Stuttgart: Steinkopf Verlag. 1999.
Klages, Ludwig. *Goethe als Seelenforscher.* 3rd edn. Zürich: Hirzel, 1949.
Prinzipien der Charakterologie. Leipzig: Barth, 1910.
Kleist, Heinrich von. "Aufsatz, den sichern Weg des Glücks zu finden, und ungestört, auch unter den größten Drangsalen des Lebens, ihn zu genießen!" In *Werke und Briefe.* Ed. Peter Goldammer. Vol. III. Berlin and Weimar: Aufbau Verlag, 1978, 433–49.
The Marquise of O – and Other Stories. Trans. and with an introduction by David Luke and Nigel Reeves. Harmondsworth: Penguin, 1987.
Knebel, Karl Ludwig von. *Literarischer Nachlaß und Briefwechsel.* 3 vols. Ed. K. A. Varnhagen von Ense and Theodor Mundt. Leipzig: Reichenbach, 1836.
Külpe, Oswald. *Philosophie der Gegenwart in Deutschland.* Leipzig: Teubner, 1902.
Kurt, N. *Wahrheit und Dichtung in den Hauptlehren Eduard von Hartmanns.* Leipzig: Friedrich Fleischer, 1894.
Lacan, Jacques. *The Seminar.* Book 2: *The Ego in Freud's Theory and in the Technique of Psychoanalysis 1954–1955.* Ed. Jacques-Alain Miller. Trans. Sylvana Tomaselli. New York and London: Norton, 1991.
The Seminar. Book 3. *The Psychoses 1955–1956.* Ed. Jacques-Alain Miller. Trans. Russell Grigg. London: Routledge, 1993.
Lange, Albert Friedrich. *Die Grundlegung der mathematischen Psychologie. Ein Versuch zur Nachweisung des fundamentalen Fehlers bei Herbart und Drobisch.* Duisburg: Falk & Volmer, 1865.
Geschichte des Materialismus: Und Kritik Seiner Bedeutung in der Gegenwart. Leipzig: Baedeker, 1896. [*The History of Materialism, and Criticism of its*

Present Importance. 3rd edn. Trans. Ernest Chester Thomas. London: Routledge and Kegan Paul, 1950.]
Geschichte des Materialismus und Kritik seiner Bedeutung in der Gegenwart. 2 vols. 2nd rev. and expanded edn. Iserlohn: Baedeker, 1873–5. Reprint in 2 vols. Ed. Alfred Schmidt. Frankfurt am Main: Suhrkamp, 1974.

Lawrence, David Herbert. *Fantasia of the Unconscious and Psychoanalysis and the Unconscious.* Harmondsworth: Penguin, 1983.

Leibniz, Gottfried Wilhelm. *Monadology.* Trans. Nicholas Rescher. Pittsburgh, PA: University of Pittsburgh Press, 1991.
Neue Abhandlungen über den menschlichen Verstand. Stuttgart: Reclam, 1993.
New Essays on Human Understanding. Ed. and trans. Peter Remnant and Jonathan Bennett. Cambridge: Cambridge University Press, 1996.
Opera Philosophica. Ed. Johann Eduard Erdmann. Aalen: Scientia, 1959.
Philosophical Essays. Ed. and trans. R. Ariew and D. Garber. Indianapolis, IN: Hackett, 1989.
Philosophical Writings. Trans. Mary Morris. London: Dent; New York: Dutton, 1956.
Theodicy: Essays on the Goodness of God, the Freedom of Man and the Origin of Evil. Ed. Austin Farrer. Trans. E. M. Huggard. London: Routledge and Kegan Paul, 1951.

Lessing, Gotthold Ephraim. *Hamburgische Dramaturgie.* Berlin: Deutscher Verlag der Wissenschaften, 1952.

Lindner, Gustav Adolf. *Lehrbuch der empirischen Psychologie als inductive Wissenschaft.* 3rd edn. Vienna: Carl Gerold's Sohn, 1873.

Locke, John. *An Essay Concerning Human Understanding.* London: Penguin, 1997.

Lukács, Georg. *Die Zerstörung der Vernunft: Der Weg des Irrationalismus von Schelling zu Hitler.* Berlin: Aufbau, 1955.

Mach, Ernst. "Über die Wirkung der räumlichen Vertheilung des Lichtreizes auf die Netzhaut." In *Sitzungsberichte der Kaiserlichen Akademie der Wissenschaften (Wien), math.-naturw. Klasse 2, Abtheilung* 52 (1865): 303–22.

Mann, Thomas. "Freud and the Future." In *Essays of Three Decades.* Trans. H. T. Lowe-Porter. London: Secker and Warburg, 1947, 411–28.
Freud und die Psychoanalyse: Reden, Briefe, Notizen, Betrachtungen. Frankfurt am Main: Fischer, 1991.

Maury, Alfred. *Le Sommeil et les rêves.* Paris: Didier, 1861.

Mendelssohn, Moses. *Philosophical Writings.* Trans. Daniel O. Dahlstrom. Cambridge: Cambridge University Press, 1997.

Mill, John Stuart. *The Collected Works of John Stuart Mill.* Ed. F. E. L. Priestley and J. M. Robson. 33 vols. Toronto: University of Toronto Press; London: Routledge and Kegan Paul, 1963–91.

Mörike, Eduard. *Mozart's Journey to Prague and a Selection of Poems.* Trans. David Luke. London: Libris and Penguin, 2003.
Sämtliche Werke. 2 vols. 6th edn. Ed. Helmut Koopmann. Darmstadt: Wissenschaftliche Buchgesellschaft, 1997.

Nietzsche, Friedrich. *Beyond Good and Evil: Prelude to a Philosophy of the Future.* Trans. Walter Kaufmann. New York: Vintage, 1966.

Briefwechsel: Kritische Gesamtausgabe. Ed. Giorgio Colli, Mazzino Montinari, *et al.* 3 parts. 24 vols. Berlin and New York: Walter de Gruyter, 1975–2004.
Daybreak. Trans. R. J. Hollingdale. Cambridge: Cambridge University Press, 1982.
Ecce Homo. Trans. R. J. Hollingdale. Harmondsworth: Penguin, 1979.
The Gay Science. Trans. Walter Kaufmann. New York: Random House, 1974.
Sämtliche Briefe. Kritische Studienausgabe. 8 vols. Ed. Giorgio Colli and Mazzino Montinari. Berlin and Munich: Walter de Gruyter and Deutscher Taschenbuch Verlag, 1986.
Sämtliche Werke: Kritische Studienausgabe. 15 vols. Ed. Giorgio Colli and Mazzino Montinari. Berlin: Walter de Gruyter; Munich: Deutscher Taschenbuch Verlag, 1980.
Philosophy and Truth: Selections from Nietzsche's Notebooks of the Early 1870s. Ed. and trans. Daniel Breazeale. Atlantic Highlands, NJ: Humanities Press, 1979.
The Birth of Tragedy and Other Writings. Ed. Raymond Geuss and Roger Speirs. Trans. R. Speirs. Cambridge: Cambridge University Press, 1999.
Thus Spoke Zarathustra. Trans. R. J. Hollingdale. Harmondsworth: Penguin, 1961.
Twilight of the Idols. In *The Portable Nietzsche.* Ed. and trans. Walter Kaufmann. New York: Viking Press, 1976.
Unpublished Writings From the Period of Unfashionable Observations. Trans. R. T. Gray. Stanford, CA: Stanford University Press, 1995.
Werke in drei Bänden. 3 vols. Ed. Karl Schlechta. Munich: Hanser, 1954.
Werke. Historisch-kritische Gesamtausgabe. Ed. H. J. Mette, Carl Koch, and Karl Schlechta. 5 vols. Munich: C. H. Beck, 1933–40.
Werke: Kritische Gesamtausgabe. 9 parts, 40 vols. Ed. Giorgio Colli, Mazzino Montinari, Wolfgang Müller-Lauter, and Karl Pestalozzi. Berlin and New York: Walter de Gruyter, 1967.
Novalis (Friedrich von Hardenberg). *Das philosophisch-theoretische Werk.* Munich and Vienna: Hanser, 1978.
Werke, Tagebücher und Briefe. Ed. Hans-Joachim Mähl and Richard Samuel. Darmstadt: Wissenschaftliche Buchgesellschaft, 1999.
Nunberg, Herman, and Ernst Federn, eds. *Protokolle der Wiener Psychoanalytischen Vereinigung.* 4 vols. Frankfurt am Main: S. Fischer, 1976–81.
Paul, Jean. *Vorschule der Ästhetik.* Ed. Wolfhart Henckmann. 4th edn. Hamburg: Felix Meiner Verlag, 1980.
Platner, Ernst. *Philosophische Aphorismen nebst einigen Anleitungen zur philosophischen Geschichte.* Leipzig: Schwickertscher Verlag, 1776.
Popper, Karl. *Conjectures and Refutations: The Growth of Scientific Knowledge.* London: Routledge and Kegan Paul, 1963.
The Logic of Scientific Discovery. London: Routledge, 2002.
Reich, Wilhelm. *Listen, Little Man.* London: Souvenir Press, 1972.
Reil, Johann Christian. *Rhapsodieen über die Anwendung der psychischen Curmethode auf Geisteszerruettungen.* Halle: Curtsche Buchhandlung, 1803.

Renan, Ernst. *L'Avenir de la science: Pensées de 1848*. Paris: Calmann-Lévy, 1923.
Rilke, Rainer Maria. *Die Gedichte*. Frankfurt am Main: Insel, 1986.
Schelling, Friedrich Wilhelm Joseph. *On the History of Modern Philosophy*. Trans. Andrew Bowie. Cambridge: Cambridge University Press, 1994.
— *Philosophie der Kunst*. Darmstadt: Wissenschaftliche Buchgesellschaft, 1976.
— *Philosophie der Offenbarung*. Ed. Manfred Frank. Frankfurt am Main: Suhrkamp, 1977.
— *Sämmtliche Werke*. Ed. K. F. A. Schelling. 2 parts, 14 vols. Stuttgart: Cotta, 1856–61.
Scherner, Karl Albrecht. *Das Leben des Traums*. Berlin: Heinrich Schindler, 1861.
Schiller, Friedrich. *Letters on the Aesthetic Education of Humanity*. Ed. Elizabeth M. Wilkinson and L. A. Willoughby. Oxford: Clarendon Press, 1982.
— *Medicine, Psychology and Literature*. Ed. Kenneth Dewhurst and Nigel Reeves. Oxford: Sandford Publications, 1978.
— *On the Naïve and Sentimental in Literature*. Trans. Helen Watanabe-O'Kelly. Manchester: Carcanet New Press, 1981.
— *Schillers Werke. Nationalausgabe*. Ed. Julius Petersen and Gerhard Fricke. 50 vols. Weimar: Hermann Böhlhaus Nachfolger, 1943.
Schiller, Friedrich and Johann Wolfgang von Goethe. *Der Briefwechsel zwischen Schiller und Goethe in den Jahren 1794 bis 1805*, ed. Manfred Beetz. 2 vols. Munich: Goldmann, 2005.
— *The Correspondence between Schiller and Goethe, from 1794 to 1805*. Trans. L. Dora Schmitz. 2 vols. London: George Bell and Sons, 1877.
Schleiermacher, Friedrich. *Dialektik (1822): Aus dem handschriftlichen Nachlaß*. Ed. L. Jonas, *Sämtliche Werke*. Part 3, vol. IV.2 (Berlin, 1839).
Schmidt, Oscar. *Die naturwissenschaftlichen Grundlagen der Philosophie des Unbewussten*. Leipzig: F. A. Brockhaus, 1877.
Schopenhauer, Arthur. *Manuscript Remains*. Ed. Arthur Hübscher. Trans. E. F. J. Payne. Oxford: Berg, 1988.
— *Prize Essay on the Freedom of the Will*. Ed. Günter Zöller. Trans. E.F.J. Payne. Cambridge: Cambridge University Press, 1999.
— *Sämtliche Werke*, ed. Arthur Hübscher. Mannheim: F. A. Brockhaus, 1988.
— *The World as Will and Representation*. Trans. E. F. J. Payne. New York: Dover, 1969.
— *Werke in zehn Bänden*. 10 vols. Zürich: Diogenes, 1977–81.
Schubert, Gotthilf Heinrich von. *Ansichten von der Nachtseite der Naturwissenschaft*. Darmstadt: Wissenschaftliche Buchgesellschaft, 1967.
— *Die Symbolik des Traumes*. Heidelberg: Lambert Schneider Verlag, 1968.
Schumann, Robert. *Schriften über Musik und Musiker*. Ed. Josef Häusler. Stuttgart: Reclam Verlag, 1982.
Simmel, Georg. *Goethe*. Leipzig: Klinkhardt und Biermann, 1916.
Spencer, Herbert. *Principles of Psychology*. London: Longman, Brown, Green and Longmans, 1855.
Spinoza, Benedict de. *Ethics*. Ed. and trans. Edwin Curley. Harmondsworth: Penguin, 1996.

Stahl, Georg Ernst. *Über den mannigfaltigen Einfluss von Gemütsbewegungen auf den menschlichen Körper.* Leipzig: Barth, 1961.
Über den Unterschied zwischen Organismus und Mechanismus. Halle, 1714.
Über die Bedeutung des synergischen Prinzips für die Heilkunde. Halle, 1695.
Überlegungen zum ärztlichen Hausbesuch. Ed. Bernward Josef Gottlieb. Leipzig: Barth, 1961.
Strümpell, Ludwig. *Die Natur und Entstehung der Träume.* Leipzig: Veit, 1874.
Sulzer, Johann Georg. *Kurzer Begriff aller Wißenschaften und andern Theile der Gelehrsamkeit, worin jeder nach seinem Inhalt, Nuzen und Vollkommenheit kürzlich beschrieben wird.* 2nd edn. 1759.
Vaihinger, Hans. *Hartmann, Dühring und Lange: Zur Geschichte der deutschen Philosophie im XIX. Jahrhundert: Ein kritischer Essay.* Iserlohn: J. Baedeker, 1876.
Volkelt, Johannes. *Das Unbewußte und der Pessimismus.* Berlin: Frommann, 1873.
Der Symbolbegriff in der neuesten Ästhetik. Jena: Dufft, 1876.
Die Traumphantasie. Stuttgart: Meyer and Zeller, 1875. Reprinted in *Traumarbeit vor Freud. Quellentexte zur Traumpsychologie im späten 19. Jahrhundert.* Ed. Stefan Goldmann. Gießen: Psychosozial Verlag, 2005, 99–240.
"Mein philosophischer Entwicklungsgang." In *Die Deutsche Philosophie der Gegenwart in Selbstdarstellungen.* Ed. R. Schmidt. Leipzig: Meiner, 1921, 201–28.
Wagner, Richard. *Dichtungen und Schriften: Jubiläumsausgabe in zehn Bänden.* 10 Vols. Ed. Dieter Borchmeyer. Frankfurt am Main: Insel Verlag, 1983.
Windelband, Wilhelm. *Lehrbuch der Geschichte der Philosophie.* 3rd edn. Tübingen and Leipzig: J. C. B. Mohr, 1903. [*A History of Philosophy.* Trans. James H. Tufts. New York: Harper and Row, 1958].
Wolff, Christian. *Gesammelte Werke.* Ed. Jean École *et al.* Hildesheim and New York: Olms, 1962.
Psychologia empirica. Frankfurt and Leipzig: Renger, 1732.
Wundt, Wilhelm. "Die Psychologie im Beginn des zwanzigsten Jahrhunderts." In *Die Philosophie im Beginn des zwanzigsten Jahrhunderts: Festschrift für Kuno Fischer.* Ed. Wilhelm Windelband. Heidelberg, 1904.
Vorlesungen ueber die Menschen- und Thierseele. 2nd edn. Hamburg: Verlag von Leopold Voss, 1892.
Zweig, Stefan. *Das Geheimnis des künstlerischen Schaffens: Essay.* Ed. Knut Beck. Frankfurt am Main: S. Fischer, 1984.
Gesammelte Werke in Einzelbänden. Ed. Knut Beck. Frankfurt am Main: S. Fischer, 1984.

SECONDARY SOURCES

Abeln, Reinhard. *Unbewußtes und Unterbewußtes bei C. G. Carus und Aristoteles.* Meisenheim am Glan: Anton Hain, 1970.
Adler, Hans. "Fundus Animae – der Grund der Seele: Zur Gnoseologie des Dunkeln in der Aufklärung." In *Deutsche Vierteljahrsschrift für Literaturwissenschaft und Geistesgeschichte* 62 (1998), 197–220.

Adler, Jeremy. "Science, Philosophy and Poetry in the Dialogue between Goethe and Schelling." In *The Third Culture: Literature and Science*. Ed. Elinor S. Schaffer. Berlin: Walter de Gruyter, 1998, 66–102.
Alexander, Franz. "The Development of Psychosomatic Medicine." In *Psychosomatic Medicine* 24 (1962): 13–24.
Althans, Birgit and Jörg, Zirfas. "Die unbewusste Karte des Gemüts – Immanuel Kants Projekt der Anthropologie." In *Das Unbewusste*. 3 vols. Ed. Michael B. Buchholz and Günter Gödde. Gießen: Psychosozial Verlag, 2005, vol. I, 70–94.
Andreas-Salomé, Lou. *Friedrich Nietzsche in seinen Werken*. Ed. Thomas Pfeifer. Frankfurt am Main: Insel, 2000.
Angelloz, Joseph-François. *Goethe*. Trans. R. H. Blackley. New York: The Orion Press, 1958.
Armstrong, John. *Love, Life, Goethe: How to Be Happy in an Imperfect World*. London: Allen Lane, 2006.
Arntzen, Helmut. "An den Mond." In *Goethe Handbuch*. 4 vols. in 6. Ed. Bernd Witte *et al*. Stuttgart: Metzler, 1996, vol. I/I, 180–7.
Assoun, Paul Laurent. *Freud and Nietzsche*. Trans. Richard L. Collier. London: Continuum, 2000.
— *Freud: La Philosophie et les philosophes*. Paris: Presses Universitaires, 1976.
Augé, Marc. *Pour une anthropologie des mondes contemporains*. Paris: Flammarion, 1994.
Barnouw, Jeffrey. "Goethe and Helmholtz." In *Goethe and the Sciences: A Reappraisal*. Ed. Frederick Amrine, Francis J. Zucker, and Harvey Wheeler. Dordrecht: Kluwer, 1987, 45–82.
Becker-Cantarino, Barbara, ed. *German Literature of the Eighteenth Century: The Enlightenment and Sensibility*. Volume V of *The Camden House History of German Literature*. Rochester, NY: Camden House, 2005.
Beiser, Frederick. *Schiller as Philosopher: A Re-examination*. Oxford: Clarendon Press, 2005.
Bell, Matthew. "Psychological Conceptions in Lessing's Dramas." In *Lessing Yearbook* 28 (1996), 53–81.
— *The German Tradition of Psychology in Literature and Thought, 1700–1840*. Cambridge: Cambridge University Press, 2005.
Benn, Maurice. "Goethe and T. S. Eliot." In *German Life and Letters* 5, no. 3 (1952): 151–161.
Bensch, Hans-Georg. *Perspektiven des Bewußtseins: Hegels Anfang der Phänomenologie des Geistes*. Würzburg: Königshausen & Neumann, 2005.
Berlin, Isaiah. *The Roots of Romanticism*. Ed. Henry Hardy. London: Pimlico, 1999.
Bernays-Freud, Anna. "My Brother, Sigmund Freud." In *American Mercury* 51, no. 203 (1940): 335–42.
Bernfeld, Siegfried. "Freuds früheste Theorien und die Helmholtz-Schule." In *Bausteine der Freud-Biographik*. Ed. Siegfried Bernfeld and Suzanne Cassirer Bernfeld. Frankfurt am Main: Suhrkamp 1981, 54–77.
Bettelheim, Bruno. *Freud and Man's Soul*. New York: Knopf, 1982.

Bishop, Paul. *Analytical Psychology and German Classical Aesthetics*. 2 vols. London and New York: Routledge, 2008–9.
"Goethe on the Couch: Freud's Reception of Goethe." In *Goethe at 250: London Symposium/Goethe mit 250: Londoner Symposion*. Ed. T. J. Reed, Martin Swales, and Jeremy Adler. Munich: Iudicium, 2000, 156–68.
Bittner, Günther. *Metaphern des Unbewussten: Eine Kritische Einführung in die Psychoanalyse*. Stuttgart: Kohlhammer, 1998.
Blackwell, Richard J. "Christian Wolff's Doctrine of the Soul." In *Journal of the History of Ideas* 22, no. 3 (1961): 339–54.
Bloom, Paul. *Descartes' Baby: How the Science of Child Development Explains What Makes Us Human*. London: Heinemann, 2004.
Boadella, David. *Wilhelm Reich: The Evolution of his Work*. London: Arkana, 1985.
Borch-Jacobsen, Mikkel, and Sonu Shamdasani. *The Freud Report: An Inquiry into the History of Psychoanalysis*. Cambridge: Cambridge University Press, forthcoming.
Borchmeyer, Dieter. *Weimarer Klassik: Portrait einer Epoche*. Weinheim: Beltz Athenäum, 1994.
Bovet, E. "Die Physiker Einstein und Weyl: Antworten auf eine metaphysische Frage." In *Wissen und Leben* 15, no. 9 (1922): 901–6.
Bowie, Andrew. *Aesthetics and Subjectivity from Kant to Nietzsche*. 2nd edn. Manchester: Manchester University Press, 2003.
From Romanticism to Critical Theory. London: Routledge, 1997.
"German Idealism's Contested Heritage." In *German Idealism. Contemporary Perspectives*. Ed. Espen Hammer. London: Routledge, 2007, 309–30.
Music, Philosophy, and Modernity. Cambridge: Cambridge University Press, 2007.
Schelling and Modern European Philosophy. London: Routledge, 1993.
Brehony, Kevin J. *The Origins of Nursery Education: Friedrich Froebel and the English System*. London: Routledge, 2001.
Buchholz, Michael B. and Günter Gödde, eds. Das Unbewusste, 3 vols. Vol. I: *Macht und Dynamik des Unbewussten: Auseinandersetzungen in Philosophie, Medizin und Psychoanalyse*; Vol. II: *Das Unbewusste in aktuellen Diskursen: Anschlüsse*; Vol. III: *Das Unbewusste in der Praxis: Erfahrungen verschiedener Professionen*. Gießen: Psychosozial Verlag, 2005–6.
Buchwald, Jed Z. "Electrodynamics in Context: Object States, Laboratory Practice, and Anti-Romanticism." In *Hermann von Helmholtz and the Foundations of Nineteenth-Century Science*. Ed. David Cahan. Berkeley, CA: University of California Press, 1993, 334–73.
Buggle, Franz and P. Wirtgen. "Gustav Theodor Fechner und die psychoanalytischen Modellvorstellungen Sigmund Freuds." In *Archiv für die Geschichte der Psychologie* 121 (1969): 148–201.
Caldwell, W. "The Epistemology of Ed. v. Hartmann." In *Mind* 2 (1893): 188–207.
"Von Hartmann's Moral and Social Philosophy I – The Positive Ethic," and "Von Hartmann's Moral and Social Philosophy II – The Metaphysic." *Philosophical Review* 8 (1899): 589–603 and 465–83.

312 Works cited

Canguilhem, Georges. *The Normal and the Pathological*. Trans. C. Fawcett. New York: Zone Books, 1989.

Clark, Maudemarie: *Nietzsche on Truth and Philosophy*. Cambridge: Cambridge University Press, 1990.

Clark, Ronald W. *Freud: The Man and the Cause*. London: Paladin, 1982.

Crawford, Claudia. *The Beginnings of Nietzsche's Theory of Language*. Berlin and New York: Walter de Gruyter, 1988.

Curran, Jane V. and Christophe Fricker, eds. *Schiller's "On Grace and Dignity" in its Cultural Context: Essays and a New Translation*. Rochester, NY: Camden House, 2005.

Dallmayr, Fred R. *Life-World, Modernity and Critique: Paths between Heidegger and the Frankfurt School*. Cambridge: Polity Press, 1991.

Damasio, Antonio. *Descartes' Error: Emotion, Reason and the Human Brain*. London: Vintage, 2006.

Darnoi, D. *The Unconscious and Eduard von Hartmann*. The Hague: Martinus Nijhoff, 1967.

Davey, Nicholas. "Baumgarten's Aesthetics: A Post-Gadamerian Reflection." In *British Journal of Aesthetics* 29 (1989): 101–15.

Davidson, Donald. *Problems of Rationality*. Oxford: Clarendon Press, 2004.

Davis, William Stephen. "Subjectivity and Exteriority in Goethe's 'Dauer im Wechsel.'" In *The German Quarterly* 66 (1993): 451–66.

Dehrmann, Mark-Georg. "Die problematische Bestimmung des Menschen: Kleists Auseinandersetzung mit einer Denkfigur der Aufklärung im 'Aufsatz, den sichern Weg des Glücks zu finden', im 'Michael Kohlhaas' und in der 'Herrmannsschlacht.'" *Deutsche Vierteljahrsschrift für Literaturwissenschaft und Geistesgeschichte* 81, no. 2 (2007): 193–227.

Dewhurst, Kenneth and Nigel Reeves. "The Emergence of the Psychological Sciences." In Friedrich Schiller. *Medicine, Psychology and Literature*. Ed. Kenneth Dewhurst and Nigel Reeves. Oxford: Sandford Publications, 1978, 109–41.

Diemer, Alwin. "Bewußtsein." In *Historisches Wörterbuch der Philosophie*. 12 vols. Ed. Joachim Ritter *et al*. Basel: Schwabe, 1971–2004, 1:888–96.

"Die Begründung des Wissenschaftscharakters der Wissenschaft im 19. Jahrhundert." In *Beiträge zur Entwicklung der Wissenschaftstheorie im 19. Jahrhundert*. Ed. A. Diemer. Meisenheim am Glan: Verlag Anton Hain, 1968, 3–62.

"Die Differenzierung der Wissenschaften in die Natur- und die Geisteswissenschaften." In *Beiträge zur Entwicklung der Wissenschaftstheorie im 19. Jahrhundert*. Ed. A. Diemer. Meisenheim am Glan: Verlag Anton Hain, 1968, 174–221.

Dorer, M. *Historische Grundlagen der Psychoanalyse*. Leipzig: Meiner, 1932.

Dörr, Volker C. *Weimarer Klassik*. Paderborn: Fink, 2007.

Dudley, Will. *Understanding German Idealism*. Stocksfield: Acumen, 2007.

Edwards, David and Michael Jacobs. *Conscious and Unconscious*. Buckingham: Open University Press, 2003.

Ehrenstein, Walter H. and Addie Ehrenstein. "Psychophysical Methods." In *Modern Techniques in Neuroscience Research*. Ed. U. Windhorst and H. Johansson. Berlin: Springer, 1999, 1211–41.

Eissler, Kurt: *Goethe: A Psychoanalytic Study.* Detroit, MI: Wayne State University Press, 1963.
Ellenberger, Henri F. *The Discovery of the Unconscious: The History and Evolution of Dynamic Psychiatry.* New York: Basic Books, 1970.
Erikson, Erik H. "Growth and Crises of the Healthy Personality." In *Identity and the Life Cycle.* New York and London: Norton, 1980, 51–107.
Felber, Werner and Otto Bach. "Carl Gustav Carus und das Unbewußte: Ein philosophisch-psychologisches Entwicklungskonzept im 19. Jahrhundert." In *Carl Gustav Carus: Opera et efficacitas: Beiträge des wissenschaftlichen Symposiums zu Werk und Vermächtnis von Carl Gustav Carus am 22. September 1989.* Ed. Günter Heidel. Dresden: Carus-Akademie, 1990.
Figl, Johann. *Interpretation als philosophisches Prinzip: Friedrich Nietzsches universale Theorie der Auslegung im späten Nachlaß.* Berlin and New York: Walter de Gruyter, 1982.
Frank, Manfred. *Das Sagbare und das Unsagbare.* Frankfurt am Main: Suhrkamp, 1989.
Frankl, George. *The Social History of the Unconscious.* London: Open Gate, 1989.
Friebe, Cord. *Theorie des Unbewußten: Eine Deutung der Metapsychologie Freuds aus transzendental-philosophischer Perspektive.* Würzburg: Königshausen & Neumann, 2005.
Fullenwider, Henry F. "The Goethean Fragment 'Die Natur' in English Translation." In *Comparative Literature Studies* 23, no. 2 (1986): 170–7.
Furness, Raymond: *Zarathustra's Children: A Study of a Lost Generation of German Writers.* Rochester, NY: Camden House, 2000.
Gardner, Sebastian. "Psychoanalysis and the Personal/Sub-Personal Distinction." In *Philosophical Explorations* 3 (2000): 96–119.
"Schopenhauer, Will, and the Unconscious." In *The Cambridge Companion to Schopenhauer.* Ed. Christopher Janaway. Cambridge: Cambridge University Press, 1999, 375–421.
Gardner, Sebastian and W. Bischler. "Schopenhauer and Freud: A Comparison," *Psychoanalytic Quarterly* 8 (1939): 88–97.
Gasser, Reinhard. *Nietzsche und Freud.* Berlin: Walter de Gruyter, 1997.
Gay, Peter. *Freud: A Life for Our Time.* New York and London: Norton, 1988.
Gerber-Münch, Irene. *Goethe's Faust: Eine tiefenpsychologische Studie über den Mythos des modernen Menschen. Beiträge zur Psychologie von C. G. Jung.* Series B. Vol. VII. Küsnacht: Verlag Stiftung für Jung'sche Psychologie, 1997.
Gerratana, Federico. "Der Wahn jenseits des Menschen. Zur frühen Eduard von Hartmann-Rezeption Nietzsches (1869–1874)." In *Nietzsche-Studien* 17 (1988): 391–433.
Ginsburg, Lev. *Giuseppe Tartini.* Trans. from Russian into German by Albert Palm. Zürich: Eulenburg Verlag, 1976.
Gödde, Günter. "Das Unbewußte als Zentralbegriff der Freudschen Metapsychologie und seine philosophischen Wurzeln." In *Traum, Logik, Geld: Freud, Husserl und Simmel zum Denken der Moderne.* Ed. Ulrike Kadi, Brigitta Keintzel, and Helmuth Vetter. Tübingen: edition diskord, 2001, 33–60.
"Die Öffnung zur Denkwelt Nietzsches – eine Aufgabe für Psychoanalyse und Psychotherapie." In *Psychoanalyse. Texte zur Sozialforschung* 4 no. 7 (2000): 91–122.

"Dionysisches – Triebe und Leib – 'Wille zur Macht': Nietzsches Annäherungen an das 'Unbewusste'." In *Das Unbewusste*. Ed. Michael Buchholz and Günter Gödde. Vol. I: *Macht und Dynamik des Unbewussten: Auseinandersetzungen in Philosophie, Medizin und Psychoanalyse*. Gießen: Psychosozial Verlag, 2005, 203–34.

"Freuds 'Entdeckung' des Unbewussten und die Wandlungen in seiner Auffassung." In *Das Unbewusste*. Ed. M. B. Buchholz and G. Gödde. Vol. I: *Macht und Dynamik des Unbewussten: Auseinandersetzungen in Philosophie, Medizin und Psychoanalyse*. Gießen: Psychosozial Verlag, 2005, 325–60.

"Freuds philosophische Diskussionskreise in der Studentenzeit." In *Jahrbuch der Psychoanalyse* 27 (1991): 73–113.

"Nietzsches Perspektivierung des Unbewussten." *Nietzsche-Studien* 31 (2002): 154–94.

Traditionslinien des "Unbewussten": Schopenhauer, Nietzsche, Freud. Tübingen: edition diskord, 1999.

Gode von Aesch, Alexander. *Natural Science in German Romanticism*. New York: Columbia University Press, 1941.

Goldmann, Stefan. *Via regia zum Unbewußten: Freud und die Traumforschung im 19. Jahrhundert*. Gießen: Psychosozial Verlag, 2003.

"Von der 'Lebenskraft' zum Unbewussten: Stationen eines Konzeptwandels der Anthropologie." In *Das Unbewusste*. Ed. M. B. Buchholz and G. Gödde. Vol. I: *Macht und Dynamik des Unbewussten: Auseinandersetzungen in Philosophie, Medizin und Psychoanalyse*. Gießen: Psychosozial Verlag, 2005, 125–52.

ed. *Traumarbeit vor Freud: Quellentexte zur Traumpsychologie im späten 19. Jahrhundert*. Gießen: Psychosozial Verlag, 2005.

Good, Bryon. *Medicine, Rationality, and Experience: An Anthropological Perspective*. Cambridge: Cambridge University Press, 1994.

Görner, Rüdiger. "Dialog mit den Nerven: Stefan Zweig und die Kunst des Dämonischen." In *Stefan Zweig und das Dämonische*. Ed. Matjaž Birk and Thomas Eicher. Würzburg: Königshausen & Neumann, 2008, 36–44.

Gould, Stephen Jay. *Ontogeny and Phylogeny*. Cambridge, MA: Belknap Press, 1977.

Grau, Kurt Joachim. *Bewusstsein, Unbewusstes, Unterbewusstes*. Munich: Rösl, 1922.

Gray, Richard T. *About Face: German Physiognomic Thought from Lavater to Auschwitz*. Detroit, MI: Wayne State University Press, 2004.

Grossman, Karl M. and Sylvia Grossman. *The Wild Analyst: The Life and Work of Georg Groddeck*. New York: George Braziller, 1965.

Grünbaum, Alfred. *The Foundations of Psychoanalysis: A Philosophical Critique*. Berkeley, CA: University of California Press, 1984.

Gupta, R. K. "Freud and Schopenhauer." In *Schopenhauer: His Philosophical Achievement*. Ed. Michael Fox. Sussex: Harvester, 1980, 226–35.

Gurisatti, Giovanni and Klaas Huizing. "Die Schrift des Gesichts: Zur Archäologie physiognomischer Wahrnehmungskultur." In *Neue Zeitschrift für systematische Theologie und Religionsphilosophie* 31 (1989): 271–87.

Hadot, Pierre. *N'oublie pas de vivre: Goethe et la tradition des exercices spirituels*. Paris: Albin Michel, 2008.

"'The Present Alone is our Joy': The Meaning of the Present Instant in Goethe and in Ancient Philosophy." In *Diogenes* 133 (1986): 60–82.
Heidelberger, Michael. "Beziehungen zwischen Sinnesphysiologie und Philosophie im 19. Jahrhundert." In *Philosophie und Wissenschaften. Formen und Prozesse ihrer Interaktion*. Ed. Hans Jörg Sandkühler. Frankfurt am Main: Peter Lang, 1997, 37–58.
Die innere Seite der Natur: Gustav Theodor Fechners wissenschaftlich-philosophische Weltauffassung. Frankfurt am Main: Klostermann, 1993. [*Nature from Within: Gustav Theodor Fechner's Psychophysical Worldview*. Trans. Cynthia Klohr. Pittsburgh, PA: University of Pittsburgh Press, 2004].
"Fechner's (Wider) Conception of Psychophysics – Then and Now." In *Fechner Day 2004: Proceedings of the Twentieth Annual Meeting of The International Society for Psychophysics*. Ed. Armando M. Oliveira, Marta Teixeira, Graciete F. Borges, and Maria J. Ferro. Coimbra: International Society for Psychophysics and Institute of Cognitive Science of the University of Coimbra, 2004, 18–25.
"Räumliches Sehen bei Helmholtz und Hering." In *Philosophia Naturalis* 30, no. 1 (1993): 1–28.
"The Mind-Body Problem in the Origin of Logical Empiricism: Herbert Feigl and Psychophysical Parallelism." In *Logical Empiricism: Historical and Contemporary Perspectives*. Ed. Paolo Parrini and Wesley Salmon. Pittsburgh, PA: University of Pittsburgh Press, 2003, 233–62.
Heinrichs, Heinz. *Die Theorie des Unbewußten in der Psychologie von Eduard von Hartmann*. Bonn: Verein Studentenwohl, 1933.
Hemecker, Wilhelm H. *Vor Freud: Philosophiegeschichtliche Voraussetzungen der Psychoanalyse*. Munich: Philosophia Verlag, 1991.
Henry, Michel. *The Genealogy of Psychoanalysis*. Trans. Douglas Brick. Stanford: Stanford University Press, 1993.
Hermann, Imre. "Goethes Aufsatz *Die Natur* und Freuds weitere philosophisch-psychologische Lektüre aus den Jahren 1880–1900." In *Jahrbuch der Psychoanalyse* 7 (1974): 77–100.
Hill, David, ed. *Literature of the Sturm und Drang*. Volume VI of *The Camden House History of German Literature*. Rochester, NY: Camden House, 2002.
Hinderer, Walter. "Schiller's Philosophical Aesthetics in Anthropological Perspective." In *A Companion to the Works of Friedrich Schiller*. Ed. Steven D. Martinson. Rochester, NY: Camden House, 2005, 27–46.
Hirschmüller, Albrecht. *Freuds Begegnung mit der Psychiatrie: Von der Hirnmythologie zur Neurosenlehre*. Tübingen: edition diskord, 1991.
Hödl, Hans Gerald. *Nietzsches frühe Sprachkritik: Lektüren zu "Über Wahrheit und Lüge im außermoralischen Sinne."* Vienna: Wiener Universitätsverlag, 1997.
Hoffer, Peter T. "The Legacy of Phylogenetic Inheritance in Freud and Jung." In *Journal of the American Psychoanalytic Association* 40 (1992): 517–30.
Hofmann, Johann Nepomuk. *Wahrheit, Perspektive, Interpretation: Nietzsche und die philosophische Hermeneutik*. Berlin and New York: Walter de Gruyter, 1994.

Hoffmeister, Gerhart, ed. *A Reassessment of Weimar Classicism.* Lewiston, Queenston and Lampeter: Edwin Mellen, 1996.
Hogrebe, W. *Prädikation und Genesis: Metaphysik als Fundamentalheuristik im Ausgang von Schellings "Die Weltalter."* Frankfurt am Main: Suhrkamp, 1989.
Holub, Robert C. "From the Pedestal to the Couch: Goethe, Freud and Jewish Assimilation." In *Goethe in German-Jewish Culture.* Ed. Klaus Berghahn and Jost Hermand. Rochester, NY: Camden House, 2001, 104–20.
Holzhey, Christoph. "On the Emergence of Sexual Difference in the 18th Century: Economies of Pleasure in Herder's *Liebe und Selbstheit.*" In *The German Quarterly* 79 (2006): 1–25.
Hühn, H., S. Meier-Oeser, and H. Pulte. "Wissenschaft." In *Historisches Wörterbuch der Philosophie.* 12 vols. Ed. Joachim Ritter *et al.* Basel: Schwabe, 1971–2004, vol. XII, 902–47.
Jansen, Marga-Elfriede. *Die ausdruckskundlichen Studien Schillers und ihre Beziehung zu Ludwig Klages.* Braunschweig: Technische Hochschule Carolo-Wilhelmina, 1944.
Jauss, Hans Robert. "Deutsche Klassik – eine Pseudo-Epoche?" In *Epochenschwelle und Epochenbewußtsein.* Ed. Reinhart Herzog and Reinhart Koselleck. Munich: Fink, 1987, 581–5.
Jolles, Matthijs. "Goethes Anschauung des Schönen." In *Deutsche Beiträge zur geistigen Überlieferung* 3 (1957): 89–116.
Jolley, Nicholas. *Leibniz.* London: Routledge, 2005.
Jones, Ernest. *The Life and Work of Sigmund Freud.* 3 vols. New York: Basic Books, 1953–7.
Kaiser-El-Safti, Margret. "Unbewußtes, das Unbewußte." In *Historisches Wörterbuch der Philosophie.* 12 vols. Ed. Joachim Ritter *et al.* Basel: Schwabe, 1971–2004, vol. XI, 124–133.
Kanzer, M. "Freud, Theodor Lipps and Scientific Psychology." In *Psychoanalytic Quarterly* 50 (1981): 383–410.
Keulartz, Jozef. *Die verkehrte Welt des Jürgen Habermas.* Trans. Inge van der Aart. Hamburg: Junius, 1995.
Kinsbourne, Marcel. "Taking the *Project* Seriously: The Unconscious in Neuroscience Perspective." In *Annals of the New York Academy of Sciences* 843 (1998): 111–115.
Klatte, Jürgen, Hans Göbbel, and Heinz Schott, eds. *Justinus Kerner, Medizin und Romantik: Kerner als Arzt und Seelenforscher.* Weinsberg: Stadt Weinsberg and Justinus-Kerner-Verein, 1990.
Klein, Dennis. *The Unconscious: Invention or Discovery? A Historico-Critical Inquiry.* Santa Monica, CA: Goodyear, 1977.
Kleinman, Arthur. *The Illness Narratives: Suffering, Healing, and the Human Condition.* New York: Basic Books, 1988.
Kleinschmidt, Erich. *Die Entdeckung der Intensität: Geschichte einer Denkfigur im 18. Jahrhundert.* Göttingen: Wallstein Verlag, 2004.
Koch, Christoph. *The Quest for Consciousness: A Neurobiological Approach.* Englewood, CT: Roberts & Co., 2004.
Koestler, Arthur. *The Act of Creation.* London: Penguin, 1964.
Kofman, Sarah. *Nietzsche and Metaphor.* Trans. Duncan Large. Stanford, CA: Stanford University Press, 1993.

Köhnke, Klaus Christian. *Entstehung und Aufstieg des Neukantianismus: Die deutsche Universitätsphilosophie zwischen Idealismus und Positivismus.* Frankfurt am Main: Suhrkamp, 1986. [*The Rise of Neo-Kantianism: German Academic Philosophy Between Idealism and Positivism.* Trans. R. J. Hollingdale. Cambridge: Cambridge University Press, 1991].

Kondylis, Panayotis. *Die Aufklärung im Rahmen des neuzeitlichen Rationalismus.* Stuttgart: Klett-Cotta, 1981.

Kris, Ernst. "The Nature of Psychoanalytic Propositions and Their Validation." In *Freedom and Experience: Essays presented to Horace M. Kallen.* Ed. Sidney Hook and Milton R. Konvitz. New York: Cooper Square Publishers, 1947, 239–59.

Kuehn, Manfred. *Kant: A Biography.* Cambridge: Cambridge University Press, 2001.

Lampert, Laurence. *Nietzsche and Modern Times: A Study of Bacon, Descartes, and Nietzsche.* New Haven: Yale University Press, 1993.

Lampl, Hans Erich, ed. *Zweistimmigkeit – Einstimmigkeit: Friedrich Nietzsche und Jean-Marie Guyau.* Cuxhaven: Junghans, 1990.

Lange, Victor. "Goethe in psychologischer und ästhetischer Sicht." In *Psychologie in der Literaturwissenschaft: Viertes Amherster Kolloquium zur modernen deutschen Literatur, 1970.* Ed. Wolfgang Paulsen. Heidelberg: Stiehm, 1971, 140–56.

Lehmann, Herbert. "A Conversation between Freud and Rilke." In *The Psychoanalytic Quarterly* 35 (1966): 423–7.

Lenoir, Timothy. "The Eternal Laws of Form: Morphotypes and the Conditions of Existence in Goethe's Biological Thought." In *Goethe and the Sciences: A Reappraisal.* Ed. F. Amrine, F. J. Zucker, and H. Wheeler. Dordrecht: D. Reidel, 1987, 17–28.

Livingstone Smith, David "'Some Unimaginable Substratum': A Contemporary Introduction to Freud's Philosophy of Mind." *Psychoanalytic Knowledge.* Ed. Man Cheung Chung and Colin Feltham. Houndmills, Basingstoke: Palgrave Macmillan, 2003, 54–75.

Lütkehaus, Ludger, ed. *Dieses wahre innere Afrika: Texte zur Entdeckung des Unbewußten vor Freud.* Frankfurt am Main: Fischer, 1989; 2nd edn. Gießen: Psychosozial Verlag, 2005.

MacIntyre, Alasdair. *The Unconscious: A Conceptual Analysis.* London: Routledge and Kegan Paul, 1958.

Magee, Bryan. *The Philosophy of Schopenhauer.* 2nd edn. Oxford: Oxford University Press, 1998.

Makkreel, Rudolf A. "The Confluence of Aesthetics and Hermeneutics in Baumgarten, Meier and Kant." In *The Journal of Aesthetics and Art Criticism* 54 (1996): 65–75.

Malherbe, Michel. "Bacon's Method of Science." In *The Cambridge Companion to Bacon.* Cambridge: Cambridge University Press, 1996, 75–98.

Mandelkow, Karl Robert. "Die Anfänge der Goethe Philologie." *Goethe in Deutschland: Rezeptionsgeschichte eines Klassikers.* 2 vols. Munich: Beck, 1980–9, 1: 157–8.

Margolis, Joseph. "Goethe and Psychoanalysis." In *Goethe and the Sciences: A Reappraisal.* Ed. Frederick Amrine, Francis J. Zucker, and Harvey Wheeler. Dordrecht: Kluwer, 1987, 83–100.

Marquard, Odo. *Transzendentaler Idealismus, romantische Naturphilosophie, Psychoanalyse*. Cologne: Dinter, 1987.
Martinson, Steven D. "'Maria Stuart': Physiology and Politics." In *A Companion to the Works of Friedrich Schiller*. Ed. Steven D. Martinson. Rochester, NY: Camden House, 2005, 213–26.
Mayr, Ernst. "Teleological and Teleonomic: A New Analysis." *Methodological and Historical Essays in the Natural and Social Sciences*. Ed. Robert S. Cohen and Marx W. Wartofsky. Dordrecht: Kluwer, 1974, 91–117.
Mazlish, Bruce. *The Uncertain Sciences*. 2nd edn. New Brunswick, NJ: Transaction, 2007.
McDowell, John. *Mind and World*. Cambridge, MA: Harvard University Press, 1994.
McGrath, William. *Freud's Discovery of Psychoanalysis: The Politics of Hysteria*. Ithaca, NY: Cornell University Press, 1986.
Meijers, Anthonie. "Gustav Gerber und Friedrich Nietzsche: zum historischen Hintergrund der sprachphilosophischen Auffassungen des frühen Nietzsche." In *Nietzsche-Studien* 17 (1988): 369–90.
Meijers, Anthonie and Martin Stingelin. "Konkordanz zu den wörtlichen Abschriften und Übernahmen von Beispielen und Zitaten aus Gustav Gerber: Die Sprache als Kunst (Bromberg 1871) in Nietzsches Rhetorik-Vorlesung und in 'Über Wahrheit und Lüge im außermoralischen Sinne'." In *Nietzsche-Studien* 17 (1988): 350–68.
Merlan, Phillip. *Monopsychism, Mysticism, Metaconsciousness: Problems of the Soul in the Neoaristotelian and Neoplatonic Tradition*. The Hague: Martinus Nijhoff, 1963.
Micale, Mark, ed. *Beyond the Unconscious: Essays of H. F. Ellenberger in the History of Psychiatry*. Princeton, NJ: Princeton University Press, 1993.
Mies, Thomas and Holger Brandes. "Unbewußte, das." *Europäische Enzyklopädie zu Philosophie und Wissenschaft*. Ed. Hans Jörg Sandkühler. Vol. II. Hamburg: Felix Meiner, 1999, 1657–65.
Molnár, Geza von. *Goethes Kantstudien*. Weimar: Hermann Böhlhaus Nachfolger, 1994.
Montinari, Mazzino. *Reading Nietzsche*. Trans. Greg Whitlock. Champaign, IL: University of Illinois Press, 2003.
Mörchen, Hermann. *Adorno und Heidegger: Untersuchung einer philosophischen Kommunikationsverweigerung*. Stuttgart: Klett-Cotta, 1981.
Macht und Herrschaft im Denken von Heidegger und Adorno. Stuttgart: Klett-Cotta, 1980.
Moser, Tilmann. "Parsifals Weg vom Es zum Ich: Wagners Bühnenweihfestspiel aus psychoanalytischer Sicht." In *Frankfurter Allgemeine Zeitung/Bilder und Zeiten*, November 23, 1985.
Müller-Lauter, Wolfgang. *Heidegger und Nietzsche*. Berlin and New York: Walter de Gruyter, 2000.
Murray, David. "A Perspective for Viewing the History of Psychophysics." In *Behavioral and Brain Sciences* 16, no. 1 (1993): 115–86.
Nager, Frank. *Goethe: Der heilkundige Dichter*. Frankfurt am Main and Leipzig: Insel, 1994.

Naumann, Barbara. *Philosophie und Poetik des Symbols: Cassirer und Goethe.* Munich: Wilhelm Fink, 1998.
Neubauer, John. "Goethe and the Language of Science." In *The Third Culture: Literature and Science.* Ed. Elinor S. Schaffer. Berlin: Walter de Gruyter, 1998, 51–65.
Nicholls, Angus. *Goethe's Concept of the Daemonic: After the Ancients.* Rochester, NY: Camden House, 2006.
  "On Science and Subjectivity." In *History of the Human Sciences* 18, no. 1 (2005): 143–58.
  "The Hermeneutics of Scientific Language in Goethe's Critique of Newton." In *Sprachkunst. Beiträge zur Literaturwissenschaft.* 36, no. 2 (2005): 203–226.
  "The Subject-Object of *Wissenschaft*: On Wilhelm Dilthey's *Goethebilder.*" In *Colloquia Germanica* 39, no. 1 (2006): 69–86.
Nisbet, Hugh Barr. *Goethe and the Scientific Tradition.* London: Institute of Germanic Studies, 1972.
Nitzschke, Bernd. "Goethe ist tot, es lebe die Kultur." In *Über das Pathologische bei Goethe.* Ed. Paul Julius Möbius. Munich: Matthes & Seitz, 1983, 9–75.
  "Liebe – Verzicht und Versöhnung: Das Ethos der Entsagung im Werk des Goethepreisträgers Sigmund Freud." In *Liebe und Gesellschaft: Das Geschlecht der Musen.* Ed. Hans-Georg Pott. Munich: Fink, 1997, 139–53.
Noë, Alva and Evan Thompson. "Are There Neural Correlates of Consciousness?" In *Journal of Consciousness Studies* 11, no. 1 (2004): 3–28.
Oberlin, Gerhard. *Goethe, Schiller und das Unbewusste: Eine literaturpsychologische Studie.* Gießen: Psychosozial Verlag, 2007.
Oberthür, Johannes. "Verdrängte Dunkelheit des Denkens. Descartes, Leibniz und die Kehrseite des Rationalismus." In *Das Unbewusste.* Ed. Michael B. Buchholz and Günter Gödde. Vol. I: *Macht und Dynamik des Unbewussten: Auseinandersetzungen in Philosophie, Medizin und Psychoanalyse.* Gießen: Psychosozial Verlag, 2005, 34–69.
Orsucci, Andrea: "Unbewusste Schlüsse, Anticipationen, Übertragungen: Über Nietzsches Verhältnis zu Karl Friedrich Zöllner und Gustav Gerber." In *Centauren-Geburten: Wissenschaft, Kunst und Sprache beim frühen Nietzsche.* Ed. Tilman Borsche, Federico Gerratana, and Aldo Venturelli. *Texte und Monographien zur Nietzsche-Forschung* 27. Berlin and New York: Walter de Gruyter, 1994, 193–207.
Parkes, Graham. "Nietzsche and Jung. Ambivalent Appreciation." In *Nietzsche and Depth Psychology.* Ed. J. Golomb *et al.* Albany, NY: State University of New York Press, 1999.
Peters, Uwe Henrik. "Goethe und Freud." In *Goethe Jahrbuch* (1986): 86–105.
Pfäfflin, Friedrich, ed. *Justinus Kerner, Dichter und Arzt 1786–1862.* 2nd edn. Marbach am Neckar: Deutsche Schillergesellschaft, 1990.
Pippin, Robert. *Idealism as Modernism.* Cambridge: Cambridge University Press, 1997.
  The Persistence of Subjectivity. Cambridge: Cambridge University Press, 2005.

Plänkers, Tomas. "'Vom Himmel durch die Welt zur Hölle': Zur Goethe-Preisverleihung an Sigmund Freud im Jahre 1930." In *Jahrbuch der Psychoanalyse* 30 (1993): 167-81.
Prawer, Siegbert S. "A Change of Direction? Sigmund Freud between Goethe and Darwin." In *Publications of the English Goethe Society* 76, no. 2 (2006): 103-17.
Proctor-Gregg, Nancy. "Schopenhauer and Freud." In *Psychoanalytic Quarterly* 25 (1956): 197-214.
Prokhoris, Sabine. *The Witch's Kitchen: Freud, "Faust," and the Transference.* Trans. G. M. Goshgarian. Ithaca, NY, and London: Cornell University Press, 1995.
Reed, T. J. "Weimar Classicism: Goethe's Alliance with Schiller." In *The Cambridge Companion to Goethe.* Cambridge: Cambridge University Press, 2002, 101-15.
Reeves, Joan Wynn. *Body and Mind in Western Thought: An Introduction to Some Origins of Modern Psychology.* Harmondsworth: Penguin, 1958.
Regenbogen, Arnim and Holger Brandes. "Unbewußte, das." In *Europäische Enzyklopädie zu Philosophie und Wissenschaften.* Ed. Hans Jörg Sandkühler. Vol. IV. Hamburg: Felix Meiner, 1990, 647-61.
Rennie, Nicholas. *Speculating on the Moment: The Poetics of Time and Recurrence in Goethe, Leopardi, and Nietzsche.* Göttingen: Wallstein, 2005.
Reuter, Sören. "Reiz – Bild – Unbewusste Anschauung: Nietzsches Auseinandersetzung mit Hermann Helmholtz' Theorie der unbewussten Schlüsse in Über Wahrheit und Lüge im außermoralischen Sinne." In *Nietzsche-Studien* 33 (2004): 351-72.
Rey, Georges. "Unconscious Mental States." In *The Routledge Encyclopedia of Philosophy.* London: Routledge, 1998, 522-7.
Richards, Robert J. "Christian Wolff's Prolegomena to Empirical and Rational Psychology: Translation and Commentary." In *Proceedings of the American Philosophical Society* 124, no. 3 (1980): 227-39.
The Romantic Conception of Life: Science and Philosophy in the Age of Goethe. Chicago: University of Chicago Press, 2002.
Richter, Simon, ed. *The Literature of Weimar Classicism.* Volume VII of *The Camden House History of German Literature.* Rochester, NY: Camden House, 2005.
Riedel, Wolfgang. *Die Anthropologie des jungen Schiller: Zur Ideengeschichte der medizinischen Schriften und der "Philosophischen Briefe."* Würzburg: Königshausen & Neumann, 1985.
Roazen, Paul. "Review of Matthew von Umerth: 'Freud's Requiem'." In *The American Journal of Psychiatry* 163, no. 2 (2006): 333-4.
Ronell, Avital. *Dictations: On Haunted Writing.* 2nd edn. 1986; Lincoln, NE: University of Nebraska Press, 1993.
Rossi, Paolo. "Bacon's Idea of Science." *The Cambridge Companion to Bacon.* Cambridge: Cambridge University Press, 1996, 25-46.
Rousseau, George S. "Psychology." In *The Ferment of Knowledge: Studies in the Historiography of Eighteenth-Century Science.* Ed. George S. Rousseau and Roy Porter. Cambridge: Cambridge University Press, 1980, 143-210.

Rupke, Nicolaas A. "Richard Owen's Vertebrate Archetype." *Isis* 84 (1993): 231–51.
Russell, Bertrand. *A Critical Exposition of the Philosophy of Leibniz*. London: Routledge, 1992.
Safranski, Rüdiger: *Romantik: Eine deutsche Affäre*. Munich and Vienna: Hanser Verlag, 2007.
Salaquarda, Jörg. "Studien zur Zweiten Unzeitgemäßen Betrachtung." In *Nietzsche-Studien* 13 (1984): 1–45.
Sandler, Joseph, Alex Holder, Christopher Dare, and Anna Ursula Dreher. *Freud's Models of the Mind: An Introduction*. London: Karnac, 1997.
Scheerer, Eckart. "The Unknown Fechner." In *Psychological Research* 49 (1987): 197–202.
Schivelbusch, Wolfgang. "Der Goethe-Preis und Sigmund Freud." In *Intellektuellendämmerung: Zur Lage der Frankfurter Intelligenz in den zwanziger Jahren*. Frankfurt am Main: Insel, 1982, 77–93.
Schlimgen, Erwin. *Nietzsches Theorie des Bewußtseins*. Berlin and New York: Walter de Gruyter, 1999.
Schmidt, Jochen. *Die Geschichte des Genie-Gedankens in der deutschen Literatur, Philosophie und Politik, 1750–1945*. 2 vols. Darmstadt: Wissenschaftliche Buchgesellschaft, 1985.
Schmitz, Hermann. *Goethes Altersdenken im problemgeschichtlichen Zusammenhang*. Bonn: Bouvier, 1959.
Schönau, Walter. *Sigmund Freuds Prosa: Literarische Elemente seines Stils*. Stuttgart: Metzler, 1968.
Schulz, Walter. *Philosophie in der veränderten Welt*. Pfullingen: Neske, 1972.
Segaller, Stephen and Merrill Berger. *The Wisdom of the Dream: The World of C. G. Jung*. London: Weidenfeld & Nicolson, 1989.
Seifert, Friedrich. "Psychologie. Metaphysik der Seele." In *Mensch und Charakter*. Ed. Alfred Baeumler and Manfred Schröter. Munich and Berlin: Oldenbourg, 1931, 72–85.
Selbmann, Rolf. *Deutsche Klassik*. Paderborn: Schöningh, 2005.
Sepper, Dennis L. *Goethe Contra Newton: Polemics and the Project for a New Science of Colour*. Cambridge: Cambridge University Press, 1998.
Shamdasani, Sonu. "Automatic Writing and the Discovery of the Unconscious." In *Spring: A Journal of Archetype and Culture* 54 (1993): 100–31.
——— "Encountering Hélène: Théodore Flournoy and the Genesis of Subliminal Psychology." In *From India to the Planet Mars: A Case of Multiple Personality with Imaginary Languages* by Théodore Flournoy. Princeton, NJ: Princeton University Press, 1994, xi–li.
——— *Jung and the Making of Modern Psychology: The Dream of a Science*. Cambridge: Cambridge University Press, 2003.
Simpson, James. *Goethe and Patriarchy: Faust and the Fates of Desire*. Oxford: Legenda, 1998.
Smith, N. *Reading McDowell's "Mind and World."* London: Routledge, 2002.
Smith, Roger. *Being Human: Historical Knowledge and the Creation of Human Nature*. New York: Columbia University Press, 2007.
——— "Does Reflexivity Separate the Human Sciences from the Natural Sciences?" In *History of the Human Sciences* 18, no. 4 (2005): 1–25.

Spitz, Lewis W. "Natural Law and the Theory of History in Herder." In *Journal of the History of Ideas* 16 (1955): 453–75.
Steiner, George. *Grammars of Creation*. London: Faber and Faber, 1991.
No Passion Spent: Essays 1978–1996. London: Faber and Faber, 1997.
Stephenson, Roger. *Goethe's Conception of Knowledge and Science*. Edinburgh: Edinburgh University Press, 1995.
Steuer, Daniel. *Die stillen Grenzen der Theorie. Übergänge zwischen Sprache und Erfahrung bei Goethe und Wittgenstein*. Cologne: Böhlau, 1999.
"In Defence of Experience: Goethe's Natural Investigations and Scientific Culture." In *The Cambridge Companion to Goethe*. Ed. Lesley Sharpe. Cambridge: Cambridge University Press, 2002, 160–78.
Sulloway, Frank J. *Freud, Biologist of the Mind*. New York: Basic Books, 1979.
Thomé, Horst. "Goethe-Stilisierung bei Sigmund Freud: Zur Funktion der enigmatischen Persönlichkeit in der psychoanalytischen Bewegung." In *Klassik und Moderne: Die Weimarer Klassik als historisches Ereignis und Herausforderung um kulturgeschichtlichen Prozeß*. Ed. Karl Richter and Jörg Schönert. Stuttgart: Metzler, 1983, 340–55.
Unwerth, Matthew von. *Freud's Requiem: Mourning, Memory, and the Invisible History of a Summer Walk*. New York: Riverhead Books, 2005.
Urbach, Peter. "Francis Bacon as a Precursor to Popper." In *British Journal for the Philosophy of Science* 33 (1982): 113–32.
Venturelli, Aldo. "Nietzsche in der Berggasse 19: Über die erste Nietzsche-Rezeption in Wien." In *Nietzsche-Studien* 13 (1984): 448–480.
Vidal, Fernando. "Le Sujet cérébral: Une esquisse historique et conceptuelle," *PSN: Revue de Psychiatrie, Sciences humaines et Neurosciences* 3, no. 11 (2005): 37–48.
Völmicke, Elke. *Das Unbewusste im Deutschen Idealismus*. Würzburg: Königshausen & Neumann, 2005.
Wegener, Mai. "Das Psychophysische Unbewusste – Gustav Theodor Fechner und der Mond." In *Das Unbewusste*. Ed. Michael B. Buchholz and Günter Gödde. Vol. I: *Macht und Dynamik des Unbewussten: Auseinandersetzungen in Philosophie, Medizin und Psychoanalyse*. Gießen: Psychosozial Verlag, 2005, 240–61.
Wessell, Leonard P. "Alexander Baumgarten's Contribution to the Development of Aesthetics." In *Journal of Aesthetics and Art Criticism* 30 (1972): 333–42.
Whyte, Lancelot Law. *The Unconscious before Freud*. London: Julian Friedmann, 1978.
Wilkinson, Elizabeth M. and L. A. Willoughby. "Missing Links or Whatever Happened to Weimar Classicism?" In *Erfahrung und Überlieferung: Festschrift for C. P. Magill*. Ed. Hinrich Siefken and Alan Robinson. Cardiff: Trivium Special Publications, 1974, 57–74.
Williams, Robert C. "The Russian Soul: A Study in European Thought and Non-European Nationalism." In *Journal of the History of Ideas* 31 (1970): 573–8.
Wittels, Fritz. *Sigmund Freud, der Mann, die Lehre, die Schule*. Leipzig, Vienna, and Zurich: Tal, 1924, 13–14.

Wolff, Hans Matthias. *Friedrich Nietzsche. Der Weg zum Nichts.* Bern: Francke, 1956.
Wollheim, Richard. *Freud.* 2nd edn. London: Fontana, 1991.
Wucherer-Huldenfeld, Augustinus von. "Freuds Umsetzung der Philosophie in Metapsychologie." In *Ursprüngliche Erfahrung und personales Sein: Ausgewählte philosophische Studien I*. Vienna: Böhlau, 1994, 179–95.
Young, Christopher and Andrew Brook. "Schopenhauer and Freud." In *International Journal of Psychoanalysis* 75 (1994): 101–18.
Zammito, John H. *Kant, Herder and the Birth of Anthropology.* Chicago: University of Chicago Press, 2002.
Zentner, Marcel R. *Die Flucht ins Vergessen: Die Anfänge der Psychoanalyse Freuds bei Schopenhauer.* Darmstadt: Wissenschaftliche Buchgesellschaft, 1995.
Zimmermann, Rolf Christian. *Das Weltbild des jungen Goethe: Studien zur hermetischen Tradition des deutschen 18. Jahrhunderts.* 2 vols. Munich: Fink, 1969–79.

Index

Abel, Jakob Friedrich 35
Adelung, Johann Christoph 20
Adler, Hans 8
Adorno, Theodor W. 54, 80, 81, 82–6, 124
Alighieri, Dante 4
Althans, Birgit 18
Andreas-Salomé, Lou 41
Aquinas, Thomas 4, 31
Aristotle 36, 156, 158, 159, 160, 164, 165, 166, 167, 170
   De Anima 164
Arnim, Achim von
   The Guardians of the Crown 130
   The Mad Invalid at the Fort of Ratonneau 130
Augustine, St. (Augustinus) 4

Bacon, Francis 33, 105, 115–17
Baer, Karl Ernst von 164
Bahnsen, Julius 186, 245
Bain, Alexander 33
Baldwin, James Mark 173, 290
Balzac, Honoré de
   Louis Lambert 137
Baumgarten, Alexander 8–9, 18, 38
Beethoven, Ludwig van 79, 245
Bell, Matthew 108
Berliner physikalische Gesellschaft 93
Berlioz, Hector
   Symphonie fantastique 132, 137, 138
Bernheim, Hippolyte 291–2
Bishop, Paul 108
Böhme, Jakob 4
Börne, Ludwig 51
   The Sulfur Baths near Montmorency 130
Bowie, Andrew 17, 141
Brandom, Robert 70, 77
Brentano, Clemens
   Godwi 130
Brentano, Franz 50, 102, 180, 265–6, 267–8, 270, 271, 273
Breuer, Josef 268

Brücke, Ernst 50, 51, 92, 94, 102, 265, 276
Brühl, Carl 26, 51, 92, 100, 101
Buchholz, Michael B. 18
Büchner, Georg
   Lenz 137–9
Buddha, Gautama 4
Byron, Alfred Lord 109

Carpenter, William 287
Carus, Carl Gustav 19, 43, 89, 101, 109, 123, 182, 265, 276
   Lectures on Psychology 157, 164, 165, 169
   Mnemosyne 163
   Psyche 156, 157, 158, 168, 170, 263
Cassirer, Ernst 39
Chamisso, Adelbert von
   Peter Schlemihl's Miraculous Story 130
Clarke, Maudemarie 243
Colli, Giorgio 243
Cudworth, Ralph 156
Cuvier, Georges 157
Czermak, Johann Nepomuk 249

Dennett, Daniel 177
Darwin, Charles 51, 100, 101, 120, 157, 178–9
   On the Origin of Species 92, 100, 101
Davidson, Donald 58
De Quincey, Thomas 132
defense (*Abwehr*) 19
Descartes, René 4, 18, 31–2, 34, 62, 87, 159, 160–1, 162, 168, 190, 214, 215, 220
Dilthey, Wilhelm 90, 93
Dostoevsky, Fjodor 158
drive (*Trieb*) 36, 256, 277, 281, 283
Du Bois-Reymond, Emil 50, 51, 92, 93, 95, 98–9, 101, 102, 109
Dudley, Will 76, 77
Dühring, Eugen 186, 203

Index

Ebbinghaus, Hermann 290
Ebner-Eschenbach, Marie 122
Eckermann, Johann Peter 95, 109, 111
Eichendorff, Joseph Freiherr von
  A Sea Voyage 131–2, 136
Einstein, Albert 216
Eliot, Thomas Stearns 40
Ellenberger, Henri F. 3, 22, 108, 288
Empedocles 197
Erikson, Erik 47
Eros 26, 46, 49, 278, 284
Euripides 244

Fabricius, Johann Albert 48
Falk, Johannes Daniel 46
Fechner, Gustav Theodor 23, 203–40, 262, 269, 272–3, 276
  Elements of Psychophysics 221, 226, 233–4
  Zend-Avesta 221
  Vorschule der Ästhetik 230–1
  Some Ideas Concerning the Creative and Developmental History of Organisms 235
Ferguson, Adam 34
Feuerbach, Ludwig 46, 50, 51, 68
Fichte, Johann Gottlieb 19, 68, 69, 71, 72, 80, 89–102, 126–7, 186, 208, 263
Ficino, Marsilio 156
Figl, Johann 256
Fliess, Wilhelm 101, 102, 103, 111, 269, 272, 273
Foucault, Michel 87, 91, 118
Frauenstädt, Julius 186
Freud, Sigmund 1–2, 19, 20, 21, 22, 23, 26, 27, 30, 39–56, 58, 62, 87, 92–5, 109–11, 118–20, 124, 142–3, 158, 171, 172, 184–5, 199, 258, 269–70, 292
  "A Childhood Recollection from *Dichtung und Wahrheit*" 107
  "Address Delivered in the Goethe House at Frankfurt" 91, 94, 95, 103–7, 110
  "An Autobiographical Study" 40, 91, 143
  "An Outline of Psychoanalysis" 52
  Beyond the Pleasure Principle 278
  "Civilization and its Discontents" 53, 284
  condensation (*Verdichtung*) 275
  counter-transference (*Gegenübertragung*) 119
  displacement (*Verschiebung*) 275
  ego (*Ich*) 278, 279, 281, 283, 285
  id (*Es*) 46, 158, 278, 279, 281, 282, 283–4, 285
  Introductory Lectures on Psycho-Analysis 52, 275
  "Leonardo da Vinci and a Memory of His Childhood" 42
  metapsychology 261, 276, 282
  "On Transience" 40–2, 45, 55
  pleasure principle 46, 275
  "Project for a Scientific Psychology" 49–50, 94, 95, 102–3, 114
  reality principle 276
  "Recommendations to Physicians Practising Psychoanalysis" 119
  "Something about the Unconscious" 278
  Studies on Hysteria 46
  super-ego (*Über-Ich*) 278, 279
  "The Ego and the Id" 279–81
  The Interpretation of Dreams 50, 51, 94, 111, 119, 261, 272, 274–5
  Three Essays on the Theory of Sexuality 277–8
  Totem and Taboo 165
Friedrich, Caspar David 157
Froebel, Friedrich 158

Gadamer, Hans-Georg 22
Gardner, Sebastian 141, 142
Garve, Christian 34
Gay, Peter 40
genius 17, 96, 97, 98, 109, 120
George, Stefan 242
Gerber, Gustav 249, 250
Gerratana, Federico 246
Gödde, Günter 18, 22–3, 24, 100, 108, 109, 245, 262–3
Goethe, Johann Wolfgang von 19, 26, 37, 38, 90–120, 141, 157, 159, 164, 171, 201, 263, 265
  "Empirical Observation and Science" 105
  "Ephemerides" 48–9
  Faust 23, 30, 42–3, 94, 104, 105, 106, 107, 108, 111, 162, 171, 278
  "Fortunate Encounter" 112
  "Judgement Through Intuitive Perception" 105
  "Lasting Change" 43–4
  Maxims and Reflections 45
  "On Nature" 26, 38–40, 49, 53, 56, 93, 101, 120, 264
  "On the Lake" 55–6
  Pandora 170
  Poetry and Truth 95, 98, 109, 111
  "Study after Spinoza" 97
  "Testament" 45
  The Elective Affinities 141
  "The Experiment as Mediator between Object and Subject" 112–13, 115
  "The Godlike" 43

326 Index

Goethe, Johann Wolfgang von (*cont.*)
  The Sorrows of Young Werther 28, 92, 98, 123
  Theory of Color 93, 94, 98, 106, 113–14, 116–18
  "To the Moon" 106–7
  Wilhelm Meister's Journeyman Years 47
Gould, Steven Jay 165
Grau, Kurt Joachim 20
Groddeck, Georg 158, 280
Grün, Karl (Ernst von der Haide) 51

Habermas, Jürgen 54
Hadot, Pierre 45, 46
Haeckel, Ernst 51, 101, 164, 217, 287
Hall, Granville Stanley 165
Haller, Albrecht von 35
Hamann, Johann Georg 263
Hamilton, William 21
Hartley, David 33, 169
Hartmann, Eduard von 1–2, 24, 60, 64, 142, 157, 171, 204, 231, 246, 247, 263, 276, 289, 290–1
  Philosophy of the Unconscious 173–99, 200, 201–3, 240, 245, 267–8
Haym, Rudolf 200–1, 202, 240
Hegel, Georg Wilhelm Friedrich 46, 68, 76–9, 81, 82, 85, 89, 99, 124, 174, 185–8, 190, 191, 192, 193, 194, 201, 263, 267
  Phenomenology of Mind 76, 122, 125–6
Heidegger, Martin 54, 65, 80, 243
Helmholtz, Hermann von 50, 51, 89–91, 92, 93, 95, 98, 109, 120, 182, 201, 219–20, 249, 250, 263, 265, 276
Hemecker, Wilhelm 18, 22, 50, 100
Heraclitus 197
Herbart, Johann Friedrich 23, 206–9, 210–11, 220, 223–5, 239, 262, 266, 269, 270, 272–3
Herder, Johann Gottfried 37, 61, 96–7, 108, 109, 123, 164, 201, 263
  Sculpture 38
Hering, Ewald 219, 220, 287
Herrick, Robert 45
Hobbes, Thomas 33
Hoffmann, Ernst Theodor Amadeus 130
  The Life and Opinions of Kater Murr 136
Hofmann, Johann Nepomuk 256
Hogrebe, Wolfram 75
Homer 17
Horace 45
Horkheimer, Max 54, 282

Huch, Ricarda 123
Hufeland, Christoph Wilhelm 276
Hume, David 5, 33, 159, 161, 169
Husserl, Edmund 77

Immermann, Karl
  Three Days in Ems Spa 130

Jacobi, Friedrich Heinrich 72, 201
James, William 213, 223, 289, 292
  Principles of Psychology 291, 293–4
Janet, Pierre
  Psychological Automatism 136
Jaspers, Karl 242
Jerusalem, Wilhelm 271, 276
Jung, Carl Gustav 1, 142, 158, 165, 169, 171, 172, 258, 260
  "Mind and Earth" 165
  "Psychological Types" 53

Kant, Immanuel 9–18, 19, 21, 32, 34, 46, 47, 60, 64–7, 75, 96, 99, 102, 104, 111, 112, 113, 114, 120, 141, 145, 149–50, 159, 161, 162, 163, 177–8, 179, 180, 189, 200
  Anthropology from a Pragmatic Point of View 10–16, 20, 24, 116
  Attempt to Introduce the Concept of Negative Magnitudes into Philosophy 10
  Critique of Judgment 16–18, 23, 81, 88, 103, 105, 175
  Critique of Pure Reason 14, 129, 161, 170
  Groundwork of the Metaphysics of Morals 13
  Metaphysical Foundations of Natural Science 88
  Prolegomena to Any Future Metaphysics 15
Kepler, Johannes 89
Kerner, Justinus 122
Klages, Ludwig 108, 158, 172
Kleist, Heinrich von 124
  The Marquise of O – 129
  Prinz Friedrich von Homburg 129
Kondylis, Panayotis 159
Köselitz, Heinrich (Peter Gast) 252
Kris, Ernst 53
Külpe, Oswald 290
  The Philosophy of the Present in Germany 290

Lacan, Jacques 52, 60
Lamarck, Jean-Baptiste 287
Lange, Friedrich Albert 180, 201, 203
  History of Materialism 195, 202, 249

Index

Lawrence, David Herbert 121
Lehmann, Herbert 41
Leibniz, Gottfried Wilhelm 5–7, 9–10, 13, 18, 20, 32–3, 51, 59, 63, 156, 159, 160, 161, 162, 164, 166, 168, 180, 214, 262, 277
  on *petites perceptions* 6–7, 10, 20, 32, 59, 262
Lenz, Michael Reinhold 139
Lessing, Gotthold Ephraim 34
Lindner, Gustav Adolf 264
Lipps, Theodor 263, 273–4, 276, 277
  Fundamental Facts of the Inner Life 274
  "The Concept of the Unconscious in Psychology" 274
Locke, John 5, 6, 11, 33, 239
Lütkehaus, Ludger 4, 12

Mach, Ernst 220
madness 58, 140, 152
Margolis, Joseph 94
Marquard, Odo 18, 19–20, 22, 159
Marx, Karl 68
Maudsley, Henry 165
Mayr, Ernst 235
Mazlish, Bruce 110, 118
McDowell, John 77, 82
McGrath, William 51
Medicus, Friedrich Casimir 276
Meister Eckhart 4
Mendelssohn, Moses 34
Meynert, Theodor 276
Micale, Mark 288
Mill, James 33
Mill, John Stuart 33, 56
monad 5
Montinari, Mazzino 243
Mörike, Eduard 139
  Mozart on his Journey to Prague 133–6
Mozart, Wolfgang Amadeus 109
  Don Giovanni 134, 135
Müller, Georg Elias 223
Müller, Johannes 92

Napoleon Bonaparte 109
Neubauer, John 112
Newton, Isaac 64, 93, 98, 100, 112, 113–14, 204
Nietzsche, Friedrich 1, 3, 19, 24, 90, 142, 198, 263, 266–7, 276, 282, 284–5, 286
  Apollonian/Dionysian distinction 244, 259

Beyond Good and Evil 197–8
Daybreak 252, 253–4
Ecce Homo 241
Human, All Too Human 247, 251
Genealogy of Morals 284
On Truth and Lies in an Extra-Moral Sense 243, 247–9, 250–1, 252, 253
The Birth of Tragedy 128, 242, 244, 245, 246, 247, 251, 258–9, 260
The Gay Science 252, 254, 259–60
Thus Spoke Zarathustra 130, 252
Twilight of the Idols 260
Untimely Meditations 242, 244, 246, 250, 260, 268
will to power 241, 243, 255–7, 263
Nisbet, Hugh Barr 115, 116
nominalism 21
Novalis (Friedrich von Hardenberg) 66, 121, 122, 124, 126
  Heinrich von Ofterdingen 128
  Pollen 127–8
  The Apprentices of Sais 128

Oberlin, Gerhard 92
obscure thoughts, obscure representations (*dunkle Gedanken, dunkle Vorstellungen*) 8, 9, 10–13, 15, 16, 20, 32
Owen, Richard 157

Paneth, Josef 50, 266
Pater, Walter 79
Paul, Jean (Johann Paul Friedrich Richter) 12, 21, 60, 130, 136, 139
  Prolegomena on Aesthetics 126
Peirce, Charles Sanders 231
Pfister, Oskar 47
Pippin, Robert 70, 79, 86
Platner, Ernst 7, 9, 10, 13, 18, 20
Plato 4, 34, 156, 175, 197, 245
Plotinus 4, 156, 161
Popper, Karl 116, 118

Reading Group of the German Students in Vienna 266
Regenbogen, Arnim 3, 14
Reich, Wilhelm 48
Reil, Johann Christian 123, 167
Renan, Ernest 289
Rennie, Nicholas 43
repression (*Verdrängung*) 19, 51, 61, 62, 72, 261, 270, 278, 280
resistance (*Widerstand*) 19, 61, 270

Rilke, Rainer Maria 41
Ronsard, Pierre de 45
Rorty, Richard 77
Rousseau, Jean-Jacques 64

Sallust 36
Schelling, Friedrich Wilhelm Joseph 19, 20, 57, 89, 99, 101, 109, 114, 125, 156, 157, 158, 162, 163, 168, 170, 171, 178, 179, 184, 186, 187, 188, 190, 191, 192, 193, 194, 197, 201, 214, 231, 240, 263, 265
  On the Essence of Human Freedom 75
  On the History of Modern Philosophy 63
  Philosophy of Art 126
  Philosophy of Revelation 61
  System of Transcendental Idealism 37, 68–9, 71–6, 77, 78, 80, 82, 141–2
Schiller, Friedrich 19, 27, 28–9, 35–7, 90, 96, 97, 98, 99, 105, 111
  Aesthetic Letters 36
  Essay on the Connection between the Animal and the Spiritual Nature of Man 35
  "Nänie" 42
  "On Grace and Dignity" 35, 36
  "On Naïve and Sentimental Literature" 29, 36
  On the Aesthetic Education of Man 29, 35
  Philosophy of Physiology 35
Schlegel, Friedrich
  Lucinde 129
Schleiermacher, Friedrich 65, 132
Schmidt, Oscar 203
Schopenhauer, Arthur 19, 24, 60, 80, 156, 159, 161, 174, 179, 185–8, 190, 192, 193, 197, 199, 203, 204, 241, 244, 245, 246, 247, 263, 266, 267, 276, 281, 282–4, 285, 286, 290, 291
  On the Fourfold Root of the Principle of Sufficient Reason 249
  The World as Will and Representation 140, 141, 144–55
Schubert, Gotthilf Heinrich 133
Schumann, Robert 132, 137
Seifert, Friedrich 31
Sellars, Wilfrid 77
Shakespeare, William 4, 109
Silberstein, Eduard 50
Simmel, Georg 90
Smith, Roger 118
Socrates 244–5, 251

Sophocles 62
Spencer, Herbert 21
Spinoza, Benedict de 48, 71, 97, 101, 108, 109, 120, 190, 197
Spitz, Lewis W. 38
Stahl, Georg 34
Steiner, George 136
Storm and Stress (*Sturm und Drang*) 27, 29–30, 39, 43, 48, 56, 111
Strauss, Friedrich 101
Sulloway, Frank J. 269
Sulzer, Johann Georg 8

Tait, Peter 250
Taylor, Charles 81
Thanatos (death-drive) 26, 49, 278, 284
Thomsen, William 250
Tobler, Georg Christoph 93, 101, 264–5
Turing, Alan (Turing Test) 218

unconscious / *unbewusst* (concept of)
  and associated terms
    bewusstlos 20, 228, 245
    Bewusstlosigkeit 144
    preconscious 230, 269, 275, 276, 277, 279, 285
    sub-conscious 21, 121–2
    unterbewusst 7, 20, 122
    Unbewusstsein 9, 20, 222, 230
  conceptual history 1–3, 18–25
  epistemology of 2–3, 57–63, 72–4, 288, 294–6
Unsworth, Matthew von 41, 42

Vaihinger, Hans 201, 203
Vidal, Fernando 296
Viennese Psychoanalytic Society 46
Volkelt, Johannes 186, 267
Völmicke, Elke 19, 20, 21, 22

Wagner, Cosima 245
Wagner, Richard 79, 139, 244, 245, 266
  Parsifal 133
  The Artistry of the Future 133
Weber, Ernst Heinrich 221
Weber, Wilhelm 249
Weimar classicism 28–30, 39, 43, 48, 56, 111
Whyte, Lancelot Law 22, 108
Windelband, Wilhelm 195–6
Wittels, Fritz 40
Wittgenstein, Ludwig 198, 293
Wolff, Christian 7, 10, 13, 18, 20, 33, 34, 156, 159, 161, 163, 167, 206
  Empirical Psychology 159

Index

Wucherer-Huldenfeld, Augustinus Karl 270
Wundt, Wilhelm 205, 212, 273
 Lectures on Human and Animal Psychology 292–3

Young, Thomas 249

Zammito, John H. 13
Zentner, Marcel R. 282
Zirfas, Jörg 18
Zöllner, Karl Friedrich 217, 249, 250
 On the Nature of Comets 249
Zweig, Stefan 125

For EU product safety concerns, contact us at Calle de José Abascal, 56–1°,
28003 Madrid, Spain or eugpsr@cambridge.org.

www.ingramcontent.com/pod-product-compliance
Ingram Content Group UK Ltd.
Pitfield, Milton Keynes, MK11 3LW, UK
UKHW040609070825
461487UK00005BA/323